The Age of Communication

The Age of Communication

WILLIAM D. LUTZ

Goodyear Publishing Company, Inc.,   Pacific Palisades, California

Current printing (last digit: 10987654321)
ISBN: 0-87620-013-7
Library of Congress Catalog Card Number:
72-97279
Y-0137-3

Printed in the United States of America.

Contents

Preface

I believe that no one ever reads the preface of any book; no one, that is, except the author who writes it and the editor who edits it. Just think of the great volume of prefaces that exist, for the most part, unread. Why do I write this preface if I believe that no one will read it? Because there are a few things that I would like to say before plunging into the main part of the book.

I would like to say something about the thinking behind this book. I, of course, do not consider it just another textbook, and I certainly hope that anyone who uses this book in a class would not consider it as such either. I hope this is an interesting book, one that is fun to read. I also hope it is a valuable book for classroom use, one that will effectively aid in teaching that most difficult of subjects, rhetoric. I have taken rhetoric in a very broad definition and applied it to the contemporary world. There is a rhetoric of advertising just as there is a journalistic rhetoric. And I think I can say there is a definite rhetoric in such

cultural manifestations as rock music, movies, and television. The subject matter of this book is the rhetoric of the world of everyday life.

One final thing remains to be said before I end my brief prefatory note and that is my thanks to those who helped with the preparation of this book. David Grady was always at hand to lend good cheer and advice whenever I needed it. Barbara Blader was indispensible in the preparation of the manuscript and continually demonstrated her remarkable efficiency. Gail Weingart and Sally Kostal are responsible not only for the handsome physical appearance of this book but also for giving me innumerable helpful suggestions to improve the contents. My wife Kris served as first reader and critic on all materials in the text giving me suggestions and ideas for revisions. To all these people I am indebted.

Advertising

Advertising surrounds us in almost every aspect of our lives. Inside and outside our homes we are continuously assaulted by some kind of advertising. Television, radio, magazines, newspapers, signs, billboards, and labels on packages all feed a steady and unrelenting stream of commercial and noncommercial messages to us. Even our churches advertise. There is no escaping advertising, and perhaps on some distant future date archeologists will label our age the Age of Advertising. To understand America, our culture, our values, and to some extent ourselves, we need to understand advertising.

Some experts have estimated that over 40 billion dollars a year is spent on advertising. Obviously the economic impact of advertising is enormous, both in the resources it consumes and in the power it commands to channel the spending of the American consumer. Whenever we buy a product, whether we are responding to advertising or not, we are paying part of that 40 billion dollars a year.

Modern advertising is highly sophisticated and employs every art form available, and even invents some more. Advertising appeals to our known and hidden strengths and weaknesses, our conscious and subconscious desires and needs. It reflects, affects, and, some would contend, to a certain extent creates our attitudes toward love, sex, happiness, politics, society, business, health, and other significant aspects of our lives. Whether we want to admit it or not, our lives are very much affected in some way or other by advertising.

This section deals with some aspects of advertising, both internally and externally. That is, the essays in this section discuss something of how advertising is devised, how it works, and how it influences our society and our lives. The first part of this section is a collection of some contemporary advertisements for various products. There is an inherent limitation that must be recognized immediately in this collection of advertisements. Since this is a book, advertisements from radio and television could not be included. Thus it is necessary to point out that the collection of advertisements in this section are not representative of the full range of advertising as it exists in our society. But it should be possible, after analyzing the advertisements presented here, to extend that analysis to other forms of advertising.

The essays in this section present as broad a picture of advertising as possible. They begin by discussing the various techniques that advertisers use. These techniques are not necessarily acceptable to everyone, as evidenced by the dissenting essays in this section. The substance of advertising, the language it uses, is discussed in some detail in order to give you some insight to the sophisticated use of rhetoric found in a large portion of modern advertising. Other essays in this section discuss some of the problems and implications of advertising. Since advertising plays such an important role in our economy there are certain economic implications and problems which arise. There are certain political issues which arise and which we must also consider.

Finally, the section ends with the inevitable question, should advertising be abolished? Hopefully, at this point you will be able to formulate a more informed and thoughtful response to this question.

Throughout this section there are numerous questions for discussion. They are designed to promote discussion of not only the content of each advertisement and essay, but also the rhetorical aspects. These questions should be considered starting points. Certainly any consideration of the selections here should not be limited to the questions included in the text.

Finally, you should not consider this section a definitive discussion of so complex and interesting a subject. Advertising is too large, too fascinating a subject to discuss satisfactorily in a few brief essays. Every attempt should be made to go beyond the confines of the text to learn more about this subject. Advertising can teach us much, but before we approach it we should know something of it. Hopefully this section provides the basic tools necessary to an extended analysis of advertising and thus provides exploration of the very effective use of rhetoric as employed by advertising.

DEWAR'S PROFILES

(Pronounced Do-ers "White Label")

BLENDED SCOTCH WHISKY • 86.8 PROOF • © SCHENLEY IMPORTS CO., N.Y., N.Y.

BILL DRAKE

HOME: Bel Air, California

AGE: 33

PROFESSION: Designs the format for pop music programs on radio stations around the country.

HOBBIES: Pool. Monitoring his radio stations.

LAST BOOK READ: "The Godfather."

LAST ACCOMPLISHMENT: Created "Solid Gold Rock and Roll" and "Hit Parade 71," two of the most successful musical formats on radio today.

QUOTE: "You can't dismiss the rock groups as 'far-out'. The fact that their music succeeds, suggests that their ideas are widely circulated and probably accepted by a lot of people. I think more attention should be paid to them. Listening might give everybody a better idea about what's on young people's minds."

PROFILE: Intuitive. Shrewd. Disarmingly casual. His sometimes abrasive manner has helped make him the most powerful force in broadcast rock.

SCOTCH: Dewar's "White Label"

Authentic. There are more than a thousand ways to blend whiskies in Scotland, but few are authentic enough for Dewar's "White Label." The quality standards we set down in 1846 have never varied. Into each drop goes only the finest whiskies from the Highlands, the Lowlands, the Hebrides. **Dewar's never varies.**

Dewar's

Topics for Discussion

1. Advertisers often have famous people endorse their products. Is this such an advertisement?
2. Why is the text of this advertisement presented in a formal outline? What effect is achieved with this format?
3. Why is only part of this advertisement in color?
4. What is the appeal of this advertisement?
5. Is this the same kind of advertisement as the one for *Pub* cologne? What are the differences between the two advertisements?

Rhetorical Considerations

1. What information are you given about the man endorsing *Dewar's*? How pertinent is this information?
2. Parts of this advertisement look like an official document. Why?
3. The advertisement states "there are more than a thousand ways to blend whiskies" but *Dewar's* is authentic. What is the fallacy here? How do you know *Dewar's* is "authentic"? What does "authentic" mean?

New England Life

Topics for Discussion

1. What product is advertised? Where is the product mentioned in the advertisement? Why is the mention of the product so understated?
2. How does the cartoon help sell insurance? Is the cartoon morbid? Is there any humor here?
3. Is life insurance concerned with life or death? Why is it called life insurance and not death insurance?
4. Do you consider this an effective advertisement? Why?

Rhetorical Considerations

1. Look carefully at the arrangement of this advertisement. Why is there so much white space? How does the arrangement of the advertisement lend emphasis to the point it is making?
2. The caption of the advertisement is an answer to a question not stated in the advertisement. How does the cartoon make clear who has asked the question and who is answering? How does the cartoon make clear what the unstated question is?

"My insurance company? New England Life, of course. Why?"

Advertisement for New England Life Insurance Co., from *Newsweek*, June 12, 1972. Copyright 1971 by New England Life Insurance Co. Reprinted by permission.

Get a taste of what it's all about.
Get the full taste of Viceroy.

VICEROY
FILTER CIGARETTES

18 mg. "tar," 1.3 mg. nicotine av. per cigarette, FTC Report Aug. 72.

© 1972, BROWN & WILLIAMSON TOBACCO CORP.

Advertisement for *Viceroy* cigarettes. © 1972 Brown & Williamson Tobacco Corporation. Reprinted by permission.

The Age of Communication

Ford Mustang: Control, balance, style.

And new Sprint colors!

There's a new Mustang option package at your Ford dealer's that just may be the ultimate in personal sporty style.

The Sprint color scheme is classic white with bold blue panels, red pin-striping, color-matched interior. You also get dual racing mirrors, white sidewall tires, and red, white and blue bodyside insignia.

Combine that with Mustang's independent front suspension, floor-mounted stick shift, bucket seats, and panoramic instrument panel —and you're in for a beautiful driving experience. Inside and out.

Mag wheels, raised white letter tires and competition suspension are also available.

Put a little Sprint in your life!

1972 Ford Mustang SportsRoof shown with Sprint Decor Option.

FORD MUSTANG

FORD DIVISION *Ford*

1972 Ford Mustang Hardtop shown with Sprint Decor Option.

Advertisement for *Ford Mustang* from *Time*, June 12, 1972, reprinted by permission of Ford.

VICEROY

1. Why would a race driver have the word *Viceroy* on his driving suit?
2. What relevance does a race driver have to cigarettes? Does he have any special knowledge about cigarettes? What appeal is being made here?
3. Would the advertisement be more effective if the driver were holding a package of cigarettes? Why?
4. Why is there so little text with this advertisement? How does the advertisement achieve its effect?
5. How much information does this advertisement give you about *Viceroy* cigarettes?
6. Do you think this advertisement appeals only to men? Would it appeal in any way to women?

Rhetorical Considerations

1. The advertisement says to "get a taste of what it's all about." What does this statement mean? What is the antecedent of the pronoun "it"?
2. How can you get "the full taste of *Viceroy*"?
3. Does the word "taste" mean the same thing in both sentences?
4. The sentences here are in the form of commands. What effect does this create? Would it be better if these sentences were written differently?

FORD MUSTANG

Topics for Discussion

1. What relationship is there between surfing and driving a *Mustang*?
2. If you had never surfed, could you understand this advertisement?
3. What audience is this advertisement directed to? What is the basis of the appeal of the advertisement?
4. Why is there no mention of the price as in the advertisement for the *Honda Coupe*?
5. Why is the picture of the surfer dark, hazy, and indistinct while the picture of the *Ford* cars is clear and distinct?

Rhetorical Considerations

1. What is the implied comparison in this advertisement?
2. Note the use of adjectives in the text. Why are such adjectives as "personal," "sporty," "classic," and "panoramic" used?
3. How does the composition of the advertisement create impact while drawing the reader's attention to the text?

RAVEEN MUSK OIL

A very special
Christmas gift selection
for that very special
someone in your life

Don't Say We Didn't Warn You

It can start a sensuous, silent conversation between man and woman.

Down through the ages women have searched for new, exciting ways to be more alluring, more exciting, more basically sensuous and exotic.

It lingers, it pulses, it stimulates passion. It releases the animal instinct and creates a spell . . . your own irresistible spell.

Just a drop on elbows, behind the knees, on your wrists and at the temples creates a haunting essence that's all your own.

While you scarcely notice the subtle aroma, those around you respond to its magic. A magic your body chemistry and RAVEEN Musk Oil create together.

RAVEEN MUSK OIL

Wear This Mysterious Fragrance With Care.

Topics for Discussion

1. What product is advertised here? How do you know exactly?
2. Why isn't the woman in the advertisement wearing a wedding ring?
3. To whom is this advertisement directed—men or women?
4. What catches your eye first—the man and woman or the bottle of perfume? Where is the center of the advertisement?
5. Is there any difference between musk oil and perfume? Would the advertisement be the same if it were for perfume?
6. Is there too much text with this advertisement? Do you think the average reader will read all of this advertisement?
7. What are the sexual overtones in this advertisement?
8. What does this advertisement imply about the relationship between men and women?

Rhetorical Considerations

1. What is the advertisement's warning? Is it stated anywhere? What does this warning imply?
2. Examine all the adjectives used in this advertisement. What effect do they achieve?
3. Read the text out loud. How does it sound?
4. *Raveen* is called a "mysterious fragrance," a "subtle aroma," and a "haunting essence." What appeal is being made here?
5. Does this advertisement depend on words or pictures?

Now that you've decided to be beautiful

Make the choice beautiful people make more often than any other—Afro Sheen. Three beautiful choices are Afro Sheen Comb Easy Conditioner, Afro Sheen Hair Spray for Sheen and Afro Sheen Holding Hair Spray.

Start with Afro Sheen Comb Easy, the special lotion that conditions your hair while it takes the hassle out of combing and styling. Then, after you finish styling your natural, glorify it —with the shimmering lustre only Afro Sheen Hair Spray for Sheen can give. Now, hold that beautiful style all day with Afro Sheen Holding Hair Spray. It's protein enriched, non-sticky, and never dulls or flakes.

Your beauty is in your realness. So, express your realness beautifully with the finest products available—Afro Sheen.

watu wazuri use afro sheen®

JOHNSON PRODUCTS CO., INC. CHICAGO, ILLINOIS 60620 1972

Advertisement for *Afro Sheen* reprinted by permission of Johnson Products Company, Inc.

afro sheen

Topics for Discussion

1. How specialized is the product advertised here?
2. Would you expect to find this advertisement in *Time* or *Newsweek*? What audience is this product directed to?
3. Who are the beautiful people mentioned in the advertisement? How do you know?
4. What is the appeal of this advertisement? How similar is this appeal to other advertisements for cosmetics?
5. Why is the picture of the people at the bottom of the advertisement? Can you think of a better arrangement for this advertisement?
6. What, if anything, do you find different or unusual about this advertisement?

Rhetorical Considerations

1. What does "Watu Wazuri use *Afro Sheen*" mean? How does this reflect the specialized audience of the advertisement?
2. The advertisement says "Your beauty is in your realness." What does this mean? How can *Afro Sheen* contribute to your realness?
3. The lead on this advertisement is a sentence fragment. What does it leave unsaid? Does the rest of the advertisement state what is implied in this?
4. How can you "glorify" your natural with *Afro Sheen*?
5. How much concrete information does this advertisement offer?

Pub Cologne

Topics for Discussion

1. Who is the man pictured in this advertisement? Where have you seen him before? Why do you think he was chosen for this advertisement? Do you think he knows any more about men's cologne than you?
2. What is the basic appeal of this advertisement? Is this appeal directed at men or women?
3. Why is the man in the advertisement fully clothed? Do you think it would have been more effective if he had been pictured in the bath room just after shaving?
4. Why is the text of the advertisement put almost in the middle of the page? Should the text go at the bottom or the top of the advertisement? What do you notice first about the advertisement, the text, the man, or the picture of the bottle of cologne? What do you think the advertiser wants you to notice first?
5. Why isn't the man in the advertisement holding the bottle of cologne?

Rhetorical Considerations

1. What "kind of guy" uses *Pub* cologne? How do you know? How do you know what kind of guy he is? What are the implications of the text of this advertisement? What assumptions does the text make?
2. Why is "guy" used and not "man"?
3. How precise is the use of language in the text of the advertisement?
4. What effect is achieved by having the text of the advertisement in white print?
5. What does the organization of this advertisement tell you the advertiser wants to emphasize?

The kind of guy who uses it doesn't need it.

Pub Cologne.

After Shave, After Shave Balm, Deodorant Spray, too.
Created for men by Revlon.

Advertisement for *Pub* Cologne reprinted by permission of Revlon, Inc.

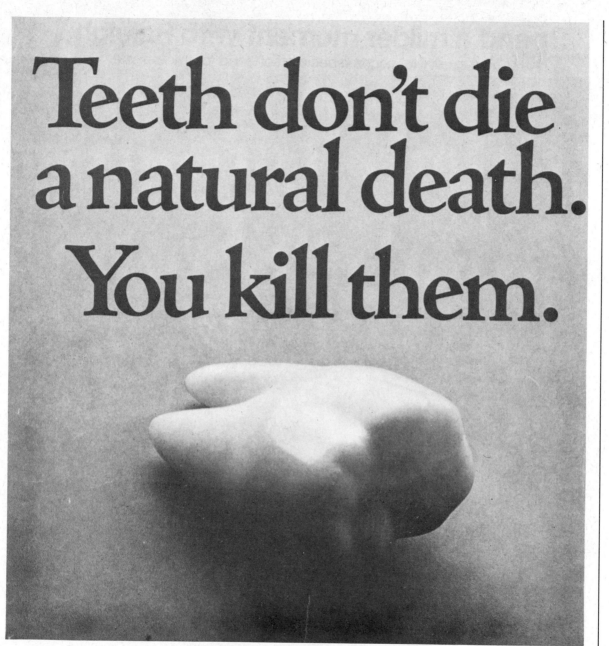

Teeth don't die a natural death. You kill them.

Chances are, when you lose a tooth, it's because you killed it with neglect. By not eating the right foods, or seeing the dentist often enough, or brushing properly. Such neglect can lead to cavities, and cavities can lead to tooth loss. In fact, the average person loses 6 to 9 teeth in a lifetime *simply* due to cavities.

Crest with fluoride fights cavities. So, besides seeing your dentist and watching treats, make sure you brush with Crest.

Because the more you fight cavities, the less your teeth have to fight for their lives.

Fighting cavities is the whole idea behind Crest.

"Crest has been shown to be an effective decay-preventive dentifrice that can be of significant value when used in a conscientiously applied program of oral hygiene and regular professional care." Council on Dental Therapeutics, American Dental Association.

Advertisement for *Crest* toothpaste from Life, July 7, 1972 reprinted by permission.

Crest

Topics for Discussion

1. What do you notice first in this advertisement—the tooth or the headline?
2. Why isn't *Crest* mentioned in the headline of the advertisement?
3. A picture of a tooth is certainly appropriate to an advertisement for toothpaste. How does it differ from others?
4. What is the basis of the appeal of this advertisement? Is this advertisement like others you have seen for toothpaste? How does it differ from others?

Rhetorical Considerations

1. Note the words used in the headline. Three of the words refer to death. What effect does this have?
2. Does the text at the bottom of the advertisement have a paragraph structure?
3. The second sentence in the text at the bottom is a fragment. How does this fragment function in context?
4. What is the tone of the text in this advertisement?
5. What is more noticeable about the headline in the text, what it says or how large the type is? Why is the type in the headline so large?

Geritol

Topics for Discussion

1. What is *Geritol*? Does the advertisement tell you what it is?
2. Why is the man's wife "incredible"? What does this have to do with *Geritol*?
3. This advertisement has been cited as one that demeans women. Do you agree with this charge? What is the picture of woman presented here?
4. Is this advertisement directed only at women? Does the advertisement suggest at any place that men should take *Geritol* also?
5. The advertisement says that "she looks better than any of her friends. And they're all about the same age." How do you know she looks better? How do you know this is due to taking *Geritol*?

Rhetorical Considerations

1. Why is the caption "My wife is incredible" at the top of the picture? Would it be as effective placed at the bottom of the picture?
2. At the bottom of the advertisement it says "Take care of yourself. Take *Geritol*." Does this mean that if you don't take *Geritol* you aren't taking care of yourself?
3. "*Geritol* has more than twice the iron of ordinary supplements." What is an ordinary supplement? How much iron does an ordinary supplement contain? How much iron does *Geritol* contain?
4. Why is "Take care of yourself. Take *Geritol*" repeated at the bottom of the advertisement in bold face type?

"My wife is incredible."

"The way she takes care of the kids, the house, a job and me—it's incredible. And look at her. She looks better than any of her friends. And they're all about the same age."

Aren't those nice words for a woman to hear? But to be able to get all of those compliments, you have to take care of yourself.

You should eat the right foods, get plenty of rest, exercise. And to make sure you get enough iron and vitamins, take Geritol every morning. Geritol has more than twice the iron of ordinary supplements. Plus seven vitamins.

Take care of yourself. Take Geritol.

Take care of yourself. Take Geritol.

Advertisement for *Geritol* reprinted by permission of The J. B. Williams Company, Inc.

The phone company wants more installers like Alana MacFarlane.

Alana MacFarlane is a 20-year-old from San Rafael, California. She's one of our first women telephone installers. She won't be the last.

We also have several hundred male telephone operators. And a policy that there are no all-male or all-female jobs at the phone company.

We want the men and women of the telephone company to do what they want to do, and do best.

For example, Alana likes working outdoors. "I don't go for office routine," she said. "But as an installer, I get plenty of variety and a chance to move around."

Some people like to work with their hands, or, like Alana, get a kick out of working 20 feet up in the air.

Others like to drive trucks. Some we're helping to develop into good managers.

Today, when openings exist, local Bell Companies are offering applicants and present employees some jobs they may never have thought about before. We want to help all advance to the best of their abilities.

AT&T and your local Bell Company are equal opportunity employers.

Eyes are the mirror of the soul.
Wordless communication is established.
Silence becomes a spiritual symphony.
The serene perpetual gaze of
a Buddha image signifies mute
supplication to seekers after truth.

Photographed by Ken Domon

Japan is beauty. And Japan is industry. One of its largest integrated manufacturers of heavy machinery is **IHI**
Ishikawajima-Harima Heavy Industries Co., Ltd., Tokyo, Japan

MARTIN MARIETTA MOVES *in cement,* *aggregates,*

Our aluminum subsidiary (formerly Harvey) has taken the Martin Marietta name. Now it's Martin Marietta Aluminum. As before, 82.7 percent-owned by Martin Marietta Corporation.

The other companies in our family are 100 percent-owned. Cement manufacture. Crushed stone, sand and gravel. Products for textile dyers, chemical admixtures for concrete and refractories for steel makers. Space and defense systems.

Plus aluminum.

MARTIN MARIETTA CORPORATION
New York Stock Exchange symbol: ML
1971 Sales: $958,843,000
Earnings before interest and taxes:
$110,291,000
Net Earnings: $56,466,000

MARTIN MARIETTA CEMENT
1971 Sales: $122,124,000
Operates 10 cement plants in the
Rockies, the Midwest, the Southeast,
the Middle Atlantic states and
New England.

MARTIN MARIETTA AGGREGATES
1971 Sales: $90,009,000
Shipped 48 million tons of crushed
stone, construction sand and gravel
from 209 locations in 1971.

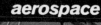

MARTIN MARIETTA
Ishikawajima-Harima
Heavy Industries Co., Ltd.

Topics for Discussion

1. What comes to your mind when you think of "heavy industry"? How does your mental picture compare with the picture in the advertisement for *Ishikawajima-Harima Heavy Industries*?
2. Why does the advertisement for heavy industry use a picture with muted colors? What effect does the advertisement aim to achieve?
3. How does the text of the heavy industries advertisement relate to the picture?
4. What is the purpose of both these advertisements? Is there any particular product advertised here?
5. What audience do you think these advertisements are designed for?

Rhetorical Considerations

1. What is the implication in the two sentences "Japan is beauty. And Japan is industry"?
2. How does the composition of the *Ishikawajima-Harima* advertisement emphasize the poem in the advertisement?
3. "*Martin Marietta* Moves" not only alliterates but implies something in the use of the verb "moves." What does it imply? How does this fit in with the rest of the advertisement?
4. What does each of the pictures in the *Martin Marietta* advertisement emphasize?
5. The text of the *Martin Marietta* advertisement is very factual. How does this relate to the purpose of the advertisement?

Marlboro

Topics for Discussion

1. What relevance do cowboys have to an advertisement for cigarettes? What appeal is being made here?
2. Why do you think one package of cigarettes is red and white while the other is gold and white?
3. Why are the cowboys riding toward you? What effect does this create?
4. What does this advertisement tell you about *Marlboro* cigarettes?

Rhetorical Considerations

1. Why is one kind of *Marlboro's* called *Longhorn 100's*? What is the connotation of the word *Longhorn*?
2. The caption in the advertisement tells the reader to "come to Marlboro country." How can the reader obey that command? Where is Marlboro country?
3. How do you "get a lot to like"? A lot of what? Why is the statement deliberately vague?

Advertisement for *Marlboro* cigarettes, from *Life*, July 7, 1972, reprinted by permission.

If your menthol isn't smooth enough, come all the way up to KOOL.

Advertisement for *Kool* cigarettes, © 1971 Brown & Williamson Tobacco Corporation. Reprinted by permission.

In 1907, Maggie Trude discovered that the best time to sneak a cigarette without her husband finding out was when he took his bath. Mrs. Trude insisted he bathe at least once a day.

You've come a long way, baby.

VIRGINIA SLIMS.

Slimmer than the fat cigarettes men smoke.

Fashions by Giorgio di Sant' Angelo

Regular: 17 mg."tar,"1.1 mg. nicotine—
Menthol: 18 mg."tar,"1.2 mg. nicotine av.
per cigarette, FTC Report Aug.'71

VIRGINIA
SLIMS
FILTER

BENSON & HEDGES
PARK AVENUE, NEW YORK
20 CLASS A CIGARETTES

Warning: The Surgeon General Has Determined That
Cigarette Smoking Is Dangerous to Your Health

Advertisement for *Virginia Slims* cigarettes, from *Woman's Day,* June 1972. Reprinted by permission of Philip Morris, Incorporated.

KOOL

Topics for Discussion

1. Why would a cigarette be named *Kool*? What effect does this name have? What similar names for cigarettes can you think of?
2. What is the appeal of this advertisement? How relevant is this appeal to cigarettes?
3. Is *Kool* a menthol cigarette? How does the advertisement reveal whether *Kool* is or not? Why is menthol mentioned in the advertisement?
4. What mood and effect are created by the dominance of the color green? Why are there no people in the advertisement?

Rhetorical Considerations

1. The caption of the advertisement is brief and ambiguous. Why does the caption refer to "your menthol" and not to "your menthol cigarette"?
2. The advertisement says to "come all the way up to *Kool*." Come up from where? Does this caption really say anything?
3. How does color function rhetorically in this advertisement?

VIRGINIA SLIMS

Topics for Discussion

1. Is this advertisement based on women's liberation, or does it exploit women? Base your answer on specific references to the advertisement.
2. Why is the modern woman smiling and partially covering her face?
3. What is the appeal of the advertisement? Is this advertisement directed only to women? Would a man smoke *Virginia Slims*?
4. The advertisement states that these cigarettes are "slimmer than the fat cigarettes men smoke." What does this statement imply about men and women? Why would women supposedly want a slim cigarette?
5. Is the right to smoke a mark of women's liberation? Why?
6. What is there in this advertisement that states why *Virginia Slims* are good cigarettes?

Rhetorical Considerations

1. Is this advertisement well organized?
2. The advertisement states that "you've come a long way, baby." Who is the "you" addressed? What does "come a long way" mean? From where? To where?
3. If the advertisement is addressed to women, why is a woman referred to as "baby"? Who normally calls a woman "baby"? Does this reveal anything about the advertisement?

The less you spend on a car, the more you can spend on other things.

This car gets up to 40 miles to the gallon.

Up to 75 miles an hour.

Overhead cam engine, rack and pinion steering, 4-speed synchromesh transmission, power-assisted front disc brakes, front bucket seats, radial tires, tachometer, racing mirror. All standard equipment.

Oh, it doesn't have automatic transmission, air conditioning, and a 400-horsepower engine.

But which would you rather have? Automatic transmission, air conditioning, and a 400-horse-power engine?

Or Michelle and Tammy and Alison?

The Honda Coupe. Under $1700.*
It makes a lot of sense.

Advertisement for *Honda Coupe,* from *Playboy,* May 1972, reprinted by permission of American Honda Motor Co., Inc., © 1972.

Honda

Topics for Discussion

1. What do you notice first in this advertisement—the car, the young women, or the headline at the top? What part of the advertisement do you think the advertiser wants you to notice?
2. Why is there no background color or design to this advertisement?
3. How does the text of the advertisement stress economy? Is the text consistent with the picture in the advertisement?
4. Why is no man in this advertisement, either behind the steering wheel of the car or standing next to it?
5. What is significant about the costume of the young woman on the left?
6. What does this advertisement imply about the relations between men and women?

Rhetorical Considerations

1. What are the "things" referred to in the headline?
2. What is the effect of using the exclamation "oh" in the text?
3. Many sentence fragments are used in the text. Why? What would happen if all the fragments were complete sentences?
4. Only certain parts of the text are in boldface type. What information do these parts stress?
5. The advertisement addresses the reader as "you." How do you know the "you" addressed is a man?

Nice 'n Easy

Topics for Discussion

1. What is your first reaction to this advertisement? Do you find this advertisement sexy? Why?
2. To whom do you think this advertisement appeals more, men or women?
3. This advertisement has been cited as an example of those advertisements that demean women. Do you agree with this charge? Why?
4. Why is the text not included in the picture but set off by itself at the bottom of the page?
5. This is an advertisement for hair coloring, or hair dye. What relation does this picture have to the product it advertises?

Rhetorical Considerations

1. What does "It lets me be me" mean? To what does "it" refer? To whom does "me" refer?
2. "In hair color, as in make-up, clothes, love, work . . . a woman wants to be herself." What is the significance of the order of items in this sentence? Why use three dots in the middle of this sentence and not another punctuation mark?
3. The caption of the advertisement refers to "me" while the text of the advertisement refers to "you." Why is there a shift in person?

It lets me be me:

Color that becomes part of you (not the other way around!)— that's what you get with Nice 'n Easy, from Clairol. Whether you want to color or conceal, to change a little or a lot, choose Nice 'n Easy, for beautiful coverage, healthy-looking hair and honest-to-you color.

Nice 'n Easy haircolor
It sells the most.

Advertisement for *Nice 'n Easy* hair coloring, from *McCall's* Magazine, October 1971. Reprinted by permission of Clairol Incorporated.

Advertisement for *Chanel No. 5* reprinted by permission of Chanel, Inc.

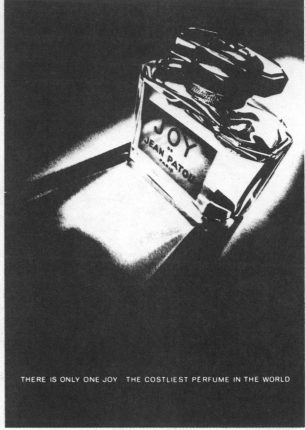

THERE IS ONLY ONE JOY   THE COSTLIEST PERFUME IN THE WORLD

Advertisement for *Joy* perfume, from *Playboy,* November 1972, reprinted by permission.

CHANEL JOY

Topics for Discussion

1. Does the use of color make the advertisement for *Chanel* more effective and appealing?
2. Does the use of lighting and composition make the advertisement for *Joy* more dramatic?
3. Why is there no text with the *Chanel* advertisement?
4. *Joy* perfume is called "the costliest perfume in the world." What appeal does this have?
5. Both advertisements use a black background. What effect does this background create?
6. Which advertisement appeals to you more? Why?

The phone company wants more operators like Rick Wehmhoefer.

Rick Wehmhoefer of Denver, Colorado, is one of several hundred male telephone operators in the Bell System.

Currently, Rick is a directory assistance operator. "So far, my job has been pleasant and worthwhile," he says. "I enjoy assisting people."

We have men like Rick in a lot of different telephone jobs. Both men and women work as Bell System mechanics, truck drivers, installers and engineers.

We want the men and women of the telephone company to do what they want to do, and do best.

Today, when openings exist, local Bell Companies are offering applicants and present employees some jobs they may never have thought about before. We want to help all advance to the best of their abilities.

AT&T and your local Bell Company are equal opportunity employers.

AT&T

Topics for Discussion

1. What is the purpose of these two advertisements?
2. What audience is each advertisement directed at?
3. How important is the picture in each advertisement? Would the texts be as effective without the pictures?
4. Alana MacFarlane is pictured by herself while there is someone next to Rick Wehmhoefer. Is there any reason for this?
5. How many similarities are there in these two advertisements?
6. Why is Alana MacFarlane called an "installer" and not a "lineman"?
7. Why does the headline on each advertisement refer to "the phone company" and not to *AT&T*?

Rhetorical Considerations

1. Why do the advertisements refer to "male telephone operator" and "woman telephone installer"? Why is it necessary to emphasize the sex of each job holder?
2. Compare the text in each advertisement. What similarities do you find?
3. Each advertisement contains a quotation by the person pictured. Why?
4. The advertisements refer to *AT&T* as "we" and "our." What effect does this achieve?

AIR FORCE

Topics for Discussion

1. Is the space program run by the U.S. Air Force? What relevance does the picture in this advertisement have to enlisting in the Air Force?
2. What is the appeal of this advertisement? How effective is it?
3. Although there is little color in this advertisement, it is printed in color and not black and white. Why?
4. Is there any danger this advertisement could become quickly out of date?
5. The text of the advertisement states that "the Air Force guarantees you a choice of jobs before you enlist." Do you think that choice includes astronaut? Does the advertisement imply there is this choice?

Rhetorical Considerations

1. Is there any particular order or composition to the picture in this advertisement? What elements are emphasized in the picture?
2. What is the ambiguity in the headline on this advertisement?
3. What audience is this advertisement directed at?

The Age of Communication

FIND YOURSELF IN THE AIR FORCE.

SCOTT, IRWIN & WORDEN DID.

Now the Air Force guarantees you a choice of jobs before you enlist. For more information, call 800-631-1972 toll free*. (*In New Jersey call 800-962-2803.)

Advertisement for Air Force Recruiting reprinted by permission.

Topics for Discussion

1. After reading David Ogilvy's essay "How to Write Potent Copy," apply Ogilvy's principles to one or two of the advertisements in this section.

2. According to law, cigarette advertisements must state the tar and nicotine content of the cigarette brand advertised. Also, the advertisement must carry the warning statement that cigarette smoking is dangerous. Compare the *Kool, Marlboro,* and *Virginia Slims* advertisements and see how each advertisement fulfills the law. Which one does it more effectively?

3. Compare the *Ford Mustang* and *Honda Coupe* advertisements. How do they differ in their appeal? Why does the *Honda* advertisement mention the price of the car while the *Ford* advertisement does not?

4. The advertisements for *AT&T, Martin Marietta,* and *Ishikawajima-Harima Heavy Industries* are corporate advertisements designed not to sell a product but to advance the corporation itself, to improve the corporation's "image." Compare these four advertisements. What is the purpose of each advertisement? Are there any similarities in the advertisements? Which advertisement do you find more effective? Why?

5. Both the *New England Life* advertisement and the public service advertisement against forest fires leave much unstated. Compare these two advertisements and determine which one leaves the more unstated. Do both advertisements use the same techniques to imply what they do not state?

6. Which advertisement in this section did you find most effective? Which advertisement did you find least effective? Compare the two advertisements and point out their comparative strengths and weaknesses.

7. Many people are upset by what they call bad taste in advertising. Do you find any of the advertisements in this section in bad taste?

8. Note the use of color in the advertisements in this section. Does the use of color make an advertisement more effective? Note particularly the advertisements for *Joy* and *Chanel No. 5.*

9. Which advertisements in this section have sexual overtones? In which ones is the sexual overtone more subtle? Do you think the use of sex to sell products is going out of style?

10. Choose any advertisement in this section and compare it to a current advertisement for a competing brand. You might, for example, compare the *Crest* advertisement with an advertisement for *Colgate.* What similarities and differences do you find?

Worriers, Swingers, Shoppers

'Psychographics' Can Tell Who'll Buy Crest, Who'll Buy Ultra Brite

By Daniel Henninger

SCENE: A typical American family—father, mother, and teen-aged daughter—is watching "The Every Night Movie" on television. A commercial appears showing a beautiful young girl walking through a rainstorm. A close-up reveals tears in her eyes. She stops and from her shoulder bag takes a small canary-yellow cylinder of "Can Dew" mouth spray. She pumps a few jets into her mouth and turns to greet a handsome young man. He smiles. She smiles. They embrace, kiss, and depart into the misting rain, followed by a deep male voice: "When you can't, Can Dew. Always."

Sitting with the family is a research specialist in "psychographics," an increasingly popular marketing science that uses psychology, sociology, and computers to help advertisers sell their products. He asks each family member's reaction to the commercial.

Daughter: "It looks pretty good. I've never used a mouth spray, but I think I'll try Can Dew."

Mother: "It's awful. Ads like this are the work of a bunch of subliminal sneaks who are teaching our kids aerosol emotions."

Father: "What commercial?"

The psychographics man is thrilled: All responded just as his computer predicted. He knew that the ad might enrage Mom and miss Dad. But the commercial sold its "target," their daughter. Although Can Dew is a fictional product, the ad is based on reality. The girl is a "target" because she belongs to a specific group of consumers identified by the computer as "a segment of the youthful population which has an active, socially oriented life style, is inclined to accept changing values and mores, and prefers personal-care products that promise cosmetic appeal rather than personal hygiene."

Identifying Life Styles

All that in a 30-second commercial? Yes, say the psychographics researchers. They maintain that the current TV audience, or "consumer market," has split into many disparate "segments." General commercial appeals to "the average consumer" are now less than successful, they say. What appeals to one segment of the market may annoy or disinterest other segments.

Psychographics (which has other imposingly murky names, such as "segmentation research" and "activity and attitude variables") tries to identify the personal values, attitudes, emotions and beliefs—the life style—common to a particular market segment. It then directs that segment, through finely tuned advertising, to a product that fits the group's psychographic portrait.

For example, everyone expects his tooth paste to prevent cavities, but people choose specific brands for other reasons. Russell Haley of Appel Haley Fouriezos, Inc., New York City, is a leading proponent of segmentation research. He describes four possible psychographic segments in the tooth-paste market: Worriers, Sociable, Independents, and Sensory.

Haley says the Worriers contain "a disproportionately large number of families with children." They are concerned about cavities and prefer fluoride tooth paste. "This is reinforced by their personalities," he says. "They tend to be a little hypochondriacal and, in their life styles, they are less socially oriented than some of the other groups." Their brand is Crest, whose ads portray a Responsible Father dedicated to his son's healthy teeth.

The Sociables, Haley says, "is where the swingers are." They are young marrieds, active, and probably smoke a lot. To assure teeth that are Ali MacGraw white they use Plus White, Macleans, or Ultra Brite, which "gives your mouth—sex appeal!"

'Voyeurs Into the Psyche'

Price-conscious men dominate the Independents. They "see very few meaningful differences between brands," says Haley. They think for themselves, trust their judgment when buying, and shop for tooth paste on sale.

The Sensory segment prefers tooth paste pleasing in flavor and appearance. Most Sensories are

Daniel Henninger, "Worriers, Swingers, Shoppers," *The National Observer* (June 10, 1972), vol. 2, no. 24, pp. 1 & 19.

Advertising

children who choose Stripe and Colgate.

Haley suggests that advertising for the Sociable and Sensory segments should be light; for the Worriers, serious; for the Independents, "rational, two-sided arguments."

Shirley Young, director of research services for Grey Advertising, Inc., New York City, says psychographic analysis includes "attitudes about the product category, about brands, as well as attitudes which reflect personality and attitudes about life style. The personality and life-style data, of course, are what's relatively new. It provides the juicy stuff that captures the imagination of the researcher and marketer alike. It allows us to become voyeurs into the psyche of the consumer."

Are we really that tough to sell, or is Madison Avenue substituting psychographics for its failed imagination? Long-time TV viewers may recall an old commercial in which a band of pixies hopped around the bathroom sink and tub, polishing and singing: "So use Ajax, bum, bum, the Foaming Cleanser. Floats the dirt right down the drain." That commercial first appeared in 1948, but it still sticks in the minds of many people.

It is possible, though, that no one would notice or remember that ad if it appeared for the first time today. The pixies would fall victim to the ad world's worst nemesis, the "perceptual screen." Americans watch endless hours of television, and to survive the accompanying commercial flood they have developed perceptual screens: They watch the ads without letting them register. Dad's perceptual screen was up when he answered "What commercial?" to the Can Dew mouth-spray ad.

Researchers have shown volunteers a 30-minute film of a drama or comedy broken by three commercials. The next day many of the volunteers could not recall seeing any commercials. The Quaker Oats Co. recently telephoned several hundred viewers of six popular programs one day after they appeared and found only 3 per cent remembered brands advertised on specific shows.

Confounding the Demographers

In the past advertisers tried (and some still try) to penetrate the screens by tailoring ads to broad population segments sharing common demographic characteristics—income, sex, age, and residence. But advertisers often find demographic data to be unreliable or incomplete.

For example, many middle-aged fathers still conform to a demography of high income and conservative taste in fashion and leisure interests. But today several men on the same block—the conservatives' demographic peers—may have adopted their children's fashions. The kids in turn throw away *their* bright clothes, resurrect dad's GI jacket, and all wear blue denim. Yet the young spend $9 a week on gas, one survey shows, and 50 per cent of them use mouthwash.

This family defies conventional demography. How do I reach such people? the advertiser wonders. More importantly, how and where do I find them?

Enter the psychographics researcher carrying a market basket full of sharply defined "segments."

Of Cars and Potions

A psychographics study by MPI Marketing Research, Inc., for American Motors Corp. found that new-car buyers worry most about having problems during the first year of ownership. American Motors' Guaranteed Car Campaign resulted, guaranteeing the free repair or replacement of any defective part, except tires, for one year or 12,000 miles.

Benton and Bowles, Inc., a New York City ad agency, did a psychographic study of housewives' attitudes and divided the drug market into four categories:

Realists "view remedies positively, want something that is convenient and works, and do not feel the need for a doctor-recommended medicine."

"Authority Seekers are doctor- and prescription-oriented" and "prefer the stamp of authority on what they do take."

"Skeptics have a low health concern, are least likely to resort to medication, and are highly skeptical of cold remedies."

Conversely, Hypochondriacs "regard themselves as prone to any bug going around and tend to take medication at the first symptom."

Translating their findings into possible advertising strategies, Benton and Bowles said that Realists "could be reasoned with on practical terms" and "should not be depicted as either overly sick or overly concerned." Authority Seekers "would be receptive to claims that specify doctor's approval, laboratory testing, to advertising with an ethical aura or prescription look." Admen sometimes call this "man-in-the-white-coat information."

Authority Seekers. The Sociables. Psychographics. It sounds as if the Viennese psychologists are still mixing their motivational theories with the daily horoscope. "You are buying a red convertible because you can't afford a mistress."

In fact, psychographics is the product of statisticians, sociologists, and psychologists trying to figure out how a shifting market of finite consumption capacity can absorb an endless proliferation of goods and services. For them, computers have replaced the couch.

Psychographics researchers obtain their information from large population samples through personal interviews or mail questionnaires. Motivational researchers such as Ernest Dicter [The National Observer, Nov. 13, 1971] rely on in-depth interviews with individuals or small groups. Proponents of psychographics admit that the motivational people can sometimes identify market segments similar to theirs, but they say large-sample statistical analysis is more reliable than a psychologist's judgment, which may be influenced unintentionally by subjective factors.

'Conscientious Vigilants'

Benton and Bowles mailed questionnaires to 2,000 housewives for its study of their product attitudes. A computer analysis of the 1,600 responses received classified some of the women, for example, as Conscientious Vigilants who tend to be "conscientious, rigid, meticulous, germ-fighting, with a high cleanliness orientation." They have "sensible attitudes about food. They have a high cooking pride, careful shopping orientation, tend not to be convenience-oriented."

In a TV commercial this Conscientious Vigilant might be portrayed sniffing out household odors, killing them with disinfectant spray. Her war on bacteria might amuse some women, but it might also draw other Vigilants to the product.

Correctly identifying distinct consumer segments such as the Conscientious Vigilant is acutely important because many product categories—analgesics, breakfast cereals, toiletries, deodorants—are filled with products that all do pretty much the same thing. What imposes order on product chaos is "positioning."

If brands A, B, and C are almost identical, they must establish some product distinction in the consumer's mind. They must assume different "positions" in the market and appeal to specific segments of it. Otherwise there may be little basis for customer loyalty to any of the products. Avis, for example, "positioned" itself in the car-rental market by saying, "We're Number Two."

Seeking Holes in the Screen

In seeking open positions a company may turn to the psychographics people, whose research chops up the market and tells the company what segments are available. Sometimes the studies turn up a previously unidentified segment. "That's the ideal," says the market-research director of a large analgesic manufacturer. "Take one of your established brands and tap that market or come up with another product and go after that group."

Some years ago, while at Grey Advertising, Russell Haley made a psychographic study of the cigaret market for the P. Lorillard Co., whose brand sales had leveled off. Haley discovered a segment of highly independent smokers, and an ad campaign stressing independence was developed for Old Gold cigarets. In one ad, says Haley: "A guy driving on a crowded throughway would turn off and drive on another road by himself. That was for the man who likes to make up his mind." Old Gold's sales increased.

It is estimated that the "average consumer" encounters about 300 commercial messages of all types daily. Day after day these commercial suitors pour out their promises to millions of unnervingly fickle consumers. Like a computerized dating service making matches less by love than logic, the psychographics man rummages through the market place, searching with his questionnaires and computers for consumer segments statistically compatible with his client's product. For his services the psychographics researcher may charge between $30,000 and $300,000. We segments are expensive.

Topics for Discussion

1. What is your reaction to the hypothetical advertisement described in the opening of this article? Have you seen similar advertisements on television?
2. What brand of toothpaste do you use? Were you influenced by advertising in choosing your present brand? Are you loyal to a particular brand or do you simply buy any brand that is convenient or on sale? Would you classify yourself a Worrier, Sociable, Independent, or Sensory toothpaste user?
3. Psychographics enables researchers "to become voyeurs into the psyche of the consumer." What does this mean? As a consumer, what is your reaction to this function of psychographics?
4. Henninger says that every day the average consumer encounters some 300 commercials. As a result, consumers have developed what is called a "perceptual screen" to block out certain commercials. How does your perceptual screen operate? What commercials do you "turn off"? What commercials can you remember right now?
5. What current commercials do you like best? Why? Do you use the products they promote?

Rhetorical Considerations

1. How effective is the opening of this article? Could Henninger have used a more effective opening? Suggest at least one other technique for beginning this article.
2. Psychographics is certainly a very technical subject for a newspaper article. What devices does Henninger use to simplify a difficult subject?
3. Examine the vocabulary used in this article. What kind of readers do you think make up Henninger's audience?
4. Look at the final sentence of the article. What is significant about the use of the pronoun "we"?

Advertising and Intensional Orientation

S. I. Hayakawa

Among the forces in our present culture contributing to intensional orientation, advertising must be counted as one of the most important. The fundamental purpose of advertising—the announcing of products, prices, new inventions, or special sales—is not to be quarreled with: such announcements deliver needed information, which we are glad to get. But in national advertising directed to the consumer, the techniques of persuasion are rarely informative. As stated in the previous chapter on "Poetry and Advertising," the main endeavor is to "poeticize" or glamorize the objects you wish to sell by giving them brand names and investing those names with all sorts of desirable affective connotations suggestive of health, wealth, popularity with the other sex, social prominence, domestic bliss, fashion, and elegance. The process is one of creating intensional orientations toward brand names:

> If you want love interest to thrive, then try this dainty way. . . . For this way is glamorous! It's feminine! It's alluring! . . . Instinctively, you prefer this costly perfume of Verona Soap. . . . It's a fragrance men love. Massage each tiny ripple of your body daily with this delicate, cleansing lather. . . . Thrill as your senses are kissed by Verona's exquisite perfume. Be radiant.

Advertisers further promote intensional habits of mind by playing on words: the "extras" of skill and strength that enable champions to win games are equated with the "extras" of quality that certain products are claimed to have; the "protective blending" that harmonizes wild animals with their environment and makes them invisible to their enemies is equated with the "protective blending" of whiskies.

There is another subtle way in which advertising promotes intensional habits: through the practice of making slogans out of commonplace facts, advertisers make the facts appear to be unique to particular products. Rosser Reeves, head of Ted Bates and Company advertising agency, cites with admiration a number of phenomenally successful campaigns using this technique—the parenthetical comments are his own: OUR BOTTLES ARE WASHED WITH LIVE STEAM" ("His client protested that every other brewery did the same"); "IT'S TOASTED" ("So, indeed, is every other cigarette"); "GETS RID OF FILM ON TEETH" ("So, indeed, does every other toothpaste"); "STOPS HALITOSIS" ("Dozens of mouth-washes stop halitosis"); "STOPS B.O." ("All soaps stop body odor").[1] The skill that advertisers and propagandists often display in this kind of slanting reminds us of William Blake's famous warning:

> A truth that's told with bad intent
> Beats all the lies you can invent.

When advertising by verbal hypnotism succeeds in producing these intensional orientations, the act of washing with Verona Soap becomes, in our minds, a thrilling experience indeed. Brushing our teeth with Colgate toothpaste becomes a dramatic and timely warding off of terrible personal calamities, like getting fired or losing one's girl friend. The smoking of Marlboros becomes an assertion of masculinity (instead of a possible invitation to lung cancer)—making one a rugged, outdoor, he-man type, like a telephone line-man or a paratrooper—even though in actuality one may be simply a clerk at a necktie counter. The taking of unnecessary (and even dangerous) laxatives becomes "following the advice of a world-renowned Viennese specialist." We are sold daydreams with every bottle of mouthwash and delusions of grandeur with every package of breakfast food.

Advertising, then, has become in large part the art of overcoming us with pleasurable affective connotations. When the consumer demands that, as a step toward guiding himself by facts rather than by affective connotations of brand names, certain products be required by law to have informative labels and verifiable government grading, the advertising industry raises a hue-and-cry about "government interference with business."[2] This is the sort of argument presented against grade-labeling, *in spite of the fact that business-men, both retailers and wholesalers, rely extensively on grading according to federally established standards when they do their own purchasing.*

In other words, many advertisers *prefer* that we be governed by automatic reactions to brand names rather than by thoughtful consideration of the facts about their products. An important reason for this preference lies in the me-chanics of present-day retail distribution. Most of the buying of groceries, for example, is done at supermarkets, where the housewife must make choices among huge and dazzling displays of packaged merchandise, with no clerk to explain to her the advantages of one choice over another. Therefore, to use the terminology of the trade, she must be "pre-sold" *before* she gets to the market—and this is done by getting her to remember, through tireless reiteration on radio and television commercials, a brand name, and by invest-ing that name with nothing but pleasant connotations.

Thoughtful purchasing is the last thing many merchandisers want. Once the customer is hooked on a brand name, all sorts of tricks can be played on him (or her). A currently widespread practice is to reduce the contents of a package without reducing its size or price; many items traditionally bought in one-pound and half-pound packages now come in such sizes as 15 oz., 14½ oz., 7 oz., and 6¾ oz. These figures arre usually printed in tiny letters on the package in places where they are least likely to be seen. For the unwary housewife, the costs of "brand loyalty" can be high.[3]

Within recent years, the advertising of brand names has climbed to a higher level of abstraction. In addition to the advertising of specific products by their brand name, there is now *advertising of advertising*. As the pamphlet of the Brand Names Research Foundation urges, "So it's up to you as a salesman for a brand name to keep pushing not only your BRAND, but brands in general. *Get on the Brand Wagon!*" A whisky advertisement says: "AMERICA IS NAMES . . . Seattle, Chicago, Kansas City . . . Elm Street, North Main, Times Square . . . Wrigley, Kellogg, Squibb, Ipana . . . Heinz, Calvert . . . Goodrich . . . Chevrolet. Names [the American has] always known . . . names of things he's bought and used . . . believed in. . . . Yes, America is names. *Good* names. Familiar names that inspire confidence. . . . For America *is* names . . . *good* names for good things to have. . . ." This sort of advertising of advertising has become increasingly common. The assumption is dinned into us that if a brand name even *sounds* familiar, the product it stands for must be good ("The best in the land if you buy by brand.") *A graver example of systematic public miseducation can hardly be imagined. Intensional orientation is elevated to a guiding principle in the life of the consumer.*

Sometimes it seems as if the conflict between the aims of the advertiser and those of the educator is irreconcilable. When the teacher of home economics says, "Buy wisely," she means careful and reflective purchasing in the light of one's real needs and of accurate information about the product. When the advertiser says, "Buy wisely," he often means, "Buy our brand, regardless of your special situation or special needs, because DUZ DOES EVERYTHING!" The teacher's job is to encourage intellectual and moral self-discipline. The job of the advertiser often seems to be to encourage thoughtlessness ("impulse buying") and self-indulgence, even at the cost of life-long bondage to finance companies.

However, I am far from certain that the conflict between the aims of the advertiser and the educator is inevitable. It is inevitable *if* advertising cannot perform its functions *except* through the promotion of mistaken reactions to words and other symbols. Because advertising is both so powerful and so widespread, it influences more than our choice of products; it also influences our patterns of evaluation. It can either increase or decrease the degree of sanity with which people respond to words. Thus, if advertising is informative, witty, educational, and imaginative, it can perform its necessary commercial function and contribute to our pleasure in life without making us slaves to the tyranny of affective words. If, however, products are sold largely by manipulating affective connotations—"*pin-point* carbonation," "*activated* chlorophyll," "*dual-filter* Tareytons," "contains *RD-119*," "*tired blood*"—the influence of advertising is to deepen the already grave intensional orientations widely prevalent in the public. The schizophrenic is one who attributes a greater reality to words, fantasies, daydreams, and "private worlds" than to the actualities around him. Surely it is possible for advertising to perform its functions without aggravating our all-too-prevalent verbomania! Or is it?

---

[1] Rosser Reeves, *Reality in Advertising* (1961), pp. 55–57.

[2] For example, a pamphlet called "Your Bread and Butter: A Salesman's Handbook on the Subject of Brand Names," prepared by "Brand Names Research Foundation" (no address given), undertakes to explain "What's Behind All the Smoke" of the consumer movement which, for many years, has demanded grade-labeling of consumer goods. Most of the members of women's organizations in the consumer movement, the pamphlet says, are "honestly concerned with solving the perennial problems of common sense buying," but a "vocal minority" of "self-appointed champions of the consumer" are the "spokesmen." This minority, it is explained, "want to standardize most consumer goods, to eliminate advertising and competing brands, to see government controls extended over production, distribution and profits. They believe in a planned economy, with a government brain trust doing all the planning."

[3] Not all proprietors of brand names do this sort of thing, of course. The following comments from readers published in *Consumer Reports* give the other side of the picture: "It has always impressed me how the *Wheatena* cooked-cereal boxes are filled so close to the top that they can hardly be opened without running over. What a happy experience to encounter in today's world of commerce." "I am happy to call attention to the *Hi Ho* crackers package. A one-pound size, so designated in large type on the front and back, was a welcome relief."

Topics for Discussion

1. What does Hayakawa mean when he defines advertising as "the art of overcoming us with pleasurable affective connotations"? Does this definition mean anything to you? Does Hayakawa explain his definition?
2. Hayakawa lists at least three ways in which advertisers promote brand loyalty. What are these three ways?
3. Are you "pre-sold" on any particular brands of products? That is, do you shop for certain products by brand name? How "brand loyal" are you?
4. Hayakawa says that many products that were once sold in 1-pound and ½-pound packages are now sold in such odd sizes as 15 oz., 7 oz., and 6½ oz. Is such a parctice honest? Do you check the contents of a package, or do you simply buy by brand name?
5. Look at the last paragraph of this article. Is Hayakawa "anti-advertising"? What changes would he make in advertising?

Rhetorical Considerations

1. This selection is an excerpt from a college textbook. How is this reflected in Hayakawa's vocabulary, sentence style, and paragraph structure?
2. Note the use of such transitional words and phrases as "in other words," "then," and "however" to give this selection coherence and unity. What other devices are used?
3. The last paragraph is Hayakawa's conclusion yet he uses the word "if" three times. Does this affect the definiteness of his conclusion?
4. What effect does the last sentence of the final paragraph have? Is it good writing to end an essay with a question?

The Built-in Sexual Overtone

Vance Packard

THE POTENCY of sex as a sales promoter was not, of course, an original discovery of the depth merchandisers. Sex images have long been cherished by ad men purely as eye stoppers. But with the depth approach, sex began taking on some interesting twists, ramifications, and subtleties. Penetration to deeper levels of consciousness was sought. Simple cheesecake and get-your-man themes of old, while used for routine selling, were regarded as limited-penetration weapons.

One shortcoming of get-your-man themes was that they frequently left the buyer disappointed and resentful. Perfume makers, in straining to outpromise each other in the early fifties with sex-drenched titles and themes, had trouble getting women to buy a second bottle when the first bottle, rich in sexual promise, had failed to deliver a satisfactory man into their arms. The Institute for Motivational Research, after exploring this problem, reported finding many women's dressers cluttered with "dead enthusiasm"—stale jars, unopened bottles, half-used boxes of cosmetics. It found that there is a dismally low rate of brand loyalty among users and that the industry has had to combat disappointment and raise new hopes by constantly bringing out new products, an expensive and discouraging process. (Ad men at conventions tell the story of the wistful girl who surveyed all the passionate labels on a perfume counter and asked bashfully if the store perhaps had something for beginners.) In 1955 more than 250 new trade-marks were issued in the toilet preparation field. Another difficulty harassing the cosmetics people was that modern women were no longer bewitched by a mere get-your-man or sexual enchantment promise. They wanted something more: to be accepted and respected by men as *partners,* and that of course was something a little more difficult for a mere perfume merchant to promise. It would take thought. In the words of the institute the situation called for "more subtle and more passive sex symbols than was the case a generation ago" with careful emphasis on such ingredients as poetry, fantasy, whimsey, and a distinct soft-pedaling of pure sex.

While sex was soft-pedaled for marketing in depth, its use as a simple eye stopper took more daring forms. The public had become jaded and permissive. The brassière and girdle appeals, for example, became bolder, with overtones of masochism, body exhibitionism, and so on. One ad widely exhibited showed a lovely girl with blond tresses, dressed only in her bra and girdle, being dragged by the hair across the floor by a modern caveman. The gay title was "Come out of the bone age, darling!" Another girdle ad showed a girl and her boyfriend at a Coney Island type of wind tunnel with the wind blowing her skirt above her head and exposing her entire mid-section, which, of course, was encased in the girdle being offered for sale. She was giggling modestly.

The most controversial of the eye stoppers of this sort was the "I Dreamed I Stopped Traffic in My Maidenform Bra" campaign. The situations varied but always the girl involved, dressed fully except that she wore only a bra above the waist, was wandering about among normally dressed people. The theory was that since she was dreaming, her undressed state was permissible. The ad men themselves argued about the wisdom of this ad and the deep-down effect it had on women seeing it. Some were convinced, after talking with their psychological consultants, that the scene depicted would simply produce an anxiety state in women since it represented a common oneiric, or dream, expression of the neurotic anxieties experienced by many women. Others in the trade, however, became convinced after checking their psychologists that the ad was sound because the wish to appear naked or scantily clad in a crowd is "present in most of us" and "represents a beautiful example of wish fulfillment." This view evidently prevailed because the campaign was intensified and Maidenform began offering the public prizes up to $10,000 for ideas on dream situations that could be depicted.

The twists given sex in the hands of the depth merchandisers took some odd forms. A study was made for a major fountain-pen company in the Midwest on the sensuality and sexual connotations of pens. R. R. McMurry, psychological consultant of Chicago, made the study into the motivation for buying fountain pens and concluded that the pen is experienced as a body image by men—which is why they will pay up to fifteen dollars for a pen with an image particularly satisfying to them even though a cheaper one might write just as well.

An evidence of the extent to which sexual appeals have been carried is available in the so-called sport of wrestling. The discovery was made that the grunt-and-groan spectacles of professional wrestling, supposedly a sweaty he-man sport, survive only because of the feminine fans. A Nielsen check of TV fans watching wrestling matches revealed that ladies outnumbered men two to one. The promoters of the matches, shrewdly calculating the triggers that produced the most squeals from feminine fans, stepped up the sadism (men writhing in torture), the all-powerful male symbolism (chest beating and muscle flexing), and fashion interest (more and more elegant costumes for the performers).

A classic example of the way motivation analysts found merchandising possibilities in our deeper sexual yearnings was a study Dr. Dichter made for Chrysler Corporation in the early days of M.R. His study is now known as "Mistress versus Wife."

Dr. Dichter was called upon to explain a fact puzzling marketers of the auto. While most men bought sedans and rarely bought convertibles they evidently were more attracted to convertibles. Dealers had found that they could draw more males into their showrooms by putting convertibles in the window. After exploring the situation Dr. Dichter concluded that men saw the convertible as a possible symbolic mistress. It set them daydreaming of youth, romance, adventure just as they may dream of a mistress. The man knows he is not going to gratify his wish for a mistress, but it is pleasant to daydream. This daydreaming drew the man into the auto salesroom. Once there, he finally chose a four-door sedan just as he once married a plain girl who, he knew, would make a fine wife and mother. "Symbolically, he marries the sedan," a spokesman for Dr. Dichter explained. The sedan is useful, practical, down to earth, and safe. Dr. Dichter felt that the company would be putting its best foot backward if it put its main emphasis on sedans simply because that was the car most men ended up buying. Instead, he urged the company to put the hope of mistress-adventure a little closer to males by giving most prominent display to the convertibles. The spokesman went on to explain Dr. Dichter's line of thinking: "If we get a union between the wife and mistress—all we sought in a wife plus the romance, youth, and adventure we want in a mistress—we would have . . . lo and behold, the hardtop!" The hardtop was soon to become the most successful new auto style introduced in the American market for several years, and Dr. Dichter's organization takes full credit for inspiring it by its "Mistress versus Wife" study.

The motivational analysts began finding that a major sexual need of both men and women in America at mid-century was sexual reassurance. Women by the millions were yearning for evidence that they were still basically feminine; and men by the millions were yearning for evidence they were still indisputably and virulently masculine. Merchandisers were quick to see the possibilities of offering both products that would serve as reassurance symbols.

Women were in need of evidences of reassurance because during the first half of the century their role in life had been undergoing radical changes: they had lost many of their old functions, had taken over many male functions, and in business had often fought to be accepted on the same basis as men.

During one of the psychiatric brain-storming sessions conducted at the Weiss and Geller agency the conferees began speculating on the fact that much of the "sex business" in cosmetic advertising seemed to be bringing inadequate responses and one of the consultants offered this insight: "I think the modern ad should place more emphasis on one term Erich Fromm [the noted analyst] pointed out, one that is almost missing in our society. That is tenderness." And he went on to explain: "I mention that because of what Fromm points out as the tremendous mark on the part of the woman who is constantly trying to get ahead and who pays such enormous penalty for it by her failure to be tender."

The agency began applying this line of thinking to its merchandising of lingerie and hair preparations for women. This meant quite a change. As one official explained its efforts to sell hair preparations: "We used to handle it by having a guy's nose stuck in the dame's hair." Under the new thinking the guy's nose went completely out of the picture. Get-your-man themes became outmoded. The new emphasis was on themes that would reassure the woman of her own femininity. The agency made a depth study on the problem of marketing lingerie and concluded that when it comes to approval symbols the woman first of all wants to be able to look approvingly at herself and feel assured she is fully feminine, and second she wants the approval of other women. Approval of the male—as typified in ad symbology by the admiring glance of a romantic-looking male—was judged to be the least effective way of the three to sell lingerie. Upon arriving at this insight the agency mapped an ad strategy for its lingerie that consisted simply of showing a woman admiring herself in the lingerie in a full-length mirror, and urged all women to do the same. Such an appeal, of course, had strong overtones of narcissism. It proved a strong sales booster, and the sales of the lingerie in question climbed in two years far ahead of the industry trend.

Professor Smith, in his book on M.R., reports incidentally, that this agency saved itself from hitting a hidden reef, in trying to sell a hair preparation to women, by getting timely counsel from social scientists. The idea, and it had seemed a brilliant one, was to sell a home permanent by showing identical hairdos of mother and daughter with the headline, "A Double Header Hit with Dad." It was cute, and when they asked wives casually—and at the conscious level—if the wives would resent the idea of being compared with their daughter in competition for the husband-father's admiration, they dismissed the possibility that such a competition could exist. The agency was apprehensive, however, and decided to explore the question in depth interviews. There it became quickly evident that women would indeed deeply resent a double "hit with Dad" theme. It was dropped.

As for men and their need for sexual reassurance, it was discovered that reassurance symbols would be appealing to them because women had been invading so many domains that they were being hard put to demonstrate that they were still he-men. After all, women were wearing trousers and standing up at bars.

One publication that thrived by offering a product strongly pervaded with masculine sexual reassurance was *True Magazine*. It grew to 2,000,000 circulation largely by offering assurance to men at bay. It addressed its 2,000,000 male readers, the bulk of whom obviously had sedentary lives, as if they were all hairy-chested sourdoughs who had just returned from a tramp in the woods. And it voiced man's resentment at woman's "creeping equality." Its editorial director Ralph Daigh told a group of men in early 1956 that man in "unprecedented numbers" had turned to *True* because it "stimulates his masculine ego at a time when man wants to fight back against women's efforts to usurp his traditional role as head of the family."

The problem of marketing razors and shaving preparations can be simplified, depth merchandisers discovered, if man's feelings toward his beard are understood. The psychologists on the staff of a New York advertising agency found in a study that the beard is very important symbolically to man. Investigators found that for some men the mere daily act of cutting off this symbol of manliness is a kind of daily castration. Some men admitted that they perspired when they shaved, and many complained about what a chore and bother it was. In a test survey, however, a number of men were given this hypothetical question: If a cream was offered for sale at a reasonable price which in three applications would rid you of your beard forever so that you would never need to shave again, would you buy it? The response? Practically none of the men was interested. Only 3 per cent of them showed any interest in buying such a wondrous product. One of those few men who did show interest explained, "It would be O.K., because I've got hair on my chest."

The fact that cigar makers have been enjoying the heaviest sales in a quarter century (6,000,000,000 cigars in 1955) has been credited by some to the man-at-bay market. The cigar certainly is one of the potent symbols of masculinity available, certainly the most potent available for a dime. When men assemble at stag parties or "smokers" where women are barred, they all light up stogies, even those who have difficulty suppressing a fit of coughing. The cigar, in our minds, is a symbol of masculine toughness: it is favored by gangsters and hardboiled bankers. An ad agency, Young and Rubicam, found in a depth study that young men feel uneasy smoking cigars, presumably because cigars are such virility symbols that they feel a bit presumptuous trying to smoke them. A study made by a Chicago ad agency (Weiss and Geller) turned up the fact that cigars appeal both to men who are very strong, and to men who are basically weak and small. A cigar helps the little guy feel big. When a new father passes out cigars to his friend the true meaning of this, according to one depth study, is that he is in effect trying to crow: "What a man am I to have produced a child!"

And when a man politely asks ladies if they mind if he smokes a cigar, according to one theory, he is being less than sincere. He actually is defiantly asserting his masculinity. As Edward Weiss explained it, "He knows darned well he is going to stink up the room."

Mr. Weiss became intrigued with the symbol meanings of cigars when a cigar campaign that showed a woman beaming as she offered cigars to men backfired. Mr. Weiss ordered a depth study to find out why. The conclusion was that men smoke cigars to assert their masculinity and like to think the habit is objectionable to women. Any message that runs counter to this deprives the man of one of his main reasons for smoking cigars.

Despite these warnings from Mr. Weiss it appears that the cigar makers as a whole intend to try to get women into the picture. There are sound marketing reasons for this. It seems that when women are shopping in supermarkets they can be persuaded to pick up a handful of cigars to take home to their husbands. The possibilities of cigars as impulse items for wives are so appealing that the Cigar Institute of America began featuring, in 1956, a woman approving her husband's cigar smoking in a $200,000 campaign to be used on Father's Day. News reports stated that the Cigar Institute had its "eye on the woman shopper" and that a move was afoot to build good manners into cigar smoking. The cigar, evidently, was about to be demasculinized, for the sake of volume.

The motivational analysts began finding that products have fundamental differences of meaning for men and women. This knowledge soon was enabling the merchandisers hiring them to be more precise in shaping and aiming their appeals. The attitude of a man and woman toward their new car, for example, shows a gap in motivations. Whereas the woman can't wait to ride in it, the man can't wait to start polishing and taking care of it. Women in recent years have attained an increased voice in determining what car will be purchased. Their voice is particularly persuasive in deciding the color and styling of the family chariot. Car makers are taking this into account. As one maker proclaimed in 1956: "You never had it so safe and so stylish!"

Dr. Dichter brought the auto-servicing industry to attention in the early fifties by pointing out that it was gearing its sales messages to the wrong sex. Marketers had been gearing their sales messages for filling station products to the man of the family exclusively since he was well known to be the practical one in the family. Dr. Dichter, however, reported (and most of us upon thinking about it know he is right): "When we conducted our study we found something had happened—particularly in suburban areas. Apparently the woman has taken over and she has taken over quite thoroughly. She is really the one who has the car fixed; she is the one who discovers the first rattle; and she is the one who knows Charlie, the mechanic, much better than her husband does. . . ."

In our buying of homes our motivation evidently varies considerably depending upon our sex. Several years ago a large community development near Chicago faced the problem of selling a thousand houses quickly. To expedite the seemingly formidable task it retained a depth-oriented ad agency in Chicago. The agency called in several psychiatrists for counsel, and a depth study was made to find the triggers of action that would propel prospects into a home-buying mood. The task of selling the houses was complicated, the probers found, by the fact that men saw home in quite a different light from women. Man sees home as a symbolic Mother, a calm place of refuge for him after he has spent an abrasive day in the competitive outside world, often taking directions from a boss. He hopes wistfully to find in his idealized home the kind of solace and comfort he used to find as a child when at his mother's side.

Women on the other hand see home as something quite different since they already are symbolic Mothers. A woman sees home as an expression of herself and often literally as an extension of her own personality. In a new home she can plant herself and grow, re-create herself, express herself freely. As a result of these insights the agency devised several hard-hitting themes to reach both men and women. One ad that was drawn up to appeal especially to men showed a small home with two feminine arms stretching out, seemingly beckoning the troubled male reader to the bosom of her hearth. Mom would take care of him!

During the mid-fifties many different products that were judged by motivational analysts to be maladjusted sexually began undergoing a planned transvestism. These changes in sex were felt to be necessary often in order to cope with changing buying habits.

Whisky, gin, and beer for example had traditionally been garbed in two-fisted male vestments in keeping with the assumed sex of the buyer. *Vogue*, the ladies' fashion magazine, became suspicious of this assumption in the mid-fifties and surveyed four hundred retail liquor stores. It found 38 per cent of the dealers reporting that more than half of their liquor customers were women. The women evidently were ignoring many of the old taboos about liquor, perhaps because liquor stores were starting to be grouped in shopping centers. Dorothy Diamond, an advertising writer, took her male colleagues to task for being so outdated. "If I were to become acquainted with American drinking habits merely from advertising I would assume that whisky and gin are consumed solely by men. Clubmen, sportsmen, men in evening clothes . . . but women, never." She conceded there were still some taboos with potency, but felt the liquor people could do a much better job of appealing to the little woman, especially in gift items. "Actually many hostesses prefer it to candy," she said, and she exhorted the industry to do something to "make the average liquor store a more attractive place to shop," with festive windows and well-styled interiors. In catering merely to men the liquor stores had neglected *décor* so that the average liquor store, she felt, was as listless as a leftover highball.

Fleischmann's Gin, in seeking to cope with the sexual revolution, turned to Louis Cheskin for guidance. He suggested a slight change in the label design which probably wasn't even noticed by the average buyer but which, he claims, distinctly modified its sex appeal and brought a great increase in business for the company. The old label was a plain rectangle with sharp right-angle corners. Mr. Cheskin merely rounded the corners, which reportedly made the label more feminine.

One big trend of 1956 in liquor merchandising, the race to bring out whisky in decanters, was also partly a response to the new sexual situation. Women, it was found, like nice decorative bottles. This trend developed troubles in depth, however, that gave the marketers grave second thoughts. Studies showed that many people who had bought decanter-type liquor bottles felt a sense of guilt about seeing old whisky bottles sitting around the house as lamp bases, or if they hadn't converted them into something attractive such as lampshades they again felt guilty because they hadn't gotten their full money's worth from the bottle.

The beer brewers, too, had been caught napping. In 1955 the United States Brewers' Foundation exhorted members to stop assuming the average beer buyer was an older man. The average beer buyer, it said after researching the subject, was a woman between twenty-five and thirty-six who buys beer out of her weekly food budget and is particularly prone to female-oriented ads, nice packaging, and display.

The beer packagers began tampering with their can's sex

appeal in ways that must have made some he-man customers uneasy. Pabst began stressing fashion as a selling lure by using the selling line "The finest is always in fashion," and its ads began showing stylish young people of both sexes partaking of beer. Budweiser, meanwhile, came out with a slim new beer can aimed at the woman buyer. The merchandising director explained that the can was being made "high style" to "appeal to the woman buyer. . . . We believe that the innate preference of women for grace, beauty, and style carries over to the purchase of beer."

A spectacular transvestism in the opposite direction was carried out in 1956 by Marlboro cigarettes, which used to be lipstick red and ivory tipped, designed primarily for women. Marlboro felt a little unhappy about its sexual designation because men smokers still outnumbered women two to one. When the cancer scare drove millions of men to show interest in filter tips, the Marlboro people decided to do a sexual flip-flop and go after the men, while holding onto as many women as they could. Their first move was to have Louis Cheskin, of the Color Research Institute, design a more masculine package. He did, in bold red and white. But that was only one of several significant changes. The Marlboro ads began featuring rugged, virile-looking men deep in work. To get the virile look desired the company used many nonprofessional models for the pictures (sailors, cowboys, and, reportedly, some men who worked at the company's ad agency). And the headlines of the ads began talking of Marlboro's "man-sized flavor."

Perhaps the most fascinating innovation was that all the rugged men shown in the long series—whether they were cowpokes, fishermen, skiers or writers—had one mark in common: they wore man-made stigmata. By an amazing coincidence they all had "tattoos," and still more amazing all the tattoos just happened to be on the back of the men's hands so that they showed in close-up photos. This tattoo motif puzzled some people since the tattoo is a common phenomenon among delinquents in reformatories. Marlboro, however, decided the tattoo was just what was needed to give its men a virile and "interesting past" look. The Marlboro people in fact became so pleased with this symbol of virility that they began distributing millions of transfer pictures of tattoos that men could stamp on their wrists just as children have long done.

Interestingly, first reports showed that Marlboro was, with this campaign, holding onto many women, while recruiting males. Many women seemed to enjoy gazing at the dashing-looking men in the ads. And Marlboro was still careful to call itself "A man's cigarette that women like too."

Motivational expert Pierre Martineau hailed the Marlboro campaign as investing its brand with a "terrifically exciting personality." He felt the highly masculine figures and the tattoo symbols set the cigarette "right in the heart of some core meanings of smoking: masculinity, adulthood, vigor, and potency. Quite obviously these meanings cannot be expressed openly. The consumer would reject them quite violently. The difference between a top-flight creative man and the hack is this ability to express powerful meanings indirectly. . . ."

Topics for Discussion

1. The use of a young woman in a bikini to sell a product is probably the most obvious use of sex in advertising. But Packard speaks of much more subtle uses of sex in advertising. What are some of these uses?

2. Name at least three products whose advertising is based on sex.

3. Packard says that the public has become "jaded and permissive." Do you agree with this? Consider current advertising for brassieres, girdles, and "feminine" deodorants before you answer this question.

4. Do you agree with Packard that men feel threatened and thus respond favorably to masculine sexual reassurance advertising? Can you cite any examples of current advertising that seeks to assure men of their masculinity?

5. What effect do you think women's liberation has had and is having on advertising? Be specific and cite examples from current and past advertising to illustrate your answer.

6. Packard gives the impression in this article that most advertising is designed to appeal to women. How true do you think this is?

Rhetorical Considerations

1. Examine the first paragraph of this essay. Does it adequately state the thesis idea of the essay?

2. Packard quickly moves into the use of examples in the second paragraph to illustrate his ideas. Why does he do this?

3. How adequate is the final paragraph of the essay? Does it conclude the essay or does it leave you with unanswered questions?

4. Look at the essay and note how well Packard uses facts, figures, and quotations to illustrate and back up his ideas. Yet note also that all of these blend into his sentences without interrupting the flow of the prose. Choose one or two quotations and explain how Packard has worked them into his prose.

NOW Says:
TV Commercials
Insult Women

By JUDITH ADLER HENNESSEE
and JOAN NICHOLSON

The bride and groom have run directly from their wedding without bothering to change their clothes or go on their honeymoon, to the appliance store. The salesman is telling the groom (not the bride) how terrific the G.E. Toaster-Oven is. The bride is standing around in a daze, having just achieved the greatest ambition of her life—a husband. The two men decide that the groom should buy the product and then, as a polite afterthought, they turn to the bride and ask her what she thinks. Oblivious to everything she replies, "I do."

THE New York Chapter of the National Organization for Women (N.Y.-NOW) has just filed a petition with the Federal Communications Commission in Washington, asking that it take the American Broadcasting Company's flagship station, WABC-TV of New York, off the air. The legal action is based on three grounds: discrimination against women in employment; failure to ascertain women's needs and interests in programing and violation of the F.C.C. Fairness Doctrine, which requires that both sides be presented in "an issue of controversial public importance." The petition asks formally for F.C.C. denial of WABC-TV's application for the renewal of the station's three-year license to broadcast. WABC-TV is currently preparing an answer. NOW believes the ABC network is equally guilty but the only legal way to get at it is through the local affiliate. The Government may

decide the case upon receipt of the answer, or it may order hearings. In the interim, the station has requested a meeting to negotiate with N.Y.-NOW and NOW lawyers at the Center for Constitutional Rights, a non-profit group of attorneys who have volunteered their services. Meanwhile the TV company declines public comment except to say that it believes it does not discriminate against women.

THE legal action results in part from NOW's monitoring of television programs during the course of a year and half. At first, the monitoring seemed to show that all TV programs portray women equally—that is, in an equally bad light. But in the over-all studies conducted by more than 100 monitors, WABC-TV came out considerably worse than other stations. In news programs, women in the movement are made to seem ridiculous, snide remarks trailing after them like broken arrows. In sports coverage of the Olympics, when women won seven out of eight U.S. medals, reporter Doug Johnson led off his 40-second story with "Thank heaven for little girls." The "little girls" remained anonymous—although, rest assured, the women in Clifford Irving's life were covered in loving and lengthy detail. In public affairs programs women's needs and issues—divorce and alimony, the Equal Rights Amendment, child-care centers, the earnings gap, abortion—are for the most part ignored.

Compared with its rival, the printed word, television is an ostrich. A generalized contempt for women is implicit in the entire pattern of programing. From "The Courtship of Eddie's Father" to "The Young Lawyers," women are domestic drudges and office ancillaries, dependent on men emotionally and economically, their extraordinary incompetence exceeded only by their monumental stupidity. Decision-making positions of power and leadership, authority and status in the community—these are the province of men only.

Nowhere is this more evident than in commercials. As part of its challenge, N.Y.-NOW did a study of 1,241 commercials. Almost all of them showed women inside the home. In 42.6 per cent they were involved in household tasks; in 37.5 per cent they were domestic adjuncts to men, and in 16.7 per cent they were sex objects. That doesn't leave very many, and a lot of commercials don't even have people in them. Only 0.3 per cent showed women as autonomous people, leading independent lives of their own.

The majority of commercials sell either domestic or cosmetic products, and in these, of course, women are the stars. Above and beyond their consumer function (to keep the economy breathing), they play two stock roles—the housewife-mother or the sex object. In both, they are viewed solely in their relation to men. Biologically, the wife-mother is there to serve the species, socially, her purpose is to serve men, children and animals. Psychologically, she's an obsessive-compulsive. Her life alternates between the kitchen and the bedroom, persecuting the germs, guarding the wax on "her" floor, scrubbing dirt off collars, manufacturing delicious little miracles on the stove and coloring her hair to make it look more natural. The Downey Fabric Softener commercial offers an explicit definition of a wife. "Honey, here's your laundry," the new bride says brightly. "Did I wash it right?" Her husband registers his approval and she is fulfilled. "He noticed," she says euphorically. "I'm a wife!"

THIS sort of thing may seem absurdly funny to those of us who fancy ourselves above it, but when it goes on day after day and well into the night, endlessly repeating the same unnerving message to 40 million viewers, it's not so funny anymore. Last year, a Good House-

"But, K. M.—we can't do a commercial that's not false, misleading or deceptive."

Sydney Harris, cartoon from *Playboy*, May, 1972, p. 242. Reproduced by special permission of *Playboy* Magazine; copyright © 1972 by *Playboy*.

keeping Survey reported more than a third "of all respondents have, on occasion, been so offended by a commercial that they've turned it off." Our own monitors, most of whom were not feminists, found 40 per cent of the commercials objectionable. Watching commercials is like being blasted by some casually malevolent propaganda machine dedicated to the humiliation of women.

The woman in the Anacin commercial doesn't even have a headache to call her own. She takes Anacin to stay on her feet longer in order to serve her family. "No headache is going to make me explode at my husband," she says, gritting her teeth and vibrating with pain. The point isn't that Anacin will make her feel better but that it will spare her husband. No wonder the man in the Geritol ad is complacent. The product has given his wife the energy to take care of the baby, go to a school meeting, shop for groceries and cook dinner. Through it all she has still managed to stay attractive for him. "My wife, I think I'll keep her," he says. Who wouldn't?

In most ads women's lives are dreary. It's the men, children and even the family dog who have the fun while women do the work. In 54.4 per cent of the food commercials and 81.2 per cent of the cleaning commercials men are the beneficiaries. Maxim Freeze Dried Coffee shows a woman in a galley making coffee while her husband and son (not daughter—a daughter would be helping) are on deck enjoying themselves sailing. Fleischman's Margarine uses the same theme. This time, the husband and son are out playing ball while Mom is in the kitchen worrying about their eating habits. She doesn't get a vacation, either. She unpacks in the hotel room while her husband complains about how he can't sleep — and she stops unpacking to get him some Nytol. There's something inherently illogical in all this. A woman's main goal is supposed to be to catch a man, but once she's got him she spends her life slaving away in the kitchen.

Maybe she ought to rethink her goals?

The television industry perhaps feels it has a vested interest in encouraging a conventional role for women. Keep women in the kitchen and you won't have to hire them, or worry about raising their pay. According to a Time magazine article: "If women workers got as much as men, wage costs would rise by some $109-billion — more than all pretax corporate profits last year." Women who are seen engaging in mad dusting contests with Endust provide their own justification for not being hired, much less being paid decent wages — incompetence and lack of intelligence. Even in their traditional roles as housewives women are put down.

In a Head and Shoulders Shampoo commercial a touching blind devotion is exhibited by Michael's wife, whose thinking apparatus seems to have dried up and flaked away since her marriage. Her delivery is naively sincere. "When I met Michael," she confides, "he was using Head and Shoulders. . . . When we don't have three tubes, I have to run out to the store to get that third tube." She laughs. "It works," she says, staring out with big brown, blank eyes. "Michael says it works."

But Michael's wife has no credibility. Females rarely do. Her small voice is followed by a male voice-over, the voice of authority, which confers the stamp of approval on the product. Male authority is a built-in assumption, and it teaches women to look up to men as experts; 89.3 per cent of the voice-overs are male. The consumers, who might normally be expected to know something about the products they use, are not granted

even that slight margin of knowledge. Women *never* tell men what to do, but men are forever telling women what to do. And how to do it. Even in their own private beauty realm, women aren't quite with it. "I'm all thumbs," the helpless woman in the Revlon Fabuliner ad says. "It won't skip? It won't run?" The male voice-over keeps telling her, with decreasing patience, that no matter how clumsy and inept she is, she just can't mess herself up because "it draws a perfect line every time." She finally learns the lesson and repeats, with slow, dawning comprehension: "It draws a perfect line every time."

She really ought to haul off and sock him, but the need for male approval, implicit in 33.9 per cent of these commercials, stops her. Women, who have been traditionally dependent on the approval of men in order to survive, are frequently made to play the fool as the price.

Submissiveness is one way. It shows up in 24.3 per cent of commercials. Take the Maxwell House Coffee ad with Danny and Doubting Thomas. The one thing she doesn't doubt is male superiority. As she rattles away with her spiel, she says something he doesn't like—"Test my Instant Maxwell House Coffee" — and he pounces. "Hold it, young lady," he says, in mock sternness, having supervised her performance from the sidelines. It's her commercial, but he just can't resist taking over. And she lets him. "Our coffee?" she asks meekly, divining his purpose on the spot. And smiles. And smiles. Women smile a lot. It goes with the shuffle.

Even more devastating is the new-Mr.-Clean-with-lemon commercial which features a marionettelike woman whose strings are pulled by an avuncular voice-over. "Nice nose," he says, touching it presumptuously. As if he had clicked a switch, her face lights up with a huge grin. "Thanks," she says gratefully. "Let's test it," he says—an order, not a question — and she acquiesces cheerfully and obediently, like a child. Even with all of her previous odor-sniffing experience she guesses wrong. But he is there to tell her the right answer while she listens, wide-eyed and respectful.

Can't these pursuits be presented with dignity? Taken by itself, there needn't be anything degrading about housework or caring for a family. Advertising agencies claim that they are in business to sell products and that their primary responsibility is to the client. In other words, if the manufacturers who advertise on television decide they won't approve any ads showing women driving station wagons, then the agency won't create any such ads. Last year, we met with the market - research people at B.B.D.&O. to convince them that they had some social responsibility toward the public in the area of image-making. They disagreed. At any rate, in most commercials the image of woman is an inferior one, and image makers have made housework a pejorative word. When men do the same work as women, the work is upgraded because they earn money at it. In two separate scenes, Campbell's Vegetable Soup shows a male chef and a housewife. She is the family cook, but cooking is his profession. The implication is that even a lowly housewife can make as good a bowl of soup as a professional cook can.

Yet not even the few pro-fessional women whose lives definitely do not revolve around the stove escape. In a Dove commercial, a professional actress is shown hand-washing the dirty dinner dishes of 150 people. The important thing is not that she is an actress but that she is a female, and females wash dishes. Her career, her real work, is valueless. Eve Arden is actually in the kitchen demonstrating Roast 'n Boast, but you don't see Durward Kirby, who represents Ivory Liquid, washing the dishes with it. As a man, all he has to do is hand down the word. His identity and status are conferred on the product. A woman, who has none, derives hers from the product.

People tend to imitate the roles they see, to become what is expected of them. When they are given only one socially acceptable "choice," it inhibits them from choosing freely what they want to be. For the millions of women painfully breaking out of their traditional roles, the persistent television stereotypes are like a knock on the head telling them to stay in line. The psychological damage is immeasurable.

"Feedback," a WBAI series about television, discussed the problem: "Societies develop images about themselves, their purposes and their objectives. The system of such images forms a society's mythology and governs its actions, thoughts, and attitudes. . . . The passive viewer lets the TV image subvert his own . . . and the viewer is removed from the possibility of alternatives." The big concern of ad agencies is something they call "the reality of the market place." Bill Ballard, a Madison Avenue copywriter, says, "Ads are a reflection of society as the people who are responsible for advertising see it." But most ads reflect only one aspect of the life of the middle-class housewife. There are other realities. The life-style and problems of working women—43 per cent of adult women—are virtually ignored on commercials. They are still perceived primarily in their relationship to men, as wives who happen to be working. The working woman crops up occasionally, still close to the hearth, as in the Reynolds Aluminum ad, wrapping a quick gourmet dinner that cooks itself while she dresses for the dinner party she and her husband are giving. Reynolds hasn't yet got to the point where the husband, who also works, shares or—perish the thought —takes full responsibility for the dinner. In fact, television takes a positively reactionary moral stance toward women. On the rare occasions when they are let out of the house, they are generally chaperoned, as if all were Victorian virgins. They don't do anything alone. In commercials, they never buy airplane tickets or travel by themselves. If they use a camera, there is always a man taking pictures alongside them. If they go to a restaurant, they are accompanied by their family. If they smoke, the tobacco is offered to them by a man.

Looking at these capsule dramatizations of male fantasies, you would never know that 42 per cent of the first million Mustangs sold were bought by women. Ads for cars, banks and insurance were only 3.2 per cent of daytime commercials, as opposed to 19.1 per cent in prime time, when the men are home. These sex-segregated ads are saying in effect that women are incapable of making important decisions alone. Important decisions are decisions that cost a lot of money. In the bank ads, women who do use banks do so for frivolous reasons—the checks are pretty, or you don't have to bother about your balance because the bank will cover your overdraft anyway. As for cars, a woman by herself neither buys them nor has them serviced, and she is rarely shown behind the wheel. If she is with her husband, he is driving. Goodyear Tires has a stacked commercial showing a man driving along happily on a sunny day and a woman driving in the pouring rain at night, worried and nervous. Despite the fact that insurance tables show that women have fewer accidents than men, the woman is still imagined as the mechanically inept hairbrain who manages to run over a suitcase twice in the middle of her own driveway.

Just as women are barred from the world of money and power, so men are revealed as incompetent on the domestic scene. Since the things men do are socially and economically more valuable than the things women do, a man is not supposed to know his way around the house. There's something wrong with him if he *can* cope. If he is in the kitchen, he is usually filling in sloppily while his wife is out performing another of her sex functions—having a baby. Comet, which features Jane Withers as Josephine the Plumber, has a sink piled high with a week's worth of filthy pots, which the man asks her to clean for him. He wouldn't dare ask a male plumber to scrub those pots. Josephine, who looks more like a nurse than a plumber, is a fraud. All she ever does is clean sinks; you never see her actually take on a leaking faucet.

With all the work she has to do and with the small amount of intelligence allotted to her, the woman who will "always be a Maxwell housewife" certainly doesn't need an education. Education anyway is for the purpose of getting a job, to earn more money; and money, along with mental activity, is male territory. All of the ads for educational opportunities and careers invite only men to participate—except for one, the U.S. Auto Club Driving School. "There is a special division for women students," the male voice-over says patronizingly. Women are some strange subspecies whose coordination is questionable at best.

FOR women, self-betterment has nothing to do with education or training. Rather, it is generally synonymous with sex appeal, and the pitch is to fear, a veiled threat that women won't be acceptable to men. Skinny Dip Cologne has a woman rejected by a group of men until she splashes on the scent. Then they welcome her. It is assumed that men are naturally acceptable to women because they are men. They may occasionally have to rinse their mouths with Listerine or spray their unruly locks with Command, but the object is polygamous fun, not the serious business of monogamy. For a woman, anything goes. As a physical entity, she commands no more respect than she does as an economic entity. Maybe less. Consider the Playtex bra ad, in which a woman, wearing the bra, runs into a male friend who had ignored her charms in the past. The man, his popping eyes fastened on her chest, says in disbelief: "Is it really you?"

We all know what "Fly Me" really means, and why all the men in the office cluster around the Olivetti Girl. She is a plaything, a sex object. With the typewriter fixing up all the errors, she will have more time to entertain her bosses. "Two brains are better than one," says Olivetti, but she doesn't really need a brain at all. In the marketplace of television, women are just another commodity, peddling their wares like the model in the Shop-Rite pantyhose commercial who becomes the product. She sits there in the grocery cart like a big doll, smiling, her legs in one of the classic cheesecake positions, waiting to be picked up and bought.

There's no denying that sex sells, but it's safe to say that the male broadcasting oligarchy would be revolted at the sight of men perpetually displaying their bodies. It would strike them as obscene. But it hasn't occurred to them to consider whether a female sex symbol, selling not only a product but herself, strikes women as obscene. Maybe the best consciousness-raiser would be to turn the ads around in a kind of reverse degradation, and show men slinking around in tight bikinis being ogled by appraising female eyes, or eating spoonfuls of Light 'n Lively in the reducing salon while the camera panned slowly up their legs. "Minute by minute, you become a man again," a condescending female voice-over would tell him as he soaked in the tub with his Softique.

Only 2.2 per cent of all commercials are for male personal-care products. And the image of the male is quite different from that of the female. He is rarely seen inside the home. In more than 70 per cent of the ads, men are engaged in a wide range of activities from politics to fishing, and the advertisers' approach to them is both serious and informative—in a word: adult. Provocative poses are out. The man in the Proteen 29 commercial barely glances in the mirror as he talks, merely a quick check for neatness and grooming. There isn't a hint that he is prettying up for a woman or that he is in love with his own image. There's a brisk, snappy efficiency about him, in contrast to the helpless woman in the Twice As Nice Shampoo commercial who turns down her date because she can't do a thing with her hair. A magic man materializes to tell her what to do, but the Proteen 29 man already knows, and he's telling us.

Women are forever put under the microscope, singled out for male scrutiny. Virginia Woolf noticed it, looking through the titles in the British Museum and seeing all the books about women written by men. Things haven't changed that much since 1928. A woman's anatomy is fair game. A man's sex is unmentionable. Even in the health ads, Blue Cross/ Blue Shield talks about the pap test, never about prostate trouble. But if biology is destiny for one sex, then it has to be destiny for the other, too.

It is taken for granted that men perspire, but women are victims of their own bodies. "Emotions make a woman different from a man," the male voice-over insinuates, but he's got it all backward. If the female body were the norm for the whole human race—and the fact that the fetus starts out as a female strongly suggests that it is— the reasoning would be quite the opposite. Men, who are frequently shown engaging in strenuous sweaty activities, are the ones who need a "special" deodorant. It depends on whether you consider excessive perspiration to be normal. But women's needs are measured against the "normal" standard of male

needs, and where those needs diverge, it is the woman, not the man, who is judged to be lacking, or peculiar, or delicate, or inferior. Her own standards don't apply. Indeed, it isn't recognized that she has any.

This subhuman creature, defective mentally and physically, has been endowed by men with a hypothetical need for extra iron, a gentler laxative, a thinner cigarette, a smaller car (presumably so she can park it alongside a man's without denting his fender). But now the final blow. She is the victim of an ancient taboo, a primal flaw in her sex. "It makes you feel fresh and it lasts all day," one woman tells another in one commercial. Women, obsessed with cleanliness, are unclean themselves. There are similar genital products for men, but they're not advertised on television. In fact, in ad-agency product categories, male deodorants are listed under "cosmetics" and female deodorants under "hygiene." This idea goes all the way back to the prejudices of the men who wrote Leviticus, a book of the Bible which reflects primitive beliefs that women, during their menstrual periods, are unclean, and must be isolated from other members of the group. Leviticus took it one step further—women were also unclean after they had borne a child, and anyone who went near them risked defilement. This is tantamount to telling black people that their skin color is naturally dirty. No advertiser in his right mind would think of doing that, but it's all right to say it to women. The message is sadistic. And some of the products may be dangerous. They con-

tain talc, which is under Government investigation as a possible cancer - producing agent.

IT is naive to expect spontaneous changes. The National Association of Broadcasters' code, the Ten Commandments of the industry, says, thou shalt not violate "the sanctity of marriage and the value of the home." No other life-style is valid. Marriage, home and children are television's hottest-selling items. In today's overpopulated, polluted world, this value is open to question. Ellen Peck, author of "The Baby Trap," accuses broadcasters of a "pronatalist" bias in their programing, which, she feels, discourages women's career aspirations. She suggests that television is the only medium that has access on a scale large enough to educate the public about these social issues. But discussion of this, and other socially pressing problems, according to the industry's own guidelines, is in bad taste. It is precisely this lack of information and lack of choices that motivated the N.Y.-NOW challenge.

The sad thing is that products can be sold without insulting people. Last year, Clairol received an "old-hat" award from NOW for its sexist advertising. Its new ad demonstrates what new habits of thought can do. One woman is shown as a jockey, another is congratulated by her husband and child on receiving her college diploma, a third is working competently and with aplomb in a professional capacity. All of them are away from home. If the corporate mind of Clairol, a bastion of genteel sexism, can do it, so can everyone else. ■

Topics for Discussion

1. Is this article anything more than an attack on the image of woman portrayed by television advertising?
2. According to this article, television advertising vigorously promotes male chauvinism. Based upon your observations of current television advertising, do you agree with this statement? Why?
3. "Only 2.2 percent of all commercials are for male personal-care products." Why are there so few commercials for men's products and so many for women's products?
4. This article finds few, if any, television commercials that portray women properly. Do you agree with this? Can you cite any commercials which you think do portray women accurately?
5. Choose some of the commercials mentioned in this article and rewrite them in a way that you think would be acceptable to women.
6. How important do you think it is to change the image of woman portrayed in commercials?

Rhetorical Considerations

1. What is the thesis of this essay? Is it stated or implied in the essay?
2. What is the effect of citing example after example of commercials that demean women? Is the effect cumulative or repetitive? Could the examples have been used more effectively?
3. At the beginning of the essay, there is a discussion of the petition filed against a New York television station. Is this discussion relevant to the rest of the essay?
4. Is the tone of this essay too strong? Would the essay be more effective if the tone were more restrained and less outraged? Or is the tone of anger proper to the subject matter?

'Bugs Bunny Says They're Yummy'

Dawn Ann Kurth

Do TV commercials take unfair—and even dangerous—advantage of children? Dawn Ann Kurth, 11, of Melbourne, Fla., thinks they do. Miss Kurth was a surprise witness at a recent Senate subcommittee hearing in Washington on the effects of TV advertising. Here is her statement to the committee.

MR. CHAIRMAN:

My name is Dawn Ann Kurth. I am 11 years old and in the fifth grade at Meadowlane Elementary School in Melbourne, Florida. This year I was one of the 36 students chosen by the teachers out of 20,000 5th-through-8th graders, to do a project in the Talented Student Program in Brevard County. We were allowed to choose a project in any field we wanted. It was difficult to decide. There seem to be so many problems in the world today. What could I do?

A small family crisis solved my problem. My sister Martha, who is 7, had asked my mother to buy a box of Post Raisin Bran so that she could get the free record that was on the back of the box. It had been advertised several times on Saturday morning cartoon shows. My mother bought the cereal, and we all (there are four children in our family) helped Martha eat it so she could get the record. It was after the cereal was eaten and she had the record that the crisis occurred. There was no way the record would work.

* * * * * *

Martha was very upset and began crying and I was angry too. It just didn't seem right to me that something could be shown on TV that worked fine and people were listening and dancing to the record and when you bought the cereal, instead of laughing and dancing, we were crying and angry. Then I realized that perhaps here was a problem I could do something about or, if I couldn't change things, at least I could make others aware of deceptive advertising practices to children.

To begin my project I decided to keep a record of the number of commercials shown on typical Saturday morning TV shows. There were 25 commercial messages during one hour, from 8 to 9 A.M., not counting ads for shows coming up or public service ads. I found there were only 10 to 12 commercials during shows my parents like to watch. For the first time, I really began to think about what the commercials were saying. I had always listened before and many times asked my mother to buy certain products I had seen advertised, but now I was listening and really thinking about what was being said. Millions of kids are being told:

"Make friends with Kool-aid, Kool-aid makes good friends."

"People who love kids have to buy Fritos."

"Hershey chocolate makes milk taste like a chocolate bar." Why should milk taste like a chocolate bar anyway?

"Cheerios make you feel groovy all day long." I eat them sometimes and I don't feel any different.

"Libby frozen dinners have fun in them." Nothing is said about the food in them.

"Cocoa Krispies taste like a chocolate milk shake only they are crunchy."

"Lucky Charms are magically delicious with sweet surprises inside." Those sweet surprises are marshmallow candy.

I think the commercials I just mentioned are examples of deceptive advertising practices.

Another type of commercial advertises a free bonus gift if you buy a certain product. The whole commercial tells about the bonus gift and says nothing about the product they want you to buy. Many times, as in the case of the record, the bonus gift appears to be worthless junk or isn't in the package. I wrote to the TV networks and found it costs about $4,000 for a 30-second commercial. Many of those ads appeared four times in each hour. I wonder why any company would spend $15,000 or $20,000 an hour to advertise worthless junk.

The ads that I have mentioned I consider deceptive. However, I've found others I feel are dangerous.

Bugs Bunny vitamin ads say their vitamins "taste yummy" and taste good.

Chocolate Zestabs says their product is

"delicious" and compare taking it with eating a chocolate cookie.

If my mother were to buy those vitamins, and my little sister got to the bottles, I'm sure she would eat them just as if they were candy.

I do not know a lot about nutrition, but I do know that my mother tries to keep our family from eating so many sweets. She says they are bad for our teeth. Our dentist says so too. If they are bad, why are companies allowed to make children want them by advertising on TV? Almost all of the ads I have seen during children's programs are for candy, or sugar-coated cereal, or even sugar-coated cereal with candy in it.

I know people who make these commercials are not bad. I know the commercials pay for TV shows and I like to watch TV. I just think that it would be as easy to produce a good commercial as a bad one. If there is nothing good that can be said about a product that is the truth, perhaps the product should not be sold to kids on TV in the first place.

I do not know all the ways to write a good commercial, but I think commercials would be good if they taught kids something that was true. They could teach about good health, and also about where food is grown. If my 3-year-old sister can learn to sing, "It takes two hands to handle a whopper 'cause the burgers are better at Burger King," from a commercial, couldn't a commercial also teach her to recognize the letters of the alphabet, numbers, and colors? I am sure that people who write commercials are much smarter than I and they should be able to think of many ways to write a commercial that tells the truth about a product without telling kids they should eat it because it is sweeter or "shaped like fun" (what shape *is* fun, anyway?) or because Tony Tiger says so.

I also think kids should not be bribed to buy a product by commercials telling of the wonderful free bonus gift inside.

I think kids should not be told to eat a certain product because a well-known hero does. If this is a reason to eat something, then, when a well-known person uses drugs, should kids try drugs for the same reason?

Last of all, I think vitamin companies should never, never be allowed to advertise their product as being delicious, yummy, or in any way make children think they are candy. Perhaps these commercials could teach children the dangers of taking drugs or teach children that, if they do find a bottle of pills, or if the medicine closet is open, they should run and tell a grown-up, and never, never eat the medicine.

I want to thank the Committee for letting me appear. When I leave Washington, the thing that I will remember for the rest of my life is that some people *do* care what kids think. I know I could have led a protest about commercials through our shopping center and people would have laughed at me or thought I needed a good spanking or wondered what kind of parents I had that would let me run around in the streets protesting. I decided to gather my information and write letters to anyone I thought would listen. Many of them didn't listen, but some did. That is why I am here today. Because some people cared about what I thought. I hope now that I can tell every kid in America that when they see a wrong, they shouldn't just try to forget about it and hope it will go away. They should begin to do what they can to change it.

People will listen. I know, because you're here listening to me.

The Age of Communication

Topics for Discussion

1. This article is the statement Dawn Ann Kurth read before a United States Senate subcommittee on the effects of television advertising. How effective do you think her statement is? Does her age contribute anything to the effectiveness of her statement?

2. ". . . I think commercials would be good if they taught kids something that was true." Does this mean that current commercials do not tell the truth? What examples of children's commercials does Kurth offer to illustrate her contention?

3. Do you see any relationship between commercials for children and commercials for adults? Are the appeals used in both kinds of commercials the same?

4. Have you ever purchased anything because of the "free gift" you could get with the product? Was the "gift" worth anything? What is the appeal used in such offers?

5. Kurth says that "it would be as easy to produce a good commercial as a bad one." If that is true, why aren't there more good commercials produced?

6. Why do you think there are twenty-five commercials during one hour of children's programs but only ten to twelve commercials during adult programs?

Rhetorical Considerations

1. Dawn Ann Kurth's mother and teacher insist that she received no help in preparing her statement. What do you think of this essay as an example of the writing ability of an eleven-year-old fifth-grade student?

2. In her introduction, Kurth describes the family crisis involving her sister Martha. How effective is this introduction? How relevant is it to the rest of the article?

3. This statement was prepared as a speech to be read. What makes this read like a speech and not an essay? Try reading parts of it aloud. How does it sound?

4. How effective are the last two paragraphs? Do they really conclude the speech?

5. Look at the vocabulary used in this speech. Are there any big or technical words? Is the speech less or more effective because of the kind of words used?

THE FACE THAT LAUNCHED A THOUSAND SHIPMENTS

Terry Galanoy

Look at yourself as others see you. As the admen look at you.

From the top of your dandruff-salted head to the corns on your splayed feet, you're a mess. Your face looks like a shattered windshield. Your clothing like rummage rejects. Your table manners would upset a zoo guard. Your voice sounds like teaspoons in a garbage disposer. Your breath and ten other parts of you stink. Your nose and hose run. And your grammar could be corrected by a Brooklyn cab driver.

And so's your old man and your old lady. The kids are even worse because they have pimples too late and bunions too soon and say things like, "Golly, Mary-jane, use this mouthwash and the football team will take you to the dance at the gym . . . or maybe into the bushes behind it."

Is the ugly American the real American?

According to a lot of the advertising writers, art directors, and commercials producers, he or she is. They're convinced that the average American is a lump, his wife is a frump, and they live in a dump. They believe that most Americans are dreary drudges with intellectual horizons limited to the distance they can throw a beer can. They're sure that the television audience thinks *chic* is a kind of Arabian gang leader, that *high fashion* is anklets with high heels, and that *taste* is what you do to chicken soup before you turn it off.

In trying to reach you, they insult not only your intelligence to your face but your face as well.

"Listen," they say in agency meetings, "this product is for the average ordinary basic number 24 American home. Y'know, wrinkled housewife—skin and clothes. Breakfast dishes on the table—from Sunday. Dirty kids. Curdled milk in the cat's bowl. Honest, real folks. The sort of thing your wife and mine'd laugh at but describes the rest of the country pretty well."

A couple of years ago I took a complete camera crew into northern Oregon. Our job was to get a testimonial for a brand of dog food from the operators of

Terry Galanoy, "The Face That Launched a Thousand Shipments." Reprinted from *Down the Tube* by Terry Galanoy, published by Henry Regnery Company, Chicago. Copyright © 1970 by Terry Galanoy. Reprinted by permission.

a kennel who raised champion-stock collie dogs. The advertising manager for the dog food company had found a kennel he wanted to use. As he said, "I can tell they're great people, sight unseen, because they're good customers."

We took his word for it.

They looked pretty good. They looked great. The man was about 30, slim, wore tweeds, a tie, and a vest all the time. His wife was tall, had the facial angles and Scandinavian good looks of a New York model, and dressed in well-cut slacks and Brooks Brothers shirts while she did her chores.

"Who's that?" asked the ad manager, when he arrived a little later the first day.

"That's the couple we're supposed to shoot," I answered smugly. It isn't often we find more than we had anticipated.

"My God, get rid of them!" he said, his mouth twitching.

"Why?"

"Why? Why?" he spluttered. "They're too pretty, that's why!"

"But they're real. He's a graduate vet. She has a degree in animal husbandry. They've been raising champion dogs for four or five years now," I argued, reading from my worksheets.

"I don't care if they're Mr. and Mrs. American Kennel Club. They're not going to be in *my* commercial," he said decisively.

"Give me one good reason," I asked. "One good reason."

"Because," he said slowly, "they're not real."

It was his commercial, so we skipped it. In their stead, we sent out for two professional actors. The wife we cast had the profile of a Goodyear blimp wrapped in calico. The replacement husband had a corrugated face and wattles that shook when he talked. We dressed her in Indian-head bedroom slippers. He put on bib overalls.

"Now that's what I call real believable kennel folks," the advertising manager said just before we made the spot.

Another time, a friend of mine was assigned to work on a commercial for face soap. This particular spot had a bride-to-be talking to her father as she washed her face with the product. The father tells the girl what a beautiful bride she is.

The film studio producing the commercial called in the prettiest models in town for auditions.

"Nothing doing," said the agency producer turning them away. "We want a believable girl. A homely one who got the guy because she used our soap."

They set out to find one. They finally located her working as a receptionist for a dental supply company. She was so unattractive the agency receptionist refused to believe she was there for a modeling interview.

"Perfect," said the agency producer.

"Ideal," said the soap advertising manager.

"Ugh," said the film director, a bachelor. "Listen, I don't know anybody who would marry that broad even if her father owned the soap company."

Which shows how much bachelor-directors know. That commercial ran hundreds of times on the air and sold a great deal of soap. More importantly, according to research figures, it gave heart and encouragement to a lot of plain girls, who identified with the plain model. The only casualty, besides the director, was the long-standing commercials tradition that every American bride is an American beauty: that got a swift kick in its satin bustle.

Those are just two of maybe a thousand examples of how the advertising business has moved from the "Beautiful People" to the "Believables." (Some agencies call them the "Real People"; others call them the "Uglies"; all of the agencies call them successful.)

"The reason unattractive people are highly successful in commercials," agent Charlie Stern once said to me, "is because most people identify with them. They feel close to them. They feel friendly and warm toward them—because they are no threat, real or implied. Once we discovered this psychological fact in relationship to casting, it became a simple matter to gain that empathy for our actors and actresses, and through them, for the product."

"Not true," counters Max Komer, an agency executive. "There's no diabolical scheme to downgrade the American in manner or appearance. It's the pressures. If we put a pretty girl who looks like a model into a commercial we get mail asking why she isn't more representative of American womanhood. If we use a girl with a midwestern accent, people complain it's too regional. If the girl is dressed in a topcoat for an outdoor scene, there will be a pile of mail pointing out we're running a winter commercial in the summertime. While people are looking at that they're not looking at the commercial. The agency's only solution is to draw the American woman as a one-dimensional, noncontroversial little gray mouse who won't attract attention to herself and *away from the product.*"

"They're both wrong," says a researcher. "The main reason for using the uglies is simply because research audiences which say go or no-go for commercials are made up of real-life uglies and they'll kill the commercial and the model if she's too pretty."

Whichever reason is correct, the mud hens outnumber the beauties in casting agencies these days. One talent agency owner estimates that agency calls run three to one "for the believables over the gorgeous." Another says, "The real beauties are just about restricted these days to commercials for hair coloring or for cosmetics. Other products and services—airlines, soaps, soft drinks, tires—want people who look like the people next door—providing you don't live next door to the Richard Burtons."

There is one more reason. There was a time—and it was not so long ago—when everybody looked alike on commercials. "But that isn't how people look in Brooklyn," was the philosophy of agency president Bill Bernbach, who lived in Brooklyn Heights. "And that isn't how people on the subway look." He knew, because he took the subway to work. At that time, he was the only agency president who did.

"People look Jewish," said the Jewish copywriters at Young & Rubicam.

"And Italian," said the Italian art directors at Papert, Koenig & Lois.

"And Irish," said the Irish film directors at MPO and VPI studios.

"And black," said the Black janitors, quietly at first but increasingly louder.

"And they're fat and skinny and have warts and moles and double chins, and guess what, some of the men are going bald . . ." one memo from the agency head producer to his staff ran on.

"Watch! I will make a star out of that bum walking down the street over there," said a highly publicized creative man. "You, sir," he approached the derelict type, "how would you like to appear on television in a commercial?"

"You'll have to ask the William Morris agency. They handle my commercial work," he smiled back.

Agencies like WRG, Doyle Dane, Carl Ally, and others began casting on the spot—in delicatessens, dime stores, at Nathan's Coney Island hot-dog stands. They pulled drivers out of cabs, cops off motorcycles, and timekeepers out of navy yards. Burnett used a New York Giants quarterback for one of their Marlboro men and then followed him by using airline pilots for their rugged, father-image look.

At the same time, seasoned legitimate actors were discovered by the agencies and the film houses. Stubby Kaye, the blocky star of *Guys and Dolls*, was suddenly starring in a musical *soap* opera. Jack Guilford, one of the great comedy talents of *A Funny Thing Happened on the Way to the Forum* could also be seen in Cracker Jack commercials. Bert Lahr appeared for potato chips. The Great Talent Hunt was under way.

It was only in the early 1960s that common sense replaced common practice. The common practice, until then, had been for legitimate and name actors and personalities to turn down commercials.

"One commercial and you'll never get a decent part on the stage or in a picture," was the prevailing folk tale. Talent agents said it. Studios hummed it. Even starring actors sang the chorus.

Good, slick professionals turned down commercials to wait for their big break on Broadway or at MGM. A lot of them are still waiting. A few, more practical—or more hungry—took commercials and were thumbed out of readings at the Schubert Theatre.

The only exceptions to the non-name commercials rule before the new dispensation were threatrical personalities who did commercials within the framework of their individual television shows. If Red Skelton wanted to do a commercial within the Red Skelton hour, why, that was fine. But if those commercials appeared in other time periods or in other shows, or if he had made commercials for products that did not sponsor his show, the rumors would have been out fast that he was in financial or professional trouble and probably both, and his top banana reputation would have peeled off. Bob Hope, Dinah Shore, Jack Benny, Loretta Young, George Burns and Gracie, Perry Como either did within-the-show spots for the sponsors or plugged the sponsors' products heavily in the monologues or acts in the shows or somehow were so identified with the products that they gave the impression of doing commercials. To millions, Perry Como will always be the Chesterfield salesman, Dinah Shore will be Miss USA in her Chevrolet, Bob Hope the big talent for the big Chrysler.

Still, the few recognized personalities getting into commercials encouraged others. That is, they were either encouraged or they were desperate for income. Some even had a friend at the agency or with the advertiser. One of them had a particularly good friend at home. He was Alfred Steele, and he was the head of Pepsi-Cola; she was Joan Crawford, and she was married to Steele, so she did a series of commercials for the Pepsi company.

Most casting people agree that the major breakthrough for theatrical personalities occurred when the Benton & Bowles agency wheedled, cajoled, pleaded, and sold four top stars—Claudette Colbert, Lauren Bacall, Jason Robards, Jr., and Edward G. Robinson—

into doing commercials for Maxwell House coffee.

At the end of his spot, Robinson cocked his thumb and forefinger like a gun and said in a semi-serious voice, "Now, do what I tell you, hear?"

Listening—and looking—was other talent.

Actors and actresses dropped their coffee cups with a clatter in Walgreen's on Broadway. In Hollywood, yogurt malted milks were left half-finished at Schwab's. Dozens of top names stormed into agent's offices asking for equal time: the 60-second commercial—and, more importantly, the money that went with it.

Even the unknowns who had grown stale waiting in the wings for their big chance began to envy Barbara-come-lately. Her last name was Felden. This stage-trained actress had done a deodorant commercial and then was cast as a purring female on a tiger rug selling a men's hair product for the Revlon Company. "Sic 'em, Tiger," Barbara Felden said at the end of that spot, and tigers in producers clothing sicced themselves onto this lamb with motion-picture contracts, a leading role in a television series, and instant-success contracts for additional commercials and endorsements. Paul Richards stood on the wing of a Braniff airplane and talked about it, and when he climbed down, he had expensive offers to do Pontiac commercials, to do plays, motion pictures, to have his own television show. Sandy Duncan, the star of the TV series *Funnyface* had earned the job starring in commercials.

Suddenly, ad agencies couldn't beat the talent off with a deodorant stick. And in many cases, they didn't want to. Bette Davis was signed to do a commercial for Awake breakfast drink and later said that she loved the job. Jane Russell popped up in commercials. So did leggy Betty Grable, suave David Niven, pretty Lena Horne, tough Richard Boone, sincere Peter Lawford. The nation's television watchers were surprised but not overly startled to turn their sets on one night and see the king, Albert Francis Sinatra, doing commercials for a beer.

"There's no more negativity about doing commercials," says one casting director. "For enough money you can get just about anybody you want. You want established stars like Cary Grant? I can probably get him for you, if you're prepared to pay through the nose. Or, if you want the new stars, how about Ruth Buzzi from *Laugh-in*? You can have her for a $5,000 advance as Ruth or a $50,000 advance if she dresses and plays the part of Gladys, the dame she played on the *Laugh-In* TV show. All the kids from that show went on to commercials. Park Lockwood and Gene Powell from the Banquet Food Corporation gave Jo Anne Worley, I don't know, $20-30,000, I understand, for about seven-eight hours on-camera work for frozen dinners commercials. That's pretty good but I've seen better."

He probably has. In-demand, high-popularity stars can get $100,000 or more for one commercial. Some have multiple appearance deals that run higher. In many cases, only part of the total fee is paid at the time the commercial is filmed or video-taped; the remainder comes to the performer in residuals checks. Residuals can make the difference between an actor driving a Volkswagen or a Ferrari. An ordinary actor making an ordinary filmed commercial for the television screen works under the minimum payment rules of his union, the Screen Actors Guild. He gets paid about $140 for a day's work, and that's all he gets right away.

When "his" commercial starts running, however, the actor begins getting additional money. Even if the commercial does not run or runs for a while and is then taken off for a period, he still gets paid. This is called a "holding" payment and is considered the Screen Actors Guild's best extortion ploy to date. A SAG spokesman says, "As long as that commercial is off the air our member isn't making a cent from it but he is blocked from making commercials for products in that same category."

There are two unions for commercial actors and actresses, SAG and the American Federation of Television and Radio Artists; most professionals belong to both groups. SAG's turf since 1953 has been any commercial made on film; AFTRA controls appearances in commercials done live or on video tape. By the time television began using film, SAG, which goes back to the early 1930s, had the numbers and the names and the organization to demand repayment for their members. Most talent leaned toward them. With the signing of each new name SAG became stronger. AFTRA could only pick up the crumbs. Rates for actors in tape commercials are lower than rates for the same actor doing the same commercial on film. And, today, the great majority of national, big-residual commercials are done on film because creative men consider it a more flexible and glamorous medium.

Most of the performer's money comes from "residuals," which are based on what is really a very simple idea: payment for additional use of a program —in this case, the commercial. If a guy on the production line earned residuals, he'd get a check in the mail each time you drive your Mustang. So why does the actor deserve it and not the machinist?

"For two very good reasons," said SAG executive John L. Dales a short while ago. "Television is a medium not so much for entertainment as for selling products. Actors and actresses are the frosting on the cake mix, the medicine show that comes with the cough syrup. As salesmen, then, they deserve to be paid each time they help the advertiser sell a product."

The 40,000 words of fine type in the residuals code reads like a repair book for a Chinese computer; it has more mathematical formulas in it than the U.S. space program. What the code basically says is that it is unfair to pay an actor the same rate when his commercial is shown in Akron as when it is shown in Los Angeles, because of the population difference. The more population, the more money. Cities under 1 million count as one unit; cities of 1-2 million count as two; and so on. New York and Los Angeles and Chicago are the three largest cities and count as about seven units each. This way, depending upon where a commercial is going to be seen and how often and for how long, an ordinary actor doing an ordinary commercial can start out with his $140 for one day's work in front of the camera and easily end up with $10,000 without doing any more work. As long as the commercial runs, the talent in it gets paid. Some are paid exceptionally well. The story goes that Frank Sinatra received a very lucrative beer distributorship for his Budweiser commercials.

Charlie Stern's California-based talent shop provides Leslie Nielsen, Keenan Wynn, Barry Sullivan, Agnes Moorehead, Mickey Rooney, and Morey Amsterdam for commercials. Stern says that many noted talents make over $100,000 a year from commercials and that some of his little-knowns make $35-45,000 a year doing spots. Charlie also points out that the pot at the end of the rainbowed peacock has gold for voice talents, too. There are a handful of people who make yearly fortunes with their voices alone. They are specialists. Paul Frees is one. June Foray is another. Frees does Jolly Green Giant, Kellogg's, Pillsbury commercials and about 20 other products. Frees admits to making over $250,000 a year. People close to him say that he does a lot better than that, like $500,000. Frees is a brilliant voice mimic. He was once asked to do an imitation of Milton Cross: "Milton Cross doing the opera or a commercial?" asked Frees and proceeded to prove to the group that Cross did indeed sound different at varying times in his program.

Supplying a voice for commercials is now in just about everybody's day's work. This *voice-over* activity (so called because it is the sound of a voice over an action on the film) is popular with name stars because it gives them a degree of anonymity and keeps them from being overexposed.

Some voices you might have listened to in the past

were Maureen Stapleton and Ruby Dee, the great Broadway actresses, for Minute rice; David Wayne for Chrysler and American Airlines; Van Johnson for Cranapple juice; Joel Gray for Yuban coffee; Dane Clark for Chef-Boy-ardee; Howard Duff for American Airlines and Chesterfields; and the star of the Broadway hit, *Fiddler on the Roof*, Herschel Bernardi, for just about everything including Jell-O, Burlington Mills, Star-Kist tuna, Bugles, and A.T.&T. There are many more. Dana Andrews, Burgess Meredith, Joseph Cotton (who also *appeared* in a commercial), Hal Holbrook, who made Mark Twain famous the second time around, and Alfred Drake have all stopped by a recording studio for an hour or two to help make their world and ours a better place in which to live. One voice that makes a great deal of money just being itself belongs to deep-throated, mellifluous Alexander Scourby. If you have not heard him as the narrator on the famous television documentary series, *Victory at Sea*, you have definitely listened to him as the voice of Eastern Airlines.

There are over 16,000 members of SAG and close to half of their work is in commercials. The membership has cut up close to $50 million dollars in residuals for these televised advertisements. Their payment for appearing on regular filmed television shows is not more.

Watching this gold drain result from commercials created in *their* brains, many agency boys have begun to cast themselves in spots. They write in a part for themselves, do it, and then join SAG to get residuals. They also make deals to cast each other in commercials. "These are real people," they say, justifying the use of a co-worker to their bosses.

Sometimes the advertiser insists on the adman's appearance in his commercials. He gets used to the sound of the adman's voice or the look of his face and suggests that the creative person also be the talent in the spot. Mary Agnes Schroeder wrote Maybelline commercials and read them in final form. Alice Westbrook was the creative lady for Toni's agency; she was also their spokeswoman. A creative director at Leo Burnett did a Gallo wine commercial featuring himself.

Another group is the one-man show. These people write the commercial, put music to it, produce it, direct it, star in it, and even do the choreography and make out the invoices. Pop painter Andy Warhol does this kind of commercial. So does Peter Max, the painter. The most self-promoted and expensive one-man show is an ex-television voice talent and pop song satirist named Stan Freberg. Freberg's motto is "Art for money's sake," and it exactly describes his approach to making commercials. Just recently Freberg turned a two-day commercial into a two-week job. When faced with the sevenfold increase in cost, the advertiser asked why. "To make sure they were right," Freberg answered. Freberg not only charges a very hefty creative fee, and producer's fee but gives himself a huge fee ($2,000 for a job that has been known to be worth $300) for the use of his nasal whine on commercials— and he makes sure that he is in all of them. One of Freberg's most recent *tours de farce* was the one minute takeoff he did on early Hollywood song-and-dance films. The commercial starred a cast of chorus girls and 1940's star Ann Miller tap-dancing on top of a giant can of Heinz soup. Every time Miss Miller and her ladies of the chorus get tapped to appear on your television screen, so does the till at Heinz get tapped for additional residuals.

The residual has become so taxing to advertising budgets that some agency creative assignments deliberately call for avoiding them. There are several ways to do this. One is called "table top" or "hand" photography. In these commercials, the camera shoots the product only or shoots people from the back or up to the shoulders only. Another way to avoid on-camera residuals is to use drawings, puppets, or animated cartoons, but even then the voice owners must be paid residuals. One agency figured out that some commercials were costing so much in residuals that they might as well make new ones each time the residuals were due.

The use of personalities for commercials makes good martini-time talking.

"It's a cop out," said the great adman George Hawkins. "Whenever a copywriter or an agency can't come up with an idea for a product, they go the star route, hoping the name will attract some attention."

Agreeing with him, partially, was Ron Holland, the copy chief at the Lois Holland Calloway agency, who was once quoted as saying, "There is no particular value in just saying Tuesday Weld, for example, uses a certain kind of soap . . . the main thing is to make sure that the personality and the product jibe."

Holland's agency made a classic commercial, which perfectly bears out Ron Holland's point of view, for a stock brokerage called Edwards & Hanley. In it was ex-heavyweight champion Joe Louis, whose rags-to-riches-to-rags story is well known. "Where were you when I needed you?" Louis says to the brokerage house.

Proper casting of personalities is important. Using Zsa Zsa Gabor to promote AAMCO transmission shops in television was a bad case of miscasting. It was obviously based on the "garage mechanics nudie calendar" concept, or else it was designed to give a dubious type of prestige to transmission repair stores. How much more believable and effective would it have been if race car drivers Dan Blocker or Steve McQueen or even Dan Gurney had done the spots.

Benton & Bowles came up with brilliant casting when the agency produced a series of spots for Texaco gasoline. These commercials stressed Texaco mileage. They talked Jack Benny into doing them. Another example of ideal casting was the use of comedian Louis Nye for Rath meats. These commercials had a fumbling, prissy, affected public relations man always apologizing for the product's bad manners in disappearing from dinners and parties.

The president of one very large agency forbids his creative department to hire name talents for spots. "Our commercials make stars, not the other way around," he said in a widely circulated memo.

It is true. Commercials do make stars. Like Barbara Felden. Like Pam Austin, the ex-Dodge girl. Like Sandy "Funnyface" Duncan. A star of tomorrow could easily be Bill Fiore, the Jack Lemmon-type you've seen in Vitalis commercials, in Dristan spots, and speaking for Nyquil and Right Guard. Oh, *him*. Yep. Him. There are dozens of young talents like Fiore who do not distract from the commercial message while their warm, familiar faces are welcome in the living room. Too often, according to agency experts, the too-famous face has the viewers yelling to each other, "Hey, look who's doing commercials," and paying no attention to the sales copy. The moment the audience is more interested in the people of the commercial than the product, everybody loses.

In the early 1960s the people who create and make commercials began to get written orders to start using "colored people." The first official notice to do so that I remember was a copy of a letter from the National Association for the Advancement of Colored People to the president of a gasoline company. The letter pointed out, as I remember, that over 10 percent of the country was Negro, that the 10 percent used gasoline, that it was tired of being ignored, and that the NAACP would encourage Negroes to use the products of companies that fairly and accurately reflected this minority group in its commercials—and also helped provide employment for black actors and actresses in television commercial work.

It was about this same time that human rights commissions and local and national advertising agency associations began to push a drive to hire "colored" copywriters and art directors and film makers. In New York, Chicago, Los Angeles, and other cities advertising personnel agencies were suddenly turning red ink into black on their ledgers by turning black hopefuls into black employed. The ad agencies were hiring anyone dark. They would merge with a one-man ad agency in the ghetto that had been handling hair straightener and grits. They hired young writers from underground newspapers and artists from garrets in Greenwich Village, Chicago's West Side, and Watts. Those who were hired were placed in outside offices near doors where Fair Employment Practices people and Negro group representatives could see them. The running gag about these people was that they were "show spades," and one producer built on that phrase to call Negro actors and actresses, "Show-show spades". Most of the first black creative people in white agencies were marginally talented and the black actors needed much more training to be truly professional. Most had very little background and very little opportunity to develop their abilities.

For a while, if the writer included a black in his commercial, that person had to have a dignified position, live in a middle-class neighborhood, and look well fed instead of welfared. Except for skin color, the models in the soap commercials were interchangeable.

A group called Negro Actors Guild complained bitterly. Enough is enough, they protested. Their officials pointed out that eliminating shoeshine boys and janitors from commercials also cut out a lot of jobs for their black actors. They took the stand that the Negro actor would play any part as long as it was written and shot with authenticity and dignity and taste.

The National Urban League, however, felt that the advertising industry was still giving the back of the hand to Negroes, putting black actors only in token commercials in token roles.

Some agencies and advertisers actually produced commercials in two versions: an all-white version to be shown in the South and an integrated commercial for the rest of the country. Some wag thought up a labeling code on the reel to tell the agency traffic people which was which. For northern audiences commercials shot in black and white were listed as "B & W—Color"; those shot in color were tagged "Color—B & W." For the South, it was the other way around.

Meanwhile, the almost all-white creative departments pecked away absentmindedly on standard Royals, trying to find a fresh way to include black talent in their commercials. Most of the writers began including crowd scenes with background blacks in them. For a period every soap commercial that had more than three women had one black. The group of commercials called testimonials (in which people endorse a product) would have three whites and a black in separate scenes. Kids are naturally integrated in schools, so many products were set in child situations. Peter Pan peanut butter and Post cereals and Armour and many other food and soap companies set their products in kids' playgrounds or school yards. Mattel toys got around the "un-naturalness" of black and white kids playing together inside the house by resetting some of their toy commercials outside. Polaroid integrated. So did Ford and Chevrolet. Airlines and bus companies, beer and cigarette advertisers began to demand a black or two in every spot. Some agencies began making four or five commercials at a time with one of them having an all-black cast. For example, Crest toothpaste has a black child interrupting a black father to point out that he has no cavities. The same spot was also shot all-white.

Finally, the Broadcast Committee of the American Association of Advertising Agencies began to examine the problem of blacks in commercials. They measured how much work black talent was getting in commercials and also *how* the Negro appeared in these spots. A survey they made in 1967 showed that less than 3 percent of the more than 8,000 commercials surveyed had Negro talent in them. A year later Gordon Webber, chairman of that group, estimated that between 8 and 9 percent of all commercials being made included Negro talent. By the end of 1971 the figure was way over 15 percent, according to Joy McLellan, head of the A+ model agency.

"I expect it to go higher and higher with time," she commented, "to the point where viewers won't even distinguish between blacks and whites on the screen."

A couple of years ago, a research firm took a closer look at the Negro-black market and found that this group spent more money than whites of the same income on beverages, some foods, soaps, and cleanser. The surprising thing they found was that the studied group had very firm attitudes toward brand name products. Some brands had an accepted image and were bought; others were considered bad buys or white folks' foolishness and were ignored completely. An additional study by a supermarket group showed that Negroes tended to buy products that were expensive ("for image") or very cheap ("for value"). They drank Cutty Sark scotch or dollar wine, drove loaded Cadillacs or stripped Fords. The black model's main job was to encourage his black brothers and sisters to start buying mediocre products made for middle-class consumption.

One copy supervisor at McCann-Erickson commented, "Everybody's up tight about using blacks in commercials. If I call a model agency and say that we want to look at some girls because we have a hair-coloring commercial for a long-haired blonde, they'll send over two or three Afro-headed blacks. Not only that, the producer'll try to fit one in somewhere."

Barbara Proctor, owner of a black-oriented ad agency, is against using "white" commercials for blacks. She says, "It doesn't work. Blacks have their own aura, environment, patois, and interrelationships that are natural and believable. None of this appears in black-populated white commercials. In fact, black commercials today are really black-face commercials."

She feels that this approach not only does not turn on the country's more than 23 million blacks but actually turns them against certain products.

In Kansas City a strong personality named Inez Kaiser runs her own advertising and public-relations company. She agrees with Barbara Proctor, goes on to say that New York and Chicago ad agencies are out of touch. For example, she says, the big city agencies use models in commercials sporting Afro haircuts' whereas most Negroes in the country have nothing to do with the Afro look or any radical or unusual form of dress.

One other type of black commercial has had a fair degree of success. In these, noted black personalities do testimonials for products. Ethel Waters did Jell-O; Lena Horne did Schaefer beer; comedian Flip Wilson did what the agency called the "first really non-token black commercial," a spot made for Sea & Ski suntan lotion and addressed to a generally white audience. The theme that pushed the virtues of Sea & Ski was "Brown is beautiful."

The impact of blacks on and in advertising was used as the basis for a no-punches-pulled motion picture called *Putney Swope*. Audiences, especially black ones and admen, stayed away by the millions. It finally putt-putneyed out.

For the "personality" commercial the writer usually comes up with an idea for Eve Arden, the art director changes it to Phyllis Diller, and the producer wants to use Carol Burnett. Telephone calls are made to agents, and the creative team waits.

"Eve wants $30,000 to do it," the Coast agent calls back about Miss Arden.

"Phyllis has a product conflict and can't do it," New York telephones.

"Carol isn't doing commercials for anybody," her agent reports back.

"Okay, now we go to work," says the producer. He places a call to California.

"Harry?" he says. "Harry, you know how I wanted to use your client Eve Arden in these new commercials, but what could I do? Phyllis's agent wanted them for her. Carol's agent is mad for them, feels they give her a whole new image. What could I do, Harry?"

He listens for a moment. "No, Harry, nothing is signed yet, Harry but it's all set, y'know? . . . I don't know, Harry . . . Sure money is important to the client but more important is a good commercial, y'know? . . . Listen Harry, I wouldn't do this for anybody but only Eve because she's such a sweetheart and I really want her because she'll make these spots sing, Harry, sing! . . . Okay, call me back. And . . . uh . . . Harry . . . listen, I think the old man could be talked out of Phyllis and Carol if Eve could see her way clear to doing it for let's say, ten?"

Says Harry, calling Eve, "Listen, honey, I got ten for you against double scale residuals for two spots. Let's grab it before he changes his mind. Naw, he doesn't have anybody else. Sure we woulda done it for five if he hadn't out-cuted himself."

"Those agency jerks are all alike," somebody in Harry's office says. They all laugh.

The deal is made. Eve Arden (or whoever) shows up for work on the day the commercial is being shot.

The second method of casting is the open interview. These are run for the benefit of everyone involved in the production. (A small representation would have to include the copywriter, the copy chief or creative director, the art director and maybe the senior art director, the agency producer and his assistant, the account executive, the account supervisor, the assistant account executive, the advertising manager for the client, his assistant, and the marketing director.) The interviews are held at the agency or in a conference room at the film studio. They go something like this:

"Hi, honey, let's see your pictures. That's Allan the director and over there Willie and Chick and Tom and Nate from the agency and Maurie and Jack from the Jersey City plant of the client and show your back to Willie. Let's see you've done a Palmolive and a Ford and your agent says you have no conflicts with this product on the air. I see you played the part of Annie in *Oklahoma* third road show company. Well listen this script's about a new prepared dinner that you bake right in the refrigerator and you read the part of woman number one just down to where she puts it in the bowl. No go ahead and take a minute to look it over. Uh-huh, a little faster please. No honey that's woman number one reads that line. Yeah well thanks for coming in and are you available next Thursday. We'll be in touch with your agent honey and thanks for coming in. Next Maurie."

Every day in maybe 25 film studios across the country this monologue or one close to it parades models and talents to the pimpled wonders who stamp out cigar butts in their Dixie cup coffee and think about their new suede slacks. In they come. The Korduroy Kids from the Pasadena Playhouse with a cracked, stained picture of themselves as Othello in their back pocket. And the mini-skirts with talent to match. And the stand-ups who do five minutes of Las Vegas lounge to show what great guys they are and the I'd-do-anything-for-the-job hustlers and the I've-been-sick and the I've-never-been-better.

Another version of this is the Cattle Call. It's exactly the same except that somebody—the writer, the advertiser, the director—has said, "Let's see lots of people."

"Send 'em over by the busload," the film-studio girl tells the model and talent agencies.

They're supposed to arrive every couple of minutes to keep traffic moving. They don't. Three or four arrive at once. Then 22 are lined up in the hall. A half-hour later, 74 are jamming the waiting room and the corridor making a wallow-wallow noise like a backward-run soundtrack. Some come in smiling and some with their toes turned in and some with their legs astride their defiance. And when the door opens and closes and Maurie yells, "Who's next?" you can tune in to an alien world:

"There's an Un-cola at Lacy."

"I got a Miracle White."

"Another strike and I'm going to Rome."

There might be another Garbo sitting out there. Right next to the carhop. They both won beauty contests at home. They both have mothers who budgeted and hid money from the old man to buy them their first Angel Pageant costume, to give them a makeup kit for their birthday, to help send them to the state finals at Evansville. They're both studying dramatics: one with the extra money she makes hustling drunks at a Santa Monica bar, the other second-hand from a theater arts major at UCLA. Tonight, they'll do a scene from *Detective Story* before they go to bed. The men are getting different. Less pretty. More talented. A square face and a pear-shaped tone and a well-rounded wardrobe isn't enough anymore. Crooked teeth, a broken nose, interesting scars, voices full of broken glass: these are what the agency boys look for. They want another John Cassavetes, Paul Richards, Peter Falk—and—every once in a while, they find him, too.

For all of them—the untrained pretties and the theater guild pros—there must be a better way to make a living. Most of this group make under $1,500 a year from commercials; a few exceptions make $15,000. They bunk up four to a one- or two-bedroom apartment in the Valley or in the Village and hustle each other for food and carfare, for cigarettes and soap powder and a false eyelash to match the one that didn't get lost. There's the Snowmobile King fresh from his triumph in the Ford Festival industrial film. Next to him Miss Hurst Golden Shifter runner-up who just knows she'll be picked as next year's Dodge girl—if there is a Dodge girl next year, if there is a next year.

Bellevue and Los Angeles County Hospitals get a lot of them. They pump out their stomachs or sew up their wrists, clean up the abortion, patch up the knife cuts, put something on the belt buckle welts. Sometimes all they do is call the coroner.

In the meantime, between starvation and stardom, they are there and they are young and they are beautiful. And because they are beautiful and because they are hungry, they use what they have. After all, so does everybody else.

"He'll want to see my legs again. He always does."

He usually gets to see them, too. Later.

"There is nothing secret about working steadily in commercials," says an ex-Gaslight Club waitress. "You have to show some personal interest in the project—like taking the producer or the director or both of them to bed."

Another queen of the 60-second movies says, "If I'd realized that underneath their button-down beards, agency men are just men, I wouldn't have wasted two years at the neighborhood playhouse."

I remember one casting session. A very pretty young Texas lady who had been in town for only a few days looked deadeyed at the table and said, "I'd do anything for anybody here for this part." Instead of being embarrassed, the art director was intrigued.

Another time a girl said, "Thanks, fellas, and listen, whether I get the part or not, why don't you come by my place for a drink later?"

She admitted she gets one out of three commercials that way. "Why not?" she says. "Out of town agency men are bright, interesting and fun to be with. They have big expense accounts, stay at the best places, eat at the best restaurants. When an agency guy invites me out for the evening I even take along my toothbrush. Why stay at my crummy pad when he has a suite—a suite!—at the Plaza?"

For the agency creative man, it's hard to say no. Surrounded by temptation in assorted Clairol colors, he has to keep biting his lip and holding onto the snap of the wife and kiddies out in the country, some country. Sometimes he wakes up in the middle of the night and stares straight ahead. He suddenly realizes why the boys who make the print ads hate him so much.

The ladies get it, too, the lady producers and girls who cast for large agencies. Every male model and actor in the city knows them, knows who they're sleeping with, and knows his chances of getting something from her—even if it's just a ten-second local spot. He knows what it will cost him. Most of the casting girls are overly ugly, overly snotty, and overly indulged. They are highly opinionated, underqualified, salary-and-space drones who keep trying to slip their sleeping buddies, male or female or both, into productions and running to the head of the department and crying if her people aren't used. The boss backs her up. He has to. She won't fix him and *his* boss up with pretty ladies anymore if he doesn't.

Of course, there are some pretty babies around who won't play. Experienced admen can spot them in a minute.

One type carries her pictures in a big leather portfolio, along with two or three shots of a handsome male stuck in the back. "Oh," she says when the interviewer reaches those. "He's a friend and I take his pictures around." This girl is out to make a name for herself—Mrs. whatever his name is. She works only to support *his* Corvette: the one she bought to keep him from moving out. The other group turns off the room by flashing a wedding band or talking a lot about her children. The play succeeds with most admen who suddenly think of the little folk at home and get a case of advanced quiet.

What do agency men really think of the models and actors they hire for commercials? Not too much.

How can they?

They hire them and makeup and wardrobe them and get them on a $1,000-a-minute stage and say, "Camera. Action," and point at them and the actors still say things like: "Always ask for Texaco Fire Chief gasoloon."

Or, "Next time don't forget Phillips Milk of Amnesia."

Or, talking about old-fashioned pot scrubbing, "Once you don't like it, you always will." Or, for a mattress spot, "Does your husband wake up dill and lustless?" Or, "This is typical of the scare and kill shown by the chemical company."

It's little wonder that during a casting session, one director turned to a copywriter and said, "I want to talk to you about this commercial."

"Go ahead," said the writer.

"Not in front of the talent," the director answered.

"Well, spell it then."

Topics for Discussion

1. Do you agree with Galanoy that advertisers think "the average American is a lump, his wife is a frump, and they live in a dump . . . most Americans are dreary drudges with intellectual horizons limited to the distance they can throw a beer can." If advertisers believe this, can you see this attitude reflected in current advertisements? Can you cite any current advertising which would refute Galanoy's contention?
2. Do you find some or all advertising insulting? Are you insulted when advertising tells you that you smell and need deodorant or mouthwash, or that you don't look nice and need to use a hair dye, makeup, or shampoo? Do you feel, as Galanoy says advertisers do, that the average American is ugly?
3. At first, famous actors and actresses refused to do commercials. Why? What made them change this attitude? How often do you see commercials with famous people endorsing products? Have you ever used a particular product because someone famous endorsed it?
4. If there is a great demand for famous people to do commercials, how do you reconcile this with Galanoy's contention that advertisers want to use "unattractive," "plain," or "ugly" people in their commercials?
5. "Commercials do make stars," says Galanoy, and he mentions Barbara Feldon and Sandy Duncan as two examples. Can you think of anyone famous you see only in commercials?
6. Galanoy mentions the increasing use of black actors and actresses in advertising. Have you noticed any change in the racial content of advertisements?
7. Does Galanoy picture advertising as a "glamorous" business? What kind of people does Galanoy picture as working in advertising?
8. Make a brief survey of current television commercials. What type of commercial is dominant—famous person endorsement, plain people, hidden camera, or some other?

Rhetorical Considerations

1. Galanoy discusses many aspects of advertising in this essay, but what is his thesis? Does he state his thesis at any point in the essay?
2. Much of this essay is humorous, but some of it isn't. Speaking of the young people who try for jobs in advertising, Galanoy says that "Bellvue and Los Angeles County Hospitals get a lot of them. They pump out their stomachs or sew up their wrists, clean up the abortion, patch up the knife cuts, put something on the belt buckle welts. Sometimes all they do is call the coroner." How does this fit in with the humorous tone of the article?
3. Look at the prose style of this article. Note the use of such sentence fragments as "Honest, real folks," and "Oh, him. Yup. Him." Why does Galanoy use this style? What effect is he trying to achieve?
4. How well organized is this essay? Many aspects of advertising are discussed—financial, aesthetic, racial. How has Galanoy organized all his disparate elements?
5. Does this essay go anyplace? That is, does it lead to some kind of conclusion about advertising or does it merely discuss some interesting aspects of the business?
6. Galanoy has a wealth of anecdotes in his essay. Does he use too many? If you were to eliminate half or all of these anecdotes what would remain? What does this tell you about the essay?

Sweet Talk— The Rhetoric of Advertising

Walker Gibson

More than one observer has remarked that the freshest writing going on nowadays comes from the ad agencies on Madison Avenue. If there is anything to that, we should be able to say what's fresh about it, and what kinds of voice are produced by such freshness. More, we should be able, by comparing details of Madison Avenue style with those of Tough Talk, to indicate some rhetorical techniques by which the adwriter characteristically makes his devastating pitch.

The first thing to do is look at some ads. I offer eight of them below—that is, I reproduce the first hundred words or so (often the whole) of eight ads plucked out of magazines. I make no apology for the arbitrary choice: these simply seemed to me interesting rhetorically. First to knock, first admitted. They offer a grabbag of goods and services: a bank, a magazine, a whisky, a telephone gadget, a bath soap, a prepared dinner, a refrigerator, and a car. But you needn't buy a thing to enjoy the rhetoric, and no salesman will call.

For convenience I label this chunk of language Advertising Rhetoric of Madison Avenue, or AROMA for short.

AD #1

For a better way to take care of your nest egg, talk to the people at Chase Manhattan. So many otherwise well-ordered people unaccountably lose their touch when the subject is personal investments.

If you're letting investment cares compete with the quiet hours—don't. Get hold of The Chase Manhattan Bank's Personal Trust Division right away and let it take over.

And, if you're interested, the Personal Trust Division will also go out of its way to act as your Executor and Trustee, advise you on your estate with you and your lawyer.

AD #2

People listen to people who *know*. Years ago Newsweek broke the language barrier by publishing straight facts in plain English. The effect on communications was startling. Today, more people know what they're talking about. And because these people have made up their own minds, they can communicate more meaningfully to other people. Advertisers are aware of this communications chain-of-command. They have found that through Newsweek it also moves goods. We can elaborate on this subject with all sorts of compelling statistics. But we'd much rather try it first in plain English: More *news*—more *straight news*—in NEWSWEEK.

AD #3

You can't tell one scotch from another. Or can you? Identifying a scotch is a rare skill confined to the rarefied and mysterious world of the connoisseur. The layman, however, is content with his limited but perfectly adequate ability to know what he likes. (Every man his own connoisseur.) It happens that out of the many brands of Scotch available most people choose Johnnie Walker—the Scotch of Scotch. They have made it the world's best-selling scotch. It is specially and delightfully different. Different in a way that most people prefer.

AD #4

They're all on the telephone!

It's the new Bell Speakerphone. It's a hands-free, group-talk, across-the-room kind of telephone. About as flexible as a phone can be. Perfect for "conference" conversations. Ideal when you need both hands free for writing or filing or searching. Just right when it's more convenient for you to talk from another part of the room.

Of course, you can regulate volume, move the microphone or speaker anywhere on your desk or a table, switch to the handset for privacy, or use it for intercom calls. Think of the people on your staff who can benefit from this versatile new Speakerphone. Then call your Bell Telephone Business Office for full particulars.

AD #5

Dry skin? Not me, darling.

Every inch of little me is as smooth as (well, you know what).
   Because I never, never bathe without Sardo.
Sardo bathes away dry skin. Gives my skin precious moisture
         (moisture is really a girl's best friend).
And Sardo works from bath to bath to keep moisture in,
      dryness out. Rough heels? Chapped knees?
   Flaky elbows? Itchy skin? Not me! I'm an
      old smoothie. (You'd never guess how old.) Next bath,
why don't you add a capful of wonderful Sardo?
   You'll be deliciously smooth all over again.
   Where do you get Sardo? At any drug
   or cosmetic counter. Where else?

AD #6

You may have tried Kraft Dinners before and been delighted at how quick and easy they are—and how unusually good. Well, wait till you taste these *new* Dinners from Kraft. They're complete, the finest of their kind, made with all the best Kraft ingredients.

Tomorrow, help yourself to the new Kraft Pizza with Cheese. Complete, from crispy crust to tomato cheese topping. Or the Spaghetti with Meat Sauce. Lots of tender juicy beef—more beef than you'd ever expect in a sauce.

Of course they're homemade good because you cook them up fresh, yourself! When *you* do that important final cooking, everything comes out fresh and full of flavor—the way you like it.

AD #7

Hollow legs love Foodarama living.

Your family will love it too!

With Foodarama's supermarket selection of foods on hand, your family enjoys better meals. You save time by shopping less . . . save money by having room for "specials." Entertaining's more fun because you can prepare everything in advance.

You never defrost Foodarama—either the refrigerator or freezer.

And Kelvinator's "No-Frost" Foodarama costs less to buy and operate than a separate refrigerator or freezer. So much better living and savings are possible because of the Kelvinator Constant Basic Improvement program. It's another way American Motors brings you more *real value* just as in Rambler cars.

AD #8

Here's the car that's all brand-new in a pleasing new size! We made Chevelle for people who like the way a small car handles and parks—yet still want wide-open spaces inside, with a good-sized trunk to match. So we put together refreshing new styling, stretch-out interior room, big choice in performance, a huge 27-cu.-ft. trunk—all in a size that's a good foot shorter than the big cars! Inside, you'll find foam-fashioned seats topped with the newest in expensive vinyls and fabrics. In most models there's a thick color-keyed carpeting that wears like iron. And a wide range of new decorator colors.

What about the eight personalities we have just met? Are they hard men who have been around? Clearly they are not. (One, #5, is not a man at all, but a particularly silly female. More of her later.) These people simply do not present themselves as *hard,* nor do they give any hint of a violent world they could have been around in. Do they subtly *imply* an intimacy with the reader? No: their intimacy with you and me is decidedly *explic-*

it. The voices talk as if they knew us exceedingly well, and they characterize us, the reader, in specific ways. (We own a nest egg in Ad #1; we are a business executive in #4; we run the family kitchen in 6 and 7.) Do these voices tend to ignore us in favor of paying attention to their own thoughts and feelings? They do not. In fact they scarcely *have* any thoughts and feelings except as these relate to *our* needs and desires. Very polite voices we have here, whose central interest is their effort to be nice to you and me.

Words, their size. To be statistical about our tiny samplings, the frequency of monosyllables in AROMA comes to 68 per cent of the total words used. This may seem a little surprising, since one hardly thinks of advertising as complex prose. Partly we can point to the adwriter's polysyllabic tradenames (Kelvinator, Speakerphone) and perhaps his taste for terms with a speciously scientific look to them. But there also seems to be some willingness on the part of AROMA voices to use words just a little elaborate, words that could not possibly appear on the first pages of *Farewell to Arms* or *All the King's Men*. There are mouth-filling adverbs like *unaccountably, meaningfully, delightfully, deliciously*. Sometimes we read a windy cliché whose faded elegance we seem invited to appreciate, like *the rarefied and mysterious world of the connoisseur* in Ad #3. You do not sell the goods, evidently, by extreme simplicity of diction.

Modifiers. An adwriter is inconceivable without modification; his product has got to be called *best-selling, delightfully different, finest, all brand-new*. It therefore follows that AROMA contains more adjectives. But the attentive reader will notice something peculiar about the way nouns are modified in AROMA, a particular trick of coining phrases that deserves a longer look.

One of the traditional ways in which modifiers have come into being historically is of course by transfer from other parts of speech, notably from nouns. Children who attend school become school children; trees that bear fruit become fruit trees; lamps that illuminate streets are street lamps. By this process a clumsy phrase can be shortened, perhaps strengthened. The technical name for this use of words is the "noun adjunct." Many noun adjuncts like *fruit trees* have so thoroughly entered the language that we treat them practically as single names, and some of them eventually come to be written as one word, like *landlord.*

The distinction I am making here is between a true adjective (*tall children*) and a noun adjunct (*school children*), and my method of discriminating between the two is borrowed from the practice of contemporary linguists. It is simple enough: you call a particular modifier an adjective when you can transpose the construction in which it appears into a sentence pattern using *be* or *seem.* Thus "the tall children" can be transposed into "the children are tall" or "the children seem tall." Furthermore you can inflect the modifier: *taller* children, *tallest* children. *Tall* then is a true adjective. But the noun adjunct *school children* won't work. "The children were school." "Schooler children." "The schoolest children seemed school."

There are several noun adjuncts in our samples of AROMA. The use of this particular construction is fashionable in our time—further evidence for the point noted by scholars that the language is increasing in "nominalization" and decreasing in "predication." But why should this development be taking place? To take an example from AROMA, why do we say *decorator colors* rather than "colors preferred by decorators" or "colors invented by decorators" or "colors manufactured under the supervision of decorators"? If it's brevity we're after, the brevity has been purchased at considerable cost in clearness, for the relation between *decorator* and *colors* is woozily ambiguous.

I myself don't believe it is brevity we're after. We don't want to be brief, we only want to appear brief, we want to *seem* businesslike. Besides, there are practical advantages to ambiguity. To explain our fascination with the noun adjunct, I suggest our fascination with naming. And why do we like names? Why is it evidently more satisfactory, in our society, to name something than to say what the thing does or what it is like? Do we suffer from some mass compulsion to act as if we knew the name, in an era when our lack of absolute knowledge is a commonplace assumption? Are we compensating, in some obscure way? In any case there is no doubt that this elliptical process of name-calling has been accelerated in our time, and that many familiar noun adjuncts are associated exclusively with modern life. Here are some examples from passages we have already considered in this book: *business district, highway patrolman, Jim Crow town, dirt shoulder, world brotherhood.* Occasionally other parts of speech are similarly shifted into noun modifiers, as in *a must book*, from "Unrequired Reading."

Many of AROMA's noun adjuncts are phrases that have similarly become familiar items of modern life, like *drug counter, stock rights, decorator colors.* (I find very few of the older kinds of phrases, no street lamps, no fruit trees, no school children.) But the great difference is this: the adwriter does not confine himself to phrases with which our culture is already familiar. He himself puts into play the traditional technique of displacing nouns (or other parts of speech) in order to cook up entirely new phrases. *Foodarama living. Communications chain-of-command. Supermarket selection.* Chevrolet speaks of its *stretch-out interior room.* The Bell Company, advertising a gadget for *conference conversations* and *intercom calls,* praises the beauties of a *hands-free, group-talk, across-the-room kind of telephone.* This is all very poetical and imaginative (I'm not saying, of course, that you have to like it). Most important, though, is the fascination with naming. Consider the implication. If one says "Hungry people love the kind of living that is associated with owning a Foodarama refrigerator," one has made more or less the point that Kelvinator makes at the beginning of Ad #7. But this is not the language of the actual ad, which reads "Hollow legs love Foodarama living." Putting aside the forced whimsy of the opening phrase, the use of *Foodarama living* as a name seems to me significant. It is not an explicit metaphor, as if one were to say that a kind of living might be associated with a kind of refrigerator. Not at all: it is a named living. It exists! We have no way of knowing whether such manipulation of nouns sells refrigerators and other nice things, but somebody must think it does, because this naming device is repeated again and again throughout AROMA.

Similarly, if you speak of "the barriers that separate people because of their difficulties with language," you are referring to a familiar problem whose perplexities will continue to disturb us, probably forever. But if you coin the phrase *language barrier,* you make the problem precise and simple, by naming it, and of course by implying an analogy with "sound barrier." You can then go ahead, as Ad #2 does, and say you've broken it, and no doubt somebody will believe you.

Modifiers of adjectives. Some adverbs, like *very* or *extremely,* serve the lowly purpose of beefing up the failing force of an adjective. They are called "intensifiers," and their use may be a key to attitudes about modification. It is as if the speaker were saying that a mere adjective (*good, fine*) were not enough to describe the beauties in question, and the phrasing has to be *very fine, extremely good.* AROMA has several clear-cut examples (*just right, much better*), and it follows that the AROMA writers are generally liberal with the modifying of modifiers—that is, with the prefixing of an adverb to the noun-modifying adjective. *Specially and delightfully different* is a nice double example, while *homemade good* displays again the adwriter's cavalier attitude toward conventional grammar. There are very few of these piled-up modifications in our other passages, though there is a nice one—*perturbingly moving*—in "Unrequired Reading." I take it that the practice of heaping adverbs onto adjectives in this manner is characteristic of AROMA.

The definite article. The determiner *the* implies a relation of common understanding between speaker and reader. The adwriter too must set up an intimate relation with his reader and force assumptions on him. He *does* have to set it up, he forces the assumptions. The AROMA writer *states* it, works on it, and leaps right into our laps. He does not do this with a high proportion of definite articles. (Articles in the ads: 4 per cent of all words.) He does it with a battery of other weapons, which we may now consider.

Tone. In adwriting, tone is everything. The writer's problem is to fabricate an assumed reader who has to be an attractive person with whom the real reader may be expected to identify cheerfully. Second, he must be an admirer or user, or highly prospective admirer or user, of the writer's product. The assumed reader is specifically defined, with considerable detail. "Of course they're homemade good because you cook them up fresh, yourself! When *you* do that important final cooking, everything comes out fresh and full of flavor—

the way you like it." (Ad #6.) That, of course, is a crude example, in which the rejoinder "I do? Are you sure? What if I hate cooking?" is unthinkable.

We are directly assaulted. Not only are we addressed personally by the pronoun, but we are frequently commanded in imperative verbs, or forced to respond to rhetorical questions ("Why not try . . .?"). Meanwhile every linguistic device known to man is brought to bear on the language to secure intimacy with the reader. For example we have a whole punctuation system appropriate to informal, colloquial expression. There are dashes, parentheses, exclamation marks. The physical layout of an ad, with its spacing and colors, functions also as a kind of punctuation, and of course in the whole appearance and pictorial matter of an ad there are enormous unconventional resources for informality simply not available to conventional writers. The sentence structure in AROMA is exceedingly flexible and free-swinging; there are 20 instances of "sentences" that have either no subject or no main verb, what the schoolmarm calls a sentence fragment. (*Dry skin? Not me, darling.* #5.) The length of sentences has been reduced almost to the disappearing point. (Average length of AROMA sentences: 11 words. Average of Ad #5: less than 6 words.) Finally, the oral-speech-intimate-tone is supported by contractions (*you'll, you've*).

The Sweet Talker may now be defined more closely. A Sweet Talker is not at all a hard man who has been around. He addresses me directly ("you"), and when he says "you" he doesn't mean just anybody, he means *me*. He is not a passionate or self-centered man, more concerned with his own feelings than with my needs and desires. On the contrary, he goes out of his way to be nice to me. He defines me as a very particular person with identifiable qualities. (This of course is a problem, for they may not be qualities I possess or desire.) He may use the rhetorical devices of informal speech (contractions, fragments, eccentric punctuation) to secure his intimacy with me. His sentence structure is simple but his vocabulary is not. He modifies generously. He has no great love for the definite article.

On the other hand, he loves to name things. If he is an adwriter he loves to make up new names for things and call things by those names. Foodarama living, that's

The Age of Communication

the life. Precisely because we have been forced into positions of such intimacy, we are impelled to accept the names. And to accept the names is to buy the product, to get rid of that old refrigerator, the one that failed to provide Foodarama living.

But having said that, I add an unconventional opinion. The adwriter's rhetoric may not be so dangerous as it is often alleged to be. The know-it-all intimacy of AROMA offends me, at least, less violently than fictitious omniscience in newswriting. For one thing, of course, we recognize it's an ad; our guard is up. For another, the best ads are done with such dash and good humor that some of them have built into them their own self-irony. The tone is pushed to such extreme chumminess (Not me, darling!) that it becomes parody. (Of course we may still buy the product for all that.) Many ads are composed in language that surely suggests, at least to most readers, that the words were composed in a spirit of frolicsome exaggeration.

An example of such a frolic is Ad #1, one of the famous series of nest-egg ads. (An enormous egg, elegantly chained, is pictured in the possession of a man of means, who is engaged in some expensive leisure-time pleasure often involving boats.) "For a better way to take care of your nest egg [the ad begins], talk to the people at Chase Manhattan. So many otherwise well-ordered people unaccountably lose their touch when the subject is personal investments." The whole ad depends for its startling effect upon a time-honored and witty literary technique, that of bringing a dead metaphor (nest egg) to life. And the pictured egg is wonderfully outsize, polished, clad in its golden chain. The prose of the ad is similarly elegant and similarly exaggerated. The rather fancy adverb *unaccountably* helps set the tone. There will be no prying here into the reasons why people are so sloppy with their investments, and if you are that way too, rest assured that you are "otherwise well-ordered." "Such nuisance details as stock rights and record keeping, call dates and coupons are Chase Manhattan's dish of tea."

The assumed reader of such prose is an almost incredible character—or so it seems to me. The bland gayety with which speaker and reader dismiss stock rights and record keeping as "nuisance details" is magnificently aristocratic. *La dolce vita.* Let 'em eat cake. For all the gestures of warm intimacy, the tone is contrived and stylized. Somebody is kidding somebody, more or less in the spirit of the flashy nest-egg photograph that heads the ad. There are, no doubt, thousands of real-life people who think of stock coupons as nuisance details, but the ad's bravado in accepting such privileged sloth as perfectly normal is almost delightful. The assumptions are so extreme that the ad contains its own parody. I see this assumed author as a complex wit capable of laughing at his own language as he utters it. In fact, he could fairly be called "unreliable."

An ad aimed at an entirely different buying audience, but with a narrator more spectacularly unreliable, is the charming #5. Here a pert young lady is pictured in her bath, holding to her ear one of those old-fashioned new-fashionable telephone handsets. Her left hand postures affectedly somewhere in the vicinity of her just-invisible bosom. Her hair is gaily blond and sports a pink ribbon; her amused eyes, looking right offstage at you and me, are thoroughly made up; her lipstick is delicious. In sum, this kitten is just a little absurd, and perhaps the artificial frivolity of her style suggests that she knows it. Or that somebody knows it. Of course what she is saying over the phone, to an acquaintance unidentified, is far more absurd.

Dry skin? Not me, darling.
Every inch of little me is as smooth as (well, you know
what).
Because I never, never bathe without Sardo.
Sardo bathes away dry skin. Gives my skin precious
moisture
(moisture is really a girl's best friend).

Here is a case, surely, where at least some readers, if not most readers, are expected to laugh at the young lady while maintaining a sympathetic touch with an assumed author who is also laughing at his creation. At the same time the assumed author is frankly selling a product! It is all quite complicated. The lady's dated clichés and general silliness are intolerable except as parody, though, doubtless, many readers of the *Ladies Home Journal* (where it appeared) read the ad, took the language straight, and bought the stuff. But the adwriter has ingeniously produced such an exaggerated

The Age of Communication

tone that readers of a more critical turn of mind (you and I, dear assumed reader?) may also enjoy the ad. *And buy the stuff!* The assumed author is a very slippery fellow, with something for everybody. Even the young lady in the ad seems to have some sense of AROMA's tired phrases, and she kids them as she utters them. "Where do you get Sardo? At any drug or cosmetic counter. Where else?" We can scarcely imagine anyone, outside of an ad, actually saying "any drug or cosmetic counter." That is ad-language. But her flip question, "Where else?" undercuts it, and forces us to reconsider this young lady. Who *is* she? Is she terribly bright or terribly dumb? Who is her assumed author, how much of this is *he* making fun of? The intricacies of unreliability here are worthy of a novelist.

Questions about the narrating voice in an ad are even more pressing on television. There a voice literally speaks, and our response is governed not only by its rhetoric but by audible tone, visible facial expression, gesture, and most of the other forces of face-to-face communication. Even in an ad in which the speaker does not appear on the screen, his manner of speech conveys personality and attitude—sometimes an attitude that expresses irony about his own "message."

Take the recent series of Rheingold Beer commercials, well known in New York, whose final line—we must be doing something right—has become a national cliché. A characteristic ad in this series gives us some quick shots of a Greek-American wedding, full of mirth and old-world jollity. Gay dancers of various ages are seen cooling off with bottles of New York's favorite beer. "In New York City," the voice intones (I quote from memory), "where there are more Greeks than in Sparta, more people drink Rheingold than any other brand. How come so many Greeks prefer Rheingold? We don't know, but we must be doing something right."

The illogic here must be at least subconsciously apparent to any listener; it becomes obvious if we reduce it to a syllogism.

> Lots of Greeks live in New York.
> Lots of New Yorkers prefer Rheingold.
> Lots of Greeks prefer Rheingold.

The loophole in this line of argument is big enough to drive a beer truck through. Known to the logician as the Fallacy of the Undistributed Middle, it is a familiar type of chicanery, but rarely is it so ostentatious. I suspect that is just the point. The voice that utters all this does so with such dry urbanity that we can hardly believe he expects us to be taken in, at least by his logic. "You and I are men of this world," he *may* be saying, "and we recognize that the reasoning in this commercial is absurd. What else would we expect? But how good-humored we are about it all, how charming the Greeks are at their convivial high jinks, how charming *I* am to entertain you not only with that Greek folderol but with the very absurdity of my argument! On the whole, considering the easy gayety of this little show I've put on for you, you may as well drink Rheingold too. I mean, it can't be *that* bad!" He may be saying all that, to some of his listeners. On the other hand he may not.

The language of modern fiction and the language of modern advertising, while obviously different, and certainly paid at different rates, share at least this in common: both are produced with more care and energy and talent than any other prose in our time. If there are fresh and imaginative uses of language to be discovered, they should be here—and they are, in their different ways. And in both genres one finds *some* uses of words so self-conscious and contrived that the reader can be unsure where he is, unsure, that is, of the speaker's voice and its relation to the assumed author. Is it possible that both these arts, the novelist's and the adwriter's, are entering a rococo phase? Who's talking? Not me, darling.

John Hart, cartoon, "B.C." August 6, 1972. By permission of John Hart and Field Enterprises, Inc.

The Age of Communication

Topic for Discussion

1. Is Gibson serious when he calls the language of advertising AROMA for short? What implications are there in his acronym?
2. Gibson says that our language is "increasing in 'nominalegations' and decreasing in 'predication'." What does he mean?
3. It becomes evident at the end of the essay that the language of advertising is only one aspect of Sweet Talk. What are some of the elements of Sweet Talk?
4. What does Gibson mean when he says that adwriting may be entering a "rococo phase"?
5. Gibson points out the illogic in the Reingold Beer commercials. Can you cite any current commercials which are also illogical?

Rhetorical Considerations

1. Gibson states his thesis immediately in his opening paragraph. How well does he develop his thesis in the essay?
2. Dashes, parentheses, and exclamation marks are used to "secure intimacy with the reader." Find two or three advertisements which rely heavily upon such punctuation to create the feeling of intimacy. How does such punctuation create this feeling?
3. Modifiers play an important role in all writing as well as advertising. Select an advertisement from a newspaper or magazine and analyze the use of modifiers in it according to the method Gibson uses.
4. Gibson says that "in advertising, tone is everything." What does he mean by tone. Give an example of two different kinds of tone in two different advertisements.
5. Look at the last two sentences in the essay. What do they mean? Are they effective as a conclusion?

How to Write Potent Copy

David Ogilvy

I. HEADLINES

THE headline is the most important element in most advertisements. It is the telegram which decides the reader whether to read the copy.

On the average, five times as many people read the headline as read the body copy. When you have written your headline, you have spent eighty cents out of your dollar.

If you haven't done some selling in your headline, you have wasted 80 per cent of your client's money. The wickedest of all sins is to run an advertisement *without* a headline. Such headless wonders are still to be found; I don't envy the copywriter who submits one to me.

A change of headline can make a difference of ten to one in sales. I never write fewer than sixteen headlines for a single advertisement, and I observe certain guides in writing them:

(1) The headline is the "ticket on the meat." Use it to flag down the readers who are prospects for the kind of product you are advertising. If you are selling a remedy for bladder weakness, display the words BLADDER WEAKNESS in your headline; they catch the eye of everyone who suffers from this inconvenience. If you want *mothers* to read your advertisement, display MOTHERS in your headline. And so on.

Conversely, do not say anything in your headline which is likely to *exclude* any readers who might be prospects for your product. Thus, if you are advertising a product which can be used equally well by men and women, don't slant your headline at women alone; it would frighten men away.

(2) Every headline should appeal to the reader's *self-interest*. It should promise her a benefit, as in my headline for Helena Rubinstein's Hormone Cream: HOW WOMEN OVER 35 CAN LOOK YOUNGER.

(3) Always try to inject *news* into your headlines, because the consumer is always on the lookout for

David Ogilvy, "How to Write Potent Copy" from *Confessions of an Advertising Man,* copyright © 1963 by Atheneum Publishers.

new products, or new ways to use an old product, or new improvements in an old product.

The two most powerful words you can use in a headline are FREE and NEW. You can seldom use FREE, but you can almost always use NEW—if you try hard enough.

(4) Other words and phrases which work wonders are HOW TO, SUDDENLY, NOW, ANNOUNCING, INTRODUCING, IT'S HERE, JUST ARRIVED, IMPORTANT DEVELOPMENT, IMPROVEMENT, AMAZING, SENSATIONAL, REMARKABLE, REVOLUTIONARY, STARTLING, MIRACLE, MAGIC, OFFER, QUICK, EASY, WANTED, CHALLENGE, ADVICE TO, THE TRUTH ABOUT, COMPARE, BARGAIN, HURRY, LAST CHANCE.

Don't turn up your nose at these clichés. They may be shopworn, but they work. That is why you see them turn up so often in the headlines of mail-order advertisers and others who can measure the results of their advertisements.

Headlines can be strengthened by the inclusion of *emotional* words, like DARLING, LOVE, FEAR, PROUD, FRIEND, and BABY. One of the most provocative advertisements which has come out of our agency showed a girl in a bathtub, talking to her lover on the telephone. The headline: *Darling, I'm having the most extraordinary experience . . . I'm head over heels in DOVE.*

(5) Five times as many people read the headline as read the body copy, so it is important that these glancers should at least be told what brand is being advertised. That is why you should always include the brand name in your headlines.

(6) Include your selling promise in your headline. This requires long headlines. When the New York University School of Retailing ran headline tests with the cooperation of a big department store, they found that headlines of ten words or longer, containing news and information, consistently sold more merchandise than short headlines.

Headlines containing six to twelve words pull more coupon returns than short headlines, and there is no significant difference between the readership of twelve-word headlines and the readership of three-word headlines. The best headline I ever wrote contained *eighteen* words: *At Sixty Miles an Hour the Loudest Noise in the New Rolls-Royce comes from the electric clock.* [1]

When the chief engineer at the Rolls-Royce factory read this, he shook his head sadly and said, "It is time we did something about that damned clock."

NOT BAD, HOW'S IT GOING?

(7) People are more likely to read your body copy if your headline arouses their curiosity; so you should end your headline with a lure to read on.

(8) Some copywriters write *tricky* headlines—puns, literary allusions, and other obscurities. This is a sin.

In the average newspaper your headline has to compete for attention with 350 others. Research has shown that readers travel so fast through this jungle that they don't stop to decipher the meaning of obscure headlines. Your headline must *telegraph* what you want to say, and it must telegraph it in plain language. Don't play games with the reader.

In 1960 the *Times Literary Supplement* attacked the whimsical tradition in British advertising, calling it "self-indulgent—a kind of middle-class private joke, apparently designed to amuse the advertiser and his client." Amen.

(9) Research shows that it is dangerous to use *negatives* in headlines. If, for example, you write OUR SALT CONTAINS NO ARSENIC, many readers will miss the negative and go away with the impression that you wrote OUR SALT CONTAINS ARSENIC.

(10) Avoid *blind* headlines—the kind which mean nothing unless you read the body copy underneath them; most people *don't*.

II. BODY COPY

When you sit down to write your body copy, pretend that you are talking to the woman on your right at a dinner party. She has asked you, "I am thinking of buying a new car. Which would you recommend?" Write your copy as if you were answering that question.

(1) Don't beat about the bush—go straight to the point. Avoid analogies of the "just as, so too" variety. Dr. Gallup has demonstrated that these two-stage arguments are generally misunderstood.

(2) Avoid superlatives, generalizations, and platitudes. Be specific and factual. Be enthusiastic, friendly, and memorable. Don't be a bore. Tell the truth, but make the truth fascinating.

How long should your copy be? It depends on the product. If you are advertising chewing gum, there isn't much to tell, so make your copy short. If, on the other hand, you are advertising a product which has a great many different qualities to recommend it, write

long copy: the more you tell, the more you sell.

There is a universal belief in lay circles that people won't read long copy. Nothing could be farther from the truth. Claude Hopkins once wrote five pages of solid text for Schlitz beer. In a few months, Schlitz moved up from fifth place to first. I once wrote a page of solid text for Good Luck Margarine, with most gratifying results.

Research shows that readership falls off rapidly up to fifty words of copy, but drops very little between fifty and 500 words. In my first Rolls-Royce advertisement I used 719 words—piling one fascinating fact on another. In the last paragraph I wrote, "People who feel diffident about driving a Rolls-Royce can buy a Bentley." Judging from the number of motorists who picked up the word "diffident" and bandied it about, I concluded that the advertisement was thoroughly read. In the next one I used 1400 words.

Every advertisement should be a *complete* sales pitch for your product. It is unrealistic to assume that consumers will read a *series* of advertisements for the same product. You should shoot the works in every advertisement, on the assumption that it is the only chance you will ever have to sell your product to the reader—*now or never*.

Says Dr. Charles Edwards of the graduate School of Retailing at New York University, "The more facts you tell, the more you sell. An advertisement's chance for success invariably increases as the number of pertinent merchandise facts included in the advertisement increases."

In my first advertisement for Puerto Rico's Operation Bootstrap, I used 961 words, and persuaded Beardsley Ruml to sign them. Fourteen thousand readers clipped the coupon from this advertisement, and scores of them later established factories in Puerto Rico. The greatest professional satisfaction I have yet had is to see the prosperity in Puerto Rican communities which had lived on the edge of starvation for four hundred years before I wrote my advertisement. If I had confined myself to a few vacuous generalities, nothing would have happened.

We have even been able to get people to read long copy about gasoline. One of our Shell advertisements contained 617 words, and 22 per cent of male readers read more than half of them.

Vic Schwab tells the story of Max Hart (of Hart, Schaffner & Marx) and his advertising manager, George L. Dyer, arguing about long copy. Dyer said, "I'll bet you ten dollars I can write a newspaper page of solid type and you'd read every word of it."

Hart scoffed at the idea. "I don't have to write a line of it to prove my point," Dyer replied. "I'll only tell

you the headline: THIS PAGE IS ALL ABOUT MAX HART."

Advertisers who put coupons in their advertisements *know* that short copy doesn't sell. In split-run tests, long copy invariably outsells short copy.

Do I hear someone say that no copywriter can write long advertisements unless his media department gives him big spaces to work with? This question should not arise, because the copywriter should be consulted before planning the media schedule.

(3) You should always include testimonials in your copy. The reader finds it easier to believe the endorsement of a fellow consumer than the puffery of an anonymous copywriter. Says Jim Young, one of the best copywriters alive today, "Every type of advertiser has the same problem; namely to be believed. The mail-order man knows nothing so potent for this purpose as the testimonial, yet the general advertiser seldom uses it."

Testimonials from celebrities get remarkably high readership, and if they are honestly written they still do not seem to provoke incredulity. The better known the celebrity, the more readers you will attract. We have featured Queen Elizabeth and Winston Churchill in "Come to Britain" advertisements, and we were able to persuade Mrs. Roosevelt to make television commercials for Good Luck Margarine. When we advertised charge accounts for Sears, Roebuck, we reproduced the credit card of Ted Williams, "recently traded by Boston to Sears."

Sometimes you can cast your entire copy in the form of a testimonial. My first advertisement for Austin cars took the form of a letter from an "anonymous diplomat" who was sending his son to Groton with money he had saved driving an Austin—a well-aimed combination of snobbery and economy. Alas, a perspicacious *Time* editor guessed that I was the anonymous diplomat, and asked the headmaster of Groton to comment. Dr. Crocker was so cross that I decided to send my son to Hotchkiss.

(4) Another profitable gambit is to give the reader helpful advice, or service. It hooks about 75 per cent more readers than copy which deals entirely with the product.

One of our Rinso advertisements told housewives how to remove stains. It was better read (Starch) and better remembered (Gallup) than any detergent advertisement in history. Unfortunately, however, it forgot to feature Rinso's main selling promise—that Rinso

SAY HELLO TO MY WIFE.

YOU TOO!

The Age of Communication

washes whiter; for this reason it should never have run. [2]

(5) I have never admired the *belles lettres* school of advertising, which reached its pompous peak in Theodore F. MacManus' famous advertisement for Cadillac, "The Penalty of Leadership," and Ned Jordan's classic, "Somewhere West of Laramie." Forty years ago the business community seems to have been impressed by these pieces of purple prose, but I have always thought them absurd; they did not give the reader a single *fact*. I share Claude Hopkins' view that "fine writing is a distinct disadvantage. So is unique literary style. They take attention away from the subject."

(6) Avoid bombast. Raymond Rubicam's famous slogan for Squibb, "The priceless ingredient of every product is the honor and integrity of its maker," reminds me of my father's advice: when a company boasts about its integrity, or a woman about her virtue, avoid the former and cultivate the latter.

(7) Unless you have some special reason to be solemn and pretentious, write your copy in the colloquial language which your customers use in everyday conversation. I have never acquired a sufficiently good ear for vernacular American to write it, but I admire copywriters who can pull it off, as in this unpublished pearl from a dairy farmer:

> Carnation Milk is the best in the land,
> Here I sit with a can in my hand.
> No tits to pull, no hay to pitch,
> Just punch a hole in the son-of-a-bitch.

It is a mistake to use highfalutin language when you advertise to uneducated people. I once used the word OBSOLETE in a headline, only to discover that 43 per cent of housewives had no idea what it meant. In another headline, I used the word INEFFABLE, only to discover that I didn't know what it meant myself.

However, many copywriters of my vintage err on the side of underestimating the educational level of the population. Philip Hauser, head of the Sociology Department at the University of Chicago, draws attention to the changes which are taking place:

> The increasing exposure of the population
> to formal schooling . . . can be expected to

---

[2] The photograph showed several different kinds of stain—lipstick, coffee, shoe-polish, blood and so forth. The blood was my own; I am the only copywriter who has ever *bled* for his client.

effect important changes in . . . the style of advertising. . . . Messages aimed at the "average" American on the assumption that he has had less than a grade school education are likely to find themselves with a declining or disappearing clientele.[3]

Meanwhile, all copywriters should read Dr. Rudolph Flesch's *Art of Plain Talk*. It will persuade them to use short words, short sentences, short paragraphs, and highly *personal* copy.

Aldous Huxley, who once tried his hand at writing advertisements, concluded that "any trace of literariness in an advertisement is fatal to its success. Advertisement writers may not be lyrical, or obscure, or in any way esoteric. They must be universally intelligible. A good advertisement has this in common with drama and oratory, that it must be immediately comprehensible and directly moving."[4]

(8) Resist the temptation to write the kind of copy which wins awards. I am always gratified when I win an award, but most of the campaigns which produce *results* never win awards, because they don't draw attention to themselves.

The juries that bestow awards are never given enough information about the *results* of the advertisements they are called upon to judge. In the absence of such information, they rely on their opinions, which are always warped toward the highbrow.

(9) Good copywriters have always resisted the temptation to *entertain*. Their achievement lies in the number of new products they get off to a flying start. In a class by himself stands Claude Hopkins, who is to advertising what Escoffier is to cooking. By today's standards, Hopkins was an unscrupulous barbarian, but technically he was the supreme master. Next I would place Raymond Rubicam, George Cecil, and James Webb Young, all of whom lacked Hopkins' ruthless salesmanship, but made up for it by their honesty, by the broader range of their work, and by their ability to write civilized copy when the occasion required it. Next I would place John Caples, the mail-order specialist from whom I have learned much.

These giants wrote their advertisements for newspapers and magazines. It is still too early to identify the best writers for television.

[3] *Scientific American* (October 1962).
[4] *Essays Old And New* (Harper & Brothers, 1927). Charles Lamb and Byron also wrote advertisements. So did Bernard Shaw, Hemingway, Marquand, Sherwood Anderson, and Faulkner—none of them with any degree of success.

Topics for Discussion

1. After reading this essay do you feel it would be easy to write an advertisement? Write two advertisements, one long and one short. Then compare your advertisements with the principles of good copy listed by Ogilvy.
2. Select three different advertisements from newspapers or magazines and analyze them according to Ogilvy's principles. How closely do the advertisements follow these principles?
3. Ogilvy says "there is a universal belief in lay circles that people won't read long copy." Do you read long advertisements? Would you read an advertisement of 700 or 1,000 words? Why or why not?
4. "Fine writing is a distinct disadvantage. So is unique literary style. They take attention away from the subject." What does this say about advertising writing? What attitude toward advertising writing does Ogilvy have?
5. Look at the collection of advertisements in the front of this book. How many have copy? How many depend more on visual effects? Which advertisements do you prefer? Why?

Rhetorical Considerations

1. This is a factual, step-by-step, how-to essay. But is it interesting to read? How does Ogilvy hold your attention?
2. Could Ogilvy have chosen a better method of organization than the mechanical method of enumeration? Why do you think he chose to list his points numerically rather than some other way?
3. This selection is divided into two parts. Is there any transition between the parts? How are the two parts joined? Is this consistent with Ogilvy's technique in the entire essay?
4. Is there any introduction or conclusion to this essay? After reading Ogilvy's philosophy of writing are you surprised to find that his prose style is so bare and unadorned? How does this relate to Gibson's contention that advertising relies heavily on modifiers?

The Creative Life

Jerry Della Femina

There are talented people all over New York today who are capable of turning out advertising that doesn't drive people crazy and does sell the product. Problem is whether the people can sell their advertising to their agencies and their accounts. Within every big agency there's a pocket of good people who for some reason manage to save the situation, make the advertising and do it well. Within every agency. When I went to Bates my team was, I modestly believe, that quality pocket of advertising. We turned out some excellent advertising at Bates. In one year, we literally turned the Panasonic Electronics account around.

* * *

The first day they had a meeting on the Japanese electronics company, Panasonic, and there must have been six or seven guys there: the account supervisor, the account executive, the executive art director, and a couple of others. I figured I'd keep my mouth shut for a few minutes, like it was my first morning in the place. One guy said, "Well, what are we going to do about Panasonic?" And everybody sat around, frowning and thinking about Panasonic. Finally, I decided, what the hell, I'll throw a line to loosen them up—I mean, they were paying me $50,000 a year plus a $5,000-a-year expense account, and I thought they deserved something for all this bread. So I said, "Hey, I've got it, I've got it." Everybody jumped. Then I got very dramatic, really setting them up. "I see a headline, yes, I see this headline." "What is it?" they yelled. "I see it all now," I said, "I see an entire campaign built around this headline." They all were looking at me now. "The headline is, the headline is: 'From Those Wonderful Folks Who Gave You Pearl Harbor.'"

Complete silence. Dead silence. And then the art director went into hysterics, like he was hitting the floor. To him it was funny. One of the account guys who was smoking a pipe—well, his mouth opened up at the line and his pipe dropped all over him, and he spent the next five minutes trying to put out the sparks. The rest of them looked at me as if to say, "God, where are we, what did we do?" They looked very depressed. I was pretty pleased. I thought it wasn't too bad a line. Later in the day I repeated the line to the guy who hired me, did the same bit for him. The feeling wasn't as spontaneous as all that the second time around but it served its purpose. I know why I do these things: it sets the pace, it really tells people who I am, what I feel.

Now advertising is a small business, with a lot of gossip, and there are a lot of guys sitting around in their offices with not too much to do, so when they hear a funny story or a crazy line they sit and call each other up to pass it on. I became known as the Pearl Harbor guy at Panasonic.

* * *

I really don't think creative people are afraid of losing their jobs at the whim of the agency, but there is one thing that drives them up the wall: fear of losing their talent, their abilities. Everybody I know feels this pressure. Is this ability something like magic? Will it ever just disappear? Will the day come when you sit down and suddenly you don't feel the same thing working in you the way you used to? You can't write any more. The words don't go together.

* * *

Listen, somebody is paying you thirty-five, forty grand a year to do this thing, copywriting, or being an art director, and you're bound to have this fear of going dry.

* * *

Most writers and art directors become impatient when they've got a tough problem, and that's where they get into trouble. They play, they dance, they do everything in their power to look as though they're producing advertising. And the minute they come in your office you know they're pretending. They're cold and they're dry and they know it and you know it and they know you know it.

* * *

Another problem with copywriters and art directors is the problem of recognition. There are a lot of copywriters who get mixed up and think they're Faulkner or Hemingway. They sit there and they work and they mold and they play and when it's over they've written something that's absolutely beautiful but they forget one thing. It's within the confines of a page that's bought by a media director. What kills most copywriters is that people don't buy *Life* magazine to read their ads. People don't buy *Gourmet* magazine to read their ad for Bombay Gin. People are buying *Gourmet* to read the recipes, and the ads are just an intrusion on people's time. That is why it is our job to get more attention than anything else. Nobody buys any magazine to read an ad. But a lot of guys act as though this is what is happening. This guy sat there, he's written this thing, and as far as he's concerned, this is it. Then he meets someone at a party and is explaining with a great deal of pride that he is a copywriter and the person says, "Oh, you put the captions on the bottom of the pictures."

I've had account executives who sit down and practically cry, asking me to change something because the client's going to yell. "We're going to lose the account." That's the big word all the time from the account executives to the copywriters and the art directors.

Once a year the New York copywriters hold a party. Last year it was held in a photographer's studio with maybe five hundred people jammed into a room that can really only hold about two hundred. With a rock-and-roll band that's blasting so you can't hear yourself think. Copywriters aren't the kind of people who usually go to parties. But this is the party they all go to, this is where they're going to get that job or they're going to meet that guy or they're going to do something that is going to change their lives.

They try to make their contacts. Any creative director who walked from one end of the room to the other had at least eight people tell him, "Can I bring my portfolio up and see you on Monday?" One after another. "Hi, how are you? I hear things are going very good. Can I bring my book up to see you on Monday? The place I'm at is really terrible; can't stand it, I can't stay there another day."

Then I met a guy at the party, and I knew him fairly well. He's a very good writer and kind of a strange kid, very quiet, but nothing unusual about him. He was making about thirty thousand a year. At that party he was very uptight.

What was it all about? He'd been fired that morning. And he said, "I've got five hundred dollars in the bank, I make thirty thousand a year, and I pay two hundred and eighty-four dollars a month in rent." Who knows where his money went? Clothes, apartment, chicks, I don't know. But he'd blown all his money and there he was, thirty-one or thirty-two, and I tell you he was a desperate kid, he really was. I had never seen him like that. "What am I going to do?" he asked. "How about some free-lance?" I said. He shook his head. He must have made twenty calls that day because every time I said, "Did you call Ned, did you call Ron, did you call Ed?" he'd shake his head yes. He'd called everybody worth calling. So he's run out of names to call and he's only one day out of a job. Now he starts with the headhunters and asks them to start setting up appointments for him.

He's a good writer. That's the scary part of it. He blew his last job essentially because he's a very tough sport. He won't take any garbage. He had been working for Leber, Katz & Paccione, and Patch finally couldn't take any more lip from him. So out he went.

* * *

On about the fourth job out, he's not going to be so quick to be such a smart-ass. He mentioned to me that he had called a small agency which is really not an advertising agency but rather a dress house; they do all of that Seventh Avenue advertising you see in *Women's Wear Daily* and the Sunday *Times* magazine section. Very big on girdle and bra ads. Anyhow, the owner of the agency told him to come on by on Monday, that is, the guy said, "I'll see you Monday if you want to come in and say hello." Now this agency is one of the all-time bad places—it may be the worst agency in America. And he's thinking seriously of going there for a lot of bread—if they'll have him. So he's scared, he's got a bad weekend ahead of him, and when I left him he was quaking he was so scared.

Paccione already had replaced this guy. He found a twenty-two-year-old who thought advertising was the living end and hired her for eight grand a year. I had talked to her a couple of times about coming to work for us. No sooner do I finish talking to the guy who's out of work when I run into this kid. "Hi," she says, full of life, "I got my job. I'm working. I'm starting with Leber, Katz, Paccione on Monday." "That's terrific," I said, and I started to figure it out. Patch hired this kid for eight grand, and he's saving twenty-two grand a year already by getting rid of the thirty-grand guy. Plus he's gotten rid of somebody who was a pain in the ass to him. And this young chick now is on her way to making a lot of money. Her next job she'll be able to grab off ten grand, the one after that fifteen grand, then twenty-one and then up to thirty a year. And then she'll find herself in the same position as the guy who just got fired. And she'll start to get a little nervous because there will be somebody else hot coming up.

It's really not unlike baseball. You don't have that many good years to perform in. You've got about seven, eight, or maybe nine years when you're hot and everything you do works and they're calling you for a job and the headhunters are crying for you, and then there's that long downhill slide. Which is why the shrinks are making out so well. And everybody knows that day is going to come to them. It used to kill me that I never saw a copywriter over forty. Very, very few. There are one or two guys worth mentioning but that's it. I can't figure out where they go after forty. But they leave. There must be an island somewhere that is populated only by elephants, copywriters and art directors. I can see it now. One tiny island jammed with old elephants, burned-out copywriters and art directors. That must be where they go.

I wonder what happened to most of the guys I started out in business with. I began in the mailroom of Ruthrauff & Ryan, and the only guy that I know of still in advertising from those days is Evan Stark, who is now at Doyle, Dane. Forget about where the guys are. Where are the agencies? Ruthrauff & Ryan is gone. I once went looking for a job at the Biow Agency. Gone. Donahue & Coe. Gone. Cecil & Presby. You ever hear of that one? Lennen & Newell used to be Lennen & Mitchell. You'd better amend that thought about the island with the elephants and the ex-copywriters: they also got on that island one hell of a lot of dead agencies.

Fashions change. So does advertising. The physical look of advertising changes from year to year. Last year's ads don't look as good as this year's. I get tired of looking at my old ads. They bore me. The kids are changing everything—language, clothes, style, and the visual arts.

The schools are breeding kids like nobody's business. Don't you think that when Patch got rid of that thirty-two-year-old guy that a lot of guys felt a cold draft down their necks? Of course they did. I know a $40,000-a-year art director working for Patch who's thinking about that eight-grand-a-year copywriter and he's saying to himself, "What if Patch goes out and finds an eight-grand-a-year art director—where do I go with my forty grand a year?" Phones are ringing all over town. Everybody's changing jobs. It's like musical chairs—you can't keep up. The kids are death on forty-grand-a-year art directors and copywriters. Pure death.

* * *

At that annual copywriter's party I went to last year, there was a lot of fear and the whole room was kind of nervous. What is happening is simply that there aren't enough jobs to go around. There have been periods in this business when phones were always ringing and you couldn't keep up with all of the openings. Not today—and I wonder if it is going to get even worse. It's interesting that in that room of five hundred people—mostly copywriters—there were only four or five people I would hire. Forget about the party; in the entire city there are maybe twenty-five copywriters worth mentioning. The whole city. You're talking about an agency like J. Walter Thompson which had only one writer whose work I admire—Ron Rosenfeld—and he just quit there after one year. Forget it after that. An agency like Compton must have fifty or sixty copywriters. The only guy whose stuff I can look at is my ex-partner's—Ned Tolmach. Four years ago I went to that party and this year it was an entirely different group of people. I found about ten or fifteen standbys who always show up, and the rest, you know, it's tall, gangly kids with pimples and girls who have decided it's the most glamorous business in the world and they're really out to make it.

The same sort of fear that copywriters show in public— like at the party—bugs them in private. For example, if a writer's campaign is killed, forget it, the guy is lost for a couple of months. And these campaigns are like babies. These guys sit there and they love their campaigns and they look at their ads and they take them out and mount them. You're talking about a piece of paper, and the copywriter puts it on a piece of mounting board and wraps it in cellophane and he carries it around to show people.

The dilemma is that the good writers in this town are those who are really not afraid. You've got to be loose. It's the one business where you've got to be so loose when you're sitting down to work that you can't sit there and worry about what's going on next door or am I going to lose my job. And there are very few people like that in the creative end of advertising. Practically none. Most copywriters have the same background: middle class to lower middle class. All the copywriters in town have read *Portnoy's Complaint* and they all say, "That's my life. I was Portnoy except that I would never do such a thing to a piece of liver."

Everybody in advertising is mixed up—but especially the creative people. Your whole life is screwed up. You're not the same kind of guy once you get into the business. It's hard to describe a business that really gets into your blood the way advertising does. After you've worked in it for a while, you're not the same person that you ordinarily would be. I often wonder how I would have been or how I would behave if I had gone into the aluminum-siding business.

* * *

In New York, advertising is changing drastically and rapidly. Creative people are getting more clout. It is a provable fact that the so-called creative agencies are the ones that are growing the fastest. But I also have the feeling that life for the creative side of an agency will always be tough. Now you've got creative review boards made up of red noses and blue veins. Who knows? In twenty years perhaps pot will be legalized. It depresses me to think that in twenty years there still will be creative review boards, except that the board will not be made up of red noses. Instead, you'll have a bunch of old guys with very funny pupils looking at your work. A bunch of dilated pupils checking you out. *That* kind of nonsense will never change.

Topics for Discussion

1. Does Femina's essay make life in the advertising business seem appealing? Based on this description, would you like to work in the advertising business? Why?
2. Femina says that "ads are just an intrusion on people's time." Is this how you feel about advertisements? If Femina feels this way why do you think he stays in advertising?
3. There are no copywriters over forty, according to Femina. What happens to them? What does this reveal about the advertising business?
4. "You're not the same kind of guy once you get into the business." Does Femina give any suggestion as to what it is in advertising that changes the people who work in the business?
5. What is the implication of Femina's suggestion that the headline for the advertising campaign for *Panasonic* be "From Those Wonderful Folks Who Gave You Pearl Harbor"? Can you suggest what the possible public reaction would be to such an advertising campaign?
6. Femina says that he doesn't think that "creative people are afraid of losing their jobs at the whim of the agency," but then he later tells the story of the young copywriter who lost his $30,000-a-year job. How does Femina reconcile this seeming contradiction?

Rhetorical Considerations

1. How would you characterize the prose style of this essay—formal, casual, or scholarly? Why do you think Femina chose this approach? Is it appropriate for his subject matter?
2. Is this a well-organized essay? How does the organization, or lack of it, contribute to what Femina is saying?
3. Reread the first and last paragraphs of the essay. Is there any relation between the two? Do you see how Femina went from the first paragraph to the last? Can you follow his development?
4. Would you say Femina's style and approach to writing reflects his profession?

Advertiser Control

Peter M. Sandman, David M. Rubin, and David B. Sachsman

Newspapermen are not easy to embarrass, but this time the Denver *Post* offices were filled with red faces. Someone had spirited an inter-office memorandum from the newspaper's files and published it. Addressed to the managing editor, the memo read as follows:

> Regarding "editorial" commitment on advertising schedules for Villa Italia Shopping Center. . . .
>
> I'm open to review on figures, based on Hatcher's [retail advertising manager] stated commitment of 25 per cent free space ratio to advertising, but believe this is reasonably accurate. . . .
>
> We have since Feb. 2 . . . published in various sections of the *Post* 826 column inches of copy and pictures directly related to Villa Italia, through March 7.
>
> Coverage beyond Monday (three days of grand openings . . . which we can't ignore and must cover with pix and stories) won't come close to the total commitment, but probably would put it over the half-way mark. If we did a picture page each day of the opening . . . we would be providing another 546 column inches and thus be beginning to get close to the commitment figure. . . .

Why is this memo so damning? All it reveals, after all, is that the *Post* had promised the shopping center one inch of free "news stories" for every four inches of paid advertising—and that the paper was having trouble finding the necessary news angles. Such a commercial arrangement is straight-forward, legal, and very common. It is also typical of the way advertisers influence the content of the mass media. The Villa Italia Shopping Center did not bribe the *Post* to support a particular political candidate, or even to fight for a zoning change it might have wanted. It simply purchased a little free space along with its ads. That seems harmless enough.

Nonetheless, the loss to Denver *Post* readers is clear. For one thing, they were falsely led to believe that the newspaper's editors considered Villa Italia an important news story. Moreover, in just over a month 826 column inches of genuinely important stories (roughly 30,000 words, the equivalent of a short novel) were eased out of the paper to make room for this disguised advertising.

[1] "News for Advertisers: A Denver Case," *Columbia Journalism Review*, Summer, 1966, p. 10.

The Age of Communication

WHO PAYS THE PIPER

Almost all American mass media are commercial. Some, like the book and motion picture industries, earn their revenue directly from the consumer. Most earn it—or at least the bulk of it—from advertising.

Newspapers: Sixty percent of the space in the average newspaper is devoted to ads, which account for three-quarters of the paper's income.

Magazines: A little over half of all magazine income is derived from ads, which fill just about half the available space.

Broadcasting: One quarter of the nation's air time is reserved for commercial messages, which pay the entire cost of the other three quarters.

In 1968 advertisers spent $5.24 billion on newspapers; $3.14 billion on television; $2.07 billion on magazines and business papers; and $1.15 billion on radio. Each year the figures are larger. It is obvious that none of these media could exist in the form we know them without advertising.

Imagine that you are the Vice-President for Advertising of Procter & Gamble, which in 1970 spent over $120,000,000 on television advertising alone, much of it for daytime serials. Imagine also that the script for one of your serials calls for an episode in which the heroine goes swimming in detergent-polluted water and suffers a psychotic breakdown because of the slime. You would almost certainly feel tempted to ask the producer to skip that part, and you might well feel cheated if he refused. As far as we know P&G does not monitor TV shows before broadcast. But then, as far as we know no soap opera has ever featured the dangers of detergent pollution. With $120,000,000 of Procter & Gamble's money at stake, no soap opera is likely to do so.

The advertiser pays the piper. If he wants to, he can more or less call the tune.

IDEOLOGY VERSUS BUSINESS

In the late 1950s, General Motors signed with CBS to sponsor a series of television documentaries. When it was learned that the first program would be entitled "The Vice-Presidency: Great American Lottery," the company guessed that the show might attack V.P. Richard Nixon. Nixon was a great favorite of many GM executives, so GM withdrew from the entire series.[2]

This anecdote has been told and retold many times over, and for good reason: It is rare. Advertisers almost never exercise their power, as GM apparently did, purely for ideological reasons. Their goal, after all, is to sell a product, and they pick their outlets on commercial grounds, not

---

[2] William L. Rivers and Wilbur Schramm, *Responsibility in Mass Communication,* rev. ed. (New York: Harper & Row, 1969), p. 107.

political ones. No matter how conservative a company may be, if it wants to sell to young people it will be pleased to have an ad in the middle of "Laugh-In." Wherever the market is, that is where the advertiser hopes to be. In a 1962 speech, conservative business editor Donald I. Rogers described (and criticized) this devotion to circulation:

> When businessmen place their advertising in Washington, where do they place it?
>
> They place 600,000 more lines per month with the liberal, welfare-state loving *Post* than in the *Star*, and the poor old conservative *News* runs a poor—a very poor—third. . . .
>
> The picture is no different here in New York. We find that the greatest amount of advertising placed by businessmen goes into the liberal *Times*. . . .
>
> The influential conservative New York papers, the *Herald Tribune* and the *World Telegram & Sun*, get very sparse pickings indeed from the American business community which they support so effectively in their editorial policies. [3]

Rogers considered the ideological neutrality of advertisers shortsighted. Perhaps it is, but it is also very fortunate for the democratic process. Because of this neutrality, a publisher or broadcaster who attacks the business establishment will be kept in business *by* the business establishment so long as he can attract an audience. In the early 1940s, Marshall Field owned two Chicago businesses: a giant department store and a liberal newspaper, the *Sun*. While the *Sun* battled the conservative *Tribune* for the morning market, the department store continued to advertise in the *Tribune*—for business reasons. A decade later the Milwaukee *Journal* led the nation in advertising linage, despite its opposition to Red-baiting Joseph McCarthy and its support for Democrat Adlai Stevenson. Advertisers agreed that the *Journal* was "anti-business," but Hearst's conservative Milwaukee *Sentinel* was a loser in the circulation race—and so the ads stayed with the *Journal*. [4]

Every underground newspaper today, from the Berkeley *Barb* to the (N.Y.) *East Village Other*, depends for its survival on advertisements from the business establishment, especially record and film companies. The ideological tension between the underground paper and the large corporation is obvious. Even open hatred, apparently, does not often prevent businessmen from putting their ads where they will help sales the most.

PATTERNS OF ADVERTISER CONTROL

The fact that most advertisers are ideologically neutral does not mean

---

[3] Donald I. Rogers, "Businessmen: Don't Subsidize Your Enemies," *Human Events*, August 11, 1962, pp. 599–600.

[4] Vern E. Edwards, Jr., *Journalism in a Free Society* (Dubuque, Ia.: William C. Brown Company, 1970), p. 176.

that they ignore the content of the programs they sponsor or the publications they appear in. Some companies, of course, are satisfied to pay for their ads and let it go at that. But many like to have at least a little say over what comes before and after.

There are four major types of advertiser control over the content of the mass media:

1. The ads themselves.
2. Connecting the product to nonadvertising content.
3. Making the company and product look good, never bad.
4. Avoiding controversy at all costs.

We will discuss each of these in turn.

1. The Ads Themselves. It may be obvious, but it is worth emphasizing that roughly half the content of the mass media is written directly by advertisers—the ads. The average American adult is exposed to well over a hundred separate advertising messages each day. Many find their way into the language as symbols of our culture—"The Pepsi Generation," "The Dodge Rebellion," "Progress Is Our Most Important Product." Besides selling goods, these ads undoubtedly have a cumulative effect on American society. Philosopher Erich Fromm has defined Western Man as *Homo consumens*—Man the Consumer. If the description fits, the institution to blame is advertising.

Legally, a publisher or broadcaster is free to reject most kinds of ads if he wishes, but as a practical matter only the most egregiously dishonest or offensive specimens are ever turned away. It is a strange paradox that advertisers have more power over the content of the media than the media have over the ads.

2. Connecting the Product to Non-advertising Content. The clearest example of the blurred line between advertising and non-advertising is the common newspaper custom of trading free "news stories" for paid ads, as in the Denver *Post* case already discussed. A parallel practice in the magazine world is the disguising of advertisements as editorial copy. The November, 1967, issue of the *Reader's Digest,* for instance, contained a special section advocating the use of brand-name drugs instead of the cheaper generic versions. The whole section was laid out to look like standard *Digest* fare. Only a small box at the end informed readers that it was paid for by the Pharmaceutical Manufacturers Association. Are readers confused by such ads? Evidently advertisers think so, for they pay dearly for the privilege of running them.

Nearly every newspaper has a department or two whose main purpose is to keep advertisers happy by giving them something "appropriate" to appear next to. Frequent offenders include the real estate section, entertainment page, church page, and travel and dining pages. There is nothing evil about a newspaper deciding to run a weekly ski page. But if the only function of the page is to give skiing advertisers a place to locate—and if the page disappears when the ads fall off—then the editor's news judgment has been replaced by the business manager's. In his book *The Fading American Newspaper,* Carl Lindstrom calls these sorts of articles "revenue-related reading matter." [5] Many newspaper executives use another term: BOMs, or Business Office Musts. The reader, of course, pays the price—a steady diet of pap and puffery.

In broadcasting, the best way to connect paid and unpaid content is to hire the performer to do his own ads. It was Dinah Shore herself who sang, at the end of every show, "See the U.S.A. in your Chevrolet." Between monologues and interviews, Johnny Carson tells millions of viewers what to buy.

Almost from the beginning, network television newscasters refused to do commercials, believing that it was unfair and misleading to slide from a review of the day's action in Vietnam to a review of the reasons for taking Excedrin. Many local TV newsmen are not so conscientious, and nearly all radio announcers are willing to alternate between news and commercials. Even on network TV news, some combination is permitted. NBC's coverage of the 1964 political conventions, for example, was sponsored by Gulf Oil. At the company's request, the luminous orange Gulf disc was installed behind every commentator's desk. Blurring the line between news and advertising is intended to strengthen the credibility of the ads. It may also lessen the credibility of the news.

3. Making the Company and Product Look Good, Never Bad. Advertisers go to a great deal of trouble to look good in their ads; wherever possible, they would like to look good between ads as well. It is often possible. CBS newsman Alexander Kendrick recalls the case of a cigarette sponsor that "dictated that on none of its entertainment programs, whether drama or studio panel game, could any actor or other participant smoke a pipe or cigar, or chew tobacco, or even chew gum that might be mistaken for tobacco. Only cigarettes could be smoked, and only king-sized, but no program could show untidy ashtrays, filled with cigarette butts. . . ." [6]

Though cigarettes are no longer advertised on television, other companies have similar policies. If Bufferin sponsors a television drama, the hero is unlikely to take a plain aspirin for his headache. If Jello sponsors a family comedy, the desserts served on the show will rarely be layer cakes. If TWA sponsors a spy story, the CIA man will not fly the friendly skies of United—though the Communist agent might. Needless to say, neither plane will crash.

When a plane does crash, newspapers and news broadcasts must report it, and they even mention the name of the airline (though there was a time when they didn't). But if an airline ad is scheduled next to the news show, it is quietly moved to another spot. And even the newspapers are unlikely to report which airlines have the worst crash records.

The following additional newspaper practices are designed to preserve the "good image"—and therefore the goodwill—of advertisers and

[5] Carl E. Lindstrom, *The Fading American Newspaper* (Gloucester, Mass.: Peter Smith, 1964).

[6] Alexander Kendrick, *Prime Time* (Boston: Little, Brown & Co., 1969), p. 449.

potential advertisers:

- When someone dies or commits suicide in a downtown hotel, the name of the hotel is rarely mentioned.
- When a big advertiser gets married, the story is almost certain to receive big play on the society page; when he gets divorced the story is often ignored—no matter how juicy.
- The names of shoplifters and embezzlers are printed, but whenever possible the names of the stores and businesses they stole from are not.
- Government suits against advertisers, especially those that involve consumer protection, are sometimes killed or quietly buried.

When an entertainment show is "rigged" to make an advertiser look good or to keep him from looking bad, the problem is a petty one. When news is similarly affected, the danger to democracy is great.

4. Avoiding Controversy at All Costs. A major advertiser of break- fast foods once sent the following memo to the scriptwriters of the televi- sion series it sponsored:

> In general, the moral code of the characters in our dramas will be more or less synonomous with the moral code of the bulk of the Ameri- can middle class, as it is commonly understood. There will be no mate- rial that will give offense, either directly or by inference, to any organized minority group, lodge or other organizations, institutions, residents of any state or section of the country, or a commercial organization of any sort. . . . We will treat mention of the Civil War carefully, mindful of the sensitiveness of the South on this subject. . . . There will be no material for or against sharply drawn national or regional controversial issues. . . . There will be no material on any of our programs which could in any way further the concept of business as cold, ruthless and lacking in all sentiment or spiritual motivation. [7]

The goal of this broad coat of whitewash is to give advertisers an antiseptic environment in which to peddle their goods—an environment that nobody could possibly find offensive. This is especially important on television, which caters to an audience of millions.

In a celebrated incident in 1969, CBS was quick to edit out of the Merv Griffin talk show an appeal by actress Elke Sommer for postcards and letters to be sent to Mrs. Martin Luther King calling for world peace. Comedienne Carol Burnett made a similar appeal on the Christmas Day show and it, too, was censored. Peace, apparently, is a controversial issue. In his book *Television and The News,* critic Harry Skornia of the University of Illinois, Chicago Circle, lists these noteworthy subjects which he believes the broadcast media have ignored over the years in deference to advertisers: poverty in America; public utilities bilking the public; the harmful effects of liquor, tobacco, and coffee; air and water

[7] Dallas Smyth, "Five Myths of Consumership," *The Nation,* January 20, 1969, p. 83.

pollution; and the problems of labor in labor-management disputes.[8]

The aversion of advertisers to controversy is largely responsible for the homogenized quality of most television entertainment. More important, it is a factor in the consistent avoidance by the news media of many problems of national importance.

THREATS, BRIBES, AND UNDERSTANDINGS

When the average citizen thinks of advertiser influence, two images are likely to come to mind: the sumptuous party at which newsmen are wined and dined into the "right" attitude, and the irate businessman who storms into an editor's office and threatens to withdraw all advertising unless. . . . Both images—the bribe and the threat—have some truth to them. There isn't an editor, reporter, or broadcaster of experience who hasn't experienced both at one time or another. But such tactics are too gauche, and so they tend to fail as often as not. In the mid-1950s, the *Wall Street Journal* managed to get the details on the new General Motors cars before the information was officially released. GM quickly cancelled $11,000 worth of advertising in retribution. The *Journal* was not intimidated, and published the story anyhow.[9]

More recently, St. Louis Cardinal owner Gussie Busch fired his radio commentator Harry Caray. The word went out that any station that hired Caray would not only get no ads from Busch's Budweiser beer, but also no business from the two largest advertising agencies in town. Months later Caray was back on the air in St. Louis—sponsored by Schlitz.

More subtle techniques are more effective, and always have been. During the oil pipeline wars of the 1890s, the Ohio press was highly critical of John D. Rockefeller's Standard Oil Company. The boss assigned his trusted "fixer," Dan O'Day, to sweeten the sour press. O'Day did not threaten anybody, nor did he offer any outright bribes. Instead, he planned a heavy advertising campaign for Mica Axle Grease, a very minor Standard product. Huge ads were purchased on a regular basis in every Ohio newspaper. Editors got the point: Don't bite the hand that feeds. After a year of receiving monthly checks from the axle grease subsidiary, most had quit knocking John D. and the parent corporation. Mica, by the way, became a top seller.[10]

Even this indirect sort of bribe is not often necessary. Over the years, editors have come to know what advertisers expect, and they supply it without questioning. Nobody has to tell the copy editor of a newspaper to cut the name of the car out of that traffic accident article. He understands without being told that including the name might embarrass the manufacturer. He understands that embarrassing the manufacturer would be in "bad taste" for the newspaper. He understands that that

[8] Harry Skornia, *Television and the News* (Palo Alto, Calif.: Pacific Books, 1968), pp. 87–90.
[9] Rivers and Schramm, *Responsibility*, pp. 108–9.
[10] Will Irwin, "Our Kind of People," *Collier's*, June 17, 1911, pp. 17–18.

just isn't the sort of thing one business (publishing) does to another business (automotive). He doesn't have to be threatened or bribed; such tactics would only offend and bewilder him.

Can you call this advertiser control? Only in the sense that in the back of every editor's mind is the need to keep advertisers happy. The local auto dealer, after all, does not even know that the newspaper copy editor is "censoring" the name of the car. Should the name slip in, he would probably take no action whatever; at worst he might mention the matter to his friend the managing editor at the country club or the next Chamber of Commerce meeting. Certainly he would be most unlikely to threaten to withdraw his ads. He needs the newspaper at least as much as the newspaper needs him. The important point is that this conflict of wills seldom takes place. The copy editor knows his job, and so the name of the car rarely gets into the traffic accident report. . . .

BROADCASTING: A SPECIAL CASE

American television is designed to attract advertising, and advertising is designed to influence the largest possible audience. It follows that the great majority of TV programming must be aimed at the "mass market," at the lowest common denominator of public viewing tastes. The potential audience for a classical opera may be, say, one million viewers. The potential audience for a soap opera in the same time slot may be ten million. Naturally television will choose the soap opera, not the classical opera, to broadcast. The classical opera will not even be allotted one-tenth as much broadcast time as the soap opera (though it has one-tenth the potential audience)—for what advertiser would be willing to sponsor such a minority-interest program?

Even when advertisers can be found for small-audience shows, television stations are reluctant to broadcast them. A single "highbrow" program can force millions of viewers to switch to another channel; once switched, they may stay there for hours or even days. The ratings on adjacent shows are therefore lowered. Other advertisers begin to complain, and station profits begin to drop.

Exactly this happened to the Firestone Hour in the early 1960s. Sponsored by the Firestone Tire & Rubber Company, the classical music program had a consistently low rating. Firestone did not mind; it wanted an "elite" audience for its ads. But adjacent mass-market programs were suffering. After moving the show around a few times in an effort to reduce the adjacency problem, the network finally gave up and refused to continue the show. Companies like Bell Telephone and Xerox, which like to sponsor documentaries and cultural programs, have had similar difficulties finding a time slot.

More recently, United Press International moved the following news item: "Armstrong Cork Co., whose Circle Theater was one of television's best known dramatic shows, said . . . it has dropped video advertising because the networks offer only childish programming." [11] Apparently

[11] United Press International, April 8, 1970.

Armstrong was unable to find a network willing to produce another Circle Theater.

Advertising revenue is at the heart of the debate over the quality of television programming. In the 1959–60 season NBC and CBS tried an experiment, offering several "high quality" music and drama shows. ABC, financially weakest of the three networks, refused to go along. Instead, it chose that season to introduce its gory detective series "The Untouchables," plus ten westerns a week. Ratings were excellent and ABC closed the gap on its older rivals. The next season, NBC and CBS followed the ABC lead, with detective and western series galore. The experiment was over.

Comments critic Robert Eck: "In the audience delivery business, you do not have the luxury of setting either your standards or those of your audience. Instead, they are set for you by the relative success of your competitors." [12] This is another way of saying what NBC President Robert Kintner answered in response to the question "Who is responsible for what appears on network cameras?": "The ultimate responsibility is ours," Kintner replied, "but the ultimate power has to be the sponsor's, because without him you couldn't afford to run a network." [13]

[12] Robert Eck, "The Real Masters of Television," *Harper's*, March, 1967, p. 49.
[13] "The Tarnished Image," *Time*, November 16, 1959, pp. 72–80.

Topics for Discussion

1. "The advertiser pays the piper. If he wants to, he can more or less call the tune." But if the advertiser is calling the tune, is there any way for the public to know it? Does this lessen your trust in the mass media?

2. "Critic Harry Skornia . . . lists these noteworthy subjects which he believes the broadcast media have ignored over the years in deference to advertisers: poverty in America; public utilities bilking the public; the harmful effects of liquor, tobacco, and coffee; air and water pollution; and the problems of labor in labor-management disputes." How accurate is this statement? Why would advertisers want the media to avoid these subjects?

3. In 1968 advertisers spent $11.6 billion on newspapers, television, magazines, and radio. Without this income none of these media could exist. How much control do you think this gives advertisers over the media? Can you offer a better way to finance these media?

4. If you were an advertiser, would you be concerned with the content of the programs on which you advertised? Why? Why do you think Xerox sponsors only special programs which are generally considered intellectual or sophisticated?

5. "Over the years, editors have come to know what advertisers expect, and they supply it without questioning . . . in the back of every editor's mind is the need to keep advertisers happy." Is this a form of censorship? Does this mean that advertisers interfere with freedom of the press?

6. Why is broadcasting a "special case"?

Rhetorical Considerations

1. What is the tone of this essay? How does it differ from the tone in other selections in this section?

2. What is the purpose in beginning the essay with an anecdote? What use do the authors make of the anecdote?

3. Is the organization of the section on "Patterns of Advertiser Control" too mechanical? Can you suggest a better approach to presenting the same material?

4. Examine the prose style of this selection. What devices do the authors use to make their sentences read easily? Note, for example, the use of transitional words and phrases.

Freedom to Advertise

On this page today we publish a small selection from the several hundred letters The Times has received in protest against two advertisements that appeared in this newspaper on May 31 and June 6 respectively. The first of these advertisements, signed by a group of citizens calling themselves "The National Committee for Impeachment," denounced President Nixon for continuing to prosecute the war in Vietnam in alleged violation of law and the Constitution, and demanded his removal from office. The second of the two advertisements consisted of an open letter to the President signed by one Norman F. Dacey, bitterly attacking Mr. Nixon for a Middle East policy in allegedly "blind support" of Israel.

While many of the letter writers limited themselves to discussion of the issues, many others leveled their criticism primarily at The Times itself for carrying such emotionally worded and politically impassioned advertisements, with whose sentiments this newspaper (not to mention a very large part of its readership) is obviously in disagreement. This criticism of The Times for accepting such advertising was expressed so frequently and with such deep sincerity that we believe it desirable to state once again the principles that have always guided The Times in this respect.

*   *   *

As we see it, the issue goes to the very heart of the freedom and the responsibility of the press. The Times believes it has an obligation to afford maximum reasonable opportunity to the public to express its views, however much opposed to our own, through various outlets in this newspaper including the advertising columns.

The Times does, of course, make every attempt to insure that the advertisements it carries are truthful and in good taste. Such standards are relatively easy to enforce in respect to commercial products — though even here sharp differences of opinion frequently arise over the precise applicability of our rules. But political advertising— the presentation of a point of view of an individual or a group through a paid announcement in our columns— presents a more difficult problem than the advertising of a commercial product. Here we feel that the widest possible latitude must be given the public to express

Editorial: "Freedom to Advertise," in *The New York Times,* June 16, 1972. © 1972 by The New York Times Company. Reprinted by permission.

what from our point of view may be even the most objectionable of opinions. There are indeed limits; we would not knowingly publish an advertisement containing a direct incitement to violence or other illegal action, or a clear misstatement of fact or a distorted quotation.

While The Times makes every effort to detect such violations and to eliminate them from the political advertising that it does accept, our screening process does fail us on occasion when, usually due to the pressures of time and deadlines, human error manages to nullify even the most carefully conceived administrative controls. Just such a regrettable lapse occurred in connection with the Dacey advertisement; in any event, it was the general tenor of this diatribe, rather than any of its specific charges, that gave offense to so many of our readers.

Times policy in this important question is not new. On this page nearly three years ago (Aug. 29, 1969) we stated:

"We at The New York Times have always felt an obligation to keep our advertising columns open to all comers, refusing ads only on the grounds of fraud or deception, vulgarity or obscenity and incitement to lawbreaking or to racial or religious hatred. In pursuit of that policy, The Times has printed many advertisements setting forth ideas we abhor but feel no right to censor."

More than a decade ago, on Dec. 28, 1961, we discussed the issue in these words, which we feel are as applicable today as the day they were written:

"Subject of course to the laws of libel and the bounds of decency and good taste and the requirements of factual accuracy, we think the principle of freedom of the press not only requires us to report events and occurrences of which we disapprove . . . but also imposes on us the obligation to accept advertising of books whose contents we reject and of political parties and movements whose goals we despise. . . .

"The political and other opinions of The New York Times—that is, our editorial policies—are expressed daily and exclusively in the editorial columns on this page. Our policy on 'Letters to the Editor' is to print communications from our readers of general interest and of all shades of opinion. Our news policy is 'to give the news impartially, without fear or favor, regardless of any party, sect or interest involved.' . . . Our policy with respect to political advertising is to keep our columns open to those who wish to express a particular point of view, no matter how widely divergent it may be from our own.

"These policies, as we see them, comprise the essence of the freedom and the responsibility of the press."

Topics for Discussion

1. What limits does the *New York Times* place on the advertisements it accepts for publication? Are these limits reasonable?
2. Why would there be sharp differences of opinion whether an advertisement was in good taste?
3. Should a newspaper be required to accept all advertisements placed with it, if the advertisements are factual and in good taste?
4. Does a newspaper have the responsibility to present all points of view?
5. What is a diatribe?

Rhetorical Considerations

1. Although concerned with a specific case, this editorial is a statement of general principle and policy. How does the editorial move from the specific to the general?
2. At the end of the editorial the *Times* repeats two previous statements of advertising policy. Do these quotations repeat what has already been stated, or do they develop the policy statement further?
3. Is the prose style of this editorial the kind you normally associate with journalism? Why is the prose style of an editorial different from the prose style used in reporting the news?

The Right to
Turn Down Advertising

RICHARD L. TOBIN

The right of every newspaper publisher to decline advertising, with or without explaining his reasons for doing so, was recently upheld in a vital decision of the Supreme Court of the United States. Briefly, the Court ruled that a newspaper is not a common carrier, therefore does not have to sell its space to everyone who requests it. In other words, it's up to each individual publisher to print what *he* thinks is in the public interest and to be able to turn down advertisements unsuited to his audience, for all manner of reasons including libel, vulgarity, bad taste, or because they are misleading. It is one of those milestone decisions that come out of the Supreme Court affecting the very innards of the newspaper business.

The fundamental difference between publishing a newspaper and owning a radio or television station is, to be obvious, that one medium operates entirely inside the concept of free enterprise and the other two are, to some degree, government-controlled. Anyone can start a newspaper anywhere at any time. All he needs is a great deal of money, which he is certain to lose in the first few years of operation, a printing plant, and some sort of fixed audience. Most cities in the United States are now monopoly newspaper towns, alas, but not because other publishers have not been allowed to operate there. It's strictly a matter of economics in the highly competitive age of electronic news. On the other hand, the number of radio and TV stations is limited to the available channels and assignments must come through the Federal Communications Commission. This simple fact of applying to the government for a "publishing" outlet makes all the difference between printing a daily paper and owning a local broadcasting station.

A septuagenarian Japanese press lord, Matsutaro Shoriki, once boasted that he made a lot more money from his television network than from his great newspaper, *Yomiuri Shimbun*, and that he did it with a small fraction of the people he needed to put out the paper. Yet, just before his death two years ago, when asked if he had to do it all over again, which would he give up, his newspaper or TV chain, he replied: "I would never give up my newspaper. A newspaper means power." Lord Thomson, the powerful British press-TV-radio lord, fully agrees with this assessment, as would most, if not all, of those lucky Americans capable of owning properties in both fields.

It is this sense of power, we believe, that has always been the lodestone of the newspaper business, less so now that radio and television skim the cream off the top of the news, but still a valid magnet. Within the laws of libel a newspaper can publish or refuse virtually anything it pleases, including advertisements, under the new Supreme Court ruling. This has never been so and probably cannot be in any situation where a government agency like the FCC must license stations. *Ipso facto*, the licensing dampens if not kills the enthusiasms for and expressions of free enterprise available to public print. A newspaper editor, or publisher, is beholden only to himself and his audience, and even the social mirror does not always inhibit a courageous, or a stupid, publisher. In other words, it's entirely up to him what he says and how he says it in his news columns (and now with his advertisements, too). This simply is not true of government-assigned electronic media.

In the past two months this column has been devoted, in order, to the right to know and the right to protect a news source. The newest Supreme

Richard L. Tobin, "The Right To Turn Down Advertising," from *Saturday Review*, June 12, 1971, pp. 55–56. Copyright 1971 Saturday Review, Inc. Reprinted by permission.

Court ruling involves the right to decline advertising, with or without a stated reason for doing so. It may, in the long run, be as important a journalistic freedom as either of the other two. It is, in a fundamental sense, closely related to both. It all began when a suit was brought by the Amalgamated Clothing Workers of America against several Chicago newspapers after they had rejected an ad explaining the union's reasons for picketing the Marshall Field department store two years ago. A United States district court dismissed the suit on grounds that a newspaper is a private enterprise, not a common carrier, and that its publisher and editor have a perfect right to turn down advertising with or without telling anyone why. The fact that the Chicago press were probably trying to protect one of their largest sources of revenue had no bearing in court. All appeals sustained dismissal of the suit.

Freedom of speech and freedom of the press include the right to refrain from speaking and publishing, to omit or turn down something for publication. If this were not the intent of the Bill of Rights, no newspaper could function since it would be forced to print everything anyone submitted to it. An editor (or publisher) would have no function in a society where everything submitted had to be put into type. Again, no editor exists in the true sense of the word on such totalitarian publications as *Izvestia* and *Pravda*. Mimics, yes; editors, no. And the Supreme Court is now saying to us that this right to publish and to refuse to publish extends beyond news to the advertising content that helps keep every paper in business—a milestone decision in every way.

The Age of Communication

Topics for Discussion

1. Do you agree that a newspaper should have the right to turn down any advertisement without explanation?
2. If owning a newspaper means power, shouldn't there be some kind of government regulation of newspapers?
3. Would Tobin agree with the *New York Times* statement on the "Freedom to Advertise"?
4. Were the Chicago papers correct, in your opinion, to turn down the advertisements from the Amalgamated Clothing Workers of America?
5. If newspapers arbitrarily refuse to run certain advertisements, can these same newspapers claim they are a part of the "free press" in America?

6. Compare the style of this essay with the style of the editorial from the *New York Times.*

Rhetorical Considerations

1. Is there a fallacy in this statement: "An editor (or publisher) would have no function in a society where everything submitted had to be put into type."
2. What is the thesis of this essay? Where is it stated?
3. Tobin never directly states his approval of the Supreme Court decision, but he clearly indicates his approval in several places in the essay. How does he do this? Why is this more effective than a clear statement of approval?

A Newspaper Says No to 'Orange'

Some 30 American newspapers now have a policy of declining advertising for films rated X by the Motion Picture Association of America. One of the largest is the Detroit News, which instituted its policy with Stanley Kubrick's "A Clockwork Orange." Here are the Detroit News editorial of March 19, explaining its stand, and a challenge to that stand by Mr. Kubrick, which the Detroit News ran on April 9.

The Detroit News announces today that, effective next Sunday, it no longer will publish display advertising—or give editorial publicity to—X-rated motion pictures and those other unrated pictures which, in our judgment, are of a pornographic nature.

Delayed for one week to give theaters time to find alternative advertising space, a new Detroit News code includes:

Rejection of display advertising, regardless of copy content, from general entertainment movie houses when such advertising is in support of films carrying the X rating of the Motion Picture Association of America (MPAA);

An "information only" restriction applicable to our daily Movie Guide under which houses periodically showing X films will be permitted to list only the name of the theater and picture, the cast, the fact of the X rating and the hours of performance;

Complete exclusion from display advertising and the Movie Guide of all material from those movie houses which habitually show only unrated "adult" films or those with MPAA's X rating;

Removal from our entertainment pages of all publicity stories, reviews and other promotion material (including listings in The News' own film ratings) of both X-rated and the unrated pornographic films. General news developments concerning such pictures, of course, will be reported.

We anticipate varied objections to this program.

Some will fault us as "not with it," as defenders of a defunct moral code. Our answer is that, in our view, a sick motion picture industry is using pornography and an appeal to prurience to bolster theater attendance; quite simply, we do not want to assist them in the process.

It may be said that we are restricting the exhibitors' "rights" to publicize films which the courts have refused to ban as obscene. Disregarding our views on the "nothing can be done about it" court approach to obscenity, we would reply that no judge so far has said that a newspaper is required to help sell tickets for such films.

Many will feel we are not going far enough, that the X rated should be barred from our Movie Guide and that similar bans should apply to many films with R or other ratings which also may be offensive. Our answer is that we will continue the Movie Guide listing so that neighborhood movie patrons who do not wish to attend an X film can be advised and avoid it. We agree that some R and other movies also are offensive but, for the time being, we plan to concentrate our restriction on those films which the industry itself classifies as unsuitable for non-adult viewers.

We anticipate no movie industry cleanup as a result of our decision. Although we are the largest newspaper in the country to have taken such a step, we recognize that other advertising vehicles are available to the exhibitors both within and outside Detroit. Perhaps the only result will be in our own satisfaction in a modest declaration against the theory that makes hardcore sex, voyeurism and sadistic violence the prime ingredients of art and entertainment in the 1970's.

Stanley Kubrick Replies

To the Editor

The Detroit News terms its decision to refuse to give space to advertising, publicizing or reviewing X-rated or unrated films "a modest declaration." To me, it seems rather to be an irrational diktat.

In its emphasis on protection and purification, on purging the public mind of what, "in our judgment," are motion pictures of a pornographic nature, it recalls the words of another arbiter of public morals and national taste who said: "Works of art which cannot be understood and need a set of instructions to justify their existence, and which find their way to neurotics receptive to such harmful rubbish, will no longer reach the public. Let us have no illusions: we have set out to rid the nation and our people of all those influences threatening its existence and character."

The speaker was Adolf Hitler, commenting on two art exhibitions in Munich, in 1937, one of "approved" German art, and other of so-called "degenerate" art. In this day and age, the Detroit News censors may feel better equipped to make such fine distinctions—though I do not envy them their task. But what they are doing is, in essence, the same.

A film is made to be seen by the public. In order for this to be done, the public must be made aware of its existence. When you decide to see a film you do not turn on the radio or the television, hoping to find it advertised; you look in the newspaper. There is no adequate substitute for newspaper advertising in informing the public of a film's existence and its whereabouts. If a newspaper denies some films of which it does not approve the right to advertise, while allowing competing films to purchase as much advertising space as they like, then the newspaper is effectively suppressing the films it does not like.

For all practical purposes, a film is

banned when the public is prevented from knowing of its existence or whereabouts. To start to ban films—or books, or plays, or any medium of free expression—on the grounds of offensiveness is to take the first step on a course that history has shown to end in a suppression of many other liberties.

For any newspaper to deliberately attempt to suppress another equally important communications medium seems especially ugly and shortsighted. I am not a Constitutional expert, but I should guess this is a violation of the First Amendment. It is certainly an act inimical to the principles of freedom without which the newspaper itself could not exist.

It is important to understand that the X rating is designated by the Motion Picture Association of America, and it does not stigmatize or condemn a film, but merely places it in the adult film category, allowing no one under 17 (18 in some states) to view it. This category is consistent with the United States Supreme Court opinion that only the morals of minors are vulnerable and must be protected.

There is no power, legal or otherwise, which should be exercised against the rights of adults to select their own entertainment.

In addition to the antidemocratic principles involved in the position of the Detroit News, the indiscriminateness and arbitrariness of its edict is illustrated by the banning of my film, "A Clockwork Orange," from its display advertising and editorial pages. The film has been awarded the New York Film Critics prizes for Best Film of the Year and Best Director of the Year, and it was nominated for Academy Awards as "Best Picture," "Best Director," "Best Screenplay" and "Best Editor." Yet the Detroit News censors would indiscriminately defame and discredit all X films because they do not conform to what they judge to be the standards of their readers.

But even if they are so sure of the rightness of their judgments of a vast variety of films, are they so overwhelmingly certain, in this age of diverse social attitudes, of what their readers regard as "offensive" to them? Many readers may find their purification program offensive. They may find that they are censoring their readers rather than their advertisers; that they are imposing their judgment in an arbitrary and exclusive fashion upon the right to be informed, yet at the same time, to exercise free choice which is one of the reasons—and by no means the least important one—why one buys a newspaper.

High standards of moral behavior can only be achieved by the example of right-thinking people and society as a whole, and cannot be maintained by the coercive effect of the law. Or that of certain newspapers.
STANLEY KUBRICK

Topics for Discussion

1. The *Detroit News* calls X-rated films "films which the industry itself classifies as unsuitable for nonadult viewers." Why should such a rating prompt the *News* to refuse to advertise it? Is the *News* reading anything into the X-rating? What does the editorial imply about X-rated films?

2. What is an "appeal to prurience"? How could it bolster theater attendance?

3. Is the *Detroit News*'s decision to refuse to advertise all X-rated movies, including "A Clockwork Orange," the same kind of decision as that of the Chicago newspapers refusal to publish the advertisement by the Amalgamated Clothing Workers of America?

4. Does a newspaper have a right, or an obligation, to protect public morals? What does Stanley Kubrick think of the *Detroit News*'s decision?

5. Is the refusal of the *Detroit News* to carry any advertisements for X-rated films a form of censorship? How do you think the *Detroit News* would react if someone told them what they could and could not print?

6. Stanley Kubrick quotes Adolph Hitler. How appropriate and relevant is the quotation?

7. Do you agree with Kubrick that "high standards of moral behavior can only be achieved by the example of right-thinking people and society as a whole, and cannot be maintained by the coercive effect of the law?"

8. What does Kubrick mean when he calls the *Detroit News* editorial an "irrational diktat"?

Rhetorical Considerations

1. Which selection do you think is better written, the editorial or Kubrick's letter? Why?

2. Examine the editorial and list as many emotional words and phrases as you can, such phrases as "hardcore sex" and "sadistic violence" for example. Then do the same with Kubrick's letter. What effect do such words and phrases create?

3. Which selection is more logical? Point out the illogic you find in both selections.

4. Compare the introduction and conclusions of both selections. Which do you find more effective? Why?

The Economics of Advertising

Peter M. Sandman, David M. Rubin, and David B. Sachsman

In 1954 the net profits of Revlon, Inc., a cosmetics company, stood at $1,297,826. In 1955 CBS introduced a new TV quiz program, "The Sixty-Four Thousand Dollar Question." Revlon sponsored the show, as well as its twin: "The Sixty-Four Thousand Dollar Challenge." Both programs were on the air until 1958, when it was proved that they were rigged. During those four years, Revlon's net profits rose to $3,655,950 in 1955, $8,375,502 in 1956, and $9,688,307 in 1958. When a Senate committee asked Martin Revson, owner of Revlon, whether his phenomenal success was due to sponsoring the two shows, he answered musingly: "It helped. It helped."[1]

In 1963 the Clark Oil and Refining Company spent its entire $1.6 million advertising budget on television. Until then, Clark had limped along with annual earnings of $1.5 million or so. The first year following the TV campaign, the company earned $2.1 million. It committed itself permanently to television—and in 1969 Clark Oil earned $13.0 million. Said one Clark executive: "That's really advertising power."[2]

ADVERTISING AND BUSINESS

American business spends over $20 billion a year on advertising, most of it in the mass media. This figure represents only the raw cost of time and space. It does not include the salaries of the nation's 400,000 advertising men, or the expense of preparing and producing the ads. The actual cost of advertising is closer to $40 billion a year—$200 for every man, woman, and child in the country.

What does American business get in return? Increased sales, of course. The "success stories" of Revlon and Clark are two of thousands that could be told. Frederick R. Gamble, former president of the American Association of Advertising Agencies, puts it this way:

> Advertising is the counterpart in distribution of the machine in production. By the use of machines, our production of goods and services has been multiplied. By the use of the mass media, advertising multiplies the selling effort. . . . Reaching many people rapidly at low cost, advertising speeds up sales, turns prospects into customers in large numbers and at high speed. Hence, in a mass-production and high-consump-

[1] Meyer Weinberg, *TV in America* (New York: Ballantine Books, 1962), pp. 46–47.
[2] Lawrence B. Christopher, "Clark Oil Finds Out TV Really Works," *Broadcasting*, March 2, 1970, pp. 42–44.

tion economy, advertising has the greatest opportunity and the greatest responsibility for finding customers.[3]

The purpose of nearly all advertising is to induce the buyer to purchase something that the seller has to sell—a product, a service, a political candidate, or whatever. A successful ad is an ad that sells—and most ads are successful.

Advertising can boost sales in two ways: by winning a bigger share of the market, or by increasing the size of the market itself (perhaps creating the market to start with). The first technique may be called competitive advertising; it says "Buy our brand of aspirin instead of the brand you're using now." The second is noncompetitive advertising; it says simply "Buy more aspirin." Most ads are a combination. They urge the consumer to switch brands and to buy more.

Business competition is not limited to advertising, of course. A manufacturer or a store may compete by cutting its prices, improving its products, or offering superior service. It is not hard to find examples of ads that are essentially "informational"—telling the public about a genuine competitive edge. But these tactics have limited value. Aspirin is aspirin. It is nearly impossible to make a better aspirin. And price-cutting may lose more in profits than it gains in sales; how many people would switch brands to save a nickel? Competitive ads for aspirin—and many other products—have no real differences to talk about. The competition is not in the products, but in the ads themselves. Meyer Weinberg describes the big-money television advertisers this way:

> Having eschewed competition by cutting prices, the Top Fifty instead go all out to attract the consumer's attention by amusement or entertainment. There is no other way of driving consumers to prefer one substantially identical item over another. Thus advertising agencies specialize in the manufacture of spurious individuality. . . .[4]

So much for competitive advertising. If the only way a manufacturer could earn a dollar was by stealing it from some other manufacturer, America's gross national product would be at a standstill. Fortunately or unfortunately, this is not the case. Industry grows by creating new consumer needs. Wigs, cigarettes, electric washers, power lawnmowers, toiletries, fur coats, and aluminum cans are not really essential to life, liberty, and the pursuit of happiness. But manufacturers have convinced us that they are. They did it with advertising.

Consider the TV ad budgets of the top twenty advertisers on network television in 1969.

Procter and Gamble	$120,540,700
Bristol-Myers	58,632,900
Colgate-Palmolive	53,709,000
R. J. Reynolds	50,756,000

[3] Theodore Peterson, Jay W. Jensen, and William L. Rivers, *The Mass Media and Modern Society* (New York: Holt, Rinehart and Winston, Inc., 1965), p. 191.

[4] Weinberg, *TV in America*, p. 194.

General Foods	49,642,300
American Home Products	42,144,800
General Motors	40,999,000
Sterling Drug	38,196,000
Warner-Lambert	37,756,900
American Brands	37,278,100
Phillip Morris	32,491,100
Gillette	31,521,300
Ford Motor	30,636,300
Miles Laboratories	30,261,100
General Mills	29,172,000
British-American Tobacco	28,414,000
Lever Brothers	26,846,500
J. B. Williams	26,302,500
Chrysler	26,025,100
Loews Theaters	25,821,700

Aside from wealth, what do these twenty corporations have in common? They all manufacture nonessential goods. The needs they serve are, in the words of John Kenneth Galbraith, "psychological in origin and hence admirably subject to management by appeal to the psyche." Galbraith goes further. "The individual serves the industrial system," he says, "by consuming its products. On no other matter, religious, political, or moral, is he so elaborately and expensively instructed."[5]

The overarching goal of all advertising is to get the consumer to consume. Communications researcher Dallas Smythe recalls an ad in the New York *Times* which filled an entire page with the message: "Buy Something." Smythe comments: "The popular culture's imperative—'Buy Something'—is the most important educational influence in North America today."[6] Erich Fromm sums it all up in a phrase. American man, he says, is no longer *Homo sapiens*, but *Homo consumens*—Man the consumer.[7]

America is the wealthiest nation in the world. It is also the most wealth-conscious, the most materialistic. Advertising deserves some of the credit and much of the blame.

ADVERTISING AND THE MEDIA

If Big Business as we know it couldn't exist without advertising, neither could the mass media. Television and radio earn all of their money from advertising, which fills some 20 percent of the total air time. Newspapers and magazines earn well over three-quarters of their income from advertising, which occupies roughly 60 percent of the available space.

[5] John Kenneth Galbraith, *The New Industrial State* (Boston: Houghton Mifflin Co., 1967), pp. 37–38, 201.

[6] Dallas Smyth, "Five Myths of Consumership," *The Nation,* January 20, 1969, p. 82.

[7] Erich Fromm, *Escape from Freedom* (New York: Farrar & Rinehart, Inc., 1941).

Of all the mass media, only books and movies are completely independent of advertisers.

Newspapers, magazines, television, and radio compete for every advertising dollar. As of 1968, newspapers had 29 percent of the total. Television had 17.5 percent; magazines had 11.5 percent; and radio had 6.5 percent. The other 35.5 percent went to direct mail, billboards, and the like.[8] This division of the spoils is not a constant. The development of radio ate significantly into the percentage shared by newspapers and magazines. The development of television did a lot of damage to radio and magazines.

But as long as advertising continues to grow, there is plenty of money to go around. In 1941, the total cost of all advertising was less than two billion dollars. Today, that figure is over twenty billion dollars. A minute of time on network radio may now cost up to $8,000. A full-page ad in a major newspaper may run as high as $10,000. A full page in a national magazine may sell for more than $60,000. And a minute on network television may go for a phenomenal $100,000 or more. Advertisers willingly pay the going rates, and all four media are earning good money.

ADVERTISING AND THE PUBLIC

The influence of advertising over media content has already been discussed in considerable detail (see Chapter 5). Direct threats and outright bribes are not unknown, but they are far less common than tacit "mutual understandings." The mass media, after all, are completely dependent on advertisers for their profits. They don't have to be threatened or bribed to keep the advertisers happy. It comes naturally.

None of this is inevitable. Take British television, for example. There are two networks, one commercial and the other government-sponsored. On the non-commercial network, no ads are permitted. On the commercial network, advertisers have only one choice—which station to give the ad to. Station managers schedule the ads as they please, and no commercials are permitted in the middle of a program. Unable to choose their show (much less to produce it), British advertisers have next to no influence on British programming.

The American mass media not only adjust their content to meet the needs of individual advertisers. They also adjust their attitudes to promote the interests of the business community as a whole. In an essay entitled "Mass Communication, Popular Taste and Organized Social Action," sociologists Paul Lazarsfeld and Robert Merton put the case this way:

> Since the mass media are supported by great business concerns geared into the current social and economic system, the media contribute to the maintenance of that system. This contribution is not found merely in the effective advertisement of the sponsor's product. It arises, rather, from

[8] "Ad Volume Increased 6.3% in 1968," *Marketing/Communications*, February, 1969, p. 60.

the typical presence in magazine stories, radio programs and newspaper columns of some element of confirmation, some element of approval of the present structure of society. . . .

Since our commercially sponsored mass media promote a largely unthinking allegiance to our social structure, they cannot be relied upon to work for changes, even minor changes, in that structure. . . . Social objectives are consistently surrendered by the commercialized media when they clash with economic gains.[9]

As we have already said several times, American business spends $20 billion a year on advertising. Naturally, this cost is not absorbed by advertisers in the form of reduced profits. It is passed on to the consumer in the form of increased prices. A bar of soap that sells for 30¢ might cost only 26¢ if Procter and Gamble didn't spend $120 million a year on television. Harry Skornia has computed the cost of television advertising alone to a family with disposable income of $5,000. The annual "tax" for free TV, he found, is $53. It breaks down this way.[10]

Cosmetics and toiletries	$12.00
Patent medicines and drugs	10.00
Car	10.00
Food	6.00
Cigarettes	5.00
Gasoline, oil, tires	3.00
Soaps and detergents	3.00
Other	4.00
	$53.00

A similar computation could be made for radio, newspapers, and magazines.

Defenders of advertising point out, however, that by increasing the demand for consumer goods advertising makes possible the economies of mass production and mass distribution—economies that may be passed on to the consumer. Economists have disagreed for decades as to the net effect of these opposing influences: Advertising both costs us money and saves us money.

Whatever its effect on the economy, the effect of advertising on the media is clear. The content of newspapers, magazines, television, and radio is determined by corporate interests, in an unending effort to turn People into Consumers.

[9] Bernard Rosenberg and David Manning White, eds., *Mass Culture, The Popular Arts in America* (New York: The Free Press, 1957), pp. 465–66.

[10] Harry J. Skornia, *Television and Society* (New York: McGraw-Hill Book Company, 1965), p. 96.

Topics for Discussion

1. Before you read this essay did you realize so much money was spent on advertising each year? Do you think too much money is spent on advertising?
2. Would you favor changing American television to a system similar to the British television system described in this essay? Why? What are the strengths and weaknesses of each system?
3. ". . . the effect of advertising on the media is clear. The content of newspapers, magazines, television, and radio is determined by corporate interests. . . ." Does this mean that because of advertising there is no true freedom in the media? Before answering, consider the previous articles in this section.
4. "Of all the mass media, only books and movies are completely independent of advertisers." In view of the *Detroit News* editorial, is this statement accurate?
5. Advertising costs $200 for every man, woman, and child in the country and in return for this expenditure of money American business gets increased sales and profits in return. But what does the American public get in return?
6. Do you agree that in addition to being the wealthiest nation in the world America is also the most materialistic? Explain your answer.

Rhetorical Considerations

1. This essay is filled with facts and figures. How well do the authors blend them into their sentences? Do you feel overwhelmed by all the numbers? Why?
2. Note the use of quotations throughout this essay. Besides providing necessary information what else do the quotations do?
3. Is the introduction too filled with figures? What effect do the authors hope to achieve in these first two paragraphs? Are they successful?
4. Are the final two paragraphs satisfying as a conclusion? Do they leave too much unsaid?

The Absorption of Surplus: The Sales Effort

Paul Baran and Paul Sweezy

The fact that advertising expenditures in the American economy have experienced a truly spectacular secular rise is unquestionable. A century ago, before the wave of concentration and trustification which ushered in the monopolistic phase of capitalism, advertising played very little part in the process of distribution of products and the influencing of consumer attitudes and habits. Such advertising as did exist was carried on mainly by retailers, and even they did not attempt to promote distinctive brands or labeled articles. The manufacturers themselves had not yet begun to exploit advertising as a means of securing ultimate consumer demand for their products. By the 1890's, however, both the volume and the tone of advertising changed. Expenditures upon advertising in 1890 amounted to $360 million, some seven times more than in 1867. By 1929, this figure had been multiplied by nearly 10, reaching $3,426 million.[1]

Thus as monopoly capitalism reached maturity, advertising entered "the state of persuasion, as distinct from proclamation or iteration."[2] This new phase in the work of the advertiser was already fully described as early as 1905 in *Printer's Ink:*

This is a golden age in trademarks—a time when almost any maker of a worthy product can lay down the lines of a demand that will not only grow with years beyond anything that has ever been known before, but will become to some degree a monopoly. . . . Everywhere . . . there are opportunities to take the lead in advertising—to replace dozens of mongrel, unknown, unacknowledged makes of a fabric, a dress essential, a food with a standard trademarked brand, backed by the national advertising that in itself has come to be a guarantee of worth with the public.[3]

[1] *Historical Statistics of the United States: Colonial Times to 1957,* Washington, 1960, p. 526.

[2] E. S. Turner, *The Shocking History of Advertising,* New York, 1953, p. 36.

[3] Quoted in David M. Potter, *People of Plenty,* Chicago, 1954, pp. 170-171.

Accordingly, the advertising business has grown astronomically, with its expansion and success being continually promoted by the growing monopolization of the economy and by the effectiveness of the media which have been pressed into its service—especially radio, and now above all television. Total spending on advertising media rose to $10.3 billion in 1957, and amounted to over $12 billion in 1962.[4] Together with outlays on market research, public relations, commercial design, and similar services carried out by advertising agencies and other specialized firms, the amount now probably exceeds $20 billion. And this does not include the costs of market research, advertising work, designing, etc., carried on within the producing corporations themselves.

This truly fantastic outpouring of resources does not reflect some frivolous irrationality in corporate managements or some peculiar predilection of the American people for singing commercials, garish billboards, and magazines and newspapers flooded with advertising copy. What has actually happened is that advertising has turned into an indispensable tool for a large sector of corporate business. Competitively employed, it has become an integral part of the corporations' profit maximization policy and serves at the same time as a formidable wall protecting monopolistic positions. Although advertising at first appeared to corporate managements as a deplorable cost to be held down as much as possible, before long it turned into what one advertising agency has rightly called "a must for survival" for many a corporate enterprise.[5]

● ● ●

The strategy of the advertiser is to hammer into the heads of people the unquestioned desirability, indeed the imperative necessity, of owning the newest product that comes on the

[4] *Statistical Abstract of the United States: 1963*, Washington, p. 846.
[5] An extreme case of this "must for survival" principle is presented by a proprietary drug called Contac recently launched by one of the country's largest pharmaceutical firms. This drug's advertising budget is estimated at a "breathtaking $13 million, spent in probably one of the most elaborate drug product campaigns ever devised. Most of the budget is in television." For this outlay, the pharmaceutical firm "is said to be deriving about $16 million in drug store sales, expressed in wholesale prices." (*New York Times*, January 9, 1964.) Allowing for a handsome profit margin, which of course is added to selling as well as production cost, it seems clear that the cost of production can hardly be more than a minute proportion of even the wholesale price. And when the retailer's margin is added, the fraction of the price to the consumer must be virtually invisible.

market.[6] For this strategy to work, however, producers have to pour on the market a steady stream of "new" products, with none daring to lag behind for fear his customers will turn to his rivals for their newness.

Genuinely new or different products, however, are not easy to come by, even in our age of rapid scientific and technological advance. Hence much of the newness with which the consumer is systematically bombarded is either fraudulent or related trivially and in many cases even negatively to the function and serviceability of the product. Good examples of fraudulent newness are admiringly described by Rosser Reeves, head of the Ted Bates advertising agency, one of the country's largest:

Claude Hopkins, whose genius for writing copy made him one of the advertising immortals, tells the story of one of his great beer campaigns. In a tour through the brewery, he nodded politely at the wonders of malt and hops, but came alive when he saw that the empty bottles were being sterilized with live steam. His client protested that every brewery did the same. Hopkins patiently explained that it was not *what* they did, but what they *advertised* they did that mattered. He wrote a classic campaign which proclaimed "OUR BOTTLES ARE WASHED WITH LIVE STEAM!" George Washington Hill, the great tobacco manufacturer, once ran a cigarette campaign with the now-famous claim: "IT'S TOASTED!" So, indeed, is every other cigarette, but no other manufacturer has been shrewd enough to see the enormous possibilities of such a simple story. Hopkins, again, scored a great advertising coup when he wrote: "GETS RID OF FILM ON YOUR TEETH!" So, indeed, does every toothpaste.[7]

These examples could of course be endlessly multiplied. But from our present point of view the important thing to stress is not the ubiquity of this phenomenon but that it is confined entirely to the marketing sphere and does not reach back into the production process itself.

It is entirely different with the second kind of newness. Here

[6] Vance Packard quotes the research and marketing director of the *Chicago Tribune* (which styles itself "The World's Greatest Newspaper") as saying that "tradition bores us now. Instead of being an asset, it is virtually a liability to a people looking for the newest—the newest—always the newest!" *The Waste Makers*, New York, 1960, p. 165. Packard's works, like those of many other latter-day muckrakers, provide a great deal of useful information and at the same time show, in Marx's words, "the strength and the weakness of that kind of criticism which knows how to judge and condemn the present, but not how to comprehend it." *Capital*, Volume 1, Chapter 15, Section 8e.

[7] Rosser Reeves, *Reality in Advertising*, New York, 1961, pp. 55-56. This book is reputed to be the most sophisticated guide to successful advertising.

we have to do with products which are indeed new in design and appearance but which serve essentially the same purposes as old products they are intended to replace. The extent of the difference can vary all the way from a simple change in packaging to the far-reaching and enormously expensive annual changes in automobile models. What all these product variations have in common is that they do reach back into the process of production: the sales effort which used to be a mere adjunct of production, helping the manufacturer to dispose profitably of goods designed to satisfy recognized consumer needs, increasingly invades factory and shop, dictating what is to be produced according to criteria laid down by the sales department and its consultants and advisers in the advertising industry. The situation is well summed up by the McGraw-Hill Department of Economics:

Today, the orientation of manufacturing companies is increasingly toward the market and away from production. In fact, this change has gone so far in some cases that the General Electric Company, as one striking example, now conceives itself to be essentially a marketing rather than a production organization. This thinking flows back through the structure of the company, to the point that marketing needs reach back and dictate the arrangement and grouping of production facilities. [8]

Vance Packard adds the information that "whenever engineers in the appliance industry assembled at conferences in the late fifties, they frequently voiced the lament that they had become little more than pushbuttons for the sales department," and he quotes Consumers Union to the effect that "a good deal of what is called product research today actually is a sales promotion expenditure undertaken to provide what the trade calls a profitable 'product mix.'" [9] And even this is not all. Researchers for *Fortune* magazine, that faithful chronicler of the mores and virtues of Big Business, looking into the Research and Development programs of large American corporations, found that this multi-billion-dollar effort is much more closely related to the production of salable goods than to its much touted mission of advancing science and technology. [10]

As far as the consumer is concerned, the effect of this shift in

[8] Dexter M. Keezer and associates, *New Forces in American Business*, p. 97.

[9] *The Waste Makers*, p. 14.

[10] Eric Hodgins, "The Strange State of American Research," *Fortune*, April 1955. A similar conclusion is suggested by D. Hamberg, "Invention in the Industrial Research Laboratory," *Journal of Political Economy*, April, 1963.

the center of economic gravity from production to sales is entirely negative. In the words of Dexter Masters, former director of Consumers Union, the largest and most experienced organization devoted to testing and evaluating consumers goods:

When design is tied to sales rather than to product function, as it is increasingly, and when marketing strategy is based on frequent style changes, there are certain almost inevitable results: a tendency to the use of inferior materials; short cuts in the time necessary for sound product development; and a neglect of quality and adequate inspection. The effect of such built-in obsolescence is a disguised price increase to the consumer in the form of shorter product life, and, often, heavier repair bills.[11]

But for the economy as a whole, the effect is just as surely positive. In a society with a large stock of consumer durable goods like the United States, an important component of the total demand for goods and services rests on the need to replace a part of this stock as it wears out or is discarded. Built-in obsolescence increases the rate of wearing out, and frequent style changes increase the rate of discarding. (In practice, as Masters points out, the two are inextricably linked together.) The net result is a stepping up in the rate of replacement demand and a general boost to income and employment. In this respect, as in others, the sales effort turns out to be a powerful antidote to monopoly capitalism's tendency to sink into a state of chronic depression.

The emergence of a condition in which the sales and production efforts interpenetrate to such an extent as to become virtually indistinguishable entails a profound change in what constitutes socially necessary costs of production as well as in the nature of the social product itself. In the competitive model, given all the assumptions upon which it rests, only the minimum costs of production (as determined by prevailing technology), combined with the minimum costs of packaging, transportation, and distribution (as called for by existing customs), could be recognized by the market—and by economic theory—as socially necessary costs of purveying a product to its buyer. That product itself, although under capitalism not produced with a view to its use value but as a commodity with a view to its exchange value, could be legitimately considered an object of utility satisfying a genuine human need. To be sure, even during capitalism's competitive phase, to which this model approximately applies, socially necessary costs exceeded

[11] Quoted by Vance Packard, *The Waste Makers*, p. 127.

what they would have been in a less anarchic system of production, but there was no real problem of selling costs and certainly no interpenetration of the production and sales efforts. Socially necessary costs could be unambiguously defined, and at least in principle measured, as those outlays indispensable to the production and delivery of a useful output—given the attained state of development of the forces of production and the corresponding productivity of labor. And once costs had been defined, the social surplus was easily identifiable as the difference between total output and costs. [12]

● ● ●

The question is: what are socially necessary costs when, in Veblen's words, the distinction between workmanship and salesmanship has been blurred? This question does not arise from the mere existence of selling costs. As long as the selling "industry" and the sales departments of producing enterprises are separate and do not impinge upon the production departments, everything is plain sailing. In that case, selling costs, like rent and interest, can be readily recognized as a form of surplus to be subtracted from aggregate costs in order to arrive at the true socially necessary costs of production. But how should we proceed when selling costs are literally indistinguishable from production costs, as is the case, for example, in the automobile industry? No one doubts that a large part of the actual labor which goes into producing an automobile—how much we shall examine presently—has the purpose not of making a more serviceable product but of making a more salable product. But the automobile, once designed, is a unit which is turned out by the combined efforts of all the workers in the shop and on the assembly line. How can the productive workers be distinguished from the unproductive? How can selling costs and production costs be separated?

The answer is that they cannot be distinguished and separated on the basis of any data entering into the books of the automobile companies. The only meaningful procedure is to compare the actual costs of automobiles as they are, including all their built-in sales features, with what would be the costs of automobiles designed to perform the same functions but in the

[12] Capitalist accounting methods treat rent and interest as costs for the individual firm. If the total costs of social output are calculated by adding up the costs of the individual producers, rent and interest will be included as costs and excluded from the surplus. Both classical and Marxian economics, however, had no difficulty in seeing through this appearance to the reality that rent and interest are as much components of the social surplus as profits.

safest and most efficient manner. The costs of the latter would then be the socially necessary costs of automobiles, and the difference between these hypothetical costs and the actual costs of automobiles would be labeled selling costs. If we generalize from this example, it will be seen that on a social scale the identification of that part of the social product which represents sales costs, and should therefore be included in surplus, necessarily involves a comparison of the hypothetical costs of a hypothetical product mix with the actual costs of the actual product mix.

● ● ●

Modern economics of course sees matters quite differently. For it, whatever is produced and "freely" chosen by consumers is the only relevant output; all costs incurred in the process are on a par and all are by definition necessary. From this starting point, it is only logical to reject as unscientific any distinction between useful and useless output, between productive and unproductive labor, between socially necessary costs and surplus. Modern economics has made its peace with things as they are, has no ideological or political battles to fight, wants no confrontations of reality with reason.

Not the least deplorable result of this attitude is that the energies of economists and statisticians have been directed away from the subjects here under consideration, though their elucidation is clearly of crucial importance to an understanding of the working principles of monopoly capitalism. To be sure, the required research work is beset with formidable conceptual and practical difficulties. Drawing up specifications of a hypothetical product mix and estimating its cost call for much ingenuity and good judgment; information on the cost of actual output is often shrouded in secrecy and at best can be obtained only by piecing together scattered and incomplete bits of evidence. Nevertheless, that much can be accomplished in this area has been proved beyond any doubt by a brilliant and methodologically path-breaking study of the costs of automobile model changes by Franklin M. Fisher, Zvi Grilliches, and Carl Kaysen.[13] A brief summary of this study will serve to define more sharply the nature of the questions with which we are concerned, to give some idea of the orders of magnitude

[13] "The Costs of Automobile Model Changes Since 1949," *Journal of Political Economy*, October 1962. An abstract, omitting details of estimating procedures, was presented at the 1961 annual meeting of the American Economic Association and appears in the *American Economic Review*, May 1962, beginning at page 259. Our quotations are from the latter version.

involved, and to suggest lines along which further research is urgently needed.

The principal problem—the necessity of comparing the cost and quality of actual output with the cost and quality of a hypothetical output—is solved by Fisher, Grilliches, and Kaysen by taking 1949 as their point of departure and using the model of that year as the standard of quality and cost. The authors emphasize that the 1949 model was chosen as a standard not because of any particular merits but simply because that was the earliest year for which all necessary data were available. Conceptually, it would clearly have been possible to adopt as the standard a more rationally conceived and constructed model than that of 1949—safer, more durable, more efficient, more economical to operate. Perhaps such an automobile actually exists somewhere in the world, perhaps it would be necessary to have a team of experts blueprint one. From a methodological point of view, either could be substituted for the 1949 model, and such a substitution would undoubtedly result in much higher estimates of the costs of model changes. But even taking the imperfect product of 1949 as its yardstick, the investigation leads to an estimate of costs which the authors themselves consider to be "staggeringly high."

They "concentrate on the cost of the resources that would have been saved had cars with the 1949 model lengths, weights, horsepowers, transmissions, etc., been produced in every year. As there was technological change in the industry, [they] were thus assessing not the resource expenditure that would have been saved had the 1949 models themselves been continued but rather the resource expenditures that would have been saved had cars with 1949 specifications been continued but been built with the developing technology as estimated from actual car construction cost and performance data." These calculations showed that the cost of model changes "came to about $700 per car (more than 25 percent of purchase price) or about $3.9 billion per year over the 1956-1960 period."

And this is by no means the whole story, since "there are other costs of model changes which are not exhausted with the construction of the car but are expended over its life." Among these are costs resulting from accelerated obsolescence of repair parts, higher repair costs stemming from certain changes in car design and construction, and additional gasoline consumption. Confining themselves to estimating the last of these items, the authors found that whereas actual gasoline mileage fell from 16.4 miles per gallon in 1949 to 14.3 miles per gallon ten years later, then rising to about 15.3 in 1960 and 1961, the gasoline mileage of the average 1949 car would have *risen* to 18.0 miles per gallon in 1959 and 18.5 in 1961. This meant that the owner of the average 1956-1960 car was paying about $40 more per 10,000 miles of driving (about 20 percent of his total gasoline costs) than would have been the case had 1949 models been continued.

The additional gasoline consumption due to model changes was estimated to average about $968 million per year over the 1956-1960 period. And in addition, the authors estimated that "since such additional expenditure continues over the life of the car, . . . even if 1962 and all later model years were to see a return to 1949 specifications, the 1961 present value (in 1960 prices) of additional gasoline consumption by cars already built through 1961 discounted at 10 percent would be about $7.1 billion."

Summing up the costs of model changes proper and of additional gasoline costs caused by model changes, the authors concluded: "We thus estimated costs of model changes since 1949 to run about $5 billion per year over the 1956-1960 period with a present value of future gasoline costs of $7.1 billion. If anything, these figures are underestimates because of items not included."

All these calculations take for granted that the costs of automobiles include the enormous monopoly profits of the giant automobile manufacturing corporations (among the highest in the economy) and dealers' markups of from 30 to 40 percent of the final price to the purchaser. If these were omitted from costs, it appears that the real cost of production of a 1949 automobile built with the technology of 1956-1960 would have been less than $700. If we assume further that a rationally designed car could have been turned out at a cost of, say, $200 less than the 1949 model, and assume further the existence of an economical and efficient distributive system, we would have to conclude that the final price to consumers of an automobile would not need to exceed something like $700 or $800. The total saving of resources would then be well above $11 billion a year. On this calculation, automobile model changes in the late 1950's were costing the country about 2.5 percent of its Gross National Product!

It comes as a surprise that such a crucial component of the sales effort as advertising amounted to no more than $14 per car, about 2 percent of the cost of model changes. While automobiles are unquestionably an extreme case, this nevertheless may be taken as an indication of the scope and intensity of the interpenetration of sales and production activities, of the vast amount of selling costs that do not appear as such but are merged into the costs of production. In the case of the automobile industry, and doubtless there are many others that are similar in this respect, by far the greater part of the sales effort is carried out not by obviously unproductive workers such as salesmen and advertising copy writers but by seemingly productive workers: tool and die makers, draftsmen, mechanics, assembly line workers.

But what we would like to stress above all is that the Fisher-Grilliches-Kaysen study definitively establishes the feasibility in principle of a meaningful comparison between an actual and a hypothetical output, and between the costs incurred in producing the actual output and those that would be incurred in producing a more rational output. If carried out for the economy as a whole, such a comparison would provide us with an estimate of the amount of surplus which is now hidden by the interpenetration of the sales and production efforts.

This is not to suggest that a full-scale computation of this kind could be adequately carried out at the present time. No group of economists, no matter how imaginative, and no group of statisticians, however ingenious, could, or for that matter should, attempt to specify the structure of output that could be produced under a more rational economic order. It would certainly be very different from the structure with which we are familiar today; but, as so often, it is possible to see clearly what is irrational without necessarily being able to present the details of a more rational alternative. One need not have a specific idea of a reasonably constructed automobile, a well planned neighborhood, a beautiful musical composition, to recognize that the model changes that are incessantly imposed upon us, the slums that surround us, and the rock-and-roll that blares at us exemplify a pattern of utilization of human and material resources which is inimical to human welfare. One need not have an elaborate plan for international cooperation and coexistence to perceive the horror and destructiveness of war. What is certain is the negative statement which, notwithstanding its negativity, constitutes one of the most important insights to be gained from political economy: an output the volume and composition of which are determined by the profit maximization policies of oligopolistic corporations neither corresponds to human needs nor costs the minimum possible amount of human toil and human suffering.[14] The concrete structure of a rational social output and the optimal conditions for its production can only be established in the fullness of time—by a process of groping, of trial and error—in a socialist society where economic activity is no longer dominated by profits and sales but instead is directed to the creation of the abundance which is indispensable to the welfare and all-round development of man.

[14] That products designed according to the dictates of profit maximization can be in the most literal sense inimical to the elementary need for survival is illustrated by a report in the *New York Times* (March 3, 1964), according to which the American Automobile Association finds the automobile manufacturers guilty of grossly neglecting safety considerations for the sake of body glamor. Recommendations of competent engineers, said Robert S. Kretschmar, a national director of the AAA and head of its Massachusetts branch, "have been over-ridden by the body stylists and the merchandising people." And he continued: "The manufacturers look upon an automobile as 'glamor merchandise,' not as a mechanism that should be made as safe as possible." Among safety shortcomings were listed "a lack of fail-safe brakes, faulty tires, poor interior design, poor steering design, and weak and thin construction." And yet the automobile industry spends many millions of dollars every year on research and development!

Topics for Discussion

1. Do Baran and Sweezy feel that advertising saves the average American money?
2. Footnote five gives the story of the cold remedy called *Contac*. Does advertising add significantly to this product's costs?
3. Do a brief survey of a current newspaper or magazine and list all the advertisements which advertise products as new or different. What proof is offered that the product is in fact new or different?
4. Baran and Sweezy point out that today it is perfectly possible to produce automobiles which cost $800 instead of $3,000 to $5,000. However, what would be the difference between such automobiles and current automobiles? Would the elimination of advertising be the only difference?
5. This essay is critical not only of advertising but the economic system of capitalism as well. What in the essay indicates this?
6. What is an oligopolistic corporation?
7. What is built-in obsolescence?
8. Baran and Sweezy point out that automobiles are sold on the basis of newness in design and not on the basis of an improved and more serviceable product. Do you agree with this? Examine some advertising for new automobiles. What qualities of the automobile are stressed? Is it necessary to change the design of automobiles almost every year? What qualities are stressed in a *Volkswagen* or *Toyota* advertisement compared to an advertisement for *Cadillac* or *Lincoln Continental*?

Rhetorical Considerations

1. Examine the prose style of this essay. Do you find it easy or difficult to read?
2. How well organized is this essay? What is the principle of organization?
3. How clearly do Baran and Sweezy present their argument and analysis? Do they use too many figures or too few?
4. What kind of vocabulary is used in this essay, concrete or abstract? Do you find it easy or difficult to understand most of the words in this essay? Why?
5. Can you summarize briefly the argument of this essay? If you cannot, why do you think you have trouble doing it?

The Unseemly Economics of Opulence

John Kenneth Galbraith

THERE IS a deeply held belief, the Puritan antecedents of which are clear, that if a wealthy man admits even to himself that he can afford a measure of recklessness in his expenditures, an angry God will strike him dead — or certainly take away his money. This holds also for nations. The utmost reticence must be observed in talking about the affluence of the United States. It is permissible to concede, even with a certain amount of pride, that the United States is a wealthy country. But to conclude that in peacetime this opulence excuses a certain amount of social waste is to invite the divine fury that immolated Sodom and Gomorrah. Yet a great many things about the United States can be explained only by its wealth. Although economists have long respected the tabu on drawing conclusions from it, in the service of science certain risks must now be run.

Not even the genius of the adman has been wholly equal to the task of proving that the paper, ether and skills employed in, say, cigarette advertising are related to any urgent public need. As with cigarette advertising so, presumably, with highway billboards, redundant service stations, glossy packages, bread that is first denatured and then fortified, high-pressure salesmanship, singing commercials and the concept of the captive audience. All, in one way or another, are apparently the result of incentives which guide the energies of men not toward but away from maximum social efficiency. Few would insist that these activities are in response to any very pressing desire of the American people. This is the criterion of efficiency of the competitive model. By this standard the American economy is undoubtedly a wasteful one.

However, much of the criticism of the vast activity of selling and advertising in the American economy — that which concerns economics rather than taste or the devastation of the countryside by billboards — has missed the point. Economists and a good many others have pointed to the energies devoted to it with shock or alarm. Those who make their living by it have replied, both in anger and in sorrow, that it isn't wasteful at all. Some bold spirits, with a knack for generaliza-

John Kenneth Galbraith, "The Unseemly Economics of Opulence," from *American Capitalism,* copyright 1956 by Houghton Mifflin Co. Reprinted by permission.

tion, have said that all critics of selling expenditure are subversive. The truth does not lie in between but elsewhere. Our proliferation of selling activity is the counterpart of comparative opulence. Much of it is inevitable with high levels of well-being. It may be waste but it is waste that exists because the community is too well off to care.

II

In a country where, as the result of maximum exertion of all, only a bare minimum of food, clothing, fuel and shelter can be provided, it would indeed be intolerable to have some firms or industries tacitly restricting production and sustaining prices. The price of such a monopoly in, say, the coal-mining industry would be an insufficiency of coal in relation to what consumers desperately need. This might be partially offset by a somewhat greater supply of food. The men and resources who, under more ideal circumstances, would be employed in the mines, would, as the result of the restriction there, find employment in agriculture. But the consequences for the insufficiently heated public would be far from ideal.

Similarly such a community could ill afford to have any considerable fraction of its labor force concocting sales slogans for its limited supply of bread, writing advertising copy for its meager stock of clothing, putting its few vegetables into cellophane packages or otherwise bringing the arts of direct salesmanship to bear on its poverty-stricken consumers. In such a land the whole force, male and female, of J. Walter Thompson, Du Pont Cellophane, and the market research firm of Mr. Elmo Roper should without question be at work producing potatoes, beans and coal so that people might be slightly less hungry and cold.

In fact, in such a community, this labor (perhaps after an appropriate rehabilitation for manual employments) would have no choice but to seek these utilitarian occupations. It is not necessary to advertise food to hungry people, fuel to cold people or houses to the homeless. No one could make a living doing so. The need and the opportunity to persuade people arise only as people have the income to satisfy relatively unimportant wants, of the urgency of which they are not automatically aware. In other words the social inefficiency of a wealthy community grows with the growth in wealth that goes far to make this inefficiency inconsequential.

Thus, while the forty-two million dollars worth of skill,

art and paper spent in 1949 for cigarette advertising and the twenty-nine million dollars devoted to alcoholic beverages served no urgent social purpose the same is true of the cigarettes and the liquor. It is not clear that the community would be better off if those now engaged in selling tobacco and liquor were employed instead in the production of more and cheaper cigarettes and whiskey. (Both the alcoholic and the cigarette hangover seem now to be sufficiently institutionalized.) It is not certain, always assuming peace, that Mr. James H. Blandings [1] and the other employees of Banton and Dascomb are needed in any alternative employment — they are not needed, as recent history has shown, in the production of wheat. The alternative use of the resources which a wealthy community appears to use frivolously will always be in other frivolous employments. It will be in the production of things of no very great consequence by any standards.

III

It will be worth while to examine a little more closely the relation of advertising and selling expenditures to a state of relatively high opulence. These expenditures are made for a variety of purposes. The department stores advertise for no more complex purpose than to let customers know what they have, what they would especially like to sell at the moment, and at what prices. The same motive lies behind an appreciable amount of consumers' goods selling in general. In one way or another the vendor has always had to cry his wares; the modern techniques that are brought to the service of this particular task may be no more costly or no more raucous than those that have been used throughout time.

This kind of salesmanship invites no comment on grounds of social efficiency. Indeed the New York housewife who was forced to do without Macy's advertising would have a sense of loss second only to that from doing without Macy's. However, in a consumers' goods industry shared by a comparatively small number of sellers — the characteristic industry of the contemporary American economy — advertising and selling activity is assumed in modern economics to be undertaken for one or both of two further purposes. It may be, simply, an instrument of commercial rivalry. Price com-

---

[1] For those so unfortunate as not to have encountered him, Mr. Blandings is an advertising man of incredibly complex personality who lives in the pages of two wise and joyful novels by Eric Hodgins.

petition having been foresworn as self-destructive, the firm turns to its salesmen and advertising agency to find new customers and to win customers away from its rivals. The firm is seeking, in the economist's terms, to move its demand curve to the right. Such an effort to get more is necessary, in a world where others are doing the same, if the firm is merely to hold its own. Only the very disingenuous can suppose, or argue, that this form of selling effort is just to make the customer aware that the firm has something to sell. Americans would indeed be mentally retarded if they still had to be advised that the American Tobacco Company has Lucky Strikes to dispose of.

It is also generally agreed that the firm may be seeking, often implicitly, through its advertising and salesmanship so to establish its own personality that it will be protected in some measure from other firms which do not reliably observe the convention against price competition. If a firm is able to persuade the public that its brand of toothpaste, pancake flour, razor blades or aspirin has qualities that are unique, or if it can merely get shoppers to name its brand without thought when they go into a store, then it is somewhat protected from the rivalry of other firms who sell the same product at a lower price. In so enhancing the market power which it has over its own brand, it acquires some freedom to move its own price without inviting loss of custom. The price cuts of other firms can be viewed with some equanimity. Economic theory has given much attention to this process of "product differentiation" in recent times. As a motive, either overt or implicit, for advertising and other selling expenditure its importance has been considerably exaggerated. Simple rivalry between firms is almost certainly far more important. Still, it is a recognizable phenomenon and the wastes associated with efforts to build up brand monopolies have been greatly deplored.

There could be no great volume of selling expenditure of either of these sorts, except in a wealthy community. In such a community the money dispensed in any given purchase is not of high importance to the person spending it — in the language of economics, the marginal utility of money is low. In such a community, also, a great many different purchases are made by each individual. The result is that no single purchase is worth a great deal of thought; there are too many of them for each to be considered in detail. Accordingly the purchaser is a ready subject for the attentions of the advertiser and the salesman. He even allows himself to be influenced by imaginary or contrived virtues, because he is not sufficiently under the pressure of want to learn whether or not these virtues are imaginary. He yields to the influence of suggestion because he is not obliged, by want, to think about his actions. On going into a store he repeats a brand name that has been iterated and reiterated over the radio or on television because the money he is spending is not of sufficient importance to justify his ascertaining whether there are better and cheaper alternatives. Those who are persuaded that the buyer is victimized need to realize that, in the first instance, he is the victim of his own comparative well-being.

The opportunity for product differentiation — for associating monopoly power with the brand or personality of a particular seller — is almost uniquely the result of opulence. A hungry man could never be persuaded that bread that is softened, sliced, wrapped and enriched is worth more than a cheaper and larger loaf that will fill his stomach. A southern cropper will not, as the result of advertising, develop a preference for one brand of cooked, spiced and canned ham over another. He will continue to buy plain sidemeat. No one would advertise the sound-effects of processed breakfast foods striking the milk to Scottish crofters who have only the resources to buy oatmeal. In such communities all the commercial advantages lie with the producers of plain bread, sidemeat and oatmeal.

The tendency for other forms of commercial rivalries, as substitutes for price competition, to be channeled into advertising and salesmanship would disappear in a poor community. One cannot be certain that the convention against price competition itself could be maintained. The nicotine addict, who now automatically buys one or another of the standard brands of cigarettes, would, under the whiplash of necessity, become an inviting market for a cheaper product. The firm that provided it would acquire customers with a rush. Something very like this happened during the early years of the depression when millions of impoverished smokers turned enthusiastically to the ten-cent brands of cigarettes. In any case, for maintaining the convention against price competition, it is a great help to have customers who do not care — even if, on occasion, they think they do.

There is a legend, with a great appeal to simple men, that

The Age of Communication

Americans are a nation of salesmen because they have some peculiar virtuosity in this craft. There are more salesmen, and salesmanship is more highly developed, in the United States than elsewhere in the world. But the explanation lies not with national character but with national wealth. The latter means, of course, that there are more goods to be sold. But even more, it means that psychological, not physical, considerations control desire. The biological minimums are covered. As a result that modern practitioner of applied psychology, the salesman, gets his opportunity. Sent to practice on Indians or Chinese or even French peasants the most brilliant American vendor would be a dismal failure.

Many of my fellow economists will have difficulty in sharing the equanimity with which I here view selling costs and the so-called wastes of distribution. Economics began in the eighteenth and nineteenth centuries when men were really poor. Two of its great pioneers, Malthus and Ricardo, held that grinding poverty was the fate of man — any surplus wealth, above the requirements for bare subsistence, would be promptly absorbed into the additional mouths that wealth itself would spawn. In such a society inefficiency was, indeed, an evil thing. It denied bread to the hungry and clothing to the naked even though, if these became available, they launched a new cycle of conception and birth that re-established the common poverty. Western man, as the result of an unsuspected preference for comfort over procreation, and aided by some inexpensive appliances, has escaped from this cycle of poverty. In the United States, in recent times, for most people the biological minimums of food, clothing and even shelter have been covered as a matter of course. By comparison, the further wants are comparatively unimportant. Economists, nonetheless, have stuck firmly to their conviction that anything that denies the community additional goods or services, however casual their significance, is the greatest of sins. They have brought the mentality of nineteenth-century poverty to the analysis of twentieth-century opulence.

The result is an inefficient deployment of the economist's own resources. He is excessively preoccupied with goods *qua* goods; in his preoccupation with goods he has not paused to reflect on the relative unimportance of the goods with which he is preoccupied. He worries far too much about partially monopolized prices or excessive advertising and selling costs for tobacco, liquor, chocolates, automobiles and soap in a land which is already suffering from nicotine poisoning and alcoholism, which is nutritionally gorged with sugar, which is filling its hospitals and cemeteries with those who have been maimed or murdered on its highways and which is dangerously neurotic about normal body odors.

Topics for Discussion

1. Discuss what Galbraith means by the comment that "a great many things about the United States can be explained only by its wealth." Can you think of some things which can be explained because of America's wealth?
2. "However, much of the criticism of the vast activity of selling and advertising . . . has missed the point." What is the point according to Galbraith?
3. Galbraith says that only a wealthy country can afford advertising. Why would this be so? Do you agree with this? Go to the library and look up advertisements in foreign newspapers and magazines. What products are advertised?
4. What does Galbraith mean by opulence?
5. Galbraith says that our biological minimums are covered and therefore it is psychological considerations that control our desire. What does he mean? Do you agree with this?
6. Are Americans "dangerously neurotic about normal body odors" as Galbraith states? If so, why are we so concerned?
7. Galbraith says that if the buyer is victimized "he is the victim of his own comparative well-being." What does he mean? Do you agree?
8. Although he never directly states his position, can you infer from this essay whether Galbraith is for or against advertising?

Rhetorical Considerations

1. What is the thesis of this essay? Is it stated anywhere or is it simply implied?
2. What is Galbraith's basis for dividing his essay into three parts?
3. Galbraith is a professional economist, yet he uses very few figures in this essay. How does he make his point without using impressive and overwhelming statistics?
4. How easily does this read? That is, do you find Galbraith's sentences smooth and well written and his vocabulary understandable?

WANTED:
Responsible Advertising Critics

James Webb Young

I learned my trade as a writer of advertisements in a religious publishing house, selling books by mail to Methodist ministers. My first big success was with a book called "Personal Evangelism," which had the worthy purpose of telling these ministers how to increase the membership of their church and, as the saying had it, to "bring more souls to Christ."

In such an activity I had no suspicion that I was entering upon what—much later—President Angell of Yale told me was a "*déclassé* profession." And I dare say the present writer of an effective series of advertisements, now being published by the Knights of Columbus for the Catholic faith, would have been as astonished as I was when I heard this.

My first warning on the status of the advertising man came on another campus. Early in the 1920s, in the midst of a busy advertising life, I had undertaken to get a solid physiological base for the study of psychology. And the famous Anton J. Carlson at the University of Chicago had agreed personally to give it to me in his laboratory.

One day Dr. Carlson introduced me to the late C. Judson Herrick, notable for his researches on the brain and nervous system, whose latest book I had been given to study. I said: "Dr. Herrick, it may surprise you to know that an advertising man is finding your new book on the brain of the greatest interest." Said Dr. Herrick, looking at me sourly over his glasses: "I am not only surprised; I am chagrined. As far as I can see there is no connection between brains and advertising."

Since then, through the years, in my notes on many kinds of human behavior, I have recorded other equally sweeping generalizations about advertising, made by faculty members of Harvard, Columbia, Princeton, Cornell, Wisconsin, Johns Hopkins, and McGill.

But sweeping generalizations about advertising are not confined to the academic groves, nor to recent times. A notable piece on the subject came from the pen of Dr. Samuel Johnson, in the mid-eighteenth century. And currently, triggered by the revelation of rigged TV quiz shows, any number of people have gotten into the act.

Thus, for example, in a recent column Walter Lippmann seems to transfer the responsibility for this rigging wholly to the shoulders of "advertisers"—not to particular advertisers, and not in any degree to those of the educator-idol whose feet of clay furnished all the drama.

Note, too, the adverbs used by Father P. P. Harbrecht, S.J., in a recent booklet issued by the Twentieth Century Fund on his excellent study, "Toward the Paraproprietal Society." Speaking of such big corporations as General Motors, du Pont, U.S. Steel, Alcoa, and General Electric, he says (italics mine): "Their research and innovations transform our lives, *quietly* with home

James Webb Young, "Wanted: Responsible Advertising Critics." From *Saturday Review,* April 23, 1960, pp. 35–40, 56. Reprinted by permission.

appliances or *dramatically* with atomics and space flight; *brashly* with TV advertising or *culturally* with subsidies to education." Is all the TV advertising of all these firms done "brashly"?

Now, let me say clearly that advertising needs, is entitled to, and can profit from criticism of the most public kind. It needs it more than ever today because advertising has become one of the most potent forces in our culture— ranking as an "institution" with the church and education, according to Professor Potter of Yale, in his book "People of Plenty."

But it needs that criticism in the form that the dictionary defines as "the act of passing judgment on the merits of anything"; that is, discriminating criticism, which applauds the goods and damns the bad.

No one is more concerned about the misuses of advertising than the responsible people in advertising. And, in fact, they have been trying for a very long time to do something about these misuses. If any of the shoot-from-the-hip critics of this activity would take the same trouble to understand my specialty as I was taking to understand that of Dr. Herrick, these are some of the things they would find:

First, that the technical literature of advertising is currently filled with the kind of "good-and-bad" criticism advertising needs.

Second, that advertising people have promoted and secured the adoption of "Truth in Advertising" laws in over half our states, and have supported the work of Better Business Bureaus in policing these laws.

Third, that they have supported the purposes, if not always the methods, of the Federal Trade Commission, to prevent the use of advertising in ways unfair to competition.

Fourth, that in their various trade and professional organizations advertising men have drafted any number of codes of "ethical" practices—and have been busy reactivating these lately!

Fifth, that many important advertising media refuse to accept advertising for certain classifications of products; and that the largest advertising agency in the world has never undertaken advertising for "hard" liquors—all at a considerable cost to their revenues.

All these things have, in fact, brought improvements in the use of advertising, as a recent writer noted. "In front of us," he says, "is a 1913 advertisement pointing out the advantages of Postum over Brazilian coffee. Among the ills attributed to coffee: 'Sallow Complexions; Stomach Trouble; Bad Liver; Heart Palpitations; Shattered Nerves; Caffeine, a Drug; Weakness from Drugging.' We doubt if the present owners of Postum would O.K. copy like this today. Even if they didn't own Maxwell House."

But all this is not enough, and nobody knows it better than those hard-working creators of much of our advertising, inaccurately stereotyped as "Madison Avenue."

The reason why it is not enough is that, as developed in America, the set of facilities and techniques called advertising has become the most powerful single means that the world has ever seen for informing, persuading, and inspiring a people to action. As such, it becomes vital that its potentialities for good or ill become fully recognized; that the responsibilities for its use be squarely shouldered; and that the magnificent opportunities for its use in the public service, as now amply demonstrated in the work of the Advertising Council, be fully exploited.

It is therefore my thesis that what advertising now needs is to be given, in public print, the same kind of continuing, knowing, responsible criticism as that given to the theatre, music, the arts, books, and other major aspects of our culture. It needs a "career critic," keeping a steady spotlight on both the good and the bad in the uses of advertising, and on its unexploited social potentialities.

What would be the qualifications for such a public critic of advertising—assuming the judicial temperament of the responsible man?

First, he should know that "advertising" is a set of facilities and techniques as impersonal as electricity or atomic energy, and thus equally usable for noble ends or shabby ones. Hence he will avoid the "pathetic fallacy" of animating the inanimate, into which so many critics of advertising fall. It is *advertisers* who need criticism—not advertising.

Second, he will understand clearly the economic necessities which brought advertising into existence, and still control its use. These were well stated in 1870 by Walter Bagehot in his classic work "Lombard Street." Said Bagehot:

> Our current political economy does not sufficiently take account of *time* as an element in trade operations. But as soon as the division of labour has once established itself in a community, two principles at once begin to be important, of which time is the very essence. These are—
>
> *First*, that as goods are produced to be exchanged, it is good that they should be exchanged as quickly as possible.
>
> *Secondly*, that as every producer is mainly occupied in producing what others want, and not what he wants himself, it is desirable that he should always be able to find, without effort, without delay, and without uncertainty, others who want what he can produce.

These words are even truer today than when Bagehot wrote them. To understand the workhorse job of advertising in a high production-consumption economy such as ours is primary for any intelligent criticism of its uses.

Third, he must understand that the methods by which advertising gets the workhorse job done in today's economy have been greatly developed since Bagehot's day; and why in these methods are to be found some of the roots of the criticisms of advertising.

. . . early in the expansion of the use of advertising it was discovered that the mere repetition of a name or trademark could produce a preference for one product over another. Remember "Gold Medal flour—Eventually, Why Not Now?" This sort of advertising worked because mere familiarity is a *value* to the human being. It satisfies one of his deepest needs: for a sense of "at-homeness" in this world. You can check this, perhaps, by recalling when, in a crowd of strangers, you have found yourself gravitating toward one familiar face—possibly even that of a person not well liked. Familiarity is a value, and no advertising works which does not, in some form, deliver a value to somebody.

Then it was discovered that there is a function for advertising merely as a "re-minder" of something we are already "minded" to do. For example, to "Say it with flowers!" when you have a wedding anniversary coming up. A service, surely, in the cause of domestic tranquillity!

After this, as railroads made a national market possible, came a development in the *news* use of advertising. Just as the Associated Press came into being to gather and transmit general news, so the advertising agency came into being to gather and transmit commercial news, thus making possible the announcement, say, of a new model automobile on the same day everywhere.

But there is also another kind of "news," in the advertising sense. It is the kind of news you pay no attention to until you need to know it. In our long march from the cradle to the grave we pass into, and out of, many areas of experience. And as we do, our receptivity to all sorts of news changes. Thus the young woman who ignores the infant-feeding advertisement of today may become its most eager reader next year.

Then, along the way, came the discovery that advertising could be used to overcome human inertia. Hell is indeed paved with many good intentions, toward such things as making a will, taking out adequate life insurance, seeing the dentist regularly, and so on. In all such things the reward for action taken, or the punishment for action postponed, is remote and delayed. Advertising, by making more vivid such rewards or punishments, can often overcome the inertia—to the profit of the reader or listener as well as the advertiser.

Religions have always had to deal with this problem in the training of ministers, and here it seems always to have been a moot question whether portrayal of the rewards of heaven or of the punishments of hell converted more sinners.

Then, finally, came the discovery that advertising could *add a value not in the product*. And because these values were subjective ones (such as status symbols; or, say, the luxury of bathing with the same soap the movie stars use; or what Edith Wharton once called "the utility of the useless"), here advertising really got into trouble. For in this area of subjective values, one man's meat is definitely another man's poison.

In this area, too, our critic will come face to face with one of his most difficult problems. Advertising, like editing, politics, and even to some extent education, always operates within the context of the culture of its day. One irony of its present situation is that some of the people who are most vocal in their negative attitudes toward advertising may themselves have contributed to some aspects of it which they most deplore. By supporting liberal policies for the wider distribution of wealth in this country, they have helped bring into existence a mammoth class of *nouveau riche*, whose incomes have improved faster than their tastes and subjective values.

In addition to such an understanding of the ways in which advertising works, our critic must grasp some of the trends in our economy which have major impacts on the creation of advertising.

The most important of these lie in our technology. Innovation has become an industry, as Dr. Sumner Slichter pointed out. Theoretically, our accelerated rate of innovation should produce more and more advertising news about distinction in products. But counter forces produce in some considerable degree an opposite effect.

One of these counter forces is governmental pressure for the preservation of competition. This tends to force a cross-licensing of patents which rapidly spreads any given innovation throughout an industry. Thus, for instance, when one manufacturer of television sets produces a more compact tube, soon many of his major competitors have the benefit of it.

Then, too, innovation often comes, not from the end-producer of the product or service, but from the supplier of an ingredient or part, whose interest is to gain its adoption by as many end-producers as possible. See, for example, the current jet plane advertising of our airlines.

Added to these we have, in this country, a widespread "free trade" in technological ideas, through such channels as the Society of Automotive Engineers and numerous trade and technical journals. The result is that innovating ideas get "in the air," and soon all our automobiles, for example, become more and more alike.

All these forces result in the reverse of a distinction between competitive products and services. But the advertising man is expected to present each of them as one with important differences, leading to the manufacture of mountains out of molehills in the advertising. Our critic must be knowledgeable about this problem, and about the constructive ways to deal with it.

Finally, and most importantly, our critic should be conscious of the still underdeveloped use of advertising as a social force outside the exchange of goods and services.

He must know of the remarkable results that the Advertising Council has produced over the last fifteen years for some fifty "good causes"—through the voluntary services of advertising men, and with contributions of come $180 million annually, in time and space, from advertisers and media.

And he should know, too, of the following-up of this lead in such fine corporation advertising campaigns as:

    a. The striking campaign of the Standard Oil Company (N.J.) in the interest of international friendship.

    b. The Weyerhaeuser Company's campaign for the preservation of our forests and for conservation through tree-farming.

c. The campaign for better schools, safer highways, forest fire prevention, and other useful purposes of the Caterpillar Tractor Co.

d. The campaign of the New York Life Insurance Company to help parents guide their children in career choices, or the notable campaign of the Metropolitan Life Insurance Company on behalf of better health.

e. The campaign for citizen responsibility of Nationwide Insurance.

An alert critic might see, too, in such uses of advertising, potentialities for our great foundations; for the use of some of their funds in the *distribution* of knowledge, through this most modern high-speed means of communication.

In all this let our critic be not only objective but specific. Let him deal, not with "advertising," but with its uses, good and bad. Let him examine:

Whether there is too much crowding of advertising in time and space—such as commercials per TV program, and billboards per scenic mile?

Whether there is too much stridency and bad manners in some advertising, now that it can project personal salesmanship into the living room?

Whether the paucity of real buying information, and the superfluity of adjectives in some advertising is, not a crime, but worse—a mistake?

Would such a critic have any real effect on the advertising scene? All I know is that the genius of advertising is reiteration, and that its prophet, Isaiah, said: "Whom shall he teach knowledge? and whom shall he make to understand doctrines? . . . For precept must be upon precept; precept upon precept; line upon line; line upon line; here a little, and there a little."

What I am looking for is a publisher or editor with the insight and courage to enter this new field of criticism—and for the competent critic to aid him. Such a publisher or editor will have to take some risks with his advertisers, yes. But he will, I believe, make a major contribution to the better and wiser use of advertising in our day; he will find himself attracting a surprising volume of mail from his readers; and, in the longer haul, profiting from the sharp attention given his publication by advertisers and advertising men.

Are there any takers in the house?

Topics for Discussion

1. Young says that "it is *advertisers* who need criticism—not advertising." Do you agree?
2. ". . . the set of facilities and techniques called advertising has become the most powerful single means that the world has ever seen for informing, persuading, and inspiring a people to action." But does Young say what kind of action; and whether that action is good?
3. Young mentions that advertising has "unexploited social potentialities." Does he mention what these might be? Can you think of any?
4. Advertising can add a value not in the product, such as status, says Young. Is this really adding value to a product? Are you willing to pay extra for the status value of a product? Why?
5. The advertising industry annually donates some $180 million in time and space for "good causes." Advertising is a $40-billion-a-year business. Discuss the implications of these figures.
6. Do you think such a critic as Young proposes would be very effective? Can you think of anyone who would give such a critic a job?
7. One of the functions of advertising is "the manufacture of mountains out of molehills." Do you agree with this? Can you cite any examples of this in current advertisers?
8. What is a "declassé profession"?

Rhetorical Considerations

1. How effective is Young's introduction based on his personal background and experiences? What effect does it have on you?
2. Where does Young state his thesis? Is it too far into his essay? Is everything that comes before it an introduction?
3. Examine the paragraph structure of this essay. Why do you think Young writes such brief paragraphs? Are his paragraphs too brief to really develop an idea?
4. Young ends his essay with a question. Is this a good rhetorical device? Does it really conclude his essay? What is he trying to achieve by concluding this way?

Should Advertising Be Abolished?
David Ogilvy

NOT long ago Lady Hendy, my Socialist elder sister, invited me to agree with her that advertising should be abolished. I found it difficult to deal with this menacing suggestion, because I am neither an economist nor a philosopher. But at least I was able to point out that opinion is divided on the question.

The late Aneurin Bevan thought that advertising was "an evil service." Arnold Toynbee (of Winchester and Balliol) "cannot think of any circumstances in which advertising would not be an evil." Professor Galbraith (Harvard) holds that advertising tempts people to squander money on "unneeded" possessions when they ought to be spending it on public works.

But it would be a mistake to assume that every liberal shares the Bevan-Toynbee-Galbraith view of advertising. President Franklin Roosevelt saw it in a different light:

> If I were starting life over again, I am inclined to think that I would go into the advertising business in preference to almost any other. . . . The general raising of the standards of modern civilization among all groups of people during the past half century would have been impossible without the spreading of the knowledge of higher standards by means of advertising.

Sir Winston Churchill agrees with Mr. Roosevelt:

> Advertising nourishes the consuming power of men. It sets up before a man the goal of a better home, better clothing, better food for himself and his family. It spurs individual exertion and greater production.

Almost all serious economists, of whatever political color, agree that advertising serves a useful purpose *when it is used to give information about new products.* Thus Anastas L. Mikoyan, the Russian:

> The task of our Soviet advertising is to give people exact information about the goods that are on sale, to help to create new demands, to cultivate new tastes and requirements, to promote the sale of new kinds of goods and to explain their uses to the consumer. The primary task of Soviet advertising is to give a truthful, exact, apt and

striking description of the nature, quality and properties of the goods advertised.

The Victorian economist Alfred Marshall also approved of "informative" advertising for new products, but condemned what he called "combative" advertising as a waste. Walter Taplin of the London School of Economics points out that Marshall's analysis of advertising "shows indications of those prejudices and emotional attitudes to advertising from which nobody seems to be completely free, not even classical economists." There was, indeed, a streak of prissiness in Marshall; his most illustrious student, Maynard Keynes, once described him as "an utterly absurd person." What Marshall wrote about advertising has been cribbed by many later economists, and it has become orthodox doctrine to hold that "combative"—or "persuasive"—advertising is economic waste. Is it?

My own clinical experience would suggest that the kind of informative factual advertising which the dons endorse is more effective, *in terms of sales results,* than the "combative" or "persuasive" advertising which they condemn. Commercial self-interest and academic virtue march together.

If all advertisers would give up flatulent puffery, and turn to the kind of factual, informative advertising which I have provided for Rolls-Royce, KLM Royal Dutch Airlines, and Shell, they would not only increase their sales, but they would also place themselves on the side of the angels. The more informative your advertising, the more persuasive it will be.

In a recent poll conducted among thought-leaders, Hill & Knowlton asked, *"Should advertisers give the facts and only the facts?"* The vote in favor of this austere proposition was strikingly affirmative:

	YES
Religious leaders	76%
Editors of highbrow publications	74
High school administrators	74
Economists	73
Sociologists	62
Government officials	45
Deans of colleges	33
Business leaders	23

Thus we see that factual advertising is very widely regarded as a Good Thing. But when it comes to "persuasive" advertising for one old brand against another, the majority of economists follow Marshall in condemning it. Rexford Tugwell, who earned my undying admiration for inspiring the economic renaissance of Puerto Rico, condemns the "enormous waste involved

in the effort to turn trade from one firm to another."
The same dogma comes from Stuart Chase:

> Advertising makes people stop buying Mogg's
> soap, and start buying Bogg's soap. . . . Nine-
> tenths and more of advertising is largely
> competitive wrangling as to the relative merits of
> two undistinguished and often undistinguishable
> compounds. . . .

Pigou, Braithwaite, Baster, Warne, Fairchild, Morgan, Boulding, and other economists say essentially the
same thing, many of them in almost the same words,
except that they leave Mogg & Bogg to Stuart Chase,
substituting Eureka & Excelsior, Tweedledum & Twee-
dledee, Bumpo & Bango. Read one of them, and you
have read them all.

I will let these dons in on a curious secret. The com-
bative-persuasive kind of advertising which they condemn is not nearly as *profitable* as the informative kind
of advertising which they approve.

My experience has been that it is relatively easy for
advertising to persuade consumers to try a *new* product.
But they grow maddeningly deaf to the advertising of
products which have been around for a long time.

Thus we advertising agents get more mileage out of
advertising new products than old ones. Once again,
academic virtue and commercial self-interest march
together.

Does advertising raise prices? There has been too
much sloppy argument on both sides of this intricate
question. Few serious studies have been made of the
effect of advertising on prices. However, Professor Neil
Borden of Harvard has examined hundreds of case
histories. With the aid of an advisory committee of five
other formidable professors, he reached conclusions
which should be more widely studied by other dons
before they pop off on the economics of advertising. For
example, "In many industries the large scale of operations made possible in part through advertising has
resulted in reductions in manufacturing costs." And,
"the building of the market by means of advertising
and other promotional devices not only makes price
reductions attractive or possible for large firms, it also
creates an opportunity to develop private brands, which
generally are offered at lower prices." Indeed they are;
when I am dead and opened, you shall find not "Calais"
lying in my heart, as Mary Tudor prophesied would be
found in hers, but "Private Brands." They are the natural enemies of us advertising agents. Twenty per cent
of total grocery sales are now private brands, owned by
retailers and not advertised. Bloody parasites.

Professor Borden and his advisers reached the conclusion that advertising, "though certainly not free from criticism, is an economic asset and not a liability."[1] Thus did they agree with Churchill and Roosevelt. However, they did not support all the shibboleths of Madison Avenue. They found, for example, that advertising does not give consumers sufficient information. My experience at the working level leads me to agree.

It is worth listening to what the men who pay out huge sums of their stockholders' money for advertising say about its effect on prices. Here is Lord Heyworth, the former head of Unilever:

> Advertising . . . brings savings in its wake. On the distribution side it speeds up the turnover of stock and thus makes lower retail margins possible, without reducing the shopkeeper's income. On the manufacturing side it is one of the factors that make large scale production possible and who would deny that large scale production leads to lower costs?

Essentially the same thing has recently been said by Howard Morgens, the President of Procter & Gamble:

> Time and again in our company, we have seen the start of advertising on a new type of product result in savings that are considerably greater than the entire advertising cost. . . . The use of advertising clearly results in lower prices to the public.

In most industries the cost of advertising represents less than 3 per cent of the price consumers pay at retail. But if advertising were abolished, you would lose on the swings much of what you saved on the roundabouts. For example, you would have to pay a fortune for the Sunday *New York Times* if it carried no advertising. And just think how dull it would be. Jefferson read only one newspaper, "and that more for its advertisements than its news." Most housewives would say the same.

Does advertising encourage monopoly? Professor Borden found that "in some industries advertising has contributed to concentration of demand and hence has been a factor in bringing about concentration of supply in the hands of a few dominant firms." But he concluded that advertising is not a *basic cause* of monopoly. Other economists have proclaimed that advertis-

[1] *The Economics of Advertising,* Richard D. Irwin (Chicago, 1942) pages xxv-xxxix.

ing contributes to monopoly. I agree with them. It is becoming progressively more difficult for small companies to launch new brands. The entrance fee, in terms of advertising, is now so large that only the entrenched giants, with their vast war chests, can afford it. If you don't believe me, try launching a new brand of detergent with a war chest of less than $10,000,000.

Furthermore, the giant advertisers are able to buy space and time far more cheaply than their little competitors, because the media owners cosset them with quantity discounts. These discounts encourage big advertisers to buy up little ones; they can do the same advertising at 25-per-cent less cost, and pocket the saving.

Does advertising corrupt editors? Yes it does, but fewer editors than you may suppose. The publisher of a magazine once complained to me, in righteous indignation, that he had given one of my clients five pages of editorial and had received in return only two pages of advertising. But the vast majority of editors are incorruptible.

Harold Ross resented advertising, and once suggested to his publisher that all advertisements in *The New Yorker* should be put on one page. His successor exhibits the same sort of town-and-gown snobbery, and loses no opportunity to belittle what he calls "ad-men." Not long ago he published a facetious attack on two of my campaigns, sublimely indifferent to the fact I have filled 1,173 pages of his magazine with uncommonly ornamental advertisements. It strikes me as bad manners for a magazine to accept one of my advertisements and then attack it editorially—like inviting a man to dinner and then spitting in his eye.

I have often been tempted to punish editors who insult my clients. When one of our advertisements for the British Industries Fair appeared in an issue of the *Chicago Tribune* which printed one of Colonel McCormick's ugly diatribes against Britain, I itched to pull the campaign out of his paper. But to do so would have blown a gaping hole in our coverage of the Middle West, and might well have triggered a brouhaha about advertising pressure on editors.

Can advertising foist an inferior product on the consumer? Bitter experience has taught me that it cannot. On those rare occasions when I have advertised products which consumer tests found inferior to other products in the same field, the results have been disastrous. If I try hard enough, I can write an advertisement which will persuade consumers to buy an inferior product, *but only once*—and most of my clients depend on repeat purchases for their profit. Phineas T. Barnum was the first to observe that "you may advertise a spurious article and induce many people to buy it once, but they will gradually denounce you as an impostor." Alfred Politz and Howard Morgens believe that advertising can actually accelerate the demise of an inferior product. Says Morgens, "The quickest way to kill a brand that is off in quality is to promote it aggressively. People find out about its poor quality just that much more quickly."

He goes on to point out that advertising has come to play a significant part in product improvement:

> Research people, of course, are constantly searching for ways to improve the things we buy. But believe me, a great deal of prodding and pushing and suggestions for those improvements also comes from the advertising end of the business. That's bound to be, because the success of a company's advertising is closely tied up with the success of its product development activities.
>
> . . . Advertising and scientific research have come to work hand-in-glove on a vast and amazingly productive scale. The direct beneficiary is the consumer, who enjoys an ever-widening selection of better products and services.

On more than one occasion I have been instrumental in persuading clients not to launch a new product until they could develop one which would be demonstrably superior to those already on the market.

Advertising is also a force for sustaining standards of quality and service. Writes Sir Frederic Hooper of Schweppes:

> Advertising is a guarantee of quality. A firm which has spent a substantial sum advocating the merits of a product and accustoming the consumer to expect a standard that is both high and uniform, dare not later reduce the quality of its goods. Sometimes the public is gullible, but not to the extent of continuing to buy a patently inferior article.

When we started advertising KLM Royal Dutch Airlines as "punctual" and "reliable," their top management sent out an encyclical, reminding their operations staff to live up to the promise of our advertising.

It may be said that a good advertising agency represents the consumer's interest in the councils of industry.

Is advertising a pack of lies? No longer. Fear of becoming embroiled with the Federal Trade Commission, which tries its cases in the newspapers, is now so great that one of our clients recently warned me that if any of our commercials were ever cited by the FTC for dishonesty, he would immediately move his account to another agency. The lawyer at General Foods actually required that our copywriters *prove* that Open-Pit Barbecue Sauce has an "old-fashioned flavor" before he would allow us to make this innocuous claim in advertisements. The consumer is better protected than she knows.

I cannot always keep pace with the changing rules laid down by the various bodies that regulate advertising. The Canadian Government, for example, applies one set of rules to patent medicine advertising, and the United States Government a totally different set. Some American states prohibit the mention of price in whiskey advertisements, while others insist upon it; what is forbidden in one state is obligatory in another. I can only take refuge in the rule which has always governed my own output: never write an advertisement which you wouldn't want your own family to see.

Dorothy Sayers, who wrote advertisements before she wrote whodunits and Anglo-Catholic tracts, says: "Plain lies are dangerous. The only weapons left are the *suggestio falsi* and the *suppressio veri.*" I plead guilty to one act of *suggestio falsi*—what we on Madison Avenue call a "weasel." However, two years later a chemist rescued my conscience by discovering that what I had falsely suggested was actually true.

But I must confess that I am continuously guilty of *suppressio veri*. Surely it is asking too much to expect the advertiser to describe the shortcomings of his product? One must be forgiven for putting one's best foot forward.

Does advertising make people want to buy products they don't need? If you don't think people need deodorants, you are at liberty to criticize advertising for having persuaded 87 per cent of American women and 66 per cent of American men to use them. If you don't think people need beer, you are right to criticize advertising for having persuaded 58 per cent of the adult population to drink it. If you disapprove of social mobility, creature comforts, and foreign travel, you are right to blame advertising for encouraging such wickedness. If you dislike affluent society, you are right to blame advertising for inciting the masses to pursue it.

If you are this kind of Puritan, I cannot reason with you. I can only call you a psychic masochist. Like Archbishop Leighton, I pray, "Deliver me, O Lord, from the errors of wise men, yea, and of good men."

Dear old John Burns, the father of the Labor movement in England, used to say that the tragedy of the working class was the poverty of their desires. I make no apology for inciting the working class to desire less Spartan lives.

Should advertising be used in politics? I think not. In recent years it has become fashionable for political parties to employ advertising agencies. In 1952 my old friend Rosser Reeves advertised General Eisenhower as if he were a tube of toothpaste. He created fifty commercials in which the General was made to read out hand-lettered answers to a series of phony questions from imaginary citizens. Like this:

Citizen: Mr. Eisenhower, what about the high cost of living?
General: My wife Mamie worries about the same thing. I tell her it's our job to change that on November 14th.

Between takes the General was heard to say, "To think that an old soldier should come to this."

Whenever my agency is asked to advertise a politician or a political party, we refuse the invitation, for these reasons:

(1) The use of advertising to sell statesmen is the ultimate vulgarity.
(2) If we were to advertise a Democrat, we would be unfair to the Republicans on our staff; and vice versa.

However, I encourage my colleagues to do their political duty by working for one of the parties—as individuals. If a party or a candidate requires *technical* advertising services, such as the buying of network time to broadcast political rallies, he can employ expert volunteers, banded together in an *ad hoc* consortium.

Should advertising be used in good causes of a non-political nature? We advertising agents derive modest satisfaction from the work we do for good causes. Just as surgeons devote much of their time to operating on paupers without remuneration, so we devote much of our time to creating campaigns for charity patients. For example, my agency created the first campaign for Radio Free Europe, and in recent years we have created campaigns for the American Cancer Society, the United States Committee for the United Nations, the Citizens Committee To Keep New York City Clean, and Lincoln Center for the Performing Arts. The professional services we have donated to these causes have cost us about $250,000, which is equivalent to our profit on $12,000,000 of billing.

In 1959 John D. Rockefeller III and Clarence Francis asked me to increase public awareness of Lincoln Center, which was then in the planning stage. A survey revealed that only 25 per cent of the adult population of New York had heard of Lincoln Center. When our campaign was concluded, one year later, 67 per cent had heard of Lincoln Center. When I presented the plans for this campaign, I said:

> The men who conceived Lincoln Center, and particularly the big foundations which have contributed to it, would be dismayed if the people of New York came to think of Lincoln Center as the preserve of the upper crust. . . . It is, therefore, important to create the right image: Lincoln Center is for *all* the people.

A survey conducted at the conclusion of the campaign showed that this democratic objective had been fulfilled. Those interviewed were presented with statements, and asked which they agreed with. Here are their votes:

> *Probably most people living in New York*
> *and its suburbs will visit Lincoln Center at*
> *one time or another* 76%
> *Lincoln Center is only for wealthier people* 4%

Most campaigns for good causes are contributed by one volunteer agency, but in the case of Lincoln Center, BBDO, Young & Rubicam, and Benton & Bowles volunteered to work in harness with us—a remarkable and harmonious quartet. The television commercials were made by BBDO, and New York stations donated $600,000 worth of time to running them. The radio commercials were made by Benton & Bowles, and the radio stations donated $100,000 worth of time to running them. The printed advertisements were made by Young & Rubicam and ourselves; *Reader's Digest, The New Yorker, Newsweek,* and *Cue* ran them free.

When we volunteered to take over the campaign to Keep New York City Clean, the number of streets rated clean had already increased from 56 per cent to 85 per cent. I concluded that those still littering must form a hard core of irresponsible barbarians who could not be reformed by amiable slogans like the previous agency's "Cast Your Ballot Here for a Cleaner New York."

A poll revealed that the majority of New Yorkers were not aware that they could be fined twenty-five dollars for littering. We therefore developed a *tough* campaign, warning litterbugs that they would be hauled into court. At the same time we persuaded the New York Sanitation Department to recruit a flying squad of uniformed men to patrol the streets on motor scooters, in search of offenders. The newspapers and magazines donated an unprecedented amount of free space to running our advertisements, and in the first three months the New York television and radio stations gave us 1,105 free commercials. After four months, 39,004 summonses had been handed out, and the magistrates did their duty.

Is advertising a vulgar bore? C. A. R. Crosland thunders in *The New Statesman* that advertising "is often vulgar, strident and offensive. And it induces a definite cynicism and corruption in both practitioners and audience owing to the constant intermingling of truth and lies."

This, I think, is now the gravamen of the charge against advertising among educated people. Ludwig von Mises describes advertising as "shrill, noisy, coarse, puffing." He blames the public, as not reacting to dignified advertising; I am more inclined to blame the advertisers and the agencies—including myself. I must confess that I am a poor judge of what will shock the public. Twice I have produced advertisements which seemed perfectly innocent to me, only to be excoriated for indecency. One was an advertisement for Lady Hathaway shirts, which showed a beautiful woman in velvet trousers, sitting astride a chair and smoking a long cigar. My other transgression was a television commercial in which we rolled Ban deodorant into the armpit of a Greek statue. In both cases the symbolism, which had escaped me, inflamed more prurient souls.

I am less offended by obscenity than by tasteless typography, banal photographs, clumsy copy, and cheap jingles. It is easy to skip these horrors when they appear in magazines and newspapers, but it is impossible to escape them on television. I am angered to the point of violence by the commercial interruption of programs. Are the men who own the television stations so greedy that they cannot resist such intrusive affronts to the dignity of man? They even interrupt the inauguration of Presidents and the coronation of monarchs.

As a practitioner, I know that television is the most potent advertising medium ever devised, and I make most of my living from it. But, as a private person, I would gladly pay for the privilege of watching it without commercial interruptions. Morally, I find myself between the rock and the hard place.

It is television advertising which has made Madison Avenue the arch-symbol of tasteless materialism. If governments do not soon set up machinery for the regulation of television, I fear that the majority of thoughtful men will come to agree with Toynbee that "the destiny of our Western civilization turns on the issue of our struggle with all that Madison Avenue stands for." I have a vested interest in the survival of Madison Avenue, and I doubt whether it can survive without drastic reform.

Hill & Knowlton report that the vast majority of thought-leaders now believe that advertising promotes values that are too materialistic. The danger to my bread-and-butter arises out of the fact that what thought-leaders think today, the majority of voters are likely to think tomorrow. No, my darling sister, advertising should not be abolished. But it must be reformed.

Topics for Discussion

1. Do you agree or disagree with Ogilvy? Are you convinced by his argument? Why?
2. Ogilvy says that if you "disapprove of social mobility, creature comforts, and foreign travel you are right to blame advertising for encouraging such wickedness. . . . I can only call you a psychic masochist." What is a psychic masochist? What does Ogilvy mean here?
3. What evidence does Ogilvy offer to prove that advertising does not raise prices? Is his evidence sufficient? Is it convincing?
4. What is a brouhaha?
5. Why does Ogilvy say that he doubts whether advertising can survive "without drastic reform"? What reform is he concerned with? Why does he think reform is necessary?
6. ". . . advertising serves a useful purpose *when it is used to give information about new products.*" Why does Ogilvy limit his definition of advertising this way? What other kinds of advertising are there?
7. What is "flatulent puffery"? Find one example of it in current advertising.

Rhetorical Considerations

1. Ogilvy mentions his sister at the beginning and end of his essay. Does this help unify his essay? How?
2. Ogilvy refers to a consumer as "she." Why does he do this?
3. Ogilvy uses the device of question and answer to present most of his material. What are the strengths and limitations of this device?
4. Throughout the essay Ogilvy uses the personal pronoun "I" and talks directly to the reader. What effect does he hope to achieve by doing this?
5. The thesis of this essay is stated in its title. Is it stated or implied anywhere in the essay itself?

Topics for Discussion

1. Has your attitude toward advertising changed in any way after reading all the essays in this section? In what way did your attitude change? Which essay was most responsible for changing your attitude?

2. Which essay did you enjoy most? What in particular did you enjoy about the essay? Which essay did you enjoy least? Why?

3. Compare Gibson's analysis of the rhetoric of advertising with Ogilvy's essay on how to write advertising copy. Do both essays deal with the same aspects of advertising? Which essay do you find more effective in revealing the rhetoric of advertising?

4. The *New York Times* defends the right of the public to advertise in newspapers. Tobin, on the other hand, defends the right of newspapers to turn down advertising for any reason whatsoever. Which argument do you find more convincing? Which is presented more effectively? Do you agree with the *Detroit News*'s decision to reject advertising for Stanley Kubrick's movie "A Clockwork Orange"?

5. Baran and Sweezy along with Galbraith present economic arguments against advertising. Young and Ogilvy both defend advertising, but not on an economic basis. Do you think that economics is the central argument against advertising? Do Young and Ogilvy raise any other pertinent issues in the arguments against advertising? Which of these four essays do you agree with? Why?

6. Packard speaks of the sexual overtones in advertising. Look at the advertisements in the first part of this text and locate the sexual overtones they contain. Are the sexual overtones in these advertisements the same kind that Packard speaks of? Are there any differences?

7. Do you see any relation between psychographic and intensional orientation?

8. Galanoy's essay is a humorous account of some adventures in the world of advertising. Yet beneath all the humor are some serious observations about advertising. What points does Galanoy make? Compare Galanoy's approach and prose style to Femina's. Is there any similarity?

9. Compare the prose style of the *New York Times* editorial with the style of the *Detroit News* editorial. What similarities and differences are there?

10. Advertising is a big and influential business, as many of the essays in this section have shown. Discuss some of the impact of advertising on various aspects of society, such as economical, cultural, social, and esthetic.

The News Media

Perhaps more than ever before Americans are aware of the news media. And perhaps more than ever before the news media have more impact on American life. The credit for all this can be given to television. While newspapers do continue to play an important role in the news media, it is to television that the greatest number of Americans turn for their news. But to oversimplify the matter, news is news, whether communicated by television, radio, newspaper, or magazine.

Vice-President Spiro Agnew made headlines when he launched his attack on television news. But subsequent surveys of public opinion revealed that he was voicing an opinion held by many Americans. Are the news media objective? Do they report all the facts all the time? Do they distort or suppress certain stories? Critics of the news media, from the John Birch Society to Students for a Democratic Society, believe that the news media does serve special interest groups and is not in fact free and unbiased. In a democracy the news media

play an important role in the political process by informing the public so that voters can make choices based upon knowledge. Should the news media be controlled so that the full truth were not being made available to the public, then we would indeed have a serious crisis on our hands.

This section presents essays dealing with various problems of the news media. Beginning with the fundamental problem of the economic freedom of the press, the section proceeds to another basic problem, the definition of what constitutes news. Other essays in this section deal with problems in news gathering and presentation, particularly television news. Then, too, there are problems of technique and approach which at first glance may seem uninteresting but upon closer examination are discovered to be of more than passing interest to the layman. The final part of this section presents two brief case studies in news coverage of two important recent events. My Lai 4 was more than a small Vietnamese village suddenly thrust into the public spotlight. The My Lai 4 massacre reveals much about the way the news media handled the Vietnam war. So do the Gulf of Tonkin incidents.

The news media, like the advertising industry, is large and influential. The essays in this section present only a brief outline of a very complicated industry. The news media are so important to American life that some understanding of their composition, function, and problems is necessary to appreciate the special role they play. With the news media under attack more than ever before, we should make every attempt to critically evaluate their performance. The essays in this section should serve as a starting point for forming critical judgment of the function and performance of the news media, and developing some ability to analyze the rhetoric of the news media.

In this section as in the previous section there are questions for discussion. Again remember that these questions should be treated only as a starting point for analysis and discussion.

A FREE PRESS?

A. J. Liebling

I think almost everybody will grant that if candidates for the United States Senate were required to possess ten millions dollars, and for the House one million, the year-in-year-out level of conservation of those two bodies might be expected to rise sharply. We could still be said to have a freely elected Congress: anybody with ten million dollars (or one, if he tailored his ambition to fit his means) would be free to try to get himself nominated, and the rest of us would be free to vote for our favorite millionaires or even to abstain from voting. (This last right would mark our continued superiority over states where people are compelled to vote for the government slate.)

In the same sense, we have a free press today. (I am thinking of big-city and middling-city publishers as members of an upper and lower house of American opinion.) Anybody in the ten-million-dollar category is free to buy or found a paper in a great city like New York or Chicago, and anybody with around a million (plus a lot of sporting blood) is free to try it in a place of mediocre size like Worcester, Mass. As to us, we are free to buy a paper or not, as we wish.[1]

In a highly interesting book, "The First Freedom," Morris Ernst has told the story of the increasing concentration of news outlets in the hands of a few people. There are less newspapers today than in 1909, and less owners in relation to the total number of papers. In 1909 there were 2,600; today 1,750.[2] Ernst refrains from any reflection on the quality of the ownership; he says merely that it is dangerous that so much power should be held by so few individuals. I will go one timid step further than Ernst and suggest that these individuals, because of their economic position, form an atypical group and share an atypical outlook.

[1] "A Free and Responsible Press," the published report of a committee head by Robert Maynard Hutchens in 1947, says, "Although there is no such thing as a going price for a great city newspaper, it is safe to assume that it would cost somewhere between five and ten million dollars to build a new metropolitan daily to success. The investment required for a new newspaper in a medium-sized city is estimated at three-quarters of a million to several million." Prices have gone up very considerably since this was written. The rise underlines my thesis.

Earl L. Vance, in an article in the *Virginia Quarterly Review* (summer 1945) cited in "Survival of a Free, Competitive Press," a publication of the Senate Committee on Small Businesses, says, "Even small-newspaper publishing is big business. *Time* magazine recently reported sale of the Massillon, Ohio, *Independent* (circulation 11,858) for 'around $400,000,' the Spartanburg, S.C. *Herald* (17,351) and *Journal* (8,678) for $750,000—all smaller d ilies. In contrast, William Allen White paid only $3,000 for the Emporia *Gazette* in 1892. A metropolitan daily now represents an investment of many millions. Scripps-Howard in 1923 paid $6,000-

Roger Bolen, ANIMAL CRACKERS. Reprinted through the courtesy of the Chicago Tribune–New York News Syndicate, Inc.

The newspaper owner is a rather large employer of labor. I don't want to bore you with statistics, but one figure that I remember unhappily is 2,867, the number of us who lost jobs when the Pulitzers sold the *World* for salvage in 1931. He is nowadays forced to deal with unions in all departments of his enterprise, and is as unlikely as any other employer to be on their side. As owner of a large and profitable business, he is opposed to government intervention in his affairs beyond the maintenance of the subsidy extended to all newspapers through second-class-mail rates. As an owner of valuable real estate, he is more interested in keeping the tax rate down than in any other local issue. (Newspaper crusades for municipal "reform" are almost invariable tax-paring expeditions.) A planned economy is abhorrent to him, and since every other nation in the world has now gone in for some form of economic planning, the publisher has become our number-one xenophobe. His "preference" for Socialist Britain over Communist Russia is only an inverse expression of relative dislike.[3] Because of publishers' wealth, they do not have to be slugged over the head by "anti-democratic organizations" to force them into using their properties to form public opinion the N.A.M. approves. The gesture would be as redundant as twsting a nymphomaniac's arm to get her into bed.[4] I am delighted that I do not have to insinuate that they consciously allow their output to be shaped by their personal interests. Psychoanalytical after-dinner talk has furnished us with a lovely word for what they do: they rationalize. And once a man has convinced himself that what is good for him is

000 for the same newspaper that had been offered in 1892 for $51,000; the Philadelphia *Inquirer* sold for $18,000,000 in 1930; the Kansas City *Star* for $11,000,000 in 1926."

I hadn't seen either of these publications before I wrote my Alumni Magazine article; I cite them here to show I wasn't dreaming my figures. The only recent instance I know of a man buying a newspaper for under five figures and making it go occurred in Las Vegas, Nevada. There in 1950, the typographical unions struck the only paper. It was a long stubborn strike, and the unions started a small paper of their own, which lost so much money, for such a small strike, that they agreed to sell it to a young publicity man for gambling halls named Hank Greenspun for $1,000. Hank bought it and then found a bank account with $2,500 in it among the cash assest. He thus made an immediate profit of $1,500, which must be a record. Within three years Greenspun built it into a rough, spectacularly aggressive and quickly profitable newspaper, the *Sun,* and it is, or should be, a mighty moneymaker today. This was, however, possible only because Las Vegas, in a decade, has quadrupled or quintupled its population, and the older paper remains without interest, a small-town sheet. There was therefore created an instantaneous vacuum, and the *Sun* filled it. The same thing could happen in another boom town, as it used to in the Gold Rush days, but there has been only one Las Vegas in a half century.

[2] Now 1,763 but the number of ownerships has decreased.

[3] He likes Conservative Britain rather better, except for its Socialized Medicine.

[4] "A Free and Responsible Press," that result of the collaboration

good for the herd of his inferiors, he enjoys the best of two worlds simultaneously, and can shake hands with Bertie McCormick, the owner of the Chicago *Tribune*.[5]

The profit system, while it insures the predominant conservative coloration of our press, also guarantees that there will always be a certain amount of dissidence. The American press has never been monolithic, like that of an authoritarian state. One reason is that there is always important money to be made in journalism by standing up for the underdog (demagogically or honestly, so long as the technique is good). The underdog is numerous and prolific—another name for him is circulation. His wife buys girdles and baking power and Literary Guild selections, and the advertiser has to reach her. Newspapers as they become successful and move to the right leave room for newcomers to the left. Marshall Field's Chicago *Sun,* for example, has acquired 400,000 readers in five years, simply because the *Tribune,* formerly alone in the Chicago morning field, had gone so far to the right.[6] The fact that the *Tribune's* circulation has not been much affected indicates that the 400,000 had previous to 1941 been availing themselves of their freedom not to buy a newspaper. (Field himself illustrates another, less dependable, but nevertheless appreciable, factor in the history of the American press—the occasional occurrence of that economic sport, the maverick millionaire.) E. W. Scripps was the outstanding practitioner of the trade of founding newspapers to stand up for the common man. He made a tremendous success of it, owning about twenty of them when he died. The first James Gordon Bennett's *Herald* and Joseph Pulitzer's *World,* in the eighties and nineties, to say nothing of the Scripps-Howard *World-Telegram* in 1927, won their niche in New York as left-of-centre news-

of thirteen bigwigs, which I again cite lest you think I am flippant, says:

"The agencies of mass communication are big business, and their owners are big businessmen. . . . The press is a large employer of labor. . . . The newspapers alone have more than 150,000 employees. The press is connected with other big businesses through the advertising of these businesses, upon which it depends for the major part of its revenue. The owners of the press, like the owners of other big businesses, are bank directors, bank borrowers, and heavy taxpayers in the upper brackets.

"As William Allen White put it: 'Too often the publisher of an American newspaper has made his money in some other calling than journalism. He is a rich man seeking power and prestige. . . . And they all get the unconscious arrogance of conscious wealth.'

"Another highly respected editor, Erwin D. Canham of the *Christian Science Monitor,* thinks upper-bracket ownership and its big-business character important enough to stand at the head of his list of the 'shortcomings of today's American newspapers.'"

"A Free and Responsible Press" was published after the appearance of my article.

[5] McCormick died in 1955. If he is not in Heaven he is eternally astonished.

[6] The *Sun-Times,* having become almost equally prosperous, has by now, 1961, gone almost equally as far. Poor Mr. Field is dead and his son is a Republican. Mavericks seldom breed true.

papers and then bogged down in profits.

Another factor favorable to freedom of the press, in a minor way, is the circumstances that publishers sometimes allow a certain latitude to employees in departments in which they have no direct interest—movies, for instance, if the publisher is not keeping a movie actress, or horse shows, if his wife does not own a horse. Musical and theatrical criticism is less rigorously controlled than it is in Russia.[7]

The process by which the American press is pretty steadily revivified, and as steadily dies (newspapers are like cells in the body, some dying as others develop), was well described in 1911 by a young man named Joseph Medill Patterson, then an officer of the Chicago *Tribune*, who was destined himself to found an enormously success- ful paper, the *Daily News* of New York, and then within his own lifetime pilot it over the course he had fore- shadowed. The quotation is from a play, "The Fourth Estate," which Patterson wrote in his young discontent.

"Newspapers start when their owners are poor, and take the part of the people, and so they build up a large circulation, and, as a result, advertising. That makes them rich, and they begin most naturally, to associate with other rich men—they play golf with one, and drink whisky with another, and their son marries the daughter of a third. They forget all about the people, and then their circula- tion dries up, then their advertising, and then their paper becomes decadent."

Patterson was not "poor" when he came to New York eight years later to start the *News;* he had the McCormick- Patterson *Tribune* fortune behind him, and at his side Max Annenberg, a high-priced journalist condottiere who had already helped the *Tribune* win a pitched battle with Hearst in its own territory. But he was starting his paper from scratch, and he did it in the old dependable way, by taking up for the Common Man—and sticking with him until 1942, by which time the successful-man contagion got him and he threw his arms around unregenerated Cousin Bertie's neck. The *Tribune* in Chicago and the *News* in New York have formed a solid front ever since. Patterson was uninfluenced by golf, whisky, or social am- bitions (he was a parsimonious, unsociable man who cherished an illusion that he had already hit the social peak). I think it is rather the complex of age, great wealth, a swelled head, and the necessity to believe in the Heaven- decreed righteousness of a system which has permitted one to possess such power that turns a publisher's head. The whisky, weddings, yachts, horse shows, and the rest (golf no longer sounds so imposing as it did in 1911)[8] are

[7] There is, however, no theater to write about, except in New York, and provincial critics of music lean over backward to be kind, because it is hard enough to get people to subscribe for concerts without underlining their deficiencies.

[8] There has been a revival since the first Eisenhower inaugural. I attribute it to the invention of the electric go-cart, in which, I am informed, the golfers now circulate, obviating ambulation. It

symptoms rather than causes.

Unfortunately, circulations do not "dry up" quickly, nor advertising fall away overnight. Reading a newspaper is a habit which holds on for a considerable time. So the erstwhile for-the-people newspaper continues to make money for a while after it changes its course. With the New York *Herald* this phase lasted half a century. It would, moreover, be difficult to fix the exact hour or day at which the change takes place: it is usually gradual, and perceptible to those working on the paper before it becomes apparent to the outside public. At any given moment there are more profitable newspapers in being than new ones trying to come up, so the general tone of the press is predominantly, and I fear increasingly, re-actionary. The difference between newspaper publishers' opinions and those of the public is so frequently expressed at the polls that it is unnecessary to insist on it here.

Don't get me wrong, though. I don't think that the battle is futile. I remember when I was a freshman, in 1920, listening to a lecture by Professor Mecklin in a survey course called, I think, Citizenship, in which he told how most of the newspapers had misrepresented the great steel strike of 1919. The only one that had told the truth, he said, as I remember it, was the old *World*. (I have heard since that the St. Louis *Post-Dispatch* was good, too, but he didn't mention it.) It was the first time that I really believed that newspapers lied about that sort of thing. I had heard of Upton Sinclair's book "The Brass Check," but I hadn't wanted to read it because I had heard he was a "Bolshevik." I came up to college when I was just under sixteen, and the family environment was not exactly radical. But my reaction was that I wanted someday to work for the *World*, or for some other paper that *would* tell the truth. The *World* did a damned good job, on the strikes and on the Ku Klux Klan and on prohibition and prison camps (in Florida, not Silesia), and even though the second-generation Pulitzers let it grow namby-pamby and then dropped it in terror when they had had a losing year and were down to their last sixteen million, it had not lived in vain.

I think that anybody who talks often with people about newspapers nowadays must be impressed by the growing distrust of the information they contain. There is less a disposition to accept what they say than to try to estimate the probable truth on the basis of what they say, like aiming a rifle that you know has a deviation to the right. Even a report in a Hearst newspaper can be of considerable aid in arriving at a deduction if you know enough about (*a*) Hearst policy, (*b*) the degree of abjectness of the correspondent signing the report.[*]

Every now and then I write a piece for the *New* sounds like the most fun since the goat-wagon.

[*] Albert Camus, the brilliant and versatile young French novelist, playwright, and critic, who was also editor of *Combat*, a Paris daily, once had an idea for establishing a "control newspaper" that would come out one hour after the others with estimates of the

Yorker under the heading of the Wayward Press (a title for the department invented by the late Robert Benchley when he started it early in the *New Yorker's* history). In this I concern myself not with big general thoughts about Trends (my boss wouldn't stand for such), but with the treatment of specific stories by the daily (chiefly New York) press. I am a damned sight kinder about newspapers than Wolcott Gibbs[10] is about the theatre, but while nobody accuses him of sedition when he raps a play, I get letters calling me a little pal of Stalin when I sneer at the New York *Sun*. This reflects a pitch that newspaper publishers make to the effect that they are part of the great American heritage with a right to travel wrapped in the folds of the flag like a boll weevil in a cotton boll. Neither theatrical producers nor book publishers, apparently, partake of this sacred character. I get a lot more letters from people who are under the delusion that I can Do Something About It All. These reflect a general malaise on the part of the newspaper-reading public, which I do think will have some effect, though not, God knows, through me.

I believe that labor unions, citizens' organizations, and possibly political parties yet unborn are going to back daily papers. These will represent definite, undisguised points of view, and will serve as controls on the large profit-making papers expressing definite, ill-disguised points of view. The Labor Party's *Daily Herald,* in England, has been of inestimable value in checking the blather of the Beaverbrook-Kemsley-Rothermere newspapers of huge circulation. When one cannot get the truth from any one paper (and I do not say that it is an easy thing, even with the best will in the world, for any one paper to tell all the truth), it is valuable to read two with opposite policies to get an idea of what is really happening. I cannot believe that labor leaders are so stupid they will let the other side monopolize the press indefinitely.[11]

percentage of truth in each of their stories, and with interpretations of how the stories were slanted. The way he explained it, it sounded possible. He said, "We'd have complete dossiers on the interests, policies, and idiosyncrasies of the owners. Then we'd have a dossier on every journalist in the world. The interests, prejudices, and quirks of the owner would equal Z. The prejudices, quirks, and private interests of the journalist, Y. Z times Y would give you X, the probable amount of truth in the story." He was going to make up dossiers on reporters by getting journalists he trusted to appraise men they had worked with. "I would have a card-index system," he said. "Very simple. We would keep the dossiers up to date as best we could, of course. But do people really want to know how much truth there is in what they read? Would they buy the control paper? That's the most difficult problem." Camus died without ever learning the answer to this question. His energies were dissipated in creative writing and we lost a great journalist.

[10] Gibbs is dead too. Shortly after his funeral I got a letter from a *New Yorker* reader in Hico, Texas, previously unknown to me, that began: "Well, Gibbs is dead and soon the whole damn lot of you will be."

[11] To reread this paragraph makes me glum. Mergerism has hit Britain with a sudden rush; the *News-Chronicle* is gone and the *Herald* looks to be for it.

I also hope that we will live to see the endowed newspaper, devoted to the pursuit of daily truth as Dartmouth is to that of knowledge. I do not suppose than any reader of the *Magazine* believes that the test of a college is the ability to earn a profit on operations (with the corollary that making the profit would soon become the chief preoccupation of its officers). I think that a good newspaper is as truly an educational institution as a college, so I don't see why it should have to stake its survival on attracting advertisers of ball-point pens and tickets to Hollywood peep shows. And I think that private endowment would offer greater possibilities for a free press than state ownership (this is based on the chauvinistic idea that a place like Dartmouth can do a better job than a state university under the thumb of a Huey Long or Gene Talmadge). The hardest trick, of course, would be getting the chief donor of the endowment (perhaps a repentant tabloid publisher) to (*a*) croak, or (*b*) sign a legally binding agreement never to stick his face in the editorial rooms. The best kind of an endowment for a newspaper would be one made up of several large and many small or medium-sized gifts (the Dartmouth pattern again). Personally, I would rather leave my money for a newspaper than for a cathedral, a gymnasium, or even a home for streetwalkers with fallen arches, but I have seldom been able to assemble more than $4.17 at one time.[12]

[12] Professor Michael E. Choukas, of the Dartmouth faculty, summing up after the last article of the Public Opinion in a Democracy series, commented: "Mr. Liebling's 'endowed newspaper' would probably be free from direct pressure, but it would be unable to avoid the indirect efforts of the propagandists." I think that Professor Choukas, a sociologist who has specialized in the study of propaganda, has developed an exaggerated respect for the opposition. Albert Camus's plan for the "control newspaper," which I have briefly described in another footnote, is an example of the ingenuity a good newspaperman can bring to bear, and men like Vic Bernstein, Paul Sifton, and Edmond Taylor in this country (to cite only a few—there are hundreds of others) would certainly bring into the ring with them more perspicacity than anyobdy the National Association of Manufacturers could hire. A man who thinks he can fool other men is always a little a fool himself. His assumpton that he can do it presupposes a foolish vanity—like that of the recidivist con man who spends most of his life in jail. His contempt for the truth marks him as a bit sub-human. Professor Choukas did not mention my hopes for strong labor papers.

The professor's own remedy for the dilemma, however, is worthy of citation. I hope somebody makes a good hard try at it.

"I frankly do not believe that any indirect assault would have much effect as a check against those who deliberately set out to mislead us," he wrote. "A direct attack could be launched against them by a privately endowed, independent agency whose main task would consist of compiling a list of all the propaganda groups in the country, analyzing their techniques, discovering their goals, and releasing the available information to government officials, to men responsible for our channels of communication, to men who measure public opinion, to colleges and universities, and to those pathetically few groups in the country who have undertaken to fight the battle of Democracy in a positive manner.

The above piece, written 14 years ago, was in manner laboriously off-hand, but represented my serious thought. I erred badly on the side of optimism. The postwar euphoria that lingered in the air like fall-out must have trapped me. There has been no new competition in any large American city since the piece was written, and now it seems infinitely less likely that there ever will be.

The period between the two wars, while it marked a great diminution in the number of newspapers in New York, had brought at least one tremendously successful newcomer, the *Daily News,* which changed the whole physiognomy of Metropolitan journalism. When I wrote in 1947 the two Marshall Field entries, *PM* in New York and the *Sun* (the *Sun-Times* to be) in Chicago, were both still in there battling. *PM,* which was destined to fail, had been founded in 1940, and the *Sun,* fated to succeed financially, had begun in 1942. It did not seem to me, therefore, that the times already precluded new starts, although, as I noted, they were harder than before.

The suggestions I made about where new papers might find sponsors now sound infantile, but at the time I thought, wrongly, that labor retained some of the intelligence and coherence of the Roosevelt days, and it seemed to me not inconceivable that some financial Megabelodon might fancy a good newspaper as a more distinctive memorial than the habitual foundation for research into some disease that had annoyed the testator during life. (These bequests always seem to me to mark a vengeful nature, and the viruses they are aimed at profit by them almost as much as the doctors. They eat tons of cultures, play with white rats, and develop resistance by constant practice, as slum children learn to get out of the way of automobiles.) Megabelodon, however, although a huge creature, had a brain cavity about as big as the dime slot on a telephone coin box, and most men who could afford to endow a newspaper seem to be rigged the same way.

Silliest of all, as I read back now, is the line about the profit system guaranteeing a certain amount of dissidence. This shows, on my part, an incurable weakness for judging the future by the past, like the French generals who so charmed me in 1939. I still believe that "there is always important money to be made by standing up for the underdog," but the profit system implies a pursuit of *maximum* profit — for the shareholders' sake, distasteful though it may be. That it is theoretically possible to make money by competition in the newspaper field is therefore immaterial, since there is a great deal more money to be made by

    a) Selling out and pocketing a capital gain
    b) Buying the other fellow out and then sweating the serfs.

"This I feel should be done before our crisis reaches climatic proportions—before the next depression."

Topics for Discussion

1. How free can a newspaper or magazine be if it is a business that must make a profit and depend upon advertising for three-fourths of its income?
2. Can you think of any newspaper which crusades for the common man? Do you think the editorial positions a newspaper takes are influenced by the fact that it is a business?
3. Is Liebling against the profit system for newspapers? Are there any benefits to be gained from this system?
4. What is a "high-priced journalist condottiere"?
5. Liebling says there is a growing distrust of newspapers. Do you agree with this? Do you believe everything you read in newspapers? Why?
6. Liebling suggests reading two newspapers with opposing policies "to get an idea of what is really happening." Is this a good idea? Have you ever done it? Can you suggest two papers which have opposing views which you could read?
7. As a counter to the profit-making press, Liebling suggests privately endowed papers. What is his plan? Do you think it would work?
8. The last four paragraphs of this essay were written fourteen years after the rest of the essay had been written. Does Liebling recant or alter any of his ideas in the first part of the essay?

Rhetorical Considerations

1. How would you characterize the style of this essay?
2. Liebling puts a lot of information in footnotes, some of which are very long. Do you think he could have handled this information better? Could he have incorporated it into the body of his essay? Are the footnotes distracting?
3. What analogy is Liebling making in the first two paragraphs? Is the analogy valid?
4. This essay is a blend of personal reminiscence and factual research. How well has Liebling blended these two elements together in his essay?
5. Examine Liebling's vocabulary. Is there any consistency to it?

What's Wrong with News? It Isn't New Enough

Max Ways

Europe never thrilled to what happened in 1492. Columbus' return from the New World set no fast horses galloping between the great cities. No awed crowds gathered in the streets. The news seeped around so slowly that years later most Europeans probably had only a vague notion of the event. Giant leaps in communication are measured by the contrast with 1969 when a fifth of mankind saw simultaneous TV pictures of explorers walking on the moon and could hear and read lucid explanations of how the feat was accomplished along with shrewd speculation as to what it might mean for the future.

Yet today's network of news may serve the times less effectively than did the fifteenth century's. Then, 99 percent of knowledge was far from new. Basic information, basic economic and social skills, basic beliefs and values descended from parent to child. Against this static and familiar background news could be readily isolated; prodigies of nature, interventions by supernatural or political powers, the novel speculations of savants—these exceptions to the normal course were news. But now this kind of news has been outstripped by reality. The pace, breadth, and depth of twentieth-century change have dissolved the static background. Today's novelty is tomorrow's normality, doomed to be soon discarded. A high proportion of the basic information used by society is new information. The father's skill may be useless in the son's time. Even values and creeds are in flux. Where so much is new, what is news?

Journalism has not fully adjusted itself to the transformed situation. Conditioned by its own past, journalism often acts as if its main task were still to report the exceptional and dramatically different against a background of what everybody knows. News today can concentrate with tremendous impact on a few great stories: a moon landing, a war, a series of civil disorders. But meanwhile, outside the spotlight, other great advances in science and technology, other international tensions, other causes of social unrest are in motion. Yet today's inadequately reported trends will shape tomorrow's reality.

Again and again the twentieth century has been ambushed by crisis. Looking back from the midst of some

Max Ways, "What's Wrong with News? It Isn't New Enough," *Fortune Magazine* (October, 1969), pp. 110, 111, 112, 113, 155, 156, 158, 161. Reprinted by permission.

tumult, like a race riot, or of some quietly desperate frustration, like the present condition of the cities, we are able to see how disaster might have been avoided by more timely and more effective communication. But we have not yet been able to use such hindsight as a spur to foresight.

The most biting and perilous irony of our civilization turns upon knowledge. Expanding knowledge has multiplied power, which has proliferated into the hands of millions of organizations and hundreds of millions of individuals. Now that everyone has some power to effect change, every aspect of life from economics to religion has been set in motion. But at any moment the significance of any specific change will depend in part upon knowledge of other changes that are in train. If communication lags, then the sum of all the changes will seem random and confused. Obviously, the need for better communication does not fall upon journalism alone. The present challenge to education, for instance, is even more severe. But journalism's role, less discussed than education's, is critical in a society that can no longer depend upon tradition to tell it what it is and how it operates.

Certainly news has not declined in quality. Journalists are better trained, more skillful, more serious about their work than they ever were. They have marvelous new media for reaching a larger, better educated audience, which senses its own dependence upon news. With painstaking care and admirable artistry news today brings information about this change or that one. But in actual life these specific changes are colliding and combining with one another, often in ways undreamed of by their originators—and not alertly reported in the news. A relatively simple compound—automobile plus mass prosperity—brings mass ownership of automobiles, a phenomenon that can ruin cities, alter familial relations, and demand new forms and techniques of government. Adequate news analysis of this particular compound is about fifty years overdue and not yet in sight.

When news fails to add up the permutations of change the best-informed men lack confidence that they know what's going on. Many of those who most confidently assert that they know, don't. Radicals and reactionaries both tend to ignore actual change and to derive their passionately held views from a simpler, more static society that isn't here. The noisiest debates tend to be irrelevant because their informational backgrounds are fragmentary and out of date.

Even the most powerful nation, with the highest production of new knowledge, thus becomes pervaded by a sense of its own ignorance and helplessness because it feels—correctly—that it has no adequate view of its own direction. Lack of confidence in the quality of news could be fatal in our kind of society, as it could not possibly have been in the Europe to which Columbus returned.

A fly on the wall?

In the last few years there has been a noticeable public disenchantment with news media. It's true that the avidity for news increases and the prosperity of news organs continues on a long upgrade. Nevertheless, many consumers of news voice doubts that the news adds up to an accurate picture of what's going on.

The understandable public anxiety about the adequacy of news cannot by itself be counted upon to generate improvement. The public uneasiness now contributes, for instance, to pressure for greater governmental intervention in television news, an irrelevant therapy that would correct no present defects and create new ones. Nor is public criticism of print journalism more shrewdly aimed. It tends, for instance, to overestimate the distorting effect of the commercial motives of publishers, motives that today do not influence news nearly as much as they formerly did. On the other hand, the public underestimates both the objective difficulty of telling today's news and certain rigidities that are deeply embedded in the craft of journalism itself, as distinguished from the commercial context in which most of it operates.

Among the areas of change that are inadequately discussed is the new situation of journalism. While eagerly reporting and critically appraising the ballerina, the bishop, and the federal budget, journalism has been almost silent about its own performance and its own problems. The pretense that it is an unseen witness, a mere fly on history's wall, becomes less and less plausible as the role of news expands. From the demonstrator on the street to the President of the United States the behavior of the actors in the news is affected by journalism. All the subjects of news tend to conform to journalism's standards of what is reportable.

Many of these standards, mysterious to outsiders, are in fact obsolete in the sense that they were developed to fit a world that exists no more. Why so much of journalism stubbornly clings to outdated patterns and practices is a question that needs analysis. Before turning, however, to this and other imperfections internal to journalism, a closer look at its present environment, at its position in today's world, may be useful.

Strangers and brothers

"Journalism" is used here in a broad sense encompassing newspapers, newsmagazines, radio and television newscasts or "documentaries," press services, trade magazines, corporate house organs, labor-union periodicals—in short, the enormous variety of publications that describe or comment upon the current scene or some segment of it. Along with education and the arts, journalism is one of the three great information systems that account for the bulk of "the knowledge industry," the most rapidly expanding part of every advanced society.

One reason why journalism expands is the amazing diversity of contemporary society. All the nonsense about regimentation to the contrary, there has never been a time when men varied so much in their work, pleasures, beliefs, values, and styles of life. In part, this growing diversity in life is a reflection of the specialization in knowledge and in education. To be "an educated man" no longer denotes participation in a common, circumscribed body of knowledge. Though the total of extant knowledge has multiplied many times, that part of it which "everybody knows" has increased much more slowly. Society cannot afford to imitate the university, where communication between departments is either perfunctory or non-existent. Outside the university, the world becomes smaller in terms of interdependence while it becomes larger in terms of the difficulty of communicating between heterogeneous groups and diverse individuals. Every year we become more like strangers—and more like brothers.

To deal with this difficulty, contemporary journalism has developed along a scale that ranges from publications addressed to as few as a thousand readers up to television and magazine audiences ranging around fifty million. Even in a highly specialized scientific journal some subscribers will have difficulty comprehending an article by a colleague who, in pursuit of the scientific goal of precision, may be developing a different vocabulary to express new concepts. The practitioners of each subspecialty also need to know what's going on in the nearest subspecialty, and beyond that one ad infinitum. As the circles widen, the communication difficulty increases.

FORTUNE, for instance, works in the intermediate range of the scale. Its subject, business, is a valid unit in the sense that its parts are interdependent and have many patterns, practices, problems, and interests in common. A fantastic variety is embraced within this unity. It's a far cry, apparently, from Manhattan's garment trade to the research scientists who developed the laser and the high-technology industries which first used it outside the laboratories. Yet the men on Seventh Avenue needed to be promptly and effectively informed about so fundamental an invention; lasers for cutting fabrics are already in commercial development. To convey such information requires bridging huge gaps between different kinds of information, different habits of mind.

Today every public question—national defense, water pollution, educational policy—involves highly specialized kinds of knowledge. The citizen cannot be adequately informed unless his education and, later, his journalism, give him some access to that essential part of a public question that lies outside his own immediate sphere of interest and competence.

Equally daunting is the journalistic difficulty that arises out of the way contemporary change originates. In a totally planned society (if one were possible) journalism's job would be to focus on the planning authority, reporting its decisions; the sum of these would be the sum of change. But not even the Soviet Union, rigidly authoritarian in theory, works that way. Some shots that the planners call are never made, and new conditions, unforeseen by planners, arise spontaneously.

The dissemination of power implicit in all contemporary society defeats the fondest dreams of centralizers. In the U.S. the decisions of government, important though they are, add up to only a small fraction of the whole impetus of change. Most of the great new government policies of recent decades—social security, welfare, civil-rights programs, increased regulation of business—are secondary changes, efforts to cushion new conditions that had their primary source outside of government. Nor is there in the private sector any one source of change, any establishment of concentrated power, where journalism can find the conscious, deliberate origin of most changes that sweep us onward.

For many years some newsmen and some of their customers have suspected that Washington was overcovered relative to the rest of the American scene. Journalistic tradition partly explains this. In the centuries when political intervention was one of the few sources of what little was new and different, news properly concentrated upon government. Journalism still clings to the legislative act and the presidential decision because they are relatively easy to get into focus. By contrast, such gradual and multicentered changes as the loosening of parental authority or the increase of consumer credit or public acceptance of a new technology of contraception or the rising resentment of black Americans are much more difficult to pinpoint. They are not "events." They didn't happen "yesterday" or "today" or "last week." They do not fit the journalist's cherished notions of a "story."

Losing the thread

Insofar as journalism solves the problem of where to look for change, it is then confronted with another set of difficulties: the subject will be more complex, intrinsically harder to tell, than news used to be. A scientific advance, for instance, is harder to convey than an explorer's geographical discovery. There was no great communication difficulty in saying that Columbus sailed west for seventy days, that he found a land peopled by naked men. It's all wondrous but it's not opaque. Everybody recognized the terms "sail," "day," "land," "naked." On the other hand, the discovery of deoxyribonucleic acid is, to a non-biologist, more opaque than wondrous. Yet DNA, by unlocking secrets of genetics, may cause more social change than did the age of exploration. And the consequences may follow far more quickly.

In the last ten or fifteen years journalism, thanks to a few very able science reporters, has made tremendous strides in the techniques of communicating to the public the major advances of pure science. A knowledgeable reporter, skilled in translating scientific languages, can sit down with the discoverer and his colleagues and seek ways to penetrate the opacity that surrounds any scientific discovery. Greater difficulty—and less journalistic success—comes when the new discovery begins to move out into use, mingling with technological, economic, psychological, and even moral factors. As a source of information to the reporter the original discoverer may not be of much use at this point. Members of other academic disciplines may not be interested or adroit in bringing their knowledge to bear on the meaning of the change. Journalism may lose the thread because the change has become complex in a way that goes beyond any academic discipline.

Journalism, for instance, has not done well with the economic and social implications of the greatest technological advance of the last twenty years—the computer, symbol of automation. Since its effects spread out to every part of society, everybody needs to know quite a lot about the computer.

In the Fifties, when computers and other devices for automating work were coming in, there was an almost hysterical belief that they would sharply increase unemployment. Thousands of economists and social historians were in a position to know better. They not only failed to reach the general public with a more realistic view of automation's impact on employment, they did not even get the message to the rest of the academic community. Even though U.S. employment has increased 36 percent since 1950, millions of people, including many of the best educated, are still walking around with bad cases of computerphobia.

In 1965, Charles E. Silberman, an economist and journalist, undertook in FORTUNE a careful analysis of the actual and probable future effects of computers on the number and kinds of jobs. It would have been possible—though admittedly difficult—to parallel Silberman's explanation at levels of mass-circulation journalism. Newspapers and television have made little effort to explain the economic and social meaning of the computer. Such a subject simply does not fit their working definitions of news. But if in the years ahead there occurs, for some reason unconnected with computers, a sharp and prolonged rise in unemployment, then the press will feel obliged to carry the mouthings of any demagogue who blames computers for the shortage of jobs. A lot of Americans would fall for this because education and journalism, between them, are not getting over to the public enough timely information about the significance of this sort of change.

The invisible Americans

In recent decades journalism has missed changes more important and more complex than the effect of the computer. From the end of the post-Civil War Reconstruction period to the mid-Fifties, American journalism was virtually silent on the subject of how black Americans lived. Lynchings were reported and deplored, as were race riots and the more sensational crimes committed by blacks against whites. But crimes by blacks against blacks were regularly ignored as a matter of explicit news policy on most newspapers. This was symptomatic of an implicit journalistic assumption that blacks were not a significant part of the American scene. Journalism bears a considerable share of responsibility for white society's disengagement from the Negro and his problems.

Yet journalists were aware that the position of the blacks in American life was building up tensions. The huge northward migrations during the two world wars created new conditions that seldom got into the news. Much of the material in Gunnar Myrdal's 1944 sociological classic, *An American Dilemma*, came from interviews with American journalists who were interested as individuals in the plight of the Negro, but who collectively and professionally did not consider facts about the condition of Negro life to be news.

In the last few years journalism has been widely denounced for giving undue attention to extreme black militants and to civil disorders arising from racial tension. No doubt there has been some shift over the years in the personal attitudes of newsmen toward racial inequality. But not nearly enough shift to account for a 180° reversal that moved the racial problem from the bottom to the top of the news. One difference is that black militancy found a way to pass the gate of news standards. In the light of the urban riots and fires, newsmen, especially those with TV cameras, suddenly found blacks eminently reportable.

The contrast in news between the past invisibility of blacks as people and the recent hypervisibility of black militants brings us to certain characteristics inherent in the craft of journalism. Why doesn't it try harder to expand its definition of news? Why does so much of journalism remain trapped in "the story," the dramatic, disruptive, exceptional event that properly formed the corpus of news in the generations when the broad background of society was shifting very slowly? Why is journalism still so wrapped up in the deadline, the scoop, the gee-whiz—and so seemingly unable to notice that most of what is new will not fit into a narrative pattern of what happened in the last twenty-four hours?

"The story," and all the bang-bang that went with it, used to be the way "to sell papers" in the days when newsboys crying "Extra" formed the sales force of the press. The business need for this kind of razzle-dazzle has disappeared. The editorial reason for it has diminished to the vanishing point. Yet much of journalism still operates as if its circulation and its usefulness depended on the second hand of the clock rather than the depth of its perception, the accuracy of its report, the relevance of its coverage, and the balance of its judgment.

To understand why news is trapped in its own past, journalism must be looked at in relation to the third great system of social communication mentioned above, the arts. Though most journalists are loath to admit it, what they practice is an art—crude and unbeautiful, but nevertheless an art. Even in the fine arts, where individual originality lies close to the heart of excellence, nearly all artists are influenced by traditions, canons, "schools." Descending the ladder of art toward craftsmanship, originality and novelty become less prominent and tradition becomes stronger. The artifact is acceptable because its design is more or less familiar. This may be especially true of the verbal arts of our day. Language is, after all, a huge network of conventional meanings, a heritage. In slow-moving societies language may have changed as rapidly as the realities it described. In our day, language may be a "conservative" element, lagging behind social change, forcing us to perceive today in terms of the past.

The artistic bias

The sublanguages of the sciences and other highly specialized activities do change rapidly. But most journalism cannot use these terms because it must transmit information outside the specialized group. In his overriding desire to communicate efficiently, the journalist tends unconsciously to be ruled by precedent in his choice of subject and in the form of presentation. That which is familiar can be communicated more easily than that which is really new. The simple subject is more communicable than the complex. Dramatic conflict, especially when it can be reduced to two sides, is a well established form of communication.

Thus journalism in our time has what might be called a formal bias that causes news to distort reality. Preference for "the story" that journalism *knows* can be communicated leads it to neglect the changes that need to be told but do not fit the standards of familiarity, simplicity, drama. This artistic bias has nothing to do with the ideology or partisanship of the journalist himself. He may take sides concerning the substance of a news story, but such substantive bias will often be overridden by his formal bias. A journalist who sees a story that is attractive—artistically speaking—will tell it even if it runs contrary to his political prejudices, hurts the interests of his friends, and brings sorrow to his mother's heart. This laudable independence exacts, however, a heavy price: if the artistic standards by which the story is selected and shaped are themselves out of phase with reality the consequent distortion may be greater than that produced by a journalist's substantive bias toward one "side" of an issue.

Probably most journalists who handled news produced by the late Senator Joe McCarthy opposed the substance of what he was doing. But McCarthy got enormous attention in the press before he had a large popular following because he played up to the journalistic desire for simplification and dramatization, and had a keen sense of that seven o'clock deadline. On the other hand, most journalists who dealt with John Gardner probably approved of the substance of his influence on public affairs. Yet Gardner, who was Secretary of Health, Education, and Welfare during a critical period, never became a vivid figure in the news. He tended to see life "in the round." Though he recognized the puzzles and problems that engulf government today, he tackled them with an energy derived from a sense of modern society's immense material, intellectual, and moral resources. He did not cast himself as St. George versus the Dragon. He was out of touch with news precisely because he was in touch with contemporary social reality. Gardner's name would have become familiar to every American if, after resigning his post, he had gone along with newsmen who importuned him to launch a series of public attacks on President Johnson.

Ideology and extreme partisanship attract the attention of journalists who are not themselves ideologues or partisans. If news can be simplified into a framework of Cold War or of black extremists against white extremists or of poor against rich, journalists as communicators will be happy although as men and citizens they—along with everybody else—will be depressed at the picture they paint.

Both local and national

In terms of this general view of contemporary journalism's mission, its external difficulties and its internal inhibitions, let us briefly examine some specific media, starting (as a journalistic canon requires) with the most familiar.

Daily newspapers in general do not present an inspiring spectacle of vigorous effort to meet the challenge of change. Most of them go on emphasizing specific events—a crime, an accident, a resolution of the city council—in ways not very different from the journalism of a hundred years ago. Even though crime's incidence has increased to the point where it is a substantial part of the new normality, only a few papers have made a serious effort to explain this change, more important and potentially more interesting than any single crime.

A shift of attention has occurred from local news to national and international news. On most papers this seems to take the heart out of local coverage, while leaving national and international news to the Associated Press and the United Press International, which are the least innovative, most tradition-bound of all journalistic institutions.

Few papers have discovered the category of news that is both local and national. The problems of each city are in some sense unique. Since early in the Johnson Administration, Washington has been aware that decisions made by Congress and carried out by a national Administration will be fruitless unless they are meshed with vigorous and knowledgeable local efforts. Yet each city's problems of transportation, housing, education, poverty, have a wide area of overlap with other cities' problems. The obvious need is for local reporting that will examine what's going on in Pittsburgh and San Francisco in an effort to clarify the problems of Buffalo. Communication, through journalism, between the cities and regions of the U.S. has never been so desperately needed or in worse shape. Efforts to develop a "new federalism" are handicapped by journalism's tradition-bound rigidity that sees national news as one category and local news as an entirely separate category.

The sorry condition of daily newspapers is often blamed on the trend toward local monopoly, a diagnosis that is too easy. In many cities, before mergers occurred, all the papers lacked distinction and leadership. In cities with competing papers journalism is not notably more vigorous than in the monopoly cities. Such notable smaller city papers as the Louisville *Courier-Journal*, the Cleveland *Plain Dealer*, the Minneapolis *Tribune*, and the Charlotte *Observer* are among the very few that really keep trying to improve service to the community.

Away from the traditional "story"

Of yesterday's best-known newspapers the Chicago *Tribune*, the St. Louis *Post-Dispatch*, the New York *Daily News* seem less relevant than they used to be. The most improved large daily (it had lots of room for improvement) is probably the Los Angeles *Times*. In recent years it has developed an ability to cover trends, as well as events, and to relate local subjects to the regional and national scenes. Its intelligent reporting of educational trends, for instance, enabled it to evince clear superiority over the San Francisco press when campus "stories" erupted in the Bay area, at Berkeley and San Francisco State. Because the Los Angeles *Times* was aware of the moving background behind the sensational campus disorders, it reported the events themselves with a far steadier hand than the San Francisco papers.

Two national dailies, the *Christian Science Monitor* and the *Wall Street Journal*, have largely freed themselves from the tyranny of "the story" as traditionally defined. The *Monitor's* interpretive articles are, in fact, more timely than many a front page sprinkled with the words "yesterday" and "today." The *Wall Street Journal's* two leading front-page articles add up in the course of a year to a better report of what's going on than all the bulletins of the wire services. "Kelly Street Blues," a four-part series on a block in a New York ghetto, put together a mosaic of detail that helps one part of society, the *W.S.J.*'s readers, understand how a very different part lives. Neil Ulman's roundup of protests across the nation against sex education in the schools was an

example of the kind of report that conventional newspapers miss. The *W.S.J.*'s foreign news can discuss basically interesting subjects, such as how Soviet citizens can invest their savings or anti-Franco trends in Spain, that are not pegged to any events.

A long way from the *Wall Street Journal* lies the "underground press" that has sprung up in recent years. Its chief significance is to demonstrate that, economically, the proliferation of many publications is now feasible. Unhappily, it cannot be said that the underground press displays much innovative muscle. Its ideology seems moored in nineteenth-century anarchism, and from that viewpoint it can dislike whatever the "straight" press likes. But that hardly helps the job of reducing the lag between journalism and reality. The underground papers are as similar, one to another, as the square papers. An admittedly incomplete survey of underground papers indicates that none of them has invented a new four-letter word.

In a class by itself stands that most aboveground of American newspapers, the New York *Times*. Its influence is by no means confined to its readers. Most journalists, including broadcasters, start their day with it and each journalist assumes that the others have read the *Times* attentively. In the important matter of day-to-day decisions on which stories deserve top play, the *Times* is the greatest single national influence. Its preeminence goes back a long way and it is still steeped in conventional news judgment and traditional journalistic forms. Nevertheless, in recent years the *Times* has produced more and more innovative journalism. Its development of daily biographical sketches of figures in the news abandons the old elitist assumption that everybody knows who these people are. The new managing editor, A. M. Rosenthal, is among those chiefly responsible for an emphasis on "in depth" reporting that breaks away from yesterday's developments. A landmark of this genre was Anthony Lukas' 5,000-word account of a suburban girl who had been found murdered in an East Greenwich Village basement; Lukas' detailed narrative transformed an incomprehensible horror into a memorable insight into the shifting values and life patterns that touch even the most seemingly secure homes. In August, when 300,000 youngsters suddenly converged on Bethel, New York, to hear rock music, the *Times* reports, departing from the conventional emphasis on the disorderly aspects of the scene, made a real effort to understand what had drawn the kids there, what they got out of it, what their values were.

Because of the *Times'* immense influence on journalism that paper's recent willingness to break out of conventional molds is one of the most hopeful signs of long-range improvement of the press. But it may be years before most papers follow such pioneering. They haven't the reporting staffs to do so. Bright, concerned young men and women are loath to go to work for papers that are clearly not alive, not relevant to the great changes and stresses that are sweeping through society.

Broadening the scope of news

Newspapers have been slow to adjust to the liveliness of good TV reportage and the broad-spectrum coverage of newsmagazines.

From its beginning the great distinction of *Time*, the weekly newsmagazine, was not the much-parodied sentence structure of its early years but its broadened concept of news. For example, it looked at religion as a moving part of the total scene. No future historian of the twentieth century's middle decades could possibly omit from an account of the total change the tremendous shifts of religious and ethical belief that color contemporary life. Yet most conventional newspaper journalism still virtually ignores such subjects, except when they surface as dramatic confrontations. The newsmagazines continue to broaden the concept of news. *Newsweek* has added departments on "Life and Leisure" and "The Cities." *Time's* recent addition of "Behavior" and "Environment" treats other areas that the older journalism assumed to be static. The departmentalization of news itself is more than an orderly convenience for the reader. The departmental structure forces editors to look where they know news ought to be, rather than passively waiting for news to "flow" at them—an attitude that results in today's news being defined as whatever is most like yesterday's news.

All journalism has something to learn from the pioneers of a new journalism of ideas. The quarterly *Daedalus*, under the sensitive editorship of Stephen Graubard, has reached an impressive circulation of 70,000; it provides for a highly educated readership a forum where voices from many disciplines converge in each issue upon a single subject. *The Public Interest*, another quarterly, edited by Daniel Bell and Irving Kristol, is less formidably academic in style, more directly attuned to current problems. One of the most extraordinary publications is the *Kaiser Aluminum News*, whose editor, Don Fabun, delights in translating, primarily for the company's employees, the most difficult contemporary thought into lucid, poetic words and pictures. Fabun never runs a conventional "audience-building story"; and yet the demand for his magazine continues to build because people are fascinated by what he has to say.

Not one of these magazines pursues an ideological shortcut. All are basically periodicals of explanation. They work on the assumption that relevant truths about contemporary society are difficult—but not impossible—to convey.

The special bias of TV

At the other end of the spectrum lies television journalism with its mass audience. Most of its faults have descended from print journalism; it multiplied its inheritance while finding some distortive formal biases of its own. The artistic bias inherent in the TV medium affects the behavior of the actors in the news. The "demonstration" becomes a dominant form of social action rather than the petition, the political debate, the lawsuit. Other media are drawn toward covering, as best they can, the disorderly scenes that television covers so superlatively. There have been months when a consumer of news might wonder whether anything except demonstrations was going on in the U.S. Such overconcentration on one kind of news in a society where thousands of currents are running is a sure way of walking into another ambush, perhaps more grave than that represented by today's disorderly products of yesterday's inattention.

Television is exerting another, more indirect, bias upon news. The generation now of college age is the first that was introduced to news through a medium mainly devoted to dramatized entertainment. The drama is usually highly simplified and one side is morally right, the other wrong. The young viewer expects the news to fall into the same dramatic pattern. It is not surprising if he later becomes a recruit to the new anti-intellectualism apparent in the impatience of campus protesters who regard complex facts as distractions from the "gut commitment," which they hold to be a morally superior approach to public questions. Public expectation of moralistic drama presses all media toward defining news in terms of simple conflict. But what the public needs to know may lie in just the opposite direction. Society's ability to avoid ambush may depend on receiving information before the dramatic conflict develops.

Yet some of the most hopeful signs of tomorrow's journalism are also to be found in television. It has an incomparable ability to convey the integrated *quality* of a personality or of a social situation. Eric Hoffer unobtrusively interviewed by Eric Sevareid was an experience in communication that print journalism could hardly match. C.B.S. also recently did a "documentary" (that blighting word) on Japan as interpreted by former Ambassador Edwin Reischauer, which told more people more about the subject than millions of printed words, including Reischauer's own fine books.

Conventional journalism despairs of communicating such an intrinsically interesting subject as old age in contemporary society. What's the story? What's the event? What's the conflict? What's the issue? Lord Snowdon's beautifully sensitive *Don't Count the Candles* ignores those conventional journalistic questions and brings unforgettable information of what it's like to be old.

Such examples compel the conclusion that television has a great constructive role to play in the journalism of the future upon which society must depend for its sense of cohesion and for the intelligent choice of its own direction.

That poverty in America should have been "discovered" in 1962 by Michael Harrington, an impassioned polemicist, is proof that journalism was not fulfilling its mission. Where were the journalists in the years when Ralph Nader was working on *Unsafe at Any Speed*, an exaggerated indictment of auto manufacturers that is now generally conceded to contain a lot of truth about a matter of universal interest? Nader lately has broadened his attack to other products and services where the buying public is ill-protected and ill-informed. He and Harrington both tend toward governmental remedies for the ills they identify. But the informational problem is more fundamental than the political issue. If society doesn't know about poverty it cannot deal with it governmentally or otherwise; if the consuming public doesn't know enough about what it's buying it cannot protect itself, governmentally or otherwise. The way to defend the market system is to be sure that information, an essential ingredient of any healthy market or any healthy democracy, is adequate.

It's up to the newsmen

It ought to be plain, but seemingly it is not, that the quality of journalism depends primarily on journalists—not on government and not on the legal owners of media. Publishers and executives of networks and broadcasting stations now have only a small fraction of the influence on news that owners used to exercise. As commercial bias diminishes, what counts now, for better or worse, is the bias of reporters, cameramen, editors. Their ideological bent is far less important than their artistic bias, the way they select and present what they regard as significant.

Journalism will always need artistry to reach the public's mind and heart. Indeed, what is now required is a higher level of art, a boldness that will get journalism unstuck from forms of communication developed in and for a social context very different from the present. Nobody except journalists can develop such forms. All the public can do is to be wary of existing distortions and appreciative of such efforts as appear to get closer to the current truth.

Topics for Discussion

1. At the end of his second paragraph, Ways asks the question, "What is news?" Does he answer this question? What is his answer?
2. Ways maintains that "journalism clings to outdated patterns and practices. . . ." What are some of these? Why are they outdated?
3. The *New York Times* is "in a class by itself?" and is "the greatest single national influence" on newsstories, according to Ways. Have you ever read the *New York Times*? Why does the *Times* have such great influence? If you have not read the *New York Times*, go to the library and read a few issues.
4. Speaking of television, Ways calls the word "documentary" "blighting." Why?
5. Ways charges that for the most part newspapers are not "alive, not relevant to the great changes and stresses that are sweeping through society." What are some of these changes and stresses? Do you agree that newspapers are concerned with them?
6. How adequately does your local newspaper cover local news? Does it keep its readers informed of what is occurring in the local community?
7. Is it true that "today's network of news may serve the times less effectively than did the fifteenth century's"? In what way could it be true?

Rhetorical Considerations

1. How effective is the comparison of the news coverage between Columbus and the first man to walk on the moon? How legitimate is the comparison?
2. How much of this essay is informed opinion and how much is factual information? Can you easily distinguish between the two? Does Ways separate the two or blend them?
3. What is the thesis of this essay? Can you say that the title adequately expresses the thesis, or is the thesis more fully stated in the essay?
4. How does Ways conclude his essay—on a note of hope or despair, or a suggestion for change? What is the purpose of such a conclusion?
5. How many major divisions can be made of this essay? What do they reveal about how Ways has ordered his material?

WHAT IT'S LIKE TO BROADCAST NEWS

WALTER CRONKITE

When Vice President Agnew, in November 1969, unleashed his attack upon the news media, he was following, albeit with unique linguistic and philosophic departures, a long line of predecessors. Somewhere in the history of our Republic there may have been a high government official who said he had been treated fairly by the press, but for the life of me, however, I can't think of one.

Mr. Agnew's attacks, of course, were particularly alarming because of their sustained virulence and intimidating nature. But the Vice President was simply joining the chorus (or, seeing political opportunity, attempting to lead it) of those who have appointed themselves critics of the television medium. Well, I don't like everything I see on television either, but I am frank to say I'm somewhat sick and mighty tired of broadcast journalism being constantly dragged into the operating room and dissected, probed, swabbed, and needled to see what makes it tick.

I'm tired of sociologists, psychologists, pathologists, educators, parents, bureaucrats, politicians, and other special interest groups presuming to tell us what is news or where our responsibilities lie.

Or perhaps I'm phrasing this wrong. It is not those who squeeze us between their slides and hold us under their microscopes with whom my patience has grown short. The society *should* understand the impact of television upon it. There are aspects of it that need study so that the people can cope with an entirely revolutionary means of communication. Those who disagree with our news coverage have every

Walter Cronkite, "What It's Like to Broadcast News," *Saturday Review* (December 12, 1970), pp. 53, 54, 55. Copyright 1970 by Saturday Review, Inc. Reprinted with permission.

right to criticize. We can hardly claim rights to a free press and free speech while begrudging those rights to our critics. Indeed, that would seem to be what some of them would like to do to us. So believing, it clearly cannot be the responsible critics or serious students of the TV phenomenon with whom I quarrel. I am provoked more by those in our craft who, like wide-eyed country yokels before the pitchman, are losing sight of the pea under the shell.

We must expose the demagogues who would undermine this nation's free media for personal or partisan political gain. That is news. And we should not withhold our cooperation from serious studies of the medium. But we must not permit these matters to divert us from our task, or confuse us as to what that task is.

I don't think it is any of our business what the moral, political, social, or economic effect of our reporting is. I say let's get on with the job of reporting the news—and let the chips fall where they may. I suggest we concentrate on doing our job of telling it like it is and not be diverted from that exalted task by the apoplectic apostles of alliteration.

Now, a fair portion of what we do is not done well. There are things we are not doing that we ought to do. There are challenges that we have not yet fully met. We are a long way from perfection. Our problems are immense, and they are new and unique.

A major problem is imposed by the clock. In an entire half-hour news broadcast we speak only as many words as there are on two-thirds of one page of a standard newspaper. Clearly, the stricture demands tightness of writing and editing, and selection, unknown in any other form of journalism. But look what we do with that time. There are twenty items in an average newscast—some but a paragraph long, true, but all with the essential information to provide at least a guide to our world that day. Film clips that, in a way available to no other daily medium, introduce our viewers to the people and the places that make the news; investigative reports (pocket documentaries) that expose weakness in our democratic fabric (not enough of these, but we're coming along), feature film reports that explore the byways of America and assure us that the whole world hasn't turned topsy-turvy; graphics that in a few seconds communicate a great deal of information; clearly identified analysis, or commentary, on the news—I think that is quite a package.

The transient, evanescent quality of our medium—the appearance and disappearance of our words and pictures at almost the same instant—imposes another of our severe problems. Most of us would agree that television's greatest asset is the ability to take the public to the scene—the launch of a spaceship, a Congressional hearing, a political convention, or a disaster (in some cases these are not mutually exclusive). Live coverage of such continuing, developing events presents the radio-television newsman with a challenge unlike any faced by the print reporter. The newspaper legman, rewrite man, and editor meet the pressure of deadlines and must make hard decisions fast and accurately. But multiply their problems and decisions a thousandfold and you scarcely have touched on the problems of the electronic journalist broadcasting live. Even with the most intensive coverage it still is difficult and frequently impossible to get all the facts and get all of them straight as a complex and occasionally violent story is breaking all around. We do have to fill in additional material on subsequent broadcasts, and there is the danger that not all the original audience is there for the fuller explanation.

When a television reporter, in the midst of the riot or the floor demonstration or the disaster, dictates his story, he is not talking to a rewrite man but directly to the audience. There is no editor standing between him and the reader. He will make mistakes, but his quotient for accuracy must be high or he is not long for this world of electronic journalism. We demand a lot of these on-the-scene television reporters. I for one think they are delivering in magnificent fashion.

Directors of an actuality broadcast, like newspaper photo editors, have several pictures displayed on the monitors before them. But they, unlike their print counterparts, do not have ten minutes, or five, or even one minute to select the picture their audience will see. Their decision is made in seconds. Theirs is a totally new craft in journalism, but they have imbued it with all the professionalism and sense of responsibility and integrity of the men of print. Of course we make mistakes, but how few are the errors compared to the fielding chances!

Our profession is encumbered, even as it is liberated, by the tools of our trade. It is a miracle—this transmission of pictures and voices through the air, the ability to take the whole world to the scene of a single event. But our tools still are somewhat gross. Miniaturization and other developments eventually will solve our problem, but for the moment our cameras and our lights and our tape trucks and even our microphones are obtrusive. It is probably true that their presence can alter an event, and it probably also is true that they alter it even more than the presence of reporters with pad and pencil, although we try to minimize our visibility. But I think we should not be too hasty in adjudging this as always a bad thing. Is it not salutary that the government servant, the politician, the rioter, the miscreant knows that he is operating in the full glare of publicity, that the whole world is watching?

Consider political conventions. They have been a shambles of democratic malfunction since their inception, and printed reports through the years haven't had much effect in reforming them. But now that the voters have been taken to them by television, have sat through the sessions with the delegates and seen the political establishment operate to suppress rather than develop the democratic dialogue, there is a stronger reform movement than ever before, and the chances of success seem brighter.

I would suggest that the same is true of the race rioters and the student demonstrators, whatever the justice of the point they are trying to make. Of course they use television. Hasn't that always been the point of the demonstrator—to attract attention to his cause? But the *excesses* of the militants on ghetto streets and the nation's campuses, shown by television with almost boring repetition, tend to repel rather than enlist support, and this is a lesson I hope and *believe* that rational leaders are learning.

Scarcely anyone would doubt that television news has expanded to an immeasurable degree the knowledge of many people who either cannot or do not read. We have broadened the interests of another sizable group whose newspaper reading is confined to the headlines, sports, and comics. We are going into homes of the untutored, teaching underprivileged and disadvantaged who have never known a book. We are exposing them to a world they scarcely knew existed, and while advertisements and entertainment programing whet their thirst for a way of life they believe beyond them, we show them that there are people and movements, inside and outside the Establishment, that are trying to put the good things within their reach.

Without any intent to foster revolution, by simply doing our job as journalists with ordinary diligence and an extraordinary new medium, we have awakened a sleeping giant. No wonder we have simultaneously aroused the ire of those who are comfortable with the status quo. Many viewers happily settled in their easy chairs under picture windows that frame leafy boughs and flowering bushes and green grass resent our parading the black and bearded, the hungry and unwashed through their living rooms, reminding them that there is another side of America that demands their attention. It is human nature to avoid confronting the unpleasant. No one *wants* to hear that "our boys" are capable of war crimes, that our elected officials are capable of deceit or worse. I think I can safely say that there are few of us who want to report such things. But as professional journalists we have no more discretion in whether to report or not to report when confronted with the facts than does a doctor in deciding to remove a gangrenous limb.

If it *happened*, the people are entitled to know. There is no condition that can be imposed on that dictum

without placing a barrier (censorship) between the people and the truth—at once as fallible and corrupt as only self-serving men can make it. The barrier can be built by government—overtly by dictatorship or covertly with propaganda on the political stump, harassment by subpoena, or abuse of the licensing power. Or the barrier can be built by the news media themselves. If we permit our news judgment to be colored by godlike decisions as to what is good for our readers, listeners, or viewers, we are building a barrier—no matter how pure our motives. If we permit friendship with sources to slow our natural reflexes, we also build a barrier. If we lack courage to face the criticism and consequences of our reporting, we build barriers.

But of all barriers that we might put between the people and the truth, the most ill-considered is the one that some would erect to protect their profits. In all media, under our precious free enterprise system, there are those who believe performance can only be measured by circulation or ratings. The newspaper business had its believers long before we were on the scene. They practiced editing by readership survey. Weak-willed but greedy publishers found out what their readers *wanted* to read and gave it to them —a clear abdication of their duties as journalists and, I would submit, a nail in the coffin of newspaper believability.

Today, before the drumfire assault of the hysterical Establishment and the painful complaints of a frightened populace, there are many in our business who believe we should tailor our news reports to console our critics. They would have us report more good news and play down the war, revolution, social disturbance. There certainly is nothing wrong with good news. In fact, by some people's lights we report quite a lot of it: an anti-pollution bill through Congress, a report that the cost of living isn't going up as fast as it was last month, settlement of a labor dispute, the announcement of a medical breakthrough, plans for a new downtown building. There isn't anything wrong either with the stories that tell us what is right about America, that reminds us that the virtues that made this nation strong still exist

The Age of Communication

and prosper despite the turmoil of change.

But when "give us the good news" becomes a euphemism for "don't give us so much of that bad news"—and in our business one frequently means the other—the danger signal must be hoisted.

It is possible that some news editors have enough time allotted by their managements to cover all the significant news of their areas—much of it, presumably, in the "bad" category—and still have time left over for a "good news" item or two. But for many and certainly those at the network level, that is not the case. To crowd in the "happy" stories would mean crowding out material of significance. Some good-news advocates know this, and it is precisely what they want: to suppress the story of our changing society in the hope that if one ignores evil it will go away.

Others simply are tired of the constant strife. They would like a little relief from the daily budget of trouble that reminds them of the hard decisions they as citizens must face. But can't they see that pandering to the innocent seeking relief is to yield to those who would twist public opinion to control our destiny?

It is no coincidence that these manipulative methods parallel those adopted half a century ago by Russian revolutionaries also seeking the surest means to bend the population to their will. You will not find bad news in Russian newspapers or on broadcast media. There are no reports of riots, disturbances of public order, muggings or murders, train, plane, or auto wrecks. There are no manifestations of race prejudice, disciplinary problems in army ranks. There is no exposure of malfeasance in public office—other than that which the government chooses to exploit for its own political purposes. There is no dissent over national policy, no argument about the latest weapons system.

There is a lot of good news—factories making their quotas, happy life on the collective farm, successes of Soviet diplomacy, difficulties in the United States. The system works. Without free media—acerbic, muckraking, irreverent—the Soviet people are placid drones and the Soviet Establishment runs the country the way it wants it run.

Since it is hard to know the real motives in others' minds—indeed, it is hard sometimes to know our own motives—and since few are likely to admit that they would seek to suppress dissent from Establishment norms, it would be wrong to ascribe such Machiavellian connivance to the good-news advocates. The only trouble is that the other, more likely motive—profiting from the news by pandering to public taste—is almost as frightening. To seek the public's favor by presenting the news it wants to hear is to fail to understand the function of the media in a democracy. We are not in the business of winning popularity contests, and we are not in the entertainment business. It is not our job to please anyone except Diogenes.

The newsman's purpose is contrary to the goal of almost everyone else who shares the airwaves with us, and perhaps we should not be too harsh with those executives with the ultimate responsibility for station and network management. We are asking a great deal of them. For seventeen of the eighteen hours during an average broadcast day their job is to win friends and audience. They and we live on how successfully they do this difficult job.

But then we ask them to turn a deaf ear to the complaints of those dissatisfied with what we present in the remaining minutes of the day. We ask them to be professionally schizoid—and that would seem to be a lot to ask. But is it, really? After all, in another sense, as journalists we live this life of dual personality. There is not a man who can truthfully say that he does not harbor in his breast prejudice, bias, strong sentiments pro and con on some if not all the issues of the day.

Yet it is the distinguishing mark of the professional journalist that he can set aside these personal opinions in reporting the day's news. None of us succeeds in this task in all instances, but we know the assignment and the pitfalls, and we succeed far more often than we fail or than our critics would acknowledge. We have a missionary duty to try to teach this basic precept of our craft to those of our bosses who have not yet learned it. We in broadcasting, at least, cannot survive as a major news medium if we fail.

We were well on the way before the current wave of politically inspired criticism. In my twenty years in broadcasting I have seen more and more station owners taking courage from their news editors, tasting the heady fruit of respect that can be won by the fearless conveyer of the truth. Some years ago William Allen White wrote that "nothing fails so miserably as a cowardly newspaper." I suspect he spoke not only of commercial failure but of the greater failure: not winning the confidence of the people. A radio or television station also can fail this test of courage, and when it does its owner wins not a community's respect and gratitude but its contempt.

Broadcast management is going to need a stiff backbone in the days ahead —not only for its own well-being but for the good of us all. We are teetering on the brink of a communications crisis that could undermine the foundation of our democracy that is a free and responsible press. We all know the present economic background. We in radio and television with our greater impact and our numerous outlets have forced many of our print competitors out of business. It is a rare American city today that has more than one newspaper. And yet I think most of us will acknowledge that we are not an adequate substitute for the newspapers whose demise we have hastened. We cannot supply the wealth of detail the informed citizen needs to judge the performance of his city, county, or state. If we do our jobs thoroughly, however, we can be a superb monitor over the monopoly newspaper, assuring that it does not by plot, caprice, or inadvertence miss a major story.

We *can* be, that is, if we are left alone to perform that essential journalistic function. The trouble is that broadcast media are not free; they are government licensed. The power to make us conform is too great to lie forever dormant. The ax lies there temptingly for use by any enraged administration, Republican, Democrat, or Wallaceite. We are at the mercy of the whim of politicians and bureaucrats, and whether they choose to chop us down or not, the mere existence of their power is an intimidating and constraining threat.

So on one side there is a monopoly press that may or may not choose to present views other than those of the domineering majority, on the other side a vigorously competitive but federally regulated broadcast industry, most of whose time is spent currying popular—that is, majority—favor. This scarcely could be called a healthy situation. There is a real danger that the free flow of ideas, the vitality of minority views, even the dissent of recognized authorities could be stifled in such an atmosphere.

We newsmen, dedicated as we are to freedom of press and speech and the presentation of all viewpoints no matter how unpopular, must work together, regardless of our medium, to clear the air while there is still time. We must resist every new attempt at government control, intimidation, or harassment. And we must fight tenaciously to win through Congress and the courts guarantees that will free us forever from the present restrictions. We must stand together and bring the power of our professional organizations to bear against those publishers and broadcast managers who fail to understand the function of a free press. We must keep our own escutcheons so clean that no one who would challenge our integrity could hope to succeed.

If we do these things, we can preserve, and re-establish where it has faded, the confidence of the people whose freedom is so indivisibly linked with ours.

Topics for Discussion

1. What does Cronkite mean when he says, "our profession is encumbered, even as it is liberated, by the tools of our trade"?
2. Do you agree with Cronkite that it is none of the newsman's business "what the moral, political, social, or economic effect" of his reporting is?
3. "If it *happened,* the people are entitled to know." Do you agree with Cronkite that this should be the guiding principle of journalism? Can you think of anything the public is not entitled to know?
4. Is it true that the broadcast media are not free? What does Cronkite mean?
5. Cronkite pictures newsmen as an embattled group desperately fighting off attacks by a variety of critics, governmental and others. Is this an accurate picture?
6. List your major criticisms of the news media, particularly broadcast journalism. How do you think Cronkite would answer your criticisms?
7. Does Cronkite tell you what it's like to broadcast the news? What is the purpose of this essay?

Rhetorical Considerations

1. What is the thesis of this essay? Is the title accurate or misleading?
2. Cronkite is, of course, a journalist by profession. Is the prose style of this essay what you would expect of a journalist?
3. Pick one or two paragraphs at random and analyze them. Does Cronkite follow the standard expository paragraph form—topic sentence, development, conclusion? Are his paragraphs clearly organized?
4. Look at the first two and last two paragraphs of the essay. Cronkite begins by mentioning Vice-President Agnew's attacks on the news media and ends up speaking of government control, intimidation, and harassment. What jump in logic has he made?
5. Does Cronkite make any unsubstantiated generalizations? Do you find any instances of illogic?
6. How well organized and well presented is Cronkite's argument? Is he convincing?

You'll Laugh!
You'll Cry!
You'll Watch Them Die!

Michael Arlen

LES MIDGLEY, who is the executive producer of the *CBS Evening News* and therefore the man operably responsible for what 20,000,000 Americans watch as news each evening, six days a week, 52 weeks a year, is seated at the desk in his office, which is on the ground floor of the CBS News Building on West 57th Street in New York. The CBS News Building, one should say, is not much of a building as buildings go these days, certainly nothing like the CBS setup in Los Angeles nor the austere and meticulous, plant- and Brancusi-filled CBS Building that Frank Stanton has erected on Sixth Avenue. From the outside, it is a nondescript three-story rectangle of red brick—a warehouse, perhaps, or an Eisenhower post office. Inside—well, it's clearly not a post office. Guards. Endless narrow corridors. Small offices. Large rooms full of teletypes, desks, typewriters, men in shirt sleeves. A room full of tape machines. Banks of tape machines. Television screens. The CBS News people take pleasure in that they are not in Mr. Stanton's building, in that they are over here on the wrong side of Ninth Avenue, in a warehouse of a building, in their shirt sleeves, putting out an electronic evening newspaper.

On the other side of the glass in Midgley's office is the newsroom where the Cronkite show is done—a real newsroom, real desks, real people working at the desks. "We don't use a studio like NBC," says one of the CBS people. The time is four o'clock in the afternoon. A November day; 1971. There are six desks in the room, ordinary gray metal desks, bunched together into three rows. In the far row, two men sit typing. The

Originally appeared in *Playboy* Magazine. Reprinted with permission.

man in the red shirt is the chief national-news writer. The man in the beard writes the foreign news. On the near side, one man, who seems to be in his early 20s, is holding a phone to his ear and typing at the same time. The man behind him is also typing. At the front desk in the middle row sits Walter Cronkite. He has a pile of copy in front of him. His lips move as he intones the copy in a low voice. He holds a stop watch in his hand. He pauses in his reading, scribbles corrections. Men in shirt sleeves pass in and out of the room. Girls with clipboards. Engineers. Inside Midgley's office, the Boston tape is over, although *Gomer Pyle* is still running silently on the top two screens.

"You can take out Henagan," says Midgley. "He doesn't make any sense."

Stan Gould, associate producer, is writing on his clipboard. "I can use the priest," he says.

"The priest doesn't make any sense, either," says Sandy Socolow, who is Midgley's assistant, a youngish, plump man in glasses and a suit.

"It may be understandable in Boston, but not here," says Midgley. "What do you have down for it?"

"A couple of minutes," says Gould.

A man runs into the office. "No audio from Atlanta."

A phone rings. Socolow picks it up. "Have you seen your film? Well, was it good, bad or indifferent?"

Midgley is listening in on the other phone. "Are you positive he was *there*?" he asks.

Socolow says, "OK, what kind of production problems are you going to give us? It's a self-contained run of track."

"No Shakne fore and aft," says Midgley.

"No Shakne," says Socolow.

Gould is on his way out of the office. "It's an R-three," says Socolow to Gould.

A girl in a black pants suit comes in,

leaves the latest revised line-up for the evening: *1. Open; 2. Cronkite . . . live; 3. Ft. McPherson / Medina / Morton . . . VTR . . . 3.00 Atlanta; 4. Cronkite . . . live; 5. First commercial (Absorbine and Pontiac) . . . VTR 8 . . . 1.05; 6. Cronkite . . . live; 7. Washington / Living costs / Benton . . . Washington . . . 1.45—*

In the newsroom, some kind of flurry is going on. Cronkite is standing. The man in the red shirt and one of the other writers are standing at his desk. "Goddamn it, get on the phone and find out," Cronkite is saying.

Ron Vonn, another associate producer, steps into Midgley's office. Midgley is sipping a milk shake from a paper cup. He looks up. "I talked to Bruce Morton. He'll give us voice-over at the end of the trial." Vonn leaves.

Socolow says, "Threlkeld's on two-forty-six." Then, "Let me caution you, Mr. Midgley. Ron is going to run over."

Midgley picks up the phone. "Ron, is there anything that's going to raise a question of taste with us? Is there any problem with the mother or the children?" He nods and puts the phone down. "Two-thirty?" he says to Socolow.

"We have him down for three o'clock," says Socolow.

"OK, two-forty-five. We'll split the difference."

Vonn comes back in. "It doesn't look like the logistics are against us on jurors." Midgley reaches for a switch on his desk. The lower TV screen lights up.

Bruce Morton is leaning against a railing, looking at the ground. He looks up. "I'm ready whenever you are," he says with some impatience. "Well, what's the matter?" he says. "Bullshit," he says.

One of the writers comes in from the newsroom. "When are we going to hear from Kalb?" he asks.

"Kalb is supposed to call in by six," says Midgley. Out in the newsroom, Cronkite is standing talking, or apparently arguing, with Socolow.

Socolow comes back to Midgley. "It's the 'secret meeting' on Kalb's file. He says we have to have more on it or we ought to skip it until we do."

"I don't blame him," says Midgley. He picks up a phone. "Try to get me Marvin Kalb in Washington," he says.

To get to the taping room, you walk out of Midgley's office, past the newsroom, down a corridor, through a door marked NO ADMITTANCE, past a secretary, past another NO ADMITTANCE door and into a large room filled with banks of machines. They are very much the new machines, our new 20th Century machines—no rows of seamstresses and sewing machines, no looms, no great clanking wheels, iron, pistons, ugly things. These are trim, spare, rectilinear. Taller than a man. Gray and white. Now and then, a small red or green light. Dials. Oscilloscope screens. It is a large room, maybe 80′ x 80′. There are about 20 of these machines. In rows. At each of them, on a small swivel stool, sits an operator. Above his head, on the machine, a large roll of tape is unwinding. The dials read, COLOR HOLD . . . GREEN GAIN . . . BLUE GAIN . . . V HOLD . . . V SIZE . . . RED . . . PLAYBACK CONTROL . . . BLUE. The operator throws a switch. The tape roll moves in the opposite direction. On a TV screen in the machine, the face of F. Lee Bailey appears, talking into a microphone.

"More," says Vonn. Bailey is making a speech, although it's hard to hear his voice on the machine because of all the other machines. Behind Vonn, Gould is standing beside another machine, watching Henagan in Boston. "OK," says Vonn. The operator stops the tape. Bailey is still there on the screen in mid-sentence. Another man is beside him at the microphone. "I want to use the Morton audio bridge to get to where *this* guy starts to talk," Vonn says. "I want to take it from where Bailey goes over to this man and then cut to this close-up." The tape operator throws a switch, the tape spins backward, the voices making a kind of speeded-up Disney-cartoon sound. Then forward: Bailey walking to the microphone, speaking, arm extended. Stop, backward. Forward. Backward. Vonn stands behind the operator.

Somebody comes by. "Are we going with the San Francisco stuff?"

"I don't know," says Vonn. "We're going to see it at six."

A phone rings. Gould picks it up. Listens. Puts it down. "San Francisco won't be ready until six-fifteen," he says.

"What about Boston?" says Vonn.

"How do I know?" says Gould. "I don't see how they have time for it, but I'm going to get it ready until they tell me to dump it."

The operator at Vonn's machine has the tape positioned at the point where

Bailey is extending his arm toward the man on the left. "There?"

Vonn looks. "Back it off twelve seconds and we'll lay video only for that."

Bailey's voice comes up: *"I've never gotten an acquittal for a nicer guy. . . ."*

"OK," Vonn says. "Now I want the cut to the head to come in right. OK?"

On Gould's machine, Boston school children are running down a street. On the machine next to him, Chinese soldiers are marching in a parade.

On another bank, Muhammad Ali is speaking at a press conference. "I've never felt better," he says against the sound of the Chinese military band.

"I don't *care* if we don't hear Bailey talking," says Vonn.

At six o'clock, the face of Jim Jensen, the local CBS newsman, appears on the top screen; an NBC man appears on the second screen—both without audio. On the lower screen, Midgley and Socolow are watching Bob Shakne interview a convict recently released from Attica.

"What bothers me," says Socolow, "is the guy coming out so strong, saying he was in the uprising."

Vonn sticks his head in the door. "What about San Francisco?"

Midgley says to Socolow, "You're in great shape. Relax." To Vonn, "They're putting in the last San Francisco splices."

"Jesus," says Vonn.

Midgley says to Socolow, "Cammerbandge has the guy in his apartment, doesn't he? He says he has no doubt about his being in cell block D."

Gould comes into the office. "Is your piece ready?" asks Midgley.

"Attica? Or Boston?" says Gould.

"Boston."

Gould shrugs. "I was just given a good night on Boston."

A phone rings. Socolow says to Midgley, "San Francisco is coming on." A picture of a woman and two children appears on the lower screen. The voice of Dick Threlkeld of the San Francisco CBS station. The two kids are apparently victims of a mysterious killing disease. A third kid has already died. These two are now becoming sick. It's a sad story. The woman talks about her belief in God and about how she knows the kids won't die. Threlkeld's voice tells us there is no chance that they will live. Close.

"Two-twenty," says Socolow.

"Damn good piece," says Midgley.

"Any problems with San Francisco?"

asks Vonn.

"None," says Midgley. "It's good. Two-twenty."

Outside in the newsroom, there is a good deal of activity. Two cameras are being wheeled in. One directly in front of Cronkite's desk, the other off to his right, just in front of Midgley's office. Cronkite is still working at his desk, editing copy. The writers are still on the telephone or typing. A bank of lights is suddenly turned on overhead. The two writers in the far row of desks get up. A woman comes over and tidies up the surface of their desks. Another woman is taking the sheets of copy from in front of Cronkite and feeding them into the prompting machine, an ingenious device that has also been moved onto the floor, beside one of the cameras, and which consists of a TV camera that transmits each page of copy onto a TV screen attached to the large camera that's now facing Cronkite, where, by an arrangement of mirrors, is displayed the typewritten copy, complete with last-minute corrections, directly on the lens of the camera that Cronkite looks into. A third woman comes in with a tray of make-up, which she puts down on the desk behind Cronkite, which has been entirely cleared of papers. Somebody calls, "Three minutes to air."

Cronkite gets up and goes into Midgley's office. "What about Kalb?" he says.

"Kalb is standing by," says Midgley.

"Let's forget Kalb," says Socolow.

Midgley looks at Cronkite. "Well, we don't need it," he says. "Let's dump it."

"Two minutes," someone calls. Cronkite goes back to his desk. He puts on his jacket, opens a drawer of his desk, takes out a pair of glasses, puts them on. The woman is dabbing his face slightly with make-up. The last two writers have gotten up and are standing out of the way. Cronkite is sitting down now. Socolow goes over, puts a piece of paper on his desk. Cronkite is working on it. On Midgley's screen, there is the familiar clatter of the wire-services machines. A voice says, "And now, from our newsroom in New York, the *CBS Evening News* with Walter Cronkite." Cronkite is still working at his desk. On the screen, he appears behind the lettering, still working on something. Midgley gets up, closes the door to his office. Socolow sits in a chair by the telephone. A girl sits on the couch with a clipboard. The newsroom is bright with lights. On the screen, Cronkite looks up and, without missing a beat, moves into the opening rhythms of the evening news.

● ● ●

News. Right now in America, there are morning newspapers. There is news radio. Afternoon newspapers. Evening newspapers. *The 11 O'clock News. The Noon News. Eyewitness News. Action News.* Newsmagazines. Newsletters. Five minutes of news. Two minutes of news. Round-the-clock news. Cronkite. Brinkley. *The News of the Week in Review.* Harry Dalrymple wrapping things up at the news desk at station KPGT. "And so this was Wednesday, November third. . . ."

One thing is clear: Americans are getting an awful lot of news beamed at them, printed for them, yelled into their ears, tossed into the mailbox. Another thing also seems clear: Generally speaking, news is supposed to be a good thing. Television stations announce pridefully that they are expanding their 30-minute news show to a full hour. Networks take expensive ads in newspapers in order to proclaim their total number of news hours. People talk of hard news and soft news. Radio in many cases has expanded its news coverage to a full 24 hours: the all-news station. News is a meliorative word these days. A meliorative concept. Many print ads are now presented in the form of news reports. *Sports Illustrated* has been taking ads in newspapers to promote itself as the "third newsmagazine." Opposed to news, which is good, there is presumably opinion, which is biased and unreliable; and analysis, which is intellectual; and criticism, which is self-serving and unconstructive; or fiction, which is irrelevant.

If it's true, though, that Americans are on the receiving end of an unparalleled amount and velocity of news communication, then it must also be true that something is seriously wrong with our news-communication services, because, as a nation (and also as states, as townships, as individuals), we keep getting ourselves into such serious messes—

messes that result in good part, anyway, from our having been told the wrong thing or from our having an evidently complex situation communicated to us in a simplistic way, which in effect amounted to our being told the wrong thing.

Consider the classic communication debacle: Vietnam. Today, of course, everybody has the message about Vietnam. It's a lousy war, right? We had no business going in there, right? Or, if we did, it certainly all went wrong and we should have pulled out. Right? But what, one asks, was the news in 1964? Or 1965? Or 1966? Or 1967? Or even much of 1968? That is a long, long time, and there was a lot of news. To be sure, one understands what happened. The Government said certain things were true that were not always true. Americans have generally been brought up to have faith in their Government. Besides, for a generation we have been exhorted to fight communism there, and there, and there . . . so why not *there*? One understands. Last year, I think, Cronkite declared in a magazine article that he had come round from being a moderate hawk on the war to wishing us out of it, to being a dove. Recantations over the Vietnam war somehow have a curious ring—as if the process of learning were more important than the thing learned, which is sometimes true and sometimes not. Walter Cronkite recants; Pete McCloskey recants; 203,000,000 Americans recant. But from what to what? And what is it they were told all those years by all that news?

Consider some of the other matters that have resulted in the country's experiencing the real and severe malaise that it is surely now experiencing—and will obviously have to live with and suffer with for some time to come. Consider the most important and troubling of all our problems: race. Black and white. Black versus white. Segregation. Integration. Whatever you call it. What was the news on that? Until Dr. King and James Meredith and Little Rock and the integration of the University of Georgia and Medgar Evers and Selma and all the other far-off, seemingly long-ago events, what was the news telling us? Joe Louis, the Brown Bomber? Race riots in Detroit? Harry Truman integrating the Armed Forces? When the news-absorbing public woke up one morning to find the National Guard rumbling into some village square, or Watts aflame, or some frightened school kids being turned away from, or thrust into, some school—where had all that news communication left us the night before? At what spot on the map? How good was the map?

Pollution. Ecology. Did nobody look at Lake Erie until 1967? I read in the paper that a large metals smelter on the West Coast had filed suit with the Government, protesting that, if forced to comply with a certain pollution ruling by a certain date, it would be driven perilously close to bankruptcy. The executives of the company doubtless have a point. So, doubtless, do the citizens of the nearby town who have been choking on smelter gases for the past—well—how many years? What did the news tell them about that? Where were *these* citizens on the map?

Do I seem to be saying that our news systems—our network news, our newspapers, etc.—have served us badly? In fact, I think that is only incidentally so. I think it is indeed true that, as in the case of Vietnam, a highly complex political situation was treated for many years by television news as a largely military operation—the dramatic battle for Hill 937, and so forth. Not only that, but the whole war was presented to us in isolated, disconnected bits of detail—a 30-second bombing raid here, a two-minute film clip of Khe Sanh there, another minute of President Johnson at the Manila Conference, 30 seconds of a helicopter assault—with the result that, even if we had been given the real information we needed to try to come to terms with the war, the way we were given it made it doubly difficult. I think it's true that television news is usually superficial. I think it's true that most news is superficial. I think there are a lot of things wrong with all the news systems. Radio news is often nothing more than chopped-up wire-service copy (already chopped up) and then burbled onto the airwaves by a recommissioned disc jockey. Television news is also usually chopped up. And superficial. And tends to get its big ideas from newspapers. Newspapers, with a couple of exceptions, are often mind-blowingly pa-

rochial. Newsmagazines are less parochial, but only one 50th of the people in this country buy them and, even so, they mostly *follow* certified events, like everyone else.

Yet, having said all this, I'd like to say what I believe is more to the point: I think the people of this country, in a way, get better than they deserve from their news systems. Network news may be superficial, and it may have a slight Eastern bias, but—considering that it has to have some kind of businesslike relationship with its audience—the TV people put out a basically high level of afternoon newspaper. Better, anyway, than most afternoon newspapers. Morning newspapers vary hugely, and some are little more than paste-ups of the A. P. and the U. P. I. and a couple of syndicated columnists; but the A. P. and the U. P. I., despite their haste and superficiality, manage to move an awful lot of stuff in a given day, manage to tell this country more detail about itself than is true of most other countries.

The problem is, I think, that our concept of news is increasingly false, and *that* is what is serving us badly. This news, of which network X is going to give us 45 minutes more this year than last, may not be as useful a thing as we consider it to be. This news, which our newspapers take such pride in bringing us, and propose, in fact, to bring us more of, perhaps isn't as good a thing as we *say*, as we think it to be. Consider, for example, the thrust of change that has swept through virtually every aspect of modern life. Religion. Sex. Clothes. Consider the change that has swept through art forms. Look at the novel, which has always been a form of news, and observe its inner changes. How in the 18th Century it was a news of adventure, of the great migrations from the country to the city, the churning of urban and rural classes, *Clarissa*, Smollett, Defoe. How in the 19th Century it changed to provide the news of the new middle class, the manufacturing class, the new world of Dickens, George Eliot, Arnold Bennett, William Dean Howells. It told readers about the new people, how they lived, what they wore, how vicars had tea, what lawyers did at the office, all that *furniture*. And the 20th Century novel—

while admittedly struggling with the furniture-describing heritage of the 19th, not quite sure where it's going, finding narrative shot away by movies and TV—s ¹ moves toward telling us what we intuitively need to know about our world, about the inside of people's heads (no longer furniture), about how men and women are in bed together, how they really are, how, at any rate, they think they are.

But news—newspapers, TV news, wire-service news—is still telling us of plane crashes. Hotel fires. The minister from such and such said this and that to so-and-so. A strike. A flood. "HUB MAN KILLS THREE." "SOCIALITE NABS BANDIT." And it does that because we seem to think we want that: fires, strikes, plane crashes, Hub man kills three. And the reason we think we want that, I think, is that we aren't nearly so serious about news as we allege. Or look at it this way: We say we're serious about news, so right away CBS and ABC and NBC and *The New York Times* and *Time* and *Newsweek* and all the rest of them rush to provide us with news—but time after time, it turns out to be the wrong news. It doesn't—apparently—much help us. It rarely tells us where we really are, because history is constantly appearing on our doorstep and telling us we're nowhere near where our map said we were. Admittedly, there is no news system one can conceive of that would provide us all with perfect maps; but our maps are *so* inaccurate, and require so much trouble, and tears, and often bloodshed to correct.

Clearly, the news we say we want is the old news. It somehow makes us feel good to read about a plane crash off Japan. It connects us to some ancient folk need, and maybe that is very strong, too strong, and maybe Armageddon will come mysteriously one afternoon, having been foretold by no less than four associate professors in Denver, a Swiss observatory and the *Berkeley Barb*, while the people of the most advanced nation in the world are still reading about a bus accident in Rangoon. Or Rome. Or Rochester, New York. It's perfectly likely—or so it seems to me—that we're never going to get a useful news system. In fact, in my darker moods, I can well imagine a situation developing in which the people of this country get so out of touch with what is actually going on beneath the surface that real trouble erupts, *real* trouble, and repression results, *real* repression (it certainly wouldn't be the first such cycle in history), and then, when the tanks are in place, and the guards are at their posts, and the trains are on time, and loudspeakers, or perhaps TV sets, are at the street corners—then we will have, or be given, a news system that finally will be properly attuned to the situation. Relevant.

But now, in the meantime, I think it might at least be worth while saying this much aloud: The news we congratulate ourselves on receiving, the news that our news systems congratulate themselves on transmitting, while allowing that in a more perfect world they would transmit *more* of it for us if only they could, if only they had a half hour instead of 15 minutes, 50 minutes instead of a half hour, a whole hour, a whole day, maybe, a whole week of—what? Folk entertainment. What? you say. Police-bribe scandal, rape, drowning—entertainment? I guess so. Two minutes of combat film from Vietnam—entertainment? I guess so—although maybe describing it as providing a kind of release, while giving the illusion of involvement, would be closer to it. The news we get, I think, is mostly this release, this kind of entertainment, no matter how grisly the subject, how much we even may weep at the result. We don't get it that way because *they* give it to us, nor because *they* are bad. We get it that way because we want it so. We call, they respond. Good luck, I say, to all of us.

• • •

The clock on Midgley's wall ticks toward seven. Seven is when the *CBS Evening News* goes on the air. Cronkite is still on the screen. He is winding up the taping. A commercial. During the commercial, Socolow steps into the newsroom, whispers something to Cronkite. Steps out again. The commercial is over. Cronkite is shuffling his papers. "And that's the way it is," he says. The familiar voice. The familiar inflection. "Wednesday, November third." End. People stream back into the newsroom. A writer sits back down at his desk. Cronkite walks into Midgley's office. Sits down in a chair. "I wish we could have done more with Kalb," he says.

"We couldn't reach Kalb in time," says Midgley. The Cronkite show is now on the air. Cronkite is on the third screen. Chancellor on the second. Reasoner on the top. Cronkite and Midgley watch the three screens. NBC comes on with something about China. Midgley turns up the NBC audio.

Cronkite says, "We're still one day ahead of them." The three networks carry the same report about Treasury Secretary Connally. Commercials. NBC and CBS have something on the dock strike. ABC is covering Lindsay.

Chancellor sits on his studio chair, detached, helpful. He runs through four quick items. Cronkite's face oncamera is backed by what seems to be a map of Vietnam. He tells us again about the DMZ. Then Dan Rather, Washington. The monetary crisis. Reasoner speaks about a copper crisis in Chile. Midgley sips another milk shake. Cronkite sits in his chair, swiveling it a bit from time to time. Then NBC comes on with its finale, a thing about the departure of the Washington Senators. Long. Weird. Arty camera shots of the empty stadium. "Jesus Christ," says Midgley. Then Cronkite is saying good night. Chancellor. Howard K. Smith. Good night, good night. The script girl closes her log sheet. The screens are dark. Midgley stands. He has a dinner to get to. Cronkite seems in no hurry to leave. He stretches his legs. His brow furrows. Midgley looks at him, on his way out. "I have to be uptown by seven-thirty," he says.

Cronkite looks at him. "You know," he says, "the thing that really breaks my heart is we never have enough time." Cronkite waves his hand. Midgley heads out the door.

Topics for Discussion

1. What is the meaning of the title of this essay? Where does it come from? What does Arlen mean when he calls news "a meliorative concept"?
2. Arlen charges that "something is seriously wrong with our news-communication services." What does he mean?
3. Why is Vietnam "the classic communication debacle"?
4. Arlen charges that "Our news systems . . . have served us badly." Do you agree? What evidence does Arlen offer to back up this charge?
5. Television news is chopped up and superficial, says Arlen. In view of his description of how the *CBS Evening News* is put together, is Arlen's charge valid? Do you agree with him?
6. "The problem is . . . that our concept of news is increasingly false . . ." What is your concept of news? Is it the same as Arlen's? How has this false concept of news caused problems with news communication?
7. In what way is news entertainment?

Rhetorical Considerations

1. Compare the prose style used in the description of the preparation of the *CBS Evening News* program in the first part of the essay and the prose style of the second part of the essay. How does the prose style differ? How is each style suited to the subject it discusses?
2. Throughout the essay Arlen uses sentence fragments. What effect does he achieve with their use?
3. What contrast does Arlen achieve in his description of the CBS News Building and the other CBS buildings?
4. How often does Arlen use the pronoun "I" in this essay? What tone does it give the essay?
5. What point does Arlen make in his concluding paragraphs? Is his conclusion effective?

Problems in the AP

Fred Powledge

NEW YORK—The Associated Press, according to official sources, may have problems communicating with its own people, but it is not out of touch with reality, as some critics have charged...

In the center of Rockefeller Plaza, a few feet from the Rockettes and the rink and the other attractions that tourists take as the real New York, stands the Associated Press Building. It is nondescript in a tall, gray, Rockefeller Plaza way, except for the fact that there is a glass bubble at its entrance where the day's news unreels before your eyes.

The flow of news is endless, fast and dynamic, not unlike the pace of life in New York City. And yet The Associated Press is no more *of* New York than Burlington Industries or Qantas Airways. It suffers its headquarters to be here because somewhere else would be embarrassing. But somewhere else is where its mind is: out among the Middle Americans where the news used to be, along the railroad tracks and the telegraph lines where tornadoes strike and corn and Carson grow and where it is supposedly easy to distinguish all the good there is about this country.

All of which is fine except for one problem: The Associated Press is the largest and most powerful information machine we have. It has been estimated that 900 million people around the world are exposed to The AP's product, which runs to three million words a day, transported into newspaper offices and broadcasting studios by electric typewriters hooked up to long-distance lines. Literally millions of people, including decision-makers of all sorts, rely on The AP for an approximation of what's happening—for the raw materials on which they base their thoughts, opinions and actions.

If this information machine is functioning imperfectly—if it's so concerned with the cornfields that it ignores the city streets—then The AP, and we who rely on it, are in trouble. And there are those in the news business, and in The Associated Press itself, who say this is exactly what's happening.

Not surprisingly, many of those who think The AP's in trouble are younger staff members. Not surprisingly, their major argument is that the wire service is not relevant enough. Where the organization should be attempting to explain the nation's many and complex social pressures, from race to youth to Vietnam to environment, they say, instead it is meekly adhering to a fundamental newsgathering principle that has long been discredited: the principle of getting the news from official, "respectable" sources and transmitting their version as objective fact.

The principle has been incorporated into The AP's very structure. Only about one-fourth of AP's editorial employees are actual reporters—newsmen who get out of the office to see people and ask live questions. (The ratio is about the same at many newspapers.) Three-quarters are deskmen—those who sit at a typewriter, their heads plugged into telephones, and who get the "news" from a public-relations man, a government public information officer, a desk sergeant, or a part-time correspondent who may or may not have gotten the story firsthand. The product of this work is transmitted as fact to almost 1,300 newspapers and about 3,300 radio and TV stations in the United States. (United Press International, which is AP's major domestic competitor, services about the same number, but still is considered by newsmen generally to be the lesser wire service.)

The key word in this whole operation is "objectivity," and it is fundamental to The AP's philosophy. The Associated Press started out in 1848 as

Fred Powledge, "Problems in the AP," *New York* Magazine (November 15, 1971), pp. 55, 56, 58–64. Reprinted by permission.

little more than a mutual protection society for six New York newspapers, all of whose names are now only memories. As the service grew, so did the belief that if lots of newspapers, with varying shades of editorial policy, contributed lots of news to a cooperative distributing agency, the result would be "objectivity."

By 1900, when The AP was incorporated as an association of newspapers, it was claiming that this "union for a common aim and purpose of representatives of all shades of thought and opinion—political, social, economic, religious—is assurance that news gathered and distributed by The Associated Press shall be as objective and complete as human endeavor can make it."

In seventy years' practice, however, the formula has turned out to be less than a perfect system of newsgathering. AP men, past and present, say the constant emphasis on "objectivity" has meant the toning down or avoidance of stories that might be considered, by someone in the Establishment, as "controversial." An official spokesman—a President, a senator, a governor—may say or do something that is surprising, shocking, and new, and the story will run. But someone outside the Establishment will not get the same break. (The same could be said of almost any newspaper in the nation, of course; the difference is that The AP is the closest thing we have to a national journalistic backbone.)

On stories that cannot be toned down or avoided, the cult of objectivity dictates that an AP newsman must *get the other side*. This of course implies that there are only two sides to an issue. If someone says the war is evil, it is good to secure a comment from someone who says the war is not evil (but in practice, the reverse does not necessarily apply). The rule is so basic that an AP newsman, tapping out a story about an airplane crash, is subject to an almost involuntary desire to get a quote from someone who says the plane *didn't* crash.

Newspaper editors who are on the receiving end of AP copy often ridicule the cult of objectivity and the rule of getting the other side. Gene Roberts, the national editor of *The New York Times*, and before that an old hand at

editing AP copy on Southern newspapers, says editors frequently crack jokes about The AP. But, he says, "every newspaper in the country wants a basic meat-and-potatoes kind of news agency, one that touches as many bases as possible and gives both sides of the question. If AP weren't providing that, they'd look elsewhere."

It is likely that 98 per cent of the experienced editors and reporters in the nation would agree with Roberts, but it also is quite likely that a significant proportion of the young newspaper reporters and AP newsmen, the ones who speak of relevance, view the reliance of the press on meat and potatoes as a dangerous diversion. The formula, they argue, has led The AP and newspapers generally into the comfortable and secure position of dodging the tough questions.

A militant demonstration is broken up by the cops, they say: AP gives the meat-and-potatoes of it all, and that traditionally has meant that you call up the police (because nine-to-one you were not there to see it) and take their word for what happened, and throw in a line or two of denials from the demonstrators. And this is still being done at a time when the reliability of the police and other authorities is being, and ought to be, seriously questioned. (An AP story on a civil disturbance in Chattanooga, for example, ran eleven paragraphs in one newspaper. Ten times the story attributed information to public officials; five of those times the phrase was "Police said." The "other side" was quoted once: "Several persons arrested said they had nothing to do with the disorders . . . .")

The question of what police said, at AP as at other news emporia, is part of a really big question in journalism these days. If we report just the bare bones of the news, the reasoning goes —the statistics, the body counts, the official statements—are we not misleading the public? [1] And have not the liars among our Establishment—the govern-

[1] *Sometimes, however, such reporting turns out to be less misleading. Witness The AP's performance on the September 13 Attica prison uprising. AP bulletins and*

ment publicists, the political candidates, the elected officials—taken advantage of this weakness of the press and used the media to blanket the nation and world with their deceptions?

Increasingly, at AP and elsewhere, newsmen involved in the relevance question are demanding of their editors that the formula be forgotten and that the real news be obtained by sending reporters out there where it's happening.

The man in charge of relevance at The AP is the man in charge of almost everything else there, the general manager, Wes Gallagher. Like every other AP executivè, the 60-year-old Gallagher started out as a newsman. He joined The AP in 1937, served as a foreign correspondent in 26 countries, and covered World War II in Europe. He became general manager in 1962 and works now in a corner office of The Associated Press Building in Rockefeller Plaza. In a closet in his office, muffled Teletypes punch out the news constantly on long rolls of paper. Occasionally Gallagher shows symptoms of a common AP-man's malady: he drums his fingers or taps his foot at the rate of approximately 66 words per minute, which is the speed of the national news wire in the closet.

Gallagher claims to be, and undoubtedly is, concerned with the question of relevance. He has instituted

wrapups throughout that confusing day carefully avoided conclusion-jumping, and when it was possible to attribute "information" about the state's assault on the prison, the wire service did so. A bulletin at 10:02 a.m., when the attack started, said there were gunshots but added that "it was not immediately known which side was doing the shooting." By 1:23 p.m., when word of the prisoner and hostage deaths (some of it in the form of official lies) was coming out of the prison, The AP quoted "a spokesman for the State Correction Department" as saying "Several of the hostages had their throats slashed." "The New York Times," on the other hand, which had all day to think about it, ended up with the flat statement that "several of the hostages . . . died when convicts slashed their throats with knives."

several changes that, in the context of what had been a rather unchanging institution, look like reforms. In the foreign field, for example, he asked AP correspondents to worry less about the day-to-day developments of governments and concentrate more on "putting the world in sort of a perspective for the American reader."

Domestically there have been several changes. Young AP reporters traditionally have complained about the long waiting time for good assignments and about the amount of trivia that has to be written while one is waiting. Gallagher attacked both problems three years ago when he set up a ten-man Special Assignment Team, based in Washington. These reporters, most of them young fellows, do no spot news; they can take weeks or even months to develop investigative and interpretative stories about what's really happening. Team member James Polk turned out more than twenty stories on campaign spending; there was a series on medical costs; Ken Hartnett did a series on the "Alternative Society," which probed the youth culture and which got extraordinarily good play across the country.

Gaylord Shaw, until recently the top man on the team, calls it "the best thing that's ever happened" to The AP. The wire service, Shaw said, is going to continue providing news of hailstorms and airplane crashes, but innovations such as the team "will enable us to get out and get those stories that don't surface by themselves."

About a year and a half ago Gallagher formed another team of reporters, most of them women in their twenties, and called it the New Establishment Department; this unfortunate title quickly gave way to "the Mod Squad." "These young reporters," said The AP, "will tell contemporary America about itself and will provide a bridge between the two sides of the generation gap." There have been Squad pieces on women's lib, abortion reform and Charles Reich, among others.

The AP has no intention of abandoning its role as the "service of record," as Gallagher likes to call it, or the service of meat and potatoes, as

Gene Roberts puts it; but it is aware of a "shifting emphasis in the news," a shift toward "people's concerns about how they live, what effect things have on *them*." So The AP is trying to put some gravy on the meat and potatoes, via the special teams, increased use of computers and more emphasis on the cities. Gallagher says, "My personal feeling is that the biggest story that we'll have in the years to come is covering the cities. Can the cities govern themselves? That question's going to wipe out the war and everything else. It's getting to be the main subject."

It's a difficult undertaking and as the reforms proceed at The AP, some staffers are saying that the changes are a day late and a dollar short.

Criticizing The Associated Press is very easy. It's big, dependable, wide open and thus extremely vulnerable. When The AP makes a mistake, as it does from time to time, the error is transmitted almost instantly across the nation and the world and frequently it is enshrined in print and rarely corrected. And as the wire service has gone into more sophisticated technology, chances are better that once a mistake is made, it will stay made.

For example: wire service clients receive stories via printout from a machine that resembles an electric typewriter, as before, but now many newspapers use attachments to convert the electrical impulses to perforated tape, which is fed directly into Linotype machines. Thus money-conscious publishers (there is no other kind) are not going to be happy with a telegraph editor who fools around with an AP story, whether it's to correct an error or to insert a clarifying fact, since every line he changes represents type that must be set by a human being who draws a paycheck.

There are some other mistakes that are not so forgivable. One of the more dramatic recent ones was the Arnett Affair. In May, 1970, AP's highly competent war correspondent, Peter Arnett, a young Pulitzer Prize-winning New Zealander, was covering the U.S. invasion (or incursion, as The AP would have it) of Cambodia. He entered one town with U.S. troops; they looted the town; Arnett filed the story. When it got to New York for relay to domestic newspapers, the desk deleted references to the looting. A cable went from New York to an angry Saigon bureau:

WE ARE IN THE MIDST OF A HIGHLY CHARGED SITUATION IN UNISTATES REGARDING SOUTHEAST ASIA AND MUST GUARD OUR COPY TO SEE THAT IT IS DOWN THE MIDDLE AND SUBDUES EMOTION. SPECIFICALLY TODAY WE TOOK LOOTING AND SIMILAR REFERENCES OUT OF ARNETT COPY BECAUSE WE DON'T THINK IT'S ESPECIALLY NEWS THAT SUCH THINGS TAKE PLACE IN WAR AND IN PRESENT CONTEXT THIS CAN BE INFLAMMATORY.

The exchange got out, of course, and when *Newsweek* called Wes Gallagher for comment, the general manager termed it an "error in judgment," took personal responsibility, and said, "The episode is over."

For some staffers, though, the episode is not at all over. One of them, a respected AP newsman, said: "Does the decision mean The Associated Press is in the business of helping governments keep some kind of lid on? I mean, if you know something, and you know that to report it would create trouble, what are the guidelines for *not* reporting it? Is Gallagher saying that there should be *no* suppression of news and that we made a mistake, or is he saying that there *is* a time for suppression but that this particular story shouldn't have been suppressed?"

Incidents of this sort, coupled with the tendency of younger staffers at AP, as in many other places, to view the world with a more radicalized eye, have led to a greater degree of internal rumbling at The AP. One manifestation of this was the appearance in the summer of 1970 of two issues of *The AP Review*, an anonymous newsletter put together by AP employees.

In a general statement about why there was a need for an underground journal at The AP, *The Review*'s editors said: "AP's coverage is not even adequate in many of the important areas of news today: race relations, youth, radical and black politics, feminism and homosexuality. Our 'in-depth' stories are momentously shallow. Our dependence on official sources for the greatest part of our information is inexcusable." In addition to a piece on the suppression of the looting story, *The Review* carried stories on women's lib (the Mod Squad, it said, was "this year's garnish"); the sad lack of blacks in the organization (there are about fifteen black reporters at The AP now; only one, Austin Scott, "holds a writing position of any prestige"); and the allegation that "The Associated Press makes a practice of providing police and the FBI with information its reporters gather."

That last charge, if true, would seriously damage the reputation of The Associated Press. Management says it is not true. There are, in fact, examples of AP's resistance to the FBI. Stephen Green, formerly in The AP's Philadelphia bureau, says an FBI agent tried to get information by telephone from him after he had written a story quoting someone who took credit for a raid on a draft board. Green refused the request, and his supervisor backed him up. An FBI agent arrived at the office 45 minutes later with grand jury subpoenas; AP's New York lawyers were called, and "they backed me up 100 per cent," said Green. The agent left, returning half an hour later to retrieve the writs.

It is a certainty, though, that a substantial number of younger AP staffers *believe* there are collaborators in their midst: editors, deskmen and supervisory people who have close liaisons with the FBI and who use the good name of The AP and the "covers" of its reporters to collect information that is destined not for news stories but for the dossier-keepers. Some staffers feel that the New York City bureau is a focus of such activity and that Doug Lovelace, the chief of the bureau, is especially friendly with the feds.

Lovelace denies this. "My relations with the FBI are strictly professional," he said not long ago. "I know who the key people are there. We're pleasant with each other, I try to get things out of them, and I guess we get the same treatment everybody else gets. I say this categorically: I have never been asked to do anything by the FBI, and I have not served as any kind of a conduit. As a matter of fact, I won't *permit* the FBI to harass any of my reporters."

But the belief persists. A former staffer, Terri Shaw, says she found it strange that, after the 11th Street townhouse bombing last year, The AP started to collect information on the Weathermen, and Lovelace came up with the address of a Bronx commune the police were watching and even drove her there in his car. Says Lovelace now: "It was one of those things I kept an eye on. I was able to obtain—and I'm not going into the background of it—the addresses of places which had been communes." Pressed on where he got the addresses, he replied: "I'm just not going to answer that question. I will say that the list wasn't up to date."

Another former staffer says Lovelace goes to FBI office parties. Lovelace: "I have never been at an FBI office party. I have been to those annual Police Department-FBI steak fries on City Island, at the police shooting range."

Joel Dreyfuss, another former staffer, was sent by the New York bureau to a gathering of the Young Lords back when they were first becoming newsworthy. "I was asked [by a bureau supervisor] for a list of their leaders and their titles," he said. "I never thought anything of it. I guess I supposed it was going into a story. I never saw the story or the list again. After that, when I'd work on a story, I'd warn people. I'd say, 'I work for The AP; don't give me any more information than you want the police to have.'"

Lovelace: "I would assume that we'd want to find out what the structure of a new organization is—who you contact. I see nothing sinister in that. I would assume the FBI has much better information than we could possibly have. We want to know whom to call if something comes up."

Another former staffer, Ruth Mac-Naughton, was working in The AP's photo library in the summer of 1968 when violence broke out during the Democratic National Convention. "The library assistants were asked to gather all negatives pertaining to the demonstrations in Chicago," she recalled, "and those negatives were in turn loaned to the FBI for a short period." What was wanted, she said, were pictures that otherwise had not been used by The AP. "It was clear what they wanted," she said. "We were told by our supervisors that they were going to the FBI." Miss MacNaughton thinks "at least a hundred" negatives were involved.

Wes Gallagher, asked about the allegations in general, replied: "There's not one bit of truth in that at all. We don't cooperate with them." He said he had never heard of the story about the Chicago negatives. "As a matter of fact," he said, "when this business came up about subpoenaing reporters' notes and photographs, they got instructions to destroy any negative that we didn't use. Anything that we *have* is something that's been published. If they want it, they can get it out of the newspapers. As a protective measure we just don't keep those unused negatives around any more."

Miss Yvanna Mundell is a supervisor in The AP photo library, has been for 28 years, and was mentioned by Miss MacNaughton as one of those who told her to pull negatives. Miss Mundell was asked about the allegation.

"You know," she started out, "our files can be subpoenaed at any time. From time to time we *have* had the police coming by, asking for specific pictures—demonstrations, and so on. So they can see them better. This has happened at various and sundry times —oh, maybe once in a great while. Maybe ten times in the 28 years I've been here.

"It's true that we have had requests from the FBI. We're a news *service*. We sell pictures to people who're writing stories in magazines and other places. If the FBI calls and asks for something, we treat them the same as if somebody who's anti-FBI calls. We cannot be partial here."

Miss Mundell said she couldn't remember whether any police had sought pictures after the Chicago demonstrations. She was asked about the policy of destroying unused negatives.

"Absolutely not true," she replied. "*All* negatives are kept. Whoever said that is wrong."

She was told that Wes Gallagher had said it.

"Well," she said, "Mr. Gallagher is wrong."

It is difficult to tell whether the paranoia over the FBI is founded in reality or fantasy; whether there is a general pattern of cooperation or some foolish isolated examples. As you may have noticed, what was written in the paragraphs above was written according to the AP Formula: charges and denials. You didn't really learn very much. What the argument might boil down to is, in the words of one cynical staffer, the fact that "We don't really have anything to give to the FBI. In 99 per cent of the cases, The AP gets *its* information from the cops, or the FBI, or some agency like that." And that, said the staffer, is "even scarier than some guy in the office playing cops and robbers."

But even if that specific issue were removed, the level of discontent at The AP would probably be high because the question of relevance still would not be resolved. Nor should the discontent be explained away as a simple clash between the necessarily competitive younger and older members of the organization. More than that, it is a clash of ideology between the institution and its younger members. A biased listing of the issues would include:

☐ A reliance on official sources to a degree approaching reverence. With this goes a lack of mechanisms for questioning the veracity of people in official positions. The AP still refers to one of its star reporters as a "friend of Presidents." There is no one who is called a "friend of malcontents" or "friend of the poor."

☐ A tendency (ground into every newsman's brain from his first days in a newsroom, by simple stimulus-response technique; the good reporters, people like Homer Bigart of *The Times,* constantly resist it) to have more *respect* for certain news situations than for others. And the greatest degree of respect is always reserved for the System.

☐ A fundamentally small-town view of America, with its attendant distrust of cities and of laboring men who belong to unions and/or work inside factories, and of black people. A trust in the allegedly simple things, like farm-land, suburbs, small towns, farmers, general practitioners in medicine, and people who work out-of-doors. An AP reporter who has won the Pulitzer Prize for his reporting of Southern civil rights news, and who lives in New York City, once stated unashamed-ly in barroom conversation that his wife had dragged him to a performance of the New York City Ballet and that he had become very upset at the sight of a black male dancer with his arms around a white ballerina.

☐ A deep fear, approaching hatred, of "advocacy journalism," coupled with an inability to come up with a clear definition of advocacy journalism ex-cept as something that isn't impartial and objective, together with the refusal to admit that there is no such thing as workable impartiality and objec-tivity.

The young reporters, many of them, represent a different set of ideals:

☐ The assumption that people in of-ficial positions are not endowed with any special immunity, extraordinary grace, or surplus honesty, and that, by the process of getting into the posi-tions they now occupy, such people have accumulated *prima facie* creden-tials as liars.

☐ Feelings about the System that range from distrust to skepticism to outright hatred.

☐ A cosmopolitan view of America, based on the belief that there is a lot wrong with the country, and it's just as wrong in small towns and sub-urbia as it in the cities.

☐ The younger reporters are not sold on advocacy journalism, either, if by advocacy journalism you mean the license to render summary personal judgments in print. They do believe in a re-evaluation of what constitutes news and what constitutes getting it; they want the time, money, and re-sources to pursue complicated, impor-tant stories.

☐ Despite The AP's stated commit-ment to cover some of those impor-tant stories, it's not doing the job at anything approaching its potential. The cities, for instance: the New York bureau has 54 to 60 newsmen, about half of whom work on the desk. The man covering Brooklyn, a borough of 2,570,624 souls, is not a full-time staffer but a "stringer," who also reports for other publications. At the moment, the New York bureau reports, there are no staffers in the city who "consider them-selves specialists in race relations." The last one was Austin Scott, but he's in Washington now.

Scott, *the* black reporter, is a mem-ber of the Special Assignment Team, and a good young reporter, and an out-spoken one. He takes frequent ad-vantage of the AP rule that any em-ployee can write directly to the gen-eral manager and get a reply, and he has conducted a fair-sized correspond-ence with Wes Gallagher on the sub-ject of hiring more black reporters and being more relevant. (There aren't many blacks, says the head office, be-cause it's a "seller's market" in black journalists.)

Scott travels much of the time, be-cause there are a lot of stories that require the services of a black reporter. Ordinarily, a wire-service specialist who's on the road will check in with local bureaus and ask the men there for an update. Scott rarely does this, he says, because few people in the bureaus know or care about what's happening in race relations.

"We do have people who keep abreast of the Establishment political trends," he said. "We *don't* have peo-ple who keep up with that sort of thing on the urban scene, or the mi-nority affairs scene. I think it's ex-tremely essential that we have that, because whatever areas you move in in this country, there's a lack of in-formation. East Palo Alto, California, put together a very interesting com-munity school. Washington, D.C., put together a very interesting community school. Boston has school problems. Neither the mayor nor the black ac-tivists nor most other people in Bos-ton, unless they have direct personal lines of contact, know what's happen-ing in the other two situations.

"The AP, to me, is *the* place to do this kind of reporting, because it's the only good nationwide medium, aside from UPI and television, and television has its own problems. The thing that hurts me the most about AP is that it's got so goddam much potential."

Of course, if the members of AP—the newspapers and broadcasters whose assessments keep the organization running—were to demand the sort of reporting that Scott and others want, the situation might be different. But they don't, and that is one of the troubles with a cooperative. There is a certain amount of common-denomi-nationalism in a cooperative, and the common denominator of the American press is shamefully low—not really interested in the deeper issues and, more than anything else, *afraid* to admit that those deeper issues exist, because that would require tackling them.

Back in the corner office at Rockefeller Plaza, with the Teletypes pounding away in the closet, Wes Gallagher toyed with a question about the mission of The AP. He wasn't satisfied with his verbal answers; a few days later he put it in writing:

The Associated Press' task is to gather and distribute daily as continuous and as complete a picture as possible of individuals and societies in action. This can and does on occasion include virtually every human endeavor from war to peace marches, stock market averages to art exhibits, poverty protests to corporate profits, and the activities of anyone from murderers to good samaritans. Having said that, something will come up tomorrow that will be outside that definition.

The phrase at The AP for newsmen who go beyond the limits of objectivity and impartiality is "activist reporters." To some members of management, it's a nasty phrase. To some of the reporters in question, it's a compliment. To others among the reporters in question, it's irrelevant. Said one of those in the last category, a young man who worked on *The AP Review:* "If an organization comes to the point of becoming a propaganda outfit, then perhaps you should destroy its credibility."

Gallagher said he hasn't had too much trouble with the activists, despite *The AP Review* and his correspondence with Austin Scott, at least compared with what's going on at some other newsgathering organizations.

"I have no quarrel with activist reporters or editors," he said, "but The AP is not the place for advocacy for any particular subject. If they want to go into that, they can go to anything from *The Nation* to *The National Review* and any variation in between. But it isn't The AP's function, and I think it's destructive of journalism. The AP cannot be an activist in the sense of advocacy journalism; cannot be and must not be. I think it would destroy this organization.

"I think you'll find on any paper a lot of young reporters who criticize what's put into that paper. We have exactly that same criticism throughout this organization. And if we didn't we'd be a damn lousy organization. *Damn* lousy. You have to have that sort of thing. If you can come up with a solution as to how we can communicate with what's on all these people's minds, I'd love to have it. It's very difficult. It's an ironic thing that one of our problems is communicating with our own people.

"I don't know of a single news organization that isn't sort of an organized anarchy, where everybody gets up and shoots in all directions. It goes with the territory, I suppose."

A few days later, and a few floors beneath Gallagher's office, in the big newsroom where the Teletypes are not muffled, a reporter who considers himself slightly radicalized (at least radical enough not to consider *The Nation* as one end of any spectrum) described a bit of what he called guerrilla warfare. He had been rewriting a story, he said, a meat-and-potatoes piece about what the U.S. was doing in Asia, and he deliberately used the word "invasion," knowing that the rule, since President Nixon had spoken on the subject, was to call it an "incursion." Said the reporter: "Sometimes you write it the way you feel it should be written, even though you know it'll be changed. Sometimes there's a sympathetic deskman who won't change it, though, and sometimes they're just too busy to notice."

Topics for Discussion

1. Why does Powledge say that the Associated Press "suffers its headquarters" to be located in New York? Why does Powledge suggest that the AP would prefer to be located elsewhere? What evidence does he offer to support this statement?
2. Younger staff members of the AP, and other critics, contend that the AP is not relevant enough and does not cover important stories. What are some of these stories? Do you agree that they are indeed important? Do you agree that they have been neglected?
3. Do you think reporters should accept as fact information they receive from public relations men, government spokesmen, or other people in official positions speaking officially?
4. Does every issue have two sides? Can you think of any issue that has more than two sides? Only one side?
5. What does Powledge mean by the AP's "cult of objectivity"?
6. Should the news media report "just the bare bones of the news"? Is such reporting misleading?
7. Select a current newsstory and compare the reporting of it by the Associated Press and United Press International (UPI). What differences in the two do you find?

Rhetorical Considerations

1. What is the thesis of the essay? Where is it stated?
2. How objective is this essay? Does Powledge give all sides of the issue? Is he guilty of the kind of false objectivity he accuses the AP of?
3. What is the initial picture of the AP Powledge paints? Does he prejudice his readers against the AP at the beginning of the essay?
4. Powledge implies a lot of things in this essay, not the least of which is his belief that, in terms of news, New York is more important than the Midwest. List other such implied beliefs. How do these influence Powledge's arguments?
5. Why does Powledge feel it necessary to summarize the issues at the end of his essay?
6. What effect does Powledge achieve by concluding his essay with a quotation from a disenchanted AP reporter?

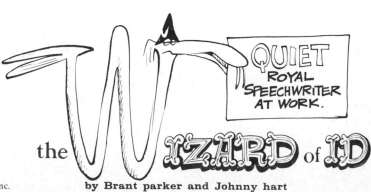

By permission of John Hart and Field Enterprises, Inc.

the WIZARD of ID

by Brant parker and Johnny hart

The Age of Communication

NOTES ON THE NEW JOURNALISM

Michael J. Arlen

It's probably easier than it should be to dismiss the articles which appeared recently in *New York* magazine on the subject of "The New Journalism." In the first place, the articles, which were by Tom Wolfe (himself a founding member of *New York* and author of *The Kandy-Kolored Tangerine-Flake Streamline Baby)*, had most of the defects of the form he was extolling—the pop sociology, the easy cultural generalities—with few of the compensating attractions—the dramatic scene-setting, the impressionistic color (such as had made, for instance, his own piece on the stock-car racer Junior Johnson so vivid and fascinating to read). "The voice of the narrator, in fact, was one of the great problems in non-fiction writing," Dr. Wolfe now intoned. Also: "The modern notion of art is an essentially religious or magical one . . ." etc. Also: "Queen Victoria's childhood diaries are, in fact, quite readable." Also: "Literary people were oblivious to this side of the New Journalism, because it is one of the unconscious assumptions of modern criticism that the raw material is simply 'there.'" And so forth. In the second place, although it must have been fun to work at the *Herald Tribune* in its last few years of existence—when and where, according to Wolfe, the birth of New Journalism mostly occurred—he manages to describe this great moment in Western cultural life with a school-boy reverence which somehow doesn't leave anyone else much breathing room, a combination of Stalky & Co. and The Day That Curie Discovered Radium. In Tom Wolfe's world, in fact (as he might say), there is perpetual struggle between a large and snooty army of crumbs, known as the Literary People, who are the bad guys, and Tom's own band of good guys: rough-and-tumble fellows like Jimmy Breslin, dashing reporters such as Dick Schaap, the savvy nonintellectuals, the aces, the journalistic guerrilla fighters, the good old boys who "never guessed for a minute that the work they would do over the next ten years, as journalists, would wipe out the novel as literature's main event."

It's easy enough to fault this sort of treatment of a complicated subject. A bit too simpleminded. Too in-groupish. Me and My Pals Forge History Together. All the same, it seems to me that beneath, or despite, the blather, Tom Wolfe is right about a lot of it. And very wrong too. And journalism is perhaps in the kind of muddle it's in today not, lord knows, because Tom Wolfe sat down at his bench one day and invented a new art form, but because people in general, editors as well as writers as well as readers, have had trouble figuring out how to deal with this terrain that he and many, many other journalists have steadily been pushing their way into over a period of a good many years.

To begin with, of course, one can say that the New Journalism *isn't* new. That's a favorite put-down: the New Journalist prances down the street, grabbing innocent bystanders by the lapels, and breathlessly (or worse, earnestly) declaiming about his "new fictional techniques," or his "neo-Jamesian point of view," or his "seeing the world in novelistic terms" and all the rest of it, while the Old Literary Person gazes out his window and mutters: "New Journalism, indeed! What about Addison and Steele, eh? What about Defoe? What about Mencken? Joe Mitchell? Hemingway? Mark Twain?" That's right in a sense, but not, I think, in the most meaningful sense. It's right, at any rate, that there's been a vein of personal journalism in English and American writing for a very long time. For example, Defoe in his *Journal of the Plague Year* developed for *his* subject the same sort of new techniques that the New Journalists discovered yesterday—namely, he wrote it in the manner of a personal autobiographical narrative, and made up the narrative (although not the details, which he got from records and interviews) since he was about five years old when the incident took place. For example, Joseph Mitchell published a remarkable series of pieces in *The New Yorker* in the early 1940s on New York fish-market life—full of impressionistic detail, and centering on a man whom he had also invented: Mr. Flood. In a prefatory note to the first piece, Mitchell wrote: "Mr. Flood is not one man; combined in him are aspects of several men who work or hang out in Fulton Fish Market, or who did in the past. I wanted these stories to be truthful rather than factual, but they are solidly based on facts."

Here, by the way, is the opening passage from "Old Mr. Flood":

"A tough Scotch-Irishman I know, Mr. Hugh G. Flood, a retired house-wrecking contractor, aged ninety-three, often tells people that he is dead set and

*determined to live until the afternoon of July 27, 1965,
when he will be a hundred and fifteen years old. 'I don't
ask much here below,' he says. 'I just want to hit a
hundred and fifteen. That'll hold me.' Mr. Flood is
small and wizened. His eyes are watchful and icy blue,
and his face is . . ."*

Here is the opening to *The Earl of Louisiana*, by A.
J. Liebling:

*"Southern political personalities, like sweet corn,
travel badly. They lose flavor with every hundred yards
away from the patch. By the time they reach New
York, they are like Golden Bantam that has been
trucked up from Texas—stale and unprofitable. The
consumer forgets that the corn tastes different where it
grows. That, I suppose, is why for twenty-five years I
underrated Huey Pierce Long . . ."*

Here is the opening to *Homage to Catalonia*, by
George Orwell, published in 1938:

*"In the Lenin Barracks in Barcelona, the day before
I joined the militia, I saw an Italian militiaman standing in front of the officers' table. He was a tough-look-
ing youth of twenty-five or six, with reddish-yellow hair
and powerful shoulders. His peaked leather cap was
pulled fiercely over one eye. He was standing in profile
to me, his chin on his breast, gazing with a puzzled
frown at a map which one of the officers had opened on
the table. Something in his face deeply moved me. It
was the face of a man who would commit murder and
throw away his life for a friend . . ."*

And here is the opening of Tom Wolfe's piece on
Phil Spector, the rock music figure:

"All these raindrops are high *or something. They
don't roll down the window, they come straight back,
toward the tail, wobbling, like all those Mr. Cool
snowheads walking on mattresses. The plane is taxiing
out toward the runway to take off, and this stupid in-
farcted water wobbles, sideways, across the window.
Phil Spector, 23 years old, the rock and roll magnate,
producer of Philles Records, America's first teen-age
tycoon, watches . . . this watery pathology . . . it is
sick, fatal . . ."*

According to Tom Wolfe and the various unoffi-
cial histories of New Journalism, something marvelous, exciting, dramatic—a light of revelation—happened to Old Journalism in the hands of the young
hotshots at *Esquire* and the *Herald Tribune*. Since
then, the novel has never been the same. A new art
form was created. And so forth.

I wonder if what happened wasn't more like this:
that, despite the periodic appearance of an Addison,
or Defoe, or Twain, standard newspaper journalism

remained a considerably constricted branch of writing, both in England and America, well into the nineteen twenties. It's true that the English had this agreeable, essayist, public-school-prose tradition of personal observation, which filtered down into their newspapers. *"As I chanced to take leave of my café on Tuesday, or Wednesday, of last week, and finding myself sauntering toward the interesting square in Sarajevo,"* the English correspondent would write, *"I happened to observe an unusual, if not a striking, occurrence . . ."* Even so, in spite of the "I," and the saunterings, and the meanderings, and the Chancellor-Schmidlap-informed-me-in-private business, English journalism was for the most part as inhibited, and official, and focused as was the society which paid for it and read it.

In America there was much of the same thing—some of it better, a lot of it worse. The American daily press didn't go in as strongly for the sauntering *I,* except for the snobbier Eastern papers, which presumably were keen to imitate the English style. The American press rested its weight upon the simple declarative sentence. The no-nonsense approach. Who-What-Where-When. Clean English, it was later called when people started teaching it at college. Lean prose. Actually, it was two things at once. It was the prose of a Europe-oriented nation trying to put aside somebody else's fancy ways and speak in its own voice. But it was also the prose of the first true technological people—Who? What? Where? When? Just give us the facts, ma'am—the prose of an enormously diverse nation that was caught up with the task (as with the building of the railroads) of bridging, of diminishing this diversity.

In those days, when something happened, an event—a hotel fire, for example—newspapers generally gave you certain facts, embedded in an official view. No matter that the reporter himself, personally, was a hotshot, a drinker, a roarer, an admirer of Yeats, a swashbuckler of the city room; in most instances he gave you the official view of the fire. Where it was. How many people got burned. How much property got damaged. What Fire Commissioner Snooks said of the performance of his men. And so forth.

Then, after the First World War, especially after the literary resurgence in the nineteen twenties—the *writers'* world of Paris, Hemingway, Fitzgerald, etc.—into the relatively straitlaced, rectilinear, dutiful world of conventional journalism appeared an assortment of young men who wanted to do it differently. Alva Johnson. John McNulty. St. Clair McKelway. Vincent Sheean. Mitchell. Liebling. And

HERE, SIRE... I JUST FINISHED IT!

god knows who else. A lot of them worked for the old *Herald Tribune*. Later, many of them connected in one way or another with *The New Yorker*. What they did to journalism I think was this: first, they made it somehow *respectable* to write journalism. A reporter was no longer a crude fellow in a fedora. He was a widely informed traveler (like Sheean), or had an elegant prose style (like McKelway), or a gusto for listening and finding out things (like Mitchell or Liebling). Second, when they looked at this same hotel fire, and how it had been covered by their predecessors and colleagues, they noted that, at the Fire Commissioner's briefing, for the most part no one started his camera, or pencil, until the Fire Commissioner came into the room, and walked to the lectern, and opened his Bible, and began to speak. One imagines that these young men saw things otherwise. Movies were already by then a part of the culture, although admittedly a lowly part of the culture. Motion was a part of the new vocabulary. And total deference to the Fire Commissioner, or to the General, or to the Admiral, had already begun its twentieth-century erosion. The *new* thing, it seems to me, that the writer-journalists of the 1930s and 40s brought to the craft was a sense, an interest, in what went on before (and after) the Fire Commissioner came into the room. What did he do when he got on the elevator downstairs? Did he drop a quarter on the floor? What were his *movements?* For the first time in conventional reporting people began to move. They had a journalistic existence on either side of the event. Not only that, but the focus itself shifted away from the Fire Commissioner or the man who owned the hotel, and perhaps in the direction of the man who pumped the water, or the night clerk at the hotel across the way. Thus: reduced deference to official figures. (For example: James Agee's *Let Us Now Praise Famous Men.*) Personal touches. Dialogue—in fact, real speech faithfully recorded. When you read a McKelway piece on Walter Winchell, for example, you found a public hero taken to task, you found out what Winchell did when he wasn't in the public view, and you heard him speak—not quotes for the press, but what he said when he was ordering a ham on rye. "I'll have a ham on rye." Few reporters had done that before. Newspapers hadn't had the space. And besides (editors said), who wants to know what Bismarck had for breakfast, or what his ordinary comments sound like.

Then time passes. The scene shifts—everybody shifts. The nineteen fifties. The nineteen sixties. Tom Wolfe writes that he came out of college, or graduate school, burdened like the rest of his generation with

the obligation to write a novel—only to discover suddenly that the time of the novel was past. I don't know whom Tom Wolfe was talking to in graduate school, or what he was reading, but back in the early nineteen fifties you didn't have to read every magazine on the newsstand to realize that a fairly profound change was already taking place in the nation's reading habits. Whether it was *Collier's, The Saturday Evening Post,* or *The New Yorker,* most magazines, which had been preponderantly devoted to fiction, were now increasingly devoted to nonfiction. It was also true, even then, that the novel itself was changing—changing, to be sure, as it had been since Henry James first gazed upward and noticed that the roof was off the cathedral. It was becoming easier, possibly, and more profitable, to become a novelist-disguised-as-screenwriter; but harder, perhaps, to become, and stay, a novelist of imagination and interior truth, which is what people increasingly seemed to be wanting of them. Mostly, in fact, one hears about the Death of the Novel from journalists, or from novelists-turned-journalists. And although there is only one *Painted Bird,* or *Separate Peace,* or *Play It As It Lays* produced in every twenty thousand books, people, the audience, still seem to be looking for *that* one; and the impress of each of those few books, I suspect, is still stronger and more lasting than nearly all the rest.

This brings us to the present state of the craft: the New Journalism. There is no getting around the point, I think, that a number of writers in the last dozen years have been exerting a steady (and often a self-dramatizing) push at the already-pushed boundaries of conventional journalism. I think of Gay Talese in many of his *Esquire* pieces, and especially in his last book, *Honor Thy Father.* I think of Terry Southern's magazine pieces, also for the most part in *Esquire.* Norman Mailer writing in *Harper's* about the peace march to the Pentagon, and the presidential campaign of 1968, and then in *Life* on the moon shot. Tom Wolfe and Breslin and Gail Sheehy and a whole lot of people who write for *New York.* Dan Wakefield in *The Atlantic.* John McPhee and Truman Capote in *The New Yorker.* A whole lot of people—sometimes they all seem to be the same person—who write in *The Village Voice.* Also: Nicholas von Hoffman, David Halberstam, Marshall Frady, Barry Farrell; and obviously a great many others. My guess is that anyone who denies that the best work of these writers has considerably expanded the possibilities of journalism—of looking at the world we're living in—is hanging on to something a bit too tightly in his own past. And on the other hand, that anyone who feels a

IT RUNS ABOUT **24** MINUTES ...WITH PAUSES.

WHAT PAUSES?

8-6

The Age of Communication

need to assert that the work, especially the whole work, of these men composes a new art form, and a total blessing, is by and large talking through his hat.

Consider the mythic hotel fire we were talking about. Today, when a New Journalist tells it, there is likely to be *no* deference to an official version—if anything, perhaps a semiautomatic disdain of one. There is virtually no interest in the traditional touchstone facts, the *numbers*—the number of people dead, or saved, or staying at the hotel, the worth of the jewelry, or the cost of damage to the building. Instead, there are attempts to catch the heat of the flames, the *feel* of the fire. We get snatches of dialogue—dialogue overheard. A stranger passes by, says something to another stranger, both disappear. Rapid motion. Attempts to translate the paraphernalia of photography—the zoom lens, film-cutting. Disconnection. And nearly always the presence of the journalist, the writer—*his* voice. Our event, in fact—the fire—has seemingly changed in the course of time from (once) existing solely as an official rectilinear fact, to (later) a more skeptically official, looser, more written, human account, to (now) its present incarnation in New Journalism as a virtually antiofficial, impressionist, nonfactual, totally personal account of a happening—which often now is only permitted to exist for us within the journalist's personality.

The chief merits and demerits of New Journalism seem then as basic as these: the merit is—who really wants to read about this fire as it is likely to be presented in the New York *Times* or in a standard newspaper report? For those who *do* want to, the standard newspaper will give you the traditional facts: the number of people in the hotel, the number of people killed, who owns the hotel, etc. The standard newspaper considers these facts important, because (apparently) the standard newspaper for the last seventy-five years or more has considered these facts important. Here is the beginning of a front-page story in the New York *Times* on the controversial and emotional subject of housing in Forest Hills: "*A compromise plan to end the fight over the Forest Hills low-income housing project has been worked out by top aides of Mayor Lindsay, including former Deputy Mayor Richard R. Aurelio, and has been discussed privately with leaders of blacks and Jews and with high-ranking officials. The plan would call for a scaling-down of the Forest Hills project by about a third and the revival of the project for the Lindenwood section of Queens that was recently killed by the Board of Esti-*

THE CALCULATED PERIODS ALLOCATED FOR APPLAUSE, SIRE.

mate. The Lindenwood project, however, would be smaller than the earlier one. . ." If this is the voice of conventional journalism speaking to us about our world, it is likely to find an increasingly restless, disconnected audience. The voice speaks too thin a language. The world it tells us about so assiduously seems but a small part of the world that is actually outside the window—seems a dead world, peopled largely by official figures, and by procedural facts, and written about in a fashion which is doubtless intended to be clear, and clean, and easy to understand, but which instead is usually flat, and inhuman, and nearly impossible to connect to.

If then the merit of New Journalism is that it affords us the possibility of a wider view of the world, a glimpse of the variousness and disorder of life, its demerits, I think, are that these possibilities are so seldom realized, or at such cost to the reality-mechanism of the reader. For instance, in the matter of our hotel fire; there is no need, it seems to me, for a journalist today to relate all the traditional facts (especially since most of them, in this sort of story, are basically concerned with Property); but if he is to tell it as a *real* story, an account of an event that actually happened, I think there is a very deep requirement on the part of the reader (usually not expressed, or not expressed at the time) that the objects in the account be real objects. If the fire took place at the Hotel Edgewater, probably one ought to know that much, and certainly not be told that it was the Hotel Bridgewater. "But what does it matter?" says the New Journalist. "That's not the important thing, is it?" In many ways it isn't, but in serious ways it is. It's a commonplace by now that contemporary life doesn't provide us with many stable navigational fixes on reality; and that we need them, and have trouble, privately and publicly, when we are too long without. Families. Schools. The Government. Movies. Television. None of these contribute much anymore to informing us of the actual objects in the actual room we move about in. Journalism *should* materially help us with this, but all too rarely does— is either too conventionally timid, or, with the New Journalist, too often (I think) gives up the task of telling us of the actual arrangement of the objects, or at any rate of trying to find out, get close to it, in favor of the journalist's *own* imposed ordering of these objects.

By no means all New Journalism is careless. Talese, for example, seems to be remarkably meticulous as to detail. Mailer's account of the march on the Pentagon seems to have been extremely faithful to

The Age of Communication

what happened. There are other examples, although not, I suspect, all that many. *A careful writer.* That was Joe Liebling's way of praising a fellow journalist, his highest praise. There are probably few careful writers around anymore. And few careful editors. Few careful generals. Few careful stockbrokers. Few careful *readers.* This doesn't seem to be a very careful period we are living in. Relationships seem to break apart . . . carelessly. Wars are waged . . . carelessly. Harmful drugs are put on the market . . . carelessly. A soldier kills ("wastes") two hundred unarmed civilians . . . carelessly; and his countrymen, when told of this, first don't want to hear, then turn away . . . carelessly. The point is not that it is a better or worse era than Liebling's, nor that there is any sure way of measuring it—but it is different.

And swirling all about us—still swirling, although the motion has somewhat abated—has been the great sexual lather of the 1960s. It was in the sixties, wasn't it, that we first had the miniskirt. Wife-swapping. Sex clubs. Swinging. The Pill. The sexuality of Kennedy politics. The new dances. Grove Press best sellers. *I Am Curious, Yellow*—and showing at a chic theater. The sexual emancipation of women. Kaffeeklatsches about the clitoral orgasm. All those strident sexy costumes—the cutout clothes, the glaring colors, the *threads* that lawyers started to wear on weekends, the big wide ties, the sideburns. Esalen. Touch therapy. Everybody (it seemed) committed to being sexy, or at any rate aware of it, or at any rate trying to deal with it. Since then, some of the stridency has quieted down a bit. Sex in writing, for instance, seems to be less insistent and obligatory. We've just had *Love Story,* haven't we? Fashion magazines have started muttering about a Return to Elegance, whatever that may mean. But it was back in the sixties that New Journalism made its big push—a debut which Tom Wolfe seems to think derived from some magic confluence of the stars, or at least from some solemn discovery of the Death of the Novel. I wouldn't say that it wasn't *at all* the way he says it was—but my guess is that a lot of what's happened in New Journalism has as much to do with the New Carelessness of the times, and the sexual stridency of writers (and of nearly everyone else), as it has to do with attempts to evolve freer journalistic techniques.

At any rate, the new journalistic techniques have produced a mightily uneven body of work. Some of it is as good as, for instance, Wolfe's own *Electric Kool-*

Aid Acid Test—but much of it—for example a recent piece in *Rolling Stone* by Hunter Thompson on the New Hampshire primaries—is slipshod and self-serving. Partly this is because of the times we live in, and how both writers and readers respond to the times. Partly, too, it's because—with one, or two, or two-and-a-half exceptions—there are virtually no prose editors anymore. Already in reporting, one notes that what used to be called a reporter is now called an "investigative reporter"; the reporter is presumably the fellow who informs us that the President is now standing in the doorway of the plane. And in editing, the person who deals with the bloody manuscript is now somebody called the "copy" or "text" editor, and works in a small office behind the broom closet; while the Editor, of course, is the man having lunch with Clifford Irving. Editors today lunch, and make deals, and assign subjects—"concepts"—and discourse airily on the "new freedom" which they now provide writers; which in fact means that the Editor can remain at lunch, and not be much bothered on his return by a responsibility to his writer's story, or to his writer's subject, because he usually has none, claims none. And writers, for their part, are just as keen to escape the strictures of traditional editing—as indeed are so many others in our society to escape the traditional strictures of *their* lives, marriages, families, jobs; and possibly for the same sort of reasons.

Writers. Writer-journalists. It is clearly a splendid thing, a sexy thing, to be a writer-journalist these days. Admirals, aviators, bishops—everyone has his day. Today it is the journalist (and some others). He declaims about the end-of-the-novel while he hitchhikes on the novel. He has small patience for the dreary conventions of the Old Journalism, although he rides upon its credibility, on the fact that most people will buy and read his work on the assumption (built up by his predecessors) that when he writes: "Startled, the Pope awoke to find the Hotel Bridgewater in flames," it was indeed the Bridgewater, not the Edgewater, and that it was, in fact, the Pope. Even so, this is not the worst of crimes. When people complain too much about inaccuracy, or inattention to detail, it seems to me they are usually talking about something else, perhaps a larger, muddled conflict of life-views.

Where I find the real failure in New Journalism, or in much of it anyway, is in the New Journalist's determination and insistence that we shall see life largely on *his* terms. Granted one knows, by now, the

pitfalls of conventional "objectivity." One is aware of the inaccuracies and timidities which so often have resulted from on-the-one-hand . . . on-the-other-hand reporting. Still, there is something troubling and askew in the arrogance—and perhaps especially in the personal unease—that so often seems to compel the New Journalist to present us our reality embedded in his own ego. A classic example of this, I thought, was Mailer's *Of a Fire on the Moon,* with its generalities about engineers and scientists—generalities which seemed less concerned with what scientists or engineers might be, even if one could generalize about them, than in the ego-ability of the writer to generalize about them. Lesser talents and egos than Mailer are less noticeable, although it seems to me that much, if not most, routine New Journalism—I am thinking of the dozens of pieces about movie stars and politicians that appear in magazines each year—consists in exercises by writers (admittedly often charming, or funny, or dramatically written exercises) in gripping and controlling and confining a subject within the journalist's own temperament. Presumably, this is the "novelistic technique." But in fact Madame Bovary is a creature of Flaubert's—regardless of whether Flaubert once spent a summer in Innsbruck with a lady who looked vaguely like her, and who expressed dissatisfaction with her husband. Whereas Phil Spector, for example, in the Tom Wolfe piece, or Bill Bonanno in *Honor Thy Father,* or George Meany in a *Harper's* piece by John Corry all are real people, *nobody's* creatures, certainly not a journalist's creatures—real people whose real lives exist on either side of the journalist's column of print. The New Journalist is in the end, I think, less a journalist than an impresario. Tom Wolfe presents . . . Phil Spector! Jack Newfield presents . . . Nelson Rockefeller! Norman Mailer presents . . . the Moon Shot! And the complaint is not that the New Journalist doesn't present the totality of someone's life, because nobody can do that—but that, with his ego, he rules such thick lines down the edges of his own column of print. Nothing appears to exist outside the lines—except that, of course, it does. As readers, as *audience,* despite our modern bravado, I don't think we show much more willingness, let alone eagerness, than we ever did to come to terms with this disorder—the actuality, the nonstorybook element in life. And it seems to me that, on the whole, the New Journalist (despite *his* bravado) hasn't risked much in this direction either; and if you think none of it matters, my guess is you're wrong. □

The "new journalism" we need

GERALD GRANT

Several months after Benjamin Bradlee left *Newsweek* to become managing editor of the Washington *Post,* a series of staff shakeups began. After the first wave one of the editors invited a dozen young city staff reporters to lunch. As he sipped his Dubonnet on the rocks we nervously wondered about our fate. Most of what he said now escapes me. But I have a vivid recollection of his curiosity about the social circles we traveled in. Whom did we see? What parties did we go to? Whom did we know? His point was that a good deal of what went on in Washington could be learned at dinner parties—or at least that those who were able to establish a social relationship with sources after working hours were most likely to be privileged to the inside story on the job. Some of the best journalists in Washington had grown in reputation as their sources had grown in responsibility; in some cases they had been lucky enough to be classmates.

At the time his message struck me as mildly offensive. Not that it was pointless; his own prominent social connections had not hurt his career. As I look back, however, his inquiry no longer strikes me as saying so much about upward mobility of journalists as about patterns of thought in journalism. His comments underscored the idea that talent in journalism is often a skill for finding out what somebody *else* thinks or knows about something. It may be an oversimplification, yet it is true that lively concern for whom a journalist knows reflects weak appreciation for how he thinks.

What separates most journalists from the few great ones is that the latter are not content with knowing what their sources think. They exhibit an independent intelligence that seeks to wrest meaning from the torrent of events rather than

Gerald Grant, "The 'New Journalism' We Need," *Columbia Journalism Review* (Spring 1970). Reprinted by permission.

acting as mere transmission belts. They ask better questions because they have a better concept of what the "story" is.

There are some journalists who think, as Richard Hofstadter has said, in terms of configuration and style, thus delineating patterns as well as describing events. One recalls the work of Philip Meyer of the Knight Newspapers, who has effectively used social science skills to analyze current issues; of the perceptive reporting of Joseph Lelyveld and Anthony Lukas of the New York *Times;* of the probing exemplified by the work of Laurence Stern's and Richard Harwood's Insight Teams on the Washington *Post.* There has been a gratifying tendency on a number of papers such as *Newsday* and the Los Angeles *Times* to give reporters the time and freedom to do serious, thoughtful journalism. But as Daniel P. Moynihan said in his brilliant eulogy for Paul Niven, "[Journalism is] that most underdeveloped, least realized of professions. Not a profession at all, really. Rather a craft seeking to become such out of the need to impose form on an activity so vastly expanded in volume and significance as desperately to need the stabilizing influence of procedure and precedent and regularity."

Max Ways, in a *Fortune* article last October entitled "What's Wrong with News: It Isn't New Enough," attributes journalism's shortcomings to its failure to adopt new forms and new definitions of "the story." As a result of applying old yardsticks to events, he says, journalism continues to focus on what can be easily measured and told, to the neglect of more complex and important events unfolding in the society. But were the yardsticks ever any good? My guess is that journalism in 1870 failed in much the same ways it does today. The underlying explanation, then as now, is the kind of mental habits and attitudes most journalists bring to bear on events.

Journalists work by a code that makes many of them moral eunuchs. The professional, in print at least, generally pretends to be without opinions or convictions. His objectivity differs from that of the scientist who demands freedom to develop a fresh hypothesis but then remains objective in the sense that he will look in an unprejudiced way at the results of his experimentation.

Reportorial objectivity has been under vigorous attack by the "New Journalists." Citing Norman Mailer and others, they rightly sense that newsroom objectivity may result in untruth. It masks feelings and stifles imagination. More importantly, it can produce a trained incapacity for thought in the young journalist. Unconsciously he comes to believe that what he thinks doesn't matter. He regards himself as a conduit. The reporter calls an expert for a quote as an unfortunate shortcut to thinking the problem through himself. He asks not what do I think, but what do they think? That can be a habit difficult to break. He seldom has a sense of personal responsibility for what he writes.

This is why Michael Arlen, writing in *Living Room War,* is right when he characterizes much current journalism as propaganda. Not that experts shouldn't be interviewed, or that reporters must be philosopher-kings; but they should be something more than tape recorders. Most journalists are caught in a nether world. They are neither men of action, forced to confront a problem by struggling with it in an operational sense, nor men of true imagination or contemplation.

Yet uncritical enthusiasm for the New Journalism of passion and advocacy may cost more in the loss of the valuable skepticism of the traditional newspaperman than can be gained through the new involvement. The trouble with advocacy may be that it leads writers who haven't thought or felt much to portray cardboard emotions. Most readers would rather hear the experts. The challenge is to make sense out of the experts and of events. We don't need a whole new breed of novelists in action; we need more cogent journalism that tells us about problems rather than sketching conflict, that gives us the arguments rather than two sets of opposing conclusions. We do not need more passion but more intellect, more understanding.

While there are heartening signs of change, it

remains depressingly true that the rewards in journalism tend not to go to the writer who painstakingly thinks a problem through and expresses the subtleties, but to the author of jazzy personality pieces, scoops, and exposés. Exposés are nominated for prizes (often rightly so, of course) while a complicated piece of analysis wins the epithet "thumbsucker." These attitudes are related to the city-room environment where keen—often counter-productive—competition encourages reporters to jealously guard their scoops and current projects even from their co-workers. There is no incentive for the kind of intellectual sharing and discussion of first drafts that is common in an academic community or in any profession where the contributions and criticisms of one's colleagues are considered essential.

Work tends to be defined as scurrying about and asking questions. It is the rare reporter who has the fortitude to sit at his desk and read a book on a subject he intends to write about. Not infrequently one reads a long newspaper series—in which hundreds of man hours of reporting and travel time have been invested—and it is glaringly obvious that some of the most basic books written in that field have not been glanced at by the writers. I once asked Nicholas von Hoffman of the Washington *Post* how he avoided the usual pitfalls of newspaper writing. His exaggerated reply: "I never read newspapers."

Interestingly, von Hoffman was in his thirties when he turned to journalism, having been a community-action organizer with Saul Alinsky. Perhaps that thought-provoking apprenticeship also protected him from learning the bad intellectual habits that are bred into many young reporters. There may be something of a pattern in his experience, although it could just as well be explained by genetic endowment. The careers of a number of exceptional journalists reveal some catalytic intellectual experience outside the newsroom: Walter Lippmann's association with Santayana and his diplomatic experience; David Broder's opportunity to break out of the usual journalistic formulas on the *Congressional Quarterly;* Nick Kotz's background of Phi Beta Kappa and study at the London School of Economics before his present assignment with the Des Moines *Register* and *Tribune;* Willie Morris' residence at Oxford before tackling the *Texas Observer,* and now the editorship of *Harper's;* Anthony Lewis' immersing himself in the Harvard Law School as a Nieman Fellow before doing his exceptional reporting on the U.S. Supreme Court; Alan Barth's sojourn with the Schlesingers while he was a Nieman; Joseph Lelyveld's Fulbright year in Southeast Asia before joining the *Times.*

Journalists pride themselves on being generalist-specialists. Ridicule of academic specialties ranks high as newsroom sport. Yet the methods by which journalists are trained tend to be extremely narrow, even though most are probably college graduates. On most large papers today reporters specialize early in fields in which few have any general background: transportation, politics, education, or perhaps even elementary education. But the academic, whose specialty or current research may be narrowly focused, usually has had a broad intellectual base that emphasizes the interrelationships of knowledge and common methods of inquiry. The journalist learns his lore on the job. He is steeped in the concrete and specific phenomena pertaining to his beat, learning in the syncretic, associative way. Thus, he often lacks a broad conceptual framework of his subject, or a method of analysis. Hence he is usually very good in predicting what will happen tomorrow, but seldom about the shape of things five years from now. Similarly, he often remains unaware of historical parallels of current events, or of cross-cultural comparisons.

The aims of journalism differ crucially from those of scholarship. The academic investigating police behavior, for instance, wants to tell it all once, thoroughly, exhaustively. His intellectual aim is to formulate a theory or model that will explain the seemingly variable surface events, and perhaps predict the shape of things to come. The newspaper has a vested interest in the concrete and specific, in telling the same story again and again in a way that makes it sound new and different. Thirteen petty robberies must be written in a way to make them sound as different and interesting as possible.

Both approaches have their strength, however. If the journalist often obscures the general truth in mountains of fact, the scholar frequently remains blinded to the specific truth of a particular situation because of his faith in his abstractions, and occasionally, his ideology. Noam Chomsky has shown in *American Power and the New Mandarins* how frequently the latter is true. He convincingly pairs Neil Sheehan's description in the New York *Times* of fetid slums in Saigon with some scholarly accounts of the supposed benefits of American-sponsored "urbanization" in Vietnam. He writes:

> Many have remarked on the striking difference between the way the press and the visiting scholar describe what they see in Vietnam. It should occasion no surprise. Each is pursuing his own craft. The reporter's job is to describe what he sees before his eyes; many have done so with courage and even brilliance. The scholarly adviser and colonial administrator, on the other hand, is concerned to justify what he has done and what he hopes to do, and—if an expert as well—to construct an appropriate ideological cover, to show that we are just and righteous in what we do, and to put nagging doubts to rest.

Paradoxically, the limited generalization characteristic of most journalism is often a great strength. It doesn't care what the general theory is, but what is true in this particular instance. Ignorance of what is supposed to be true may have the productive result of puncturing myth or forcing scholars to re-evaluate old evidence.

Much more could be said of the sins of academe —of its petty jealousies, blindnesses, and irrelevancies. My aim, however, has been to probe the roots of what Norman Isaacs of the Louisville *Courier-Journal* once called the "mental prearrangement" that passes for thought among many journalists. More weight could be given to exceptions to some of the norms cited. But the point is precisely that there are such norms, though they are increasingly being violated.

The more general question that obtrudes is how can the norms be changed? To begin with, journalism schools could profitably follow the developments of law, education, and business schools whose faculties are no longer top-heavy with former practitioners, although they have an important place. Faculty are needed from the academic disciplines who are interested in applying their knowledge to the problems of mass media and who will teach students more thoughtful modes of analysis in a realistic setting. Such new faculty could also play a vital role in strengthening journalism schools' much-neglected role of critically assessing the performance of the press.

Newspapers should also recruit from law schools and graduate schools of sociology and political science. A great many more skilled young academics in the social sciences could be attracted to new careers in the mass media if given responsibility to tackle significant issues. Newspapers need not become miniature graduate schools, but neither should they produce the kind of shabby analysis that they do of city budgets and school reading scores. Personnel practices must change. Salaries must rise. Sabbaticals should become standard. Research assistants will be needed. Change might be so drastic as to free the average reporter from drudgery and scut work in the way that the average elementary school teacher has been liberated in New York City. The costs of carrying out these suggestions might prove a considerable financial drain on many smaller papers—at least until their benefits could be established. For that reason, such programs ought to be worthy of foundation support.

But these are long-term changes. What about now? Newspapers have only begun to take advantage of outside expertise. Academic skepticism of "newspaper writing" can be overcome with the right kind of assurances from sensitive editors that copy will be responsibly handled (not to mention massage of professorial egos with promises of the right kind of display). This puts a premium on editors who are aware of the outside expert's area of competence and interest and who can frame issues in an intellectually stimulating way. Outsiders should also be involved in seminar-like lunches planning sessions and critiques of coverage. This use of experts as "consultants" has become fairly common among magazines but is employed less frequently by newspapers.

A bolder necessary step is to go beyond hiring the free-lance talents of academics to hiring the academics themselves. But the twist here is to employ them for their skill as teachers, as catalysts who would develop new concepts and methods of reporting. Distinguished teachers and thinkers could be brought to newspapers for short periods to head special projects and reporting teams. Some might come on sabbatical; others for only a semester or a few months or weeks. They might come from think tanks, foundations, publishing houses, and universities as well as from the ranks of free-lances and other diverse social critics. Why not ask Ralph Nader, Saul Alinsky, or James Baldwin as well as sociologist Nathan Glazer, psychologist Robert Coles, economist Robert Lekachman? There are scores of candidates, though perhaps not all as well known, in every large city.

Under such a system, a small team of reporters might be assigned to work for a month preparing a series on the police, or an assessment of educational programs in the slums, or a survey of changing racial attitudes. They might work with a political scientist, a sociologist, a social psychologist. They would read and jointly discuss several books and perhaps a half-dozen relevant articles, attempting to define issues, identify historical trends, decide where reportorial energies should be directed.

Instead of rushing out to interview sources, reporters might spend time digging into census documents, examining attitudinal research, and drawing some conclusions of their own. There would be some debate about what the story is—with one result that the series would not be, like so many others, merely an elaboration of the obvious. Interviews would not be sought until there was some evaluation of what had been written, what the questions were, and the kinds of sources that could best answer them. In the case of the racial attitude series, reporters would have a chance to learn about constructing a survey, how data is fed into a computer, and some elementary notions about principles of statistical inference.

David Riesman, commenting on a draft of this article, noted that more reflective social scientists are under attack today by some of their radical activist colleagues. Although generally enthusiastic about the suggestions here, he added, "I could imagine the ironies of academicians in the newsroom being more journalistic than the journalists."

One should not overlook the benefits that would accrue to academics as a result of immersion in the newsroom. They would come away with a more realistic sense of the possible, of how complicated things really are in the concrete. It might broaden the outlook of many scholars about what their fields of inquiry ought to include. It could prove an interesting testing ground for many kinds of hypotheses and have benefits in research terms, including research about the mass media. New and better academic publications might be another by-product. The hostility of many journalists toward academics—perhaps a result of their unconscious resentment at their dependence on the experts—might be reduced. There might be a similar gain in understanding on the part of the academics, who are frequently jealous of the journalists' power (and angry at what they regard as its misuse), and who sometimes resent journalists who "cream off" the fruits of their research.

The whole notion of a newspaper as an educational institution—internally as well as externally—is central to this concept. The possibilities of encouraging greater cross-fertilization within the newsroom are limitless. Outsiders would be astonished at how little information or expertise is exchanged or developed among newspaper staffs, which have an exceptional range of talent and great opportunities for such development. A consulting firm like Arthur D. Little would close tomorrow if internal staff growth processes were as moribund as those on even our largest newspapers. Newspapermen, though they would vigorously deny it, jealously guard their imagined status and small prerogatives within the newsroom, and nothing in the way the place operates is likely to encourage them to do otherwise. One way is to bring in a catalyst from whom all learn as they teach each other. The multiplier effects of such a process could be surprising. Journalism could expand your mind.

Topics for Discussion

1. How would you summarize Grant's position on the New Journalism?
2. What kind of New Journalism would Grant like to see? Does it have any relation to the New Journalism Michael Arlen is opposed to?
3. What does Grant mean when he says, "Journalists work by a code that makes many of them moral eunuchs"? Do you agree?
4. How do the aims of journalism differ from those of scholarship, according to Grant?
5. Grant accuses most papers of producing "shabby analysis." Do you agree with him? Can you cite any examples of good analytic articles that you have read in newspapers?
6. What does Grant mean when he says a newspaper will become an educational institution if his suggestions are implemented?

Rhetorical Considerations

1. Compare the prose style and approach of Grant's essay to Arlen's. What are the differences? Are there any similarities? How would you characterize the style of each essay?
2. What is the tone of this essay? How does it help advance Grant's proposals?
3. Does Grant state his thesis any place in his essay?
4. How do you react to the final sentence of the essay? Is it a good concluding sentence? Why?

Editorial Content
What's in It

Robert Glessing

In truth, from one issue to the next, the only thing that can be safely predicted is surprise.

—*Avant-Garde Magazine*[1]

A NEWSPAPER IS, IN THE FINAL ANALYSIS, ITS OWN vision of the world. The underground press in modern America has been the youthful voice of rebellion and joy struggling with its own changing vision of itself and the world. In its early days it was a flower child sometimes almost wildly messianic. Then it vacillated from frustrated, passionate, and venomous attacks on the establishment to meditation and withdrawal into astrology, poetry, prophesy, and dreams of rural utopias. It moved in cycles as did its mobile, youthful audience and against what Bob Rudnick of *EVO* claimed to be the "diarrhetic hate and scare mongering that predominates in the official (American) press."[2] Throughout the short history of the underground press, its vision often appears to be of another world altogether.

Where the establishment press has Richard Nixon, Spiro T. Agnew, and Billy Graham, the underground papers have Tom Hayden, Eldridge Cleaver, and Kirby T. Hensley. The establishment press makes folk heroes out of Dean Martin, Twiggy, and the astronauts. The underground press does the same for Tim Leary, Allen Ginsberg, and Che Guevara. The overground makes oracles of George Washington, J. Edgar Hoover, and General Westmoreland, while the underground praises Marx, Malcolm X and Marshall McLuhan. Establishment papers cover weddings, deaths, sporting events, and the stock market, while the underground concentrates on radical politics, psychedelic drugs, and religious prophecy. The establishment press fights communism, hippies, free-love, narcotics, and sexual deviations while the underground battles the police, the CIA, the university administrations, and

1. Tom Hyman, "Walter Bowart, Mild-Mannered Editor of a Great Metropolitan Newspaper, Fights a Never-Ending Battle for the Liberation of the Human Spirit," *Avant-Garde*, March 1968, pp. 25–31.

2. S. B. Rudnick, "A Fifth Estate," *Orpheus*, August 1968, p. 23.

any other spokesman for the American establishment.

The growing underground audience can best be described as young or wanting to be young and opposed to the social status quo as viewed by the establishment press. But even among the underground press itself, there is a wide split between the radically political papers and the radically cultural papers.

Defined simply, the political papers emphasize radical politics and believe the underground press should be used as tools for a political revolution. The cultural papers, on the other hand, are interested in the total complex of relations between all people in the movement and work toward a general awareness in American society.

The political papers are represented by the *Guardian* and the *Rat* in New York City, the *Free Presses* in Washington and in Philadelphia, *The Old Mole* in Cambridge, *The Black Panther* and *The Movement* in the Bay Area, and the SDS-aligned Liberation News Service, which provides much of the national political view for all of them. Underground papers more concerned with a cultural view of American society are often as radically opposed to the system but include news and writing dealing with matters other than radical politics. Among the major cultural sheets are the *East Village Other, Barb, The Seed, Kaleidoscope, The Realist, Other Scenes, Rolling Stone*, the now commercial San Francisco *Oracle* and the Underground Press Syndicate which provides the action center for such papers.

The content in both political and cultural underground papers differs most from that of their overground brothers in their view of the importance of 1) objectivity, 2) balanced reporting, and 3) advertising. Advertising in the underground press is, as noted above, just about the reverse of the 65 per cent advertising to 35 per cent nonadvertising content ratio in the establishment press.

Subjectivity is a journalistic principle among underground press staffers and they care much more about opinion than fact. A sign in the Berkeley *Barb* office, "Put down prejudice—unless it's on our side," best describes subjective reporting and, also, why the "objectivity" standard of the establishment press is rejected. Objectivity is assumed to imply a lack of involvement with the subject, and noninvolvement is a cardinal underground sin—particularly on radically political staffs. Being involved in the action and being opposed to the establishment is a formula for an exciting brand of personal journalism, even if it presents only one side of the story. Underground journalists believe readers can get all the "law and order" viewpoint they want from the daily press, and reporters see themselves first as activists and only incidentally as

journalists. Here is an example of such personal-involvement reporting from Stew Albert in the Berkeley *Barb*, a day before the
People's Park incident:

> People's Park may be a Pigs' Pen by the time you read this,
> Roger Heyns has proclaimed his eternal loyalty to cement and
> soccer and his game begins with the motor of a bulldozer and
> the barrel of a mad pig's gun.
>
> The creators of our Park wanted nothing more than to extend
> their spirits into a gracious green meandering plaything. They
> wanted to make beauty more than an empty word in a spray
> net commercial.
>
> Our Park has been the greatest success in the history of New
> Berkeley. Thousands of sisters and brothers poured their flesh
> and sweat into the Roger Heyns parking lot swamp and in an
> unfolding sod raised work to the level of art.
>
> Each morning children come smiling into their Park and are
> instant equals. The People's Park is everybody's childhood
> daydream—the big rock candy mountain in back of Telegraph
> Avenue.
>
> On Wednesday the people of the Park met in a planned-to-be
> but still dry fish pond. The majority were longhairs of the
> street and university farmer-artists out to save their land. They
> had word Roger Heyns was going to build a Berlin wall around
> their dream.[3]

or Mike Hodel on radio reporting in *Open City*:

> Dial-diddling in Los Angeles radio can result in a plethora of
> pessimism and the feeling that your ears may be drowned in a
> torrent of stupidity. But once in a while, your attention can be
> caught and concentrated on a few flowers amid the mud.[4]

And Sheila Golden reporting on a Black Panther trial in *Other
Scenes*:

> The scene of the action was the New York Criminal Court
> Building at 100 Center Street, where less than three weeks
> before over a thousand outraged students and members of the
> black community demonstrated against the jailing of 21
> Black Panthers.
>
> This time it was lawyers themselves on the picket line
> protesting not only the nationwide campaign to destroy the
> Black Panther Party, but also the perversion of the legal system
> generally.

3. Stew Albert, "Try Them In The Streets," Berkeley *Barb* (Vol.
8, No. 20), May 16–22, 1969, p. 14.
4. Mike Hodel, "On Radio," *Open City*, December 27–January
2, 1968, p. 2.

> *The theme of the demonstration, carried on simultaneously by more than a 100 law students in front of the U.S. Courthouse and New York Supreme Court in nearby Foley Square was "Confront the Courts for Criminal Justice."*[5]

None of the underground writers accept the role of detached observer since that would eliminate the element of involvement so necessary to the new left's self-identity.

If the underground press in any way mirrors a segment of disaffected American youth, that mirror reflects more than just acrid political opposition. The *Los Angeles Free Press* features a wide-ranging view of Los Angeles' hip community. Breaking the content down into news, editorials, features, comics, art, and advertising, the *Freep* allocated 11 per cent of its space to news reporting, 19 per cent to features, 12 per cent to art, 2 per cent to editorial comment, and 45 per cent to advertising. The remaining 11 per cent was inconsistently allotted to comics, poetry, a calendar of events, and promotions. These figures are based on a study of eight consecutive issues in 1967.[6]

A quick look at the now defunct *Open City* and *Los Angeles Oracle* indicate why *Freep* carried so little art and poetry and so much advertising. Over eight issues, *Oracle* and *Open City* gave 18 and 22 per cent to advertising, 41 and 22 per cent to art, 30 and 27 per cent to features and 3 and 9 per cent to news. *Oracle* carried only 8 per cent of public service materials like a community calendar or classified ads, while *Open City* ran nearly 20 per cent of such materials.[7]

Comparisons are as odious with underground papers as other things, but the willingness of *Open City* and *Oracle* to satisfy the psychedelic fringe of Los Angeles' hip audience with color and freaked-out art was undoubtedly the reason *Freep* emphasized news and features. *Freep* considers itself an alternative to the *Los Angeles Times* and has a lot more coverage of city politics than most underground papers. After the Watts upheaval in 1965 *Freep* beat all overground media with a lengthy analysis of the reasons for unrest in that community. *Freep* features an exceptionally comprehensive coverage of Los Angeles theater, both underground and legitimate, and carries a monthly 24-page insert entitled "Living Arts" with contributors like Lawrence Lipton,

---

5. Sheila Golden, "The Perversion of the Legal System," *Other Scenes* (Vol. 3, No. 6), June 1–14, 1969, p. 5.
6. Gaye Sandler Smith, "The Underground Press in Los Angeles," an unpublished master's thesis, University of California, Los Angeles, 1968, pp. 119–123.
7. Ibid.

John Carpenter, Jerry Hopkins and other well known California writers.

One of the most outstanding contributions of *Freep* to the West Coast subterranean scene are the political cartoons of Ron Cobb. Syndicated in many underground papers, Cobb draws ominous, dark sketches of America at the brink of destruction, showing dehumanization and death of the individual at the hands of technology and the bureaucratic establishment. (Plate 11)

East Village Other is a second cultural underground sheet that offers a wide and changing variety of subject matter to its readers. EVO's major distinction is the use of satirical comic strips, far-out classified ads, and bizarre poetry. Comic strips are as American as television or apple pie and were first introduced to American journalism in the late 1890s as circulation builders on newspapers. During the '30s the slapstick strips were eclipsed by storytelling panels concerned with the family, getting a job, and security. Where Establishment strips mirror the middleclass scene, EVO's comics feature sex, drugs, police brutality, and general taboo-breaking. EVO's contributions include Art Spiegelman's "Adventures of a Jolly Jack-Off, the Masturbation Fiend," Spain Rodriguez' "Trashman, Agent of the Underground Revolt," Kim Deitch's psychedelic Alice in Wonderland, "Sunshine Girl," and Bill Beskman's "Captain High," the superman defender who protects heads (drug users) from the fuzz.

Underground comics are evidence of the new media's willingness to satirize American society without taboos. They lean heavily on long hair, drugs, radical politics, sexual freedom, and anything else that will offend the establishment mentality and consequently please the underground reader. *East Village Other* was one of the first underground publications on the comics scene and there soon followed publications like *Yellow Dog*, "a nitty gritty dog pissing on the deepest symbol of American consciousness"; *Snatch Comics*, "a further assault on the American Dream"; and The *Gothic Blimp Works*, featuring such entries as "Mr. Know-it-all and his Pal Diz in *What The Fuck*." *Gothic Blimp Works* was the first underground, all color comix newspaper and was circulating 25,000 copies monthly after its first three issues early in 1969.

Ten 1969 issues of EVO devoted 46 per cent to advertising, 16 per cent to comix, 28 per cent to feature articles, 4 per cent to editorials, 2 per cent to calendars, and 4 per cent to news. Twelve per cent of the advertising space was used for the classifieds which were another EVO first in the underground press. EVO's classified ads emphasize sexual freedom for all—heterosexual, homosexual, or combinations. Katzman believes his classified ads are neither obscene nor deviant, claiming "These ads help get people together. Before we started running *Wheel and Deal* (the overline on its three pages of unclassifiable classifieds) these people had no outlets for their sexual interests. Now they're getting together and there is less loneliness in New York City." Classified advertising copy in *EVO*[8] usually reads:

> *Calling all women from 18 to 30. Let a man of 24 share the pleasures sex has to offer to one another. Call—— between 5 and 9 p.m. Ask for Barry.*

or

> *The new fad!! Color your pubic hair any shade you wish! Green, red, bright orange, light blonde or magenta! Surprise your friends. The next time your crowd gets together for a party, be known as 'the girl with the green pussy' or 'the fellow with the pink peter.' Send $5.00 today to——.*

or

> *Discreet, groovy guy, early 30's, handsome, hung and horny! Looking for similar males for uninhibited mutual delight in twosomes or threesomes! Send details and photo if possible to——.*

Paul Krassner of the *Realist* claims sexual freedom is a political thing since it involves a person's freedom to do what he or she wants with his or her body. Whatever the political implications, many underground newspapers have been sued, harassed, and even closed down by means of the obscenity laws in certain state and regional jurisdictions, and the United States Post Office authorities have disrupted mail distribution on the same grounds. Many politically inclined publications avoid obscenity simply because they want to arouse the establishment on more political issues.

A wide range of features and self-help columns set the cultural papers apart from their more politically-oriented counterparts. A column in John Wilcock's *Other Scenes* called "Phoney Facts" explained in detail how to "diddle" the telephone company. It read: "Install your own extension phones and save the rent of a Princess; for long-distance calls, record lengthy messages and play them into the mouthpiece at high speed to be decoded at the other end at normal speed."[9]

One of the most popular columns in the Los Angeles *Freep*

8. Classified Ads, *East Village Other* (Vol. 4, No. 34), July 23, 1969, pp. 21–22.

9. John Wilcock, "Phoney Facts," *Other Scenes*, June 1–14, 1969, p. 14.

and fifteen other cultural and radical underground publications is Dr. HIPPOCRATES. The good Dr. Hip is Eugene Schoenfeld, M.D., a Berkeley medical-treatment-for-pay drop-out, whose column specializes in the treatment of aberrant sexual behavior. A sort of "Dear Abby" for the hip set, Dr. Hippocrates answers questions on sex, drugs, and other non-conforming habits unlikely to be answered by the overground press' Dr. Crane. Dr. Hip answers them thoughtfully and often humorously. Typical questions are, Can pot or LSD be given safely to children, puppy dogs, or cats? Is it harmful to fart in the presence of others? Should a bent penis be straightened? Is masturbation harmful to one's eyesight? Here are a few exchanges typical with Dr. Hippocrates:

Question: *In the showers I notice all very fat men have a penis barely an inch long. Why?*

Answer: *An aroused (angered) colleague stoutly maintains this is a false observation, caused, no doubt, by lack of familiarity with obese people. Increased fat tissues covering the base of the penis accounts for this belief. Have you ever read about Fatty Arbuckle?*

Question: *Is masturbation physically harmful if I do it once a day?*

Answer: *There is a story about a little boy who was found masturbating and told that he would go blind unless he stopped. "Well," he pleaded, "can I do it until I need eyeglasses?" There is no evidence that masturbation is physically or mentally harmful whatever its frequency.*

Question: *I have been getting a rather weird high by smoking a tobacco cigarette like a joint. A drag will start me up and two cigarettes will get me totally zonked. I usually don't smoke (except grass). Do you have any idea about the medical ramifications of this habit?*

Answer: *Cigarettes are a known health hazard. Do you get them from The Friendly Stranger?*

Question: *I have a 'condition' which seems to worry my husband more than myself. Ever since my teens my inner or minor vaginal lips have hung outside my major lips. Because they are not neatly within my major lips my husband believes this could indicate some disorder. What do you think?*

Answer: *There is nothing abnormal about the labia minora protruding through the labia majora. Why, some of my best friends. . . .*[10]

10. Burton Wolfe, "Dr. HIPocrates, Will Bull Sperm Grow Hair On Me?" *Cavalier*, April 1968, pp. 38–40, 63–64, 73–74.

Dr. Hip originated in the Berkeley *Barb* and is now syndicated in fifteen underground papers. Many other underground papers pick up Dr. Hippocrates without bothering to pay when the column carries questions that interest their editors. By August 1969, the overground San Francisco Sunday *Chronicle* had picked up his column as a regular feature. Anonymous features are used widely in the underground because of the pressure put on staffers by police and narcotics agents. Along with many articles credited to the fictitious Intergalactic World Brain, the *Barb* features Sergeant Pepper's column on Vietnam and the mysterious Roving Rat Fink, a column of opinions on everything under the political and cultural sun. Sometimes entire underground staffs use aliases or put-on names to avoid being identified. Columns by Lenny the Lewd, the Grass Prophet, or William Randolph Hearst are sometimes cover-ups, sometimes put-ons, with the actual writers usually well-known to staffers and readers alike.

Another popular feature in the cultural papers is a weekly astrology guide. When radical politics became hip in 1967, many of the political papers swung away from Astrology, but it remained a mainstay in *Great Speckled Bird*, *Helix*, and *Kaleidoscope*. Entitled "the Gigantic Tent of Hermes Trismegistics," "The Aquarian Age," or simply "Using Astrology," the feature was carried as the religious prophesy of the movement. Astrology preached the unification of religions, science, and technology, and many of the NOW children of the underground audience followed it as their weekly bread.

Underground readers are not the only readers who approve of underground style or content. Joan Didion in *The Saturday Evening Post* called the underground press: "Strident and brash, but they do not irritate; they have the faults of a friend, not of a monolith." Miss Didion concluded: "They are the only American newspapers that do not leave me in the grip of a profound physical conviction that the oxygen has been cut off from my brain tissue."[11] *Look* magazine noted in an article: "What's happened is not the point (of the underground press), 'What's happening' is."[12]

Less complimentary was the following statement from *American Opinion*, the official organ of the John Birch Society:

11. Joan Didion, "Alicia and the Underground Press," *Saturday Evening Post*, January 13, 1968, p. 14.
12. John Kronenberger, "What's Black and White and Pink and Green and Dirty and Read All Over?" *Look* (Vol. 32, No. 20), October 1, 1968, p. 21.

The editorial format of the underground press calls for a Marxist message blanketed in sex and drugs. This is kneaded with four-letter words, malapropped with polysyllables, and stirred with corny revolutionary slogans that would have embarrassed an East Side anarchist of 1910. It is mixed with 'hip' language taken from the lexicons of Marx, Lenin and Chairman Mao, along with the weird vernacular of the Hindu mystics. Served with a quart of self-righteousness, the above recipe produces the nicest little revolutionary stew you ever saw.[13]

The underground press unquestionably deals with Hindu mystics, Marx, Lenin, and Chairman Mao. They also include sex, jazz, and narcotics, since that's what their editors and readers are interested in.

When asked what the underground press cared about, Tom Forcade of the Underground Press Syndicate wrote in *Orpheus*:

Radical theater, sexual freedom, the taboo against knowing who you are, communes, anarchy, draft resistance, light shows, peace and freedom, hashish and a thousand other things and non-things, real and imagined, ridiculous and sublime.[14]

Since their doings are largely ignored by the overground press, most movement members find their calendar of events on underground pages. Such calendars feature a listing of where it's going to be at on the hip scene for the coming week. Titled "Scendrome," "Happenings," or "Trips—Free and Not-So-Free" (many events are free to members of the movement) these announcements serve as social guidelines for activists and cultural hipsters alike and are followed religiously by the turned-on generation.

Coverage of musical groups, individuals, and concerts takes up much of the feature space of the papers. Electronically-controlled rock music as an intensely participational, non-linear art form has become the sound of revolution and, as such, a bridge between politically and culturally oriented papers. *Rolling Stone* in San Francisco is dedicated almost solely to the rock music scene and is a must for advertisers of rock albums. *Rolling Stone's* eleven-page analysis of Groupies, the male and female sleep-in followers of rock musicians, in a February 1969 issue was an outstanding example of what the underground press can do with in-depth reporting.[15] Dis-

13. Gary Allen, "Underground for Adults Only," *American Opinion*, December 1967, p. 4.

14. Forcade, "Underground Press Loves You," p. 18.

15. "The Groupies and Other Girls," *Rolling Stones* (No. 27, February 15, 1969, pp. 11–26.

tant Drummer is, and the now-defunct *Open City* was, largely concerned with the rock music world, with stories about individual performers as well as reviews of groups popular among the underground audience.

When reviews of rock music are included in the *Movement*, *Guardian*, or other politically-oriented new left papers, they are usually selected, analyzed, and judged according to their political value to the movement. The political sheets are more interested in the protest songs of Bob Dylan and Phil Ochs than the grinding, hipswiveling sounds of Jimmy Hendrix or Janis Joplin.

Establishment media in general are another target of the alternative press, which takes strong issue with the establishment's definition of news. The following analysis by Marty Glass in *Dock of the Bay*'s third issue in August 1969, speaks powerfully about how the underground defines news:

> There's been a lot of murder and rape in the Bay Area during the past few weeks.
>
> A pregnant woman was raped and stabbed in the throat with a butcher knife by two men in the Haight. Two San Jose girls, 14 & 15, were discovered with hundreds of stab wounds in their bodies. A 17-year old girl from Salinas found strangled with a red belt; police suspect this job was linked with the murder of eight girls in Ann Arbor, Michigan. A gang attack in the Hunter's Point section of San Francisco led to one man murdered, his girl raped, and his father slashed. And then there's the weird L.A. movie star murders of Sharon Tate, the pregnant wife of Roman Polanski, and three friends in their secluded Bel Air mansion.
>
> There have been 96 murders so far this year in the Bay Area, just six less than the total for 1968.
>
> The Bay Area newspapers blazed out the news in giant headlines. "Savage Slaying Mystery," "Shocking Murder," "A Story of Savagery," "Big Search for Knife Killer of Two San Jose Girls," "Big Hunt for Picnic Killer," and so on.
>
> There's a big lie behind all this. The stories are more or less true; the accounts bear some police-filtered relation to the truth, but there's still a big lie behind the grisly intimate details of bloody mayhem and brutal sexual assault.
>
> The lie is linked to the idea of 'news' in the daily papers. What does 'news' mean? 'News' is what stands out on the vast, flat and presumably irrelevant plain of mundane events, 'news' is what deviates from the ordinary and the normal, 'news' is what someone else decides is important.
>
> Supposedly, everything which isn't worth knowing about isn't of public concern. The daily papers convey a very strong and very indirect message; there's a normal, everyday life which is

OK and unexceptional—not worth talking about. And then there's 'news': anything which stands out, anything that doesn't happen all the time and is, therefore, of interest.

Life is good. That's the realm where things are taken care of. 'News' is when something goes wrong.

This is pure bullshit. The real news isn't in distinct, bizarre events. The real news is what happens 24 hours a day all day long everywhere. This is the news we don't read about in the daily papers because the people who control those papers don't want us to know about it and do everything they can to distract our attention from it.

Fortunately, they can't succeed. We don't need their papers to tell us about the real news. All we have to do is open our eyes.

The real news is the expression on the faces of children sitting in tenement doorways with nothing to do. The real news is the tenement itself.

The real news is the despair and humiliation on the faces of people waiting for hours for a lousy check in the welfare or unemployment offices. And it's also on the emptied faces of people who have jobs they hate, jobs where their creative potential is stifled and crushed under the weight of meaningless labor performed to make enough money to survive.

The real news is jobs created solely to provide profits for those who don't work at all, or for a corporation which is nothing but a bankbook.

The precious unredeemable time of our lives is sacrificed for numbers in bankbooks.

The real news is elderly people rotting away in dilapidated Old Folks' Homes or in spare rooms in their childrens' houses, unwanted, resented, feeling they might as well be dead. The real news is in the millions of people who don't get enough to eat, who receive inadequate medical care, who suffer and die from diseases which could be cured and should never have been contracted in the first place.

The real news is when there's a giant traffic jam on the Bay Bridge because the market economy and capitalism require profit and there's no profit in safe, comfortable, efficient, rapid public transportation. The real news is that there are hardly enough parks and playgrounds for a fraction of our children, that schools are falling apart, overcrowded, repressive, irrelevant and hated by the children imprisoned there.

The real news is that guys are getting beaten by sadistic psychopaths in prisons and army stockades all over the country, kids watch hours of obscene commercials on TV, women are forced to waste their lives in shopping and cooking because private consumption is the syphilitic deity of our society.

The real news is that people who can't take it any more—and they're mostly black or poor whites—are called mentally ill *and given shock treatment or mind-killing drugs.*

The real news is that ten thousand women die every year in the United States from slipshod expensive abortions, because this system doesn't permit half the population to decide what goes on in their own bodies, doesn't provide for any way outside of the decayed institution of marriage for children to be cared for.

The real news is that cops who murder black men are given medals and a guy found with two joints gets ten years.

The real news is that guys are being forced to kill their brothers in Vietnam.

The real news is that all the important decisions made in this country are made by maniac insects with dollar signs engraved on their beady inhuman plastic eyeballs. We see their pictures every day on the business pages in their newspapers.

The real news is that Huey Newton is in jail and Richard Nixon isn't. . . .[16]

This dramatic statement by Glass on what is and what is not news comes close to clarifying many of the differences between over- and underground publications.

Another characteristic of underground newspaper makeup is front-page photos, art, and illustrations around a single incident. The *East Village Other* photo of President Johnson's head grafted onto the body of a Nazi storm trooper has been mentioned; the *Movement* once ran a reverse line art drawing of a black fist, symbol of Afro-American demands for equality; and half-tone shots of female nudes, militant leaders, or underground oracles are common fare for the new media's covers. Because of liberal use of white space, flexibility in using colored newsprint, and a willingness to experiment with photos, type, and art work, underground front pages resemble magazine covers more than overground tabloid newspapers.

Athletics are largely ignored by underground editors, although *Seed* and *Good Times* ran irregular satirical columns on sports for a time.

Obituaries are another feature glaringly absent in the dissenting press, an omission undoubtedly related to the hippie subculture's mystical attitude towards death. Dropping out or withdrawing from society symbolizes their own death and the so-called enlightenment that comes from drugs is considered a rebirth. Thus obituaries are generally restricted to those of an office cat or someone's stray dog.

Poetry is a popular feature in many of the culturally-inclined

16. Marty Glass, "What's News," *Dock of the Bay* (Vol. 1, No. 3), August 18, 1969, p. 4.

underground papers. The poetic themes ordinarily concern movement events, psychedelic experiences, or the beauties of nature.

Liberation News Service and the Underground Press Syndicate are an extension of the political and cultural underground press, and their differences best explain the split within the medium. Strongly oriented to the politics of revolution, LNS spends most of its time gathering and disseminating news and information of a radical political nature. Bloody confrontations between students, police and college administrators are higher on LNS's value scale than psychedelic art, rock music, or drugs. LNS claims to feature "humorous art work, satirical poetry and cultural material" but a scanning of several dozen LNS packets revealed precious little to substantiate such claims. More characteristic of this somewhat humorless service are articles on "the Christian Anti-Communist Crusade," the "Revolutionary Youth Movement," "Congress Investigation of SDS," or "Berkeley—Life with National Guards."[17]

The Underground Press Syndicate identifies more strongly with the cultural papers although it makes its services available to any and all underground papers and maintains a cooperative relationship with LNS. Seriously concerned with the future of films and broadcasting, UPS covers a wider variety of underground activities than just radical or revolutionary politics.

The underground split between radical activists and nonpolitical drop-outs is in many ways a division into different cultural aspects of the same youth movement. There are powerful forces determining the quality of American life both under- and overground and it is unlikely to be improved singlehandedly by any centralization of effort on politics, culture, music, or satire. Unless the LNS and radically political papers in the underground press realize there is more to the cultural revolution than revolutionary confrontation politics, they will fall into the limbo of other American special interest publications. The cultural papers have kept at least one foot in the broader youth movement bag and in that bag there is a variety of content and life as wide as the future of American youth—over- or underground.

17. "Table of Contents," *Liberation News Service* (Issue 17), June 12, 1969, p. 1.

Topics for Discussion

1. Glessing maintains that underground papers are split into two kinds. What are these? Do you agree with this division?
2. Many of the underground papers which Glessing mentions in his essay have gone out of business. Does this say anything about the underground press?
3. What are three ways in which an underground paper differs from an establishment newspaper? How significant are these differences?
4. The underground press does not restrain itself in the use of language. Do you agree that "sexual freedom is a political thing since it involves a person's freedom to do what he or she wants with his or her body"?
5. What events and subjects does the underground press cover that are ingored by the establishment press?
6. Do you agree with Marty Glass's definition of news?
7. Glessing predicts that unless the political underground newspapers do more than just cover politics they will fail. Do you agree with this? Why?
8. Compare a copy of an underground newspaper to a copy of an establishment newspaper. Are there any similarities? What are the most significant differences? Which newspaper do you like more? Why?
9. Why do you think the underground press ignores athletics?

Rhetorical Considerations

1. There are many quotations in this essay. How well are they integrated into the essay? Note particularly the very long quotation from Marty Glass. Is this long quotation necessary? Could Glessing have simply paraphrased Glass's views?
2. Find some examples of connotative or slanted language that Glessing uses in his essay.
3. How well organized is this essay? Can you divide it into major sections?
4. How does Glessing approach his controversial subject? Does he reveal his own position toward the underground press? What is the tone of his essay?
5. Glessing concludes his essay with a prediction. Is this a good method for concluding this essay?

Press or Government: Who's Telling the Truth?

BILL D. MOYERS

No two callings are more concerned with the public interest or more satisfying to a man's sense of duty than journalism and government. This bias of mine about the press and government is colored by the fact that I am a creature of both. I criticize them with affection, having learned enough about the vices and virtues of these two institutions to know that neither is totally innocent nor totally guilty of all the charges they heap upon one another. I have not learned enough about them to propose solutions to all the questions each asks about the other. But our obligation to each and their great power in a free society compel us all to ponder, question, and probe constantly whether they are meeting their obligations.

The first point to consider is that credibility is not the government's problem alone. . . . The press also suffers from the appearance of contradiction, which is the essence of a "Credibility Gap." From my own experience at the White House, the following examples stand out.

First, when Edwin O. Reischauer resigned as United States Ambassador to Japan, he was interviewed by the press in Tokyo. The headline in the *Washington Post* the next day read: REISCHAUER BACKS U.S. VIET POLICY. The headline in the *New York Times* read: REISCHAUER CRITICAL OF VIETNAM POLICY. After a debate in the House of Commons on British support of U.S. policy in Vietnam, the headline in the *Washington Post* read: WILSON GETS SUPPORT FOR U.S. STAND. The headline in the *New York Times* read: COMMONS RESTRICTS BACKING OF VIETNAM. Perhaps both were correct, but was one more correct? To reconcile the difference is possible if one could read the full report in both papers, but for most people that is not an option. They do not have the opportunity to weigh the differences between contradictory stories.

Second, the day before the elections in South Vietnam in 1965, one commentator for CBS declared: "the armed forces have been turned loose in the get-out-the-vote movement. In the South Vietnamese army, like any other, an order is an order. But if the voters have to be driven to the polls with guns and bayonets, so to speak, it would appear that the Viet Cong has made its point about the Ky regime's popular support." The day after the election, however, another CBS commentator expressed amazement that so many South Vietnamese turned out to vote against the Viet Cong. "After all," he said, "the Government of South Vietnam is not driving the people to the polls with bayonets. . . ." If the TV viewer had

From Bill D. Moyers, "Press or Government: Who's Telling the Truth?" *Television Quarterly,* the Journal of the National Academy of Television Arts and Sciences, Vol. 7, Summer 1968. Reprinted with permission.

heard both reports, he might have asked: "What's going on here? Was one of the reporters not telling the truth? Was one right and the other wrong?" The answer is probably that each man was partially wrong and partially right, because each man saw what *he* was looking at, or looking for. "Who's telling the truth?" a correspondent friend of mine was asked when he returned from Vietnam. "Nearly everybody," he answered. "Nearly everybody out there bears true witness to his bias and his senses." . . .

I learned at the White House that of all the great myths of American journalism, "objectivity" is the greatest. Each of us sees what his own experience leads him to see. What is happening often depends upon who is looking. Depending on who is looking and writing, the White House is brisk or brusque; assured or arrogant; casual or sloppy; frank or brutal; warm or corny; cautious or timid; compassionate or condescending; reserved or callous. As press secretary, this was repugnant to me. As a publisher, there is no alternative but to accept it.

Does the press really permit its humanity to interfere in the search for truth? For example Richard Harwood, then of the *Louisville Courier-Journal* and now of the *Washington Post*, reported not too long after President Johnson was in office that several long-time correspondents at the White House, when asked why the President's honeymoon with the press had ended, gave this answer: "Although Johnson has made even more of an effort than Kennedy to cultivate and woo the press, most White House reporters don't care for him as a person. They liked Kennedy and enjoyed his company. Johnson hasn't won their affection." In response to this attitude, Ted Lewis, of the *New York Daily News*, asked: "What sort of journalism is that? It suggests that unless the President wins the 'affection' of the White House press, he is not going to get fair treatment." Ted may be right, yet in my experiences as White House Press Secretary, I rarely found that reporters were intentionally unfair to the President because he had failed to win their affection. No one begrudges a reporter his feelings, but one can lament the righteous indignation he expresses when it is suggested that he is an error-prone human being first, and a journalist second.

All of this is so obvious that the question arises, "Why discuss it?" The first part of the answer has to do with the professional longevity of the journalist. For all practical purposes we are beyond retaliation. We almost always have the last word because we are simply more durable. While the public can turn out officials whose integrity is exposed as unethical, or whose judgments are consistently wrong, or whose talents are proven to be inadequate, journalists do not operate at the end of an electorate's whim. . . .

There is an even more important reason for examining our vision. It has to do with the crisis of confidence in America today. . . . During my recent speeches at several colleges and universities I encountered a biting doubt about the veracity of both government and the press. One student in the Midwest said: "You know, Mr. Moyers, you have served in government and journalism, so it is doubly hard to believe anything you say." That remark says a great deal about the state of America today, and the state of America is disturbing. We seem on the way to becoming a nation of cynics. While skepticism is the mark of a healthy climate in a democracy, cynicism—widespread cynicism directed at the basic institutions of a society—can cripple a nation's will and undermine her spirit. A cynic, Lord Darlington told Cecil Graham, is a man who knows the price of everything and the value of nothing. And that is true of a cynical nation. Cynicism about the press and government ultimately will infect the very core of the transaction of public affairs; it will eat at the general confidence we must be able to have in one another if a pluralistic society is to work.

The fundamental issue, according to James Reston, is the question of trust. He writes: "The most serious problem in America today is that there is widespread doubt in the public mind about its major leaders and institutions. There is more troubled questioning of the veracity of statements out of the White House today than at anytime in recent memory. The cynicism about the Congress is palpable. The disbelief in the press is a national joke. . . . There is little public trust today." . . . Some of my colleagues in journalism say: "Well, they have a point, but most government officials lie deliberately—in the name of national security—while our mistakes are not intended." The reply is that a journalist can lose his credibility in the fashion many ladies lose their virtue: with the very best of intentions.

Many young people constantly point to examples of innocent discrepancy in expressing doubts about what they read. Take, as one example, the coverage last year of the protest in the United Nations Plaza. One headline read: 100,000 RALLY AT UN AGAINST WAR. Another account reported flatly that at least 300,000 had marched. One student told me, "We might forgive journalists for not being able to write, but how can we forgive you for not admitting that you can't count?" Every political reporter knows how difficult it is to assess the size of a crowd, and no one has yet to offer a sure way of improving our estimates. The fact remains that people are not willing to recognize such handicaps in judging whether we are to be believed or not. Virtue can be lost quite innocently.

As citizens we should be worried when millions of people believe the government lies. As journalists we should be equally concerned when millions of people believe the press lies, too. A number of people, especially the young, agree with the assertion that "an ambassador is a man of virtue sent to lie abroad for his country, and a journalist is a man without virtue who lies at home for himself."

If there are growing numbers of people willing to believe the worst about the press, they are supported by quite sincere men in public life ready to convince them that their worst fears are justified. Who was responsible for the plunging fortunes of George Romney last winter? Not George Romney, but the press! "One of the most unfair things that has happened in the last two and a half years," he said, "was the effort by the press to create the idea that I have been inconsistent and wobbly and didn't understand the situation. . . ."

And why do public doubts exist about the Vietnam war? Not because of the tenacity of the Viet Cong, the complexities of a brutish war, or the natural revulsion to the horrors of war. To hear military officials tell it, these public doubts can be traced to a "cynical element" of the press in Saigon. There are always people eager to prove that the press is responsible for their misfortune; the more they succeed in casting doubts on the veracity of the press, the more we have to work to clean our own house.

What specifically can we do? There is no overall cure. My suggestions are obvious and familiar. They simply need to be stated again and again as part of the vigilance that is the price of the power and obligation of the press.

First, the press should act with the same appreciation of candor about itself that it expects of public officials. This would lead to several improvements: an admission of "the subjectivity of our objectivity"; a confession that not even the press can discover the "whole truth and nothing but the truth"—that at best the press can only come up with the "bits and pieces of truth"; and an acknowledgement that its responsibility is greater than its skill.

Second, the press should either be prepared to live apart from tangling alliances with officialdom or be prepared to give up that illusion. There is considerable public skepticism about the cozy ties between the press and governments at every level, and much of this skepticism is justified. In Washington the temptation is often for both government and the press to think of themselves as brokers of the public interest rather than its guardians.

The third suggestion for improving the press's credibility is just as fundamental as a freshman journalism course. It is to make accuracy again the first rule of reporting. Nothing undermines the credibility of the press like sloppy reporting. Bad reporting creates unbelievers. When people read an inaccurate account of their own activities, they will tend to doubt everything else they read, too. It is a sad reflection on the state of our reputation today that far more readers believe the advice they get from Ann Landers than they do the advice of our editorials.

My fourth suggestion relates to one of the most common practices in Washington today—a practice that constantly afflicts the credibility of the press and government. This is the indiscriminate use of "backgrounders" as the source of hard-news stories. In order to correct this misuse, members of the Washington press must adopt some basic ground rules for "backgrounders" and must seek to get government officials to recognize and respect those rules.

The "backgrounder" is an old Washington institution—more endured than revered. The original purpose was to permit a government official to talk freely to newsmen without worry that some offhand remark would embarrass him, his agency, or the government. For that purpose it still has merit. . . .

Individual reporters, . . . constantly seek information on a "background" basis from officials. They want as complete a story as possible, and frequently, in order to receive particular pieces of a story, have to promise not to quote the man they are talking to, or even mention his agency. . . .

Formal group briefings, however, are quite another matter. They tend often to degenerate into a relationship between the public official and reporters not unlike that of an *amanuensis* to his master. The competitive pressure permits little time for cross-checking and thus contributes to uniformity—as if the press corps were a delayed-action Greek chorus. That, indeed, is what the public officials want. Their objective is to get out what the government wants to get out, as the government wants it to get out—a quite natural and understandable ambition.

The dangers in this practice should be clear to anyone. For one thing, anonymity is fearless, and if a public official wants to do so and can find a journalist willing to co-operate, he can hide behind that anonymity to grind an axe or to float a balloon, while protecting himself from possible adverse reaction by fuzzing the source. Another danger is public confusion. I was once in a television control room at a moment when we could not see who was speaking although we could hear at least a dozen voices from the studio, and I thought at the time how bewildered newspaper readers must be when they read information from a plethora of unidentified sources. How can we expect to judge the reliability of a statement if it is attributed only to an "informed source?" Suppose, just to make a point, that instead of James Reston's by-line on his column, there only appeared these words: "By a high official of the *New York Times*." . . .

All of this may appear hypocritical, coming as it does from someone who made his living by "backgrounding" the press. But I was troubled by the process, as were many of the reporters with whom I dealt, because while we knew the careful "backgrounder" to be useful and necessary, especially in the area of national security, we also felt it had become a habit of convenience, a rule rather than an exception. . . .

As Jules Frandsen, veteran head of the Washington bureau of United Press International, has said: "A lot of skullduggery in Government and in Congress would never come to light if everything had to be attributed. Employees often can't afford to risk their jobs by talking for attribution." Nonetheless, the practice is so consistently abused that some commonly accepted ground rules are in order.

A step in the right direction would be for representatives of the various press organizations to meet and try to agree among themselves on these ground rules. . . .

Having tried on several occasions to mediate between journalists and the government, I am not sanguine about the possibility of reaching agreement within or among either group on what the ground rules for "backgrounders" should be. As a point of departure for trying, here are eight principles which, in my opinion, would help to bring some order into a ritual that at the moment can only be as confusing to the public as Haitian voodoo.

ONE: "Backgrounders" should be designed to *explain* policy rather than *announce* policy. This rule would discourage the use of unattributed quotations which turn "soft news" into "hard news."

TWO: "Backgrounders" in subjects other than national security and foreign affairs should be the exception rather than the rule.

THREE: The contents of a group "backgrounder" should not be disclosed for at least one hour after the conclusion of the session. This would permit time for cross-checking. It would also reduce the possibility of a public official using a backgrounder strictly for self-serving purposes.

FOUR: The rules should be clearly stated before the "backgrounder" begins by the principal or by his press spokesman.

FIVE: There should be only two levels of concealment. Either the reporter uses the information on his own—a practice that should be reserved for the most sensitive issues of national security—or it should be attributed as stated in the following principle.

SIX: The source should be identified by his specific agency. The loose anonymity of "high U.S. official," "top government officials," "friends of the President," or "visitors who've talked to the President" would be replaced by "A Defense Department spokesman," or "A U.S. Army official," or "White House sources." The reader would still be in doubt as to the authenticity and the reliability of the information, but the burden of proof would not be on the press completely.

SEVEN: The reporters should refuse to deliberately increase the obfuscation through such tactics as withholding the information until the source has left town (as in the case of General Westmoreland's "backgrounder" last November), or by attributing the information to plural sources when it comes in fact from one source (as also happened when the correspondents changed General Westmoreland into "some U.S. officials").

EIGHT: When a public official in a "backgrounder" refuses to permit attribution material that is patently self-serving but reporters nonetheless feel obliged to carry the story, they should carry a sentence attributing the information to a Pentagon (or State or White House) official "whose name is withheld at his insistence."

These suggestions are only the starting point for serious discussions by journalists and public officials. Other men will have better proposals. The important task is for the press to make some effort to deal with the problem. A "backgrounder" is useful to a public official and to a reporter, helping the one to get his viewpoint across and the other to gain valuable insight or information that he could not get if the official were required to speak for attribution. But what is convenient to the government and to the press is confusing to the public. These ideas are put forward with the *public* in mind. . . .

Whatever rules are agreed upon, the problem will be in getting the government to respect them. But even that is not so formidable an obstacle as it appears. Government officials only call a "backgrounder" to brief a large press gathering when those officials have something to put out. If the newspapers and the media most read and watched by Washington officials—in particular, the three networks, the wire services, and the Washington and New York City press—insist that the rules by which they will transmit the information be followed, respect for rules will grow in time. And with it the credibility of the American press.

Now we come to the credibility of the Government—the "Credibility Gap." Time and time again these questions are asked: Do Presidents and press secretaries really lie? There is the obvious answer: Before there were Presidents and press secretaries, there were Adam and Eve, and there is a little of each of them in all of us.

The question, however, goes far beyond a simple affirmation that public officials are human. The press has an obligation to increase the public's understanding of the "Credibility Gap" since we have certainly increased the public's awareness of it. I have no question but that the Government overreacted to the charges of incredibility, partly because any man grows defensive when his integrity is assaulted. But if the Government has over-reacted, the press has under-explained. The "Credibility Gap" became an overworked catch phrase that many people took for granted because they heard it repeated so often. What was otherwise and imprecise and poorly defined term took on the familiarity of an established creed which people read without thinking and repeat without understanding.

There has always been a credibility problem; the term is no recent addition to our political nomenclature. Some people trace it back to the premise of Plato that "The rulers of the State are the only ones who should have the privilege of lying, either at home or abroad; they may be allowed to lie for the good of the State." Plato has his apostles to this day; but they are not legion—they do not even often wind up in high places, fortunately. We will not be able to locate enough pathological liars in official Washington to dig a very deep "Credibility Gap." . . .

No, we have to look elsewhere for a fuller understanding of the matter. I am familiar with all the charges and with the evidence: the erroneous predictions of military progress, the attempts to put the best face on every crisis, the fiscal confusion, the stories of peace feelers raised and peace feelers dashed, and so on. But it is not as simple as all that, and some things should be said to put the problem into perspective.

There were times when the Government was less than candid about important matters which were not related to national security. Never did it fool the press. The Washington press corps, by and large, is a persistent posse, and no administration will escape being called into account for its mistakes and sins.

But the problem of credibility is far more complicated. For the purpose of perspective rather than exoneration, a few observations should be made about some of the factors that make this a difficult issue.

First, some things are simply not suited for telling on the time schedule an inquisitive press prefers. At the risk of appearing to hide the facts, a President must often remain quiet. This is especially true when a President deals with a crisis over which he has little control, but for which he must assume great responsibility. . . .

I am not referring to the deep-seated propensity for clandestine conduct that led one official to put a sign on his desk which said: "The secrecy of my job does not permit me to know what I am doing." Instead I am referring to the necessity for a President to resist commenting on a situation until he can be certain his words will produce the intended result. President Harding learned this the hard way when he jeopardized the disarmament conference of 1921 by giving reporters an off-the-cuff interpretation of the treaty. What he did not know was that his Secretary of State had already given the press his own interpretation of the treaty—

The Age of Communication

and the two interpretations were at odds.

. . . Nuclear overkill is a daily concern of a President; verbal overkill ought to be, too. Reporters should do their best to find out what is going on, but they must also recognize that the President has no obligation to spoonfeed them with a full disclosure of every facet of official thinking on every subject they see fit to probe.

Second, events make lies out of the best promises. Circumstances change, and so must a President's strategy. . . . Woodrow Wilson surely meant what he said about keeping us out of war; but circumstances overtook him, and he found it necessary to do what he did not intend to do. In 1964, Lyndon Johnson declared that he sought no wider war in Southeast Asia, that he would not send American boys to do the fighting for Asian boys. One year later he widened the war and American boys were sent to fight it. For these decisions the President has been accused of breaking faith with the American people, of lying, of deliberately doing what he had said he would not do, of creating the "Credibility Gap." If it were only that simple! Even when it leads him to be at odds with his former position, a President can ill afford to have a closed mind or to fail to do what *he be-lieves* is best, no matter what *he said* or *believed* earlier.

Third, a President must sometimes reach conclusions from inconclusive evidence. There are times when a decision seems imperative before all the evidence is in. The choice may be between acting on the basis of information at hand—inconclusive though it be—or not to act at all. But Presidents know that each decision—to act or not to act—can have far-reaching consequences. No one could prove that the Marines were needed to save the lives of Americans at the Embajador Hotel in Santo Domingo, but his Ambassador was telling the President that those lives were endangered. Later the press and others, with the benediction of hindsight, would argue that they were not required.

Some of the claims of government are incredible. I used to make them —although I was gone last year when the Department of Transportation revealed how the Bureau of Public Roads was bringing God back to American life. One of the Department's press releases began:

"There are 36 churches alongside the 60-mile Interstate Beltway (I-495) which rings the Nation's capital. And half of them have been built since 1958 when the route of the circumferential highway first became known." This, according to spokesmen of the Department of Transportation's Federal Highway Administration, points up vividly "the importance of the highway transportation system to the country's community life." This is known as straining the obvious.

A more serious cause of incredibility has been raised by Ted Lewis of the *New York Daily News*. Last year he wrote a column in which he quoted the statement made in 1963 by Secretary of Defense Robert Mc-Namara that American troops could begin to be withdrawn from South Vietnam by 1965. Lewis was reprimanded by a spokesman for the Pentagon for writing that there had definitely been a "deliberate effort by Defense Secretary McNamara . . . to make things look better than they were." In quoting from the White House statement of October 2, 1963, he was told, "you have overlooked the very important final paragraph of that statement. It reads: 'The political situation in South Vietnam remains deeply serious. The United States had made clear its continuing opposition to any repressive action in South Vietnam. While such actions have not yet significantly affected the military effort, they could do so in the future.' " Lewis did not bother to reply to the spokesman, even though, at Hickam Air Force Base, six weeks after the issuance of the statement in December, Secretary McNamara had again talked about some U.S. personnel being able to "return by the end of the year." Why did the newspapers at the time latch on to prediction about troop returns? Lewis answered, "Because people wanted to know how long our boys would be over there."

"My point is," he wrote me, "that there is a natural oversimplification in news handling due to limited space and public interest. Responsible government officials should know this. If a statement is distorted out of context, it is because it was susceptible to an honest oversimplification. Why don't people in Washington realize this is the heart of the credibility problem? McNamara's own case is only one of hundreds. He promised—in effect—when he should have expressed hope it would turn out that way."

Secretary McNamara unquestionably meant well as did the others in those "hundreds" of other cases. But Ted Lewis has a point. Many good intentions have gone awry in Washington because defuscation is susceptible to honest oversimplification. With each incident the confidence of Americans in the veracity of the government has diminished.

It is not possible to restore overnight what has been lost over the years, but a few steps can be taken at the top that will establish a climate of candor which is the minimum requirement for building trust between government, press, and people. If the new President elected in November wishes to work in such an environment, he will be advised to begin with four simple but essential elements:

First, regular press conferences—at least once each month—the purpose of which should not be to announce the news but to explain the news. The timing of press conferences must fit the convenience of the President. However, they should be scheduled, and they should be frequent. And for all the short comings, they should also be televised.

Second, access for the press to second- and third-level officials in the White House and in each Department—men below the President and the Cabinet Secretaries who know the details of what is happening and who can increase a reporter's understanding or knowledge without abusing his responsibility.

Third, minimum use of "backgrounders" and unattributed quotations. The indiscriminate practice smacks of the secretiveness that Americans resist as alien to an open society.

Fourth, a willingness to live and let live. Some Presidents have regarded the press as an instrument of government, not an independent arm of the people. Some have been eager to woo the press; others to criticize it. Some have wished to make cronies of reporters; others to make cheerleaders of them. Modern Presidents have realized that they can never effectively govern unless they learn to reach the people through the mass media, and the wise ones have discovered how to go through or over the press to the people.

What the press and government should seek from each other is a mutual no-poaching agreement, for the press and the government are not allies. They are adversaries. That should be repeated. They are adversaries. Each has a special place in our scheme of things. The President was created by the Constitution, and the press is protected by the Constitution—the one with the mandate to conduct the affairs of state, the other with the privilege of trying to find out all it can about what is going on.

How each performs is crucial to the workings of a system that is both free and open but fallible and fragile. For it is the nature of a democracy to thrive upon conflict between press and government without being consumed by it.

If neither the government nor the press can take for granted the confidence of the people, each of us must guard against poorly-formed judgments about the other and against an unperturbable sense of security about our own well being.

All of this is important because we are in quite difficult straits in this country. The deepest crises are not Vietnam and the cities, but cynicism about the political order and a corroded confidence in our ability to communicate with one another and to trust one another. For such crises the requirements are large—to revive the public spirit, to restore the political vigor, and to rouse the nation from her present querulous divisions to a new sense of purpose.

The government has quite a duty, for the issues must be made plain, the truth clear, if these things are to be done. But the role of the press is no less. As William Allan White said, "This nation will survive, this state will prosper, this orderly business of life will go forward if only men can speak in whatever way given them to utter what their hearts hold—by voice, by postal card, by letters, or by press."

Topics for Discussion

1. What does Moyers mean when he says he has gone over to the enemy?
2. Moyers says that he learned that "of all the great myths of American journalism, objectivity is the greatest." What reasons does he give for this?
3. Is America on the way to becoming a nation of cynics?
4. What does Moyers suggest the press do to regain the confidence of the public?
5. What is a "backgrounder"? Why is Moyers concerned about the indiscriminate use of the backgrounder for stories? Do you think the press should even report what "an informed source" has to say? What are the dangers of this practice?
6. What relationship between the press and government would Moyers like to see? Do you think such a relationship could ever be achieved?
7. Why does Moyers say the problem of credibility in government is complicated? What does he mean by complicated?

Rhetorical Considerations

1. Why does Moyers make a point of his bias and ambivalence at the beginning of his essay? What effect does this have on what he says in the rest of his essay?
2. Many of Moyers' examples are based upon personal experiences. Does this tend to strengthen or weaken his arguments? Why?
3. Some of Moyers' paragraphs are rather long while many others are very short. Is there any reason for this seeming inconsistency in his paragraph structure?
4. Throughout his essay, Moyers frequently will list items numerically—one, two, three. Is this a good writing practice? What could he have done instead?
5. How valid and relevant are the two analogies Moyers uses in his first two paragraphs? Is this a good technique for opening his essay?

Two weeks that shook the press

JULES WITCOVER

For most of the American people, the story of the Pentagon Papers began on June 13, 1971, when copies of the New York *Times* appeared on doorsteps and newsstands bearing an unsensational two-line, three-column headline that read: VIETNAM ARCHIVE: PENTAGON STUDY TRACES 3 DECADES OF GROWING U.S. INVOLVEMENT. To the left was a particularly handsome picture of President Richard M. Nixon, his smiling daughter Tricia on his arm, at her Saturday afternoon White House wedding. The chances are that most readers saw that before they noticed the story that was to trigger one of the major government-press confrontations in American history.

Nineteen months earlier, however, readers of the *Times* had been told of the existence of the papers. In an article about former Secretary of Defense Robert S. McNamara in the New York *Times* Magazine of Nov. 9, 1969, Henry Brandon of the *Sunday Times* of London had written:

> McNamara is reluctant to comment on what he believes were his lasting accomplishments in the Department of Defense, but not as reluctant as he is to discuss his role in the Vietnam war. Even with the documents at his disposal, he says, he would not trust himself to write a history of those years. Instead, long before leaving the Pentagon, he ordered detailed historical records to be assembled, and there are now thirty to forty volumes that will be the raw material for a definitive history of that war.

And on Oct. 25, 1970, in the popular Personality Parade column in *Parade* magazine by "Walter Scott," who is Lloyd Shearer, *Parade*'s editor on the West Coast, there was this exchange:

Jules Witcover, "Two Weeks That Shook the Press." Reprinted from the *Columbia Journalism Review*, September/October, 1971 ©, pp. 7–15. Reprinted by permission.

Roger Bolen, ANIMAL CRACKERS. Reprinted through the courtesy of the Chicago Tribune–New York News Syndicate, Inc.

Q. There is a belief in this community that most quietly President Nixon has ordered a top-secret, exhaustive report on the U.S. involvement in Vietnam dating from World War II. Is there in fact such a report in the works? If so, will it be made available to the public so that we may finally learn the truth about the origin of the war? B. T. Clancy, Washington, D.C.

A. President Nixon has ordered no such report. Robert McNamara, Defense Secretary under Presidents Kennedy and Johnson, did, however. Several months before Lyndon Johnson oozed him out of the Pentagon, McNamara assigned a task force under Les Gelb to undertake the most thorough, in-depth study of U.S.-Vietnamese relations. The report was finished when McNamara was already out of the government. It runs to thirty volumes, is approximately 10,000 pages. There are relatively few copies in existence. There are no plans to make it public.

Daniel Ellsberg, one of the men who worked on the study, since then has said that he was the source of the material first published in the New York *Times*. He has not said when or how he supplied the documents, and the *Times* has said only that it obtained 7,000 pages through the investigative reporting of Neil Sheehan, a Washington reporter formerly assigned to coverage of the war in Vietnam. Sheehan obtained the papers sometime in March and informed his superiors. From the start, according to *Times Talk,* the paper's internal newsletter, their handling was a matter of utmost secrecy; *Times* employees were informed on the same strict need-to-know principle that guides internal disclosure of highly classified material within the Pentagon itself. Managing editor A. M. Rosenthal assigned foreign editor James L. Greenfield to direct the project, and Gerald Gold, an assistant foreign editor in New York, was told at the end of March he was to work with Sheehan.

Eventually, about seventy-five *Times* employees were brought into the effort and they successfully maintained the secrecy, going to remarkable pains to do so. On May 20, three weeks before publication, Nat Hentoff wrote in the *Village Voice* that the *Times* was working on a "breakthrough unpublished story concerning the White House,

Pentagon, and Southeast Asia," and, alluding to an internal debate, he asked: "Is this story going to be published?" Still, most members of the *Times* staff learned about the story when they read it in the paper.

Work on the project started in Washington, then shifted to New York when manpower and logistics problems dictated the move. Gold checked into two rooms at the Jefferson Hotel in Washington, a few blocks from the Washington *Post,* on April 5, and for two weeks worked there with Sheehan, who had been examining and assessing the material with Max Frankel, the *Times*' Washington bureau chief. Sheehan and Gold gauged the scope of the task and assembled a library of books and magazines to help them sort out what had and had not been published about the American involvement in Vietnam. They conveyed their assessment to Rosenthal, who in turn took it to publisher Arthur Ochs Sulzberger and got approval. There has been speculation since then that Sulzberger balked at publication and was persuaded by his editors, but this is denied.

Sheehan and Gold were brought to New York, to a three-room suite in the New York Hilton equipped with typewriters, filing cabinets, and two safes for the documents. Another assistant foreign editor, Al Siegal, and Muriel Stokes, a newsroom secretary, were added to the team—the first of a stream of staff members siphoned from regular duties and inserted unobtrusively into the operation. Hedrick Smith of the Washington Bureau, taking Russian lessons in preparation for a Moscow assignment, pitched in, and E. W. Kenworthy, also of the Washington bureau, was sent to New York. When colleagues asked Robert Phelps, the bureau's news editor, where they had gone, they were told: "Don't ask." Sheehan, Smith, and Kenworthy were the writers, with assistance from Fox Butterfield, who was on the New Jersey beat after having reported from both North and South Vietnam. Butterfield had to go back to Newark at one point to appear before a grand jury in-

vestigating a mugging he had suffered. All these staff members were told to stay away from the *Times'* main office. Greenfield shuttled back and forth, overseeing the project.

Eventually, the *Times* team had nine rooms on two floors of the Hilton. On the few occasions when all members of the team were out—for dinner or a meeting at Greenfield's apartment—guards from the *Times* stood watch. Members of the staff worked twelve to fifteen hours a day on the project. As the project neared completion, a makeup man went to the Hilton to lay out pages.

Meanwhile, in late May key production men were told about the effort and were instructed to plan a secret, separate composing room in miniature to handle the special copy. A recently vacated office was found on the ninth floor of the *Times'* 43rd Street building and on June 9 was stripped and renovated to accommodate heavy equipment. Additional power and light fixtures were installed. In the composing room, a page proof press was dismantled, moved to the special room and reassembled, all in eight hours. The next day, six teletypesetter perforators, a galley proof press, a printer's saw, page storage cabinet, makeup tables, proofreader's desk, and even a paper shredder to destroy extra proofs were installed. A plant patrolman was posted outside the door and given a list of those to be admitted.

On Thursday night, June 10, the first segment of the finished copy was brought from the Hilton and the first tapes were punched. The tapes then were taken to a corner of the main composing room, run through Linotypes, and type and tapes were brought back to the ninth floor, where proofs were taken and pages made up. On Friday morning, Sulzberger, who had been reading the material, gave final approval. Fifty to sixty printers in teams—also pledged to secrecy—moved in and out of the special composing room, around the clock, while the staff back at the Hilton continued to write, check, and polish copy.

At 1:30 p.m. on Saturday, June 12, associate news editor Lawrence G. Hauck laid out page 1 of the Sunday paper, slugging the section at the top NEIL. Only ten copies were Xeroxed for the makeup editors and news desks that really needed them. In midafternoon, six complete pages that had been made up on the ninth floor were rolled to the main composing room for final corrections. The page 1 copy was made up in a type galley upstairs and dropped into the page as one unit; the page was locked up and sent to the presses amid a mood of exultation. One of the great journalistic coups had been achieved, with hardly a whisper of suspicion anywhere.

In Washington, where the story probably had its greatest impact, reporter Don Oberdorfer of the Washington *Post* had heard some rumblings during the final week before publication, and on Thursday, Philip Geyelin, editor of the editorial page at the *Post,* heard that the project had something to do with Indochina, and that its publication would materially affect U.S. policy on Vietnam, possibly speeding American withdrawal. Ben Bagdikian, assistant managing editor for national news, heard Friday or Saturday that there had been a Rand Corporation study on the advisability of withdrawal from Vietnam, that all but one copy had been destroyed, and that copy may have fallen into the hands of the New York *Times.* Bagdikian called Henry Rowen at Rand and was told there had been no such study.

On Saturday night, Bagdikian was on the alert for the *Times'* story. Through an arrangement with UPI photos in New York, each night as page 1 of the *Times* comes off the press it is photostated and transmitted to the *Post;* the *Times* has the same arrangement for page 1 of the *Post.* At about 11:30 o'clock Saturday night, Bagdikian called his national desk, was read the *Times'* page 1 copy, and realized at once its importance. He phoned for staff reporters experienced on the Vietnam story—veteran diplomatic reporters Chalmers Roberts and Murrey Marder, Pentagon reporter Michael Getler and Oberdorfer, who had covered the war in Vietnam—and asked them to report to work on Sunday.

On Sunday afternoon, the group conferred with Benjamin Bradlee, the paper's executive editor, and Howard Simons, deputy managing editor, about what to do. Some thought was given to sending Roberts and Marder to New York to skim the paper as it came off the presses and do a quick rewrite job, but the notion was quickly dismissed. The story was too important and complicated; it required the most careful analysis, checking, and rewriting. The editors decided to accept a one-day beating on the story by the *Times* in favor of doing a careful description of what the *Times* printed each day, feeding in documentation from the *Times* and other sources to give the reader an intelligible package.

Meanwhile, the *Post*—and the rest of American journalism—started scrambling, either to try to get the Pentagon Papers—a dim prospect, it seemed, at that juncture—or to spin off enterprise and reaction stories based on what the *Times* was printing in New York. For most Washington bureaus, it was a period first of shock and then of frustration, until events and enterprise finally spread the story among a number of papers.

The first development in that direction, ironically, came Sunday morning when U.S. Attorney General John N. Mitchell reached outside his Watergate apartment and picked up his delivered copy of the *Times* at his doorstep. He had received no advance warning, and it is probable that the first thing that hit his eye was the picture of President Nixon and Tricia, whose wedding Mitchell and his wife Martha had attended the previous afternoon. Mitchell had gone from there to a black-tie dinner for the Japanese ambassador Saturday night, and had gone to bed blissfully unaware that American journalistic tradition and the First Amendment were about to come crashing down on him.

Mitchell's Sunday morning reading was interrupted by a call from Secretary of Defense Melvin R. Laird, who was about to appear on CBS' *Face the Nation*. He was certain to be asked about the *Times'* disclosures. What should he say? Tell them the matter has been referred to the Justice Department, Mitchell growled. Laird went on the panel show with two CBS reporters and one from the New York *Times* but, incredibly, through thirty minutes and twenty-seven questions there was not a single inquiry about or reference to the Pentagon Papers story.

Mitchell, for all his concern, did nothing on Sunday. On Sunday night the *Times* published its second installment. On Monday morning Mitchell and two assistant attorneys general, Robert C. Mardian (for internal security) and William H. Rehnquist (legal counsel), began conferring. Laird called again, to ask what he should tell the Senate Foreign Relations Committee; again he was told to say that the matter had been referred to Justice, and Mitchell asked Laird for a Pentagon memorandum indicating the national security implications of publication. About 7 p.m. Monday, Mardian met Mitchell at Mitchell's Watergate apartment and they agreed on the text of a telegram to Sulzberger asking the *Times* to desist. It was decided to phone him as well.

Mardian placed the call and was told Sulzberger was in London; he talked instead to Harding F. Bancroft, executive vice president. The papers, Mardian said, reading the telegram, contained "information relating to the national defense of the United States" bearing top-secret classification whose publication was "directly prohibited" by the Espionage Law. If the paper did not desist, he told Bancroft, Mitchell would seek an injunction. The *Times'* answer came in a statement read to Mardian two hours later and printed in the *Times* of Tuesday, June 15, along with the third installment. "The *Times* must respectfully decline the request of the Attorney General," it said, "believing that it is in the interest of the people of this country to be informed of the material contained in this series of articles." Later Tuesday, the *Times* was enjoined from further publication, pending a hearing on the Government's plea.

At the Washington *Post,* the paper's Vietnam experts still were rewriting, and scrambling to get a piece of the action on their own. On Tuesday, according to Bagdikian, the *Post* obtained "a little sliver" of the Pentagon study, but careful examination showed that the period it covered already had been broadly reported in the *Times'* Tuesday piece. The material was assessed as not unique enough to warrant *Post* publication. The *Post*'s editors anticipated that the Government's action against the *Times* would be thrown out in short order and that the *Times* would resume publication on Wednesday. Instead, U.S. District Court Judge Murray I. Gurfein granted a temporary restraining order for four days, until Saturday, June 19, at 1 p.m. Suddenly the *Times* was faced with prior restraint of publication; the scramble among the competition was bound to intensify now—and, as it turned out, segments of the Pentagon Papers soon were to become available to other newspapers. That night, Wednesday, June 16, on a New York radio show, former New York *Times* reporter Sidney Zion identified Ellsberg as the source of the *Times'* stories, and the FBI was on Ellsberg's trail.

On Thursday morning, June 17, Bagdikian arrived in a cab at Bradlee's Georgetown home, 4,400 unbound pages of the documents in hand. Bradlee, Roberts, Marder, and Oberdorfer were there; the five men went into the library and started sorting out what they had according to time periods and subject matter. Later that morning, Geyelin joined them, and two secretaries were brought in to compile a table of contents. Decisions were made as to what material was most important, and what material had not been covered in the *Times'* first three installments. Reporters took segments about which they were most knowledgeable and started writing.

Simultaneously, in the living room, a twelve-hour discussion began about whether the stories ought to be published at all. Involved were Bradlee, Bagdikian, and two of the *Post*'s lawyers, Roger A. Clark and Anthony Essaye. As the reporters labored at the raw material, not knowing that there was some question that the *Post* would publish, the debate proceeded, joined through the afternoon by Simons, Geyelin, and his deputy, Meg Greenfield, and later by Frederick S. Beebe, chairman of the board of the *Post*. Bagdikian moved between the library and the living room, overseeing the flow of copy and entering into the discussion. About 7 p.m., the writers joined the living room group for a break and a drink.

Basically, according to Bagdikian, it was the lawyers and management on one side, wary about publication, and the editors and writers on the other, zealous to print. The lawyers posed the question of legal tactics and propriety—whether it might be wiser to establish the right to publish by allowing the New York *Times* case to run its course, avoiding indication of any contempt for the court in that case; the editors and writers saw it strictly in terms of freedom of the press and journalistic responsibility to the public—if it is authentic and significant, publish it. The discussion continued through the *Post*'s small first edition run, finally ending about 9:30 p.m., in time for the main run. The decision was to publish.

A copy editor had been sent to Bradlee's house and had edited most of the first story by Roberts, and the copy had been sent to the paper in takes. Bagdikian grabbed the final three takes and took them himself by cab to the composing room. Publication seemed assured, when a call came for Bagdikian to return to Bradlee's. There the lawyers were posing a new objection. Maybe the *Post* should refrain from publication to avoid any appearance of collusion with the *Times*—which there had not been. The debate shifted to the kitchen. Calls were made to Mrs. Katharine Graham, the *Post*'s publisher. Finally, facing a 12:30 a.m. deadline, with the story set in type, the group again reached a decision to print, and the *Post* ran its first story on Friday, June 18.

All Thursday, the *Times* had been preparing its defense. The Justice Department had asked Judge Gurfein to order the *Times* to turn over the documents. While he urged the *Times* to do so, he did not so order. The paper refused to give up the papers but did supply a list of what it had. At the *Times*, its lawyers were busy educating its newsmen about the legal implications; the newsmen were educating the lawyers in the realities of how classified information, as a matter of course, is used and abused by government and press in Washington. Max Frankel now was in New York aiding in preparation of the defense, and he started to write a memo to the lawyers on how use of classification had become a self-serving government tool. It turned out to be a ninety-page affidavit, including seventy-two pages of exhibits.

On Friday, June 18, while Government witnesses in New York charged that the *Times'* publication had damaged national security and while Judge Gurfein examined the documents, the *Post* also heard from the Justice Department. Around noon, Rehnquist called Bradlee and "respectfully requested" that the paper halt publication of the study-based stories. Bradlee "respectfully declined." A telegram ensued from Mitchell to Mrs. Graham; Justice then went into the federal district court in Washington seeking a temporary restraining order. Judge Gerhard Gesell in early evening refused to grant it, and the *Post* proceeded with its second installment, by Marder. But the Government appealed, and two judges ordered Gesell to take a longer look at the case and decide by 5 p.m. on Monday. The *Post* stopped its presses, pulled off the plates containing Marder's story, and was ready to install substitute plates that had been prepared omitting the story. Just then one of the *Post*'s lawyers called; he had gone to one of the appellate judges, who said the order permitted the *Post* to complete its Monday night run. The original plates were rushed back onto the press and the full run was completed, with a delay of only about thirty minutes.

On Saturday, June 19, Gurfein ruled for the *Times*, but U.S. Circuit Court of Appeals Judge Irving R. Kaufman quickly extended the restraining order until the next Monday to enable a three-judge panel to hear the case. It was becoming clear now that a historic legal confrontation was under way that doubtless would reach the Supreme Court. *Post* editors and reporters, meanwhile, prepared affidavits of their own like Frankel's. Bradlee wrote that "President John F. Kennedy once read to me portions of a highly classified memorandum of conversation between him and Nikita Khrushchev in Vienna in 1961. I received his permission to use this material, which is still highly classified, and it appeared in *Newsweek*," where Bradlee then worked. Marder's affidavit included a story on the American intervention in the Dominican Republic in 1965 that was based "in considerable part on government cables which then were highly classified and still as far as I know remain classified," made available to him by Johnson Administration officials.

On Monday, June 21, the restraining order against the *Times* was extended another day to permit a full eight-judge panel to consider the case, and in Washington Gesell again backed the *Post* but the U.S. Court of Appeals extended the restraining order another day to allow the full nine-man appellate court to consider it.

Meanwhile, in Boston, a segment of the Pentagon Papers had come into the hands of the Boston *Globe,* and a select group of staff members were gathered in a locked room with the papers. About 5 p.m., under the direction of John Driscoll, assistant to editor Thomas Winship, they began a crash study of the papers. Matthew V. Storin, the paper's metropolitan editor—recently returned from the Washington bureau and a tour in Vietnam—checked the published *Times* and *Post* presentations to identify material that was new, and stories were suggested to and approved by Winship and Crocker Snow, Jr., the assistant managing editor. Storin was assigned the lead story, executive editor Robert Healy wrote a piece on President Kennedy's approval of covert action in North Vietnam, and Darius S. Jhabvala, the State Department reporter, wrote two stories on diplomatic and CIA involvements.

Another eventual member of the writing team, Washington bureau chief Martin F. Nolan, was not in Boston. He had a prior speaking engagement at the American University in Washington and kept it to avoid any hint that the *Globe* was about to publish stories on the Pentagon study. At one point a student asked Nolan: "Is competition among newspapers as much of an influence as it was always said to be?" Nolan replied that he knew and liked Neil Sheehan, "but I would have broken both his legs to get the story first." Then Nolan took a late-night plane to Boston. Aboard was Stuart Loory of the Washington bureau of the Los Angeles *Times,* who had returned from vacation to join the pursuit. "I look at Loory," Nolan said later, "and Loory looks at me, and we both know we're up to something." Nolan on arrival went directly to the *Globe,* started reading, and wrote a story for the final replate edition.

About three hours later, at 5 a.m. Tuesday, the phone rang in the *Globe* city room. Joseph Dineen, managing editor of the *Evening Globe,* took the call. It was Mardian asking whether the *Globe* would voluntarily cease publication—and griping about having been roused out of bed by news of the *Globe*'s stories. *Globe* editors, after conferences, called back and said that it planned to publish more. At 10.20 a.m., the phone rang in Winship's office. This time it was Mitchell himself. "Yes sir, General, Tom Winship here," the young editor said jovially. "Well," Mitchell said, "I see you're in the act." He "respectfully requested" that the *Globe* desist; Winship "respectfully declined." All right, Mitchell said, the Government would have to move against the *Globe;* otherwise the *Times* and *Post* would feel discriminated against.

In this instance, not only was the paper enjoined from further publication of its own stories based on the papers; it also was ordered to have the documents and stories impounded at the federal courthouse and was prohibited from printing stories from other newspapers or wire services based on the secret documents. The *Globe*'s lawyers swiftly appealed the rulings and won permission to store the papers and unpublished stories in a commercial bank vault, thus retaining possession. Also, after a day, the prohibition against using other stories based on the papers was lifted. Meanwhile, the bans on the *Times* and *Post* continued, amid more legal maneuvering.

The next paper to, in Mitchell's words, "get into the act" was the Chicago *Sun-Times*. About 5 p.m. Tuesday, the day Mitchell had called Winship, the *Sun-Times'* first edition had a story based, according to editor James F. Hoge, on declassified documents and "access to sources who had the papers." It concerned a contingency memorandum by then Assistant Secretary of State Roger Hilsman on the prospects for the overthrow of President Diem in 1963; the declassified memo had been dealt with much earlier in a New York *Times* Magazine article by former Johnson adviser John Roche, and was being offered around Washington by the Vietnam Veterans Against the War. At 1:30 a.m. Wednesday, June 23, a call came to Hoge from the U.S. Attorney's office in Chicago inquiring what the paper had and what it intended to print in the future. Hoge was not there but other editors reported the paper would print what was "relevant and responsible," without indicating whether it had any secret papers. Presumably for this reason, and because the paper ran no documents as such, no Justice action followed, though the paper subsequently did run stories based on the Pentagon study.

That night, as a grand jury in Los Angeles was looking into the matter of the leaked papers, two more news organizations—the Knight newspapers' and the Los Angeles *Times'* Washington bureaus —were preparing stories based on parts of the study. In each case, the same procedure was followed: careful examination of the material by teams of newsmen to determine what was significant and had not yet been published elsewhere. Knight released its story with a statement that the papers at that time did not plan further stories. No one at Justice ever called, though the Knight papers later did obtain more secret papers and did publish again. Mardian tried to call Los Angeles *Times* executives Wednesday night but was unsuccessful. On Thursday, June 24, however, the U.S. Attorney in Los Angeles, Robert Meyer, called the paper's executive editor, William F. Thomas, and was told that the *Times* had no present intention of publishing more. Subsequently, the Los Angeles *Times,* too, obtained more of the papers and ran another story. Neither Knight nor the Los Angeles *Times* was enjoined.

Throughout all this, both the New York *Times* and *Post* cases continued to occupy the courts; the appellate court in New York voted 5 to 3 to send the *Times* case back to Gurfein; the appellate court in Washington voted 7 to 2 for the *Post,* but retained the restraining order to permit the Government to take a further appeal. The *Times* asked the Supreme Court to rule in its case, and the Government appealed the *Post* case there. On Friday, June 25, the cases were consolidated and the Supreme Court voted 5 to 4 to continue the ban and hear evidence. At this juncture, primarily at issue was certain material the Justice Department had listed as damaging to national security. Under the rulings, both papers now were free to publish material not listed, but both declined, partly on principle, partly out of practicality.

In one of the great absurdities of the whole affair, Bradlee was not permitted to see the list of unpublishable items because he did not have security clearance, yet he was supposed to be free to publish what was not on the list he couldn't see! Lawyers who had seen the list would look at prepared copy, Bradlee said later, and one would say to the other: "I'm a little concerned about this." "Why?" Bradlee would ask. "I can't tell you," one of the lawyers would say. And then he would consult with his lawyer colleague.

Because the lawyers were the ones who were in conference and negotiation, and because they were approaching the case primarily from the legalistic rather than the journalistic point of view, Bagdikian said later, "we constantly were worried they might give something away. We had to educate them." George Wilson, the paper's military writer, who was considered to know the ma-

The Age of Communication

terial best, was given security clearance to work with the lawyers.

As the Supreme Court prepared to hear the combined case, still another newspaper published stories and documents from the Pentagon study— the St. Louis *Post-Dispatch,* in its afternoon editions of Friday, June 25. About 9:30 p.m., assistant managing editor David Lipman received a call from U.S. Attorney Dan Bartlett in St. Louis, asking whether the paper planned further stories. If it did, Bartlett told Lipman, or if the paper wouldn't say, the Government was going to seek a restraining order. The paper was going to print more, Lipman said, but not until Sunday; the Saturday paper was thin with small circulation.

Overnight, however, wire stories from Washington quoted the Justice Department as saying the *Post-Dispatch* was desisting pending the outcome of the Supreme Court decision in the *Times* and *Post* cases, then possibly due on Saturday. *Post-Dispatch* officials, learning of this erroneous version, called Bartlett and told him the paper's position had been misrepresented, that it appeared the *Post-Dispatch* was bowing to pressure. Hence, to protect its reputation for independence, the paper had decided to print a study-based story on Saturday. Before it could get another story in print, the *Post-Dispatch* was enjoined.

On Saturday, the Supreme Court heard arguments and then went into seclusion to vote and write opinions. On Monday, June 28, it extended its term, which was to have ended that day, and the final, most tense wait began. A brief and minor diversion came Tuesday morning, June 29, when the *Christian Science Monitor* printed the first of three articles based on the secret study. Shortly before noon, Erwin D. Canham, the paper's editor-in-chief, got a call from Herbert F. Travers, Jr., the U.S. Attorney in Boston. Travers said he was under orders to ask the *Monitor* not to publish further articles based on the study. Travers was told the paper would not voluntarily desist. Then he asked what the future stories would include, and Canham told him in a very broad way the subject matter. "I was in no sense submitting this or seeking clearance," he said later. "There was no question of clearance. It was the last thing I would have done." But the Justice Department issued a statement saying the *Monitor*'s editors "had cooperated by disclosing to (Travers) the contents of the two remaining installments they propose to publish" and hence there would be no effort to enjoin the paper.

Shortly before the Supreme Court ruling one other paper, *Newsday,* published a story based on the Pentagon study, together with a cloak-and-dagger account of how a reporter had been contacted and led through a treasure-hunt scenario to get the papers, in a shopping bag, in Boston.

Moments after 2 p.m. on Wednesday, June 30, the historic ruling of the Supreme Court finally came. The 6 to 3 verdict in favor of the *Times* and *Post* was flashed to jubilant newsrooms by reporters at the court. Cheers erupted in the *Times* newsroom when a news assistant rushed in from the wire room with a bulletin shouting, "We won!" Nowhere were the cheers louder and lustier than near the foreign news desk where Gerald Gold, who had played the central editing role from the start, sat in anticipation. Sulzberger and

Rosenthal hugged each other; at a press conference, Sulzberger expressed "complete joy and delight," and Rosenthal called it "a joyous day for the press and for American society."

At the *Post,* managing editor Eugene Patterson was in the wire room; Mary Lou Beatty, deputy national editor, was holding a line to the court reporter; and Bradlee was holding a line to the lawyers. Miss Beatty was the first to yell: "The decision is out! It looks as though we've won!" Patterson came out of the wire room and jumped on a desk. "We win, 6 to 3!" he shouted, amid general jubilation. "This whole organization was electrified," Bagdikian said later. "Even in the composing room they cheered."

In Boston, when the verdict came John Driscoll was sitting in the vault of the First National Bank of Boston, babysitting the documents and copy. Forty minutes after the Court ruled, with the Boston *Globe*'s afternoon deadlines slipping away, the *Globe* obtained a lower court order vacating the impounding of the papers and the temporary restraining order. Driscoll carried the whole batch back to the *Globe.* The stories were in the next edition.

Topics for Discussion

1. Why does Witcover call these "two weeks that shook the press"?
2. Why did the *New York Times* go to such extreme lengths of secrecy during the preparation of the articles on the "Pentagon Papers"? Do you think the strict secrecy was necessary?
3. Why did the United States Government want to stop the publication of the "Pentagon Papers"?
4. How important was the Supreme Court decision in the "Pentagon Papers" case? Do you agree that the issue involved was freedom of the press?
5. Look up these two weeks in back issues of the *New York Times*. Pay particular attention to editorial reaction by the *Times*. How does the newspaper view its confrontation with the government?
6. When you read the back issues of the *Times*, read carefully one or two of the articles based on the Pentagon Papers. Can you find anything in these articles that the government would find objectionable?
7. Do you think the *New York Times* was right in publishing the "Pentagon Papers"? How do you balance the people's right to know with the government's duty to keep some information secret?

Rhetorical Considerations

1. This article is organized chronologically. How does Witcover avoid the monotony of continually repeating dates?
2. Why does Witcover cite the quotation from the *Times* Magazine and *Parade* magazine? Are these quotations important to the rest of the article?
3. Witcover says that in his reply to Melvin Laird, John Mitchell "growled." What impact does this word have? Why couldn't Witcover just have used the word "said"?
4. Is Witcover's conclusion anticlimactic? Could the conclusion have been more forceful?

Is anything unprintable?

LEE H. SMITH

When Michael McClure's play, *The Beard*, opened in New York last fall, the daily reviews were unanimous on two points. They didn't like the play very much and they didn't want to talk about it very much. The reason for the latter seems clear. The play, a fanciful sex duel between Jean Harlow and Billy the Kid, not only contained a good deal of verbal obscenity, it also ended in one of the most startling scenes ever staged. *The New York Times* described that finale as "a highly publicized sexual act" (referring, somewhat cryptically, to the notoriety the play had received in San Francisco). The *Daily News* called it "an unorthodox sex act." The *New York Post* glided over it as "a sexual act that can't be described in a family newspaper." What the reviews couldn't say — or wouldn't say — was what the fuss was all about: an act of cunnilingus.

For better or for worse, American society has become increasingly concerned with its sex life and more and more eager to talk about it in public. The taboos against strong language and references to sex are vanishing with such staggering speed that it is often hard to remember what last year's taboos were. Two years ago, the movie *Who's Afraid of Virginia Woolf?* created a stir when Richard Burton said "hump the hostess." Today, the film *In Cold Blood* uses much earthier language and no one bothers to mention it. Norman Mailer was an iconoclast when he wrote the verb "fug" in *The Naked and The Dead*. In his latest novel, *Why Are We In Vietnam?*, he uses much more explicit obscenities much more often

Lee H. Smith, "Is Anything Unprintable?" *Columbia Journalism Review* (Spring 1968). Reprinted by permission.

and hardly anyone is surprised.

Candor is not restricted to the arts. Women hem their skirts well above their knees and trot off to cocktail parties where "The Pill" has replaced breastfeeding versus bottlefeeding as the favorite topic of conversation. Homosexuals have emerged from the shadows to parade in front of the White House and the Pentagon to demand equality, including the right to serve in the armed forces. August state legislatures openly debate the pros and cons of relaxing the laws for abortion—a word that used to be anathema almost everywhere. Schools across the country are beginning to feel the pressure to provide sex education, even for grammar school pupils.

The sexual revolution is real enough. For responsible newspapers, magazines, and radio and television stations that presents a problem: How can they report the revolution without compromising their standards? Some publications, of course, have a vested interest in cheering the revolution on. Magazines such as *Playboy* and its female counterpart, *Cosmopolitan*, often seem to be leading the way. But many more editors seem to be thoroughly confused. They want to keep up with what's happening but they aren't quite certain how to do it. More and more editors are faced with the problem of separating what is pertinent from what is simply prurient and trying to define the line between good reporting and bad taste. Some publications have been extremely bold, others far too reticent. And surprisingly, television —usually thought of as the meekest of the media—may be on its way to establishing a standard that accepts progress and yet maintains good taste; it may help the so-called "family" publications decide what can be said and what cannot.

Government censorship doesn't offer much guidance. The Supreme Court in recent years has decided it will allow just about anything short of what it considers hard-core pornography or (in the case of Ralph Ginzburg's conviction) hard-sell titillation—boundaries most editors have no intention of approaching. A few publications are exploring and exploiting that frontier, most recently the growing band of underground newspapers scattered in hippie enclaves from New York's East Village to San Francisco's Haight Ashbury district. The *East Village Other,* one of the most successful undergrounders, recently displayed, for example, a somewhat fuzzy photograph of what appeared to be an act of homosexual fellatio. And in the classified pages anyone can put his sexual appetites on the block. One ad in the same issue ran: "Attention!!! Dominant male wishes to meet docile female, gay or straight. We will have a whipping good time." As a result of such frankness, the Brooklyn District Attorney's office seized 1,000 copies of the paper and the editors of *EVO* are going to have to defend their candor in court.

The older *Village Voice,* which straddles the underground and the Establishment, draws the line at peddling perversion in its classifieds. "If you allow those," says editor Daniel Wolf, "suddenly you discover you're running an adjunct to Bellevue." But by most standards the *Voice* is unabashedly frank. "We have always been more open than most papers," observes Wolf. The *Voice* has used the common four-letter words freely for years. Lately the *Voice* has started running front-on photographs of nudes, collected by *Voice* photographers making the rounds of Greenwich Village dances and art shows. "We didn't sit around and discuss it," says Wolf. "We had the pictures and we just said 'what the hell' and shoved them in."

At other publications such decisions are momentous, even when an editor knows he is reaching a limited, sophisticated, and well-educated audience. Robert Manning, editor of *The Atlantic,* recalls pondering over a reportorial piece on Harlem in which the writer quoted a young boy sticking his head out the window and shouting, "Fuck you, white cop." Says Manning: "I looked at it, stared at it, and finally decided the only way to convey the full gut of it was to use it. The idea that a Negro boy of four, five, or six was already conditioned to that extent seemed to me to be something worth conveying. Dots would have undercut the impact."

Manning declines to allow four-letter words in fiction, but Willie Morris, editor of *Harper's,* says he will permit four-letter words in fiction or nonfiction when they are used by established authors. "This is something we would never do lightly," says Morris, "but times have changed. American readers are now infinitely more sophisticated than at any other time and they even demand more of the language than at any other time." Morris turned over the entire March issue of the magazine to Norman Mailer—an act that would make most editors shudder—for his journalistic report, "The Steps of the Pentagon." The report is witty, moving, and, in part, scatological.

Intellectual monthlies such as *Harper's* and *The Atlantic* can proceed rather boldly without worrying about offending large groups of readers. Candor becomes a real problem for general circulation newspapers and magazines that reach mass audiences. Advertising departments are particularly nervous. They diligently "ink in" clothes on unclad starlets in movie ads and edit out the explicit language underneath. When the Yugoslav film *Love Affair — Or The Case of the Missing Switchboard Operator* opened in New York in February the *Times* and the *Post* were sent an ad displaying a nude woman lying face down on a bed. Both newspapers "draped" a towel over her and the *Post* added a brassiere as well. This cover-up seemed reasonable enough. The ad was nothing but a cheap come-on.

Often, however, advertising departments are over-zealous. When the Yale University School of Drama opened its season last fall, the school routinely sent out an ad that listed the plays, including John Ford's seventeenth-century tragedy *'Tis Pity She's A Whore*. The *New Haven Register* reformed the lady somewhat and changed the title to *'Tis Pity She's Bad*. The *Hartford Courant* turned her into a mystery woman by truncating the title to read *'Tis Pity She's*. Donald Spargo, advertising director for the *Register,* explained that the wording of the ad was read to him over the phone and that if he had realized it was a title, he probably wouldn't have touched it. But Sidney Kaplan, advertising manager for the *Courant,* stood fast. "We just didn't run it, period," he snapped. "We try to run a clean newspaper."

The New York Times Book Review recently became alarmed that a deluge of ads for marriage manuals and other non-fiction works dealing with sex was giving the book review a bad image. As a result, the *Times* decided to close the *Review,* probably the country's major display case for publishers, to all non-fiction sex books—the important as well as the trivial and the titillating.

Editors are similarly fearful that the wrong word or picture is going to bring them reprisals from their readership. Over the past twenty years or so they have been slowly and cautiously scratching out such euphemisms as "social disease," "illegal operation," and "assault" and penciling in the more specific "syphilis," "abortion," and "rape." In some cases they have moved boldly. *Newsweek* magazine put a partly nude Jane Fonda on its cover in November to illustrate its special report on "The Permissive Society." *Life* magazine ran an excerpt from *The Naked Ape* in which British zoologist Desmond Morris examines man as a primate. The first paragraph of the excerpt included the sentence: "He [man] is proud that he has the biggest brain of all the primates but attempts to conceal the fact that he also has the biggest penis, preferring to accord this honor falsely to the mighty gorilla." (That same observation was to cause a considerable amount of trouble for other publications later.)

Some newspapers have been equally outspoken. Unfortunately, one of the best of them is now dead: the *New York Herald Tribune.* When Dr. William H. Masters and Mrs. Virginia Johnson published *Human Sexual Response,* a physiological study of the sexual act, in 1966, the *Herald Tribune* science editor, Earl Ubell, was unabashed in his summary and consequently helped dispel some disturbing myths about sexual performance.

In paraphasing the book's conclusions Ubell included such paragraphs as: "Neither the size of the male sex organ, the penis, nor that of its corresponding anatomical part in the female, the clitoris, has any relation to the adequacy of the man or woman as a sex partner."

The New York Times was more reticent, for which the *Times* is now apologetic. "I think we were wrong," says *Times* managing editor E. Clifton Daniel. "This was a serious work and it would have been perfectly acceptable to quote words such as penis and clitoris."

The *Times* has become more candid recently and such sensitive topics as homosexuality are reported liberally. And in its recent series on the drug-obsessed society the *Times* quoted a girl who said she took amphetamines to prolong her sexual activities. "I once stayed in bed for three days with a man," the girl was quoted as saying, "taking pills to keep going and smoking pot to enjoy myself." Still, the *Times* proceeds cautiously. When theater critic Clive Barnes reviewed *The Beard* he first wrote the word "cunnilingus." Metropolitan news editor Arthur Gelb asked him to take the word out: "It wasn't a big argument but at this time I just don't think we should use it. That might not be the case a month from now."

Other newspapers, perhaps a majority, are much more conservative. A former reporter on one of the largest papers in upstate New York says her movie reviews were consistently bowdlerized. In discussing *A Guide for the Married Man* she tried to convey the tone of the film by referring to "bouncing bosoms and fannies." The phrase was softened to read "flouncing females." In outlining the plot of *The Family Way* she said of the young bride: "After six weeks of marriage she was still a virgin." The desk changed it to read: "The marriage was not consummated"— a throwback to 1953 when the word "virgin" made *The Moon Is Blue* a "dirty" movie.

Usually, such editing is carried out quietly. But this January two of the nation's most influential publications—*The Chicago Tribune* and *The*

Washington Post—were caught editing in public. The two papers decided to recall some 1.7 million copies of *Book World,* the Sunday book review supplement they have published jointly since last September, when they spotted a page-one review they found offensive.

Peter Farb, a New Yorker who writes science books for laymen, reviewed Morris's *The Naked Ape* and paraphrased some of the book's conclusions, including: "The human male and not the gorilla possesses the largest penis of all primates; the human's preferred face-to-face mating is due to the frontal position of sexual signaling devices."

In New York, *Book World*'s editor, Byron Dobell, a former managing editor of *Esquire* magazine, approved the review and dispatched it to be printed for the *Post* in Philadelphia and to Chicago to be printed for the *Tribune. Tribune* editor W. D. Maxwell and publisher J. Howard Wood picked up copies from an early press run and apparently carried them off to the *Tribune* board of directors' meeting in Fort Lauderdale, Florida. Five days before the book review was scheduled to appear, Maxwell put in an urgent call to Thomas Furlong, managing editor in charge of features. Maxwell's order was to kill the review. Some 3,000 copies had already been sent to bookstores, libraries, and publishers, but the *Tribune* managed to collect more than a million copies that had been sent to distributors or were still in the plant. The page-one review was killed and a review that was scheduled to have run the following week was substituted. (Estimates of the cost of the kill ranged from $30,000 to $100,000.) The *Post* did not kill the review but did strike out the lines referring to penis from its 500,000 copies. (The *Post* had been much bolder in 1966 when it ran Ubell's review of *Human Sexual Response*.)

The *Tribune*'s kill seemed to be consistent with Maxwell's policy. The story goes that in 1961 he was given a copy of *The Carpetbaggers* by a well-meaning friend who thought it was a Reconstruction novel. Maxwell was so shocked that he ordered the book eliminated from the *Tribune*'s best-seller list and, to exclude similar works, he changed the name of the section to "Among the Best-Sellers." *Tribune* readers were thus "protected" from a significant — if depressing — scrap of sociology: The American public buys a lot of trash.

Because it does so much of its editing in public—"bleeping out" of offensive words—television often seems to be the most cautious of the media. But lately the bleeps have been fading and television has been growing much bolder. Five years ago, David Susskind invited a group of panelists that included *Playboy* editor and publisher Hugh Hefner and psychologist Dr. Albert Ellis to discuss "The Sexual Revolution in America." The show was taped but Bennett Korn, then a vice president of WNEW, refused to let it go on the air. Last year Susskind taped an even more delicate discussion, "Homosexuality: Perversion or Sickness?", with two psychiatrists and Dick Leitsch, president of the homosexual Mattachine Society. The show was broadcast to thirty cities across the country without objection from station managements.

Earl Ubell, who is now science editor for WCBS-TV, believes that he has been just as frank on television as he was on the *Herald Tribune* and that his only restraint is to make certain he delivers his information on sex soberly with no hint of a snicker or a raised eyebrow. And recently, Johnny Carson demonstrated that even a mass audience of network viewers will accept a serious discussion of sex. Carson interviewed Desmond Morris on *The Tonight Show* and needled *The Chicago Tribune*. "You talked about his [man's] penis," Carson said to Morris. "And they took that out of the paper in Chicago, because it would offend people . . . And I don't understand it, in this day and age, that you could not use that in a family newspaper." No bleep. No outraged phone calls to local television stations. Ernest Lee Jahncke Jr., NBC's vice president for standards and practices, explains why the network didn't bleep the reference. "This wasn't a lot of quipping and kidding around," he says. "It was a serious discussion, an adult discussion."

Television seems to be developing an "adult" standard for coping with the problem of sexual candor. Newspapers and many magazines persist in feeling inhibited by "family" standards. Even *The Wall Street Journal* — hardly a publication one passes on to the children — falls back on this excuse. When Edmund Fuller reviewed Mailer's *Why Are We in Vietnam?* for the *Journal* last fall he said: "Whether or not this newspaper is a family one depends, we suppose, on the family. But it is enough of one that we are restricted from offering you a slice of this pungent literary haggis for your own revulsion."

The premise that mass publications must be edited for "families" always seems to ignore the fact that families are growing up. Also, it begs the question of why publications should be edited for the most innocent reader. Most readers (if Marshall McLuhan is right, all readers) are adults and want to be written to as adults. Furthermore, the "family" standard is an unprofessional one that isn't applied to other areas of coverage. Any correspondent who filed from Saigon that he is witnessing a war that can't be talked about in a family newspaper would be hastily recalled.

This does not mean that editors should discard good taste and indulge themselves in titillation and gratuitous obscenity. On the contrary, it means that they should use good taste as a standard — their own good taste — and not waste their time trying to anticipate the most hysterical reaction of the most sensitive reader. The story of the candid society is too big to be ignored and from all indications it will run for a long time.

Topics for Discussion

1. What problem do you think an editor has in deciding what to print? Do you think certain words should not be allowed in newspapers and magazines? Which words? Why?
2. If a newspaper does censor certain words, who should decide which words are not allowed?
3. Cite some example to show that many of the traditional taboos against language are vanishing.
4. Can you note any changes in what is acceptable on television?
5. Many magazines carry advertisements which have a blatant sexual appeal while the magazine itself never uses certain sexual terms. How do you account for such a contradiction?
6. This essay is about printing the unprintable, yet how many unprintable or "dirty" words actually appear in the article? Why doesn't Smith use such words?

Rhetorical Considerations

1. Why does Smith open his essay with a specific example? How well does this serve as an introduction?
2. What is the thesis of this essay? Is it stated anywhere in the essay or is it simply implied?
3. When a book is bawdlerized, what happens to it?
4. What is Smith's attitude toward printing strong language and references to sex? How is this attitude revealed in the essay?
5. Does Smith use too many examples in his essay? Does his use of examples slow the essay and make it tedious?

My Lai 4 and the Press

The Day

Seymour Hersh

It was sunny and already hot when the first helicopter started its noisy flight to My Lai 4. The time was 7:22 A.M.; it was logged by a tape recorder at brigade headquarters. A brief artillery barrage had already begun; the My Lai 4 area was being "prepped" in anticipation of that day's search-and-destroy mission. A few heavily armed helicopters were firing thousands of small-caliber bullets into the area by the time Calley and his men landed in a soggy rice paddy 150 meters west of the hamlet. It was harvest season; the green fields were thick with growth.

The first platoon's mission was to secure the landing zone and make sure no enemy troops were left to fire at the second wave of helicopters—by then already airborne from LZ Dotti. As the flight of helicopters hovered over the landing area, the door gunners began spraying protective fire to keep the enemy—if he were there—busy. One of the helicopter's pilots had reported that the LZ was "hot," that is, Viet Cong were waiting below. The first platoon came out firing. But after a moment some men noticed that there was no return fire. "I didn't hear any bullets going past me," recalled Charles Hall, a machine gunner that day. "If you want to consider an area hot, you got to be fired on."

The platoon quickly formed a perimeter and secured the landing zone. Sergeant Cowen spotted an old man. Sledge was a few yards to Cowen's right: "We came to a well and there was a VC. We thought it was a VC. He was standing and waving his arms. Cowen fell back and said, 'Shoot the so-and-so.' I fired once, and then my [rifle] magazine fell out." Paul Meadlo noted that "the gook was standing up shaking and waving his arms and then he was shot." Allen Boyce saw it a little differently: "Some guy was in a rice field, doing something to a rice plant. He looked up and

Brigade headquarters, sure that there would be a major battle, sent along two men from the Army's 31st Public Information Detachment to record the event for history. Jay Roberts of Arlington, Virginia, a reporter, and photographer Ronald L. Haeberle of Cleveland, Ohio, arrived with the second wave of helicopters and immediately attached themselves to the third platoon, which was bringing up the rear.

The hamlet itself had a population of about 700 people, living either in flimsy thatch-covered huts—"hootches," as the GIs called them—or in solidly made red-brick homes, many with small porches in front. There was an east-west footpath just south of the main cluster of homes; a few yards further south was a loose surface road that marked a hamlet boundary. A deep drainage ditch and then a rice paddy marked the eastern boundary. To the south of My Lai 4 was a large center, or plaza area—clearly the main spot for mass meetings. The foliage was dense: there were high bamboo trees, hedges and plant life everywhere. Medina couldn't see thirty feet into the hamlet from the landing zone.

* * *

The first two platoons of Charlie Company, still unfired upon, entered the hamlet. Behind them, still in the rice paddy, were the third platoon and Captain Medina's command post. Calley and some of his men walked into the plaza area in the southern part of the hamlet. None of the people was running away; they knew that U. S. soldiers would assume that anyone running was a Viet Cong and would shoot to kill. There was no immediate sense of panic. The time was about 8 A.M. Grzesik and his fire team were a few meters north of Calley; they couldn't see each other because of the dense vegetation. Grzesik and his men began their usual job of pulling people from their homes, interrogating them, and searching for Viet Cong. The villagers were gathered up, and Grzesik sent Meadlo, who was in his unit, to take them to Calley for further questioning. Grzesik didn't see Meadlo again for more than an hour.

Some of Calley's men thought it was breakfast time as

they walked in; a few families were gathered in front of their homes cooking rice over a small fire. Without a direct order, the first platoon also began rounding up the villagers. There still was no sniper fire, no sign of a large enemy unit. Sledge remembered thinking that "if there were VC around, they had plenty of time to leave before we came in. We didn't tiptoe in there."

The killings began without warning. Harry Stanley told the C.I.D. that one young member of Calley's platoon took a civilian into custody and then "pushed the man up to where we were standing and then stabbed the man in the back with his bayonet . . . The man fell to the ground and was gasping for breath." The GI then "killed him with another bayonet thrust or by shooting him with a rifle . . . There was so many people killed that day it is hard for me to recall exactly how some of the people died." The youth next "turned to where some soldiers were holding another forty- or fifty-year-old man in custody." He "picked this man up and threw him down a well. Then [he] pulled the pin from a M26 grenade and threw it in after the man." Moments later Stanley saw "some old women and some little children—fifteen or twenty of them—in a group around a temple where some incense was burning. They were kneeling and crying and praying, and various soldiers . . . walked by and executed these women and children by shooting them in the head with their rifles. The soldiers killed all fifteen or twenty of them . . ."

There were few physical protests from the people; about eighty of them were taken quietly from their homes and herded together in the plaza area. A few hollered out, "No VC. No VC." But that was hardly unexpected. Calley left Meadlo, Boyce and a few others with the responsibility of guarding the group. "You know what I want you to do with them," he told Meadlo. Ten minutes later—about 8:15 A.M.—he returned and asked, "Haven't you got rid of them yet? I want them dead." Radioman Sledge, who was trailing Calley, heard the officer tell Meadlo to "waste them." Meadlo followed orders: "We stood about ten to fifteen feet away from them and then he [Calley] started shooting them. Then he told me to start shooting them. I started to shoot them. So we went ahead and killed them. I used more than a whole clip—used four or five clips." There are seventeen M16 bullets in each clip. Boyce slipped away, to the northern side of the hamlet, glad he hadn't been asked to shoot. Women were huddled against their children, vainly trying to save them. Some continued to chant, "No VC." Others simply said, "No. No. No."

* * *

By this time, there was shooting everywhere. Dennis I. Conti, a GI from Providence, Rhode Island, later explained to C.I.D. investigators what he thought had happened: "We were all psyched up, and as a result, when we got there the shooting started, almost as a chain reaction. The majority of us had expected to meet VC combat troops, but this did not turn out to be so. First we saw a few men running . . . and the next thing I knew we were shooting at everything. Everybody was just firing. After they got in the village, I guess you could say that the men were out of control."

Brooks and his men in the second platoon to the north had begun to systematically ransack the hamlet and slaughter the people, kill the livestock and destroy the crops. Men poured rifle and machine-gun fire into huts without knowing —or seemingly caring—who was inside.

Roy Wood, one of Calley's men who was working next to Brooks' platoon, stormed into a hut, saw an elderly man hiding inside along with his wife and two young daughters: "I hit him with my rifle and pushed him out." A GI from Brooks' platoon, standing by with an M79 grenade launched, asked to borrow his gun. Wood refused, and the soldier asked another platoon mate. He got the weapon, said, "Don't let none of them live," and shot the Vietnamese in the head. "These mothers are crazy," Wood remembered thinking. "Stand right in front of us and blow a man's brains out." Later he vomited when he saw more of the dead residents of My Lai 4.

The second platoon went into My Lai 4 with guns blazing. Gary Crossley said that some GIs, after seeing nothing but women and children in the hamlet, hesitated: "We phoned Medina and told him what the circumstances were, and he said just keep going. It wasn't anything we wanted to do. You can only kill so many women and children. The fact was that you can't go through and wipe out all of South Vietnam."

* * *

Carter testified that soon after the third platoon moved in, a woman was sighted. Somebody knocked her down, and then, Carter said, "Medina shot her with his M16 rifle. I was fifty or sixty feet away and saw this. There was no reason to shoot this girl." The men continued on, making sure no one was escaping. "We came to where the soldiers had collected fifteen or more Vietnamese men, women and children in a group. Medina said, 'Kill every one. Leave no one standing.'" A machine gunner began firing into the group. Moments later one of Medina's radio operators slowly "passed among them and finished them off." Medina did not personally shoot any of them, according to Carter, but moments later the captain "stopped a seventeen- or eighteen-year-old man with a water buffalo. Medina told the boy to make a run for it," Carter told the C.I.D. "He tried to get him to run but the boy wouldn't run, so Medina shot him with his M16 rifle and killed him.

Roberts and Haeberle also moved in just behind the third platoon. Haeberle watched a group of ten to fifteen GIs methodically pump bullets into a cow until it keeled over. A woman then poked her head out from behind some brush; she may have been hiding in a bunker. The GIs turned their fire from the cow to the woman. "They just kept shooting at her. You could see the bones flying in the air chip by chip." No one had attempted to question her; GIs inside the hamlet also were asking no questions. Before moving on, the photographer took a picture of the dead woman. Haeberle took many more pictures that day; he saw about thirty GIs kill at least a hundred Vietnamese civilians.

When the two correspondents entered My Lai 4, they saw dead animals, dead people, burning huts and houses. A few GIs were going through victims' clothing, looking for piasters. Another GI was chasing a duck with a knife; others stood around watching a GI slaughter a cow with a bayonet.

Haeberle noticed a man and two small children walking toward a group of GIs: "They just kept walking toward us

. . . you could hear the little girl saying, 'No, no . . .' All of a sudden the GIs opened up and cut them down." Later he watched a machine gunner suddenly open fire on a group of civilians—women, children and babies—who had been collected in a big circle: "They were trying to run. I don't know how many got out." He saw a GI with an M16 rifle fire at two young boys walking along a road. The older of the two—about seven or eight years old—fell over the first to protect him. The GI kept on firing until both were dead.

As Haeberle and Roberts walked further into the hamlet, Medina came up to them. Eighty-five Viet Cong had been killed in action thus far, the captain told them, and twenty suspects had been captured. Roberts carefully jotted down the captain's statistics in his notepad.

* * *

Now it was nearly nine o'clock and all of Charlie Company was in My Lai 4. Most families were being shot inside their homes, or just outside the doorways. Those who had tried to flee were crammed by GIs into the many bunkers built throughout the hamlet for protection—once the bunkers became filled, hand grenades were lobbed in. Everything became a target. Gary Garfolo borrowed someone's M79 grenade launcher and fired it point-blank at a water buffalo: "I hit that sucker right in the head; went down like a shot. You don't get to shoot water buffalo with an M79 every day." Others fired the weapon into the bunkers full of people.

* * *

Carter recalled that some GIs were shouting and yelling during the massacre: "The boys enjoyed it. When someone laughs and jokes about what they're doing, they have to be enjoying it." A GI said, "Hey, I got me another one." Another said, "Chalk up one for me." Even Captain Medina was having a good time, Carter thought: "You can tell when someone enjoys their work." Few members of Charlie Company protested that day. For the most part, those who didn't like what was going on kept their thoughts to themselves.

Herbert Carter also remembered seeing Medina inside the hamlet well after the third platoon began its advance: "I saw all those dead people laying there. Medina came right behind me." At one point in the morning one of the members of Medina's CP joined in the shooting. "A woman came out of a hut with a baby in her arms and she was crying," Carter told the C.I.D. "She was crying because her little boy had been in front of their hut and . . . someone had killed the child by shooting it." When the mother came into view, one of Medina's men "shot her with an M16 and she fell. When she fell, she dropped the baby." The GI next "opened up on the baby with his M16." The infant was also killed. Carter also saw an officer grab a woman by the hair and shoot her with a .45-caliber pistol: "He held her by the hair for a minute and then let go and she fell to the ground. Some enlisted man standing there said, 'Well, she'll be in the big rice paddy in the sky.' "

In the midst of the carnage, Michael Bernhardt got his first good look at My Lai 4. Bernhardt had been delayed when Medina asked him to check out a suspicious wood box at the landing zone. After discovering that it wasn't a booby trap, Bernhardt hurried to catch up with his mates in the third platoon. He went into the hamlet, where he saw Charlie Company "doing strange things. One: they were setting fire to the hootches and huts and waiting for people to come out and then shooting them. Two: they were going into the hootches and shooting them up. Three: they were gathering people in groups and shooting them. The whole thing was so deliberate. It was point-blank murder and I was standing there watching it. It's kind of made me wonder if I could trust people any more."

Those Vietnamese who were not killed on the spot were being shepherded by the first platoon to a large drainage ditch at the eastern end of the hamlet. After Grzesik left, Meadlo and a few others gathered seven or eight villagers in one hut and were preparing to toss in a hand grenade when an order came to take them to the ditch. There he found Calley, along with a dozen other first platoon members, and perhaps seventy-five Vietnamese, mostly women, old men and children.

* * *

Calley then turned his attention back to the crowd of Vietnamese and issued an order: "Push all those people in the ditch." Three or four GIs complied. Calley struck a woman with a rifle as he pushed her down. Stanley remembered that some of the civilians "kept trying to get out. Some made it to the top . . ." Calley began the shooting and ordered Meadlo to join in. Meadlo told about it later: "So we pushed our seven to eight people in with the big bunch of them. And so I began shooting them all. So did Mitchell, Calley . . . I guess I shot maybe twenty-five or twenty people in the ditch . . . men, women and children. And babies." Some of the GIs switched from automatic fire to single-shot to conserve ammunition. Herbert Carter watched the mothers "grabbing their kids and the kids grabbing their mothers. I didn't know what to do."

* * *

William C. Lloyd of Tampa, Florida, told the C.I.D. that some grenades were also thrown into the ditch. Dennis Conti noticed that "a lot of women had thrown themselves on top of the children to protect them, and the children were alive at first. Then the children who were old enough to walk got up and Calley began to shoot the children."

One further incident stood out in many GIs' minds: seconds after the shooting stopped, a bloodied but unhurt two-year-old boy miraculously crawled out of the ditch, crying. He began running toward the hamlet. Someone hollered, "There's a kid." There was a long pause. Then Calley ran back, grabbed the child, threw him back in the ditch and shot him.

* * *

In other parts of My Lai 4, GIs were taking a break, or loafing. Others were systematically burning those remaining houses and huts and destroying food. Some villagers—still alive—were able to leave their hiding places and walk away. Charles West recalled that one member of his squad who simply wasn't able to slaughter a group of children asked for and received permission from an officer to let them go.

* * *

By now it was nearly 10:30 A.M. and most of the company began drifting aimlessly toward the plaza and the command post a few yards to the south. Their work was largely over; a good part of the hamlet was in flames. The villagers "were laying around like ants," William Wyatt remembered. "It was just like somebody had poisoned the water and everybody took a drink and started falling out."

Herb Carter and Harry Stanley had shed their gear and were taking a short break at the CP. Near them was a young Vietnamese boy, crying, with a bullet wound in his stomach. Stanley watched one of Captain Medina's three radio operators walk along a trail toward them; he was without his radio gear. As Stanley told the C.I.D., the radio operator went up to Carter and said, "Let me see your pistol." Carter gave it to him. The radio operator "then stepped within two feet of the boy and shot him in the neck with a pistol. Blood gushed from the child's neck. He then tried to walk off, but he could only take two or three steps. Then he fell onto the ground. He lay there and took four or five deep breaths and then he stopped breathing." The radio operator turned to Stanley and said, "Did you see how I shot that son of a bitch?" Stanley told him, "I don't see how anyone could just kill a kid."

* * *

Other children were also last-minute targets. After the scene with the women and children, West noticed a small boy, about seven years old, staring dazedly beside a footpath. He had been shot in the leg. "He was just standing there staring; I don't think he was crying. Somebody asked, 'What do we do with him?' " At this point West had remembered there had been an order from Captain Medina to stop the shooting. "I just shrugged my shoulders," West recalled, "and said, 'I don't know,' and just kept walking." Seconds later he heard some shots, turned around and saw the boy no longer standing on the trail.

* * *

Some GIs, however, didn't hesitate to use their bayonets. Nineteen-year-old Nguyen Thi Ngoc Tuyet watched a baby trying to open her slain mother's blouse to nurse. A soldier shot the infant while it was struggling with the blouse, and then slashed at it with his bayonet. Tuyet also said she saw another baby hacked to death by GIs wielding their bayonets.

* * *

In the early afternoon the men of Charlie Company

mopped up to make sure all the houses and goods in My Lai 4 were destroyed. Medina ordered the underground tunnels in the hamlet blown up; most of them already had been blocked. Within another hour My Lai 4 was no more: its red-brick buildings demolished by explosives, its huts burned to the ground, its people dead or dying.

Michael Bernhardt later summarized the day: "We met no resistance and I only saw three captured weapons. We had no casualties. It was just like any other Vietnamese village—old papa-sans, women and kids. As a matter of fact, I don't remember seeing one military-age male in the entire place, dead or alive. The only prisoner I saw was in his fifties."

* * *

When Army investigators reached the barren area in November, 1969, in connection with the My Lai probe in the United States, they found mass graves at three sites, as well as a ditch full of bodies. It was estimated that between 450 and 500 people—most of them women, children and old men—had been slain and buried there.

The Story Everyone Ignored

Seymour Hersh

I was asked to write this article—to tell editors how they missed one of the biggest stories of the year—by an associate editor of one of the biggest newspapers in America, one of the newspapers that was very slow to fully realize the significance of the alleged massacre at Songmy. That irony, in itself, is important to me—for it convinces me that editorship, like democracy, is not dead . . . yet.

The fact that some thirty newspapers in this country, Canada, and abroad did publish my first and subsequent Dispatch News Service stories on Songmy is further proof that the nations' press is not as gutless as all that. I honestly believe that a major problem in newspapers today is not censorship on the part of editors and publishers, but something more odious: self-censorship by the reporters.

There is no doubt that many reporters had heard of the Pinkville incident (at least many have told me so). In talking to some Pentagon officials before I wrote my first story (they talked then), I was told by one general officer: "Pinkville had been a word among GIs for a year. I'll

Seymour Hersh, "The Story Everyone Ignored." Reprinted from the *Columbia Journalism Review*, Winter 1969-70 ©, with permission.

never cease to be amazed that it hasn't been written about before." Another general officer who was attached to headquarters in Saigon in 1968 said he had first heard talk of Pinkville soon after it happened. Of course, an outsider can also be amazed that generals would hear of such incidents and not demand an investigation, but the notion that *those* men thought that the press had somehow fallen on the job is, well, significant.

As everyone knows, the first mention of the incident was provided by the public information officer at Fort Benning, Ga., who released a brief item September 6 announcing that Lt. William L. Calley, Jr., had been charged with murder in the deaths "of an unspecified number of civilians in Vietnam."

The AP man in the area promptly put in a query; when the Pentagon did not gush forth with all of the details, that was that. No other questions were officially asked of the Pentagon about the Calley story until I offered some carefully hedged queries around October 23. The Washington *Post* queried the Pentagon about Calley on November 6; by that time I had arranged a number of interviews—with Calley, among others—and was well on the way. The New York *Times* also began asking some questions shortly before the first story broke early November 12 for the next morning's papers.

The initial Pentagon dispatch was put on the wire by the AP and appeared Saturday morning in many major newspapers in the country, including the Washington *Post*, the New York *Times*, and Los Angeles *Times*. It would be

wonderful to say I noticed it immediately, saw its significance, and dashed out with pencil and pad in hand. Of course not. I was tipped around October 20 by a source with Pentagon connections. My source simply told me that the military was planning to court-martial an officer at Fort Benning, Ga., for the murder of about seventy-five Vietnamese civilians.

What made me drop everything (I was then finishing *The Ultimate Corporation*, a book on the Pentagon for Random House) and begin pursuing the story? For one thing, my source was good—but certainly no better than others who must have told newsmen about the incident in the twenty months since it took place. Another, more important reason, I think, was my experiences with chemical and biological warfare (CBW). I had written a book on CBW (*Chemical and Biological Warfare: America's Hidden Arsenal*, Bobbs-Merrill) that was published in mid-1968 but somehow failed to make much of a mark at first. The public and the press seemingly did not want to believe that the United States was stockpiling nerve gas at Army commands overseas, nor did they want to believe that American military men would be capable of shipping trainloads of nerve gas through the American countryside without telling anyone. My book prompted very little investigative reporting.

So, I believed the story about Pinkville. And I also knew—or thought I knew—that newspapers would probably be the last to believe it. Thus I began my searches with an eye on *Look* and *Life* magazines. I won't tell who gave me leads, but suffice to say that I managed to find out who Calley was, and where his lawyer was located. I decided that the telephone was a bad interviewing instrument on the Pinkville story, and therefore interviewed every important witness or near-witness in person. I applied for and received a limited travel grant (about $2,000 en toto) from the Philip Stern Fund for Investigative Journalism in Washington, and began flying around to locate witnesses. (In all, I traveled more than 30,000 miles via air.)

By early November I had a pretty good picture of what had happened, at least solid enough so I could write. I knew Calley had been charged with 109 deaths and I had the precise wording from the charge sheets. I contacted *Life;* they said they weren't interested (little did I know that they had turned down Ronald Ridenhour, the twenty-three-year-old California college student whose letters first prompted the Army to study the incident). Then I went to *Look.* A senior editor there was very interested; I wrote a sketchy, but explosive, memo on what I had. They, too, decided to pass—I think, charitably, because of their four- to six-week lead time.

I really didn't know where to turn, so I simply kept doing research. David Obst, general manager of Dispatch and a Washington neighbor and fellow touch football player, had learned from me about Pinkville and was insistent on handling it. I had written a few Sunday pieces for his news service and been moderately successful; as many as six or eight responsible newspapers (including the Baltimore *Sun*)

had published one or more of my earlier works. So in the end, I turned to Dispatch and committed myself to its syndication.

Why? I was convinced that if I walked into a major newspaper and laid out my story, the editors, to verify my information, would have to repeat the painstaking interview-and-more-interview process I had gone through, and then write their own story. I could respect this, but I simply wanted my story for myself. And I wanted it to be credible, which ruled out smaller magazines. This wasn't an article for a journal of opinion, like the *New Republic,* or *National Review,* for that matter —it was hard news that should be written as such.

That left Obst and Dispatch. Amazingly, as is well known, it worked. Of about fifty newspapers contacted, thirty-two or so eventually ran my first story citing the charges against Calley. This was not done on a whim; the papers carefully checked me and as many of the facts as possible. That was to the newspaper world's credit.

What happened after the first story is not. Only the New York *Times,* which had its own story, chose to follow up independently on the story, by sending Henry Kamm from its Saigon bureau to the Pinkville area to interview survivors (ABC-TV and *Newsweek* also went along). The *Times* decided to treat Pinkville as a major story and do its own reporting from the outset. Other papers avoided any hint of investigatory research and it was left to me to seek out Ridenhour (who, after my first story, had told newspapers about his role) and to interview him in

California. Although he had first revealed his part in the story Friday, November 14, and I did not see him until the following Monday afternoon, amazingly I was the first reporter to personally interview him. The New York *Times* and AP had talked briefly to him by telephone, but the Los Angeles *Times*—barely thirty miles away in downtown Los Angeles—did not send a reporter. And none of the papers realized how important Ridenhour was—he had a list of eye-witnesses, many of whom were out of the service and willing to talk.

Ridenhour gave me the names and addresses of some of the eye-witnesses he had spoken to about Pinkville (he did not actually participate in the incident), and off I went. After personal interviews in Utah, Washington, and New Jersey—conducted within twenty-four hours—my subsequent story, for newspapers of November 20, was well received by the nation's press. After that second story, newspapers generally were still reluctant to comment editorially on Pinkville (with the New York *Times* and Chicago *Sun-Times* being notable exceptions), although they were playing the story big. It all had suddenly become much more credible when the Army announced in late November that Calley had indeed been charged with the murder of 109 Vietnamese civilians.

The last newspapers vestiges of resistance disappeared when Paul Meadlo of Terre Haute, Ind., submitted to a Dispatch interview and told how he had calmly executed, under orders, dozens of Vietnamese civilians. Dispatch provided information on Meadlo to CBS-TV, which ran a long interview on the Walter Cronkite show. It was a cash deal for Dispatch, with Meadlo, who had been fully informed of the possible dangers to him and his rights in the matter, not being paid one cent; but even more important was the fact that television was needed—that somehow just relying on newspapers to sear the conscience of America hadn't been working, or had been working too slowly. It took three newspaper stories and one television interview to make Pinkville a national issue; it shouldn't have.

After Meadlo came a flurry of newspaper stories quoting former members of Calley's platoon and his company. The newspaper industry, in one of those collective changes of mind that can only be found in the business, decided each man's testimony was important enough to play all over the front pages. The indiscriminate use of eyewitness statements was amazing to me; I had carefully attempted to get some kind of "feel" from each of my interviewees before quoting them. GIs are notorious liars (that point is based on a personal recollection), particularly when talking about their combat days. I think some of those who came forward did not tell all the truth.

This, of course, leads right into the issue of pre-trial publicity; a major dilemma facing newspapers today. I was impressed by how important this issue was for some newspapers when they were deciding whether or not to run my first few Dispatch stories; and then surprised at how quickly the same newspapers forgot about such rights and began splashing stories across their newspaper once Pinkville became a big issue. Dispatch handled the pre-trial publicity question by retaining a prominent Washington law firm and relying on it for advice. The advice generally was that the public's right to know far outweighed any disadvantages to some involved individuals. Even if a court-martial became an impossibility and some men had to be turned free, this seemed preferable to not having as full and as responsible a debate as possible—and "responsible" to me simply meant when I quoted a source I firmly believed him to be telling the truth; it was not always a question of just quoting someone accurately.

What made some responsible and careful newspapers publish my stories and others, equally as responsible and careful, not publish them? I think part of the answer is instinct, the instinct many reporters and editors feel for a story or a source. There are many blind sources one can trust, even over a telephone, while others need careful checking.

One newspaper with which I became involved was the Washington *Post*. I met with top editors of the paper early on the morning of November 12, when Dispatch broke the story. The meeting was chaired by Ben Bradlee, the *Post*'s executive editor. My story was passed around, read by all, and I answered some direct questions on the legal aspects of the charges against Calley. No one asked what seemed to me to be the obvious question: "Is this true?" After I left, I learned later, Bradlee handled that aspect by telling his staff, "This smells right." His instinct was working, at least that morning.

Nevertheless, I knew things had changed for most of the nation's press after the Meadlo interview; at least six friends in the Washington newspaper corps called me at home over the next few evenings seeking tips on where to go next or leads on involved GIs or officers who might be living in their local areas.

When the nation's newspapers begin wanting their hometown mass murderer, things are well in hand.

Topics for Discussion

1. Why did the press generally ignore the story of the My Lai 4 massacre?
2. Even though the My Lai 4 massacre became big news, most papers were reluctant to comment editorially. Why?
3. Why did Hersh think he would have to publish his original story in *Look* or *Life*? What does this say about the press?
4. The brief notice in the *New York Times* of a battle in Quang Tri in which 128 enemy soldiers were killed is really a report on the My Lai 4 massacre. How could a newspaper report be so wrong?
5. Given Hersh's account of how the press ignored and then gave great play to the My Lai 4 story, do you find yourself feeling somewhat cynical about the press? Why?
6. Hersh says some newspapers did publish his story and others didn't. The basis for the decision was partly instinct. Do you think a reporter and an editor should act on instinct? What kind of instinct would this be?
7. Hersh points out that high-ranking officers in the Pentagon and at headquarters in Saigon knew about the massacre but did not investigate it. Should the press accounts of the massacre have also revealed this?
8. Hersh says that a reporter has to be careful when using eyewitness statements, particularly with soldiers because, as he puts it, "GI's are notorious liars . . . particularly when talking about their combat days." How did Hersh compensate for this in his reporting? Is this caution obvious at all in his account of the massacre itself, "The Day"?

Rhetorical Considerations

1. Compare the styles of the three selections dealing with My Lai. Are they the same at all? What are some of the major differences? Which style do you like best? Why?
2. What is your reaction after reading the essay, "The Day"? Do you have the same reaction after reading the *New York Times* article and the other essay by Hersh? Why?
3. What is the irony of Hersh's concluding sentence in his essay, "The Story Everyone Ignored"?
4. What are the implications of Hersh's statement that "editorship, like democracy, is not dead . . . yet"? What is the effect of the ellipses in this quotation?
5. Hersh's account of "The Day" is very factual and unemotional. How does he give his account power and impact? Can you find any slanted or connotative words in this account?

The Gulf of Tonkin Incidents and the Press

RED PT BOATS FIRE AT U.S. DESTROYER ON VIETNAM DUTY

Maddox and Four Aircraft Shoot Back After Assault 30 Miles Off Coast

ATTACKERS DRIVEN OFF

American Units Undamaged —Rusk Says 'Other Side Got a Sting Out of This'

By ARNOLD H. LUBASCH

WASHINGTON, Aug. 2 —Three North Vietnamese PT boats fired torpedoes and 37-mm. shells at a United States destroyer in international waters about 30 miles off North Vietnam today.

The destroyer and four United States aircraft fired back, damaged them and drove them off.

The incident was announced here in an official statement by the Defense Department. It said that neither the destroyer nor the aircraft sustained casualties or damage.

The statement said that the destroyer, the 3,300-ton Maddox, was on a routine patrol when an

unprovoked attack took place in the Gulf of Tonkin.

Cautious on Identification

At first Government officials were cautious in commenting that the attacking boats presumably came from North Vietnam, but Secretary of State Dean Rusk said in New York tonight that the attackers were North Vietnamese.

"The other side got a sting out of this," the Secretary said. "If they do it again, they'll get another sting."

Reports received here, apparently based on close air surveillance of the attacking boats, indicated there was no doubt that they were from North Vietnam.

President Johnson was informed immediately and received reports from top Government officials at a 45-minute White House meeting. He issued no statement.

Not Regarded as Crisis

Government officials said later that the attack was not regarded as a major crisis. They said the United States Seventh Fleet had been patrolling the area for some time, would continue its patrols and had sufficient strength on hand.

Adm. U. S. Grant Sharp Jr., Commander in Chief in the Pacific, was advised of the incident by radio as he flew back to his Pearl Harbor headquarters from a visit to South Vietnam.

The Defense Department statement on the attack, issued also by the Pacific Command, said that the boats were damaged by gunfire from the Maddox and the four carrier-based jet aircraft. The statement said:

"While on routine patrol in international waters at 4:08 A.M., E.D.T., the United States destroyer Maddox underwent an unprovoked attack by three PT-type boats at latitude 19-40 north,

longitude 106-34 east, in Tonkin Gulf. The attacking boats launched three torpedoes and used 37-mm. gunfire."

"The Maddox answered with 5-inch gunfire. Shortly thereafter, four F-8 aircraft from the U.S.S. Ticonderoga joined in the defense of Maddox, using Zuni rockets and 20-MM. strafing attacks."

"The PT boats were driven off with one seen to be badly damaged and not moving and the other two damaged and retreating slowly. No casualties or damage was sustained by the Maddox or the aircraft."

The Zuni rocket-propelled missile, designed for firing from launchers carried on aircraft, has a non-nuclear warhead said to be almost as destructive as a nuclear weapon.

Defense Department officials described the incident as unwelcome but not especially serious. They observed that the most effective protest possible was made by the destroyer and four fighter planes.

The attacking boats, which displayed no flags or other identifying marks, were picked up on the destroyer's radar, kept coming and opened fire, according to the Defense Department officials.

After the attackers were driven off, they said, the United States forces resumed their patrol. No effort was made to sink the PT boats, because the fleet was not at war, they said.

The Maddox was apparently carrying out a surveillance mission, according to officials here. They said there was no ready explanation why the PT boats would in effect attack the powerful Seventh Fleet.

State Department officials noted that Seventh Fleet patrols in the area were nothing new and would continue, although shooting incidents could not be precluded. They indicated that the United States did not plan an immediate diplomatic protest as a result of the incident.

The White House declined to make any comment and would not even acknowledge that the high-level briefing for the President had taken place.

The White House meeting was attended by Secretary of State Rusk, Under Secretary of State George W. Ball, Deputy Defense Secretary Cyrus R. Vance, Gen. Earle G. Wheeler, Chairman of the Joint Chiefs of Staff, and other top military and diplomatic representatives, officials said.

Later Mr. Rusk went to New York to make a speech.

One reason the Seventh Fleet patrols the area of the incident is that it attempts to maintain surveillance on supplies that might be moving by sea from ports in Communist North Vietnam to Communist guerrillas in South Vietnam.

Distance Not Unusual

WASHINGTON, Aug. 2 (AP)—Officials said today that it was not unusual for units of the Seventh Fleet to operate at a distance of about 30 miles from the North Vietnamese coast, within what the United States considers international waters.

The fleet is normally composed of more than 125 ships ranging the far Western Pacific. Three attack carriers are in the fleet, each one the core for a task group. Eacy group has its escort of destroyers and other ships.

Destroyers in the Seventh Fleet average about 30. Two or more customarily travel with a carrier to serve as a guarding screen. Others operate more or less independently on patrol, antisubmarine and surveillance missions.

The North Vietnamese Communists are believed to have more than a dozen PT boats. The authoritative naval publication Jane's Fighting Ships reports that 12 of the boats are Soviet-built, transferred to the Vietnamese Communists severel years ago. These apparently are craft of about 50 tons, with a speed close to 50 miles an hour.

At least four others reported in the Communist force are 100-ton craft, with a 40-mile-an-hour speed. Both classes carry two torpedo-launching tubes.

Communist China's PT force may total 200 or more boats.

Attackers' Identity Confirmed

HONOLULU, Aug. 2(AP)— The United States Pacific military command confirmed today that the torpedo boats that attacked the United States destroyer Maddox off the coast of North Vietnam today were North Vietnamese.

"We have information that confirms that," said Col. Willis Helmantoler, public information officer for the Pacific military commander, Admiral Sharp. "I can't go into any more detail."

The Command said that the decision to return the fire from the PT boat probably was made by Capt. John J. Herrick of Garden Grove, Calif., commodore of Destroyer Division 192, of which the Maddox is flagship and Comdr. Herbert L. Ogler of St. Petersburg, Fla., captain of the Maddox.

The Maddox joined the Seventh Fleet March 28. Her home port is Long Beach, Calif. The ship is 376 feet long, and has a beam of 40 feet and displaces 3,300 tons. Armament includes batteries of six 5-inch and two triple tube torpedo launchers.

Admiral Sharp said at a news conference:

"This incident may well be a change in the present situation and may heighten the seriousness of the present crisis in Vietnam, but I do not know whether this will be temporary or not."

He noted that this was the first time a United States warship had been fired on in the area.

"Retaliation by the destroyer and naval aircraft did not represent any change in United States policy," he said. "If they shoot at us, we are going to shoot back at any time."

He added: "Our ships are always going to go where they need to be."

REDS DRIVEN OFF Two Torpedo Vessels Believed Sunk in Gulf of Tonkin

Arnold H. Lubasch
Special to The New York Times

WASHINGTON, Aug. 4—The Defense Department announced tonight that North Vietnamese PT boats made a "deliberate attack" today on two United States destroyers patrolling international waters in the Gulf of Tonkin off North Vietnam.

The attack came two days after North Vietnamese torpedo boats attacked the Maddox, one of the destroyers in today's incident.

The destroyers and covering carrier-based aircraft fired on the vessels in today's attack, drove them off and apparently sank at least two of them, according to the announcement. The Pentagon said there were no United States casualties or damage.

The attack was made by an "undetermined number of North Vietnamese PT boats" during darkness about 65 miles from the nearest land, the Pentagon reported. It said the attack came at 10:30 P.M., North Vietnamese time, or 10:30 A.M., Washington time.

'Fabrication,' Reds Say

[The North Vietnamese regime said Wednesday that the report of another attack on United States ships was a "fabrication."]

The second attack was described in Washington as much fiercer than the first one, which was said to have lasted half an hour. The second battle was understood to have lasted about three hours in rough sea, with bad weather and low visibility.

"We are in a very serious situation," a Government official said.

The attack came shortly before the State Department made public a stern protest about the North Vietnamese attack Sunday on the Maddox, which was then patrolling about 30 miles off North Vietnam, also in international waters in the Gulf of Tonkin.

The protest over the first incident was announced shortly after noon here, when the Government had received what one official later described as a "very preliminary" report of Tonkin. The North Vietnamese regime could not have formally received the protest by the time the second attack was launched, an official noted, although the United States announced yesterday that it intended to make a protest.

The protest contained a warning to North Vietnam that "grave consequences" would result from any further unprovoked attacks on United States military forces.

Arthur Sylvester, Assistant Secretary of Defense for Public Affairs, issued the official announcement of the second attack early tonight.

The announcement was preceded by a flurry of unconfirmed and conflicting reports on Capitol Hill indicating that a new and more serious attack had taken place.

There was concern at one point that Chinese Communist forces might have participated in the attack. State Department officials said later that they knew of no increased military activity by Communist China in the area.

Freedom of Sea Stressed

In the protest over the attack Sunday on the Maddox, the United States emphasized that its ships would continue to operate freely in international waters and would take whatever measures necessary to defend themselves.

A State Department spokesman said that the protest was the first diplomatic message that the United States Government had ever directed to the Communist North Vietnamese regime in Hanoi.

The spokesman, Robert J. McCloskey, said that the protest was sent to the United States Embassy in Saigon yesterday for transmission "through appropriate channels" to Hanoi. The United States maintains no diplomatic ties with North Vietnam.

It is believed that the protest will be transmitted by the headquarters of the International Control Commission in Saigon. The commission, composed of representatives of India, Canada and Poland, is charged with supervising the 1954 Geneva agreement that partitioned Vietnam.

The protest will be transmitted "as quickly as possible" to Hanoi, the State Department spokesman said.

In orders issued Sunday and announced yesterday, President Johnson instructed the Navy to destroy the attackers in any future incident in the Gulf of Tonkin.

The President ordered a second destroyer to join the Maddox in patrolling the area. He also ordered the Navy to provide air patrols over the destroyers.

Rear Adm. William P. Mack, Navy Chief of Information, confirmed today that the supercarrier Constellation had left Hong Kong "a little early" for operations at sea. The Constellation later helped to provide air support for the two destroyers.

The C. Turner Joy joined the Maddox yesterday in patrolling the Gulf of Tonkin, where planes from the carrier Ticonderoga were already providing air support.

A Pentagon spokesman said that the mission of the destroyers was to gather information on shipping and to conduct surveillance in international waters. He said this was their right.

Regarding the Sunday attack on the Maddox, the spokesman said there was no question that the North Vietnamese PT boats knew what they were heading for because the sea was calm and the visibility was good.

In that incident, the three PT boats attacked the Maddox about 30 miles off the coast of North Vietnam at 4:08 A.M. Eastern daylight time. They launched three torpedoes and directed gunfire at the destroyer which returned the fire, damaging the attackers and drove them off.

There were no American casualties or damage.

The Pentagon spokesman said that the Maddox and four carrier-based jet fighters had fired more than 1,000 shots at the North Vietnamese PT boats and had scored numerous hits.

The Maddox fired 151 rounds of 5-inch shells and 132 rounds of 3-inch shells, scoring numerous hits on all three attacking boats, the spokesman said. He added that the four jet fighter planes had fired eight Zuni rockets and 800 rounds of 20-mm. ammunition, scoring with at least two of the rockets and with the strafing fire.

According to Jane's Fighting Ships, North Vietnam has four Soviet-built P-6 type PT boats, displacing 75 tons and mounting two torpedo tubes and two twin 25-mm. guns, and 12 Soviet-built PA-4-type boats, of 50 tons displacement, mounting two twin 25-mm. guns.

HANOI SCORES U.S. REPORT

TOKYO, Wednesday, Aug. 5—(AP) Communist North Vietnam asserted today that the United States report of another attack by North Vietnamese torpedo boats on American destroyers in international waters yesterday was "a sheer fabrication."

A brief statement broadcast by the Hanoi radio said that the American announcement was "a sheer fabrication by the United States imperialists aimed at covering up their illegal acts which brazenly violated the security of the Democratic Republic of (North) Vietnam and are aggravating further the situation in southeast Asia." The broadcast was monitored here.

U.S. STATEMENTS ON CLASH

Washington, Aug. 4—Following are the texts of a protest by the United States to North Vietnam over an attack on an American destroyer Sunday and of a Pentagon statement on a North Vietnamese and on two American destroyers today.

Protest by U.S.

The United States Government takes an extremely serious view of the unprovoked attack made by Communist North Vietnamese torpedo boats on an American naval vessel, the U.S.S. Maddox, operating on the high seas in the Gulf of Tonkin on Aug. 2.

United States ships have traditionally operated freely on the high seas in accordance with rights guaranteed by international law to vessels of all nations. They will continue to do so and will take whatever measures

Associated Press, "Hanoi Scores U.S. Report," from *The New York Times*, August 5, 1964, p. 3, col. 3, 4. Reprinted by permission.

The Age of Communication

are appropriate for their defense.

The United States Government expects that the authorities of the regime in North Vietnam will be under no misapprehension as to the grave consequences which would inevitably result from any further unprovoked offensive military action against United States forces.

Statement by Pentagon

A second deliberate attack was made during darkness by an undetermined number of North Vietnamese PT boats on the U.S.S. Maddox and the U.S.S. C. Turner Joy while the two destroyers were cruising in company on routine patrol in the Tonkin Gulf international waters about 65 miles from the nearest land.

The attack came at 10:30 P.M. local time 10:30 A.M., Aug. 4, Washington time.

PT boats were taken under fire by the destroyers, and thereafter by attack aircraft from the Ticonderoga and the Constellation.

The attackers were driven off with no United States casualties, no hits and no damage to either destroyer.

It is believed that at least two of the PT boats were sunk and two others damaged.

Warning to Hanoi

President Johnson's response to the North Vietnamese attack on the destroyer Maddox contained the right mixture of firmness and restraint. No reprisals are being undertaken. But a strong diplomatic protest is being combined with military measures that should discourage Hanoi from further attacks, if any are planned. American naval forces in the Tonkin Gulf area are being strengthened. And they now have orders to destroy any forces that attack them, rather than merely to drive them off.

It must be hoped that this first attack by North Vietnam on the United States Seventh Fleet was an error. South Vietnam's small naval forces have staged a number of raids on the North Vietnamese coast. One theory in Washington is that the American destroyer, as seen on North Vietnamese radar, may have been taken for a smaller South Vietnamese ship. Another theory is that the incident may simply have been the trigger-happy response of a North Vietnamese patrol, or its command, to an encounter with an American vessel near coastal waters. There have been other recent indications of North Vietnamese nervousness, following talk in Saigon of extending the war.

But the possibility cannot be excluded that the torpedo boat strike was intended to be the first of a series designed, perhaps, to test Washington's determination to continue aiding Saigon. If that be the case, it is essential that Hanoi realize immediately that it has opened a Pandora's box.

North Vietnam's capability of injuring the Seventh Fleet is small. The power of the Seventh Fleet to damage North Vietnam is incalculable. Since this must be evident, nothing is more vital than for Hanoi to be left in no doubt about the American intention to remain in the Tonkin Gulf and to continue supporting South Vietnam's military effort. The President's action should convey this message clearly.

Editorial: "Warning to Hanoi," *The New York Times,* August 4, 1964, p. 28. © 1964 by The New York Times Company. Reprinted by permission.

The President Acts

President Johnson went to the American people last night with the somber facts of an enlarging crisis in Vietnam. He announced new steps in reply to "open aggression on the high seas." Air action by the United States is being executed against North Vietnam gunboats and supporting installations.

The President will put to the Congress a resolution expressing our united determination in support of the cause of freedom in Southeast Asia. He will put this grave situation before the Security Council of the United Nations. He has sought—and received—from Senator Goldwater, the Republican nominee for President, the assurance of bipartisan support in this critical hour.

The attack on one of our warships that at first seemed, and was hoped to be, an isolated incident is now seen in ominous perspective to have been the beginning of a mad adventure by the North Vietnamese Communists. After offensive action against more vessels of our Navy the President has backed up with retaliatory fire the warnings that North Vietnam chose frequently to ignore.

United States determination to assure the independence of South Vietnam, if ever doubted before, can not be doubted now by the Communists to the north or their allies. It is a grave moment, calling for open-eyed, cool-headed appraisal of all the alarming possibilities—by North Vietnam as well as others.

The President has reminded Hanoi again that, despite new provocation, the United States still seeks no wider war.

Editorial: "The President Acts," *The New York Times,* August 5, 1964, p. 32. © 1964 by The New York Times Company. Reprinted by permission.

President's Message to Congress August 6, 1964

Lyndon B. Johnson

Special to The New York Times
WASHINGTON, Aug 5—Following are the texts of President Johnson's special message to Congress today on Vietnam and of a proposed joint Congressional resolution.

Last night I announced to the American people that the North Vietnamese regime had conducted further deliberate attacks against U.S. naval vessels operating in international waters, and that I had therefore directed air action against gunboats and supporting facilities used in these hostile operations.

This air action has now been carried out with substantial damage to the boats and facilities. Two U.S. aircraft were lost in the action.

After consultation with the leaders of both parties in the Congress, I further announced a decision to ask the Congress for a resolution expressing the unity and determination of the United States in supporting freedom and in protecting peace in Southeast Asia.

These latest actions of the North Vietnamese regime have given a new and grave turn to the already serious situation in Southeast Asia. Our commitments in that area are well known to the Congress. They were first made in 1954 by President Eisenhower. They were further defined in the

The Age of Communication

Southeast Asia collective defense treaty approved by the Senate in February, 1955.

Pledged to Meet Aggression

This treaty with its accompanying protocol obligates the United States and other members to act in accordance with their Constitutional processes to meet Communist aggression against any of the parties or protocol states.

Our policy in Southeast Asia has been consistent and unchanged since 1954. I summarized it on June 2 in four simple propositions:

1. America keeps her word. Here as elsewhere, we must and shall honor our commitments.

2. The issue is the future of Southeast Asia as a whole. A threat to any nation in that region is a threat to all, and a threat to us.

3. Our purpose is peace. We have no military, political or territorial ambitions in the area.

4. This is not just a jungle war, but a struggle for freedom on every front of human activity. Our military and economic assistance to South Vietnam and Laos in particular has the purpose of helping these countries to repel aggression and strengthen their independence.

The threat to the free nations of Southeast Asia has long been clear. The North Vietnamese regime has constantly sought to take over South Vietnam and Laos. This Communist regime has violated the Geneva accords for Vietnam.

It has systematically conducted a campaign of subversion, which includes the direction, training, and supply of personnel and arms for the conduct of guerrilla warfare in South Vietnamese territory.

In Laos, the North Vietnamese regime has maintained military forces, used Laotian territory for infiltration into South Vietnam, and most recently carried out combat operations—all in direct violation of the Geneva agreements of 1962.

In recent months, the actions of the North Vietnamese regime have become steadily more threatening. In May, following new acts of Communist aggression in Laos, the United States undertook reconnaissance flights over Laotian territory, at the request of the Government of Laos. These flights had the essential mission of determining the situation in territory where Communist forces were preventing inspection by the International Control Commission.

When the Communists attacked these aircraft, I responded by furnishing escort fighters with instructions to fire when fired upon. Thus, these latest North Vietnamese attacks on our naval vessels are not the first direct attack on armed forces of the United States.

As President of the United States I have concluded that I should now ask the Congress, on its part, to join in affirming the national determination that all such attacks will be met, and that the U.S. will continue in its basic policy of assisting the free nations of the area to defend their freedom.

As I have repeatedly made clear, the United States intends no rashness, and seeks no wider war. We must make it clear to all that the United States is united in its determination to bring about the end of Communist subversion and aggression in the area.

We seek the full and effective restoration of the international agreements signed in Geneva in 1954, with respect to South Vietnam, and again at Geneva in 1962, with respect to Laos.

I recommend a resolution expressing the support of the Congress for all necessary action to protect our armed forces and to assist nations covered by the SEATO treaty. At the same time, I assure the Congress that we shall continue readily to explore any avenues of political solution that will effectively guarantee the removal of Communist subversion and the preservation of the independence of the nations of the area.

The resolution could well be based upon similar resolutions enacted by the Congress in the past to meet the threat to Formosa in 1955, to meet the threat to the Middle East in 1957, and to meet the threat to Cuba in 1962.

It could state in the simplest terms the resolve and support of the Congress for action to deal appropriately with attacks against our armed forces and to defend freedom and preserve peace in Southeast Asia in accordance with the obligations of the United States under the Southeast Asia Treaty.

I urge the Congress to enact such a resolution promptly and thus to give convincing evidence to the aggressive Communist nations, and to the world as a whole, that our policy in Southeast Asia will be carried forward and that the peace and security of the area will be preserved.

The events of this week would in any event have made the passage of a Congressional resolution essential. But there is an additional reason for doing so at a time when we are entering on three months of political campaigning. Hostile nations must understand that in such a period the United States will continue to protect its national interests, and that in these matters there is no division among us.

Proposed Resolution

Resolved by the Senate and House of Representatives of the United States of America in Congress assembled,

Whereas naval units of the Communist regime in Vietnam, in violation of the principles of the Charter of the United Nations and of international law, have deliberately and repeatedly attacked United States naval vessels lawfully present in international waters, and have thereby created a serious threat to international peace;

Whereas these attacks are part of a deliberate and systematic campaign of aggression that the Communist regime in North Vietnam has been waging against its neighbors and the nations joined with them in the collective defense of their freedom;

Whereas the United States is assisting the peoples of Southeast Asia to protect their freedom and has no territorial, military or political ambitions in that area, but desires only that these peoples should be left in peace to work out their own destinies in their own way;

Now therefore, be it resolved, by the Senate and House of Representatives of the United States of America in Congress assembled:

Section 1—The Congress approves and supports the determination of the President, as Commander in Chief, to take all necessary measures to repel any armed attack against the forces of the United States and to prevent further aggression.

Section 2—The United States regards as vital to its national interest and to world peace the maintenance of international peace and security in Southeast Asia. Consonant with the Constitution and the Charter of the United Nations and in accordance with its obligations under the Southeast Asia Collective Defense Treaty, the United States is, therefore, prepared, as the President determines, to take all necessary steps, including the use of armed force, to assist any member or protocol state of the Southeast Asia Collective Defense Treaty requesting assistance in defense of its freedom.

Section 3—This resolution shall expire when the President shall determine that the peace and security of the area is reasonably assured by international conditions created by action of the United Nations or otherwise, except that it may be terminated earlier by concurrent resolution of the Congress.

Tonkin: what should have been asked

DON STILLMAN

On the stormy night of Aug. 4, 1964, the U. S. Navy destroyers *Maddox* and *C. Turner Joy* were cruising the Gulf of Tonkin off North Vietnam when the *C. Turner Joy* reported radar detection of ships closing in fast for a possible attack. Sonarmen reported tracking torpedoes from the ships. Seaman Patrick Park, the main gun director of the *Maddox,* scanned his sensitive radar for signs of the enemy. But as the destroyers maneuvered wildly for three hours in heavy swells he detected nothing. Then suddenly he reported picking up a "damned big" target, and was ordered to fire. Park recalled later:

> Just before I pushed the trigger, I suddenly realized: that's the *Turner Joy.* This came right with the order to fire. I shouted back, "Where's the *Turner Joy?*" There was a lot of yelling "Goddamn" back and forth, with the bridge telling me to "fire before we lost contact. . . ." I finally told them, "I'm not opening fire until I know where the *Turner Joy* is." The bridge got on the phone and said, "Turn on your lights, *Turner Joy.*" Sure enough, there she was, right in the crosshairs. I had six five-inch guns right at the *Turner Joy,* 1,500 yards away. If I had fired, it would have blown it clean out of the water. In fact, I could have been shot for not squeezing the trigger. . . . People started asking, "What are we shooting at? What is going on?" We all began calming down. The whole thing seemed to end then.

But it didn't end there for Park, whose statements were reported by Joseph Goulden in his excellent book *Truth Is the First Casualty,* or for the rest of the world. Hours later, President Johnson ordered the first U. S. bombing raids against North Vietnam. Within the week, he had demanded and received a Congressional resolution that authorized him to "take all necessary steps" to "prevent further aggression" in Vietnam.

Don Stillman, "Tonkin: What Should Have Been Asked," *Columbia Journalism Review* (Winter 1969–70). Reprinted by permission.

The massive American buildup in Vietnam dates from that crucial week in the Gulf of Tonkin, and in retrospect the events there proved to be a turning point in the war. At the time of the incidents, only 163 Americans had died in action in Vietnam, and the 16,000 American troops there ostensibly were serving as "advisers" rather than full combat soldiers. But within a year President Johnson began to use a Congressionally approved "Tonkin resolution" as a functional equivalent of a declaration of war in an escalation that ultimately brought more than half a million U. S. troops to Vietnam. More than 40,000 were killed.

What really happened that dark night is unclear; but persistent digging by Senator J. W. Fulbright and his Foreign Relations Committee staff, by then-Senator Wayne Morse, and by a handful of persistent reporters like Joseph Goulden has given us a view of at least part of the iceberg of deception that remained hidden for years.

Reporting of the first attack on the *Maddox* on Aug. 2 and the second alleged attack on both the *Maddox* and the *Turner Joy* on Aug. 4 was extremely difficult because the only real sources of information were Pentagon and Navy officials and the President himself. Slowly and painfully over four years, as the private doubts of Senators and reporters became public, the American people learned that in fact the *Maddox* was not on a "routine patrol in international waters," but was on an electronic espionage mission to gather intelligence information on North Vietnamese radar frequencies. As part of that mission, the *Maddox* would repeatedly simulate attacks by moving toward the shores of North Vietnam with its gun-control radar mechanisms turned on to stimulate enemy radar activity. In addition, years after the incidents stories revealed that the territorial waters recognized by North Vietnam (twelve miles) were repeatedly violated by the *Maddox.*

Two days before the first attack on the *Maddox,* the South Vietnamese for the first time conducted naval shelling of North Vietnam. Using U. S.

"swift boats," they attacked the islands of Hon Me and Hon Ngu. The night following the raids, the *Maddox*, approaching from the same direction as the South Vietnamese, came within four nautical miles of Hon Me. The captain of the *Maddox* intercepted North Vietnamese messages reporting the possibility of "hostile action" because the enemy believed the *Maddox* to be connected with the South Vietnamese shelling of the islands. The *Maddox* cabled: CONTINUANCE OF PATROL PRESENTS AN UNACCEPTABLE RISK. That day it was attacked.

The *Maddox* was joined by the *Turner Joy* and, after again requesting termination of the mission because of the likelihood of attack, it reported two days later that the two ships had been ambushed by North Vietnamese PT boats. The black clouds and electrical storms during that night prevented any visual sightings of hostile craft, and contradictory sightings on radar and sonar added to the confusion. The commander in charge cabled:

> Entire action leaves many doubts except for apparent attempted ambush. Suggest thorough reconnaissance in daylight by aircraft.

After lengthy questioning of crew members on both ships, the doubts grew larger. The commander cabled:

> Review of action makes many reported contacts and torpedoes fired appear doubtful. . . . Freak weather effects and overeager sonarmen may have accounted for many reports. No actual visual sightings by *Maddox*. Suggest complete evaluation before any further action.

That evaluation did not occur, and hours later American bombers took off for North Vietnam.

Thus the espionage mission of the *Maddox*, its violation of territorial waters, its proximity and relationship to South Vietnamese shelling, and major questions about whether the second attack occurred all combine to give a much different picture of the incidents than the Administration fed the country through the news media. How well did the media handle reporting and interpretation of the Tonkin incidents?

Perhaps the worst excesses in reporting were committed by *Time* and *Life*. Both viewed the event as if the *Maine* itself had been sunk. The week after the encounter, *Life* carried an article headlined FROM THE FILES OF NAVY INTELLIGENCE that it said was "pieced together by *Life* correspondent Bill Wise with the help of U. S. Navy Intelligence and the Department of Defense." Wise was clearly fed only a small smattering of cables that contained none of the doubts about the second attack. He stated [Aug. 14, 1964]:

> Despite their losses, the [North Vietnamese] PTs continued to harass the two destroyers. A few of them amazed those aboard the *Maddox* by brazenly using searchlights to light up the destroyers—thus making ideal targets of themselves. They also peppered the ships with more 37 mm fire, keeping heads on U. S. craft low but causing no real damage.

Senator Wayne Morse, in a speech on the floor of the Senate Feb. 28, 1968, denounced the Pentagon's "selective leaking of confidential information" and *Life*'s gullibility in accepting it. "I don't know who leaked, but I can guess why," he said. "The 'why' is that someone in the Pentagon decided that the American people should see some of the messages confirming that an unprovoked attack had occurred on innocent American vessels. . . . The *Life* magazine reporter was taken in. He was 'used.' The press should be warned."

The next issue of *Life* went even further in embellishing events. It carried a picture spread headlined HEROES OF THE GULF OF TONKIN that praised the pilots who had bombed North Vietnam. "Most of the young Navy pilots had never seen combat before, but they performed like veterans," *Life* said. The planes, with two exceptions, "got back safely and their pilots, the nation's newest battle veterans, would be remembered as the heroes of Tonkin Gulf."

This kind of irresponsible puffery was evident in *Time*, too. Despite thorough and restrained files from its Washington bureau, *Time* [Aug. 14, 1964] constructed its typical dramatic scenario of events which, though lively, was grossly inaccurate:

> The night glowed eerily with the nightmarish glare of air-dropped flares and boats' searchlights. For three and a half hours the small boats attacked in pass after pass. Ten enemy torpedoes sizzled through the water. Each time the skippers, tracking the fish by radar, maneuvered to evade them. Gunfire and gun smells and shouts stung the air. Two of the enemy boats went down. Then, at 1:30 a.m., the remaining PTs ended the fight, roared off through the black night to the north.

Joseph Goulden, one of the few writers to interview crew members, reports that when the *Maddox* and *Turner Joy* arrived at Subic Bay several weeks after the incidents, one crew member had occasion to read both the *Life* and *Time* accounts. He quotes the seaman as stating:

> I couldn't believe it, the way they blew that story out of proportion. It was like something out of *Male* magazine, the way they described that battle. All we needed were naked women running up and down the deck. We were disgusted, because it just wasn't true. It didn't happen that way. . . .

Newsweek, which generally waved the flag far less than *Time* in its coverage of the Vietnam War, was just as overzealous in its dramatization of the second Tonkin incident [Aug. 17, 1964]:

> The U. S. ships blazed out salvo after salvo of shells. Torpedoes whipped by, some only 100 feet from the destroyers' beams. A PT boat burst into flames and sank. More U. S. jets swooped in. . . . Another PT boat exploded and sank, and then the others scurried off into the darkness nursing their wounds. The battle was won. Now it was time for American might to strike back.

Even the usually staid New York *Times* magazine was caught up in the adventure of the moment. Its Aug. 16 picture spread on the Seventh Fleet, which had launched the planes that bombed the North, had the look of a war comic book. Headlined POLICEMEN OF THE PACIFIC, it showed planes streaking through the sky, missiles being fired, and Marines landing on beaches. It carried captions such as, "A component of the Marines is always on sea duty, ready when the call comes."

The New York *Times* news sections handled the story with restraint and, after the Aug. 2 attack, even mentioned claims that U. S. destroyers like the *Maddox* "have sometimes collaborated with South Vietnamese hit-and-run raids on North Vietnamese cities." The Washington *Post,* like the *Times,* was thorough and incisive in its reporting. Murrey Marder's superb accounts even mentioned the South Vietnamese shelling on Hon Me and Hon Ngu as a possible cause for the then seemingly irrational attack on the *Maddox.*

Because transcripts of TV news shows from this period are not available it is difficult to evaluate broadcast media performance. But the accounts of TV coverage printed in government bulletins and elsewhere indicate that some perceptive reporting did occur. NBC carried an interview with Dean Rusk Aug. 5 in which Rusk was pressed on the question of whether the U. S. ships might have been operating in support of the South Vietnamese shelling units. But for the most part the broadcast media, while perhaps more responsible than some print outlets, fed viewers the same deceptive Administration leaks.

Editorial comment almost universally supported the President's response. The New York *Daily News* speculated that "it may be our heaven-sent good fortune to liquidate not only Ho Chi Minh but Mao Tse-tung's Red Mob at Peking as well, presumably with an important assist from Generalissimo Chiang Kai-shek and his Nationalist Chinese forces on Taiwan."

The Los Angeles *Times* praised U.S. actions as "fitting in selectivity, proper in application, and —given the clear, long-standing statement of U. S. intentions—inevitable in delivery." William Randolph Hearst, Jr., praised the bombing as a "fitting reply to one of the more outrageous—and implausible—aggressions committed by communism in many years." He went on to suggest that rather than limit the bombing it might be better to continue until the North Vietnamese surrendered.

The New York *Times* said: "The attack on one of our warships that at first seemed, and was hoped to be, an isolated incident is now seen in ominous perspective to have been the beginning of a mad adventure by the North Vietnamese Communists." But the *Times* did warn that "the sword, once drawn in anger, will tend to be unsheathed more easily in the future." When the Tonkin resolution went before Congress, the *Times* perceptively cautioned that "it is virtually a blank check."

The Washington *Post*'s editorial page saw the Tonkin resolution much differently. Earlier editorials mentioned "the atmosphere of ambiguity" that surrounded the first attack on the *Maddox*, but when the resolution was considered the *Post* said: "That unity [against Communist aggression] has been demonstrated despite the reckless and querulous dissent of Senator Morse. There is no substance in Senator Morse's charge that the resolution amounts to a 'predated declaration of war'. . . . This means of reasserting the national will, far short of a declaration of war, follows sound precedent. . . ."

One of the few newspapers to attack the President's account was the Charleston, W. Va., *Gazette,* which stated that the Tonkin attacks were probably caused by the South Vietnamese naval strikes and complained of the "air of unreality" about the incidents. But the overall failure of the press to raise questions about the incidents in the editorial columns, although in keeping with the mood of the country at the time, was part of the general breakdown of the media's responsibility to act as a check on the actions of the Government.

Foreign coverage of the incidents raised some of the significant points being ignored in this country. *Demokreten,* of Denmark, stated:

To create a pretext for an attack on Poland, Hitler ordered the Germans to put on Polish uniforms and attack a German guard. What the Americans did in North Vietnam was not the same. But the story sounds doubtful. . . . Why was the vessel off North Vietnamese coasts? In any case its presence there could indeed be interpreted as provocative.

New Statesman of Britain also raised doubts:

There is so little trust in official [U. S.] accounts about Vietnam that suspicion is surely understandable. . . . Is it not possible that the destroyers could not be distinguished from South Vietnamese craft that were engaged in another raiding mission?

One American journalist who raised continuing doubts about the veracity of the Administration's accounts was I. F. Stone. In his small, outspoken sheet, Stone reported the South Vietnamese attacks on Hon Me and Hon Ngu. He was the only one to cover in detail the charges raised by Senator Morse about the incidents and the Tonkin resolution, and he even raised questions about whether the second attack even occurred. While *Time* and *Life* were adding readable embellishments to the nineteenth-century theme of "they've sunk one of our gunboats," I. F. Stone was asking the crucial questions.

One of the major shortcomings of columnists and opinion writers was their failure to ask the broad question: does the punishment fit the crime? The total damage in both attacks was one bullet hole in the *Maddox*. No U. S. ships were sunk, no American boys were killed or even wounded. In turn, we not only claimed to have sunk four North Vietnamese vessels but went on to the bombing of the North, sinking the major part of the North Vietnamese navy, and wiping out more than 10 per cent of its oil storage tanks.

The overwhelming response of the editorialists was that President Johnson should be commended for his restraint in limiting the bombing. Among Washington journalists only Stone opined that indeed the American response was "hardly punishment to fit the crime." His small-circulation sheet

The Age of Communication

received little attention.

The record of the media improved measurably as public doubts about the Tonkin incidents began to grow. Senator Fulbright, who managed the Tonkin resolution through Congress for President Johnson, began to question the facts and, in May, 1966, wrote in *Look* that he had serious doubts about the Administration's account. But the media didn't follow this up very extensively. Despite the importance of the Tonkin incidents, they were content to pass over opportunities to interview crew members of the two ships—the only firsthand witnesses—some of whom had left the service or were otherwise accessible for interviews. The first real breakthrough came in July, 1967, when Associated Press sent a special assignment team headed by Harry Rosenthal and Tom Stewart to interview some three dozen crew members. Their superb 5,000-word account was the first real enterprise reporting on the Tonkin affair.

AP revealed for the first time that the *Maddox* was carrying intelligence equipment, and also cited for the first time that the *Maddox* had not fired any warning shots, as claimed by Secretary McNamara, but had shot to kill instead. The crew interviews indicated that there was a great confusion on board the two ships during the incident. At this point, however, there was little client interest in the story. Urban riots broke out the day it was to run. As a result, the AP report was not used by major metropolitan newspapers such as the Washington *Post,* Washington *Star,* New York *Times,* or others which might have given it the exposure it deserved. The story did appear in the *Arkansas Gazette,* however, where it was read by Fulbright, who by this time was devoting much of his attention to uncovering the true story of Tonkin.

The AP account was followed in April, 1968, by an article in *Esquire* by David Wise, who also interviewed the crews and cast further doubt on the Administration's account. These two reports and another AP account by Donald May were the only real enterprise stories that turned up new informa-

tion. But John Finney, the able New York *Times* reporter, raised further questions in *New Republic* early in 1968, as did John Galloway in *Commonweal.* (Galloway has just done a splendid source book, *The Gulf of Tonkin Resolution.*)

By this time Fulbright and Morse were generating much breaking news as they prepared for the Foreign Relations Committee hearings held in February, 1968. But even during those hearings the press failed to distinguish itself. When Morse, through the *Congressional Record,* released important segments of a top-secret study done by the Foreign Relations staff, based on cable traffic and new data from the Defense Department, it took the Washington *Post* two days to recognize the significance of his statements.

The final credit for tying together the whole thread of deception surrounding the incidents must go to Joseph Goulden, whose book appeared in early fall of 1969. While covering the 1968 Tonkin hearings for the Philadelphia *Inquirer,* Goulden had filed a story on the controversial testimony of Secretary McNamara, who appeared to contradict some aspects of his 1964 testimony. The *Inquirer* rewrote the lead to make it read:

> The United States did not provoke the 1964 Gulf of Tonkin incident, previously secret naval communications indicated Saturday.

Goulden left the *Inquirer,* sought out crewmen and others involved in the incident, and wrote his detailed and insightful account.

This, then, is the record on the Tonkin affair. Given its lessons, one may hope that the media will not fail so grandly if similar incidents occur. The reporting on the *Pueblo* and the *Liberty* give reason for hope. But the Fourth Estate must establish a far more independent and critical stance on government actions if hope is to become reality.

Topics for Discussion

1. The newspaper accounts of the Gulf of Tonkin incidents failed to provide important information. Why did newspapers fail so seriously to accurately and fully report what happened?

2. What sources did the wire services and the *New York Times* draw on to report what happened in the Gulf of Tonkin? How would this automatically distort the news accounts? What could the news services and newspapers have done to avoid the mistakes they made?

3. What does Stillman mean by "the iceberg of deception"?

4. The Gulf of Tonkin incidents rank among the most significant in the history of American involvement in Vietnam since the subsequent Gulf of Tonkin Resolution became the basis for full-scale American commitment to war in Vietnam. Compare the accounts of the incidents as given by the wire services and the *New York Times* with the account given by Stillman. What significant differences do you find?

5. Newspapers must meet deadlines and thus do not have the time to do careful, thorough research. What effect does this have on news reporting?

6. Stillman charges that the news reporting of the Gulf of Tonkin incidents was a failure not because news reporters lacked access to the facts, but because the news media had become too dependent and too uncritical of government actions. Do you agree with this? Do you think this is still the case today?

7. What does Stillman mean when he says that *Time* and *Life* magazines "waved the flag"? How would this affect their reporting?

8. Why is it important for reporters to ask critical, probing questions? Is it the job of a reporter to just report the facts? How does a reporter get the facts?

9. What can be learned from the press's handling of the Gulf of Tonkin affair?

Topics for Discussion

1. Liebling's essay begins this section of the text by raising the fundamental question of just how free the press is. What kind of a free press is Liebling talking about? Why does this essay come first in this section? Is there any connection between the economic impact of advertising and the problems in creating a truly free press?

2. Arlen's essay gives an inside look into the preparation and presentation of the *CBS Evening News* program. Compare Arlen's essay with Cronkite's essay. Are they about the same thing? Does Cronkite tell you what it's like to broadcast the news or does Arlen?

3. Moyers presents something of a defense of government news policy. How does Moyers' explanation of the balance between the press and the government compare with Witcover's essay describing what he sees as a direct government assault on the freedom of the press? Do Moyers and Witcover view the government and the press in the same light? Would you say either man is biased?

4. Both Ways and Arlen say that we need a new definition of what constitutes news. Do they agree on a new definition? Are there any differences between what each would like to see the news media cover?

5. Arlen and Grant both write about New Journalism. Do they agree on what the New Journalism is? Are both men opposed to the New Journalism? Why does Grant feel that there is a New Journalism needed? Does Arlen agree?

6. Glessing's analysis of the editorial content of the underground press includes a definition of what constitutes news. Does the underground press definition of news agree with Ways' and Arlen's definitions of news? In what ways does the underground press differ from the establishment press in its definition of news?

7. Are there any similarities between the news media's treatment of the My Lai incident and the Gulf of Tonkin incident? Who played a greater negative role in each incident, the government or the press?

8. Smith's essay reveals that the press is quite free in its use of language. Yet Witcover recounts a serious attempt by the government to suppress the press. Is government censorship more concerned with sexual or political matters?

9. Which essay in this section did you enjoy most? Why? Which one did you enjoy least? Why?

10. The essays in this section discuss some of the problems facing the news media. What problems are not mentioned in this section? What do you see as the major problems facing the news media?

Current Culture

At first glance this section seems out of place in this book. What possible relation could there be between advertising and the news media and current culture? As you should realize by now, advertising and the news media are not only a part of our current culture, but they also go a long way toward influencing and directing that culture. Advertising, for example, is closely tied to the quality and kind of television produced. This is true also of radio. Our cultural concepts are to a certain extent shaped and reinforced by advertising. The news media can not only reflect cultural values but can contribute to their change. Thus television coverage of the Vietnam war has certainly contributed to our changing concept of the soldier hero. It is impossible to speak of contemporary American culture without discussing also contemporary advertising and the news media.

This section is shorter than the preceding sections because only points of contact are discussed. Certainly much more can be said about current culture, and there are numerous books devoted entirely to this topic. What this section presents are only the very specific points of contact between current culture and advertising and the news media. There are other points of contact, but these are perhaps less precise, more indirect.

The first essays present some suggested ideas about current culture in general and its relationship to immediate past culture. From here the essays move on to discuss more specific aspects of culture in concrete manifestations. Our concept of the hero as expressed in spy fiction and the ever-popular western movie is analyzed. The film, as a growing cultural force, and its relation to television is discussed. The final part of this section deals with radio, rock music, and the comics, all important parts of current culture. After reading these essays, you should have some general idea of the makeup and complexity of current American culture. You should also be able to formulate some thoughts on culture and to make some statements about the forms of expression of current culture.

Culture is too often considered an abstract in our lives when it should be one of the most concrete aspects of our lives. Culture is ever with us, both shaping us and our world while giving us the means to shape our expressions and our beliefs. While we may find advertising and the news media remote from our control and influence, we find culture a personal and a manipulative thing. Culture is not an object removed from us that we can study with curiosity. We are the culture and the culture is us.

Again, as with the previous two sections, each essay in this section has a set of questions for discussion. These questions should prompt discussion, independent thinking, and the formulation of independent opinions and judgments. The student should also learn something of the rhetoric of the essays themselves, and something of the rhetoric of our culture.

The Old Culture and the New

Phillip Slater

> We shall be able to rid ourselves of many of the pseudo-
> moral principles which have hag-ridden us for two hundred
> years, by which we have exalted some of the most distaste-
> ful of human qualities into the position of the highest vir-
> tues.
>
> KEYNES

> Consider the lilies of the field, how they grow; they toil
> not, neither do they spin: and yet I say unto you, that even
> Solomon in all his glory was not arrayed like one of these.
> MATTHEW 6:28–29

> Don't you know that it's a fool
> Who plays it cool
> By making his world a little colder.
> LENNON AND MC CARTNEY

> And what's the point of revolution
> Without general copulation.
> WEISS

There are an almost infinite number of polarities by means of which one can differentiate between the two cultures. The old culture, when forced to choose, tends to give preference to property rights over personal rights, technological requirements over human needs, competition over cooperation, violence over sexuality, concentration over distribution, the producer over the consumer, means over ends, secrecy over openness, social forms over personal expression, striving over gratification, Oedipal love over communal love, and so on. The new counterculture tends to reverse all of these priorities.

Now it is important to recognize that these differences cannot be resolved by some sort of compromise or "golden mean" position. Every cultural system is a dynamic whole, resting on processes that must be accelerative to be self-sustaining. Change must therefore affect the motivational roots of a society or it is not change at all. An attempt to introduce some isolated element into such a system produces cultural redefinition and absorption of the novel element if the culture is strong, and deculturation if it is susceptible. As Margaret Mead points out, to introduce cloth garments into a grass- or bark-clad population, without simultaneously introducing closets, soap, sewing, and furniture, merely transforms a neat and attractive tribe into a dirty and slovenly one. Cloth is part of a complex cultural pattern that includes storing, cleaning, mending, and protecting—just as the automobile is part of a system that includes fueling, maintenance, and repair. A fish with the lungs of a land mammal still will not survive out of water.

Imagine, for example, that we are cooperation purists attempting to remove the invidious element from a foot race. We decide, first of all, that we will award no prize to the winner, or else prizes to everyone. This, we discover, brings no reduction in competitiveness. Spectators and participants alike are still preoccupied with who won and how fast he ran relative to someone else now or in the past. We then decide to eliminate even *announcing* the winner. To our dismay we discover that our efforts have generated some new cultural forms: the runners have taken to wearing more conspicuous identifying clothing—bright-colored trunks or shirts, or names emblazoned in iridescent letters—and underground printed programs have appeared with names, physical descriptions, and other information facilitating this identification. In despair we decide to have the runners run one at a time and we keep no time records. But now we find that the sale of stopwatches has become a booming enterprise, that the underground printed programs have expanded to include voluminous statistics on past time records of participants, and that private "timing services," comparable to the rating services of the television industry, have grown up to provide definitive and instantaneous results for spectators willing to pay a nominal sum (thus does artificial deprivation facilitate enterprise).

At this point we are obliged to eliminate the start and finish lines —an innovation which arouses angry protest from both spectators and participants, who have evinced only mild grumbling over our previous efforts. "What kind of a race can it be if people begin and end wherever they like? Who will be interested in it?" To mollify their complaints and combat dwindling attendance, we reintroduce the practice of having everyone run at the same time. Before long we observe that the runners have evolved the practice of all starting to run at about the same time (although we disallow beginning at the same place), and that all of the races are being run on the circular track. The races get longer and longer, and the underground printed programs now record statistics on how many laps were run by a given runner in a given race. All races have now become longevity contests, and one goes to them equipped with a picnic basket. The newer fields, in fact, do not have bleachers, but only tables at which drinks are served, with scattered observation windows through which the curious look from time to time and report to their tables the latest news on which runners are still going. Time passes, and we are increasingly subjected to newspaper attacks concerning the corrupt state into which our efforts have fallen. With great trepidation, and in the face of enormous opposition from the ideologically apathetic masses, we inaugurate a cultural revolution and make further drastic alterations in racing rules. Runners begin and end at a signal, but there is no track, merely an open field. A runner must change direction every thirty seconds, and if he runs parallel with another runner for more than fifteen seconds he is disqualified. At first attendance falls off badly, but after a time spectators become interested in how many runners can survive a thirty-minute race without being eliminated for a breach of these rules. Soon specific groups become so skilled at not running parallel that none of them are ever disqualified. In the meantime they begin to run a little more slowly and to elaborate intricate patterns of synchronizing their direction changes. The more gifted groups become virtuosi at moving parallel until the last split second and then diverging. The thirty-second rule becomes unnecessary as direction changes are voluntarily frequent, but the fifteen-second rule becomes a five-second one. The motions of the runners become more and more elegant, and a vast outpouring of books and articles descends from and upon the university (ever a dirty bird) to establish definitive distinctions between the race and the dance.

The first half of this parable is a reasonably accurate representation of what most liberal reform amounts to: opportunities for the existing system to flex its muscles and exercise its self-maintaining capabilities. Poverty programs put very little money into the hands of the poor because middle-class hands are so much more gifted at grasping money—they know better where it is, how to apply for it, how to divert it, how to concentrate it. That is what being middle class means, just as a race means competition. No matter how much we try to change things it somehow ends as merely a more complex, intricate, bizarre, and interesting version of what existed before. A heavily graduated income tax somehow ends by making the rich richer and the poor poorer. "Highway beautification" somehow turns into rural blight, and so on.

But there is a limit to the amount of change a system can absorb, and the second half of the parable suggests that if we persist in our efforts and finally attack the system at its motivational roots we may indeed be successful. In any case there is no such thing as "compromise": we are either strong enough to lever the train onto a new track or it stays on the old one or it is derailed.

Thus it becomes important to discern the core motivational logic behind the old and the new cultures. Knowing this would make rational change possible—would unlock the door that leads most directly from the old to the new.[1] For a prolonged, unplanned collision will nullify both cultures, like bright pigments combining into gray. The transition must be as deft as possible if we are to minimize the destructive chaos that inevitably accompanies significant cultural transformations.

The core of the old culture is scarcity. Everything in it rests upon the assumption that the world does not contain the wherewithal to satisfy the needs of its human inhabitants. From this it follows that people must compete with one another for these scarce resources—lie, swindle, steal, and kill, if necessary. These basic assumptions create the danger of a "war of all against all" and must be buttressed by a series of counternorms which attempt to qualify and restrain the intensity of the struggle. Those who can take the largest share of the scarce resources are said to be "successful," and if they can do it without violating the counternorms they are said to have character and moral fibre.

The key flaw in the old culture is, of course, the fact that the scarcity is spurious—man-made in the case of bodily gratifications and man-allowed or man-maintained in the case of material goods. It now exists only for the purpose of maintaining the system that depends upon it, and its artificiality becomes more palpable each day. Americans continually find themselves in the position of having killed someone to avoid sharing a meal which turns out to be too large to eat alone.

The new culture is based on the assumption that important human needs are easily satisfied and that the resources for doing so are plentiful. Competition is unnecessary and the only danger to hu-

This of course makes the assumption that some kind of drastic change is either desirable or inevitable. I do not believe our society can long continue on its old premises without destroying itself and everything else. Nor do I believe it can contain or resist the gathering forces of change without committing suicide in the process.

The Age of Communication

mans is human aggression. There is no reason outside of human perversity for peace not to reign and for life not to be spent in the cultivation of joy and beauty. Those who can do this in the face of the old culture's ubiquity are considered "beautiful."

The flaw in the new culture is the fact that the old culture has succeeded in hiding the cornucopia of satisfactions that the new assumes—that a certain amount of work is required to release the bounty that exists from the restraints under which it is now placed. Whereas the flaw in the old culture has caused it to begin to decompose, the flaw in the new culture has produced a profound schism in its ranks—a schism between activist and dropout approaches to the culture as it now exists. We will return to this problem a little later.

It is important to recognize the internal logic of the old culture, however absurd its premise. If one assumes scarcity, then the knowledge that others want the same things that we have leads with some logic to preparations for defense, and, ultimately (since the best defense is offense), for attack. The same assumption leads to a high value being placed on the ability to postpone gratification (since there is not enough to go around). The expression of feelings is a luxury, since it might alert the scarce resources to the fact that the hunter is near.

The high value placed on restraint and coldness (which, as the Beatles observe in the epigraph for this chapter, creates even greater scarcity) generates in turn another norm: that of "good taste." One can best understand the meaning of such a norm by examining what is common to those acts considered to be in violation of it, and on this basis the meaning of "good taste" is very clear. "Good taste" means tasteless in the literal sense. Any act or product which contains too much stimulus value is considered to be "in bad taste" by old-culture adherents. Since gratification is viewed as a scarce commodity, arousal is dangerous. Clothes must be drab and inconspicuous, colors of low intensity, smells nonexistent ("if it weren't for bad taste there wouldn't be no taste at all"). Sounds should be quiet, words should lack affect. Four-letter words are always in bad taste because they have high stimulus value. Satire is in bad taste if it arouses political passions or creates images that are too vivid or exciting. All direct references to sexuality are in bad taste until proven innocent, since sexual arousal is the most feared result of all. The lines in old-culture homes, furnishings, and public buildings are hard and utilitarian. Since auditory overstimulation is more familiarly painful than its visual counterpart, brilliant, intense, vibrant colors are called "loud," and the preferred colors for old-culture homes are dull and listless. Stimulation in any form leaves old-culture Americans with a "bad taste" in their mouths. This taste is the taste of desire—a reminder that life in the here-and-now contains many pleasures to distract them from the carrot dangling beyond their reach. Too much stimulation makes the carrot hard to see. Good taste is a taste for carrots.

In the past decade, however, this pattern has undergone a merciless assault from the new culture. For if we assume that gratification is easy and resources plentiful, stimulation is no longer to be feared. Psychedelic colors, amplified sound, erotic books and films, bright and elaborate clothing, spicy food, "intense" (i.e., Anglo-Saxon) words, angry and irreverent satire—all go counter to the old pattern of understimulation. Long hair and beards provide a more "tactile" appearance than the bland, shaven-and-shorn, geometric lines of the fifties. Even Edward Hall's accusation that America is a land of "olfactory blandness" (a statement any traveler will confirm) must now be qualified a little, as the smells of coffee shops, foreign cooking, and incense combine to breathe a modicum of sensation even into the olfactory sphere. (Hall is right, however, in the sense that when America is filled with intense color, music, and ornament, deodorants will be the old culture's last-ditch holdouts. It is no accident that hostility to hippies so often focuses on their olfactory humanity.) The old culture turned the volume down on emotional experience in order to concentrate on its dreams of glory, but the new culture has turned it up again.

New-culture adherents, in fact, often display symptoms of *under*sensitivity to stimuli. They say "Wow!" in response to almost everything, but in voices utterly devoid of either tension or affect. They seem in general to be more certain that desire can be gratified than that it can be aroused.

This phenomenon probably owes much to early child-rearing conditions. Under ordinary circumstances a mother responds to her child's needs when they are expressed powerfully enough to distract her from other cares and activities. Mothers who overrespond to the Spockian challenge, however, often try to anticipate the child's needs. Before arousal has proceeded very far they hover about and try several possible satisfactions. Since we tend to use these early parental responses as models for the way we treat our own impulses in adulthood, some new-culture adherents find themselves moving toward gratification before need arousal is clear or compelling. Like their mothers they are not altogether clear which need they are feeling. To make matters worse they are caught in the dilemma that spontaneity automatically evaporates the moment it becomes an ideology. It is a paradox of the modern condition that only those who oppose complete libidinal freedom are capable of ever achieving it.

Another logical consequence of scarcity assumptions is structured inequality. If there is not enough to go around then those who have more will find ways to prolong their advantage, and even legitimate it through various devices. The law itself, although philosophically committed to equality, is fundamentally a social device for maintaining structured systems of inequality (defining as crimes, for example, only those forms of theft and violence in which lower class persons engage). One of the major thrusts of the new culture, on the other hand, is equality: since the good things of life are plentiful, everyone should share them: rich and poor, black and white, female and male.

It is a central characteristic of the old culture that means habitually become ends, and ends means. Instead of people working in order to obtain goods in order to be happy, for example, we find that people should be made happy in order to work better in order to obtain more goods, and so on. Inequality, originally a consequence of scarcity, is now a means of creating artificial scarcities. For in the old culture, as we have seen, the manufacture of scarcity is the principal activity. Hostile comments of old-culture adherents toward new-culture forms ("people won't want to work if they can get things for nothing," "people won't want to get married if they can get it free") often reveal this preoccupation. Scarcity, the presumably undesired but unavoidable foundation for the whole old-culture edifice, has now become its most treasured and sacred value, and to maintain this value in the midst of plenty it has been necessary to establish invidiousness as the foremost criterion of worth. Old-culture Americans are peculiarly drawn to anything that seems to be the exclusive possession of some group or other, and find it difficult to enjoy anything they themselves have unless they can be sure that there are people to whom this pleasure is denied. For those in power even life itself derives its value invidiously: amid the emptiness and anesthesia of a power-oriented career many officials derive reassurance of their vitality from their proximity to the possibility of blowing up the world.

The centrality of invidiousness offers a strong barrier to the diffusion of social justice and equality. But it provides a *raison d'être* for the advertising industry, whose primary function is to manufacture illusions of scarcity. In a society engorged to the point of strangulation with useless and joyless products, advertisements show people calamitously running out of their food or beer, avidly hoarding potato chips, stealing each other's cigarettes, guiltily borrowing each other's deodorants, and so on. In a land of plenty there is little to fight over, but in the world of advertising images men and women will fight before changing their brand, in a kind of parody of the Vietnam war.

The fact that property takes precedence over human life in the old culture also follows logically from scarcity assumptions. If possessions are scarce relative to people they come to have more value than people. This is especially true of people with few possessions, who come to be considered so worthless as to be subhuman and hence eligible for extermination. Many possessions, on the other hand, entitle the owner to a status somewhat more than human. But as a society becomes more affluent these priorities begin to change—human life increases in value and property decreases. New-culture adherents challenge the high relative value placed on property, although the old priority still permeates the society's normative structure. It is still considered permissible, for example, to kill someone who is stealing your property under certain conditions. This is especially true if that person is without property himself—a wealthy kleptomaniac (in contrast to a poor black looter) would probably be worth a murder trial if killed while stealing.[2]

A recent sign of the shift in values was the *Pueblo* courtmartial. While the Navy, standing firmly behind old-culture priorities, argued that the Commander of the spy ship should have sacrificed the lives of ninety men to prevent the loss of "expensive equipment" to the enemy, the public at large supported his having put human life first. Much of the intense legal upheaval visible today—expressed most noticeably in the glare of publicity that now attaches to the activities of the U.S. Supreme Court—derives from the attempt to adapt an old-culture legal system to the changing priorities that render it obsolete.

It would not be difficult to show how the other characteristics of the old culture are based on the same scarcity assumptions, or to trace out in detail the derivation of the new culture from the premise that life's satisfactions exist in abundance and sufficiency for all. Let us instead look more closely at the relationship that the new culture bears to the old—the continuities and discontinuities that it offers—and explore some of the contradictions it holds within itself.

First of all it should be stressed that affluence and economic security are not in themselves responsible for the new culture. The rich, like the poor, have always been with us to some degree, but

---

[2] A more trivial example can be found in the old culture's handling of noise control. Police are called to prevent distraction by the joyous noises of laughter and song, but not to stop the harsh and abrasive roar of power saws, air hammers, power mowers, snow blowers, and other baneful machines.

the new culture has not. What is significant in the new culture is not a celebration of economic affluence but a rejection of its foundation. The new culture is concerned with rejecting the artificial scarcities upon which material abundance is based. It argues that instead of throwing away one's body so that one can accumulate material artifacts, one should throw away the artifacts and enjoy one's body. The new culture is not merely blindly reactive, however, but embodies a sociological consciousness. In this consciousness lies the key insight that possessions actually generate scarcity. The more emotion one invests in them the more chances for significant gratification are lost—the more committed to them one becomes the more deprived one feels, like a thirsty man drinking salt water. To accumulate possessions is to deliver pieces of oneself to dead things. Possessions can absorb an emotional cathexis, but unlike personal relationships they feed nothing back. Americans have combined the proliferation of possessions with the disruption, circumscription, and trivialization of most personal relationships. An alcoholic becomes malnourished because drinking obliterates his hunger. Americans become unhappy and vicious because their preoccupation with amassing possessions obliterates their loneliness. This is why production in America seems to be on such an endless upward spiral: every time we buy something we deepen our emotional deprivation and hence our need to buy something. This is good for business, of course, but those who profit most from this process are just as trapped in the general deprivation as everyone else. The new-culture adherents are thus not merely affluent—they are trying to substitute an adequate emotional diet for a crippling addiction.

The new culture is nevertheless a product of the old, not merely a rejection of it. It picks up themes latent or dormant or subordinate in the old and magnifies them. The hippie movement, for example, is brimming with nostalgia—a nostalgia peculiarly American and shared by old-culture adherents. This nostalgia embraces the Old West, Amerindian culture, the wilderness, the simple life, the utopian community—all venerable American traditions. But for the old culture they represent a subordinate, ancillary aspect of the culture, appropriate for recreational occasions or fantasy representation—a kind of pastoral relief from everyday striving—whereas for the new culture they are dominant themes. The new culture's passion for memorabilia, paradoxically, causes uneasiness in old-culture adherents, whose future-oriented invidiousness leads to a desire to sever themselves from the past. Yet for the most part it is a question of the new culture making the old culture's secondary themes primary, rather than simply seeking to discard the old culture's primary theme. Even the notion of "dropping out" is an important American tradition—neither the United States itself nor its populous suburbs would exist were this not so.

Americans have always been deeply ambivalent about the issue of social involvement. On the one hand they are suspicious of it and share deep romantic fantasies of withdrawal to a simple pastoral or even sylvan life. On the other hand they are much given to acting out grandiose fantasies of taking society by storm, through the achievement of wealth, power, or fame. This ambivalence has led to many strange institutions—the suburb and the automobile being the most obvious. But note that both fantasies express the viewpoint of an outsider. Americans have a profound tendency to feel like outsiders—they wonder where the action is and wander about in search of it (this puts an enormous burden on celebrities, who are supposed to know, but in fact feel just as doubtful as everyone else). Americans have created a society in which they are automatically nobodies, since no one has any stable place or enduring connection. The village idiot of earlier times was less a "nobody" in this sense than the mobile junior executive or academic. An American has to "make a place for himself" because he does not have one.

Since the society rests on scarcity assumptions, involvement in it has always meant competitive involvement, and, curiously enough, the theme of bucolic withdrawal has often associated itself with that of cooperative, communal life. So consistently, in fact, have intentional communities established themselves in the wilderness that one can only infer that society as we know it makes cooperative life impossible.

Be that as it may, it is important to remember that the New England colonies grew out of utopian communes, so that the drop-out tradition is not only old but extremely important to our history. Like so many of the more successful nineteenth century utopian communities (Oneida and Amana, for example) the puritans became corrupted by involvement in successful economic enterprise and the communal aspect was eroded away—another example of a system being destroyed by what it attempts to ignore. The new culture is thus a kind of reform movement, attempting to revive a decayed tradition once important to our civilization.

In stressing these continuities between the new culture and the American past, I do not mean to imply a process unique to our society. One of the most basic characteristics of all successful social systems—indeed, perhaps all living matter as well—is that they include devices that serve to keep alive alternatives that are antithetical to their dominant emphases, as a kind of hedge against change. These latent alternatives usually persist in some encapsulated and imprisoned form ("break glass in case of fire"), such as myths, festivals, or specialized roles. Fanatics continually try to expunge these circumscribed contradictions, but when they succeed it is often fatal to the society. For, as Lewis Mumford once pointed out, it is the "laxity, corruption, and disorder" in a system that makes it viable, considering the contradictory needs that all social systems must satisfy.[3] Such latent alternatives are priceless treasures and must be carefully guarded against loss. For a new cultural pattern does not emerge out of nothing—the seed must already be there, like the magic tricks of wizards and witches in folklore, who can make an ocean out of a drop of water, a palace out of a stone, a forest out of a blade of grass, but nothing out of nothing. Many peoples keep alive a tradition of a golden age, in which a totally different social structure existed. The Judeo-Christian God, patriarchal and omnipotent, has served in matrifocal cultures to keep alive the concept of a strong and protective paternal figure in the absence of real-life examples. Jesters kept alive a wide variety of behavior patterns amid the stilted and restrictive formality of royal courts. The specialized effeminate roles that one finds in many warrior cultures are not merely a refuge for those who fail to succeed in the dominant pattern—they are also a living reminder that the rigid "protest masculinity" that prevails is not the only conceivable kind of behavior for a male. And conversely, the warrior ethos is maintained in a peaceful society or era by means of a military cadre or reserve system.

These phenomena are equivalent to (and in literate cultures tend increasingly to be replaced by) written records of social practices. They are like a box of seldom-used tools, or a trunk of old costumes awaiting the proper period-play. Suddenly the environment changes, the tolerated eccentric becomes a prophet, the clown a dancing-master, the doll an idol, the idol a doll. The elements have not changed, only the arrangement and the emphases have changed. Every revolution is in part a revival.

Sometimes societal ambivalence is so marked that the latent pattern is retained in a form almost as elaborated as the dominant one. Our society, for example, is one of the most mobile (geographically, at least) ever known; yet, unlike other nomadic cultures it makes little allowance for this fact in its patterns of material accumula-

[3] Lewis Mumford, "The Fallacy of Systems," *Saturday Review of Literature*, XXXII, October 1949; Gideon Sjoberg, "Contradictory Functional Requirements of Social Systems," *Journal of Conflict Resolution*, IV, 1960, pp. 198–208.

tion. Our homes are furnished as if we intended to spend the rest of our lives in them, instead of moving every few years. This perhaps represents merely a kind of technological neurosis—a yearning for stability expressed in a technological failure to adapt. Should Americans ever settle down, however, they will find little to do in the way of readjusting their household furnishing habits.

Ultimately it seems inevitable that Americans must either abandon their nomadic habits (which seems unlikely) or moderate their tendency to invest their libido exclusively in material possessions (an addiction upon which the economy relies rather heavily). The new culture is of course pushing hard to realize the second alternative, and if it is successful one might anticipate a trend toward more simply furnished dwellings in which all but the most portable and decorative items are permanent installations. In such a case we might like or dislike a sofa or bed or dresser, but would have no more personal involvement with it than we now do with a stove, furnace, or garage. We would possess, cathect, feel as a part of us, only a few truly personal and portable items.

This tendency of human societies to keep alternative patterns alive has many biological analogues. One of these is *neoteny*—the evolutionary process in which foetal or juvenile characteristics are retained in the adult animal. Body characteristics that have long had only transitional relevance are exploited in response to altered environmental circumstances (thus many human features resemble foetal traits of apes). I have not chosen this example at random, for much of the new culture is implicitly and explicitly "neotenous" in a cultural sense: behavior, values, and life-styles formerly seen as appropriate only to childhood are being retained into adulthood as a counterforce to the old culture.

I pointed out earlier, for example, that children are taught a set of values in earliest childhood—cooperation, sharing, equalitarianism—which they begin to unlearn as they enter school, wherein competition, invidiousness, status differentiation, and ethnocentrism prevail. By the time they enter adult life children are expected to have largely abandoned the value assumptions with which their social lives began. But for affluent, protected, middle-class children this process is slowed down, while intellectual development is speeded up, so that the earlier childhood values can become integrated into a conscious, adult value system centered around social justice. The same is true of other characteristics of childhood: spontaneity, hedonism, candor, playfulness, use of the senses for pleasure rather than utility, and so on. The protective, child-oriented, middle-class family allows the child to preserve some of these qualities longer than is possible under more austere conditions, and his intellectual precocity makes it possible for him to integrate them into an ideological system with which he can confront the corrosive, life-abusing tendencies of the old culture.

When these neotenous characteristics become manifest to old-culture adherents the effect is painfully disturbing, for they vibrate feelings and attitudes that are very old and very deep, although long and harshly stifled. Old-culture adherents have learned to reject all this, but since the learning antedated intellectual maturity they have no coherent ideological framework within which such a rejection can be consciously understood and thoughtfully endorsed. They are deeply attracted and acutely revolted at the same time. They can neither resist their fascination nor control their antipathy. This is exemplified by the extravagant curiosity that hippie communes attract, and by the harassment that so often extinguishes them.[4] It is usually necessary in such situations for the rote-learned abhorrence to discharge itself in persecutory activity before the more positive responses can be released. This was true in the case of the early Christians in Rome, with whom contemporary hippies are often compared (both were communal, utopian, mystical, dropouts, unwashed; both were viewed as dangerous, masochistic, ostentatious, the cause of their own troubles; both existed in societies in which the exclusive pursuit of material advantages had reached some kind of dead end), and seems equally true today. The absorption of this persecution is part of the process through which the latent values that the oppressed group protects and nurtures are expropriated by the majority and released into the mainstream of the culture.

Up to this point we have (rather awkwardly) discussed the new culture as if it were an integrated, monolithic pattern, which is certainly very far from the case. There are many varied and contradictory streams feeding the new culture, and some of these deserve particular attention, since they provide the raw material for future axes of conflict.

The most glaring split in the new culture is that which separates militant activism from the traits we generally associate with the hippie movement. The first strand stresses political confrontation, revolutionary action, radical commitment to the process of changing the basic structure of modern industrial society. The second involves a renunciation of that society in favor of the cultivation of inner experience and pleasing internal feeling-states. Heightening

[4] See, for example, Robert Houriet, "Life and Death of a Commune Called Oz," *New York Times Magazine*, February 16, 1969.

of sensory receptivity, commitment to the immediate present, and tranquil acceptance of the physical environment are sought in contradistinction to old-culture ways, in which the larger part of one's immediate experience is overlooked or grayed out by the preoccupation with utility, future goals, and external mastery. Since, in the old culture, experience is classified before it is felt, conceptualization tends here to be forsworn altogether. There is also much emphasis on aesthetic expression and an overarching belief in the power of love.

This division is a crude one, and there are, of course, many areas of overlap. Both value systems share an antipathy to the old culture, both share beliefs in sexual freedom and personal autonomy. Some groups (the Yippies, in particular) have tried with some success to bridge the gap in a variety of interesting ways. But there is nonetheless an inherent contradiction between them. Militant activism is task-oriented, and hence partakes of certain old-culture traits such as postponement of gratification, preoccupation with power, and so on. To be a competent revolutionary one must possess a certain tolerance for the "Protestant Ethic" virtues, and the activists' moral code is a stern one indeed. The hippie ethic, on the other hand, is a "salvation now" approach. It is thus more radical, since it remains relatively uncontaminated with old-culture values. It is also far less realistic, since it ignores the fact that the existing culture provides a totally antagonistic milieu in which the hippie movement must try to survive in a state of highly vulnerable parasitic dependence. The activists can reasonably say that the flower people are absurd to pretend that the revolution has already occurred, for such pretense leads only to severe victimization by the old culture. The flower people can reasonably retort that a revolution based to so great a degree on old-culture premises is lost before it is begun, for even if the militants are victorious they will have been corrupted by the process of winning.

The dilemma is a very real one and arises whenever radical change is sought. For every social system attempts to exercise the most rigid control over the mechanisms by which it can be altered —defining some as legitimate and others as criminal or disloyal. When we examine the characteristics of legitimate and nonlegitimate techniques, however, we find that the "legitimate" ones involve a course of action requiring a sustained commitment to the core assumptions of the culture. In other words, if the individual follows the "legitimate" pathway there is a very good chance that his initial radical intent will be eroded in the process. If he feels that some fundamental change in the system is required, then, he has a choice between following a path that subverts his goal or one that leads him to be jailed as a criminal or traitor.

This process is not a Machiavellian invention of American capitalists, but rather a mechanism which all viable social systems must evolve spontaneously in order to protect themselves from instability. When the system as it stands is no longer viable, however, the mechanism must be exposed for the swindle that it is; otherwise the needed radical changes will be rendered ineffectual.

The key to the mechanism is the powerful human reluctance to admit that an achieved goal was not worth the unpleasant experience required to achieve it.[5] This is the basic principle underlying initiation rituals: "if I had to suffer so much pain and humiliation to get into this club it must be a wonderful organization." The evidence of thousands of years is that the mechanism works extremely well. Up to some point, for example, war leaders can count on high casualties to increase popular commitment to military adventures.

Thus when a political leader says to a militant, "why don't you run for political office (get a haircut, dress conservatively, make deals, do the dirty work for your elders) and try to change the system in that way"—or the teacher says to the student, "wait until you have your Ph.D. (M.D., LL.B.) and then you can criticize our program," or the white man says to the black man, "when you begin to act like us you'll receive the same opportunities we do"—there is a serious subterfuge involved (however unconscious it may be) in that the protester, if he accepts the condition, will in most cases be automatically converted by it to his opponent's point of view.

The dilemma of the radical, then, is that he is likely to be corrupted if he fights the *status quo* on its own terms, but is not permitted to fight it in any other way. The real significance of the New Left is that it has discovered, in the politics of confrontation, as near a solution to this dilemma as can be found: it is always a bit problematic whether the acts of the new militants are "within the system" or not, and substantial headway can be made in the resulting confusion.

Yet even here the problem remains: if an activist devotes his life to altering the power structure, will he not become like old-culture adherents—utilitarian, invidious, scarcity-oriented, future-centered, and so on? Having made the world safe for flower people will he be likely to relinquish it to them? "You tell me it's the institution," object the Beatles, "you'd better free your mind instead." But what if all the freed minds are in jail?

[5] Leon Festinger, *A Theory of Cognitive Dissonance* (Stanford, Calif.: Stanford University Press, 1965).

The dilemma is particularly clear for blacks. Some blacks are much absorbed in rediscovering and celebrating those characteristics which seem most distinctively black and in sharpest contrast to white Western culture: black expressiveness, creativity, sensuality, and spontaneity being opposed to white constrictedness, rigidity, frigidity, bustle, and hypocrisy. For these blacks, to make too great a commitment to the power game is to forsake one's blackness. Power is a white hangup. Yet the absence of power places rather severe limits on the ability of blacks to realize their blackness or anything else.

There is no way to resolve this dilemma, and indeed, it is probably better left unresolved. In a revolutionary situation one needs discipline and unity of purpose, which, however, leads to all kinds of abuses when the goal is won. Discipline and unity become ends in themselves (after the old-culture pattern) and the victory becomes an empty one. It is therefore of great importance to have the envisioned revolutionary goals embodied in a group culture of some kind, with which the acts of those in power can be compared. In the meantime the old culture is subject to a two-pronged attack: a direct assault from activists—unmasking its life-destroying proclivities, its corruption, its futility and pointlessness, its failure to achieve any of its objectives—and an indirect assault by the expansion of expressive countercultures beyond a tolerable (i.e., freak) size.

Closely related to the activist-hippie division is the conflict over the proper role of aggression in the new culture. Violence is a major theme in the old culture and most new-culture adherents view human aggression with deep suspicion. Nonviolence has been the dominant trend in both the activist and hippie segments of the new culture until recently. But more and more activists have become impatient with the capacity of the old culture to strike the second cheek with even more enthusiasm than the first, and have endorsed violence under certain conditions as a necessary evil.

For the activists the issue has been practical rather than ideological: most serious and thoughtful activists have only a tactical commitment to violence. For the dropout ideologues, however, aggression poses a difficult problem: if they seek to minimize the artificial constriction of emotional expression, how can they be consistently loving and pacific? This logical dilemma is usually resolved by ignoring it: the love cult typically represses aggressive feelings ruthlessly—the body is paramount only so long as it is a loving body.

At the moment the old culture is so fanatically absorbed in violence that it does the work for everyone. If the new culture should prevail, however, the problem of human aggression would probably be its principal bone of contention. Faced with the persistence of aggressiveness (even in the absence of the old culture's exaggerated violence-inducing institutions), the love cult will be forced to re-examine its premises, and opt for some combination of expression and restraint that will restore human aggression to its rightful place as a natural, though secondary, human emotion.

A third split in the new culture is the conflict between individualism and collectivism. On this question the new culture talks out of both sides of its mouth, one moment pitting ideals of cooperation and community against old-culture competitiveness, the next moment espousing the old culture in its most extreme form with exhortations to "do your own thing." I am not arguing that individualism need be totally extirpated in order to make community possible, but new-culture enterprises often collapse because of a dogmatic unwillingness to subordinate the whim of the individual to the needs of the group. This problem is rarely faced honestly by new-culture adherents, who seem unaware of the conservatism involved in their attachment to individualistic principles.

It is always disastrous to attempt to eliminate any structural principle altogether; but if the balance between individualistic and collective emphases in America is not altered, everything in the new culture will be perverted and caricatured into simply another bizarre old-culture product. There must be continuities between the old and the new, but these cannot extend to the relative weights assigned to core motivational principles. The new culture seeks to create a tolerable society within the context of persistent American strivings—utopianism, the pursuit of happiness. But nothing will change until individualism is assigned a subordinate place in the American value system—for individualism lies at the core of the old culture, and a prepotent individualism is not a viable foundation for any society in a nuclear age.

Topics for Discussion

1. What is the old culture Slater is talking about? Do you agree with his description of it?
2. Do you consider yourself a member of the old or the new culture? Remember that Slater says that every culture is a dynamic whole and compromise is not possible.
3. Slater says "the core of the old culture is scarcity." What does he mean by scarcity? Do you agree with this analysis?
4. Do you agree that "America is a land of 'olfactory blandness' "?
5. Slater stresses that the new culture is a product of the old culture and not simply a rejection of the old. What is the relationship between the two cultures?
6. Does Slater see the new culture as an integrated whole? What diversity, if any, does he see in the new culture?
7. If, as Slater maintains, a radical is likely to be corrupted if he fights the establishment on its own terms, what should the radical do? Does Slater offer any possible solutions?
8. Why is the old culture opposed to all direct references to sexuality? Do you agree with Slater's analysis?
9. Slater says "the law itself, although philosophically committed to equality, is fundamentally a social device for maintaining structured systems of inequality . . ." Do you agree with this? Does Slater offer any evidence to back up this statement?

Rhetorical Considerations

1. In the introduction of the essay, Slater in effect summarizes what he will develop in more detail in the rest of the essay. Is this an effective introduction? Does Slater develop all that he uses in his introduction?
2. Is Slater's parable of the race an accurate and understandable way to present his idea? How does he further clarify this point?

POPULAR CULTURE:

NOTES TOWARD A DEFINITION

Ray Browne and Ronald Ambrosetti

"Popular Culture" is an indistinct term whose edges blur into imprecision. Scarcely any two commentators who try to define it agree in all aspects of what popular culture really is. Most critics, in fact, do not attempt to define it; instead, after distinguishing between it and the mass media, and between it and "high" culture, most assume that everybody knows that whatever is widely disseminated and experienced is "popular culture."

Some observers divide the total culture of a people into "minority" and "majority" categories. Other observers classify culture into High-Cult, Mid-Cult and Low-Cult, or High-Brow, Mid-Brow and Low-Brow, leaving out, apparently, the level that would perhaps be called Folk-Cult or Folk-Brow, though Folk culture is now taking on, even among the severest critics of popular culture a high class and achievement unique unto itself. Most of the discriminating observers agree, in fact, that there are perhaps actually four areas of culture: Elite, Popular, Mass and Folk, with the understanding that none is a discrete unity standing apart and unaffected by the others.

One reason for the lack of a precise definition is that the serious study of "popular culture" has been neglected in American colleges and universities. Elitist critics of our culture—notably such persons as Dwight Macdonald and Edmund Wilson—have always insisted that whatever was widespread was artistically and esthetically deficient, therefore unworthy of study. They have taught that "culture" to be worthwhile must necessarily be limited to the elite, aristocratic, and the minority. They felt that mass or popular culture—especially as it appeared in the mass media—would vitiate real culture. This attitude persists today among some of the younger critics. William Gass, for example, the esthetician and critic, takes the extreme position that "the products of popular culture, by and large, have no more esthetic quality than a brick in the street. . . . Any esthetic intentions is entirely absent, and because it is desired to manipulate consciousness directly, achieve one's effect there, no mind is paid to the intrinsic nature of its objects; they lack finish, complexity, stasis, individuality, coherence, depth, and endurance."

Such an attitude as Gass' is perhaps an extreme statement of the elitist critic's point of view. Luckily the force of numerous critics' arguments is weakening such attitudes. Popular Culture has a dimension, a thrust and—most important—a reality that has nothing to do with its esthetic accomplishment, though that has more merit than is often given to it.

This point of view is demonstrated by the talented young stylist Tom Wolfe, who, perhaps writing more viscerally than intellectually, thumbs his nose at the prejudice and snobbery that has always held at arms length all claims of validity if not esthetic accomplishment of the "culture" of the masses.

Susan Sontag, a brilliant young critic and esthetician, is more effective in bludgeoning the old point of view. Far from alarmed at the apparent new esthetic, she sees that it is merely a change in attitude, not a death's blow to culture and art:

> What we are getting is not the demise of art, but a transformation of the function of art. Art, which arose in human society as magical-religious operation, and passed over into a technique for depicting and commenting on secular reality, has in our own time arrogated to itself a new function—neither religious,

nor serving a secularized religious function, nor merely secular or profane . . . Art today is a new kind of instrument, an instrument for modifying consciousness and organizing new modes of sensibility.

To Sontag the unprecendented complexity of the world has made inevitable and very necessary this change in the function of art. This is virtually the same attitude held by Marshall McLuhan:

A technological extension of our bodies designed to alleviate physical stress can bring on psychic stress that may be much worse . . . Art is exact information of how to rearrange one's psyche to anticipate the next blow from our own extended psyches . . . in experimental art, men are given the exact specifications of coming violence to their own psyche from their own counter-irritants or technology. For those parts of ourselves that we thrust out in the form of new inventions are attempts to counter or neutralize collective pressures and irritations. But the counterirritant usually proves a greater plague than the initial irritant like a drug habit. And it is here that the artist can show us how to "ride with the punch," instead of "taking it on the chin."

An equally important aspect of popular culture as index and corrector is its role as a comic voice. Popular humor provides a healthy element in a nation's life. It pricks the pompous, devaluates the inflated, and snipes at the overly solemn. For example, such organs of popular culture as the magazines spoofed Henry James' pomposity during his lifetime, spoofed his "high" seriousness and in general tended to humanize him.

A more reasonable attitude than Gass' and one that is becoming increasingly acceptable is that held by the philosopher Abraham Kaplan: That popular culture has considerable accomplishment and even more real possibilities and it is developing but has not realized its full potential. All areas draw from one another. The Mass area being largely imitative, draws from the others without altering much. Elite art draws heavily from both folk and, perhaps to a slightly lesser degree, popular arts. Popular art draws from Elite

and Mass, and Folk, but does not take any without subjecting it to a greater or lesser amount of creative change. That popular culture has "no more esthetic quality than a brick in the street" or at least no more esthetic potential is a contention refuted by America's greatest writers—Hawthorne, Melville, Whitman, Twain, to name only four—as well as the greatest writers of all times and countries—Homer, Shakespeare, Dickens, Dostoevski, Tolstoi, for example.

Melville provides an excellent case in point. *Moby Dick* is the greatest creative book written in America and one of the half dozen greatest ever written anywhere. Its greatness derives from the sum total of its many parts. It is a blend of nearly all elements of all cultures of mid-nineteenth century America. Melville took all the culture around him—trivial and profound Transcendentalism and the plumbing of the depths of the human experience, but also demonism, popular theater, the shanghai gesture, jokes about pills and gas on the stomach, etc., and boiled them in the tryworks of his fiery genius into the highest art.

Many definitions of popular culture turn on methods of dissemination. Those elements which are too sophisticated for the mass media are generally called Elite culture, those distributed through these media that are something less than "mass" that is such things as the smaller magazines and newspapers, the less widely distributed books, museums and less sophisticated galleries, so-called clothes line art exhibits, and the like—are called in the narrow sense of the term "popular," those elements that are distributed through the mass media are "mass" culture, and those which are or were at one time disseminated by oral and non-oral methods—on levels "lower" than the mass media—are called "folk."

All definitions of such a complex matter, though containing a certain amount of validity and usefulness, are bound to be to a certain extent inadequate or incorrect. Perhaps a workable definition can best be arrived at by looking at one of the culture's most salient and quintessential aspects—its artistic creations—because the artist perhaps more than any one else draws from the totality of experience and best reflects it.

Shakespeare and his works are an excellent example. When he was producing his plays at the Globe Theater, Shakespeare was surely a "popular" author and his works were elements of "popular" culture, though they were at the same time also High or Elite culture, for they were very much part of the lives of both the groundlings and the nobles. Later, in America, especially during the nineteenth century, all of his works were well known, his name was commonplace, and he was at the same time still High art, Popular (even mass) art and Folk art. In the twentieth century, however, his works are more distinguishable as parts of various levels. *Hamlet* is still a play of both High and Popular art. The most sophisticated and scholarly people still praise it. But *Hamlet* is also widely distributed on TV, radio and through the movies. It is a commonplace on all levels of society and is therefore a part of "popular culture" in the broadest sense of the term. Other plays by Shakespeare, however, have not become a part of "popular" culture. *Titus Andronicus*, for example, for any of several reasons, is not widely known by the general public. It remains, thus, Elite culture.

Wideness of distribution and popularity in this sense are one major aspect of popular culture. But there are others. Many writers would be automatically a part of popular culture if their works sold only a few copies—Frank G. Slaughter and Frank Yerby, for example. Louis Auchincloss also, though his works are of a different kind than Slaughter's and Yerby's, because his subject is Wall Street and high finance, and these are subjects of popular culture.

Aside from distribution another major difference between high and popular culture, and among popular culture, mass culture and folk culture, is the motivation of the persons contributing, the makers and shapers of culture. On the Elite or sophisticated level, the creators value individualism, individual expression, the exploration and discovery of new art forms, of new ways of stating, the exploration and discovery of new depths in life's experiences.

On the other levels of culture there is usually less emphasis placed upon, and less accomplishment reached in, this plumbing of reality. Generally speaking, both popular and mass artists are less interested in the experimental and searching than in the restatement of the old and

accepted. But there are actually vast differences in the esthetic achievements attained in the works from these two levels, and different aspirations and goals, even within these somewhat limited objectives. As Hall and Whannel have pointed out:

In mass art the formula is everything—an escape from, rather than a means to, originality. The popular artist may use the conventions to select, emphasize and stress (or alter the emphasis and stress) so as to delight the audience with a kind of creative surprise. Mass art uses the stereotypes and formulae to simplify the experience, to mobilize stock feelings and to 'get them going.'

The popular artist is superior to the mass artist because for him "stylization is necessary, and the conventions provide an agreed base from which true creative invention springs." It is a serious error therefore to agree with Dwight MacDonald (in *Against the American Grain*) that all popular art "includes the spectator's reactions in the work itself instead of forcing him to make his own responses." Consider, for example, the reactions of two carriers of non-Elite culture, the first of popular culture, the banjo player Johnny St. Cyr. He always felt that the creative impulses of the average person and his responses in a creative situation were immense:

You see, the average man is very musical. Playing music for him is just relaxing. He gets as much kick out of playing as other folks get out of dancing. The more enthusiastic his audience is, why the more spirit the working man's got to play. And with your natural feelings that way you never make the same thing twice. Every time you play a tune new ideas come to mind and you slip that one in.

Compare that true artist's philosophy with that of Liberace, to whom the "whole trick is to keep the tune well out in front," to play "the melodies" and skip the "spiritual struggles." He always knows "just how many notes (his) audience will stand for," and if he has time left over he fills in "with a lot of runs up and down the keyboard."

Here in condensed form is the difference between popular and mass art and popular and mass artists. Both aim for different goals. St. Cyr is a truly creative artist in both intent and accomplishment. His credentials are not invalidated merely by the fact that he works in essentially a popular idiom. Given the limitations of his medium—if indeed these limitations are real—he can still be just as great a creator as—perhaps greater than—Rubenstein. It is incorrect to pit jazz against classical music, the popular against the elite. They are not in competition. Each has its own purposes, techniques and accomplishments. They complement each other rather than compete.

Another fine example can be found among the youth of today and their rebellion against what they consider the establishment. They are obviously not a part of the static mass, to whom escape is everything. Instead they are vigorously active, and in their action create dynamic and fine works of art, as examination of their songs, their art, their movies, etc., dramatically demonstrates.

It is also unfair to give blanket condemnation to mass art, though obviously the accomplishments of mass art are less than those of "higher" forms. Liberace does not aspire to much, and perhaps reaches even less. His purposes and techniques are inferior, but not all his, or the many other workers in the level, are completely without value.

All levels of culture, it must never be forgotten, are distorted by the lenses of snobbery and prejudice which the observers wear. There are no hard and fast lines separating one level from another.

Popular culture also includes folk culture. The relationship between folk culture and popular and elite cultures is still debatable. In many ways folk culture borrows from and imitates both.

Historically folk art has come more from the hall than from the novel, has depended more upon the truly creative—though unsophisticated—spirit than the mediocre imitator. "Sir Patrick Spens," one of the greatest songs (poems) ever written, was originally the product of a single creative genius. Today's best folklore-to-be, that is the most esthetically satisfying folklore which is working into tradition today, is that of such people as Woody Guthrie, Larry Gorman and such individual artists.

To a large number of observers, however, folklore is felt to be the same as popular culture. To another large number folklore derives directly from popular culture, with only a slight time lag. To them, today's popular culture is tomorrow's folklore. Both notions are gross and out of line.

Esthetically folk culture has two levels. There is superb folk art and deficient mediocre folk art. Esthetically folk art is more nearly akin to Elite art, despite the lack of sophistication that much folk art has, than to popular. Elite art has much that is inferior, as even the most prejudiced critic must admit. In motivation of artist, also, folk art is close to Elite, for like the Elite artist the truly accomplished folk artist values individualism and personal expression, he explores new forms and seeks new depths in expression and feeling. But there are at the same time workers in folklore who are mere imitators, just trying to get along—exactly like their counterparts in mass culture.

Thus all elements in our culture (or cultures) are closely related and are not mutually exclusive one from another. They constitute one long continuum. Perhaps the best metaphorical figure for all is that of a flattened ellipsis, or a lens. In the center, largest in bulk and easiest seen through is Popular Culture, which includes Mass Culture.

On either end of the lens are High and Folk Cultures, both looking fundamentally alike in many respects and both having a great deal in common, for both have keen direct vision and extensive peripheral insight and acumen. All four derive in many ways and to many degrees from one another, and the lines of demarcations between any two are indistinct and mobile.

Despite the obvious difficulty of arriving at a hard and fast definition of popular culture, it will probably be to our advantage—and a comfort to many who need one—to arrive at some viable though tentative understanding of how popular culture can be defined.

Two scholars who do attempt a definition, following George Santayana's broad distinctions between work and play, believe that "Popular Culture is really what people do when they are not working." This definition is both excessively general and overly exclusive, for it includes much that is "high" culture and leaves out many aspects which obviously belong to popular culture.

One serious scholar defines a total culture as "The body of intellectual and imaginative work which each generation receives" as its tradition. Basing our conclusion on this one, a viable definition for Popular Culture is all those elements of life which are not narrowly intellectual or creatively elitist and which are generally though not necessarily disseminated through the mass media. Popular Culture consists of the spoken and printed words, sounds, pictures, objects and artifacts. "Popular Culture" thus embraces all levels of our society and culture other than the Elite—the "popular," "mass" and "folk." It includes most of the bewildering aspects of life which hammer us daily.

Such a definition, though perhaps umbrella-like in its comprehensiveness, provides the latitude needed at this point, it seems, for the serious scholar to study the world around him. Later, definitions may need to pare edges and change lighting and emphasis. But for the moment, inclusiveness is perhaps better than exclusiveness.

Topics for Discussion

1. What reasons does Browne give for the lack of a precise definition of the term "popular culture"?
2. What is an "elitist critic"?
3. Popular Culture, according to Browne, "has a dimension, a thrust and . . . a reality that has nothing to do with its esthetic accomplishment . . ." Do you agree with this? What examples does Browne offer to illustrate his point?
4. How valid is Browne's contention that Shakespeare is part of popular culture?
5. What is the difference between the popular artist and the mass artist? Do you agree that the popular artist is superior to the mass artist?
6. What does Browne mean by the term "total culture"?
7. Does Browne ever state his definition of popular culture? What is it? Discuss your agreement or disagreement with it.

Rhetorical Considerations

1. Does Browne quote too much from too many people for such a brief essay? What purpose do the quotations serve? How effective are they? How necessary are they?
2. What is Browne's thesis? Is it stated anywhere in the essay?
3. Toward the end of the essay, Browne writes in increasingly shorter paragraphs. Can you see any reason for this?
4. Does Browne reach any conclusion in his essay? Is it clearly and effectively stated?

James Bond: Culture Hero

George Grella

Ian Fleming's James Bond is the most famous spy since Mata Hari. The indomitable secret agent reaches every level of literacy: Presidents to popcorn chewers. Not only has the author become a kind of subliterary lion in *Time*, *The New Yorker*, and *The Saturday Review*, which have devoted interviews and articles to his work, but his opinion was solicited on a major network show about the U-2 affair, the producers seeming to consider Mr. Fleming something like the Walter Lippmann of espionage.

Yet there is no puzzle to solve, no criminal to discover, no brilliant method to reveal. Fleming has no view of a corrupt society in the manner of a Cain, a Hammet or a Chandler; his style and outlook are facile and pedestrian. Unlike Mickey Spillane, he doesn't write pornographic thrillers. Unlike Graham Greene, he offers no metaphysical or psychological insight, no significant comment on the nature of good and evil. Eric Ambler, a genuine craftsman, gives us plausible incidents, people stumbling into affairs which are complex, ambiguous, and believable. Newer writers, such as John Le Carré in *The Spy Who Came in From the Cold* or Len Deighton in the largely-unrecognized *Ipcress File*, portray the life of a professional spy as unglamorous, poverty-ridden and full of odd danger — one never knows when his own organization may betray him, or how far a competing unit of his own government will go, or if he must kill someone on his side, or even what side he is on.

To put it plainly, James Bond, despite his lean good looks, his taste in food, wine and women, his high standing in the British Secret Service, his license to kill, is stupid. He disobeys orders and blunders into situations he should have anticipated chapters in advance. He is almost always known to the enemy as soon as he arrives, undercover on the scene of action. He usually flounders around long enough for his adversaries to disrupt his elaborate plans and capture him.

His only genius lies in an infinite capacity for taking pain. He has suffered (and survived) bombing, shooting, stabbing, poisoning and automobile attack. He has managed to (barely) escape castration by carpet-beater; bisection by buzzsaw; rocket blast; shark, barracuda and octopus attack; a near-fatal increase in height on a health farm stretching apparatus; and a dose of poison from the sex glands of a rare Eastern fish. Such bizarre punishment is oddly requited: Bond has enjoyed the charms of the expensive Tiffany Case; the Bahamian nature girl, Honeychile Rider; the mystic Solitaire; and the ineffable Pussy Galore.

No secret agent could behave with such incompetence and still achieve such high renown, such titillating rewards. Fleming's characters are grotesques, the much-publicized sex is chrome-plated, not at all shocking, and the plots are repetitive from book to book. The solution of the paradox of James Bond's popularity may be, not in considering the novels as thrillers, but as something very different, as historic epic and romance, based on the stuff of myth and legend.

Thus, the affectionate fondling of brand names, which readers cite as an example of authenticity, is a contemporary version of the conventional epic catalogue. It is important for the reader to know that Bond wears Sea Island

George Grella, "James Bond: Culture Hero," from *The New Republic* (May 30, 1964), pp. 17-19. Reprinted by permission. Originally published in *The New Republic*.

cotton shirts, smokes a Macedonian blend of cigarettes, tells time by a Rolex Oyster watch, fires a Walther PPK 7.65 automatic in a Berns-Martin Triple Draw holster, drives a Mark II Bentley Continental, and so on, just as it is important for the reader of the *Iliad* to be told the immense detail of Achilles' shield. Instead of a catalogue of ships, Fleming gives us a catalogue of clothes, toilet accessories, or background material about some exotic place or some arcane field of knowledge. The catalogues reflect the culture: the long lists of brand names suggest the affluence of a capitalist civilization, just as Bond suggests the secure investment.

Bond fights epic battles, taking seriously what Pope used humorously in his mock epic, *The Rape of the Lock* — the epic game of cards. James Bond has won harrowing games of blackjack, baccarat, bridge, even canasta. Like Ulysses, he travels far, from Turkey to Las Vegas, the Mediterranean, the Caribbean, the Atlantic, even Miami Beach. He makes the obligatory trip to the underworld when he skindives in the Bahamas, travels through the sewers of Istanbul, visits the domain of Mr. Big in Harlem, negotiates Dr. No's cruel tunnel of terror. His name indicates further facets of his character: he is entrusted with the mammoth task of safeguarding an entire civilization; the free world depends on his actions.

In *Moonraker* the situation parallels the Perseus-St. George myth, an appropriate one for Bond's rescue of London from the great rocket of Sir Hugo Drax, the huge dragon menacing England. Drax has red hair, an ugly, burned face which even plastic surgery cannot mask, splayed "ogre's teeth"; the great burst of fire he hopes to turn on London is the modern equivalent of the dragon's flames. Fleming employs an ironic reversal of one aspect of the Perseus myth: instead of rescuing Andromeda from the cliff where she is chained, Bond and his Andromeda, Galatea Brand, are nearly killed when one of

the Dover cliffs, with some urging from Drax, falls on them. Of course Bond survives and, after escaping steamhosing and the lift-off of the Moonraker rocket (more fire from the dragon's nostrils), saves London. Alone among Bond novels, the hero fails to get the girl at the end: as a modern St. George, it would scarcely be appropriate for him to win the fair maiden.

In *Live and Let Die*, Bond travels to New York to confront Mr. Big, a giant Negro who controls a black brotherhood of crime, gathering gold to aid the Soviet Union. With his Negro network, his voodoo cult, his clairvoyant mistress, Mr. Big is almost omnipotent; his followers believe he is Baron Samedi, the Devil himself. He even controls the fishes of the sea, summoning shark and barracuda to defend his island. But Bond hurls the epic boast, which we know will clinch his victory, "Big Man? Then let it be a giant, a homeric slaying." His boast is fulfilled; just as he and Solitaire are to be dragged over a coral reef and shredded, Bond's mine blows up Mr. Big's boat and Big is devoured by the fish he tamed, his immense head bobbing bodyless in the sea. Bond again saves Civilization, this time from the powers of blackness.

Goldfinger is probably the most obvious reworking of early myth. Auric Goldfinger, who drives a gold car, carries his money in solid gold, dreams of robbing Fort Knox, and likes his women gold-plated all over, is a reincarnation of King Midas. Midas was tone deaf and earned a pair of ass's ears for misjudging a music contest between Pan and Apollo; Goldfinger, when Bond first meets him, is wearing a hearing aid and sunning himself with a set of tin wings resembling a pair of long, slightly pointed ears. Midas' barber, unable to contain the secret of his master's aural adornment, whispered his message into a hole. Later a reed grew and told the secret to all passersby. James Bond, in Goldfinger's captivity, must foil the planned robbery of

Fort Knox; he tapes his message to an airplane toilet seat, the only hole available, and thus transmits it to the outside world.

Fleming's best-known book, *Dr. No,* (there's a movie version too) is the most purely mythic of his works. Dr. No is the archetypal monster who casts a blight on the land and who must be conquered by the unquenchable spirit of life. He inhabits a lavish underground fortress in a guano island in the Caribbean, from which he misguides American missiles with intricate electronic apparatus. He has come to the British government's attention through complaints of the Audubon Society about the deaths of thousands of roseate spoonbills. Dr. No intimidates the natives and scares off the birds with a fire-breathing tractor made to resemble a dragon; his dragon is devastating the island of dung, killing the birds, the game wardens, all natural life. For his violation of nature, Dr. No must be punished by the grand spirit of affirmation, James Bond. Naturally Bond's mission fails at first; he is detected and captured by the evil doctor. After a rich meal and an opportunity to enumerate and use the deluxe living accommodations of the island fortress, Bond is subjected to an agonizing series of tortures in a tunnel of horrors, including an ordeal by fire and by water. He manages to crawl through the bowels of the island (anthropomorphically, the bowels of the monster as well), and kill Dr. No's pet giant octopus, displaying all the while superhuman strength and stamina. He buries Dr. No alive in a small mountain of guano. He has brought back the fertility of the land by ridding nature of the destroyer. As his reward, he spends a night with Honeychile Rider, the nymph of the Bahamas, who knows the secrets of snakes, spiders and seashells. His heroic reward is the possession of the nature spirit herself; it is richly deserved. James Bond has redeemed the Waste Land.

The much-touted background which distinguishes the Bond novel, the close attention to real places and real names, the bits of esoteric information, are all products of an expensive research organization. Aside from their epic function, the lists of names lend only a spurious authenticity which is negated by other lapses from realism. Not only do people like Dr. No and Mr. Big inhabit an unreal world, but even their surface reality is questionable. Fleming's painstaking tour of Manhattan with Bond in *Live and Let Die* proves only that he can read a New York City map. Mr. Fleming is maladroit at transcribing American English; his Negro dialect echoes *Porgy and Bess.* His Americans, from cabdrivers to CIA agents, speak like graduates of non-U public schools. In *Diamonds Are Forever*, Bond thinks the tails attached to automobile antennas are beaver tails. No one in America hunts beaver for their tails or for anything else and not even teenagers fly squirrel tails (which don't look at all like beaver tails) from their cars any more. It's been thirty years since jaded Cafe Society types slummed in Harlem; Fleming seems to think it's still fashionable.

But no matter; we are dealing with myths. Vivienne Michel, the breathless French-Canadian girl who narrates *The Spy Who Loved Me,* may be intended as a representation of the typical James Bond fan. Most of the book concentrates on her rather unexciting sexual reminiscences in an odd fusion of *True Confessions* and *McCall's.* She is rescued from a pair of gangsters in an Adirondack motel by the coincidental appearance of our agent. After first fumbling the job (he can't kill in cold blood, he explains, forgetting that he's hired for that job and that in another book he's detailed a couple of these jobs), Bond triumphs. He and Vivienne couple hygienically (in air-conditioned comfort, on Beautyrest mattresses, with Sanitized toilet facilities), and Vivienne comments on the action, "He had come from nowhere like the prince in the fairy tales, and he had saved me from the dragon . . . and then, when the dragon was dead, he had taken me as his reward." Vivienne doesn't have Bond's powerful Bentley, she drives a "cute little Vespa." She lists a variety of brand names, but hers consist of clothes and motel appliances. Her comments about the dragon indicate that she, at least, recognizes what's up.

In Fleming's most recent novel, *On Her Majesty's Secret Service*, Bond saves England from biological warfare waged by Ernst Blofeld, the elusive chief of SPECTRE. He narrowly escapes death and matrimony. Blofeld murders Bond's bride of a few hours and escapes, no doubt to reappear in a future novel. Bond, though hardly chaste, still must be unmarried, celibate in his fight against evil. Since there can be no Son of Bond, Blofeld does agent 007 a great service.

Mr. Anthony Boucher, an astute and prolific critic of thrillers, complained in a *New York Times* review of the book, that only bad shooting enabled Bond to escape his enemies. Mr. Boucher is correct, but he criticizes the book as a poor thriller, neglecting the myth: since Bond leads a charmed life, no one can ever shoot him dead.

Perhaps centuries from now, scholars will trace assiduously those references to Yardley soap, Kent brushes, Lanvin perfume, Sanitized toilet seats. Perhaps there will be a variorum Fleming, and "Fleming men" as there are "Milton men." Theses may be written on the epicene role of M, clearly a father figure (yet why unmarried? and that maternal sounding initial is rather damning). For James Bond is the Renaissance man in mid-century guise, lover, warrior, connoisseur. He fights the forces of darkness, speaks for the sanitary achievements of the age, enjoys hugely the fruits of the free enterprise economy. He lives the dreams of countless drab people, his gun ready, his honor intact, his morals loose: the hero of our anxiety-ridden, mythless age: the savior of our culture.

Topics for Discussion

1. According to Grella, why is James Bond such a culture hero?
2. Grella never defines the word hero in his essay, but based on how he uses the word, give a definition of hero as it is used in this essay.
3. Do you think James Bond is a hero? How do you define hero? Give two or three examples of people you consider heroes.
4. Do you think Grella is serious when he says that we should consider the James Bond novels not as thrillers but as "historic epic and romance, based on the stuff of myth and legend"?
5. Based on your knowledge of James Bond (from either the books or the movies), do you agree with Grella that "James Bond . . . is stupid. . . . His only genius lies in an infinite capacity for taking pain."
6. Is Grella's summarization of Bond in the last paragraph accurate?
7. Can you name any heroes (fictional or nonfictional) similar to James Bond?

Rhetorical Considerations

1. This is a well-organized essay. Write a brief outline of it dividing it into its major parts.
2. What is the thesis of this essay? Where is it stated?

Of War and Heroes

Sensing his own frailty, each man yearns for someone stronger or nobler or more certain in whom to believe. He embraces God, or he elevates mortals to the status of heroes, or he does both. The death of World War II hero Audie Murphy was a melancholy reminder that society imposes an impossible burden on those few from whom it expects so much. This is especially true of the battle hero, whose impulsiveness, perhaps sheer recklessness, and submersion of self can emerge as fatal faults in the day-by-day pursuit of peacetime success. And the hero, too, aware of his own weakness, must always fight the fear that he does not deserve all of the accolades.

The pressure has crushed many war heroes. World War II Flying Ace "Pappy" Boyington returned to take to the bottle, fall into debt and observe bitterly: "Show me a hero and I'll show you a bum." Marine Ira Hayes, one of the idolized flag raisers at Iwo Jima, died at 32 in a drunken stupor, frozen in the wintry outdoors of an Indian reservation. Similar strains tear at relatively unknown Congressional Medal of Honor winners as their wartime exploits dog them. Marine Johnny Basilone, decorated for bravery at Guadalcanal, was obsessed with the notion that someone else had done the deeds for which he was honored, refused his right to seek a Stateside assignment, and was killed at Iwo Jima. Michigan's Sergeant Dwight Johnson, whose heroics in Viet Nam verged on the suicidal, required psychiatric treatment on his return, then was fatally wounded when he tried to hold up a Detroit drive-in grocery store.

The ancient Greeks may have had a more humane idea. They were hero worshipers, too, but an individual had to die before he was enshrined. The dead, at least, cannot destroy or be consumed by their own legends.

To Hell and Not Quite Back

When Audie Murphy returned from World War II, not yet 21 and the war's most decorated hero, he held the promise of an emerald future. Winner of the Congressional Medal of Honor and 23 other

"Heroes: To Hell and Not Quite Back," p. 27 and "Of War and Heroes," p. 12, *Time*, June 14, 1971. Reprinted by permission from *Time*, The Weekly Newsmagazine; Copyright Time, Inc.

citations, credited with killing an estimated 240 Germans, the babyfaced kid from Kingston, Texas, was feted by the press and patriotic organizations, courted by business, industry and Hollywood. To an adoring public, he represented that elusive American ideal: the small-town boy who, despite seemingly insurmountable odds, goes on to perform such deeds as dreams and motion pictures are made of.

Yet the consequence of heroism, all too often, is an ego-rending compulsion to continue in a larger-than-life role, a task at which few succeed. Murphy was no exception. Faced with the need to translate acts of valor into a lifetime of virtue, he had nowhere to go but down. When his body was found last week in the crash of a light plane outside Roanoke, Va., Murphy, 46, left behind a promise that had dissolved unheroically into business failures, run-ins with the law and forgettable parts in forgettable movies.

No Talent. Still, Murphy's bravery in World War II was memorable indeed. A member of the Seventh Army, 3rd Division, 15th Infantry Regiment, Company B, he rose from private to first lieutenant in nearly 30 months of combat. He was wounded three times. On one occasion, he stormed a German-occupied hill alone, killing 15 and wounding 35; later he captured, singlehanded, an enemy machine-gun nest. In the battle for the Colmar pocket in eastern France, he mounted a burning tank destroyer and with its .50-cal. machine gun held off an attacking Nazi force of some 250 men and six tanks. It was for this action that he was awarded the Medal of Honor.

Yet in his autobiography, *To Hell and Back*—he later starred in the movie version—he recalled his pleasure at being just another soldier. Even in his Hollywood heyday, Murphy was never comfortable in his hero's role. He preferred chatting with the extras to hob-nobbing with actors and directors.

Murphy had no qualms about his lack of acting ability. "I'm working with a handicap," he told one director. "I have no talent." He was quick to admit that he was in acting simply for the money. He did make money—some $2.5 million from 40 pictures—but part of it he gave away and the rest he lost in poor investments. For the past several years he was hounded by creditors. When he died, he was on a business trip trying to close one last deal to stave off bankruptcy.

Busting Drug Dealers. One of nine living children of a Texas sharecropper, Murphy was no stranger to adversity. While Audie was still in his teens, his father left home; his mother died soon after, leaving Audie to support what was left of the family. He scraped through, working as a farm hand and doing odd jobs, but only the war saved him from becoming a Dust Bowl drifter. When he enlisted in the infantry after being turned down by the Marines and the paratroopers because he was too small, Murphy had never been more than 100 miles from home.

Murphy was twice married: the first time for a little more than a year, to Starlet Wanda Hendrix. His second marriage, to Pamela Archer, was more durable. He had two sons and was a devoted father. In his last years he and his family lived in a two-story Englishstyle farmhouse in Los Angeles, attempting to make a new start.

As the world got faster and faster in the '60s, it left him farther and farther behind. Murphy played a kind of grown-up cops-and-robbers game as a special officer of the Port Hueneme, Calif., police department and as a source of Mafia intelligence for the Los Angeles County district attorney's office. He developed a powerful aversion to the drug trade and took to riding around with the police, helping them bust drug dealers. Last year he and a bartender friend beat up a man after an argument over the treatment of a pet dog. Though Murphy was acquitted on a charge of attempted murder, the incident marked the depths to which he had fallen. Audie Murphy belonged to an earlier, simpler time, one in which bravery was cardinal and killing was a virtue.

Topics for Discussion

1. Both of these articles deal with the death of a famous war hero, but one does more and makes a comment on war heroes in general. Which article do you think is better? Why?

2. What do you think of the idea of the ancient Greeks that a hero could not be enshrined before he was dead?

3. Discuss the idea that a man becomes a hero in battle because of impulsiveness, recklessness, and subversion of self.

4. Does society impose an impossible burden on its heroes?

Rhetorical Considerations

1. Is the prose style of these two articles the same? Can you see any differences?

2. Compare the introductions and conclusions of both articles. Which do you find more effective? What are the strengths and weaknesses of each?

3. Examine the vocabulary in both articles. What kind of words are used? Is there any slanted or connotative language?

4. How objective are both articles? Can you find any subjectivity in either article?

Black Movies: Renaissance or Ripoff?

Charles Michener

moral: a baadasssss nigger is coming back to collect some dues.

—Postscript to Melvin Van Peebles's film, "Sweet Sweetback's Baadasssss Song"

What Van Peebles warned has come to pass. All over the country, "bad-ass niggers" are collecting dues with a vengeance—and, if you don't believe it, just head downtown for a movie. Outside the old silver-screen palaces on New York's Times Square, along Chicago's Loop, in downtown Detroit, the crowds are young, mostly black and bigger than they've been since Scarlett O'Hara ran off with Rhett Butler. Inside, the furious action on celluloid is pointed toward the triumph of black good over white evil; audiences are whooping it up with such glee that projectionists must jack up the volume during the climaxes, and theater owners are counting more dollars than they've handled in years. The black-movie explosion is on—and the controversial fallout is just beginning to settle.

Van Peebles set it off—and set the tone—when he vowed more than two years ago to "get the Man's foot out of all our black asses" by making a film "about a brother *getting* the Man's foot out of his ass." The result was the gritty, profane "Sweetback," a mythic opus about a black stud's successful revolt against white society, which grossed $11 million—an amazing success for a movie made and distributed completely outside established industry channels. A couple of months later, Gordon Parks came out with the equally low-budget "Shaft," about a black private eye, which by year's end had racked up $12 million in North America

and singlehandedly rescued M-G-M from near financial ruin.

Never slow to read handwriting that's punctuated with dollar signs, Hollywood quickly took note of two facts: first, whites had begun to flee the inner cities, vacating many big downtown theaters and leaving a vacuum for the burgeoning number of black moviegoers to fill; second, blacks would turn out in far greater numbers for films that featured black heroes and heroines and plenty of sex and violence than they would for white adventure flicks. In short order, the studio bosses began restocking—and revamping—their arsenals.

Talented black actors, directors and writers were suddenly plucked out of studio back rooms, modeling agencies and ghetto theaters, and turned loose on new black projects. White heroes of scripts that had been lying on the shelf were instantly converted into black heroes and sent scurrying before the cameras. Much of the white trash emerged as black trash and was quickly buried after release. But an astonishing number of black films have been paying off at a rate to put their white counterparts in the shade—and in the process have not only produced the first gold mine in years for a struggling industry, but also have split the U.S. black community into those who justify or at least discriminate among the films, and those for whom the entire phenomenon is a violent blow to black dignity and social well-being.

Of this year's Westerns, the two biggest nuggets are black—"Buck and the Preacher" ($9 million gross so far), in which Sidney Poitier and Harry Belafonte lead ex-slaves to a new life in the West, and "The Legend of Nigger Charley" ($5 million), in which ex-pro football star Fred Williamson goes from slavery to gunfighting. Tops in the action genre are "Shaft's" sequel, "Shaft's Big Score" ($10 million), which again features Richard Roundtree as the supercool John Shaft, foiling a gang of white hoods; "Melinda" ($5 million), with Calvin Lockhart as a Los Angeles disk jockey wiping out white gangsters who have murdered his girl friend; "Cool Breeze," a black remake of "The Asphalt Jungle"; "Slaughter," with Jim Brown also doing in the mob; and the just-released "Hammer," with Fred Williamson, using his old football nickname, as a boxer who won't go crooked.

American International Pictures has a bonanza in the first all-black vampire movie—"Blacula," which turns America's favorite Transylvanian bloodsucker into an accursed ex-African prince. And "Come Back Charleston Blue," the sequel to 1970's "Cotton Comes to Harlem," has already pulled in $7 million with the antics of Godfrey Cambridge and Raymond St. Jacques as Harlem cops who destroy a black dope lord. Finally there's "Super Fly," directed by Gordon Parks Jr., which in a little more than two months is up to $11 million and is currently outgrossing every other movie on the market—black or white—with its off-beat tale of a black cocaine pusher (Ron O'Neal) who not only beats the system—but gets out with a cool half-million.

All this is only the beginning. On their way in the next four months are Van Peebles's film of his Broadway musical play, "Don't Play Us Cheap," a biography of Billie Holiday, "Lady Sings the Blues," starring Diana Ross, and a score of entertainments with titles like "Blackenstein," "Black Gun," "Black Majesty," "Blackfather," "Black Christ" and "The Werewolf From Watts" as well as "Hit Man," "The Book of Numbers," "Trick Baby" and "Cleopatra Jones." In an industry that has recently been producing little more than 200 films a year, fully one-fourth of those now in the planning stage are black.

A long overdue avenue to success for black talent and a kick for hungry black moviegoers, the phenomenon has nonetheless drawn considerable fire from many black intellectuals, political leaders and laymen who are mounting protests against the industry and picketing theaters for showing the allegedly pro-drug "Super Fly." The situation has explosive potential—recently several cars were fire-bombed at the office of American International Pictures in Hollywood following a meeting with a black group, and there have been reports of an unexploded bomb at Warner Bros. and a burning shed at Fox, which Fox denies.

Many of the talented blacks who are involved in making these movies are torn between conflicting attitudes about their value and significance. Robert Hooks is a leading black actor, a co-founder and director of the outstanding Negro Ensemble Company in New York who is currently organizing the D.C. Black Repertory Company in predominantly black Washington. Like other serious actors, such as Calvin Lockhart, Rosalind Cash and William Marshall, Hooks is ambivalent about his participation in the black-movie explosion. In the forthcoming "Trouble Man," he plays T, a ghetto hustler who's hired, like a fast-sword samurai in a Japanese Western, to settle the rivalry between two racket gangs in Los Angeles. "The only interesting subject left for the American stage or screen is the black man," says Hooks. "So these producers have obviously found a good thing to make money on. But for the most part they have been doing these films in bad taste." Still, Hooks hopes that "Trouble Man" (which was directed by black actor Ivan Dixon) will be "a different kind of film."

There is no such ambivalence in the attitude of black community leaders such as Junius Griffin, head of the Beverly Hills-Hollywood branch of the NAACP. Says the angry Griffin: "We must insist that our children are not constantly exposed to a steady diet of so-called black movies that glorify black males as pimps, dope pushers, gangsters and super males with vast physical prowess but no cognitive skills." The danger of this fantasy, adds black critic Clayton Riley, is "to reinforce the ordinary black human being's sense of personal helplessness and inadequacy."

Black Panther chieftain Huey Newton finds the films dangerously counter-revolutionary (though he exempts "Sweetback" and "Buck and the Preacher"): "They leave revolution out or, if it's in, they make it look stupid and naïve. I think it's part of a conspiracy." And Tony Brown, dean of Howard University's school of communications and producer of educational television's "Black Journal," lays the blame squarely with the blacks themselves. "The blaxploitation films," he says, "are a phenomenon of self-hate. Look at the image of 'Super Fly.' Going to see yourself as a drug dealer when you're oppressed is sick. Not only are blacks identifying with him, they're paying for the identification. It's sort of like a Jew paying to get into Auschwitz." Those blacks who contribute to the making of these films, adds Brown, no matter how they rationalize it, are guilty of nothing less than "treason."

But those involved with the black films countercharge that the critics are obtuse, overwrought and condescending to their own people. "It's ridiculous," says Gordon Parks, "to imply that blacks don't know the difference between truth and fantasy and therefore will be influenced by these films in an unhealthy way. I knew a black preacher in Chicago and I remember people who wanted to kill their white bosses coming to the prayer meeting and being calmed down by the preacher. These movies are serving the same therapeutic function."

Ron O'Neal, who plays Priest, the victorious pusher in "Super Fly," argues that the film's critics are simply out of touch. "The plot is so old hat to every kid in Harlem," he says. "Blacks are no longer interested in perpetuating the old myths. The critics of 'Super Fly' want to support the myth that crime doesn't pay. But we all happen to know that crime *is* paying off for some people every day." And James Earl Jones, who plays the first black President in "The Man," says: "If they're going to put the damper on John Shaft let them put it on John Wayne too and they'll find out that there are a lot of people who need those fantasies."

Ex-footballers Jim Brown and Fred Williamson claim that they are doing no more on screen than they did on the gridiron—and, for that matter, no more than white screen heroes have been doing all along. "Where were the black critics when Cagney, Bogart and Raft were doing their thing?" growls Williamson. "When I was a kid, I played Hopalong Cassidy and nobody hit me in the mouth and said, "Don't be that way'."

When Williamson was a kid, of course, there were no black Hopalongs to imitate. Black movies had been around since the early talkies (King Vidor's 1929 "Hallelujah" was the first distinguished all-sound film) but until recently, the black image on screen ran through a short spectrum from the shuffling Stepin Fetchit, on the one hand, to the noble but amenable Sidney Poitier on the other—both outsiders in an alien society they were bound to accept, both fully acceptable to white sensibilities. Now the tables are turned. In the world of the new black film, the white man is the outsider—and rarely is he acceptable to black sensibilities.

It is a turnabout achieved with little regard for subtlety. When Jim Brown beds down with Stella Stevens in "Slaughter," the camera follows his brawny black hand across her pale white skin with almost palpable relish. The dumb white police sergeant whom Cambridge and St. Jacques dupe in "Charleston Blue" wouldn't survive a day on a real Harlem beat. In the climactic mayhem in "Melinda," Lockhart not only uses karate and guns to wipe out the white mobsters, but delivers a battery of well-placed kicks to their groins. Some of the turnabout seems merely cosmetic. Who, after all, is Richard Roundtree as John Shaft, with his seedy office, withering wisecracks and testy police relations, but a darker version of Sam Spade in "The Maltese Falcon"? And aren't Moses Gunn as the suavely malevolent black syndicate king and Drew Bundini Brown as his trigger-happy punk bodyguard really Sidney Greenstreet and Elisha Cook Jr. in blackface?

They are and—more important-ly—they aren't. For beyond the titillation of sex and violence, beyond the slick reworkings of tried-and-true formulas, what really turns on the black audience was best put by a black girl and boy after they saw "Super Fly" last week in Washington, D.C. "Super Fly," said the girl, "is what's happening right here on the street. That's the way it is." "Priest," said the boy of the film's dope-pushing hero, "is super fine and super bad."

Unlike most white escapist fare with its never-never landscapes of purple sage and alpine luxury, the strongest of the new black films are firmly rooted in the audience's own back-yards—"Super Fly," "Charleston Blue" and "Shaft" in the squalid, decayed slums of Harlem, "Melinda" in barren, bleached-out Watts. The spectacular Eldorado Cadillac driven by Priest in "Super Fly" gets quick recognition from some of the Harlem members of the audience because it actually belongs to "K.C.", a well-known Harlem pimp who plays himself in the film.

Unlike the James Bond movies' clubby repartee, the last languid gasps of Bulldog Drummond, Jimmy Valentine and their upper-crust ilk, the sardonic black dialogue is hot off the streets—funky, profane, frankly shocking to many middle-class whites in its sexual references, especially the ubiquitous "mother-f-----," but with a pun-

gent authenticity, especially in the bitter films such as "Super Fly." (With an eye toward future TV feasibility, many of the films are shot with alternate scenes and dialogue. Where Roundtree in "Shaft" says "I'm gonna kill that mother-f-----," Gordon Parks shot an alternate scene for TV in which Shaft snarls, "I'm gonna kill that granny-dodger.")

It is hard to gauge the true influence of these movies, especially on young blacks. The newest rage among black youths at one Los Angeles high school is to wear their hair straightened and flowing, to sport wide-lapeled midi coats and to adorn themselves with tiny silver crosses and "coke spoons" around their necks—all à la Priest in "Super Fly." But more important than clothes or hair is the "super bad" appeal of these movies. "A swift fist and a stiff penis, that's the Shaftian way" is how Clayton Riley sums up their morality. But there is more involved than that. Gordon Stulberg, the much-respected head of Twentieth Century-Fox, believes that "black films give blacks much more opportunity to feel vicariously in control of their environment than whites get from James Bond movies." And, indeed, control is first among virtues in these movies: grace under pressure (whether in bed or in the precinct house), mastery of self-defense (by karate or judo) and, above all, a hatred for heroin—the main tool of oppression and self-oppression.

At bottom, though, the black films may have more of a political dimension than any of the militant critics suspect. For with the exception of Jim Brown, whose prepotent Slaughter is the only black in an all-white world, the new black heroes are not odd men out in the white tradition of Cagney, Bogart and John Garfield, but odd men in—who only venture out of their close-knit black community to become invincible guerrillas in the white community.

Apart from "Super Fly" midi

coats and the like, there is little tangible evidence so far that life on the street has begun to imitate art. But Hollywood's sudden greed for black movies has aroused a sense of power among the new breed of black actors, writers and directors. Once again, the cue was given by Melvin Van Peebles, who hustled his way past studio brass and the unions to win total and final control over "Sweetback." Since then, no other black filmmaker has matched that precedent—though "Super Fly" 's makers successfully imitated Van Peebles's word-of-mouth marketing strategy by previewing the film, not to critics, but to pimps and hairdressers in Harlem.

Even so, black outspokenness about the content of their studio-controlled films is on the increase—and already there have been several notable victories. It was at actor William Marshall's insistence that his role of Blacula was changed from that of a black American paying a social visit to Transylvania to that of an African prince seeking an end to the slave trade—before he falls into the clutches of Dracula. In playing the clap-trappy part, says his co-star Vonetta McGee, "Marshall gave so much dignity that you're crying for him in the end."

Hired to direct Twentieth's "Trouble Man," Ivan Dixon discovered that the script had the leading black female character, played by Paula Kelly, jumping in and out of bed like a cat in heat, and called the NAACP in to negotiate a change. And three of the most outspoken black talents around—director Hugh Robertson, writer Lonne Elder III and actress Rosalind Cash—took one look at M-G-M's original script for "Melinda" and plunged into a battle that ended with the conversion of hopeless trash into stylish and diverting trash.

"I had to fight and fight for any human elements in the story," recalls Robertson, who previously had edited "Shaft." "They kept pushing for all sex and violence. I had to insist on the dinner scene between Melinda (Vonetta McGee) and Frankie (Calvin Lockhart) so we could see some kind of relationship between them, not just bring her into the story and suddenly have her dead the next morning. And I had to fight to keep a scene between Frankie and Terry (Rosalind Cash) that shows her as a black woman who's strong and a real person."

Says Cash, a fine stage actress: "I'm proud of what I did with Terry. When I go up to Harlem, the hard-working soul sisters come up to me and say, 'You were for real in that part; I know what that character was all about'." And Elder, who wrote the prize-winning play "Ceremonies in Dark Old Men," sums up his Hollywood experience in general by recalling what one big studio executive once said to him: "They want s--- and we're giving them s---."

It's that kind of exploitative—and racist—attitude that has so many veteran black activists up in arms, and, to combat it with more than words, they are trying to apply various kinds of pressure to the movie industry. Some of them have rallied to the idea that black films can be used as wedges to make, as one puts it, "the industry pay its dues to the black community"—in money. In Seattle, black owners of a black neighborhood theater have brought suit against a white-owned organization, claiming the right to share in the first-run distribution of "Super Fly." New York militants have made Harlem virtually out-of-bounds to major filmmakers with a variety of demands, ranging from an increased proportion of blacks on shooting crews to direct payments to "community organizations."

And in order to shoot "The Mack" (street slang for glorified pimp) in the Oakland ghetto, white producer Harvey Bernhard had to donate $5,000 to the community via the Black Panthers, hired twenty mostly black "security guards" at $10 an hour—and still ran into trouble. According to Panther leader Huey Newton, Bernhard's checks bounced and were made good only when Newton threatened to picket. (Bernhard left Oakland prematurely and is now finishing the film in Los Angeles.)

Still other activists are batting around such ideas as a separate rating system for black movies and a black review board to screen scripts before production. Internal bickering has prevented members of the newly formed Coalition Against Blaxploitation in Los Angeles from doing anything with these hot potatoes—out of mindfulness, perhaps, of Jim Brown's fierce admonition: "That's like being under Hitler. I don't want a black or a white Hitler."

Plausible or not, such pressures are having their effect on white movie moguls. M-G-M's president, James Aubrey, pointedly refused to grant NEWSWEEK an interview, leaving the impression that he wanted to lie low until all the controversy had blown over. According to actor Raymond St. Jacques, one group of executives decided to do a black film, then nervously converted all the characters into Puerto Ricans.

As Brown and several other blacks with clout see it, the key to better black films—and bigger payoff to blacks—is to get wealthy blacks involved in the capitalization of new films, just as two black dentists were in the financing of "Super Fly." "We're allowing white producers to make money off us in our major market like we've done through the years," says Brown. "We've got the capital if blacks would only give it up." Recently, Roy Innes, director of CORE, announced that his organization intended to enter the business, but the wherewithal to do so has not yet appeared. Jesse Jackson of Operation PUSH (People United to Save Humanity) has expressed hopes of organizing black artists, writers and producers into a cooperative film venture. And Robert Hooks is shaping up

"Nation Time Productions," to produce worthwhile material in films, TV, theater and music, using outstanding black talent and money—a project that could amount, he says, "to a black economic revolution in the entertainment industry."

Given the financial track record of so many recent black films—multimillion-dollar earnings on production costs of $750,000 or less—the inducement would seem a natural. But wealthy blacks are notoriously cautious when it comes to entering new fields ("They're the most nouveaux of the nouveaux-riches," complains Elder). For his upcoming "Book of Numbers," a story about the numbers racket in the 1930s, which he produced, directed and starred in, Raymond St. Jacques says he went to "every black millionaire in America"—and came up dry. Moreover, what's to guarantee that black-financed films would be any better than the present crop—or, if they were, that blacks would flock to them?

Perhaps the most hopeful portent for better black movies is the almost uniform desire of the new black pantheon of directors, writers and stars to break out of the sex-and-violence bag. "Unless black films explore other areas of black experience," warns "Melinda"'s super-hero Calvin Lockhart, "black films will wind up on the shelf and eventually stop." Sick of films like "Shaft," Gordon Parks has refused to oversee any more sequels (five more are planned). And rather than doing a sequel to their "Super Fly," his director son, Gordon Jr., and screenwriter Phillip Fenty are working on a project which, says Fenty, is "totally removed from drugs." Roundtree himself, the ex-model who is perhaps the reigning black superstar, sums up a widespread feeling among his colleagues: "What we want in our movies from now on is to show black people winning because they use their heads, not because they do violence with their hands."

The brilliant young novelist Ishmael Reed, whose novel "Yellow Back Radio Broke-Down" has had two movie options dropped, wants to see moviemakers deal with black experience as the young black novelists and playwrights have done. "We can't get that done because they want us to look dumb," he says. "The real problem is with the liberals. Jane Fonda will support the antiwar movement, but Jane Fonda will not ask for reforms in her own profession. Why don't they do more original novels by Afro-Americans instead of putting together hack original screenplays? If we could get the whole range of our experience into movies, I wouldn't mind something like 'Super Fly'."

But in the end, it is economics—not good intentions—that will decide the future of black movies. And at the moment, nearly everyone in the business sees the great black hope embodied in a moving little film called "Sounder." Directed by a white veteran, Martin Ritt, and scripted by Elder, "Sounder" stands apart from the prevailing tide in several important respects: its documentary feel for the historical context of American black experience; its lack of shrillness about white bigotry; its elevation of a black woman as played by Cicely Tyson into a complex, forceful human, not a groovy sex object, and, most of all, its quiet, almost mythical tale about a family of Louisiana sharecroppers in the Depression who, in Faulkner's famous words, not only endure but prevail.

But will "Sounder" prevail? Even here blacks are split: some, like actress Tyson and NEWSWEEK's Los Angeles bureau chief, John Dotson, seeing hope in the film's quiet dignity; others smelling ripoff in those very qualities. "Sounder," says one black actor, "was made for whites who want to believe that blacks are full of love and trust and patience. It avoids dealing with things like rage and bitterness and the need for some kind of release. That kind of people don't survive here on the streets of New York. I took a girl to see 'Sounder' who used to do laundry for white people. She wasn't going to be entertained by a film about black suffering, because she *knows* about black suffering." Replies Miss Tyson: "I think we have come far enough to look back on our lives with pride. It's because of people like those in 'Sounder' that we've come as far as we have."

In any case, the black is no longer a bit player on the American movie screen. "Just as we've done with theater and music," Ron O'Neal says, "black people will develop a new art form of movies in this country—given the time and opportunity."

Topics for Discussion

1. How many of the movies mentioned in this essay have you seen? Which ones did you like? Why?
2. Do you think such movies as *Shaft* and *Super Fly* accurately portray black people and their experiences? Do you think the James Bond movies accurately portray white people and their experiences? What similarities, if any, do you see between such heroes as Shaft and James Bond?
3. Michener contends that "in the end, it is economics—not good intentions—that will decide the future of black movies." Do you agree with this? Can you think of any forces other than economic ones that might determine the future of black movies?
4. Movie producers, according to Michener, assume that black audiences want more sex and violence in films than white audiences. Do you agree with this? Why?
5. Many critics of black movies complain that such movies always feature black heroes destroying white villains. Do you believe that such plots promote racism? Or do you agree with Gordon Parks that black audiences know the difference between truth and fantasy and are not influenced by such movies?
6. "Unless black films explore other areas of black experience black films will wind up on the shelf and eventually stop" says Calvin Lockhart. What could some of these "other areas of black experience" be?
7. What is the concept of the hero as expressed in black movies?
8. Why would some members of the black community feel that the entire phenomenon of black movies "is a violent blow to black dignity and social well-being"?

Rhetorical Considerations

1. What do you think of the term "black movies"? What does this term imply?
2. What does the word "blaxploitation" mean?
3. Who are the "nouveaux riches"? How can someone be the "most nouveaux of the riches"?
4. How does the quotation at the beginning of the essay relate to the main idea of the essay?
5. Does Michener reach any definite conclusion at the end of his essay? Does he decide whether current black movies represent a renaissance or a ripoff?

Black Movie Boom—Good or Bad?

A New Black Hero
GORDON PARKS

When, as a boy, I sat in a segregated Kansas theater, my heroes had already been cast. They were either Buck Jones, William S. Hart or Hoot Gibson. They were all white.

When the Indians won, it was a massacre. When the heroes emerged victorious, they had "put down a massacre." Later, in the North, I progressed via radio and the movies to Amos 'n' Andy, Stepin Fetchit and other eye-rolling, grinning, shuffling blacks who always sent me home hurt and embarrassed. And all of this for that 25 cents I had worked all week for.

We black kids didn't go to the motion pictures too much then. We were poor—and we were becoming weary of the shame.

So, in 1971, at 4 o'clock in the morning, I was somewhat astonished to see young black people still standing in line at a Broadway theater to see "Shaft." I walked inside. The orchestra was filled. The balcony was filled. And everything was "right on!" A new hero, black as coal, deadlier than Bogart and handsome as Gable, was doing the thing that everyone in that audience wanted to see done for so long. A black man was winning. John Shaft was "putting down the massacre" this time.

I haven't seen many black films. So I do not pass judgment on them. I did see "Sounder." It was a beautiful and important film. And I would like to feel that I could say the same of "The Learning Tree." But both films speak of an era that young black people, now in the heat of revolt, tend to reject. They do not want to endure again the cruelties and indignities inflicted on black people in the past; they cannot identify with the men and women, however gallant, who suffered that voiceless time. They refuse to look back. Their eyes are on the future.

The so-called black intellectuals' outcry against black films has been blown far out of proportion. It is curious that some black people, egged on by some whites, will use such destructive measures against black endeavors. In doing so, they once more ghettoize themselves.

They should realize that we new black filmmakers are not yet running the big Hollywood studios, that it took many hard years to even get our foot in the door. If they would have us more subservient to their wishes, then they should bestow on us the means, or more bluntly, the money.

The most important thing to me is that young blacks can now, if they work hard enough, enter an industry that has been closed to them for so long.

As for a black review board "to approve scripts and pre-edit finished films," forget it. The review board is already established and is moving from one theater line to another. Those black kids of the fierce black pride will, in the end, determine how long MGM will hire John Shaft to "put down the massacre."

Black Movies Are A Ripoff

JUNIUS GRIFFIN

At present, black movies are a "ripoff" enriching major white film producers and a very few black people. These films are taking our money while feeding us a forced diet of violence, murder, drugs and rape. Such films are the cancer of "Blaxploitation" gnawing away at the moral fiber of our community.

Some attempt to justify the portrayals of pimps, prostitutes, dope pushers and super-studs. But the constant bombardment of those images on the minds of our children is a theft far more damaging than economic loss.

Images projected on film shape the values, the expectations and the opinions of the viewers. It would be much too naïve to believe that some films are not message films. All films are molding the thoughts and actions of the young and old, men and women, black and white. Imagery expressed in film forms the minds of a people in terms of what we think of ourselves and what others think of us.

If black movies do not contribute to building constructive, healthy images of black people and to fairly recording the black experience, we shall have lost our money and our souls. We shall have contributed to our own cultural genocide by only offering our children the models of degradation, destruction and dope.

Recently, however, many of us concerned with black movies, particularly black talent, met at Chicago's PUSH Expo. We came together knowing that "blaxploitation" must stop immediately. We agreed that such exploitation in films must be rooted out now just as other forms of segregation and racism are being rooted out in our society.

Only recently the movie industry discovered that even the nation's poorest ethnic group, black people, makes the difference between profit and loss. At the same time, black people were learning that we are poor economically, yet our collective economic power can determine the future of major industries such as the movie industry.

Now the contest has turned to determining who is going to benefit from the millions of dollars spent and collected at the box offices of the nation's movie theaters. Though still in poverty, black people have escaped the despair and moral bankruptcy that would permit the continuing exploitation of our minds and our money.

We have long been known for our skill at entertaining. And our physical prowess has been praised from the cotton fields to the athletic fields. Now black men and women are coming together in Hollywood, Chicago, New York, Memphis, Seattle, and in many other cities across the nation demanding that we participate in the movie industry at all levels. Black people want to demonstrate our creative and cognitive skills along with our dramatic talents on the screens of the movie houses.

Now that the movie industry has discovered the black market, we have the obligation to insist that the door be opened all the way. We must work in the creative and production part of the industry, as well as participate in the distribution of films. Our contribution must be more than consumption at the box offices to see a few black actors. Our rewards in return should be strong images of a proud people and increased purchasing power from our investments, our creative energies and our employment.

Though black movies are presently exploiting our community, we are determined to turn them around until they benefit black people. We are wise enough to know that stopping the exploitation of black people is, in fact, a benefit to all Americans.

Imitations Of Life

MAYA ANGELOU

A few decades ago, Louise Beavers enacted white folks' fantasy of black folks' reality on the white folks' silver screen. She and her contemporaries were adept at being clumsy, brilliant in showing stupidity, and diligent in projecting laziness. Black audiences watched Stepin Fetchit, Hattie

McDaniel, Mantan Moreland, Willie Best and Eddie "Rochester" Anderson play the slack-mouthed versions of Uncle Tom without open protest.

We pacified our uneasiness by reminding ourselves that the characters were pigments of white mythology and, after all, the actors were again "putting Charlie on" and making big money in the fabulous Hollywood. We stood like dry-eyed mourners at the gravesite of a stranger, making no overt objection.

We remained quiet through "Cabin in the Sky," "Pinky," "Imitation of Life" (that title is apropos), "Green Pastures" and "Porgy and Bess." Then the Furious Fifties saw the birth of mass Black protest. Hollywood industries (never loath to change jackasses in the middle of the screen) issued in the age of the noble savage. Heroes were written—Black, handsome, witty, intelligent, well-dressed and so forth—and Sidney Poitier was chosen to bring a character to life who was no more real than those in "Birth of a Nation."

Today, Black protest has gone into another gear and Black writers are paraphrasing Langston Hughes' words, "They will sing their own blues and they will write them themselves." We are suddenly inundated with new "imitations of life," and these written by Black writers. Sections of the Black community—in an effort, they say, to protect the young—have spoke of imposing censorship.

I think we'd better admit that, while the new movies may be no more valid than their predecessors, they do represent, to the young, truer versions of this lawless society. The new heroes echo the root theme of the American ethos, i.e.: Kill for money for money is power, but value nothing for nothing is valuable.

Black Americans are American. Violence is American. Try to imagine a person today making a film in Harlem and starry-eyed enough to call it "How Green Was My Valley." Maybe in the next wave.

Approach It As Business

JIM BROWN

The so-called "black" film has made some important contributions not only to black people but to the black film industry as a whole. It has allowed black directors, black producers, black technicians, black writers, black actors to participate on a higher level than ever before.

The main problem with the situation is one which most people have overlooked—that black superstars like Richard Roundtree of "Shaft" are signed to contracts which do not enable them to make as much money as, say, Paul Newman, yet their products will gross more money than a Paul Newman picture. Black people have not yet been able to finance their own films so that they could participate in the huge grosses which black films are pulling.

These two factors deal directly with the business aspect of filmmaking which is, basically, profit and loss.

As far as sterotyped white films or general audience films, as you might call them, are concerned, they have portrayed every stereotype imaginable so why shouldn't the so-called "black films" do the same? As for violence, what film has been more violent than "The Godfather"? Or "Bonnie and Clyde"?

When you examine black audiences, you come up with some very strange facts. First of all, black audiences have accepted "Super Fly." They have accepted, to a degree, "Sounder." They have accepted "Lady Sings the Blues." They have accepted "Slaughter." They didn't accept "Cool Breeze." They didn't accept "Nothing But a Man."

If you know anything about these particular films, they fit into certain categories—some are violent, some are cheaply made, some are technically very good, some have very good stories, but still the audiences are discriminating about what they have accepted. Some of the films that were violent were accepted, some that were technically good were not accepted. In other words, black filmmakers have the same problem as white filmmakers—that of trying to find out what an audience will buy. And there is no guarantee.

The question is not black actors or black films but the type of film and whether it will sell.

My feeling is that Melvin Van Peebles is the epitome of the right attitude which all black filmmakers must have. This attitude, summed up, is that we should do our own thing—not necessarily as black people but as business people. Van Peebles made "Sweet Sweetback's Baaaadass Song," he got the financing, he was the producer, actor and director. He had a specialized distribution and made of lot of money.

There is *opportunity*. The one approach that will work is to approach movies as an industry, as a business. Black people must stop crying *"Black"* and start crying *"Business."* Business, business and business *techniques*—they hold up whether the film is black or white. When you have money, talent and a good story and you put them all together, you don't have to worry about whether the film is black or white, and we will then be a part of the mainstream of American life.

I am definitely against a Black Review Board. I don't think black people should set themselves up as an authority as to what black people should see. The present censorship laws are already too confining. No one—either white or black—should have the right to decide what a person who is of age should view.

Modern Nigger-Toys

IMAMU AMIRI BARAKA

Witness the *Mamaluke*, Ron O'Neal, hippy hair and Romantic, a funnel for the street capitalist drama white cowpokes makes us swaller. It carries in stunning complexity pathology at the following levels:

1. The anti-Ujima ethic of individualism, and petty capitalism. O'Neal is actually "civilized" in the jungle of scared or doped-up brownies. He is a great yellow hunter!

2. His physical appearance (the reason Europeans created the Mamalukes to wage war on their mothers' Black nations, their "fathers" being Europeans . . . Vide: Chancellor Wms "The Destruction of Afrikan Civilization"), which re-turns negroes to pre-Black is Beautiful, and if whitey caint be the hero, then by gawd its gotta be a yaller nigga.

3. Dopepeddler as hero, read Romantic. He can be a "man," a Roman astride the known world like the other inhabitants of white movies. And with that the value system he carries is dead white. Old solemn tortured hero, cagney style or bogart style, with heart of gold, blah blah. He wanna do the rite thang, ya unnerstan? But all around and under, singling him out, in true odyssean-hemingway-john ford style, whites and black in equal confusion to obstruct, the good. But he win, ma, he win. (And so SF, science fiction?, coats & "girl" are the rage among the subject peoples, imitating a nigger-"man".)

The truth of world condition is social conflict brought about by conflicting interests. The truth of Black colonial life in America is generally paralleled by life, in whatever slight variation, of Afrikans the world over, whether on the continent of Afrika, the carribean, or elsewhere. Afrikan people are in a struggle for their lives, their self-determination and self-respect against Europeans. Harlem or Johannesburg bear this out.

The film industry being a white cultural artifact at this point in history, what is issued is, with rare exception, poised for its meaning upon reference whites utilize to define the world.

The flashy niggers that people the "soul flick" of our times are modern nigger-toys, for colored adults and children. Black Art, as concept, without the material structures necessary to bring about the material culture and products for Black consumption at the level the 70's propose, is easily coopted, and "Black" images are utilized as new weapons of white control of Black minds.

The control of a film industry by Black people is necessary to develop truly Black films, or at least the beginning of independent films meant to educate and inspire Afrikan people wherever we are in the world. The creation of this industry is a political act, an act of self-determination by a culture, intent on explaining itself to itself.

"Buck and the Preacher," some of "Sounder," are rare. The content of our film industry would create itself through the act of being created, tho for certain, the reality of our lives, the day-to-day confrontation and struggle, precise rendering of our condition, and analyses of our enemies' plans and methods of subjugating us would have to be talked about.

But the most revolutionary Black images would be Unity, Self-Determination, Collective Work and Responsibility, Cooperative Economics (UJAMAA-Socialism), Purpose, Creativity and Faith, and in their use in defining and redefining us to us, and recreating through their continuity a revolutionary culture, would come (with all the parallel development that will go on in areas of Religion, History, Social Organization, Economic Organization, Political Organization, Creative Motif and Ethos) a revolutionary Afrikan people who would be by those acts already liberated.

I See No Difference

LENA HORNE

I see no difference between the current black films in question and their white counterparts dealing with similar dismal subjects. I have yet to see the definitive black movie.

Unlocking The Doors

MARTIN RITT

I consider myself no authority in the field of black films, but since you asked my opinions, here they are:

Films like "Super Fly" and "Shaft" do, indeed, represent a long-delayed and important recognition of black artists—important in the sense that someone actually gave said artists the money and authority to do their thing. As one who has been keenly conscious of the doors that have been locked to blacks in our industry, I can only applaud that fact.

As for "Shaft" and such films setting new stereotypes, I can't answer that. If they become the sum total of the kind of movies that are going to be made about black people, they will, of course, become stereotypes. That's why a film like "Sounder" is so important— it does display another aspect of the black experience. And since "Sounder" is now well on its way to being a commercial as well as a critical success, the possibility of broadening the spectrum of the kind of black films that a studio will finance can be realized.

I am opposed to any review board, black or white. That would smell of censorship, and I am and always have been opposed to censorship in any form, shape or color.

Why have films like "Super Fly" and "Shaft" been so smashingly successful? Because black audiences are delighted with the fact that their brothers are being given this chance. They are for the first time seeing black heroes or even anti-heroes on the screen and, incidentally, hearing in many of these films anti-white sentiment, which black audiences are only too happy to applaud. It gives vent to some of the accumulated and very understandable anger that has been stored up all these years.

A Joke On Blacks?

ROY INNIS

I view the present Black movie phenomenon with a strong suspicion that the Black youth of America are being programed in a subliminal, subtle way that, in its ultimate destruction of the minds of Black youth, is potentially far more dangerous than "step-n-fetch-it" and his lot.

Some defenders of these Black films have defended them on the ground that they are no worse than, say, John Wayne films, that Black youth recognize them as fantasy, as escapist entertainment. But these defenders will fail to point out that John Wayne—bad and escapist though his films may be—is usually portrayed as a man with guts and strength and positive aggressiveness. He is not portrayed as the psychopathic super-dude, as are the present crop of Black super-heroes.

I think that the most serious critics of these films have commented on their obnoxious glorification of some of the worst elements in the Black community. With them, I object to the justification of dope-pushing, the cancer that has been eating away at the bowels of the Black community, destroying whole generations of Black people. Dope pushers, dope pushing, pimps, postitutes, hankering for white women, psychopathic workouts, and other unsavory characters and modes of behavior portrayed in these Black films are subtle ways of promoting Black genocide in the Black community.

The psychic energies of Black youth are being drained because these youngsters act out their frustrations vicariously through the screen instead of participating in meaningful political action. These movies are anti-struggle, anti-revolutionary (so-called Black revolutionaries are usually portrayed as bungling idiots), and anti-direct involvement. Are we witnessing some kind of thought control device being promoted and approved by the American Government?

Even the heavy use of certain musical scores in these movies has the effect of creating a certain mood. This mood is intertwined with white women and Cadillacs, with selfish individualism. It creates a mood subtly charged with a veneer of sadistic violence that leaves the racist impression of the Black man as animalistic and not really human.

Is someone playing a joke on the Black community? If so, who?

We're All Human

ELEANOR PERRY

Now that we have black films which have turned out to be no different from white films, why is anyone grieved or incensed, let alone surprised? The whole controversy would be amusing if it weren't so outrageously *patronizing*. Apparently black Big Daddies are no different from white Big Daddies either. Now they are wagging fingers at black filmmakers and announcing that Daddy knows best.

All most of us have to do to rebel is to remember how hideous it was to be a child, how under Daddy's excuse of "socializing" or "civilizing," he was likely also to crush both soul and spontaneity. But here they go again with these shriveling accusations of self-hatred, these threats of self-censorship (as revolting as any other censorship) and the implication that no matter what, their kids mustn't risk trouble with the white folks.

If women suddenly got control of the film industry and made films depicting women as shrews and bitches (they exist, as do black pushers and pimps) instead of totally noble, nurturing creatures, we would probably hear the same cries of "treason" from all the Big Mommies.

Since it takes so much money to

make even modest films, anyone, except a saint or fool, will expect a return on his investment. Therefore it seems to me only three realities apply here:

1. Anyone who gets hold of the money to make a film should be able to make that film any way he wants and about any damn thing he pleases.

2. Color and gender have nothing at all to do with making films.

3. We're all human beings.

This May Seem Bitter

LONNE ELDER III

Any assessment of the current wave of exploitative, so-called black films must underline one common fact—that they are nothing more than inept "B" products by anyone's standards of excellence. And the moral concern and alarm on the part of a growing number of black people about the harmful images these films insist upon reflecting in the name of blackness, is in order, and should be supported by all black people.

However, we should be aware of the varied complexities, contradictions and rhythms to different sides of the questions. For instance, there are black actors and actresses in Hollywood who can only view the current trend of black movies as a long overdue opportunity for employment, and the road to what they like to fantasize about as stardom.

These artists are, in the main, hungry and over-ambitious—they so desperately want to be in the movies on any terms. Another side to the question is that there is also the serious black film artist who is not in the above mentioned category, who is ready to pick up his axe against the black exploitation film hustlers but who is not ready to welcome the concept of a black film rating board, as proposed by some black organizations to offset productions of the exploitation film.

Most black artists feel that such rating boards can lead to a form of censorship, and that a black review board can hardly expect to be any more effective than all of those white review boards and rating systems which have been in existence since time immemorial.

I think that one of the most important facts overlooked in our reaction to these films is that they are entirely put together, and controlled, by white film people for entirely white profit.

Take "Shaft," "Cool Breeze," "Legend of Nigger Charley," "Soul Soldier," "Blacula," "Shaft's Big Score," "Slaughter," "Hammer" and "Melinda," for instance. They are all products put on the market by white people for black people to buy and, with the exception of "Melinda," none of them had a black writer-producer-director team involved in its artistic outcome. This is a fact we have to pay special attention to.

Which brings to mind where the main nerve of the exploitation exists, and where it is vulnerable to attack. As a black writer, living in Hollywood for the past two years, who has written the screenplay for "Sounder," I can say I have had one great moment as a filmmaker. But that is all I can reflect upon with a special sense of pride, in an atmosphere where black art is expected to be less proficient than white art in order to have mass appeal.

This may all sound rather bitter, but I honestly feel that some time in the near future the serious black film artist is going to make a qualitative difference in what is yet to come.

Topics for Discussion

1. Of the ten statements collected here, which one comes closest to your position? Why?
2. Which of the ten statements do you disagree with most? Why?
3. Which of the statements deal with black films simply as an economic phenomenon? Which statements deal with other aspects of black films?
4. Do any of the statements offer any reasons for the popularity of such films as *Shaft* and *Super Fly*? Do you agree with any of these reasons?
5. What do you think of the idea of having a black review board approve scripts and rate black movies?

Rhetorical Considerations

1. There is a wide variety of writing styles in these statements. Which statement do you find easiest to read? Which do you find hardest to read? Why?
2. Compare and contrast the style of two of these statements, Baraka and Angelon, for example.
3. What is the tone of Brown's statement? What is the tone of Griffin's statement? In what ways, if any, do they differ?
4. Brief as Horne's statement is, how does it make a point?

Puritanism Revisited: An Analysis of the Contemporary Screen-Image Western

Peter Homans

One of the most noticeable characteristics of popular culture is the rapidity with which new forms are initiated and older, more familiar ones revitalized. While narrative forms of popular culture, such as the detective story, the romance, and the soap opera, have generally been less subject to sudden losses or gains in popularity, the western has within the last few years undergone a very abrupt change in this respect. Formerly associated with a dwindling audience of adolescents, who were trading in their hats and six-guns for space helmets and disintegrators, the western has quite suddenly engaged an enormous number of people, very few of whom could be called adolescent.

This new and far-reaching popularity is easily established. Whereas before, the western story was told from four to six in the afternoon, on Saturday mornings, in comic books and in some pulp fiction, now it is to be seen during the choicest television viewing hours, in a steady stream of motion pictures, and in every drug store pulp rack. At present, on television alone, more than thirty western stories are told weekly, with an estimated budget of sixty million dollars. Four of the five top nighttime shows are westerns, and of the top twenty shows, eleven are westerns. In addition to this, it is estimated that women now compose one-third of the western's heretofore male audience.

Such evidence invariably leads to attempts to explain the phenomenon. Here there has been little restraint in trying to analyse the unique status which the western has gained. Some have suggested that it is the modern story version of the Oedipal classic; others find it a parallel of the medieval legends of courtly love and adventure; while those enamoured of psychiatric theory see it as a form of wish-fulfillment, an "escape" from the realities of life into an over-simplified world of good and evil.

Such theories, I suppose, could be described at greater length —but not much. They not only betray a mindless, off-the-top-of-the-head superficiality; they also suffer from a deeper fault characteristic of so many of the opinions handed down today about popular culture—a two-fold reductionism which tends to rob the story of its concrete uniqueness.

This two-fold reductionism first appears as the failure to attend fully and with care the historical roots of any form. For example, to say that the western is a re-telling of chivalric tales is partly true. There is some similarity between the quest of the knight and the quest of the western hero—they both seek to destroy an evil

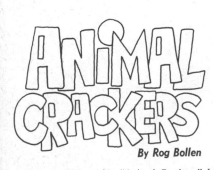

By Rog Bollen

Roger Bollen, cartoon strips, "Animal Crackers," June 11, 1972, Reprinted through the courtesy of the Chicago Tribune-New York News Syndicate, Inc.

Peter Homans, "Puritanism Revisited: An Analysis of the Contemporary Screen-Image Western," from *Studies in Communication*, no. 3, Summer, 1961. Reprinted by permission.

being by force. However, the tales of chivalry grew out of medieval culture, and any effort to account for them must consider their relationship to their culture. Similarly, the western must be seen in relation to its culture—eastern American life at the turn of the century. To relate the two forms without first considering their historical contexts is what may be called historical reductionism.

The second form of reductionism is the failure of most theories to attend the unique details of the story which set it apart from prior forms. This can also be seen in the idea of chivalric tales retold. Holders of this theory notice that both heroes are engaged in a quest, the destruction of evil, and that they both earn some kind of special status in the eyes of the communities they have served. But what is not noticed is that the modern tale betrays an intense preoccupation with asceticism and colorlessness, while the medieval one dwells upon color, sensuousness, and luxury; or, that the medieval hero exemplifies tact, manners, elaborate ceremony and custom, while his modern counterpart seeks to avoid these. Again, the western rules out women; the older story would not be a story of chivalry did not women play an important part. The refusal to attend with care specific and possibly inconsequential details is a form of reductionism which may be called textual reductionism.

Both types of reductionism rob a particular form of possible uniqueness and independence. They force it to be merely a dependent function of some prior form, whatever that form may be. Together, they have become the two main errors which have obscured analysis of many present-day forms of popular culture.

However, these two foci are more than pitfalls to be avoided. The textual and historical aspects of any popular art form are the very points which should be scrutinized most carefully and elaborately. If these points are properly attended, they will yield the greatest insight into the meaning and significance of the story.

Textual Analysis

Any effort to analyse a particular form of popular culture must begin with the problem of text. Each of us, in thinking and talking about the western, has in mind an overall understanding of it—an ordered vision of character, event, and detail shaped by all the hundreds of different versions which he has seen. Therefore, one must first set forth and defend precisely what it is he thinks the western is, before indicating what it means. Indeed, disagreements as to meaning can often be traced to disagreements as to text.

But we cannot simply lump together everything that has ever happened in every western, fearful of omitting something important. Nor can we refuse to include anything which does not appear in each and every version. For there are westerns which omit details which all critics would agree are characteristic of the story, just as there are others which include details which all would agree are of no consequence. The task consists in selecting, from the endless number of westerns we have all seen, a basic construct of narrative, character, and detail which will set forth clearly the datum for sub-

sequent analysis. This critic's basic construct can be set forth as follows:

Background

The western takes place in a stark, desolate, abandoned land. The desert, as a place deprived of vitality and life as we know it, is indispensable. The story would not be credible were it set in an equatorial jungle, a fertile lowland, or an arctic tundra. As the classical versions have told us again and again, the hero emerges from the desert, bearing its marks, and returns to it. Already we are instructed that our story deals with a form of existence deprived of color and vitality.

This desert effect is contradicted by the presence of a town. Jerry-built, slapped-together buildings, with falsefronts lined awkwardly along a road which is forever thick with dust or mud, tell us that the builders themselves did not expect them to endure. And of these few buildings, only three stand out as recognizable and important—the saloon, the bank, and the marshal's office (hero's dwelling). Recent westerns have added stores, court houses, homes, and even churches. But for the classical versions such contrived togetherness has never really been necessary.

The saloon is by far the most important building in the western. First of all, it is the only place in the entire story where people can be seen together time after time. It thereby performs the function of a meeting-house, social center, church, etc. More important, however, is its function as locus for the climax of the story, the gun-fight. Even in today's more fashionable westerns, which prefer main street at high noon, the gun-fight often begins in the saloon, and takes place just outside it.

The bank, we note, is a hastily constructed, fragile affair. Poorly guarded (if at all), it is an easy mark, there for the taking. Its only protection consists of a snivelling, timid clerk, with a mustache and a green eyeshade, who is only too glad to hand over the loot. Has there ever been a western in which a robber wondered whether he could pull off his robbery? There is a great deal of apprehension as to whether he will elude the inevitable posse, but never as to the simple act of robbery. The bank is surprisingly unprotected.

The marshal's office appears less regularly. Most noticeable here is the absence of any evidence of domesticity. We rarely see a bed, a place for clothes, or any indication that a person actually makes his home here. There is no mirror, an omission which has always intrigued me. The overall atmosphere is that of austerity, to be contrasted sharply with the rich carpeting, impressive desk, curtains, pictures, and liquor supply of the saloon owner or evil gambler. Such asceticism is not due to the hero's lack of funds or low salary; rather, because of his living habits, there is no need of anything else. Indeed, we are led to suspect that such austerity is in some way related to our hero's virtue.

The town as a whole has no business or industry. People have money, but we rarely see them make it. And we are not concerned as to how they got their money—unless they stole it. This town and

SHEEESH...

The Age of Communication

its citizens lead a derivative, dependent existence, serving activities which originate and will continue outside the town. It is expendable, and will disappear as soon as the activities it serves no longer exist.

Home life, like economic life, is conspicuous by its absence. There simply are no homes, families, domestic animals, or children. The closest thing to a home is a hotel, and this is rarely separated from the saloon. Recent westerns have included homes, along with cozy vignettes of hearth, wife, kitchen, etc. Such innovations do little more than indicate how harassed script writers have become, for these scenes do not contribute to the basic action and imagery of the story. Classically, home life in the western simply isn't.

Supporting People

As in any good form of popular culture, the number of important people is small. Such people I prefer to call "types". A type is an important figure recurring again and again, whose basic actions and patterns of relationship are relatively enduring from one version of the story to another. The particular vocation, clothing, mannerisms, personal plans, names, are all conventions—concessions to plausibility—which seemingly identify as new someone we know we've seen before. Such conventions I would like to call "role". When we refer to a particular person in a story with the preface "the"—e.g., "the" hero, or "the" good girl—we have penetrated beyond the role and identified a type.

One of the most interesting types is the "derelict-professional". He is one who was originally trained in one of the traditional eastern professions (Law, Medicine, Letters, Ministry), but who has, since his arrival in the west, become corrupted by such activities as drink, gambling, sex, or violence. Most celebrated is Doc Holliday, who trained in the east as a dentist, then came west to practice medicine whenever he was sober enough to do so. The derelict-professional sometimes appears as a judge or lawyer; sometimes as an ex-writer; in other instances he is a gun-toting preacher. The point is the same: the traditional resources of society (healer, teacher, shepherd, counselor) cannot exist in an uncorrupted state under the pressures of western life.[1]

Somewhat similar is the "non-violent easterner". He often appears as a well-dressed business man, or as a very recent graduate of Harvard, although the roles, as always, vary. Constantly forced to defend himself, he is simply not up to it. Indeed, he is usually thrashed shortly upon his arrival in town. Sometimes this is so humiliating that he tries to become a westerner. It never works. He is either humiliated even more, or killed. Another role for this type is the pastor (a recent addition) who, when the chips are down, has only a prayer to offer. The east, we soon note, is in-

WHAT **IS** IT WITH YOU KIDS AND YOUR LONG HAIR ANYWAY?

WELL...I PERSONALLY BELIEVE...

---

[1] Such TV versions as *Frontier Doctor* (Medicine), *Jefferson Drum* (Letters) and *Black Saddle* (Law) do not contradict this thesis, although they set forth professional men from the east who are hardly derelict. Close attention, however, reveals a "past" of questionable nature which these men are trying to conceal, but which is always being threatened by exposure. Such figures might best be called "covert" derelict-professionals.

capable of action when action is most needed.

The "good girl" is another supportive type. Pale and without appetites, she too is from the east. Classically represented as the new schoolmarm, she also appears as the daughter of a local rancher, someone en route to a more distant point, or the wife of a cattleman. She has her eye on the hero. While any dealings between them come about as the result of her initiative, she is rarely flirtatious or coy. She does not allow any feminine allure to speak for itself—surely one reason why she ends up doing most of the talking. The good girl fails to understand why men have to drink, gamble, punch and shoot each other, and she spends a good deal of time making this point to the hero. Usually she has some kind of protection—brother, father, fiancé, or relative—which makes it possible for her not to work. She is never independent, out in the world, with no attachments.

The "bad girl" is alone in the world, unattached, and works for her living, usually in the saloon as a waitress or dancer. She too has her eye on the hero, attracting him in a way her counterpart does not. She is often flirtatious and coy, but rarely takes the initiative in their meetings. She doesn't try to make him put away his guns and settle down. She is friendly with other men, and, like her counterpart, is unhappily stalemated in her relation to the hero.

The "attendant" is another type. The most enduring and easily recognizable role for this type is the bartender, although the snivelling bank clerk is a close second. The attendant observes the action, provides the instruments of it, but never becomes centrally involved with it. Like a child following adults from room to room, he remains passive, deferring again and again to the principals, performing the important function of appearing unimportant.

One final type, of which there are many—"the boys", those bearded, grimy people who are always "just there", drinking and gambling in the saloon, without any apparent interest in anyone or anything, except their cards, whiskey, and the occasional songstress. Their function is that of an audience. No hero ever shot it out with his adversary without these people watching. Isolated conflicts between hero and adversary are always postponed—sometimes at considerable inconvenience to both—until the "boys" have had a chance to gather. The "boys" are passive functions of the action, important primarily for their presence.

Principals and Action

The action of the screen-image western takes place in three phases: the opening, the action, and closing phases; or, everything before the fight, the fight, and everything after the fight.

The opening phase first of all introduces us to the story's setting, to the supporting types (through their roles) and principals. In doing so, however, it not only supplies us with information, but also provides the very important illusion that we are to see for the first time something which we know, in the back of our heads, we have seen many times before. It is important to believe that we are not idiots, watching the same story night after night.

... I MEAN, JUST EXACTLY **WHAT** ARE YOU TRYING TO PROVE?

FOR ONE THING...

® © 1972 NATL. News. Syn.

Secondly, the opening phase prepares us for the action by delineating the hero. He is, first of all, a transcendent figure, originating beyond the town. Classically, he rides into town from nowhere; even if he is the marshal, his identity is in some way dissociated from the people he must save. We know nothing of any past activities, relationships, future plans, or ambitions. Indeed, the hero is himself often quite ambiguous about these. There are no friends, relatives, family, mistresses—not even a dog or cat—with the exception of the horse, and this too is a strangely formal relationship.

His appearance further supports this image. In the pre-action phase the hero sets forth a contrived indolence, barely distinguishable from sloth. Lax to the point of laziness, there appears to be nothing directional or purposeful about him. Take that hat, for instance: it sits exactly where it was placed—no effort has been made to align it. His horse is tied to whatever happens to protrude from the ground—and remains tied, although little more than a lazy nod would free it. Clothes and gunbelt also betray the absence of any effort towards arrangement and order. With feet propped up on the hitching rail, frame balanced on a chair or stool tilted back on its two rear legs, hat pushed slightly over the eyes, hands clasped over the buckle of his gunbelt, the hero is a study in contrived indolence.

I have used the word "contrived" to indicate another quality—that of discipline and control—which remains latent, being obscured by apparent laxity. His indolence is merely superficial, and serves to protect and undergird the deeper elements of control which will appear in the action phase. Now he has time on his hands; but he knows his time is coming, and so do we.

The hero's coupling of laxity and control is seen in those recurrent primary images which are ordinarily referred to simply as "typical scenes". With women there is no desire or attraction. He appears somewhat bored with the whole business, as if it were in the line of duty. He never blushes, or betrays any enthusiasm; he never rages or raves over a woman. His monosyllabic stammer and brevity of speech clearly indicate an intended indifference. In the drinking scenes we are likely to see him equipped with the traditional shot-glass and bottle. The latter becomes his personal property, and therefore he is never questioned as to how many drinks he has taken. We rarely see him pay for more than one. While drinking he usually stares gloomily at the floor, or at all the other gloomy people who are staring gloomily at each other. He gulps his drink, rarely enjoys it, and is impatient to be off, on his way, hurrying to a place we are never told about. In the gambling scenes his poker face is to cards what his gloomy stare was to drink—a mask serving to veil any inner feelings of greed, enthusiasm, fear, or apprehension. We note, however, that he always wins, or else refuses to play. Similarly, he is utterly unimpressed and indifferent to money, regardless of its quantity or source, although the unguarded bank is always just around the corner.

The action phase opens with the threat of evil, and extends up to its destruction at the hands of the hero. Although evil is most

often referred to as the "villain" or "bad guy" or "heavy", I prefer the terms "evil one" or "adversary".

Of the many hundreds of seemingly different versions, each is unshaven, darkly clothed, and from the west. Little is known about him. We are not told of his origins, his relationships, habits, or customs. Like the hero, he is from beyond the town, rather than identified with the interests, problems, and resources which characterize it. All details of his personal life are withheld. We can only be sure that the evil one unhesitatingly involves himself in the following activities: gambling, drink, the accumulation of money, lust and violence. They are his vocation; with respect to these, he is a professional man. It should be noted, however, that he is inclined to cheat at cards, get drunk, lust after women who do not return the compliment, rob banks, and finally, to shooting people he does not care for, especially heroes.

The impact of this evil one on the town is electric, as though a switch had been thrown, suddenly animating it with vitality, purpose, and direction. Indeed, it is evil, rather than good, which actually gives meaning to the lives of these people—his presence elicits commitment to a cause. The townsfolk now share a new identity: they are "those who are threatened by the evil one". Unified by a common threat, the town loses its desolate, aimless quality. It becomes busy. Some hasten to protect others; some to protect themselves; some run for help; some comment fearfully. Nevertheless, they all know (as do we) that they are of themselves ultimately powerless to meet this evil. What is required is the hero—a transcendent power originating from beyond the town.

Notice what has happened to this power. Gone are the indolence, laxity, and lack of intention. Now he is infused with vitality, direction, and seriousness. Before, the most trivial item might have caught his attention; now, every prior loyalty and concern are thoroughly excluded—he drops everything—in order that he may confront with passion and single-mindedness this ultimate threat. Once this radical shift has been accomplished, the hero (and audience) are ready for the final conflict—the central part of the action phase, the climax of the story.

While the fight can take many forms (fist-fight, fight with knives, whips, etc.—even a scowling match in which the hero successfully glares down the evil one), the classical and most popular form is the encounter with six-guns. It is a built-up and drawn-out affair, always allowing enough time for an audience to gather. The two men must adhere to an elaborate and well-defined casuistry as to who draws first, when it is proper to draw, when it is not, etc. The climax also reflects much of the craft of gunplay, of which both hero and evil one are the skilled artisans (cross-draw versus side-draw, fanning versus thumbing, whether two guns are really better than one, etc.). While these issues are certainly not the main concern of the action, the prominence given them by the story as a whole tends to prolong the climax.

Although the hero's presence usually makes the fight possible —i.e., he insists on obstructing the evil one in some way—it is the latter who invariably attacks first. Were the hero ever to draw first,

...MAYBE, **YOU'RE** THE CONFORMISTS! DID YOU EVER THINK OF **THAT**?

...LET ME PUT IT THIS WAY...

6-11

The Age of Communication

the story would no longer be a western. Regardless of the issues involved, or of the moral responsibility for what is to follow, the hero's final, victorious shot is always provoked by the evil one. With the destruction of the evil one, the action phase is completed.

In the closing phase the town and its hero return to their pre-action ways. The electric quality of alarm and the sense of purpose and direction recede. People come out of hiding to acclaim their hero and enjoy his victory. He too returns to his pre-action mode of indolence and laxity. At such a moment he is likely to become immediately absorbed in some unimportant detail (like blowing the smoke from his gun), indicating for all to see that he has survived the crisis and is once again his old self.

One more event must take place, however, before the story can conclude. The hero must renounce any further involvement with the town which his victory may have suggested. In some way the town offers him the opportunity to identify with it, to settle down. Traditionally, this means marrying the schoolmarm and settling down. The hero always refuses. He cannot identify himself with the situation he has saved. He forfeits any opportunity to renounce his "beyond the town" origin and destiny. When this forfeiture has been made clear, when both savior and saved realize that it cannot be abrogated, then the story is over.

Analysis

The western is, as most people by this time are willing to acknowledge, a popular myth. And by myth I mean three things. First of all, it is a story whose basic patterns of character, plot, and detail are repeated again and again, and can be so recognized. Secondly, the story embodies and sets forth certain meanings about what is good and bad, right and wrong—meanings regarded as important by those who view and participate in the myth. And thirdly, some of these meanings are veiled by the story,[2] so that one can affirm them without overtly acknowledging them. Some part of the story (or all of it, perhaps) serves to conceal something from the participant—i.e., there is an unacknowledged aspect to the story. There is, therefore, an embarrassing question which never occurs to those in the sway of the myth—the posing of which is precisely the critic's most important task.

The meanings which the western sets forth center upon the problem of good and evil. Evil, according to the myth, is the failure to resist temptation. It is loss of control. Goodness lies in the power and willingness to resist temptation. It is the ability to remain in the presence of temptation and yet remain in control of one's desire. Five activities make up the well-known content of temptation: drinking, gambling, money, sex, and violence.

Whenever any one of these activities appears it should be seen as a self-contained temptation episode.[3] Such an episode first

... YOU THINK ANYONE WITH RESPONSIBILITY IS A SQUARE! **RIGHT?** YOU HAVE NO **USE** FOR THE OLD, TIME-TESTED TRUTHS! **RIGHT?**

IF WE EXAMINE THE...

---

[2] This point is drawn from DeRougemont's analysis of the myth of Tristan and Isolde. See Denis DeRougemont, *Love in the Western World*, New York: Pantheon Press, 1956.

[3] I am not suggesting that every western has all of these temptations, or that they appear in any given order. The subject of analysis is the repre-

of all presents an object of temptation which can be indulged, should the hero so choose; and secondly, it sets forth the hero in such a way that he can indulge the temptation in a preliminary way without becoming absorbed in it—i.e., without losing control. And, of course, it sets forth the evil one in precisely the opposite way.

In the drinking scenes the hero possesses not one drink, but a whole bottle—i.e., he has at his disposal the opportunity for unlimited indulgence and its consequent loss of self-control. Gambling is a situation over which one has rather limited control—you can lose; but the hero does not lose. He wins, thereby remaining in control (cheating simply signifies the failure to acknowledge loss of control). Wealth is not seized although it is available to him through the unguarded bank; and both good and bad girl seek out the hero in their various ways, but to no avail—he remains a hero. However, each temptation is presented in its peculiar way in order to set forth hero and evil one in their respective functions.

The temptation to do violence is more problematic, so much more so that the climax is given over to its solution. Furthermore, in the climax we find the key to the meaning of the myth as a whole—i.e., it can tell us why each type appears as he does, why the temptation episodes have their unique shape, and why certain fundamental images recur as they do.

We perceive in the evil one a terrible power, one which cannot be overcome by the ordinary resources of the town. However, he has acquired this power at great price: he has forfeited that very control and resistance which sustains and makes the hero what he is. The evil one represents, therefore, not temptation, so much as "temptation-unhesitatingly-given-into". He is the embodiment of the failure to resist temptation; he is the failure of denial. This is the real meaning of evil in the myth of the western, and it is this which makes the evil one truly evil. Because of this he threatens the hero's resistance (and that of the townsfolk, as well, although indirectly): each taunt and baiting gesture is a lure to the foreiture of control. This temptation the hero cannot handle with the usual methods of restraint, control, and the refusal to become absorbed; and it leads to a temptation which the hero cannot afford to resist: the temptation to destroy temptation.

The evil one's dark appearance is related to this threat. It tells us two things. First, that to lose control and forfeit resistance is (according to the story) a kind of living death, for black signifies death. In terms of the moral instruction of the story, and speaking metaphorically, we know that the evil one has "lost his life". But his black appearance also tells us that, speaking quite literally, this man will die—because of what he is, he must and will be executed. We are therefore both instructed and reassured.

The embarrassing question can now be posed: why must the hero wait to be attacked, why must he refrain from drawing first? Why does he not take his opponent from behind, while he is carousing, or while he is asleep? Anyone in the power of the myth would

sentative version—not any particular version or set of versions. Thus any particular western might deal with any one, or a number of such temptations.

reply that the gunfight takes place the way it does because this is the way westerns are; it's natural; this is the way it's always done—or, in the language of the myth itself, it was self-defense. But if one moves beyond the grasp of the myth, if one is no longer loyal to its rules and values, the gunfight is never inevitable. The circumstances which force the hero into this situation are contrived in order to make the violent destruction of the evil one appear just and virtuous. These circumstances have their origin in the inner, veiled need to which the story is addressed. This process, whereby desire is at once indulged and veiled I call the "inner dynamic". It is the key to the western, explaining not only the climax of the story, but everything else uniquely characteristic of it. What is required is that temptation be indulged while providing the appearance of having been resisted.

Each of the minor temptation episodes—the typical scenes setting forth hero and evil one as each encounters drink, cards, money, and sex—takes its unique shape from this need. Each is a climax-less western in itself, a play within a play in which temptation is faced and defeated, not by violent destruction, as in the climax, but by inner, willed control. Or, reversing the relationship, we may say that in the gunfight we have writ large something which takes place again and again throughout the story. It is precisely for this reason that no western has or needs to have all these episodes. Therefore westerns can and do depart radically from the composite picture described earlier. We are so familiar with each kind of temptation, and each so re-enforces the others that extraordinary deletions and variations can occur without our losing touch with the central meanings.

The inner dynamic affects the supporting types as well. The derelict-professional is derelict, and the non-violent easterner is weak, precisely because they have failed to resist temptation in the manner characteristic of the hero. Their moderate, controlled indulgence of the various temptations does not conform to the total resistance of the hero. Consequently they must be portrayed as derelict, weak and deficient men, contrasting unfavorably with the hero's virtue. In this sense they have more in common with the evil one.

Because these two types both originate in the east, they have something in common with the good girl. We note that everything eastern in the western is considered weak, emotional, and feminine (family life, intellectual life, domestic life, professional life). Only by becoming western-ized can the east be redeemed. The western, therefore, is more a myth about the east than it is about the west: it is a secret and bitter parody of eastern ways. This is all the more interesting, since it was originally written in the east, by easterners, for eastern reading. It really has very little to do with the west.

Woman is split in the western to correspond to the splitting of man into hero and evil one. Primarily, however, the double feminine image permits the hero some gratification of desire while making a stalemate ultimately necessary. To get the good girl, the story instructs us, our hero would have to become like those despicable easterners; to get the bad girl, he would have to emulate the evil one. In such a dilemma a ride into the sunset is not such a bad solution after all.

The attendant sets forth the inner dynamic by being infinitely close to the action (temptations) while never becoming at all involved in it. It is his task to provide the instruments of temptation (drink, money, cards, guns) while never indulging them himself. He is at once closer to temptation than any other type, and yet more removed than any other type.

The boys function to facilitate the action without becoming involved in it. Without them hero and adversary might find other ways to settle their differences. The boys serve to remind them of their obligations to each other and the story as a whole, thereby structuring the myth more firmly. While they are around nothing less than the traditional gunfight will do. On the other hand, because they never participate in the action, but only coerce and reenforce it, they are thoroughly resistant to this temptation as well.

In summary, then: the western is a myth in which evil appears as a series of temptations to be resisted by the hero—most of which he succeeds in avoiding through inner control. When faced with the embodiment of these temptations, his mode of control changes, and he destroys the threat. But the story is so structured that the responsibility for this act falls upon the adversary, permitting the hero to destroy while appearing to save. Types and details, as well as narrative, take their shape from this inner dynamic, which must therefore be understood as the basic organizing and interpretive principle for the myth as a whole.

Cultural Implications

The western, I believe, bears a significant relationship—both dynamic and historical—to a cultural force which, for lack of a better word, I would call "puritanism". Here I simply refer to a particular normative image of man's inner life in which it is the proper task of the will to rule, control, and contain the spontaneous, vital aspects of life. For the puritan there is little interpenetration between will and feeling, will and imagination. The will dominates rather than participates in the feelings and imagination.

Whenever vitality becomes too pressing, and the dominion of the will becomes threatened, the self must find some other mode of control. In such a situation the puritan will seek, usually unknowingly, any situation which will permit him to express vitality while at the same time appearing to control and resist it. The western provides just this opportunity, for, as we have seen, the entire myth is shaped by the inner dynamic of apparent control and veiled expression. Indeed, in the gunfight (and to a lesser extent in the minor temptation episodes) the hero's heightened gravity and dedicated exclusion of all other loyalties presents a study in puritan virtue, while the evil one presents nothing more nor less than the old New England protestant devil—strangely costumed, to be sure—the traditional tempter whose horrid lures never allow the good puritan a moment's peace. In the gunfight there is deliverance and redemption. Here is the real meaning of the western: a puritan morality tale in which the savior-hero redeems the community from the temptations of the devil.

The western is also related to puritanism through its strong self-critical element—i.e., it attacks, usually through parody, many aspects of traditional civilized life. Self-criticism, however, does not come easily to the puritan. Like vitality, it functions through imagination; and it too is in the service of the will. Therefore, if such criticism is to appear at all, it too must be veiled. The western assists in this difficult problem, for the story is well-removed from his own locale, both geographically and psychically. Because it is always a story taking place "out there", and "a long time ago", self-criticism can appear without being directly recognized as such.

It is tempting to inquire how far certain historical forms of puritanism, such as mass religious revivals, may have actually produced the western. Was it only a coincidence that the same period of 1905–1920, which saw the early emergence of the western myth, also witnessed the nationwide popularity of a Billy Sunday and an Aimee Semple McPherson? Their gospel was a radical triumph of will over feeling and vitality, through which the believer could rely wholly upon his increasingly omnipotent will for the requisite controls. And here too was the familiar inventory of vices, with its characteristic emphasis upon gambling and drinking.

Recently there has been an even more remarkable religious revival. Beginning in the early 1950's, it reached its point of greatest intensity in 1955. Here the gentle willfulness of the Graham gospel, and the more subtle (but equally hortatory) "save-yourself" of the Peale contingent permitted many respectable people to go to church and become interested in religion, without actually knowing why. However, like its earlier counterpart, this was not so much a religious movement as it was a renewed attack of the will upon the life of feeling and vitality.

That a re-appearance of the western should take place precisely at this point is certainly suggestive. For the upsurge in its popularity did occur just five years ago, beginning in the same year that the religious revival reached its height. Perhaps the present western revival has been more extensive and pervasive because the recent religious revival was equally so.

Presently, however, the religious revival has subsided, but the western remains almost as popular as ever. This could mean one of two things. On the one hand, the many changes which the western is presently undergoing—in its narrative, its types, and in its recurrent, primary images—could indicate that the religious recession has permitted the myth to be altered radically, such that it is on the way to becoming something entirely different. On the other hand, should such changes remain responsible to and be contained by the classical version, it could be that our puritanism is simply being expressed through non-religious sources: most notably through the social sciences (indeed, in the sociologist's and psychologist's denunciation of the violence, historical inaccuracies, etc. in the western, do we not hear echoes of the puritan hero himself?).

Topics for Discussion

1. What is meant by puritanism in this essay? In what way is the western hero a puritan?
2. Do you think the western is as popular today as it was previously? How many western programs are currently on television?
3. Do you agree with Homans' description of the types of people and the pattern of action in the western? Analyze a recent western movie you have seen according to Homans' descriptions.
4. Does Homans' analysis of the western apply to such classic western movies as *Shane* and *High Noon*? What about *Cat Ballou*?
5. The western is a popular myth. How does Homans define myth? How does this definition apply to the western?
6. Can you think of a western movie that does not fit Homans' analysis?
7. Does the western reflect American cultural values?
8. Did you ever have a cowboy movie star as your hero? Who was it? Why was he your hero?

Rhetorical Considerations

1. Is the thesis of this essay contained only in the title or is it stated in the essay?
2. Does Homans write with an interesting style? What do you like about it? What do you find difficult about it?
3. Cite examples of vocabulary in this essay that you find too specialized or difficult. Would Homans' audience understand his vocabulary?
4. Does Homans really reach a conclusion? Reread the final paragraph, particularly the last sentence.

Film as Environment: The Now Movie

Anthony Schillaci

The better we understand how young people view film, the more we have to revise our notion of what film is. Seen through young eyes, film is destroying conventions almost as quickly as they can be formulated. Whether the favored director is "young" like Richard Lester, Roman Polanski, and Arthur Penn, or "old" like Kubrick, Fellini, and Buñuel, he must be a practicing cinematic anarchist to catch the eye of the young. If we're looking for the young audience between sixteen and twenty-four, which accounts for 48 per cent of the box office today, we will find they're on a trip, whether in a Yellow Submarine or on a Space Odyssey. A brief prayer muttered for Rosemary's Baby and they're careening down a dirt road with Bonnie and Clyde, the exhaust spitting banjo sounds, or sitting next to The Graduate as he races across the Bay Bridge after his love. The company they keep is fast; Belle de Jour, Petulia, and Joanna are not exactly a sedentary crowd. Hyped up on large doses of *Rowan and Martin's Laugh-In*, and *Mission: Impossible*, they are ready for anything that an evolving film idiom can throw on the screen. And what moves them must have the pace, novelty, style, and spontaneity of a television commercial.

All of this sounds as if the script is by McLuhan. Nevertheless, it is borne out by the experience of teaching contemporary film to university juniors and seniors, staging film festivals for late teens and early adults, and talking to literally hundreds of people about movies. The phenomenon may be interesting, and even verifiable, but what makes it important is its significance for the future of film art. The young have discovered that film is an environment which you put on, demanding a different kind of structure, a different mode of attention than any other art. Their hunger is for mind-expanding experience and simultaneity, and their art is film.

Occasionally a young director gives us a glimpse of the new world of film as environmental art. The optical exercise known as *Flicker* came on like a karate chop to the eyes at Lincoln Center's Film Seminar three years ago. One half-hour of white light flashing at varied frequency, accompanied by a deafening sound track designed to infuriate, describes the screen, but not what happened to the audience. As strangers turned to ask if it was a put-on, if they had forgotten to put film in the projector, they noticed that the flickering light fragmented their motions, stylizing them like the actions of a silent movie. In minutes, the entire audience was on its feet, acting out spontaneous pantomimes for one another, no one looking at the flashing screen. The happening precipitated by *Flicker* could be called the film of the future, but it was actually an anti-environment that gives us an insight into the past. By abstracting totally from content, the director demonstrated that the film is in the audience which acts out personal and public dramas as the screen turns it on. The delight of this experience opened up the notion of film as an environmental art.

Critics have noted the trend which leaves story line and character development strewn along the highways of film history like the corpses in Godard's *Weekend*. The same critics have not, in general, recognized that the growing option for nonlinear, unstructured experiences that leave out sequence, motivation, and "argument" is a vote for film as environment. Young people turn to film for a time-space environment in which beautiful things happen to them. The screen has, in a sense, less and less to do with what explodes in the audience. This new scene could mean either that film is plunging toward irrelevant stimulation, or that there is a new and unprecedented level of participation and involvement in young audiences. I prefer to think the latter is the case. Young people want to talk about Ben's hang-up, why Rosemary stayed with the baby, or what it feels like to be in the electronic hands of a computer like Hal. They do not forget the film the minute they walk out of the theater.

The attention given the new style of film goes beyond stimulation to real involvement. A generation with eyes fixed on the rearview mirror tended to give film the same attention required for reading—that is, turning off all the senses except the eyes. Film became almost as private as reading, and little reaction to the total audience was experienced. As the Hollywood dream factory cranked out self-contained worlds of fantasy, audiences entered them with confidence that nothing even vaguely related to real life would trouble their reveries. As long as one came and left in the middle of the film, it was relatively non-involving as environment. When television brought the image into the living room, people gave it "movie attention," hushing everyone who entered the sacred presence of the tube as they would a film patron who talked during a movie. One was not allowed to speak, even during commercials. It took post-literate man to teach us how to use television as environment, as a moving image on the wall to which one may give total or peripheral attention as he wishes. The child who had TV as a baby-sitter does not turn off all his senses, but walks about the room carrying on a multiplicity of actions and relationships, his attention a special reward for the cleverness of the pitchman, or the skill of the artist. He is king, and not captive. As McLuhan would put it, he is not an audience, he *gives* an audience to the screen.

The new multisensory involvement with film as total environment has been primary in destroying literary values in film. Their decline is not merely farewell to an understandable but unwelcome dependency; it means the emergence of a new identity for film. The diminished role of dialogue is a case in point. The difference between *Star Trek* and *Mission: Impossible* marks the trend toward self-explanatory images that need no dialogue. Take an audio tape of these two popular TV shows, as we did in a recent study, and it will reveal that while *Mission: Impossible* is completely unintelligible without images, *Star Trek* is simply an illustrated radio serial, complete on the level of sound. It has all the characteristics of radio's golden age: actions explained, immediate identification of character by voice alone, and even organ music to squeeze the proper emotion or end the episode. Like *Star Trek*, the old film was frequently a talking picture (emphasis on the adjective), thereby confirming McLuhan's contention that technologically "radio married the movies." The marriage of dependence, however, has gone on the rocks, and not by a return to silent films but a new turning to foreign ones. It was the films of Fellini and Bergman, with their subtitles, that convinced us there had been too many words. Approximately one-third of the dialogue is omitted in subtitled versions of these films, with no discernible damage—and some improvement—of the original.

More than dialogue, however, has been jettisoned. Other literary values, such as sequential narrative, dramatic choice, and plot are in a state of advanced atrophy, rapidly becoming vestigial organs on the body of film art as young people have their say. *Petulia* has no "story," unless one laboriously pieces together the interaction between the delightful arch-kook and the newly divorced surgeon, in which case it is nothing more than an encounter. The story line wouldn't make a ripple if it were not scrambled and fragmented into an experience that explodes from a free-floating present into both past and future simultaneously. *Petulia* is like some views of the universe which represent the ancient past of events whose light is just now reaching us simultaneously with the future of our galaxy, returning from the curve of outer space. Many films succeed by virtue of what they leave out. *2001: A Space Odyssey* is such a film, its muted understatement creating gaps in the action that invite our inquiry. Only a square viewer wants to know where the black monolith came from and where it is going. For most of the young viewers to whom I have spoken, it is just there. *Last Year at Marienbad* made the clock as limply shapeless as one of Salvador Dali's watches, while *8½* came to life on the strength of free associations eagerly grasped by young audiences. The effect of such films is a series of open-ended impressions, freely evoked and enjoyed, strongly inviting inquiry and involvement. In short, film is freed to work as environment, something which does not simply contain, but shapes people, tilting the balance of their faculties, radically altering their perceptions, and ultimately their views of self and all reality. Perhaps one sense of the symptomatic word "grooving," which applies to both sight and sound environments, is that a new mode of attention—multisensory, total, and simultaneous—has arrived. When you "groove," you do not analyze, follow an argument, or separate sensations; rather, you are massaged into a feeling of heightened life and consciousness.

If young people look at film this way, it is in spite of the school, a fact which says once more with emphasis that education is taking place outside the classroom walls. The "discovery" that television commercials are the most exciting and creative part of today's programming is old news to the young. Commercials are a crash course in speed-viewing, their intensified sensations challenging the viewer to synthesize impressions at an ever increasing rate. The result is short films like one produced at UCLA, presenting 3,000 years of art in three minutes. *God Is Dog Spelled Backwards* takes you from the cave paintings of Lascaux to the latest abstractions, with some images remaining on the screen a mere twenty-fourth of a second! The young experience the film, however, not as confusing, but as exuberantly and audaciously alive. They feel joy of recognition, exhilaration at the intense concentration necessary (one blink encompasses a century of art), and awe at the 180-second review of every aspect of the human condition. Intended as a put-on, the film becomes a three-minute commercial for man. This hunger for overload is fed by the television commercial, with its nervous jump cuts demolishing continuity, and its lazy dissolves blurring time-space boundaries. Whether the young are viewing film "through" television, or simply through their increased capacity for information and sensation (a skill which makes most schooling a bore), the result is the same—film becomes the primary environment in which the hunger to know through experience is satisfied.

Hidden within this unarticulated preference of the young is a quiet tribute to the film as the art that humanizes change. In its beginnings, the cinema was celebrated as the art that mirrored reality in its functional dynamism. And although the early vision predictably gave way to misuse of the medium, today the significance of the filmic experience of change stubbornly emerges again. Instead of prematurely stabilizing change, film celebrates it. The cinema can inject life into historical events by the photoscan, in which camera movement and editing liberate the vitality of images from the past. *City of Gold*, a short documentary by the National Film Board of Canada, takes us by zoom and cut into the very life of the Klondike gold rush, enabling us to savor the past as an experience.

Education increasingly means developing the ability to live humanly in the technological culture by changing with it. Film is forever spinning out intensifications of the environment which make it visible and livable. The ability to control motion through its coordinates of time and space make film a creative agent in change. Not only does film reflect the time-space continuum of contemporary physics, but it can manipulate artistically those dimensions of motion which we find most problematic. The actuality of the medium, its here-and-now impact, reflects how completely the present tense has swallowed up both past and future. Freudian psychology dissolves history by making the past something we live; accelerated change warps the future by bringing it so close that we can't conceive it as "ahead" of us. An art which creates its own space, and can move time forward and back, can humanize change by conditioning us to live comfortably immersed in its fluctuations.

On the level of form, then, perhaps the young are tuned in to film for "telling it like it is" in a sense deeper than that of fidelity to the event. It is film's accurate reflection of a society and of human life totally in flux that makes it the liberating art of the time. We live our lives more like Guido in *8½*—spinners of fantasies, victims of events, the products of mysterious associations—than we do like Maria in *The Sound of Music*, with a strange destiny guiding our every step. Instead of resisting change and bottling it, film intensifies the experience of change, humanizing it in the process. What makes the ending of *The Graduate* "true" to young people is not that Ben has rescued his girl from the Establishment, but that he did it without a complete plan for the future. The film may fail under analysis, but it is extraordinarly coherent as experience, as I learned in conversations about it with the young. The same accurate reflection of the day may be said of the deep space relativity of *2001*, the frantic pace of *Petulia*, or the melodramatic plotting of *Rosemary's Baby*. Whether this limitless capacity for change within the creative limits of art has sober implications for the future raises the next (and larger) questions of what young people look for and get out of film.

When the question of film content is raised, the example of *Flicker* and other films cited may seem to indicate that the young people favor as little substance as possible in their film experiences. A casual glance at popular drive-in fare would confirm this opinion quickly. Nevertheless, their attitude toward "what films are about" evidences a young, developing sensitivity to challenging comments on what it means to be human. The young are digging the strong humanism of the current film renaissance and allowing its currents to carry them to a level deeper than that reached by previous generations. One might almost say that young people are going to the film-maker's work for values that they have looked for in vain from the social, political, or religious establishments. This reaction, which has made film modern man's morality play, has not been carefully analyzed, but the present state of evidence invites our inquiry.

As far as the "point" of films is concerned, young people will resist a packaged view, but will welcome a problematic one. The cry, "Please, I'd rather do it myself!" should be taken to heart by the film-maker. It is better to use understatement in order to score a personal discovery by the viewer. Such a discovery of an idea is a major part of our delight in the experience of film art. A frequent answer to a recent survey question indicated that a young man takes his girl to the movies so that they will have something important to talk about. It is not a matter of pitting film discussion against "making out," but of recognizing that a rare and precious revelation of self to the other is often occasioned by a good film. The young feel this experience as growth, expanded vitality, more integral possession of one's self with the consequent freedom to go out to others more easily and more effectively.

Very little of the business of being human happens by instinct, and so we need every form of education that enlightens or accelerates that process. While young people do not go to films for an instant humanization course, a strong part of the pleasure they take in excellent films does just this. Whether through a connaturality of the medium described earlier, or because of a freer viewpoint, young audiences frequently get more out of films than their mentors. It is not so much a matter of seeing more films, but of seeing more in a film. The film-as-escape attitude belongs to an age when the young were not yet born; and the film-as-threat syndrome has little meaning for the sixteen to twenty-four group, simply because they are free from their elders' hang-ups. A typical irrelevance that causes youthful wonder is the elderly matron's complaint that *Bonnie and Clyde* would teach bad driving habits to the young.

The performance of youthful audiences in discussions of contemporary film indicates their freedom from the judgmental screen which blurs so many films for other generations. In speaking of *Bonnie and Clyde*, late high school kids and young adults do not dwell upon the career of crime or the irregularity of the sexual relationship, but upon other things. The development of their love fascinates young people, because Clyde shows he knows Bonnie better than she knows herself. Although he resists her aggressive sexual advances, he knows and appreciates her as a person. It is the sincerity of their growing love that overcomes his impotence, and the relationship between this achievement and their diminished interest in crime is not lost on the young audience. The reversal of the "sleep together now, get acquainted later" approach is significant here. These are only a few of the nuances that sensitive ears and eyes pick up beneath the gunfire and banjo-plucking. Similarly, out of the chaotic impressions of *Petulia,* patterns are perceived. Young people note the contrasts between Petulia's kooky, chaotic life, and the over-controlled precision of the surgeon's existence. The drama is that they both come away a little different for their encounter. Instead of a stale moral judgment on their actions, one finds open-ended receptivity to the personal development of the characters.

Youth in search of identity is often presented as a ridiculous spectacle, a generation of Kierkegaards plaintively asking each other: "Who am I?" Nevertheless, the quest is real and is couched in terms of a hunger for experience. SDS or LSD, McCarthy buttons or yippie fashions, it is all experimentation in identity, trying on experiences to see if they fit. The plea is to stop the world, not so that they can get off, but so they can get a handle on it. To grasp each experience, to suck it dry of substance, and to grow in that process is behind the desire to be "turned on." But of all the lurid and bizarre routes taken by young people, the one that draws least comment is that of the film experience. More people have had their minds expanded by films than by LSD. Just as all art nudges man into the sublime and vicarious experience of the whole range of the human condition, film does so with a uniquely characteristic totality and involvement.

Ben, *The Graduate,* is suffocating under his parents' aspirations, a form of drowning which every young person has felt in some way. But the film mirrors their alienation in filmic terms, by changes in focus, by the metaphors of conveyor belt sidewalk and swimming pool, better than any moralist could say it. The satirical portraits of the parents may be broad and unsubtle, but the predicament is real and compelling. This is why the young demand no assurances that Ben and the girl will live happily ever after; it is enough that he jarred himself loose from the sick apathy and languid sexual experimentation with Mrs. Robinson to go after one thing, one person that he wanted for himself, and not for others. Incidentally, those who are not busy judging the morality of the hotel scenes will note that sex doesn't communicate without love. Some may even note that Ben is using sex to strike at his parents—not a bad thing for the young (or their parents) to know.

Emotional maturity is never painless and seldom permanent, but it can become a bonus from viewing good films because it occurs there not as taught but experienced. Values communicated by film are interiorized and become a part of oneself, not simply an extension of the womb that parents and educators use to shield the young from the world. Colin Smith, in *The Loneliness of the Long Distance Runner,* IS youth, not because he did it to the Establishment, but because he is trying to be his own man and not sweat his guts out for another. The profound point of learning who you are in the experience of freedom, as Colin did in running, is not lost on the young who think about this film a little. Some speak of Col's tragedy as a failure to realize he could have won the race for himself, and not for the governor of the Borstal. Self-destruction through spite, the pitfalls of a self-justifying freedom, and the sterility of bland protest are real problems that emerge from the film. The values that appeal most are the invisible ones that move a person to act because "it's me" (part of one's identity), and not because of "them." Because they have become an object of discovery and not of imposition, such values tend to make morality indistinguishable from self-awareness.

It should be made clear, however, that it is not merely the content, but the mode of involvement in the film experience that makes its humanism effective. In terms of "message," much of contemporary film reflects the social and human concerns that Bob Dylan, the Beatles, Simon and Garfunkel, and Joan Baez communicate. But the words of their songs often conceal the radical nature of the music in which they appear. The direct emotional appeal of the sound of "Eleanor Rigby," "Give a Damn," "I Am a Rock," or "Mr. Businessman" communicates before we have the words deciphered. Films with honest human concern, similarly, change audiences as much by their style as their message. *Elvira Madigan's* overpowering portrait of a hopeless love, *A Thousand Clowns'* image of nonconformity, *Zorba's* vitality, and *Morgan's* tragedy are not so much the content of the images as the outcome of their cinematic logic. If these films change us, it is because we have done it to ourselves by opening ourselves to their experiences.

Expo 67 audiences were charmed by the Czech Kinoautomat in which their vote determined the course of comic events in a film. Once again, we find here not a peek into the future, but an insight into all film experience. In one way or another, we vote on each film's progress. The passive way is to patronize dishonest or cynical films, for our box-office ballot determines the selection of properties for years to come. We have been voting this way for superficial emotions, sterile plots, and happy endings for a generation. But we vote more actively and subtly by willing the very direction of a film through identification with the character, or absorption into the action. The viewer makes a private or social commitment in film experience. He invests a portion of himself in the action, and if he is changed, it is because he has activated his own dreams. What happens on the screen, as in the case of *Flicker*, is the catalyst for the value systems, emotional responses, and the indirect actions which are the byproducts of a good film. Film invites young people to be part of the action by making the relationships which take the work beyond a mere succession of images. The reason why young people grow through their art is that they supply the associations that merely begin on the screen but do not end there. When parents and educators become aware of this, their own efforts at fostering maturity may be less frantic, and more effective.

It is not only the films that please and delight which appeal to the young, but also those which trouble and accuse by bringing our fears into the open. The new audience for documentary films highlights a new way of looking at film as an escape *into* reality. From *The War Game* to *Warrendale*, from *The Titicut Follies* to *Battle of Algiers*, young audiences are relishing the film's ability to document the present in terms of strong social relevance. *Portrait of Jason* is more than a voyeuristic peek into the psyche of a male whore; it is a metaphor for the black man's history in America, and this is what young people see in that film. Even the most strident dissenters will appreciate the ambiguities of *The Anderson Platoon*, which leaves us without anyone to hate, because it is not about Marines and Vietcong, but about men like ourselves. In these as in other films, the social content is intimately wed to the film experience, and together they form a new outlook. Ultimately, we may have to change our views on what film art is about.

The foregoing analysis of how young people look at film will appear to some to constitute a simplistic eulogy to youth. For this reason, we may temper our optimism by a hard look at real problems with this generation. There is a desperate need for education. Although they cannot all be structured, none of the better youthful attitudes or responses described came about by chance. Mere screening of films, for example, whether they be classics or trash, does little good. Colleges can become places where the young are taught hypocrisy, being told they "should" like Fellini, Bergman, Antonioni, or Godard. They can accept these filmmakers just as uncritically as their parents adulated movie stars. Unless there is encouragement to reflect on film experience, its impact can be minimal and fleeting. Most of the responses I have mentioned came from students who were well into the habit of discussing film. These discussions are best when they flow from the natural desire we have to communicate our feelings about a film. Nonverbalization, the reluctance to betray by treacherous abstractions the ineffable experience of the film, arises at this point. Real as it is, there must be found some middle ground between a suffocatingly detailed dissection of a film, and the noncommunicative exclamation, "like WOW!" Reflecting on one's experience is an integral part of making that experience part of one's self. Furthermore, one can see an almost immediate carry-over to other film experiences from each film discussed.

A problem more crucial than lack of reflection is the poverty of critical perspective. The young can plunge into their personal version of the *auteur* theory and make a fad or fetish out of certain films and directors. Roman Polanski has made some bad films, that is, films which do not reflect his own experience and feelings honestly as did *Knife in the Water*. Fascinating as *Rosemary's Baby* is, it suffers from an uncertain relationship of the director to his work. Some directors are adulated for peripheral or irrelevant reasons. Joseph Losey is a good film-maker, not because of a cynical preoccupation with evil, but because, like Hitchcock and Pinter, he makes us less certain of our virtue. And Buñuel, far from being a cheerful anarchist attacking church and society with abandon, is a careful surgeon, excising with camera the growths of degenerate myth on the cancerous culture.

In their own work, young people can celebrate bad film-making as "honest" and voyeuristic films as "mature." Criticism of poor films is not "putting down" the director for doing his own thing, especially if his thing is trite, dishonest, or so personal that it has no meaning accessible to others. Criticism means taking a stand on the basis of who you are. The current preferences of spoof over satire is not just another instance of cool over hot, but is symptomatic of a noncritical stance. *Dr. Strangelove* makes comic absurdity out of the cold war from a certain conviction about what mature political action should be. The *Laugh-In* has no convictions but a lot of opinions. If it is accused of favoring an idea or cause, it will refute the charge by ridiculing what it holds. The cynical, sophisticated noninvolvement of the "won't vote" movement in the recent election has its counterpart in film viewing.

A question that should perhaps have been asked earlier is: Why should we be concerned with asking how young people look at film? Tired reasons, citing *Time's* Man of the Year, the under-twenty-five generation, or the youthquake menace of *Wild in the Streets* (they'll be taking over!) are not appropriate here. Anyone who is interested in the direction taken by cinema, and its continued vitality in the current renaissance of the art, will have to take the young into account as the major shaping force on the medium. If the age group from sixteen to twenty-four accounts for 48 per cent of the box office, it means that this eight-year period determines the success or failure of most films. Fortunately, there has not yet appeared a formula for capturing this audience. *Variety* described the youth market as a booby trap for the industry, citing the surprise success of sleepers such as *Bonnie and Clyde* and *The Graduate*, as well as the supposed youth-appeal failures (*Half a Sixpence, Poor Cow, Here We Go Round the Mulberry Bush*). The list may suggest a higher level of young taste than producers are willing to admit. In any case, if the young have influenced the medium this far, we cannot ignore the fact. It is for this reason that we are encouraged to speculate on the future in the form of two developments revolutionizing the young approach to film: student film-making and multi-media experiences.

More and more, the answer to how young people look at film is "through the lens of a camera." In coming years, it will be youth as filmmaker, and not simply as audience, that will spur the evolution of the cinema. Students want a piece of the action, whether in running a university, the country, or the world; in terms of our question, this means making films. There is a strong resonance between film-making and the increasingly sophisticated film experience. Young people delighted by a television commercial are tempted to say: "I could do that!" Considering the cost and artistry of some commercials, this is a pretty naïve statement, but it doesn't stop the young from taking out their father's Super-8 or buying an old Bolex to tell their story on film. Today, anyone can make a film. Although Robert Flaherty's longed-for parousia, when film is as cheap as paper, has not yet arrived, the art has come into the reach of almost everyone. The Young Film-Makers Conference held by Fordham University last February drew 1,200 people, 740 of them student film-makers below college age. On a few weeks' notice, some 120 films were submitted for screening. Kids flew in from Richmond, California, and bussed in from Louisville, Kentucky, with twenty-seven states and Canada represented. Numbers, however, do not tell the story. One of the notable directors and actors present sized up the scene by saying: "My God, I'm standing here in the middle of a revolution!" It was the quality of the films that caused Eli Wallach to remark, only half in jest, that some day he'd be working for one of these film-makers. The young look at film as potential or actual film-makers, and this fact raises participation to an unprecedented critical level. The phenomenon also removes the last residue of passive audience participation from the Golden Forties box-office bonanza.

Foolhardy though it may be, one can predict that the new interest in film will take the direction of multi-media experimentation. Expo 67, it seems, is *now*. Our new and growing capacity to absorb images and synthesize sounds demands a simultaneity that cannot be met by traditional forms of film-making. The response so far has been the halfhearted multiple screens of *The Thomas Crown Affair*, not part of the conception of the film, but inserted as fancy dressing. The object of multiple images is not so much to condense actions as to create an environment such as the Ontario pavilion film, *A Place to Stand*. My own students have begun to relegate location shots such as street scenes or mood sequences to peripheral attention on side screens and walls, while the action takes place on the main screen.

It is symptomatic that the staged novelty of the Electric Circus is giving way to a new and interesting experiment in Greenwich Village, Cerebrum—where for a modest fee parties can set up their own media platforms equipped with projectors, tape recorders, and lights to stage their own happening. The idea being developed here is central to multi-media art, that is, the orchestration of contemporary media instruments. Young people are not afraid to carry a running projector around, spraying the images on walls and ceilings for distortions which communicate. An older generation is inclined to think of the media hardware as "machines" to be screwed to the floor or locked in a booth while they "produce" images and sounds. The young, in contrast, recognize this hardware as part of the information environment of electronic technology, and they use it accordingly. Spontaneity, the chance synchronization, overload that leads to breakthrough—these are all part of the excitement that draws people to media rather than film alone.

The young look at film is a revolutionary one, motivated more by love of the medium than hatred of the Establishment. In a sense, the new taste is liberating film for a free exploration of its potential, especially in the area of profound changes in the youth audience as people open themselves to the reality of the medium. Whether as young film-maker or multi-media entrepreneur, the young will have their say. If we take the time to cultivate their perspective, we may learn an interesting view of the future of media, and a fascinating way to stay alive.

Topics for Discussion

1. How can film be an "environment which you put on"?
2. How does Schillaci define "groove"? Do you agree with his definition? Can you give an example of "grooving"?
3. Do you agree that "television commercials are the most exciting and creative part of today's programming"? Can you give any examples of such commercials?
4. Schillaci says that film is the art that humanizes change. What does he mean by this?
5. Is it true that "young people favor as little substance as possible in their film experiences"?
6. Is Schillaci's essay nothing more than "a simplistic eulogy to youth"? How does Schillaci defend himself against this charge?
7. Do you view film as a revolutionary medium?
8. Do you share Schillaci's enthusiasm and excitement for movies? How often do you go to a movie? What kind of movies do you like to see?

Rhetorical Considerations

1. Where is the thesis of the essay stated?
2. What does the simile "like a karate chop to the eyes" mean to you? Is it a good comparison?
3. Analyze the paragraph structure of the first five paragraphs. Where does the topic sentence occur in each paragraph? What kind of paragraph structure is dominant?
4. Do you find any particular sentences difficult to understand? Why?

Films, Television, and Tennis

RICHARD E. PECK

A work of art becomes, in the hands of an historian, an artifact, a primary document which he uses to define the culture that produced it. Developments in literature, in the plastic arts, even in handicrafts, somehow help the archaeologist or historian to understand the minds and opinions of the people whose concerns fostered them. If such an approach is valid, and I think it is, consider then the delights awaiting some future historian who turns his attention to tapes or films of today's television fare. For television—not the plastic arts, not literature, not theater, not cinema—is the characteristic art form of the 1960's.

It is the child of consensus. The American love for westerns, for the fake history of a distinctively American era, gave us *High Noon* and *Shane* as well as the Lash La Rue sagas, penny dreadfuls, and Randolph Scott. The same affection keeps *Bonanza* perched securely atop the Nielsen's year after plot-repeating year. As the child of consensus, it offers the reminder that ours is not an age in which satire thrives. Inez Robb's syndicated suggestion that exterminating senior citizens would obviate the need for Medicare brought shocked replies; people persist in misunderstanding Art Buchwald's wit; and witness the undeserved demise of *That Was the Week That Was*. *The Man From U.N.C.L.E.*, a series which initially parodied itself, has responded to the time's temper and gone more or less straight. Those shows created to satirize either die aborning, turn farce, or lose their satiric edge and drift toward expressing the Grand Consensus dominant in a Great Society. Without evaluating such a drift, one must agree that television reacts to, and thereby defines, majority opinion.

Beginning as the written word, television scripts reflect literary tastes and fads as well. The fictional anti-hero, whose contrived clumsiness and gaucheries continue to enrich publishers, spawned a televised counterpart. Under several names, Dagwood bumbles through his family's problems, a charming but incompetent man who somehow fails to fit into the world, but fits snugly within the confines of a 21-inch screen. In the case of a Gomer Pyle, he finds acceptance. But—to return to an earlier point—those anti-heroes created to satirize have the survival potential of that proverbial snowball. Every week *The Fugitive* escapes being executed by an unjust society, and his audience stays with him through thin and thin. Yet an attempt to mock his plight, as in *Run, Buddy, Run,* treats satirically a man we love: an anti-hero Buddy may be, but our affection is reserved for the real thing. The romantic habit of mind which elevates to prominence a real hero and revels in black and white morality rebels at any mockery of cherished beliefs. Anyone calling George Washington a royalist fink will be shouted down without a chance to offer his evidence.

This is not to say that television defines all Americans as puri-

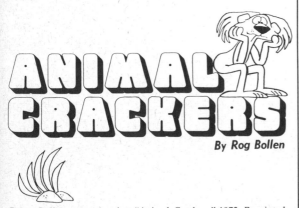

Roger Bollen, cartoon strips, "Animal Crackers," 1972. Reprinted through the courtesy of the Chicago Tribune-New York News Syndicate, Inc.

Richard E. Peck, "Films, Television, and Tennis," from *Man and the Movies*, ed. W. R. Robinson, copyright 1967 by Louisiana University Press. Reprinted by permission.

tanically stodgy. Camp, that grand phenomenon which brought back to theater screens Batman in all his serialized splendor, also eased the caped crusader and Robin into millions of homes in living, garish color. Prancing grotesquely in his snug BVD's, Batman camps through escapades designed to please the kiddies while letting all us sophisticates in on the gag to enjoy the tasteless, consciously unconscious poverty of the scripts which guide him. "Camp" becomes a national catchword; TV responds. Even *Batman's* slump in the ratings may well define the fad's finish better than anything Susan Sontag might say.

But television is not merely a mirror of the age. It is also a moving force. Just as cinema once provided for the rest of the world a specific view of American culture, television now introduces to our international neighbors the view we hold of ourselves. Some part of a national psyche is translated to television film, and such characterizing data are broadcast abroad. Broderick Crawford's *Highway Patrol* takes on new flavor dubbed in Japanese. To hear *Bonanza's* Dan Blocker addressed as "Monsieur 'oss" somehow spoils the effect of his nickname. Yet American traits survive even the silliest dubbing or translation. Foreigners learn to (mis)understand us via television. But the fondness for things American can't completely account for a show's popularity among peoples who may distrust or dislike America in the abstract; the themes treated in televised drama obviously have about them the flavor of universality. Not only our countrymen, but foreigners as well, react strongly to the strain of the heroic in televised drama. Hugh O'Brien's *Wyatt Earp,* seldom rerun any longer on domestic channels, is so popular abroad that O'Brien may be taking his life in his hands to wander unprotected through a crowd of adulatory Japanese. Captured by admiration for the heroes of American television, foreign audiences begin to identify the land which spawns these heroes as the home of violence, of cowboys and *Untouchables,* miniaturized in black and white. President Kennedy's assassination must have shocked others much less than it did us; after all, our television defines us in many eyes as gun-toting thugs.

Television's influence is equally dominant in this country, yet not entirely negative. Bill Cosby's being cast as co-lead in *I Spy* marks a significant step. A Negro, he plays a non-racial part, better educated and often more literate than his Caucasian partner-in-espionage. Initially the series did not appear on a few southern stations. Since becoming a success, it can no longer be ignored by men who react quickly to advertisers' dollars, and *I Spy* now reaches, according to *Variety,* 99 per cent of American television homes. A generation of American children, North and South, will grow up with the knowledge that Negroes are people, not merely creatures readily categorized as rapists or Uncle Toms. The impact of a national communication medium not dominated by local bias or pressure is undeniable, and healthy.

This impact makes itself felt strikingly in special circumstances. Teachers working in Project Head Start or similar programs directed toward children described by the sociologist as "culturally disadvantaged" are finding in television the greatest teaching aid yet devised. I do *not* speak of educational TV but of the garden variety of commercial programing. Children with illiterate or semiliterate parents, children from bookless homes in which newspapers or magazines

I DUNNO ... WHAT DO **YOU** WANT TO DO?

are used for kindling fires rather than for reading, have their minds stretched and hard knowledge force-fed them minute by minute as they lie in front of the television set. Nor is it only children's fare like *Discovery* or *Exploring* which exerts such strong influence. First-graders have grown up with the spectacle of the U.S. space program brought home to them in a way unavailable during their parents' childhood; the parents may still be puzzled by the basic facts of aviation. Children are more fully aware of cultural and geographic distinctions than many of their ill equipped teachers, who find themselves astounded by children's curious and inquiring minds. Their vocabularies grow at an amazing rate, as several recent series of intelligence tests testify. While critics carp about the leveling tendency of any mass medium of communication, they ignore one crucial fact: much of that "leveling" takes place in an *upward* direction. And as children learn and develop, parents share, however slightly, in the whole happy process.

Those who ignore television's power and potential quite simply fail to recognize the impact with which TV drama strikes minds seldom exposed to literature, to legitimate theater, or to any cinema other than Walt Disney's canned distortions of the world. *La Dolce Vita* and *Last Year at Marienbad* are, after all, coterie pieces, say what you will about their merits. *I Spy* and *Dr. Kildare* reach and affect more people, more beneficially, than any feature film ever made. Not merely the escapist claptrap some critics dogmatically see in it, television drama relates to and defines the world for many viewers as nothing else can. In May, 1961, Jerry McNeely's teleplay *The Joke in the Valley* appeared on *The Hallmark Hall of Fame*. In that play a popular public figure is murdered. Before the murderer can be brought to justice, he too is executed, in this case by a man who sees his own action as a noble public service. The community's problem becomes one of evaluating the second murder in light of tension between motive and action, between "public good" and overriding questions of morality unrelated to the single act. "Melodrama," one might say, and there's an end to it.

Yet the repercussions which followed that show were eventually, more than immediately, impressive. McNeely found his mailbox crammed with letters and telegrams of two sorts: One group reacted favorably to the elements of a morality play whose impact struck them at once. The other comprised, predictably, crank notes accusing him of all sorts of twisted motives or unpopular beliefs.

Nor was that the end of audience response: more than two years later, following Jack Ruby's televised "execution" of Lee Harvey Oswald, the playwright discovered how strongly people had reacted to his work, how long their memories served. He received requests that the show be rerun, somewhere, somehow, for the comment it seemed to offer about an historical event. One can assume that even the cranks who had written initially now managed to convince themselves that McNeely had known of the plot and sinned by not warning the President, or found themselves wishing that he turn his soothsaying powers to something profitable like picking the winner of the next Irish Sweepstakes.

Statistics would be helpful at this point. What percentage of viewers, on seeing Ruby's action, immediately recalled *The Joke in the Valley*? How many thought of writing but knew of no way of con-

FEEL LIKE TAKING IN A MOVIE ?

WHAT'S PLAYING ?

The Age of Communication

tacting McNeely or the show's producer? I can offer only random estimates, but it seems likely that each of the letters which actually reached the playwright represents hundreds, perhaps even thousands of viewers. The point, then, is this: while some minds resort to quotations from favorite poems or novels, to the classics, or to childhood experience for illuminating analogies, others turn just as readily to interpretations of reality driven home by TV drama. Even speech patterns are dominated by popular television. Would you believe that millions of literate adults speak in terms suggested by one running joke on *Get Smart*? Thousands of teen-agers? How about one earnest writer?

The influence is undeniable and even surpasses that of cinema, if only because television reaches a broader audience. In one evening more people saw the televised appearance of *The Bridge on the River Kwai* than had paid admission to the film during the several years of its theatrical run. The appearance on TV of feature films leads many to discuss televised drama and cinema as though the two forms were somehow interchangeable. But by considering the current relationship between these two forms I can perhaps point out the major distinctions between them and underline one of television's most striking realms of influence—the power it seems to wield over cinema itself.

Television programing has come full circle, returning for its most characteristic success to sports or variety shows, the fare of the 1939 pioneer telecasts. Sportscasts and an occasional special remain almost the only examples of live television. An insatiable public appetite for entertainment became obvious early in the game, and television production moved toward film as the major vehicle. Even those few programs which may seem live, like NBC's *The Tonight Show,* are taped for delayed broadcast. The advantages of tape or film are clear: re-runs help amortize initial production costs, bloopers can be edited out, and whole segments may be swapped between shows for better balance. It is finally cheaper to film, hiring extras ("atmosphere people," in TV jargon) for a single day's shooting, than to rehearse an entire cast for weeks before a live production.

The overwhelming majority of prime-time televised drama is now filmed. The halcyon days of *Omnibus* or *Playhouse Ninety's* error-ridden live productions are long gone and longer lamented. Critics who bemoan the loss of live televised drama, whatever its quality, and the recent dominance of filmed drama do so out of noble motives. They see two theatrical genres distinctively different in conception drifting toward one another in disappointing ways.

The similarities are unmistakable. In the most general terms technical production of a one-hour television drama differs little from that of a full-length feature film. Cameras and sound equipment, lighting techniques, processing methods in the lab, editing and scoring are identical. Even our home movies may get the same treatment. So the habit of discussing television and cinema in the same breath is understandable. Both offer a series of images which express a point of view or convey information. Actors move easily from one medium to the other. James Garner's success as Bret Maverick led to his work in motion pictures, and his apprenticeship in television gave him whatever acting skills he has. Richard Chamberlain moved from television to the Broadway stage. And Richard Burton's playing of Cali-

ban in *The Tempest* some years back lacked nothing for its being performed before TV cameras rather than on "legitimate" boards. Directors more and more often break into cinematic work through television, a medium which demands of them precision and directness not so stringently required by the relatively leisurely pace of cinema direction. A filmed narrative does not change character because of the means of its distribution—wide screen or square box.

When one turns from the media's similarities to their differences, however, one finds that television influences cinema rather than being influenced. First, television is *not* minor league cinema. Granted, many of the same techniques apply; physical equipment and processing methods are similar, if not identical. The real distinction resembles that between free verse and the sonnet. Writing free verse is, in Robert Frost's famous phrase, like playing tennis with the net down. Like free verse, cinema is more nearly an open-ended form. The restrictions which control and limit the typical teleplay are stricter, more clearly prescribed, but not necessarily debilitating. A *Tom Jones,* perhaps even more a *Dear John,* reaches the screen as the director's creation, with the merits achieved by intricate cutting and editing, fine nuance of camera work, and a shuffling of constituent parts which is impossible in the short week available for the filming, editing, and scoring of an hour teleplay. But what arbiter decides that the enormous craft demanded in the creation of an hour teleplay should be demeaned in comparison? The contrast is ridiculous, rather like the question on an aptitude test that asks which one likes better, living in the country or in the summer. I opt for the craftsman, the man who stands facing a net raised high enough for volleyball and yet plays his tennis match without begging for a change in the rules.

To use the titles *Tom Jones* and *Dear John* as I have is to approach a new attitude toward an art only now fumbling its way into prominence. *Giles Goat-Boy* is characterized in several reviews as allegory, artifice, and even craft without content. The arrangement of the material figures in random discussions of that novel much more than the material itself: What is the allegory? How many levels of meaning obtrude? Such a concern with the artifice of art dominates *Tom Jones* as well. It is impossible not to notice the techniques: speeded-up film sequences, subtitles, ornate framing, shifts into and out of brilliant color. Albert Finney even reminds the audience forcefully that they are watching a filmed narrative by hanging his hat over the lens.

To oversimplify, one can generalize about the phenomenon by suggesting that we who compose today's audience don't require "realism" any longer; we may not even respect it. Rather, we react to self-conscious art, to art forms which play with their own limitations and conventions. For that reason, television—that most stringently restricted of forms—sits perched securely atop what's happening. Perhaps by following a script from its birth as a vague idea in the writer's mind to the teleplay which results I can make my point, or at least suggest a new way of looking at a single hour of television drama.

The time necessary for revising, rewriting, editing, and correcting flaws—time which is afforded a team at work on a cinematic production—is denied the television producer. When he gets a script, he

THEY'RE SHOWING AN AWARD-WINNING FILM ABOUT TWO YOUNG PEOPLE IN LOVE ... IT SAYS,"THE MESSAGE AND CONTENT OF THIS FILM MAKE IT TRULY AN ARTISTIC TRIUMPH."!.

The Age of Communication

needs it ready to go. It may later be polished, or even rewritten, but at the cost of an expensive, ulcer-producing delay. Thus the whole process of shaping the final product for television falls more urgently into the writer's hands. He must follow a methodical plan. One of the best writers I know—"best" as opposed to "prolific"—employs the same series of steps for every script. He submits to the producer a five- or six-page "story treatment," a condensed plot. Given an OK for the idea, he moves on to a fifteen-page "step outline" in which he indicates breakdown into act and scene divisions, perhaps even a bit of dialogue for the flavor it will give his finished script. His work once more approved, he gets down to business.

Writing the finished teleplay, he finds himself entangled in the net I mentioned. There is no denying it—TV is formulaic; it has its own logic and rhetoric. Each show opens with a two- to five-minute "teaser," that capsule of drama which flashes on the screen to prevent our switching to Ed Sullivan or Lawrence Welk. In this brief span of time, the writer *must*: (1) Get our attention with a "hook" of un-explained action, striking character conflict, or a question important enough to make us eagerly await the answer; and (2) introduce the star or guest star for this particular episode. If he knows his business, he should also (1) introduce two or three other principal players, (2) distinguish the setting and historical period, (3) hint faintly at a secondary problem in the story to follow, and (4) conceal behind bright, forceful dialogue the fact that he is doing all this. If he is really good—and look to the all-too-rare scripts by names like Silliphant, Rose, McNeely, Mittleman, or the pseudonymous John Thomas James for examples—he will also make us laugh at, cry with, or hate a character on the screen. All this in the teaser, before the credits roll past and give permission for a quick trip to the pantry. A glassblower with hay fever has an easier job.

But the writer's problem has only begun. Ahead of him lies the creation of a four-act play whose acts average twelve to thirteen minutes. More, each act should ideally end as strongly as the teaser does, particularly the second, which coincides with the half-hour stroke of the clock and a viewer's recurrent impulse to catch at least the jugglers and the rock-and-roll band on the second half of Sullivan's spectacular. Once the viewer has switched channels he's gone to stay. He must be kept hooked, this time principally through effective dialogue. Each line of dialogue gets tested: Does it: (1) Define character? (2) Advance the plot? (3) Evoke emotional reaction from the audience? If it does not, out it comes. In the best scripts each line will achieve at least two of these ends.

Assuming that his muse does not desert him, the writer finishes in a matter of days—or weeks. But he has only a play, not a teleplay, and television differs even more from legitimate theater than from the cinema. The writer must now become director, sound technician, special effects man, even lighting and casting director. His completed script will contain comments unheard by any audience beyond the production staff. General camera directions are left to the director, but shots essential to creating a desired mood must be explicitly described in the script. The writer indicates essential sound cues, dramatically effective lighting, transitions between scenes—direct cut, slow dissolve, whatever paces his drama to best advantage. He includes with his script a summary description of sets and characters,

" THE FILM DEALS WITH THE SUBJECT IN A SENSITIVE AND UNDERSTANDING FASHION... A TRULY MEMORABLE AND ENRICHING EXPERIENCE."

LET'S GO!

perhaps even "typing" the characters according to what particular actor he might envision in each role.

And when he finally drops his pencil or leans back to let the typewriter cool, he has a first draft, sixty typewritten pages. Then another test: Read it aloud. To his wife, or a friend, a tape recorder, his shaving mirror, someone critical yet sympathetic. Test it. Check it. Then rewrite. And rewrite. The final version handed the director offers a full blueprint of the entire hour, subject to whatever minor changes may occur to this harried man in his tight shooting schedule.

Even after the play is filmed, editing and scoring require more time. Thus it becomes essential that a writer's ideas be explicit and readily translatable into action. Television is no medium for the improvisor who fondles and nurtures his creation to maturity; Bergman is a poor candidate for a job directing television drama. The time element assumes such major importance that a series may occasionally change because of it, shifting radically from the producer's original conception. I understand that the crew of *Maverick* found it impossible to complete episodes for that show in anything less than eight or ten days. Brother Bret, the Garner role, appeared in relief of Jack Kelly's Bart Maverick. With two production units at work on separate scripts it then became possible to meet weekly deadlines and to relieve pressure on the original company. And to many fans the show became Garner's, not Kelly's.

Given all these restrictions—time limits, formulaic act structure, economic limitations (about $140,000 for a single episode as compared with about $3,000,000 for a feature film)—television is forced into a mold. The writer exercises his craft as well as he can; an intelligent audience watches him at work, fully aware of the rhetoric he employs.

Unfortunately, that mythical "intelligent audience" does not always include men in the *business* of television or cinema. No one in the audience seriously believes any longer that feature films come off well on TV. The necessity for commercial interruptions and station breaks destroys the original tempo and mood of the film. Yet some have tried to solve the problem by writing feature-length filmscripts specifically geared to the requirements of commercial television. They do both industries a disservice. *Fame is the Name of the Game* recently fared well enough as a televised movie, but, transported into a theater as it will inevitably be, it must fail as cinema. An audience can hardly be expected to enjoy jolting through 100-plus minutes of plot in which a crisis leaps out at them every thirteen minutes to announce a commercial which never appears. And so the producers of that film define themselves as part of the group which persists in equating, and confusing, two distinct theatrical forms.

If cinema buffs complain that television turns leftover movies into Hollywood hash by mixing in liberal quantities of commercials and interruptions, how will they justify Hollywood's creating the same hash, to order? Which is now the dominant medium, cinema or television? More of these half-caste creations are promised. Perhaps their flaws will finally illustrate to all concerned that the media are essentially different. As cinema, television drama is poor stuff; just as certainly, cinema fails as television drama because it lacks the merits of conciseness, of direct and precise craftsmanship, where nothing else will serve. To consider each as *sui generis* is to recognize the

merits, and shortcomings, of each. Even more, it is to admit that by confusing them one loses the virtues of both and is left with rubbish.

The formal differences between these genres begin to disappear as television extends its influence. A new sort of audience has been trained, a generation of viewers accustomed to certain technical devices and structural patterns which dominate television drama. More recently television's influence has begun to alter the rhetoric of cinema, either because producers and directors of cinema are themselves part of that great audience and succumb to a pressure they may not recognize, or because these same men *do* recognize and pander to the audience's new-found tastes. Everyone has noticed, perhaps without remarking on it, how audience reaction to a motion picture differs from that to a glowing television screen. The psychology of audience reaction is a study in itself, yet worth a brief comment here. Having paid his money and found a seat in a darkened theater, Mr. Average Cinemaddict is free to laugh or cry in general anonymity. People seated near him—all strangers—behave similarly; a great communion takes place. I laugh, you laugh, he laughs. But the same man ensconced in his favorite chair at home, in the glaring light of his living room and surrounded by his wife and kids, is reluctant to display his emotions; he feels foolish laughing alone. Understanding such a feeling, television moguls attempt to reproduce the conditions of the theater by providing accompaniment in the form of the comforting laugh track.

But this viewer's solitary reactions developed at home go with him on his next visit to a theater. He has been acclimated to technical devices and rhetorical traditions alien to cinema in its halcyon days of pre-television monopoly. To this man's mind slow dissolves from one scene to another no longer deepen mood so effectively; they presage a commercial. A transition through a gray or black screen may lose his attention completely. Witness the restless murmur that accompanies such a transition the next time you watch a feature film in a theater. Leisurely movement prevails no longer in any but the most consciously "arty" pieces.

The close-up, once reserved to give potent impact, has become such a common shot in many recent films that its virtues are lost. Within the brief span of an hour-long television drama a close-up allows the craftsman to say, "Look. This is important. Don't ignore it." He need underline a symbolic action or object only once, rather than repeating it as he might with more time available. But the fact that close-range camera work dominates TV seems little reason for its appearance in cinematic technique. *Gengis Khan* fairly screams at the viewer with close-ups of faces, spears, hands, swords, even maps and pointers: "Look. This is where we are now." I can stand a 21-inch screen full of face; thirty feet of forehead and mascaraed eyelashes overpowers unnecessarily. The influence seems clear.

Within the past half-dozen years cinema has adopted the teaser, a device essential to the peculiarities of television but worse than useless in the theater. It's not uncommon to find eight to ten minutes of plot preceding the credits on a wide screen, certainly to the detriment of the film's structural integrity. Nothing can account for such a mannerism except its accepted presence on the TV tube and the possibility of a television-trained director's having

WE HAVE A CHOICE BETWEEN, "HANG 'EM 'TILL THEY CROAK," OR "WAR OF THE HATCHET MURDERERS...."

9-17

learned his lessons too well. In a theater the audience is already "hooked," has paid, and expects to be entertained. No one would consider leaving during the initial credits; no one can switch channels. A teaser under these circumstances satisfies expectations aroused in the audience not by the nature or traditions of cinema but by hours and hours of that other medium. Cinema, once blamed for too slavishly following a three-act structure inherited from the legitimate stage, deserves no less criticism for its currently frequent and illogical turn to the teaser-four-act structure of television.

"Don't give us a filmed stage play," critics once complained. And cinema moved outdoors to frolic in scenery, settings, and mobility unavailable onstage. But the public's insatiable demand for more and more televised drama forced TV producers back to the pattern of a small cast and few sets. Economics demands it; the audience accepts it, perhaps even considering it a new convention. But—once more—what law requires that cinema play follow-the-leader? *The Apartment* employs such a pattern. Only the opening sequence of a football game saves *The Fortune Cookie* from deserving the same criticism. The new traditions of television seem to sanction a return to theatrical patterns once happily discarded. For cinema it's a step backward, but one that offers an out to film producers: an audience which accepts filmed stage plays is also obviously more willing to accept talky drama, the too-frequently exercised option of repeating a pattern from the Greek theater—action offstage discussed onstage. Second-rate cinema runs the risk of becoming third-rate television by falling back on dialogue in place of action.

Let each do what it can do best. If TV deserves any attack in this circular mass of confusion, it is not because it too nearly approaches cinema but because it returns to formulas of the stage which film should long ago have overthrown. More, it leads cinema down the same garden path.

The influence of television, then, is pervasive, affecting certainly movies, if not *the film*—that common distinction of the culturati. Let me suggest, finally, that even *the film* benefits from the fact of television's very existence. Hollywood's self-congratulation for cinema's new maturity is misdirected praise. "Adult films" of today would have given the censors apoplexy not too long ago. Honesty is rampant. Illicit love affairs in vivid detail, frank language, visible brutality—all mark the new maturity. But it takes no cynic to suggest that all this "honesty" is also profitable. Television, as the family medium, has staked its claim on subject matter long the staple of Hollywood's output. I can see on TV more situation comedy than a normal stomach will take; Andy Hardy will never come back in a wide-screen version. Westerns abound on television. Detectives chase criminals from network to network. Film producers who expect cash customers to pay for longer versions of the same scripts misunderstand the audience and soon become agents instead of producers. Only insofar as films surpass television drama in frankness, or brutality, or "honesty" can they attract a mass audience. Whatever credit cinema claims for its honesty should be laid instead at TV's door. This is the final influence: if movies are better than ever, television made them so.

It all has to do with that net. When one recognizes that *the film* and *television* are different games, he can appreciate them both without resorting to comparisons which only cloud their differences. Let cinema play in its own backyard where television hasn't a chance to compete. And the next time you watch an hour teleplay pay attention to the net that gets in the TV playwright's way. It forces him to stretch a bit, to stay on his toes, a metaphorical exercise that might benefit all writers. A point harder won deserves more admiration. On its own court television serves up plenty of aces.

Topics for Discussion

1. Discuss the statement that "television reacts to, and thereby defines, majority opinion." What cultural and political implications does this statement have if it is true?

2. Do you agree that television is the characteristic art form of the 1970s? Peck obviously believes that films have lost their importance, and this position is in opposition to Schillaci's belief in the importance of film. Which position do you agree with? Why?

3. What does Peck mean when he says that television levels in an upward direction? Do you agree with him?

4. Do you agree that television influences the cinema? Or do you think it is the other way around? Cite specific examples to support your argument.

5. Do you agree with Peck that feature films do not come off well on television? Have you seen a movie in a theater and then later seen it on television? What were the differences? Which way did you enjoy the movie more?

6. How can movies be "coterie pieces"?

7. Television regularly shows made-for-television "movies." Are these really movies or are they just long television programs? Could such a movie succeed in a movie theater?

8. Peck says that cinema is an open-ended form while television has stricter, more clearly prescribed restrictions. Yet Peck also maintains that "if movies are better than ever, television made them so." Discuss this observation in relation to specific movies and television programs.

9. Is Peck antitelevision? What does he think about the value of television? Is television worth watching?

Rhetorical Considerations

1. What is the thesis of this essay? Is it stated anywhere?

2. Does Peck's analogy of the tennis net clearly convey his meaning? Is the tennis analogy just a gimmick or does it really help clarify his point?

3. Examine the vocabulary in the essay. List all the slang and colloquial words as well as the more formal. What effect does this create?

4. The first sentence of the second paragraph begins with the pronoun "it." Is this a good beginning for the first sentence of a paragraph? Is this particular sentence a good sentence for the beginning of a paragraph?

5. Is the long description of what it takes to write a television script necessary? Could it be shortened and still be effective?

How Much Truth Does "The FBI" Tell about the FBI?

DAVID W. RINTELS

It is our hope to convey to you our heartfelt belief that there are two related issues which fall within the scope of these hearings and which demand your most urgent attention.

First, the right of the men and women who write for television to deal in ideas and truths and realities free from the repressive censorship and program practices under which we do, in fact, write.

Second, the right of the American people to be exposed to something more than an endless cycle of programs that mislead them and distort the realities of what is happening in America today.

That these two issues are related and of grave concern to all of us should be clearly demonstrated by the following statistics taken from a recent poll of our Guild. Of all who responded:

Eighty-six (86) per cent have found, from *personal* experience, that censorship exists in television. Many state, further, that they have never written a script, no matter how innocent, that has not been censored.

Eighty-one (81) per cent believe that television is presenting a distorted picture of what is happening in this country today—politically, economically and racially.

Only eight (8) per cent believe that current television programing is "in the public interest,

convenience and necessity," as required by The Federal Communications Act of 1934.

Because these figures suggest strongly our conviction that the American people are being badly served by the television industry's use of the airwaves which they, the American people, own, it is proper to inquire as to the causes of these abuses. We approach this inquiry not, we hasten to add, in any spirit that all television must be educational or instructive or elevating, but rather from the following basis: Even granting for the moment the questionable argument advanced by those who control television, that because so many of the American people are willing to settle for non-stop lowest-common-denominator programing, television must be doing something right, must it then follow that virtually 100 per cent of all network dramatic and comedy programing must be aimed at the lowest aspirations of this audience virtually 100 per cent of the time, even to the point of disregarding any reasonable standards of balance, quality and reality? Must anything which does not amuse and titillate the majority be censored out, as it is in fact, as we shall document?

This is where we wish to join the battle and to enlist your support, over the question of whether current television programing and censorship practices and the inevitable resulting product are in the public interest, as the law requires. We believe emphatically that they are not, and that while we are the first victims of these practices, the ultimate victims are the American people.

The situation in television today—how serious is it? How well does television fulfill its legal and moral obligations to serve the public interest?

First, it must be understood how all-pervasive television has become in America. More than 95 per cent of all homes are equipped with television, a substantially larger number than have indoor plumbing. A quarter of all homes have more than one set. The average home has its television on an astounding 6.43 hours a day. At any given time between 8 and 11 P.M. not less than 75,000,000 people are watching television, with 90 per cent of them tuned to one of the three networks.

The people who control television use these figures to demonstrate their wide audience acceptance and to document their positive contributions to American life: Such love and devotion must have been earned.

We look at these same figures and are horrified because we know, first-hand, that 75,000,000 people are nightly being fed programs deliberately designed to have no resemblance at all to reality, nonsense whose only purpose is to sell snake-oil and laxatives and underarm deodorants. We know this but apparently the 75,000,000 do not. This is what is so tragic: people believe what they are being told.

"Carroll O'Connor (of 'All in the Family') is baffled by some letters which show people take TV so seriously they evidently feel the Bunkers are a real family. Some ask why he treats his wife as he does; one man called him a big, dumb S-O-B for so doing; another wrote asking why he didn't leave his wife because she was such a dumbbell!"

—VARIETY.

"Forty per cent of the poor

black children and 30 per cent of the poor white children (compared with 15 per cent of the middle-class white youngsters) were ardent believers in the true-to-life nature of the television content."

—Dr. BRADLEY S. GREENBERG, Michigan State University, reporting on his study of violence to the Kerner Commission.

With such enormous influence comes enormous power, and with such power should come—must come, in the public interest—responsibility. We agree wholeheartedly with industry spokesmen who say that television has a responsibility to entertain. But we also believe that television has a responsibility not to present one narrow view as the whole truth. A responsibility not to shy away from reality, from issues, from controversy, from substance, from public discussion of all matters in the public interest.

Yet it is our contention that in prime-time entertainment television, which most of the people watch most of the time and which has by far the largest impact of all television, these responsibilities are being shirked, willfully and totally.

From thousands of examples consider the following:

My collaborator and I interested a producer in doing a script about a magazine photographer in Vietnam who was shooting a picture essay on 18-year-olds going into their first combat. The photographer, a man who likes to incite action as much as to observe it, follows one especially cocky boy until he comes face to face with a guerrilla and then takes a picture showing terror in the boy's eyes. The boy acts

bravely; he just looks afraid.

On the next patrol the boy, who has been shown the pictures of himself by the photographer with the result that he now begins to question his own bravery, anxiously looks around to see where the photographer is and whether he is taking more damning photos. He turns once too often and is killed.

The producer liked the story well enough—a character study that would allow us to say something about truth and bravery, he kindly called it—to forward it to the network for its required approval. The network liked the story, too. They wanted only one change. Vietnam is controversial, you know.

My collaborator, wise in the ways of television, felt his heart sink. If they wanted the story moved to Korea, or Germany during World War II, the usual gambits, we were prepared to make a fight of it.

No, not at all. Keep the story fresh and contemporary by all means. Keep it in the present. Just change the locale to Spain, make it a bullfight instead of a war, and make the soldier into a matador. That way, when the bull charges, the matador can look to see whether the photographer is taking more pictures and . . .

Last year John Block was story editor on an ABC-Paramount Studios series called "The Young Lawyers." He wrote a script in which the white male Young Lawyer was to be shown having a drink in a public place with the black female Young Lawyer. Just drinking and talking, with perfect and total innocence. Six times the producer, acting under the explicit direction of the Paramount Studios censor

and network liaison man, Henry Colman, requested that the black girl be rewritten into a white girl; six times Bloch refused. Finally he was promised that the change would not be made. His option was not picked up by the studio and, after he was let go, the film was shot—with a white girl playing the part.

Norman Felton, executive producer of "Dr. Kildare," writes: "On one occasion, despite backing from the American Medical Association, the National Educational Association and the Surgeon General of the United States (who eventually sent a telegram to the network endorsing the project) we were not allowed to present a film concerned with venereal disease. It was developed with scrupulous attention to good taste. The advisers, as above, pointed out that people watched a program like 'Dr. Kildare' more than documentaries, and it would be of great benefit to the people of America for the film to be made and shown. The network, however, was afraid of 'offending.'"

Robert Collins, an established writer, tells of how he was asked three times to write episodes of "The Senator," deservedly called the boldest and best dramatic series on recent television:

"The theme of the first story I submitted was the question of possible amnesty for draft evaders. The producer refused the story on the grounds that advocacy of amnesty was not the consensus of the country and was therefore unacceptable.

"The second show I proposed concerned itself with the question of whether a homosexual in government was, by the fact of his homosexuality, a possible security risk. The producer was willing in this case—but because the treatment of the homosexual in my story was sympathetic and he was portrayed as neither nance nor psychopath, and I refused to treat him as such, the network refused the story.

"The third story I proposed, again with the producer's approval, dealt with the Pentagon's storage of nerve gas near an urban area. A one-line memo from Jean Messerschmitt of NBC to the producer said simply that this story was unacceptable to the network. She gave no reason, but the producer told me he had heard the subject would offend sponsors who had dealings with the Pentagon. I don't know about that; I do know that NBC is RCA, and RCA is one of the biggest defense contractors."

Norman Felton, again concerning his experiences as executive producer of "Dr. Kildare":

"We once did a script on 'Kildare' called 'Holiday Weekend.' A doctor had told us that holiday weekends were the worst time in a hospital due to auto crashes. We thought it would be a public service to make a show about this, dramatizing—painfully—the need for safer and saner driving, and put it on the air the Thursday before the Labor Day weekend. NBC fought us, long and bitterly, before finally giving in, on the grounds that we were an entertainment show and what, please, was entertaining about auto crashes?"

Writers by the dozens report that they have written characters who are black and have seen them changed to white; they have proposed shows about South African apartheid, Viet-nam, old folks, mental disease, politics, business, labor, students, and minorities; and they have been chased out of studios.

This year, one year after "The Senator" was canceled, ABC and Universal Studios did a show starring Anthony Quinn called "The Man and the City." Producer Stanley Rubin says: "Although the format cried out for relevancy, we were flatly forbidden to make a relevant show. On a series about a contemporary Mexican-American Mayor of a south-western city, no stories about the poor, about the old, radicals, Chicanos, Blacks—the whole field of urban life was, expressly and by fiat, forbidden."

Says Rubin, "I wanted to do one show about the refusal of a father to accept a posthumous medal for his son, killed in Vietnam. The issue of the war was background to the plot, which concerned the man and not the war. The network turned this story down. ABC does not recognize war."

There are thousands of other stories ranging from the ridiculous—as when Adrian Samish, who supervises all scripts for QM Productions, which is responsible for "The Fugitive," "The FBI," "Cannon," etc., objected to a political reference in a script of mine by slamming his fist on my desk and telling me, "We hired you to write scripts, goddam it, not to put your ideas in them"—to the marvelously sublime, as when the producer of the series "My Favorite Martian" required a writer to change a line on the grounds that "A Martian would never talk like that."

The list is so long that it is impossible to believe for one moment that these are isolated instances, temporary aberrations, foolishness on the part of a few myopic individuals. On the contrary, these instances are symptomatic of the rigorous and final institutionalization of censorship and thought control on television.

Let us now look at one whole series: ABC's "The FBI."

The "FBI" series, about to go into its eighth successful year under the official imprimatur of J. Edgar Hoover and the Federal Bureau of Investigation, formerly claimed that its programs were based on real FBI cases, when they frequently were not, and even now claims that its programs are "inspired" by real FBI cases, which they frequently are not; that although the names and places are fictitious, everything you see on the air happened and they have even broadcast official-looking file numbers on the air to prove it.

And, if this isn't enough, a narrator begins each program by announcing the exact date on which the crime was committed and ends each program by announcing, documentary-style, the Federal prison terms meted out by Federal courts to the criminals. They then show you the great seal of the FBI and thank the Bureau and Mr. Hoover for their cooperation. They strongly imply, in short, that they are telling you the truth about what the FBI does. The facts suggest something very different.

For example, I was offered a job writing on the series; when I asked them which case they wanted me to adapt, they told me to come up with a story of my own invention—no case needed. Other writers, including the president of the television branch of the Writers Guild of America, have had the same experience.

It doesn't always work this way. Sometimes the producers invent and write out, with the cooperation of the resident FBI agent assigned to the series, one-page "notions" which they then assign to writers; sometimes the shows are in fact based on real cases. But in many cases the story is not only not "based on" or "inspired by" real FBI cases, it is invented solely by the writer and/or producer, and inevitably the story details are fabricated from beginning to end. As William Randolph Hearst cabled the artist Frederic Remington in 1898 before hostilities broke out between the United States and Spain over Cuba, "You provide the pictures, I'll provide the war."

For a second example, I was asked to write another episode of "The FBI" on a subject of my choice, at about the time, five or six years ago, when four little black girls were killed by a bomb in a Birmingham church. It had been announced that the FBI was involving itself in the case and I told the producer I wanted to write a fictionalized account of it.

The producer checked with the sponsor, the Ford Motor Company, and with the FBI—every proposed show is cleared sequentially through the producing company, QM; the Federal Bureau of Investigation; the network, ABC; and the sponsor, Ford, and any of the four can veto any show for any reason, which it need not disclose—and reported back that they would be delighted to have me write about a church bombing subject only to these stipulations: The church must be in the North, there could be no Negroes involved, and the bombing could have nothing at all to do with civil rights.

After I said I wouldn't write

that program, I asked if I could do a show on police brutality, also in the news at that time. Certainly, the answer came back, as long as the charge was trumped up, the policeman vindicated, and the man who brought the specious charge prosecuted.

For a third example, and to lend credence to the second, in the seven years in which the series has been on the air, years of great change racially in this country, change in which the FBI has been centrally involved, the producers have never—not once—done a program about any aspect of the violation of the civil rights of a minority. There is dramatic material for a thousand shows in this area, and the writers would not, for a change, have to invent the details; scores of writers have asked if they could write about civil rights and each has been turned down. If you want to do a kidnapping, great; Communist espionage, wonderful; organized crime, marvelous; civil rights, never.

Fourth example: On the series no FBI agent has ever bugged a house or tapped a phone or hired a paid informant. And no writer is ever allowed to suggest that these stratagems are ever employed, or indeed that they exist. They may be invaluable to police work and the FBI certainly employs them, the argument goes, but they're bad public relations. The public can be spared these truths.

Fifth example: Should a writer want to write, say, about violations of antitrust law, he is told to go elsewhere. In seven years not one episode of "The FBI" has been allowed on this subject. The trouble is, of course, there is no other place for the writer to go in television—no

other series will touch this subject, either—so no writer can write about it on television, and nobody who depends on television for his knowledge of the world will ever know that crime in the real world is sometimes committed by respectable white-collar types.

Street crime and organized-gang crime and law-and-order crime exist because they are staples of dramatic television. Anti-trust crime does not exist, in effect, because television says it does not exist, any more than do violations of minority rights. The FBI in Washington, of course, does know that these crimes happen because it is charged with investigating them—in fact, if not on television.

There are other misrepresentations made to the American people by this purportedly realistic series. Although the director of the FBI, Mr. Hoover, has said publicly that the Cosa Nostra exists, the series chooses to call it The Organization, a criminal syndicate whose chief visible trait is that its membership is comprised of a lot of non-Italians named Smith keeping up with a lot of folks named Jones; again, although the FBI explicitly teaches its agents never to shoot except to kill, on the series nobody has been killed for years now—wounded by the carload, certainly, but never killed.

There is other, sadder evidence of the series' refusal to deal with the real world or even to acknowledge its existence. In seven years on the air, not one woman has ever been hired to write an episode, nor has any black, despite the fact that on one occasion a white writer with four credits on the series recommended a black writer and said that he would rewrite the script for free if the black writer's script was not up to par; and, a matter which will concern the members of this Subcommittee on Constitutional Rights as much as it does us, namely that the producers acknowledge privately what has long been an open secret in the industry—that all actors and writers and directors are screened by the Federal Bureau of Investigation in Washington and only those who are "politically acceptable" to the FBI are hired to work on the show.

But by now the message should be clear. The American people are being force-fed a dishonest picture of the work of a Government agency and any writer who attempts to portray the real world, suggesting that white-collar or business crime exists or that crimes against peoples' rights are as much a source of national concern as crimes against their persons, is simply not allowed to do so.

Will Marcus Welby Always Make You Well?

David Rintels

The writer has no more freedom to deviate from the official line in any *series in television: Take the omnipresent medical shows as a group—"Marcus Welby, M.D." on ABC; "Medical Center" on CBS; "The Doctors" segment of "The Bold Ones" on NBC. Anybody who watches these programs must of necessity believe the following about American medicine:*

No patient is ever denied a hospital bed or required to wait

until one is available.

No doctor ever charges for his services; no hospital ever bills a patient; no one ever has to go on charity, or do without care.

Almost every doctor cures almost every patient—if only the patient lets him. Occasionally someone does die, more likely out of boredom or pique than of the medical profession's inability to cure him; he's usually 107 when he goes.

The American Medical Association doesn't exist, and of course doesn't lobby. There's no need for it, to be sure, because no one on television ever suggests that we need more and better doctors, more and better hospitals, more and better medical schools, lower-cost health care or, heaven help us, national health insurance.

The one man with more experience than any other in producing medical shows for television, Norman Felton, has been responsible for "Dr. Kildare," "The Eleventh Hour," and "The Psychiatrist." Felton says:

"Television does not reflect truth. On the 'Dr. Kildare' series we were asked by NBC to get the approval and seal of the A.M.A. This meant that we submitted scripts for approval to the A.M.A. Although the organization gave us technical help, it goes without saying that we did not present an accurate picture of the practice of medicine, or the difficulties many people had in obtaining adequate medical care. . .

"The network's censorship extended from preventing us from tackling whole subjects to a myriad of smaller items, such as making us take out any reference to 'breast' or use of the word in a film concerned with mastectomy. Control of ideas exists down to the present in series such as 'Marcus

Welby, M.D.' and 'Medical Center.' "

At least two Senators on this Subcommittee—Senator Kennedy and Senator Scott—have strong feelings about the cost and availability of health care in this country; they stand up here, in one of the two most influential forums in the country, and they say so. It's their right, not to say their obligation. Many writers agree with them. Those who do are absolutely prohibited from standing up in the other most influential forum and suggesting that American medicine could be improved, its costs reduced, its scope expanded. Your work is more difficult because our television doctors are all heroes and above mistakes or the need for help or improvement. They're doing fine, their patients are all in splendid shape at the end of the hour, and the viewer is content—what could possibly be wrong with American health care?

The consequences of this shallow one-sidedness are tragic. No debate ensues, no national awareness of a problem which some of you and some of us believe may have reached crisis proportions. Personally, I don't know whether there is a health crisis in America; I'd like to know. I do know that it is a gross disservice to the country to refuse to discuss whether such a crisis exists.

Here, then, is the impossible situation we as writers labor under. We want desperately to write about the subjects which interest us as writers and human beings, subjects which are not very different from those which interest you. But we cannot because the men who control television have decreed, we feel in gravest error, that these matters do not interest the public.

Cops-and-robbers interest

the public; large and happy families whose worst problem is whether Gramps will find his new set of teeth before the Saturday-night wingding at the Golden Age Home interest the public; dentists with chimpanzees and priests who solve crimes and lawyers who invariably defend minority-group children without fee and never lose a case—these interest the public.

But life and truth do not interest the public and cannot be written about except in rare instances when we are allowed to explore controversial themes, and then only under the most rigidly controlled conditions and only under the expressed condition that we still "play it safe."

It is our contention that this is one of the basest and most virulent forms of censorship imaginable, that there are substantial First Amendment questions here, and that there is, as a consequence, an immediate need to examine the enormous gap between what the law requires—namely, that television program in the public interest—and the television industry's own and self-serving interpretation of the law, namely, that it feels free to put on practically anything which will attract a sufficient audience.

The broadcasters have rewritten the definition of "the public interest" as follows:

"Robert Sarnoff, in a speech while he was still chairman of corporate NBC (he has since become chairman of the parent RCA Corporation), once ventured a definition. He said the public interest was what the public was interested in. It was patently a definition to justify broadcasting's excesses in commercial entertainment. A young child may be *interested* in lighting matches and an older one in experimenting with drugs, but any parent knows that neither is in their best interest."
—Les Brown in "Television: The Business Behind the Box."

". . . a program in which a large part of the audience is interested is by that very fact . . . in the public interest."
—Dr. Frank Stanton, then president, now vice-chairman of the board of CBS, 1970.

"I believe that he [Stanton] despaired of the broadcast schedule about 1960; thereafter he did not bother to watch much of it except for news and special programs."
—Fred Friendly, former president, CBS News, now with the Ford Foundation, in "Due to Circumstances Beyond Our Control."

We do not have to watch, either; but we do write for it and under arbitrary and restrictive conditions imposed upon no other people in this country. We cannot explore, we cannot discuss, we cannot criticize. Lawyers and police and teachers and clergy all have the right to discuss their professions and criticize where they feel criticism is merited. We can only praise. The NBC Radio and Television Broadcast Standards and Practices Book, Page 8, Paragraph 1, reads:

"Respect for lawyers, police, teachers and clergy should not be diminished by undue and unnecessary emphasis on unfavorable aspects of members of these professions."

The Standards and Practices books do not spell out the many other restrictions under which we labor. Of course, they do not have to. We all know what the rules are by now and we know how to obey them if we hope to survive.

These unwritten rules, which were born out of the union between Television and Business and any parent knows that neither is in their best interest."

which limit so drastically our right to speak and your right to hear, were carved in granite long before 1959. But never have they been better expressed than in a memo of that year, when Hubbell Robinson was in charge of all programming for CBS Television. The following is a letter he received from the general manager for radio and television of a major advertising agency:

"We know that your series is striving mightily to do things that are different and outstanding so that as a series it will rise above the general level of TV drama. This is fine, but since the series is a vehicle for commercial advertisers, it must also be extremely sensitive to utilizing anything, however dramatic, however different, however well done, if this will offend viewers.

"You know that we can never lose sight of the fact that the sole purpose for which an advertiser spends money is to win friends and influence people. Anything that he might do, however meritorious in one direction, that makes enemies is a bad action and is to be assiduously avoided.

"As long as this series wishes commercial sponsorship, all of the creative people associated therewith must never forget that not to offend people must be an inviolate rule for guiding their operation. Narrow, prejudiced, ignorant, or what you will, though any part of the population may be, as a commercial vehicle the series must be ever alert not to alienate its viewers.

"I think you can gather that from the sponsor's point of view this matter is serious. We would like to hope that as a result of this second major flareup in one season you are taking such steps as may be necessary to insure that no future program in this series violates the public concept of what is right."

—Robinson, Introduction to "Electronic Drama," by Averson and White.

Dollars, ratings, sponsors, affiliates, networks—the whole economic base of television has been so thoroughly documented that it requires no elaboration here. Suffice to say that in the same year Robinson received that letter Walter Lippmann wrote, "While television is supposed to be 'free,' it has in fact become the creature, the servant and indeed the prostitute of merchandising."

What is in the sponsor's interest is clear. What is in the network's interest is also clear. We only get into difficulties when we ask, as the law invites us to, what is in the public interest?

Realistically and unsurprisingly, every writer who wants to make a living knows what the rules are; learning is the beginning of survival. As a consequence, censorship invariably and unhappily begins, like charity, at home. The unwritten rules are so well known that it is a recklessly brave and probably independently wealthy writer who attempts to buck The System in an attempt to get anything of substance on the air. The majority of writers who hope to sell know enough to come in with safe ideas.

If they do not, the network quickly tells them.

Writes William Froug: "During the two years I served as an executive producer at CBS-TV it was repeatedly made clear to me that the network was in the business of 'pure entertainment,' that nothing of a controversial, provocative or disturbing nature was to be permitted in programing.

"The philosophy, often explicitly expressed, always implicit in the day-to-day operations, was to provide the greatest number of people with the least offensive material. As noted writer Walter Brown Newman, author of the original 'Gunsmoke' script in radio from which the series originated, stated it to me: 'In television the writer's job is to write about nothing.'"

But if a writer screws up his courage and mortgages his house, he can try. Many do. They can go in and meet a producer with a story they want to do. With what prospects? What is the producer's function? Writes Froug:

"As the producer of many television series ('Twilight Zone,' 'Mr. Novak,' 'Playhouse 90,' 'Alcoa-Goodyear Theater,' 'Bewitched,' 'Dick Powell Theater,' etc.) it was a correlative of the work that a precise form of pre-censorship and self-censorship be exercised at all times. That is to say that my function was to discourage writers from thinking in areas which the networks would find too 'sensitive.'"

Froug never was given a written copy of the unwritten rules, either. He never had to be: "The rules existed and to my best knowledge still exist. They were the topic of many meetings with network officials and it was rarely necessary that they be written down. Everyone always clearly understood everyone else when it came to what could and what could not be dramatized on television. There was no chance for misunderstanding for, if a submitted story violated any of the precepts . . . it was quickly returned with a phone call to the effect that such-and-such could not be approved unless the offensive material were deleted."

Even writers who should know better censor themselves and each other when they get into positions of responsibility as producers and executives. Two weeks ago a writer-producer who serves on the Censorship Committee of the Writers Guild told another writer that he would not buy a script about the practice of some otherwise reputable drug companies which manufacture excess amphetamines for the illicit market on the grounds that, although the problem was factual and serious, "You can't get away with taking on a drug company on television and you know it." In other words, you can attack dope-pushers on television only up to the point where they become a vested interest; and then you must stop.

If the fact is that we do admittedly censor ourselves, if only to prevent the networks from doing it to us, why are we here criticizing The System and the networks?

The answer is that the network is to blame because it sets a climate, a tone, a standard which requires us to write only the material it will put on. The tone is set when they schedule only action-adventure melodramas and situation comedies and variety shows to write for; it grows through the meetings at which they expound the unwritten rules; and it reaches full flower when they hunt through our scripts looking for words and ideas and dreams to delete.

Does anyone believe for a moment that if the networks actively sought creativity, ideas, provocative themes handled with conviction, that if they encouraged writers to use logic and reason and emotion and truth in our scripts instead of three shootouts, two auto crashes and a karate chop on the neck, we would not jump at the chance?

They say they are an entertainment medium although the law says they must program in the public interest. They say they are an entertainment medium and then define entertainment to rule out the actions and passions of our time. They allow laughter but not tears, fantasy but not reality, escapism but not truth. Television chooses almost never to stretch its boundaries to include serious drama, or indeed any drama that is not melodrama; chooses not to allow points of view not "safe," not its own; chooses not to include art or music or literature in its giddy chase after what it considers entertainment.

We *want* to entertain; writers don't want to bore anyone any more than executives do. But why cannot entertainment be truthful? Free from distortion? Why cannot television ever reflect the real world? Why must it always be that television brings you a detective in a wheelchair and that is a success so next they bring you an insurance investigator who is blind and that is a success with the result that now ABC is trying to put together a new show about—I wouldn't kid about this—a sheriff in the Old West with a stiff trigger finger.

In the public interest, presumably.

Earlier we said we would challenge the whole premise that a clear majority of the people want this kind of programing and the corollary to that premise, which has become the credo and raison d'être and justification of the television industry, that the people will watch no other kind. I hate, personally, being held in such base contempt by the television industry, and I don't believe them.

When "The Senator" was on, so briefly, it had an average 29 rating share for the year, which trans-

lates into imprecise millions but means that 29 out of each 100 television sets were tuned to a show of significant content. On occasion "The Senator" went over a 35 share, meaning that more than one-third of the national audience was watching this show. Or viewed another way, probably more people watched one episode of "The Senator" on television than have seen, live in theaters, all the plays of Shakespeare produced in every language in every country of the world since they were written.

Does this not suggest that we are smarter, more aware, more eager to be informed and involved in the world around us than these men who program shows in such disregard for us can know or will admit? And isn't it vitally important to ask the question raised by former Senator William Benton, as cited by Commissioner Nicholas Johnson of the Federal Communications Commission in his book, "How To Talk Back To Your Television Set":

"I can only ask, if this alleged 'wasteland' is indeed what the American people want, is it *all* they want of television? . . . Is it all they are entitled to? . . . Are not . . . these dwellers of the wasteland . . . the same Americans who have taxed themselves to create a vast educational system. . . . Are they not the same who have established an admirable system of justice, created a network of churches. . . . When they turn their TV knobs, do they not by the millions have interests broader than the entertainment which is so complacently theirs? . . . I think the American people should expect that the greatest single instrument of human communication ever developed must make its due contribution to human security and human advancement. . . . A high common

denominator distinguishes our people—as well as a low one—and both denominators apply to the same men, women and youngsters. Television has crystallized into the low road . . ."

There is still another collateral question which must be asked. Is television really giving us what we want, as its spokesmen claim, or has it, rather, simply conditioned us to accept and even appreciate, like Pavlov's dogs, what it programs for us? We can never truly know the price we have paid and continue to pay, individually and as a nation, for television's conditioning of us and our expectations. Like babies who have been fed nothing but Pablum, our taste has been dulled to the point that dry martinis and thick steaks taste somehow wrong.

It does not have to be this way. In Elizabethan England, the popular theater of the day—their equivalent of our television—was Shakespeare and Marlowe. From the royalty in the galleries to the common people in the pits, it was what they got and it became what they wanted—or perhaps it was the other way 'round. We have not progressed culturally quite as far as we think in three-and-a-half centuries. Television is partly the evidence of this, and I suspect also partly the cause.

And yet, when they give us the few chances we get to see quality programing, as often as not we do respond. Dramatic subjects, provocative themes provocatively handled—these draw enormous audiences. Norman Lear is here to testify to that as producer of "All in the Family"—and also to the three years of difficulty he had in getting the series on the air.

The director of sales and marketing for Time-Life Films, Wynn Nathan, further substantiates the case for quality programing in a publication of the Broadcast Information Bureau, Inc. He writes:

"I have talked about 'quality' and specialized programs as though I assumed they would get poor ratings. And perhaps I have fallen into a trap I suggested the program makers have fallen into. Actually, when supposedly specialized programs have been tried in prime time lately, they have often done surprisingly well in the ratings. One good example was 'The Six Wives of Henry VIII,' a BBC-TV produced series of six 90-minute plays—quite specialized in that it was about English history and was serious drama. Television programing for only a special highbrow audience, it seemed.

"While it was plainly quality programing, 'Henry VIII' was not a safe programing idea for prime time. Here's what happened when it played: It increased CBS's audience for the time period 10 per cent over the previous four weeks, getting a 25 per cent share of the national audience; and in the key markets of Los Angeles and New York it consistently beat network A's movie in the ratings—by large margins."

So the public is truly interested in programs truly in the public interest. We can be delighted that CBS showed this series, even though someone else produced it. Still, why cannot CBS produce good television? Why did CBS, like NBC and ABC, reject the prize-winning British series "Civilisation," hosted by Sir Kenneth Clark, when it was offered to them, and let PBS—Educational Television—carry it?

It's a disgrace and a scandal but it's also something worse, a source of national sadness and concern for all of us that American television imports "Civilisation," "The Six Wives of Henry VIII" and "The Forsyte Saga," while American television exports "The Beverly Hillbillies," "Green Acres" and "Gilligan's Island." You are not the only ones in this country who have to worry about a Balance of Payments deficit.

And every year it gets worse.

Ours is not a new complaint. Television has long been delinquent in its responsibilities. Even its most ardent defenders concede that. What, if anything, is significant and new in our appeal?

The difference might be only that now the country seems of a mood to demand its rights, to ask for itself what it believes to be fair. There is a bright new spirit afoot which says that if air pollution is legal and institutionalized, it ought not to be. A protest must be made and must be listened to.

It is our belief that air pollution is no less a problem in television than it is in the automobile industry or a mill town or a crowded city, and that the public interest means that we can no more afford the one than the other.

The men who control television do not agree with us. But their view of the public interest was made painfully clear several years ago when, long after the Surgeon General issued his report conclusively linking cigarette smoking with cancer, they persisted in advertising cigarettes and stopped only when Congress passed a law forbidding it.

Their view of the public interest as being subservient to their private interests has not changed for the better. And now it seems clear that something must be done.

The solution could possibly lie in our hands as writers, if only our hands were untied. There is little wrong with television that could not be cured by diversity of ideas and programs, by the freedom to explore and discuss anything in this world free from the fears and strictures which dominate our business. At least it would be a beginning.

We are sometimes asked what we really want, why the end of censorship is so important to us. Sometimes the question is meant to imply that we are little boys who want to write dirty words on bathroom walls.

Nothing could be further from the truth. What we want is the freedom that everyone else in this country has and which we alone are denied—the freedom not to have to distort the truth as we see it.

We are also asked what difference it will make. Aren't we all writers of fiction anyway? Aren't illusion and fantasy our stock in trade? Here the answer is easier.

Perhaps among us there is a Zola or a Dickens, a man who can see a wrong and by his skill and zeal require us to right it.

Perhaps we can stimulate and excite the country to care about its deeper heritage, its drama and art and music and history and poetry and literature and science, all the glories which television now denies us.

But the real difference would be that whereas now we are required to foster, without critical examination, a mythology which states that a punch in the mouth solves all problems and doesn't really hurt anyone, that bullets wound without killing, that ours is a society hampered in its strivings to improve its acknowledged greatness only by the efforts of a few sinister malcontents who seek to undermine us for their own perverse purposes, instead of this mythology we could proceed to an honest evaluation of who we are and where we are headed.

Once we become aware that in real life the cavalry does not always arrive in time; that the good guys do not always win; that it must hurt deeply to be black and unemployed or to be hungry in a land of abundance; once we strip away the clichés and look at the problems, then we can make that new first step toward our great and shared goals.

We want desperately to aid in this effort, not hinder it.

A member of this Senate sees deep implications in refusing to make the necessary effort. Senator Robert Dole poses the following questions:

"Every day and every night for most of their lives your children and mine have watched [on television] the major problems of the universe solved in 30 to 60 minutes.

"Is it possible—and I throw this at you as a question, not a conclusion—is it possible part of the unrest in this country, part of the dissatisfaction with our leaders is that, as far as our children are concerned, they do not solve problems fast enough? The smog that is here today is here tomorrow. And so is the civil rights problem. And so is the war. And you name it.

"In real life problems are solved and go away very slowly. Are our children having trouble separating the immediacy of TV from the reality of life? Are they demanding more than we can ever deliver, or more than they will ever be able to deliver? Is TV creating a frustration with reality that can only be relieved by threats and demands for change, and, that failing, by violence?

"I don't know the answer but I suggest that we think about it."

We, too, have raised a great many questions here today and, like Senator Dole, we do not pretend to have all the answers. But is seems to us that the problems we have discussed are so grave and the consequences for America so great that a new attempt to examine the course of television, drawing on the nation's best minds, must now be made. We therefore hope that you will recommend creation of a Citizens Committee to Examine Television which can make the necessary study and detailed recommendations that will, hopefully, start us on the high road.

We ask partly for ourselves. Dostoevski has written, "There is one punishment so terrible that even hardened convicts tremble at the prospect, and that is simply this: to take a man's lifework and render it meaningless." But much more than for ourselves as writers, we ask for the country.

A Typical Daytime Hour

It's coming up 5 P.M. on Dec. 4 in Chicago. NBC affiliate WMAQ-TV is about to air the local news. But first . . .

One minute for a **Dennison Buttoneer** device, another for **Hav-A-Maid mops,** 30 seconds for **National Car Rentals,** 30 for **Heinz steak sauce,** then 10 for **Worth Parfums. A station identification** and, at last, the news.

Six minutes later, the pitches resume: half-a-minute each for **Osco Drug Store, Farah jeans, Fleischmann's margarine,** and **Selchow & Righter games.**

As the news hour progresses, the commercial breaks come with clutterful regularity:

5:11—**Norelco products** (30 seconds), **Tuborg Beer** (30), **Seiko Watches** (30), **Max Pax coffee** (30).

5:21—**Bahamas resorts** (1 min.), **True Value Stores** (10 sec.), **Wieboldt department store** (30), **American Greeting Cards** (30).

5:29—**Admiral color TV** (30), **Birds-Eye foods** (30), **Karoll's Men's Wear** (30), **Optigan Music Maker** (30).

5:35—**Stouffer frozen foods** (30), **Joy liquid detergent** (30), **Sears, Roebuck** (30), **Washington Park Jockey Club race track** (30).

5:45—**Oster cooker** (1 min.), **National Food Stores** (10 sec.), **Sunbeam iron** (30), **Shake 'n Bake** (30).

5:53—**Kodak cameras** (30), **Bayer aspirin** (30), **Martini & Rossi wines** (30), **Albolene face cream** (30).

5:58—**Nirvana bath massage** (1 min.), **Sears, Roebuck** (10 sec.), and a **station ID.**

Altogether, 30 different commercials, occupying 15-and-a-half minutes—not counting the two minutes and 10 seconds of plugs leading *into* the newscast.

And somewhere in there was the news.

The Age of Communication

Topics for Discussion

1. This article is taken from the testimony of David Rintels before a congressional committee. How effectively has he made his point to the committee?
2. Is television just an entertainment medium? If it isn't what is it? What do you think television should do besides entertain?
3. Is self-censorship the worst form of censorship? Why?
4. Should television be free from all censorship?
5. Can television programs deal with contemporary problems and people without becoming political and controversial?
6. If advertisers will advertise only on "safe" programs, what chance is there that television programming will reflect reality? Should advertisers have such control over what television programs are broadcast?
7. Besides "The FBI" and all the medical shows, what other television programs do you think distort reality?
8. What is your favorite television program? Why? Do you think it is based on reality?
9. Do you think television creates a frustration with reality and leads to discontent?

Rhetorical Considerations

1. This essay was written to be read aloud before a congressional committee. What elements do you find in the essay that indicate that it was intended to be read?
2. How much factual evidence does Rintels offer to prove that censorship does exist in television? Are his facts relevant?
3. What is the effect of concluding this essay with a quotation from Dostoevski?
4. Rintels is a professional writer. How well organized, written, and presented is this essay?
5. Rintels' argument is quite one-sided. Why does he not give the opposing views to his arguments?

TELEVISION SHOWS AND ROCK MUSIC

Carl Belz

In 1954, an unknown singer named Joan Weber appeared in a CBS television drama and sang a song called "Let Me Go, Lover." The show was part of the *Studio One* series, and its story dealt with a disk jockey. The song had existed in a different version entitled "Let Me Go, Devil," and a record of it had been issued about a year before. Joan Weber's recording of "Let Me Go, Lover" had appeared several weeks before its television exposure, and it had stimulated very little activity in terms of Pop sales. In fact, *Billboard* had given it a "60" rating, thereby predicting that it would enjoy only limited popularity. On the day after the television show, however, the record suddenly began to sell. It literally became an overnight sensation; it reached the top of the Pop charts, and it was covered by numerous Pop vocalists, including Peggy Lee, Patti Page, Teresa Brewer, and Sunny Gale.

Joan Weber never issued another hit record, but "Let Me Go, Lover" remained as a stunning example of the promotion power of the television medium. The same power also turned Tommy Sands's "Teenage Crush" into an overnight success after he appeared on NBC's *Kraft Theater* in February, 1957. Because of incidents like these, major networks and individual producers realized that there was a place for popular music and for rock music on TV. Yet, finding that place has proved to be a tricky enterprise because it has necessitated an understanding of both the television medium and the music. For popular singers—Perry Como, Dean Martin or Andy Williams, for instance—this problem has not been too acute. Their pleasing brand of entertainment has continually satisfied the tastes of the larger television audience. Each of these artists has starred in weekly or special variety shows, and each possesses a large, faithful audience. In other words, the commercial appeal of popular music has remained generally predictable. But television shows devoted to rock have been more problematic in terms of their commercial appeal. Rock programs have quickly originated and just as quickly disappeared. Few shows have been able to sustain an interest across the nation. At the same time, this pattern helps to illuminate the character of rock and the ways in which its style has changed during the past decade.

Of all the television shows that have dealt with rock, one classic has survived: *American Bandstand*. It was first seen nationally in 1957, at the most popular weekday viewing hours for teenagers, 3 to 5 P.M. It continues today, although it is limited to one day per week and one hour, generally on Saturday afternoons. *American Bandstand* presently emanates from Hollywood, and its host is the same Dick Clark who has been associated with the show for more than ten years. However, it originated in Philadelphia at the astonishingly early date of 1952. At that time it was simply called *Bandstand*, and its master of ceremonies was Bob Horn. When its national telecasts began, the show adopted a new title, and Dick Clark became a nationally recognized personality. Before that he had been merely a Philadelphia disk jockey, and he had been with *Bandstand* about a year before its network recognition.

American Bandstand was a deceptively simple show. With Dick Clark it retained the format that it had had with Bob Horn: that is, it was a teenage dance which happened to be on television. Records were played and the audience danced, and this pattern was periodically broken by the visit of a guest performer, the formation of a panel which judged new releases, and very short interviews in which the teenagers filed past the microphone, introduced themselves, and named the schools they attended. The ingredients were few, but the program became a national success which Clark parlayed into additional shows and into an extensive personal business.

The appeal of *American Bandstand* lay in its very simplicity. The program made no positive effort to "entertain" the television audience. It existed primarily for the pleasure of the audience within the television studio, as it had since its inception. In 1952, *Bandstand* consisted of a record show in which filmed performances accompanied each song and provided visual appeal. An audience of teenagers was present in the studio, and they spontaneously began dancing when the records were played. As this phenomenon persisted, the entire show unexpectedly evolved into a dance party. Ultimately, this gave the program its meaning: It was a life situation which anyone was allowed to observe. If one viewed it often enough, one became familiar with the "regulars"—that is, the kids who attended the dance four or five days a week. One knew who was dating whom, or going steady, as well as other personal details about the individuals in the audience. The folk, in other words, were the real stars of *American Bandstand*. Of course most of them remained anonymous, but their lifelike situation was immediately accessible to the television viewer. In this type of setting, rock music unconsciously performed its function: The dance was a living drama, and, although the music generally remained in the background, it nevertheless unified the audience and provided their *raison d'être*. Instead of being transformed into popular entertainment, it was permitted to maintain its inherent folk identity.

In the passive medium of television, *American Bandstand* provided an absorbing and intimate experience to which Dick Clark's personal style was perfectly suited. Clark's manner was consistently relaxed, controlled, and quiet. Unlike his radio counterparts, he introduced records with relative casualness. In his relation to the audience, he never imposed himself on the teenagers or sought to assume their dress, vocabulary or attitudes. His image was that of an attractive older brother or father; that is, a distinguished personality who understood and sympathized with teenagers, enjoyed their music, but did not assume their way of life. Dick Clark's mild style accounted for his appeal: He receded behind the music and permitted the dancing of the teenagers to describe rock's vitality and impact.

In the 1950's, Dick Clark became an idol for teenagers and a symbol of their aspirations. Like the young man described by Chuck Berry's "Too Much Monkey Business," Dick Clark married, bought a home, settled down, and wrote a book. Later he was divorced, and in 1959 and 1960 his name became unfavorably connected with the payola hearings. They publicly revealed the extraordinary breadth of Clark's commercial enterprises and showed that he was a super-entrepreneur as well as a mild-mannered disk jockey. His distinctiveness, however, has resided in his ability to balance these different roles against one another without sacrificing the rewards of either. He still conducts *American Bandstand*, for instance, although his presence on the show constitutes a tradition more than it provides a relevant insight into current television rock shows. Clark's other program, *Where The Action Is*, reflected more clearly his image during the 1960's. He rarely appeared in the half-hour show, not because its structure could not accommodate him, but because he probably realized that his style was not as meaningful to teenagers in 1967 as it had been a decade earlier.

The significance of Clark's *American Bandstand* becomes clearer when the program is compared to a more recent version of the same idea, the *Lloyd Thaxton Show*. It too was a televised dance for teenagers, featuring records, visits from guest stars, and brief conversations with members of the audience. But the distinctive feature of the *Lloyd Thaxton Show* lay in its stylization of elements which had arisen spontaneously in *American Bandstand*. Through various manipulations of the records and the audience, it transformed a folk situation into popular art. Thaxton, for instance, performed as an entertainer: He frequently mimed the lyrics of a record while it was being played, or feigned an organ or trumpet performance during the instrumental sections. Likewise, the audience became entertainers. A group of teenagers periodically mimed a current song in the Thaxton manner or entered a contest in which they actually sang with a record and had to continue its beat and lyrics when the song was unexpectedly halted. Dancing also became popular art instead of folk expression. Contests required dancers to hold their positions, like statues, when the music was interrupted; any subsequent movement automatically eliminated a couple from the competition. Even the non-contest dances possessed an aura of popular entertainment, as when a couple danced behind a screen on which the silhouettes of their bodies were projected, like lantern-slide reproductions of paintings. Because of these gimmicks and contests, the meaning of the *Lloyd Thaxton Show* became radically different from Dick Clark's *American Bandstand*. The show willfully molded the audience into a core of entertainers instead of allowing them to entertain unconsciously by being themselves; in addition, it showed less respect for the music, because it constantly interrupted records in order to force them into the structures of a contest. While the results were often amusing, they were neither as spontaneous nor as expressive as the events which characterized *American Bandstand*. In fact, they changed *American Bandstand* in the way that the Peppermint Lounge changed rock dancing, that RCA changed Elvis Presley, and that the Crew Cuts changed "Sh-Boom."

The thrust toward stylization and popular art typified most of the television rock shows of the 1960's. Both *Shindig* and *Hullabaloo* exemplified this tendency. *Shindig* originated in 1964 and lasted about one year; *Hullabaloo* quickly followed *Shindig* but survived into 1966, largely because it gradually broadened its format to include artists who were popular with adult audiences. *Shindig* performers had been more exclusively teen-oriented. Both programs initially generated an enthusiastic response within the television audience, but the response was not sustained, probably because the programs ignored the life context of *American Bandstand* and created a variety-show atmosphere instead. The programs invariably consisted of appearances by currently popular groups and individuals who performed their hit records. As they did, they were accompanied by a troop of professional dancers who did the Jerk, the Monkey, or whichever dance was best known at the time. Although these dancers performed with extraordinary enthusiasm this did not conceal their resemblance to popular art chorus lines. That is, they standardized dances and made them academic, retaining only a superficial appearance of folk excitement and involvement. Moreover, the presence of famous artists did not insure the programs' commercial success. Although a keen excitement accompanied the first appearance of a particular group or individual, this response dissipated when the audience became familiar with the new faces. The decline in interest was accentuated by the fact that neither show permitted viewer participation or empathy. The rock artists and music were merely projected at the television audience in an entertainment package that excluded the viewer's world of experience. Both *Shindig* and *Hullabaloo* failed to grasp the essential folk function of the rock music they promoted. They took their inspiration from television variety shows like Ed Sullivan's. While perennially helping to popularize rock among adult audiences, however, Ed Sullivan has always maintained a balance between rock and other kinds of entertainment. *Shindig* and *Hulla-baloo* never achieved this balance. In following the variety show format, moreover, they overlooked the crucial connections between rock and the life situations from which it originates and in terms of which it ultimately has meaning.

Several television shows of the late sixties attempted to present rock music in a more lifelike context. *Where The Action Is* and *Malibu U.*, for instance, both made effective use of video tape, extending the television medium in a way which seemed to defy the viewer's ability to separate the actual world from the world of film reproductions. *Where The Action Is* was particularly subtle in capitalizing on this ambiguity. In many ways, the show employed the same format as *Shindig* or *Hullabaloo*: Current groups performed their hit records and were accompanied by the program's own dance troupe, the "Action Kids." Instead of the television studio, however, the out-of-doors provided the setting for each record play. The scenes varied from the beach at Santa Monica to a ski resort in the Colorado Rockies, and from the San Francisco Bay to the Boston Harbor. Within the space of one show, rock music jumped from coast to coast and border to border, and video tape transformed the whole into a disarmingly immediate experience. But *Where The Action Is* seemed to operate on the assumption that rock involves pleasure exclusively: Since, however, pleasure represents only one side of the complex meaning of rock, the show was unduly restrictive. Like *Shindig* and *Hullabaloo*, *Where The Action Is* made folk art into popular entertainment.

Malibu U. was a short-lived adaptation of *Where The Action Is*. When the show appeared in 1967, it was described as a mythical university whose courses were conducted by Ricky Nelson and other popular stars. The university and its courses ostensibly provided a life situation for the music. Actually, the show consisted of a television beach film, and its only tie with the life situation of a university lay in the introduction of such performers as "our next drop-in," and "our professor of marine biology." *Malibu U.* was simply popular art. It not only standardized the music by forcing it into the categories of college courses, but it standardized fun as well. The show was crowded with bikini-clad girls who, as they scampered through forests and across beaches, were reminiscent of stale nineteenth-century paintings by French academicians such as Bouguereau, paintings which disguised a restricting aesthetic in the cloak of a supposedly natural vitality.

Television's transformation of rock into popular art reached a climax with *The Monkees*, which survived two years of network viewing before being removed in the 1968-69 season. The program was extraordinary, however, in the overtness of its commerciality. Each element of the Monkees' style was carefully and blatantly culled from existing rock groups, particularly from the Beatles. The ingredients were welded together into an image of youthful exuberance and well-meaning rebellion. The resulting style was polished and seductive, an acme of popular art perfection. But the style appealed primarily to subteens, children between the ages of six and twelve who had never seen *American Bandstand*. For older viewers, the program was too obviously an artificial pastiche. Through many years of viewing, years which began with *American Bandstand* and culminated with *The Monkees*, the rock audience had gradually become more sophisticated.

Topics for Discussion

1. Do you think television can make a song a hit today? Why?
2. Did you watch The Monkees when they were on television? Were you interested in their music or in the stories?
3. Do you agree that the rock audience has become more sophisticated?
4. Why would some viewers consider "The Monkees" television show an obvious artificial pastiche?
5. Does popular and rock music have a role on television? What is it?

Rhetorical Considerations

1. Does Belz use any slang in his essay? Is there any attempt to demonstrate to his reader that he is "hip" or "with it"? What is the tone of the essay?
2. How much information does Belz provide? How much background is necessary to understand this essay? How effectively has Belz blended background information with the new information he is providing?
3. Examine the paragraph structure of this essay. Where does the topic occur most often? How well organized are the paragraphs?

ROCK FOR SALE

Michael Lyndon

In 1956, when rock and roll was just about a year old, Frankie Lymon, lead singer of Frankie Lymon and the Teenagers, wrote and recorded a song called "Why Do Fools Fall in Love?" It was an immediate million-selling hit and has since become a rock classic, a true golden oldie of the sweet-voiced harmonizing genre. The group followed it up with other hits, starred in a movie, appeared on the Ed Sullivan Show, toured the country with Bill Haley and the Comets, and did a tour of Europe. Frankie, a black kid from Harlem, was then 13 years old. Last year, at 26, he died of an overdose of heroin.

Despite the massive publicity accorded to rock in the past several years, Frankie's death received little attention. It got a bit more publicity than the death in a federal prison of Little Willie John, the author of "Fever," another classic, but nothing compared to that lavished on the breakup of the Cream or on Janis Joplin's split with Big Brother and the Holding Company. Nor did many connect it with the complete musical stagnation of the Doors, a group which in 1967 seemed brilliantly promising, or to the dissolution of dozens of other groups who a year or two ago were not only making beautiful music but seemed to be the vanguard of a promising "youth cultural revolution."

In fact these events are all connected, and their common denominator is hard cash. Since that wildly exciting spring of 1967, the spring of *Sgt. Pepper's Lonely Hearts Club Band,* of be-ins and love-ins and flower-power, of the discovery of psychedelia, hippies and "doing your thing"—to all of which "New Rock," as it then began to be called, was inextricably bound—one basic fact has been consistently ignored: rock is a product created, distributed and controlled for the profit of America (and international) business. "The record companies sell rock and roll records like they sell refrigerators," says Paul Kantner of the Jefferson Airplane. "They don't care about the people who make rock or what they're all about as human beings any more than they care about the people who make refrigerators."

Recently, the promoters of a sleazy Southern California enterprise known as "Teen Fair" changed its name to "Teen Expo." The purpose of the operation remains the same: to sell trash to adolescents while impressing them with the joys of consumerism. But nine years into the '60s, the backers decided that their '50s image of nice-kid teenagerism had to go. In its place, they have installed "New Rock" (with its constant companion, schlock psychedelia) as the working image of the "all new!" Teen Expo.

By the time the word gets down to the avaricious cretins who run teen fairs, everybody has the message: rock and roll sells. It doesn't make money just for the entertainment industry—the record companies, radio stations, TV networks, stereo and musical instrument manufacturers, etc.—but for law firms, clothing manufacturers, the mass media, soft drink companies and car dealers (the new Opel will "light your fire!"). Rock is the surest way to the hearts and wallets of millions of Americans between 8 and 35—the richest, most extravagant children in the history of the world.

From the start, rock has been commercial in its very essence. An American creation on the level of the hamburger or the billboard, it was never an art form that just happened to make money, nor a commercial undertaking that sometimes became art. Its art was synonymous with its business. The movies are perhaps closest to rock in their aesthetic involvement with the demands of profitability, but even they once had an arty tradition which scorned the pleasing of the masses.

Yet paradoxically it was the unabashed commerciality of rock which gave rise to the hope that it would be a "revolutionary" cultural form of expression. For one thing, the companies that produce it and reap its profits have never understood it. Ford executives drive their company's cars but Sir Joseph Lockwood, chairman of EMI, the recording company which, until Apple, released the Beatles' records, has always admitted that he doesn't like their music. The small companies like Sun and Chess Records which first discovered the early stars like Elvis Presley and Chuck Berry were run by middle-class whites who knew that kids and blacks liked this weird music, but they didn't know or really care why. As long as the music didn't offend the businessmen's sensibilities too much—they never allowed outright obscenity—and as long as it sold, they didn't care what it said. So within the commercial framework, rock has always had a certain freedom.

Moreover, rock's slavish devotion to commerciality gave it powerful aesthetic advantages. People had to like it for it to sell, so rock had to get to the things that the audience really cared about. Not only did it create a ritualized world of dances, slang, "the charts," fan magazines and "your favorite DJ coming your way" on the car radio, but it defined, reflected and glorified the listener's ordinary world. Rock fans can date their entire lives by rock; hearing a "golden oldie" can instantaneously evoke the whole flavor and detail of a summer or a romance.

When in 1963-64 the Pop Art movement said there was beauty in what had been thought to be a crass excreta of the Eisenhower Age, when the Beatles proved that shameless reveling in money could be a stone groove, and when the wistful puritanism of the protest-folk music movement came to a dead end, rock and roll, with all its unabashed carnality and worldliness, seemed a beautiful trip. Rock, the background music of growing up, was discovered as the common language of a generation. New Rock musicians could not only make the music, they could even make an aesthetic and social point by the very choice of rock as their medium.

That rock was commercial seemed only a benefit. It ensured wide distribution, the hope of a good and possibly grandiose living style, and the honesty of admitting that, yes, we are the children of affluence: don't deny it, man, dig it. As music, rock had an undeniably liberating effect; driving and sensual, it implicitly and explicitly presented an alternative to bourgeois insipidity. The freedom granted to rock by society seemed sufficient to allow its adherents to express their energies without inhibition. Rock pleasure had no pain attached; the outrageousness of Elvis' gold lamé suits and John Lennon's wildly painted Rolls Royce was a gas, a big joke on adult society. Rock was a way to beat the system, to gull grown-ups into paying you while you made faces behind their backs.

Sad but true, however, the grown-ups are having the last laugh. Rock and roll is a lovely playground, and within it kids have more power than they have anywhere else in society, but the playground's walls are carefully maintained and guarded by the corporate elite that set it up in the first place. While the White Panthers talk of "total assault upon the culture by any means necessary, including rock and roll, dope and fucking in the streets," *Billboard,* the music trade paper, announces with pride that in 1968 the record industry became a billion-dollar business.

Bob Dylan has described with a fiendish accuracy the pain of growing up in America, and millions have responded passionately to his vision. His song, "Maggie's Farm," contains the lines, "He gives me a nickel, he gives me a dime, he asks me with a grin if I'm having a good time, and he fines me every time I slam the door, oh, I ain't gonna work on Maggie's farm no more." But along with Walter Cronkite and the New York Yankees, Dylan works for one of Maggie's biggest farms, the Columbia Broadcasting System.

Mick Jagger, another adept and vitriolic social critic, used rock to sneer at "the under assistant west coast promotion man" in his seersucker suit; but London Records used this "necessary talent for every rock and roll band" to sell that particular Rolling Stones record and all their other products. For all its liberating potential, rock is doomed to a bitter impotence by its ultimate subservience to those whom it attacks.

In fact, rock, rather than being an example of how freedom can be achieved within the capitalist structure, is an example of how capitalism can, almost without a conscious effort, deceive those whom it oppresses. Rather than being liberated heroes, rock and roll stars are captives on a leash, and their plight is but a metaphor for that of all young people and black people in America. All the talk of "rock revolution," talk that is assiduously cultivated by the rock industry, is an attempt to disguise that plight.

Despite the aura of wealth that has always surrounded the rock and roll star, and which for fans justified the high prices of records and concerts, very few stars really make much money—and for all but the stars and their backup musicians, rock is just another low-paying insecure and very hard job. Legend says that wild spending sprees, drugs, and women account for the missing loot; what legend does not say is that most of the artists are paid very little for their work. The artist may receive a record royalty of 2½ percent, but the company often levies charges for studio time, promotion and advertising. It is not uncommon for the maker of a hit record to end up in debt to the company.

Not surprisingly, it is the black artists who suffer most. In his brilliant book, *Urban Blues,* Charles Keil describes in detail how the blues artist is at the mercy of the recording company. It is virtually impossible, he states, for an unknown artist to get an honest contract, but even an "honest" contract is only an inexpensive way for a company to own an artist body and soul.

A star's wealth may be not only nonexistent, but actually a fraud carefully perpetuated by the record company. Blues singer Bobby Bland's "clothes, limousine, valet, and plentiful pocket money," says Keil, "are image bolsterers from Duke Records (or perhaps a continual 'advance on royalties' that keeps him tied to the company) rather than real earnings." And even cash exploitation is not enough; Chess Records last year forced Muddy Waters to play his classic blues with a "psychedelic" band and called the humiliating record *Electric Mud.*

Until recently, only a very few stars made any real money from rock; their secret was managers shrewd to the point of unscrupulousness, who kept them under tight control. Colonel Parker molded the sexual country boy Elvis into a smooth ballad singer; Brian Epstein took four scruffy Liverpool rockers and transformed them into neatly tousled boys-next-door. "We were worried that friends might think we had sold out," John Lennon said recently, "which in a way we had."

The musicians of New Rock—most of them white, educated, and middle-class—are spared much of what their black and lower-class counterparts have suffered. One of the much touted "revolutions" New Rock has brought, in fact, has been a drastic increase in the power of the artist vis-à-vis the record company. Contracts for New Rock bands regularly include almost complete artistic control, royalties as high as 10 percent, huge cash advances, free studio time, guaranteed amounts of company-bought promotion, and in some instances control over advertising design and placement in the media.

But such bargaining is at best a futile reformism which never challenges the essential power relationship that has contaminated rock since its inception. Sales expansion still gives the companies ample profits, and they maintain all the control they really need (even the "revolutionary" group, the MC5, agreed to remove the word "motherfucker" from an album and to record "brothers and sisters" in its place). New Rock musicians lost the battle for real freedom at the very moment they signed their contracts (whatever the clauses) and entered the big-time commercial sphere.

The Doors are a prime example. Like hundreds of New Rock musicians, the four Doors are intelligent people who in the early and mid-'60s dropped out into the emerging drug and hip underground. In endless rehearsals and on stage in Sunset Strip rock clubs, they developed a distinctly eerie and stringent sound. The band laid down a dynamo drive behind dramatically handsome lead singer Jim Morrison, who, dressed in black leather and writhing in anguish, screamed demonic invitations to sensual madness. "Break on through," was the message, "yeah, break on, break on through to the other side!"

It was great rock and roll, and by June 1967, when their "Light My Fire" was a number-one hit, it had become very successful rock. More hits followed and the Doors became the first New Rock group to garner a huge following among the young teens and pre-teens who were traditionally the mass rock audience. Jim Morrison became rock's number-one sex idol and the teeny-boppers' delight. The group played bigger and bigger halls—the Hollywood Bowl, the garish Forum in Los Angeles, and finally Madison Square Garden last winter in a concert that netted the group $52,000 for one night's work.

But the hit "Light My Fire" was a chopped-up version of the original album track, and after that castration of their art for immediate mass appeal (a castration encouraged by their "hip" company, Elektra Records), the Doors died musically. Later albums were pale imitations of the first; trying desperately to recapture the impact of their early days, they played louder and Morrison lost all subtlety: at a recent Miami concert he had to display his penis to make his point.

Exhausted by touring and recording demands, the Doors now seldom play or even spend much casual time together. Their latest single hit the depths; *Cashbox* magazine, in its profit-trained wisdom said, "The team's impact is newly channeled for even more than average young teen impact." "Maybe pretty soon we'll split, just go away to an island somewhere," Morrison said recently, fatigue and frustration in his voice, "get away by ourselves and start creating again."

But the Doors have made money, enough to be up-tight about it. "When I told them about this interview," said their manager, Bill Siddons, sitting in the office of the full-time accountant who manages the group's investments (mostly land and oil), "they said, 'Don't tell him how much we make.'" But Siddons, a personable young man, did his best to defend them. The Doors, he said, could make a lot more money if they toured more often and took less care in preparing each hall they play in for the best possible lighting and sound; none of the Doors lives lavishly, and the group has plans for a foundation to give money to artists and students ("It'll help our tax picture, too"). But, he said, "You get started in rock and you get locked into the cycle of success. It's funny, the group out there on stage preaching a revolutionary message, but to get the message to people, you gotta do it the establishment way. And you know everybody acquires a taste for comfortable living."

Variations on the Doors' story are everywhere. The Cream started out in 1966 as a brilliant and influential blues-rock trio and ended, after two solid years of touring, with lead guitarist Eric Clapton on the edge of a nervous breakdown. After months of bitter fighting, Big Brother and the Holding Company split up, as did Country Joe and the Fish (who have since reorganized, with several replacements from Big Brother). The Steve Miller Band and the Quicksilver Messenger Service were given a total of $100,000 by Capitol Records; within a year neither one existed in its original form and the money had somehow disappeared.

Groups that manage to stay together are caught in endless conflicts about how to make enough money to support their art and have it heard without getting entangled in the "success cycle." The Grateful Dead, who were house and bus minstrels for Ken Kesey's acid-magical crew and who have always been deeply involved in trying to create a real hip community, have been so uncommercial as to frustrate their attempts to spread the word of their joyful vision.

"The trouble is that the Grateful Dead is a more 'heard of' band than a 'heard' band," says manager Rock Scully, "and we want people to hear us. But we won't do what the system says—make single hits, take big gigs, do the success number. The summer of '67, when all the other groups were making it, we were playing free in the park, man, trying to cool the Haight-Ashbury. So we've never had enough bread to get beyond week-to-week survival, and now we're about $50,000 in debt. We won't play bad music for the bread because we decided a long time ago that money wasn't a high enough value to sacrifice anything for. But that means that not nearly enough people have heard our music."

The Jefferson Airplane have managed to take a middle route. A few early hits, a year of heavy touring (150 dates in 1967), a series of commercials for White Levis, and the hard-nosed management of entrepreneur Bill Graham gave them a solid money-making popular base. A year ago they left Graham's management, stopped touring almost entirely, bought a huge mansion in San Francisco and devoted their time to making records (all of them excellent), giving parties, and buying expensive toys like cars and color TVs. They've gone through enormous amounts of money and are now $30,000 in debt. But they're perfectly willing to go out and play a few jobs if the creditors start to press them. They resolve the commercial question by attempting not to care about it. "What I care about," says Paul Kantner, "is what I'm doing at the time—rolling a joint, balling a chick, writing a song. Start worrying about the ultimate effect of all your action, and in the end you just have to say fuck it. Everybody in the world is getting fucked one way or another. All you can do is see that you aren't fucking them directly.

But the Airplane also profess political radicalism, and, says Kantner, "The revolution is already happening, man. All those kids dropping out, turning on—they add up." Singer Grace Slick appeared in blackface on the Smothers Brothers show and gave the Black Panther salute; in a front window of their mansion is a sign that reads, "Eldridge Cleaver Welcome Here." But Kantner said he hadn't really thought about what that meant: would he really take Cleaver in and protect him against police attack, a very likely necessity should Cleaver accept the welcome? "I don't know, man. I'd have to wait until that happened."

Cleaver would be well-advised not to choose the Airplane's mansion for his refuge. For Kantner's mushy politics—sort of a turned-on liberalism that thinks the Panthers are "groovy" but doesn't like to come to terms with the nasty American reality—are the politics of the much touted "rock revolution." They add up to a hazy belief in the power of art to change the world, presuming that the place for the revolution to begin and end is inside individual heads. The Beatles said it nicely in "Revolution": "You say that it's the institution, we-ll, you know, you better free your mind instead."

Jac Holzman, president of Elektra Records, said it in businessman's prose: "I want to make it clear," he said, "that Elektra is not the tool of anyone's revolution. We feel that the 'revolution' will be won by poetics and not by politics—that poetics will change the structure of the world. It's reached the kids and is getting to them at the best possible level."

There is no secret boardroom conspiracy to divert antisocial youthful energy into rock and thus render it harmless while making a profit for the society it is rebelling against, but the corporate system has acted in that direction with a uniformity which a conspiracy probably could not have provided. And the aware capitalists are worried about their ability to control where kids are going: "There is something a bit spooky, from a business point of view," a *Fortune* issue on youth said recently, ". . . in youth's widespread rejection of middle-class styles ('Cheap is in') . . . If it . . . becomes a dominant orientation, will these children of affluence grow up to be consumers on quite the economy-moving scale as their parents?"

So the kids are talking revolution and smoking dope? Well, so are the companies, in massive advertising campaigns that co-opt the language of revolution so thoroughly that you'd think they were on the streets themselves. "The Man can't bust *our* music," read one Columbia ad; another urged (with a picture of a diverse group of kids apparently turning on): "Know who your friends are. And look and see and touch and be together. Then listen. *We* do." (Italics mine.)

More insidious than the ads themselves is the fact that ad money from the record companies is one of the main supports of the underground press. And the companies don't mind supporting these "revolutionary" sheets; the failure of Hearst's *Eye* magazine after a year showed that the establishment itself could not create new media to reach the kids, so squeamish is it about advocating revolution, drugs and sexual liberation. But it is glad to support the media the kids create themselves, and thereby, just as it did with rock, ultimately defang it.

The ramifications of control finally came full circle when *Rolling Stone,* the leading national rock newspaper, which began eighteen months ago on a shoestring, had enough money in the bank to afford a $7000 ad on the back page of *The New York Times.* Not only was this "hip rock" publication self consciously taking its place among the communication giants ("NBC was the day before us and *Look* the day after," said the 22-year-old editor), but the ad's copy made clear the paper's exploitive aim: "If you are a corporate executive trying to understand what is happening to youth today, you cannot afford to be without *Rolling Stone.* If you are a student, a professor, a parent, this is your life because you already know that rock and roll is more than just music; it is the energy center of the new culture and youth revolution." Such a neat reversal of the corporate-to-kids lie into a kids-to-corporate lie is only possible when the kids so believe the lie they have been fed that they want to pass it on.

But rock and roll musicians are in the end artists and entertainers, and were it not for all the talk of the "rock revolution," one would be led to expect a clear political vision from them. The bitterest irony is that the "rock revolution" hype has come close to fatally limiting the revolutionary potential that rock does contain. So effective has the rock industry been in encouraging the spirit of optimistic youth take-over that rock's truly hard political edge, its constant exploration of the varieties of youthful frustration, has been ignored and softened. Rock musicians, like their followers, have always been torn between the obvious pleasures that America held out and the price paid for them. Rock and roll is not revolutionary music because it has never gotten beyond articulation of this paradox. At best it has offered the defiance of withdrawal; its violence never amounted to more than a cry of "Don't bother me."

"Leave me alone; anyway, I'm almost grown"; "Don't step on my blue suede shoes"; "There ain't no cure for the summertime blues"; "I can't get no satisfaction": the rock refrains that express despair could be strung out forever. But at least rock has offered an honest appraisal of where its makers and listeners are at, and that radical, if bitterly defeatist, honesty is a touchstone, a starting point. If the companies, as representatives of the corporate structure, can convince the rock world that their revolution is won or almost won, that the walls of the playground are crumbling, not only will the constituents of rock seal their fate by that fatal self-deception, but their music, one of the few things they actually do have going for them, will have been successfully corrupted and truly emasculated.

Topics for Discussion

1. Lyndon says that "rock is a product created, distributed and controlled for the profit of American (and international) business." But other critics have maintained that rock music was created and grew because it filled a need. Which position do you think is correct?
2. "From the start, rock has been commercial in its very essence." Lyndon argues that rock is not an art form but is merely another business. What does this position do to the belief that rock lyrics are today's poetry?
3. Lyndon says that "rock fans can date their entire lives by rock." Can you cite two or three "golden oldies" that trigger memories for you?
4. What is the "New Rock" that Lyndon mentions?
5. Is there a "rock revolution"? If you think there is one, describe it.
6. Can you think of any rock singers or groups who became stars "overnight" only to disappear just as quickly? Why and how do you think all this happens?
7. Why do you think there is a revival of rock songs of the 1950s? Would this revival have anything to do with Lyndon's contention that all rock music is commercial?
8. Does Lyndon offer any hope that rock music can break away from corporate control?

Rhetorical Considerations

1. Lyndon begins his essay with a specific incident. How does this set the tone for the rest of the essay?
2. How much and how effectively does Lyndon document his charge of commercialism? Is his evidence convincing?
3. The concluding paragraph of this essay begins with quotations from four rock songs. How relevant are these quotations to the essay? To the conclusion?
4. Look at the beginning of each paragraph in this essay. What kinds of sentences begin each paragraph? How does Lyndon achieve variety in his paragraph openings?
5. Note some of the words used in this essay. What words would you consider emotionally charged? Consider, for example, such words as "trash," "schlock psychedelia," "avaricious cretins," and "slavish devotion to commerciality."

The New Sound of Radio

WILLIAM H. HONAN

Radio station WEVD in New York City is looking for a Chinese disk jockey. Applicants should be acquainted with such personalities as Poon Sow Keng (the hottest rock 'n' roll singer today in Hong Kong), be able to report the time, news and temperature in easy-going Cantonese, and quote Confucius in the original. The resulting program may be of limited appeal—beneath the notice, one might guess, of a mass-media adman worth his double martini—and yet, it is chiefly this sort of specialization, or "fractionalization of the market," as they say in the trade, that accounts for the remarkable sonic boom reverberating from radio these days.

Right now, for example, there are more radios in the United States than people—262,700,000 at the last count. Forty-seven million sets were sold last year alone. Such profusion cannot be attributed merely to teen-agers buying transistor radios with which to annoy their parents—although that is a not inconsiderable factor. But parents are buying radios like hot cakes, too. They get them nowadays built into their tractors, hairdryers, Scotch bottles and even sunglasses. And the knobs on all these instruments are being clicked and twirled with astonishing frequency.

In fact—and this may be enough to make even Marshall McLuhan gulp with wonder—a recent Trendex survey conducted for the National Broadcasting Com-

pany found that more Americans now listen to radio in the course of an average week than watch TV. The audience for individual radio programs, of course, cannot compare with that of the most popular TV shows, but on a cumulative basis the figures indicate that 90.5 per cent of the adult population tunes in a radio sometime during the week as compared with 87 per cent who flick on television. That finding, the Trendex survey supervisor reported, "puts radio right back in the league with the other major media in terms of total audience dimensions."

The robustness of radio is also illustrated by the fact that the giant advertisers, most notably such bellwethers as the soap and automotive companies which shifted from radio to TV in the early nineteen-fifties, have once again become substantial radio time buyers. Colgate-Palmolive, for example, which was not even listed among the top 100 radio spot advertisers as recently as 1964 was 23rd on the list last year. Ford, General Motors and Chrysler were first, second and third, respectively, with a total expenditure last year of $56 million—up 17 per cent over the previous year and up 56 per cent over that of the year before.

The explanation for this renaissance of a medium which many condemned to a lingering death as recently as 10 years ago lies, to a great degree, with the sought-after Chinese disk jockey. For, once radio broadcasters began to face up to the fact that television had permanently taken their place as dispenser of general entertainment for the masses, they began experimenting with new formats and discovered that, collectively, they could recapture their old audience piecemeal by directing strong ap-

peals to specific fractions of the population.

This discovery led to the development of all manner of limited-appeal programs, and the advancing trend is now doing away with even these one-hour or half-hour shows, since the stations themselves are beginning to take on the characteristics of a single, 24-hour program, narrowly addressed to a distinct slice of the population. Such broadcast parochialism is now revolutionizing the industry, with several stations almost every month dropping their old-style eclectic programing in preference for the new "continuous format."

Competition in a city like New York, where no fewer than 63 different AM and FM stations vie for attention, has naturally pushed specialization to an extreme, and some of the more popular formats appear to have been divided, subdivided and virtually pulled apart with tweezers in order that each station may find a niche (and presumably a distinct audience) it can call its own.

For example, WMCA, WABC, WJRZ and WOR-FM are all what the casual listener might consider standard rock 'n' roll stations, but connoisseurs are aware that WMCA tries to add a local hometown flavor by using such disk jockeys as Joe O'Brien, who has a Yonkers accent; WABC seeks to impart an all-American tone to the proceedings with disk jockeys like Herb Oscar Anderson, who is from Minnesota and full of corn and good cheer; WJRZ restricts itself exclusively to that close relative of rock 'n' roll known as country-Western music, and WOR-FM lays stress on the subdivision known as folk rock, which may include such controversial ballads (which the other stations would never touch)

William H. Honan, "The New Sound of Radio," *The New York Times Magazine*, December 3, 1967. © 1967 by The New York Times Company. Reprinted by permission.

as Phil Ochs's "I Ain't Marchin' Anymore" and Country Joe and the Fish's prickly L.B.J. put-on, "Super Bird."

Even in lesser cities than New York, however, format specialization has proceeded to a surprising degree. There are as many as 1,500 radio stations across the nation substantially if not exclusively devoted to country-Western music, according to the Country Music Association. And the all-talk or telephone-participation format is not only popular in New York City, where N.B.C.'s Brad Crandall and the insomniac Long John Nebel have large followings, but Philadelphians like to hear themselves gabbing over the telephone with Jack McKinney over WCAU, and nearly everybody in Salina, Kan. (pop. 43,202), listens at one time or another to Mike Cooper on KLSI to catch the latest chatter about the local school merger and to hear Cooper adding his laconic "uh-huh" to a phoned-in beef about how all the rain in June loused up the local wheat crop.

Typical of the trend is a middle-sized city like Peoria, Ill., which now has as many as six radio stations, each with its own distinctive format. WIRL, Peoria's leading outlet, is a "top-40" or predominantly rock 'n' roll station. WXCL, the local N.B.C. affiliate, is devoted to country-Western music. WMBD, the C.B.S. affiliate, is strong on conversation and plays "middle-of-the-road" music (Frank Sinatra, Peggy Lee, Vic Damone). WMBD-FM specializes in "potted-palm" fare (schmaltzy renditions of the Warsaw Concerto, and the themes from "Intermezzo" and "Gone With the Wind").

WIVC-FM has female disk jockeys—or "program hostesses," as they are known in Peoria—and plays "adult" pop, jazz and classical music. Finally, WPEO, the Mutual affiliate, having recently tried and then dropped "top-40" and "middle-of-the-road" formats, became a virtually "all-talk" station in January of this year and then in September raided WXCL's country-Western disk jockey—Cal Shrum, an old Gene Autry sidekick—and is now trying to blend the recorded yodelings of assorted farmhands-turned-vocalists with its decidedly right-leaning cast of talkers, whose ranks include Fulton Lewis 3d, the Rev. Carl McIntire and the suave pitchmen of H. L. Hunt's "Life Lines."

Such quick shifting from one format to another as practiced by WPEO is possible because the process is remarkably cheap. There is no retooling to be done, and usually disk jockeys who can handle one type of music can handle another as well. Subscriptions to the various record library services required to keep a radio station jangling with the latest tunes of whatever genre it chooses rarely run more than $300 or $400 a year. Furthermore, stations like WPEO—far from spending revenue when shifting to the seemingly expensive all-talk format—actually coin money in doing so. For every Fulton Lewis or Bill Stern whose tapes the station has to pay for, WPEO broadcasts several "Life Lines" or "20th-Century Reformation Hours" which are actually advertisements for which the station is handsomely compensated.

With specialization paying off in radio, a rise might be expected in new small stations throughout the country. Actually few new stations are being formed. As of Aug. 31, there were 4,145 AM and 1,712 FM stations—and these figures have held fairly steady for the last few years. It costs a minimum of $35,000 to start a station in a city the size of Fort Worth, Tex.—and this figure does not include promotion expenses, which are likely to be enormous.

But even that cost is not what stops people from starting new stations. The F.C.C. controls the issuance of new licenses very closely, since the radio band is now almost saturated, and thus even if an entrepreneur had the $35,000 to $100,000 to spend, he would have a tough time convincing the F.C.C. that Fort Worth, say, really needs a new radio station.

So far has format specialization progressed among radio stations throughout the United States today that local affiliates of the national networks have been ignoring network programing in preference for their own locally originated material. In response to this trend, the A.B.C. radio network has recently announced that it plans to split up its piped fare into four separate subnetworks, each of which will cater to stations with distinctly different formats. There will be one subnetwork for stations with an all-talk or music-and-news format, another for "top-40" stations, one for those with more sophisticated FM formats and another for stations still using the old-style eclectic format. A.B.C.'s hope is that its subnetworks will be more congenial to highly specialized stations and will, in addition, make possible more than one A.B.C. affiliate in a given community.

There are, of course, other possible explanations besides specialization for the come-back of radio—among them the portability and convenience of the new transistor sets, the fact that car radios have become virtually standard rather than optional equipment, the development of sophisticated techniques of audience measurement to demonstrate to advertisers the large, new, out-of-home listenership, and so forth. But the basic reason for the boom is that people are listening to the radio again because it is offering them something they want to hear and cannot find elsewhere.

Of New York City's bewildering array of radio stations, three picked more or less at random—WINS, WHOM and WBAI-FM—illustrate the latest types of specialization and to whom these new formats appeal.

In April 1965 WINS, a Westinghouse station, dramatically gave away its rock 'n' roll record library to Fordham University, kissed its disk jockeys good-by, hired 27 radio newsmen and began broadcasting news for 24 hours a day. Skeptics had said that the WINS anchor men would grow hoarse by early afternoon of the first day, and that if no worse disaster overtook the station, the babbling brook of news would simply run dry, and, on the first really slow day, WINS would be begging to get its records back from Fordham.

Neither of these eventualities came to pass. WINS provided enough anchor men so they could spell one another in half-hour shifts. And far from running out of news, a veritable geyser of gab was churned up by the station's 21 "airmen" covering New York City, by the squad of rewrite men who had access to all the major wire services and by correspondents of the Westinghouse communications network who were sending in "voice cuts" from such far-flung places as Madrid and Saigon.

As time went by, the WINS team of broadcasters developed an original and often rather exciting manner of news presentation, in which the process of news gather-

ing is exposed to the listener in an unfolding drama. In a major news break, for example, the presentation begins with a high-pitched BEEP - BEEP - BEEP - BEEP which, according to high Westinghouse policy, may even interrupt a commercial (but never has). The beeping fades and the voice of the anchor man rises over it with: "Late word has just been received at the WINS newsroom that President Johnson and Premier Kosygin will meet tomorrow in the college town of Glassboro, N.J. Stay tuned for further details as they are received in the WINS newsroom."

Whatever was cut into is then resumed, but pretty soon "Jim McGiffert at the editor's desk," who has been madly pawing through a stack of reference books dumped in front of him, whisks the anchor man a "sidebar" about Glassboro—where it is, its population, principal industry, etc. The next morning, Sid Davis tells about the President's helicopter chugging up off the White House lawn; there is a quick switch to Doug Edelson at the Soviet Mission in New York describing the departure of Kosygin's limousine; then reports from Rod MacLeish, Paul Parker and Jim Gordon in Glassboro shouldering their way through the crowds and finally telling of the arrival of the dignitaries the moment they appear.

So impressed by this dramaturgy was Angus McDermid, the B.B.C.'s U.N. correspondent, that he was moved to do a special feature about WINS for the B.B.C., in which he commented enthusiastically: "I found myself waiting for the next thrilling installment. It was better than many a fictional radio series I can think of."

More jaundiced listeners, however, may note that all too often the instant news in these "thrilling

installments" winds up having to be retracted or modified. For example, during the emergency session of the United Nations in the wake of the six-day war in the Middle East, WINS reported that a Mohawk Airlines jet bound for Washington, D.C., had crashed near Blossburg, Pa., and that many of the 34 passengers aboard were U.N. delegates. It was a thrilling installment, all right, but it later turned out to be an example of what Elmo Ellis of WSB, Atlanta, a sharp critic of broadcasting, once characterized as "rip-snorting, inaccurate news reports." No U.N. delegates had been on the flight.

WINS spokesmen argue that the Mohawk Airlines story was an unusual case. They add with pride that WINS newsmen are not merely "rip-and-read" announcers who rip off the wire-service stories and blather them uncritically into the microphone, as do the "newsmen" at other stations they say they could name. The WINS newsmen, they say, have had analytical experience—four-fifths of them are former radio or TV station news directors—and normally they "don't jump." They did not jump on the air, for example, as did WQXR, with a rumor circulated by The Associated Press during the Newark rioting to the effect that Stokely Carmichael was leading a caravan of 33 cars into Newark. WINS newsmen were on their toes and knew Carmichael was in London at the time. And it was not a WINS man, they say, whom Newsweek pictured poking his stick microphone into the anguished face of a woman felled by a bullet on a Newark street; that, too, was "a man from another station we could name"—in this case, WMCA.

The all-news format for radio was originated not by WINS but by Gordon B. McLendon, the flamboyant Texas promoter who was also one of the first to use the "top-40" or "rock-around-the-clock" format. McLendon's station XTRA in Tijuana, Mexico, which broadcasts to Southern California, in 1961 became the first to go on an all-news bender, and was followed three years later by another McLendon property, WNUS in Chicago. (Philadelphia, Washington, Denver and St. Louis now have all-news stations, too.)

The original McLendon format, however, is substantially different from that of WINS. McLendon likens XTRA and WNUS to the weather- and time-dialing services of the telephone company, and believes that they will succeed to the degree that they strictly adhere to a "monotonous" recital of the headlines, eschewing all features and commentary. The ultimate disaster for an all-news station, McLendon once remarked, would be for its listeners to turn in expecting to hear the latest bulletins and get instead a book review.

Disagreement is voiced by Charles F. Payne, the stocky, natty-looking general manager who now presides over WINS at its chic, mid-town Park Avenue headquarters. Also a Texan and, by coincidence, the manager of two McLendon stations before he joined Westinghouse, Payne explains: "It's true, of course, that we cycle the headlines every 15 minutes, do a time check every 5, weather every 7 and so forth, so when you tune in you're never far away from the bulletins. But in between we have special in-depth reports, a shopping feature, theater reviews, even editorials and sometimes a feature that continues in sections all day long—we call it a 'blitz'—on topics like the poor of New York, the overcrowded air corridors or the coming Broadway

season. Furthermore, even the news bulletins are not 'monotonous.' They're changing all the time. Someone once said we're like a newspaper with 48 separate editions every day."

"The key to our format," Payne goes on, "is being informally informative. What we try to avoid is the old H.V. Kaltenborn pompousness. We want to create the image of the working newsman, the guy who's on the scene."

Although the sound of news would seem to have a universal appeal, WINS's most faithful listeners, according to a recent Politz survey, tend to be those New Yorkers with high incomes, college educations and relatively high-status jobs. Most listeners are between the ages of 25 and 64, teenagers and senior citizens being conspicuously absent. When WINS first shifted to the all-news format, its audience, which had been accustomed to rock 'n' roll, fell off sharply. According to the latest surveys, however, the station has now more than doubled the size of its former audience—a success story which must have been read with interest across town at WCBS, which switched in August to an all-news format, too.

Another increasingly important specialization in contemporary radio is known as ethnic broadcasting, or, less euphemistically, as ghetto radio. There are now, for example, no fewer than three Negro stations broadcasting in New York City. WWRL, by far the most popular of these, anticipates that its annual revenue from advertising will rise above the $2-million mark this year, having practically quadrupled over the last four years.

WEVD, the formally all-Yiddish station which now broadcasts in 13 different tongues, including Japanese and Norwegian, says that 1966

was "the best year ever" in its 40-year history. And The Wall Street Journal recently reported that because Pepsi-Cola was the first soft drink to advertise intensively on the local Spanish stations, Pepsi now outsells Coca-Cola two-to-one among New York's 1.5 million Spanish-speaking residents—a state of affairs that Coca-Cola is now trying to rectify by plugging away over "the Spanish Main," as the three stations between 1280 and 1480 kilocycles are known, with the jingle *Todo va mejor con Coke*" ("Things go better with Coke").

Typical of the sound and format of ethnic broadcasting is that of WHOM, New York's foremost Spanish station, which is so hot-bloodedly Latin that it has, quite literally, blown its fuse. The program responsible for this occasional boiling over—called *"Debate Musical"* ("Musical Debate")—is the top-rated Spanish disk-jockey show in New York and is hosted by Juan Rodriguez Diaz, a deceptively placid-looking Puerto Rican. On the program, which is broadcast live every weekday afternoon at 4, Diaz spins a couple of Spanish pop records and then urges his listeners to call in and "vote" for whichever one they liked best. He can stimulate as many as a thousand calls on a good afternoon, working himself into a frenzy as the votes mount up and bawling into the microphone in Spanish:

"The vote is even! It's even! We don't want any sleepy-heads here! No, you have to be *awake* to listen to *this* show! Call in! My friends! Call in! Look, if you don't call in right away, I'll fall down and break 14 ribs. I'll smash my head against the wall! If I don't get 400 calls right now, I'll break 44 ribs!"

Suddenly, the lights on all the studio telephones begin to flicker,

The Age of Communication

indicating a shower of incoming calls. When this happens, Diaz puts his hands to his temples, closes his eyes and shrieks with ecstasy: *"Esto es treMENNNDO!"* WHOM's engineers, not one of whom understands Spanish, have learned to watch their volume-units meter with a hawk's eye when El Tremendo, as they call Diaz, gets lathered up and they "ride gain" on him with their volume controls like a destroyer captain in a gale. Nevertheless, on two consecutive days last summer, when Diaz was unloosing his *"Esto es treMENNNDO!"* he overloaded the station's 5,000-watt transmitter and blew out a high-voltage fuse, temporarily putting WHOM off the air.

That is overdoing it, perhaps, but the Latin sound and volatile temperament is all that WHOM has to sell, and the management evidently would rather err with too much than too little. "Language is our most important product," explains Ralph Costantino, WHOM's affable program director, who is himself of Italian extraction but survived the station's changeover in 1957 from Italian to Spanish broadcasting by virtue of his fluent Spanish. The dialect spoken over WHOM, he says, is Caribbean Spanish, interspersed with plenty of *ay benditos* and *Ave Marias!,* which are characteristic of the Puerto Rican and Cuban idiom one hears on East 125th Street.

So important is the sound of the Spanish language to the station's identity, in Costantino's opinion, that he has a rule of long standing that popular music, which constitutes from 65 per cent to 75 per cent of the station's programing, must be vocal rather than instrumental. Moreover, with the current unusual exception of *The Monkees* and *The Turtles,* vocalists who sing in

English are strictly *prohibido.* WHOM even snubbed Frank Sinatra's last big hit, "Strangers in the Night," and played instead Andy Russell's Spanish rendition *"Estraños en la Noche,"* which had more tropical zing.

It is not only the disk jockeys and vocalists one hears over WHOM who radiate Latin excitement; newscasters do, too. Last summer, for example, one of WHOM's newsmen broke into a musical program almost hysterically shouting a news bulletin. Fortune Pope, the station's co-owner, who does not speak Spanish, happened to be listening and promptly called in to find out what in blazes was going on. "Has war been declared?" he asked. No, he was told, the news bulletin merely concerned a report that Che Guevara was then rumored to have been seen somewhere in Venezuela.

"Our announcers become emotionally involved in the news when they read it," says Costantino. "It isn't that they aren't professional. It's just the Latin way. You should have heard them reporting the rioting in El Barrio the last week in July. It was . . . well, pretty loud."

Baseball games and soap opera—the latter still a great favorite with Spanish-speaking audiences—round out WHOM's regular fare, and they, too, are as popular as they are tempestuous. One of the most avidly followed "soaps" carried on WHOM is called *"Collar de Lagrimas"* ("Necklace of Tears"), and seems to consist chiefly of organ music and the sound of a woman sobbing, punctuated now and then by gunfire and commercials. (It also has an enormous audience in Cuba, and Fidel Castro will not permit Havana stations to broadcast it while he is making a speech.) The soaps are gradually

giving way on WHOM, however, to the living sound of the *boogaloo* and *la neuva ola* (rock 'n' roll with a Latin beat), since the younger generation, according to the surveys, is now the dominant group in Spanish Harlem and it would rather twist and wriggle than sniffle and sigh.

So firm is the grip of the ethnic stations on their audiences that a recent Pulse survey shows the Spanish-speaking population, for example, listening to radio for an average of four hours a day, which is almost twice as much time as other Americans devote to the medium. This audience, according to surveys, is profoundly influenced by what it hears, whether commercials, news or comment.

It is particularly regrettable, then, that WHOM has an intellectual content of zero, and offers little that might be considered of genuine public service. (A notable exception among ethnic broadcasters is WLIB, the Harlem Negro station that last year won a Peabody Award—the highest honor in broadcasting—for a telephone participation program that was believed to have served as a sort of social safety valve by permitting the frank airing of Negro grievances.) The rationale for the low level of programing by WHOM, according to Costantino, is that "most Puerto Ricans who have intellectual capacity are bilingual and thus get their stimulation from English-language sources" (which is a dodge), and that the station did in fact "give free air time to Spanish-speaking deputies of Mayor Lindsay and Cardinal Spellman to appeal for restraint during the summer rioting" (which is true enough, but surely the minimum in terms of social responsibility). A strong case can be made that ethnic radio stations like

WHOM, which exploit commercially the linguistic handicap of their listeners, actually serve to perpetuate that handicap, and therefore ought to be charged with providing special counterbalancing educational services.

Another highly specialized area of radio broadcasting is occupied by the 350-odd licensed noncommercial stations in the United States which are affiliated with schools, churches, municipalities and foundations. A good many of these have undergone as much format refinement as any all-news or rock-around-the-clock station on the dial. Perhaps the best known of them in New York is WNYC, the city-owned station.

Other local noncommercial stations specializing in fine music and thoughtful discussions and lectures include Columbia University's WKCR-FM, Fordham University's WFUV-FM, the Riverside Church's WRVR-FM and the Pacifica Foundation's listener-sponsored WBAI-FM, which is the left-leaning "free-speech" station that was put off the air for 52 hours in September when its transmitter was wrecked by vandalism. An articulate spokesman for WBAI is Larry Josephson, the hip disk jockey. Josephson, a rather corpulent, bearded, 28-year-old computer-programer by day, has for the last year and a half been conducting a far-out breakfast club for the station, irreverently called "In the Beginning," which is—in marked contrast to the usual fare at that hour—refreshingly grumpy, lusty and alienated.

Noncommercial stations have specialized just as have the commercial broadcasters, Josephson believes, not only because of the pressures of competition, which naturally affect them less, but in response to "the great diversity of life styles today." Back in the thirties, he says, cultural unity gave rise to relatively undiversified styles in the communication media. But today, in an era of cultural splintering, a great many people find themselves "disfranchised by the mass media" and they begin to seek new styles of experience elsewhere.

WBAI is attractive to at least some of these seekers—no one knows how many since its call letters have never appeared in a general audience survey—because it offers, according to Josephson, programs attuned to the new life styles, programs which are, in his words, "no longer sequential, but random, associative and parallel." Josephson cites as an example of such programing the breakfast club he convenes every weekday morning at 7 A.M. or whenever he gets around to arriving at the station (he is frequently late and sometimes never shows at all), and on which he is likely to say anything that pops into his head—it may be something fairly salacious or he may just indulge in a long spate of moaning and groaning.

Josephson points with admiration to his WBAI colleague, Bob Fass, the station's after-midnight disk jockey, who has lately been achieving remarkable effects by playing two records simultaneously—for example, pairing speeches by Timothy Leary and Lyndon B. Johnson about their respective visions; playing the voices of soldiers in a United States Army basic-training course along with a dog-training record, and so forth. Similar effects, Josephson says, were to be found in the dramatization of Christopher Morley's "The Trojan Horse," which juxtaposed cynicism and romanticism, and which the station broadcast, under the direction of Baird Searles, in a four-and-a-half-hour spree on Oct. 8 and 9.

WBAI, like its commercial counterparts, Josephson says, has its very own sound. "Some people say it is the sound of boredom," he begins, adding: "To some extent that's true. Some say it's aggression—a kind of postured hipness. That's true, too. Some say it's amateurishness. Some call it humaneness, or love, or naturalness. It's all of that. Naturalness, especially. For example, when we're running behind time, we say so. When we make a mistake, we admit it. We don't try to come up with our radio-broadcast *persona grata* intact. When we read news, we try to read it like human beings. I hate WINS. They read everything in the same excited monotone. It isn't human."

A few weeks ago, Josephson took over WBAI's regular book-review program for half an hour, and what he said as well as the manner in which his material was presented pretty well illustrates the WBAI "sound" he was trying to describe.

To begin with, the program, which was scheduled to follow a commentary by a spokesman for the Socialist Labor party at 7 P.M., did not start until about 7:07. Then the announcer, who introduced the program as "Books to Buy, Borrow or Burn," tripped over a word, and neglected to say who the reviewer was going to be or to give the titles of the books to be discussed. The next voice was that of a newscaster announcing the beginning of World War II on a scratchy old record.

When it was finished, an obviously "live" voice came on the air and explained that the recording was from a broadcast by Edward R. Murrow from London. The live voice went on to say in a very intimate and unradiolike tone that Murrow was "the best broadcaster ever produced by this country." Murrow had also been an intelligent and effective foe of McCarthy, the voice said, but he should not be mistaken for a true liberal because he had condoned the execution of Julius and Ethel Rosenberg.

In any case, the voice continued, Murrow was great because he came through on the human level and he made you stop and think. A collection of Murrow's broadcasts, the voice added, had been published by Alfred A. Knopf Inc., in a book called "In Search of Light," which might well be read along with "Due to Circumstances Beyond Our Control" by Fred Friendly, who, as everybody knows, resigned from C.B.S. after the network refused to permit him to drop a rerun of "I Love Lucy" in order to carry the testimony of George F. Kennan before the Senate Foreign Relations Committee. Taken together, the voice commented, the two books reveal what is good and what is bad about broadcasting in America. "This is Larry Josephson," said the voice, and stopped.

There was a long pause—a *very* long pause—and then an old recording of Murrow's voice came on again, this time saying that he had just been with the first wave of U.S. troops to arrive at a concentration camp in central Germany called Buchenwald. His voice trembled perceptibly as he said: "Now let me tell this in the first person." Murrow then described the terrible scene in short, clipped language, remarking at one point: "Men tried to lift me to their shoulders. They could not. They were too weak." And later: "When I came in, they applauded. It sounded like the handclapping of babies."

After describing several other such scenes, Murrow said fervently: "I *pray you* to believe what I have reported about Buchenwald!" He closed by adding: "If I have offended you by this rather mild account of Buchenwald, I am not sorry."

Then the first voice, that of the WBAI announcer, came on once more to say that "Books To Buy, Borrow or Burn" was over, and, tripping over a word again, he introduced the next program, which was in French.

Will the specialized formats such as those represented by WINS, WHOM and WBAI continue to proliferate? Most radio spokesmen say yes. In fact Timebuyer, the trade magazine, recently declared that "everyone from career girls to bird watchers to traveling salesmen could well be the special province of a particular station." Others have suggested that an important area of specialization in the future will be politics—with radio stations not only backing candidates, as did WMCA in 1960 (endorsing John F. Kennedy for President), but identifying themselves as, for example, "the National Review of the air."

These notions may not be as far-fetched as they sound, what with stations like WNCN-FM in New York broadcasting programs of special interest to physicians, to which the general public is discouraged from listening, and like KADS in Los Angeles—another Gordon McLendon creation—which has become the first radio station in the country devoted exclusively to classified advertising.

Just as radio is now going through a fractionalization previously experienced by the printed media, so television will follow, industry spokesmen agree, especially once the U.H.F. stations begin to catch on. The interesting upshot of all this specialization may then be that the mass media, only recently condemned as purveyors of a bland, regularized sameness, may be counted in the near future as a vigorous force working for cultural diversity.

The level or quality of that diversity, of course, is another question, and that remains to be seen—perhaps to be overseen.

Topics for Discussion

1. Do you think that radio is really changing and experimenting with new approaches? Give one or two examples of experimental or different radio programs.
2. Honan describes a wide variety of radio stations, mainly located in New York City. Does your city have any variety in radio stations, or are they all the same?
3. Do you own a radio? Do you listen to it very often? Which medium do you think has more impact on teenagers?
4. Do you agree with Honan that television follows radio and becomes more innovative and specialized?
5. What reason does Honan give for the comeback in radio? Do you agree with this reason?
6. Make a list of all the things that radio offers besides music. What things aren't on your list? Should radio do more than it is doing? What can radio do that television cannot do?

Rhetorical Considerations

1. Does the first sentence of the essay catch your attention? What about the rest of the opening paragraph? Is it a good introduction?
2. What function do the second, third, and fourth paragraphs play in the essay?
3. Why is the fifth paragraph of the essay important?
4. Why does Honan end his essay with a one sentence paragraph? Would it have been better to have included this sentence in the preceding paragraph?

Shazam! Here Comes Captain Relevant

SAUL BRAUN

Envision a scene in a comic book:
In Panel 1, two New York City policemen are pointing skyward with their jaws hanging open and one is saying, "Wha . . .?" They are looking at four or five men and women, shown in Panel 2 plummeting through the air feet first, as though riding surfboards. The dominant figure has a black long coat thrown over his shoulders, wears a peaked, flat-brim hat and carries a cane. As the group lands on the street and enters the "Vision Building," Panel 3, a hairy hip figure on the sidewalk observes to a friend: "Fellini's in town."

In Panel 4, an office interior, the man with the cape is saying to the secretary, "I am Federico Fellini, come to pay his respects to . . ." Turn the page and there is the Fellini figure in the background finishing his balloon: ". . .the amazing Stan Lee." In the foreground is a tall, skinny man with a black D. H. Lawrence beard, wearing black bathing trunks, long-sleeved turtleneck sweater and misshapen sailor hat. Stan Lee stands alongside a table that has been piled on another table, and on top of that is a typewriter with a manuscript page inserted in it that reads: "The Amazing Spiderman. In the Grip of the Goblin! It's happening again. As we saw last. . . ."

THIS visit, in more mundane fashion, actually took place. Stan Lee has been writing comic books for 30 years and is now editor-in-chief of the Marvel Comics line. His reputation with *cognoscenti* is very, very high.

Alain Resnais is also a Lee fan and the two are now working together on a movie. Lee has succeeded so well with his art that he has spent a good deal of his time traveling around the country speaking at colleges. In his office at home—which is currently a Manhattan apartment in the East 60's—he has several shelves filled with tapes of his college talks. An Ivy League student was once

quoted as telling him, "We think of Marvel Comics as the 20th century mythology and you as this generation's Homer."

Lee's comic antiheroes (Spiderman, Fantastic Four, Submariner, Thor, Captain America) have revolutionized an industry that took a beating from its critics and from TV in the nineteen-fifties. For decades, comic book writers and artists were considered little more than production workers, virtually interchangeable. Now Lee and his former collaborator, artist Jack Kirby of National Comics, Marvel's principal rival, are considered superstars—and their work reflects a growing sophistication in the industry that has attracted both young and old readers.

"We're in a renaissance," says Carmine Infantino, editorial director at National Comics, and he offers as proof the fact that at Brown University in Providence, R.I., they have a course, proposed by the students, called "Comparative Comics." A prospectus for the course sets out the case for comic books as Native Art:

"Comics, long scorned by parents, educators, psychologists, lawmakers, American Legionnaires, moral crusaders, civic groups and J. Edgar Hoover, have developed into a new and interesting art form. Combining 'new journalism' with greater illustrative realism, comics are a reflection of both real society and personal fantasy. No longer restricted to simple, good vs. evil plot lines and unimaginative, sticklike figures, comics can now be read at several different levels by various age groups. There are still heroes for the younger readers, but now the heroes are different—they ponder moral questions, have emotional differences, and are just as neurotic as real people. Captain America openly sympathizes with campus radicals, the Black Widow fights side by side with the Young Lords, Lois Lane apes John Howard Griffin and turns herself black to study racism, and everybody battles to save the environment."

As for Fellini, his interest in American comic books, and Stan Lee's work in particular, is no passing fancy. For an introduction to Jim

Steranko's "History of the Comics," he wrote the following lines:

"Not satisfied being heroes, but becoming even more heroic, the characters in the Marvel group know how to laugh at themselves. Their adventures are offered publicly like a larger-than-life spectacle, each search-

ing masochistically within himself to find a sort of maturity, yet the results are nothing to be avoided: it is a brilliant tale, aggressive and retaliatory, a tale that continues to be reborn for eternity, without fear of obstacles or paradoxes. We cannot die from obstacles and paradoxes, if we face them with laughter. Only of boredom might we perish. And from boredom, fortunately, the comics keep a distance."

FOR an industry that wields considerable influence, comic-book publishing has only a small fraternity of workers. There are something like 200 million comic books sold each year, a volume produced by less than 200 people, including writers, artists and letterers. The artists fall into two categories, pencilers and inkers. Pencilers are slightly more highly reputed than inkers but, with few exceptions, nobody in the business has much of a public reputation, and most are poorly compensated. Most are freelancers, paid at a page rate that the various publishers prefer not to divulge. A rate of $15 a page, however, is said to be not uncommon.

"This is a fiercely competitive business," says Infantino. "After Superman clicked in 1935 everybody jumped in; there were millions of outfits. Then one by one they all slipped away. When World War II ended, then came survival of the fittest and, boom, they died by the wayside."

As in other industries, power gradually became concentrated during the nineteen-fifties and sixties, and now the industry consists of perhaps half a dozen companies with annual sales of about 200 million. National, the leader, sells about 70 million. Marvel sells 40 million, Archie 35 million, and the next three firms—Charleton (Yogi Bear, Beetle Bailey, Flintstones), Gold Key (Bugs Bunny, Donald Duck, Mickey Mouse) and Harvey (Caspar the Friendly Ghost, Richie Rich, Sad Sack) each sell about 25 million. That is a great many copies, but doesn't necessarily reflect profitability. The index of profit and loss is not sales but the percentage of pub-lished copies that are returned unsold from the store racks. A book that suffers returns of more than 50 per cent is in trouble.

Martin Goodman, president of the Magazine Management Company, which puts out the Marvel line, recalls that the golden age of comics was the war years and immediately afterwards. By the late forties, he says, "everything began to collapse. TV was kicking the hell out of a great number of comics. A book like Donald Duck went from 2¼ million monthly sale to about 200,000. You couldn't give the animated stuff away, the Disney stuff, because of TV. TV murdered it. Because if a kid spends Saturday morning looking at the stuff, what parent is going to give the kid another couple of dimes to buy the same thing again?

"Industrywide," says Goodman sorrowfully, "the volume is not going up. I think the comic-book field suffers from the same thing TV does. After a few years, an erosion sets in. You still maintain loyal readers, but you lose a lot more readers than you're picking up. That's why we have so many superhero characters, and run superheroes together. Even if you take two characters that are weak sellers and run them together in the same book, somehow, psychologically, the reader feels he's getting more. You get the Avenger follower and the Sub-mariner follower. Often you see a new title do great on the first issue and then it begins to slide off..."

Goodman recalls with avuncular diffidence the arrival of Stan Lee at Marvel, then called Timely Comics. "Stan started as a kid here; he's my wife's cousin. That was in 1941, something like that. He came in as an apprentice, to learn the business. He had a talent for writing. I think when Stan developed the Marvel superheroes he did a very good job, and he got a lot of college kids reading us. They make up a segment of our readership, but when you play it to them you lose the very young kids who just can't follow the whole damn thing. We try to keep a balance. Because I read some stories sometimes and I can't even understand them. I really can't!"

TODAY'S superhero is about as much like his predecessors as today's child is like his parents. My recollection of the typical pre-World War II child (me) is of a sensitive, lonely kid full of fantasies of power and experiencing, at the same time, a life of endless frustration and powerlessness. Nobody knew, of course, about the hidden power, the supermuscles rippling beneath the coarse woolen suits I had to wear that itched like crazy. How I longed to rip off that suit. Shaz...

Comic book buffs will not need to be reminded that Shazam is the magic name of a mysterious bald gentleman with a white beard down to his waist, which, when spoken by newsboy Billy Batson, turns Billy into Captain Marvel. The book didn't last long, due to the swift, self-righteous reprisals of National Comics, which took Captain Marvel to court for impersonating Superman. It lasted long enough to impress upon my memory, however, that "S" stood for Solomon's wisdom, "H" for Hercules's strength, "A" for Atlas's stamina, "Z" for Zeus's power, "A" for Achilles's courage and "M" for Mercury's speed. I always had trouble remembering the last two; like many another man, I have gone through life saying "Shaz" to myself and getting nowhere.

So my childhood was one of repressed anger and sullen obedience and scratching all winter long, together with an iron will that kept me from lifting my all-powerful fist and destroying those who threatened me: Nazis, Japs, Polish kids (mostly at Easter time), older kids, teachers and parents. My personal favorite was Submariner. He hated everybody.

Actually, all of the early comic-book heroes perfectly mirrored my own condition, and even provided pertinent psychological details. The parents of superheroes were always being killed by bad men or cataclysmic upheavals over which the heroes — let me make this one thing perfectly clear—had absolutely no control. However, they then embarked on a guilty, relentless, lifelong pursuit of evildoers. So many villains in so many bizarre guises only attested to the elusiveness and prevalence of—and persistence of—superhero complicity.

Secretly powerful people, like the superheroes and me, always assumed the guise of meekness; yet even the "real" identities were only symbols. All-powerful Superman equaled all-powerful father. Batman's costume disguise, like the typical parental bluster of the time, was intended to "strike terror into their hearts." For "their" read not only criminal but child.

Infantino, whose National Comics publishes, among othe.s, the long-run superhit of the comic-book industry, Superman, believes that power is the industry's main motif:

"The theme of comic books is power. The villain wants power. He wants to take over the world. Take over the other person's mind. There's something about sitting in the car with the motorcycles flanking you back and front and the world at your feet. It motivates all of us."

FOR three decades, the social setting was an America more or less continuously at war. At war with poverty in the thirties, with Fascism in the early forties, and with the International Red Conspiracy in the late forties and in the fifties. During these years there existed simultaneously, if uneasily, in our consciousness the belief that we were uniquely strong and that nothing would avail except the unrelenting exercise of that strength. From wanting or being forced to take the law into our own hands during the thirties, we moved swiftly towards believing that our security depended on taking the whole world into our hands. That carried us from the Depression to Korea and, eventually, in the sixties, to a confused war in which it was impossible to tell whether we were strong or weak, in which irresponsible complacency existed comfortably with political and social atrocities that could spring only from secret weakness masquerading as

strength.

It is not irrelevant to note that the Vietnamese war developed without hindrance—with some few exceptions—from a generation of men flying around the world on a fantasy-power trip, and was resisted in the main by their sons, the generation that began rejecting the comic books of the fifties with their sanitized, censored, surreal images of the world: a world in which "we" were good and "they" were bad, in which lawlessness masqueraded as heroism, in which blacks were invisible, in which, according to a survey taken in 1953 by University of California professors, men led "active lives" but women were interested mainly in "romantic love" and only villainous women "try to gain power and status." A world in which no superhero, whatever his excesses, ever doubted that he was using his powers wisely and morally.

During this time the industry was adopting a self-censorship code of ethics in response to the hue and cry raised by a Congressional look into the industry's excesses of gore and by the appearance of "Seduction of the Innocent," a shrill piece of psycho-criticism by a psychiatrist named Fredric Wertham, who supported his view that the comics were a pernicious influence on children with stories like: "A boy of 13 committed a 'lust murder' of a girl of 6. Arrested and jailed, he asked only for comic books."

While it is true some publishers were printing stories with grisly and violent elements, I must confess that I to this day find myself unable to believe that the worst comic books could have corrupted the child's mind as much as the knowledge that in his own world, the world he was being educated to join, 6 million men, women and children had only recently been killed in gas ovens for no very good reason, and large numbers of others had died at Hiroshima and Dresden, for only slightly better reasons. Two of my own strongest memories of the time are of my father, who owned a candy store, denying me the treasure trove of comics ("They'll ruin your mind"), and of my father, after receiving a telegram

telling him that his family had been wiped out in some concentration camp somewhere, turning ashen and falling to his knees. So, Superman, where were you when we needed you? My mind was corrupted, yes, and so were those of countless other children of the forties and fifties.

During this time, the only comic that held its own commercially was none other than William M. Gaines's "MAD." Gaines's defense of one of his horror comics was the high point at hearings of the Senate subcommittee on juvenile delinquency. The cover, depicting the severed head of a blonde, said Gaines, would have been in bad taste "if the head were held a little higher so the neck would show the blood dripping out."

The industry response was the comics code, including provisions forbidding horror, excessive bloodshed, gory or gruesome crimes, depravity, lust, sadism and masochism; an authority to administer the code was created, with power to deny the industry seal of approval to any comic book violating its provisions. This satisfied parents and educators, but only intensified the sales slide for seal-of-approval comic books. The turnabout came in 1961, when Stan Lee metamorphosed the Marvel line and very likely saved comic books from an untimely death.

"OUR competitors couldn't understand why our stuff was selling," Lee recalls. "They would have a superhero see a monster in the street and he'd say, 'Oh, a creature, I must destroy him before he crushes the world.' And they'd have another superhero in another book see a monster and he'd say, 'Oh, a creature, I must destroy him before he crushes the world.' It was so formularized. I said to my writers, 'Is that what you'd say in real life? If you saw a monster coming down the street, you'd say, 'Gee, there must be a masquerade party going on.'

"Because sales were down and out of sheer boredom, I changed the whole line around. New ways of talking, hangups, introspection and brooding. I brought out a new magazine called 'The Fantastic

Four,' in 1961. Goodman came to me with sales figures. The competitors were doing well with a superhero team. Well, I didn't want to do anything like what they were doing, so I talked to Jack Kirby about it. I said, 'Let's let them not always get along well; let's let them have arguments. Let's make them talk like real people and react like real people. Why should they all get superpowers that make them beautiful? Let's get a guy who becomes very ugly.' That was The Thing. I hate heroes anyway. Just 'cause a guy has superpowers, why couldn't he be a *nebbish*, have sinus trouble and athlete's foot?"

The most successful of the Stan Lee antiheroes was one Spiderman, an immediate hit and still the top of the Marvel line. Spidey, as he is known to his fans, is actually Peter Parker, a teen-ager who has "the proportionate strength of a spider," whatever that means, and yet, in Lee's words, "can still lose a fight, make dumb mistakes, have acne, have trouble with girls and have not too much money."

In Parker's world, nobody says, 'Oh, a creature.' In an early story, Spiderman apprehends three criminals robbing a store, and the following dialogue ensues:

Spidey: "If you're thinking of putting up a fight, brother, let me warn you . . ."

Crook: "A fight? The only fight I'll put up is in court. I'm suin' you for assault and battery, and I got witnesses to prove it."

Second crook: "Yeah, that's right."

If it is not already perfectly clear that the last vestiges of the nineteen-forties have fallen away from the world that Spiderman inhabits, it becomes so two panels later when one crook says, right to his face, "Don't you feel like a jerk paradin' around in public in that get-up?"

After overhearing a conversation in another episode between two men who also apparently consider him a kook, Parker goes home and, unlike any superhero before him, does some soul-searching. "Can they be right? Am I really some sort of crackpot wasting my time seeking fame and glory? Why do I do it?

Why don't I give the whole thing up?"

THE 48-year-old Lee may very well have asked precisely these questions at some point in his career. He's been in the business since 1938 when, as a 16-year-old high school graduate, he held some odd jobs (delivery boy, theater usher, office boy). Then he came to Timely Comics with some scripts and was hired by editors Joe Simon and Jack Kirby.

For the next 20 years, he labored professionally, but without any special devotion, to what he thought of as a temporary job. When Simon and Kirby left, Lee took over as editor as well as writer, and all during the forties and fifties, mass-produced comic books, 40 or 45 different titles a month.

"The top sellers varied from month to month, in cycles. Romance books, mystery books. We followed the trend. When war books were big, we put out war books. Then one day my wife came to me and said, 'You've got to stop kidding yourself. This is your work. You've got to put yourself into it.' So I did. Joanie is the one you really ought to interview. She's beautiful and talented. And my daughter, Joanie, who's 21, she's also beautiful and talented. I'm a very lucky guy."

His wife, he says, is exactly the dream girl he'd always wanted, and he decided to marry her the first time he saw her. At the time she was married to another man, but that hardly deterred him. For something like 25 years, the Lees lived a quiet domestic life in Hewlett Harbor, L. I., before recently moving back into town. Lee is nothing if not a devoted family man. Among his other self-evident qualities: he enjoys talking about his work. He is in the office Tuesdays and Thursdays, editing, and at home the other five days of the week, writing. "I'm the least temperamental writer you'll ever know," he says. "I write a minimum of four comic books a month. Writing is easy. The thing is characterization. That takes time. The thing I hate most is writing plots. My scripts are full of X-outs [crossed-out words]. I

read them out loud while writing, including sound effects. 'Pttuuuu. Take that, you rat!' I get carried away."

The comic industry has treated Lee very well. He is now, he says, in the 50 to 60 per cent income tax bracket, and he has a very high-paying, five-year contract with Cadence Industries, which bought Magazine Management Company from Goodman some 2½ years ago. When the contract expires, he says, he's not sure what he'll do. He has the vague discontent of a man looking for new fields to conquer, or, to use another simile, the look of a superhero adrift in a world that no longer wants him to solve its problems.

Last year he solved a recurring problem for industry workers by helping to form the Academy of Comic Book Artists:

"I felt that the publishers themselves weren't doing anything to improve the image of the comic books, so I thought, why don't we do it? Also I wanted to leave it as a legacy to the industry that has supported me over 30 years."

The academy now has as members about 80 writers, artists and letterers. I attended one of their recent meetings, held at the Statler-Hilton Hotel in the Petit Cafe, a barren, pastel-blue and mirrored room with about 200 gray metal folding chairs with glass ashtrays on them, and a gray metal long table with glass ashtrays and a lined yellow pad on it.

Around the room, leaning on gray folding chairs, were "story boards" from comic books that have been nominated for this year's awards, which are to be called Shazams.

Sketches of the proposed designs for the Shazams were being passed around, most of them serious renderings of the jagged bolt of lightning that accompanied Billy Batson's transformation. One, however, represented a side of comic book artistry that the fans rarely see: A naked young woman, bent forward at the waist, stands upon the pedestal, while the airborne Shazam lightning bolt strikes her in the rear. She has a look of unanticipated delight upon her face.

There were about 30 men present, and one or two young women. Among the artists and writers I spoke to, there was general agreement that working in the comic-book industry was not all magic transformations of unworthy flesh. Problems mentioned as organic included the lack of economic security, the inability of the artists to keep control over their material, insufficient prestige and a catch-all category that is apparently the source of abiding resentment: publishers who do not treat them as serious artists.

As for the censorship of the Comics Code Authority, virtually everybody agreed they wanted more freedom. Younger writers, in fact, are bringing fresh ideas into the field. But, as 33-year-old Archie Goodwin, who writes "Creepy Comics" for Jim Warren Publishers, wryly observes, the real problem is self-censorship: "The truth is, maybe half the people here wouldn't do their work any different if they didn't have censorship."

It did seem to me as I observed the crowd that there was perhaps more than a random sample of serious-purposed people who spoke haltingly, with tendentious meekness. The meeting began with nominations for A. C. B. A. officers for the coming year. I gleefully anticipated some earth-shaking confrontations between good and evil, but none developed. Nobody slipped off to a telephone booth to change. The two nominations for president, Neal Adams and Dick Giordano, by coincidence, jointly draw the Green Lantern-Green Arrow book for National. Lantern and Arrow have been squabbling lately, but Adams and Giordano were not at all disputatious.

In the entire group I was able to uncover only a single secret life.

"This is my secret life," Roy Thomas admitted. "Or rather it was, when I was a teacher at Fox High School in Arnold, Mo." Thomas, a bespectacled 30-year-old who wears his corn-silk hair straight down almost to the shoulders, edits at Marvel. "After school hours, I was publishing a comics fanzine called Alter Ego. I spent all my time at night working on Alter Ego."

"The people in this business," Lee said to me after the meeting, "are sincere, honorable, really decent guys. We're all dedicated, we love comics. The work we do is very important to the readers. I get mail that closes with, 'God bless you.' Most of us, we're like little kids, who, if you pat us on the head, we're happy."

All in all, add a little touch of resentment, discontent and a pinch of paranoia to Lee's description and you have the modern-day comic book superhero. Lee himself has only one frustration in a long, satisfying career:

"For years the big things on campus have been McLuhan and Tolkien, and Stan Lee and Marvel, and everybody knew about McLuhan and Tolkien, but nobody knew about Marvel. Now our competitor is coming out with 'relevant' comics and he has big public relations people, so he's been easing in on our publicity."

RELEVANCE is currently such a lure that even industry classics like Archie are having a stab at it. John Goldwater, president of Archie Comics, says that Archie definitely keeps up with the times, and offers as evidence Xerox copies of a silver print, which is an engraver's photographic proof of an original drawing. It was of a recent six-page Archie story entitled, "Weigh Out Scene."

"This is a civil-rights story," Goldwater said. "It's done subtly. It has to do with a fat boy who comes to town who can't fit into the mainstream with the teen-agers in town. Because of his obesity, he's taunted and humiliated. You know how kids are. Then one night Archie has a dream. And in this dream he is obese and fat and everybody is taunting him and ridiculing him and now he finally realizes what happened to this poor kid. So then there is a complete turnaround. But we don't say, remember, this kid is black. We don't say that. But the subtlety is there."

Goldwater, who is also president of the Comics Code Authority is convinced that "comics don't ruin your mind." He says: "I wouldn't be in this business unless it had some value, some educational value. If you can get a kid today to read, it's quite some victory — instead of him looking at the boob tube, you know?"

Recently there were some ruffled feelings in the industry when Marvel issued a comic book without the authority seal, which was denied because the subject of drugs was alluded to in one story that showed a stoned black kid tottering on a rooftop. Goldwater felt that hinted a bit of sensationalism, and Infantino believes the subject calls for a more thorough and responsible treatment. Lee scoffs. Black kids getting stoned isn't exactly a biannual occurrence, he suggests. Goodman calls the fuss a tempest in a teapot. Goldwater, at any rate, is not inclined to be harsh:

"Goodman came before the publishers and promised not to do it again. So we're satisfied. Anybody with 15 solid years of high standards of publishing comic books with the seal is entitled to one mistake."

Subsequently the publishers agreed to give themselves permission to deal with the subject. "Narcotics addiction," says the new guideline, "shall not be presented except as a vicious habit."

GOODMAN is not so sure relevance will continue to sustain sales, but Infantino is elated at National's success with social issues.

National turned toward relevance and social commentary for the same reasons Marvel had a decade earlier. "I'd like to say I had a great dream," says Infantino, "but it didn't happen that way. Green Lantern was dying. The whole superhero line was dying. Everything was sagging, everything. When your sales don't work, they're telling you something. The front office told me, get rid of the book, but I said, let me try something, just for three issues. We started interviewing groups of kids around the country. The one thing they kept repeating:

they want to know the truth. Suddenly the light bulb goes on: Wow, we've been missing the boat here!"

In the first of National's relevant books, which came out in the fall of 1970, Green Lantern comes to the aid of a respectable citizen, besieged by a crowd, who turns out to be a slum landlord badly in need of a thrashing. Lantern is confused to discover his pal Green Arrow actually siding with The People. "You mean you're . . . defending . . . these . . . ANARCHISTS?" he says.

Following a tour of the ghetto, Green Lantern is finally brought face to face with reality by an old black man who says: "I been readin' about you, how you work for the Blue Skins, and how on a planet someplace you helped out the Orange Skins . . . and you done considerable for the Purple Skins. Only there's Skins you never bothered with. The Black Skins. I want to know . . . how come? Answer me that, Mr. Green Lantern."

This story, written by 28-year-old Denny O'Neil, is one of the nominees for the writing Shazam, and the consensus of opinion, even among rival nominees, is that he'll win it. In the following months, O'Neil had the superheroes on the road discovering America and taking up such provocative current issues as the Manson family, the mistreatment of American Indians, the Chicago Seven trial, and, finally, in a forthcoming issue, the style and substance of the President and Vice President.

Mr. Agnew appears as Grandy, a simpering but vicious private-school cook whose ward is a certain ski-nosed child-witch named Sybil. A mere gaze from Sybil can cause great pain; one look from her and even Arrow and Lantern double over in agony. That certainly is making things clear. Grandy is constantly justifying his nastiness: "Old Grandy doesn't kill. I simply do my duty. Punish those who can't respect order. You may die. But that won't be my fault."

"What we're saying here," says Infantino, "is, there can be troubles with your Government unless you have the right leaders. Sure, we expect

flak from the Administration, but we feel the kids have a right to know, and they want to know. The kids are more sophisticated than anyone imagines, and we feel the doors are so wide open here that we're going in many directions.

"You wouldn't believe whom I'm talking to. Big-name writers — and they're interested. We have innovations in mind for older audiences, and in graphics we're going to take it such a step forward, it'll blow the mind." He was so excited during our talk that he stood up. "We're akin to a young lady pregnant and having her first baby." He grinned shyly

THE artist who has produced the most innovative work for Infantino is 53-year-old Jack Kirby, about whom Stan Lee says: "He is one of the giants, a real titan. He's had tremendous influence in the field. His art work has great power and drama and tells a story beautifully. No matter what he draws it looks exciting, and that's the name of the game."

Unlike the "relevant" comic books, Kirby's new line eschews self-conscious liberal rhetoric about social issues and returns to the basic function of comic books: to describe in an exciting, imaginative way how power operates in the world, the struggle to attain it by those who lack it and the uses to which it is put by those who have it.

Kirby began to conceive his new comic books when he was still at Marvel, but felt he might not get enough editorial autonomy. He left his $35,000-a-year job at Marvel and took his new books to National. He also moved from New York to Southern California, where he edits, writes and draws the books

His new heroes are the Forever People, whom he describes as "the other side of the gap — the under-30 group. I'm over 50. I've had no personal experience of the counterculture. It's all from the imagination."

The Forever People arrive on earth through a "boom tube," which is an attempt to offer approximate coordinates for an experiential con-

junction of media wash and psychedelic trip. They are said to be "In Search of a Dream." There are five of them: one is a relaxed, self-assured, young black man who, probably not by accident, carries the group's power source, known as the "mother box"; another is a shaggy-bearded giant who overwhelms his small-minded taunters with a loving, crushing bear hug; the third, a beautiful saintly flower child named Serafin is called a "sensitive"; the fourth, a combination rock star-football hero transmogrified into one Mark Moonrider; and the fifth, a girl named Beautiful Dreamer.

The mother box, which warns them of impending danger, also transforms them — not into five distinct, ego-involved superheroes but into a single all-powerful Infinity Man, who comes from a place where "all of natural law shifts, and bends, and changes. Where the answer to gravity is antigravity — and simply done."

These new heroes, unlike the characters of the sixties, are brash, confident youngsters whose superpower lies in their ability to unify. They are also, says Kirby, "basically nonviolent."

Infantino has been asked up to Yale to talk about Kirby's new books, and to Brown, for the new course in Comparative Comics. Students in Comp. Com. I will doubtless relish Kirby's toying with words like "gravity" (and other mild Joycean puns sprinkled elsewhere) to suggest elements of his parable of culture vs. counterculture. Suffice it to say here that the Forever People are from New Genesis, where the land is eternally green and children frolic in joy, and their enemy is Darkseid, who serves "holocaust and death."

The story of New Genesis is also told in another new Kirby book called "New Gods." When the old gods died, the story goes, the New Gods rose on New Genesis, where the High-Father, who alone has access to The Source, bows to the young, saying, "They are the carriers of life. They must remain free. Life flowers in freedom."

Opposed to New Genesis is

The Age of Communication

its "dark shadow," Apokolips, the home of evil Darkseid and his rotten minions. Darkseid's planet "is a dismal, unclean place of great ugly houses sheltering uglier machines." Apokolips is an armed camp where those who live with weapons rule the wretches who built them. Life is the evil here. And death the great goal. All that New Genesis stands for is reversed on Apokolips.

· Darkseid has not, of course, been content to rule on Apokolips. He wants to duplicate that horror on, of all places, Earth, and he can do this if he manages somehow to acquire the "antilife equation." With it, he will be able to "snuff out all life on Earth — with a word."

Thus is the battle drawn, and the Forever People, notably, are not going to waste their time hassling with raucous hardhats who don't understand the crisis. When a hostile, paranoid, Middle-America type confronts them, they arrange it so that he sees them just about the way he remembers kids to have been in his own childhood: Beautiful Dreamer wearing a sensible frilly dress down to her knees, the cosmic-sensitive Serafin wearing a high-school sweater and beanie, Moonrider with hat and tie and close-cropped hair.

"What's going on here? You kids look so different—and yet so familiar."

"Why sure," says Beautiful Dreamer soothingly. "You used to know lots of kids like us. Remember? We never passed without saying hello."

In the titanic struggle against Darkseid, the Forever People have lots of help, and they are beginning to populate four different comic books: "Forever People," "New Gods," "Mister Miracle" and "Superman's Pal Jimmy Olsen." Both Superman and Jimmy Olsen are being altered to fit the evolution of Kirby's Faulknerian saga of the difficult days leading to Armageddon. Already identified in the Kirby iconography on the side of the good are the newly revived and updated Newsboy Legion, so popular in the nineteen-forties; various dropout tribes living in "The Wild Area" and "experimenting with life" after harnessing the DNA molecule; and a tribe of technologically sophisticated youths called "Hairies," who live in a mobile "Mountain of Judgment" as protection against those who would destroy them. "You know our story," says one Hairy. "We seek only to be left alone—to use our talents, to develop fully."

On the other side, in support of Darkseid are middle managers and technocrats of the Establishment, like Morgan Edge, a media baron who treats his new employe Clark Kent—now a TV newscaster—abominably.

Darkseid's lousy band also includes an assortment of grotesque supervillains. Among them are DeSaad and his terrifying "Fear Machine," and a handsome toothy character named Glorious Godfrey, a revivalist. Godfrey is drawn to look like an actor playing Billy Graham in a Hollywood film biography of Richard Nixon starring George Hamilton.

"I hear you right thinkers,"

Godfrey says to his grim, eyeless audience of true believers, "You're shouting antilife—the positive belief."

In the background acolytes carry signs: "Life has pitfalls! Antilife is protection!" And, "You can justify anything with antilife!" And, "Life will make you doubt! Antilife will make you right!"

"I HAVE no final answers," Kirby admits. "I have no end in mind. This is like a continuing novel. My feeling about these times is that they're hopeful but full of danger. Any time you have silos buried around the country there's danger. In the forties when I created Captain America, that was my feeling then, that patriotism. Comics are definitely a native American art. They always have been. And I'm feeling very good about this. My mail has been about 90 per cent positive, and sales are good."

Infantino adds:

"The kids at Yale think Kirby's new books are more tuned in to them than any other media. They're reading transcripts from 'New Gods' over their radio station. The Kirby books are a conscious attempt to show what things look like when you're out where the kids are. The collages, the influence of the drug culture. We're showing them basically what they're seeing. We're turning into what they're experiencing."

If that is true—and I am not so sure it isn't—then perhaps the rest of us had better begin choosing sides. New Genesis anyone?

Topics for Discussion

1. Do you read comic books or comic strips? Why? Which comic book or comic strip is your favorite? Why?
2. While comic books continue to struggle for existence, daily comic strips thrive. Can you account for this? Are daily comic strips as relevant as comic books? Consider, for example, such comic strips as "B.C.," "Doonesbury," "Animal Crackers," and "Pogo."
3. What does Braun mean when he says that "the theme of comic books is power"? Do you agree with him?
4. What relationship does Braun see between the Vietnamese war and comic books? Do you think there is such a relationship?
5. In what ways are comic books and comic strips relevant?
6. Do you think it is possible to have a college course on comic books and comic strips? What would you include in such a course? What would be the value of such a course?

7. What is your reaction to Braun's description of the comic book *The Forever People?*
8. Do you see any relationship between the form and content of television and the form and content of comic books?

Rhetorical Considerations

1. Why does Braun begin his essay with the description of a scene from a comic book? How effective is this as an introduction?
2. The thesis of this essay is never stated. What do you think is the thesis of the essay? State the thesis in one sentence.
3. How does Braun define "relevance"? Why is this definition important to the development of the essay?
4. Examine the paragraph structure of this essay. At various points Braun uses one and two sentence paragraphs. What function do these paragraphs serve?
5. What does the last sentence of the essay mean? How does it serve as a conclusion?

Topics for Discussion

1. Slater's essay compares old and new culture while Browne's discusses popular culture. Are all of these cultures the same? How do they differ? What is the basis of their differences?

2. Grella calls James Bond a "culture hero." What does he mean by that term? Why isn't Bond just a hero? Does the term "culture" in this essay mean the same as it does in Slater's and Browne's essays?

3. Grella and two *Time* articles all speak of heroes, but none defines the term. What is a hero? Does any essay in this section of the book describe what a hero is? How does Homans view the cowboy hero of the western movie?

4. Do Schillaci and Peck agree on the function of the film? How do both men view the future of the film? Schillaci ignores the influence of television while Peck is very much concerned with it. Is it possible to discuss the present state of film without reference to television? Why is Peck so concerned with the relationship between film and television?

5. Belz cites an incident which demonstrates the tremendous power of television in popularizing a record. Do you think rock music would have become as popular as it did without such television programs as Dick Clark's?

6. Honan believes that radio is growing in popularity because it has become more specialized. Rintels believes that television does not serve its audience and instead seeks to serve the interests only of its advertisers. Do you believe that radio serves its audience better than television does? Does radio fail in any way?

7. Do you think that in becoming more relevant the comics have lost their place in American culture? What was their place in the past? What is the place of comics in today's culture?

8. Which essay did you enjoy most? Why? Which essay did you enjoy least? Why?

9. Which essay was the easiest to read? Which essay did you find the most difficult to read? Analyze the source of your difficulty in that essay.

10. How would you define culture? Your definition should deal with specifics and avoid generalities. Do you agree with any of the definitions offered in this section?